DocBook

The Definitive Guide

DocBook

The Definitive Guide

Norman Walsh and Leonard Muellner

O'REILLY®

Beijing · Cambridge · Farnham · Köln · Paris · Sebastopol · Taipei · Tokyo

DocBook: The Definitive Guide
by Norman Walsh and Leonard Muellner

Published by O'Reilly & Associates, Inc., 101 Morris Street, Sebastopol, CA 95472.

Editor: Frank Willison

Production Editors: David Futato and Madeleine Newell

Printing History:

October 1999: First Edition.

ISBN: 1-56592-580-7 [3/00]

[M]

Table of Contents

Preface

DocBook provides a system for writing structured documents using SGML or XML. It is particularly well-suited to books and papers about computer hardware and software, though it is by no means limited to them. DocBook is an SGML document type definition (DTD). An XML version is available now, and an official XML release is in the works. Because it is a large and robust DTD, and because its main structures correspond to the general notion of what constitutes a book, DocBook has been adopted by a large and growing community of authors. DocBook is supported "out of the box" by a number of commercial tools, and support for it is rapidly growing in a number of free software environments. In short, DocBook is an easy-to-understand and widely used DTD. Dozens of organizations use DocBook for millions of pages of documentation, in various print and online formats, worldwide.

Why Read This Book?

This book is designed to be the clear, concise, normative reference to the DocBook DTD. This book is the official documentation for the DocBook DTD.

We hope to answer, definitively, all the questions you might have about all the elements and entities in DocBook. In particular, we cover the following subjects:

- The general nature of DocBook. With over 300 elements, DocBook can be a bit overwhelming at first. We quickly get you up to speed on how the pieces fit together.
- How to write DocBook documents. Where should you start and what should you do?
- Parsing and validation. After you've written a document, how can you tell if it really conforms to the DocBook DTD?

- How to publish DocBook documents. After you've written one, what do you do with it? We provide a guide to using some popular free tools to publish DocBook documents both in print and on the Web.
- Customizing the DTD. Many individuals and corporations have standardized on the DocBook DTD. Whether your subject matter is computer software documentation or not, we explain how you can write a "customization layer" to tailor DocBook explicitly for your information.
- Understanding all of the elements. Each element is extensively documented, including the intended semantics and the purpose of all its attributes. An example of proper usage is given for every element. The parameter entities and character entities are also described.
- Stylesheets. Several standard stylesheet languages are briefly described.
- XML compatability. We outline all of the points that you'll need to consider as you or your organization contemplate XML for authoring, publishing, or both.
- Additional resources and a CD-ROM. Finally, we direct you to other places you can go for all the latest info, and offer a complete set of online documentation on the CD-ROM.

This Book's Audience

We expect that most readers will have some familiarity with SGML or XML. Even if your experience goes no farther than writing a few HTML pages, you're probably in good shape. Although we provide an introduction to SGML, XML, and structured markup, this book may not suffice as your only tutorial about SGML and XML. This depends, naturally, on your needs and experience. For a list of some other good resources, consult Appendix D, *Resources*.

Some sections of this book describe tools and applications. For the most part, these are Microsoft Windows or UNIX applications, although there's nothing about DocBook that makes it unsuitable for the Mac or VM/CMS or any other operating system of your choice.

Organization of This Book

This book is divided into three parts. *Part I: Introduction* is an introduction to structured markup and DocBook:

Chapter 1, Getting Started with SGML/XML
: A quick introduction to structured markup.

Chapter 2, Creating DocBook Documents
: How to make DocBook documents.

Chapter 3, Parsing DocBook Documents
: Parsing and validating DocBook documents.

Chapter 4, Publishing DocBook Documents
: How to publish DocBook documents.

Chapter 5, Customizing DocBook
: How to customize DocBook.

Part II: Reference is a complete reference to every element in the DocBook V3.1 DTD and provides a concise summary of the parameter entities. For a detailed reference to the parameter entities, consult the online version available either on the CD-ROM or the web site (*http://docbook.org/*).

DocBook Element Reference
: A reference guide to the DocBook elements.

DocBook Parameter Entity Reference
: A reference guide to the DocBook parameter entities.

DocBook Character Entity Reference
: A reference guide to the character entities declared in DocBook.

Part III: Appendixes discusses other resources:

Appendix A, Installation
: How to install DocBook, Jade, and the stylesheets.

Appendix B, DocBook and XML
: DocBook as XML.

Appendix C, DocBook Versions
: A guide to DocBook versions, including a summary of the features expected in future releases.

Appendix D, Resources
: Other resources.

Appendix E, What's on the CD-ROM?
: What's on the CD?

Appendix F, Interchanging DocBook Documents
: An interchange checklist. Things to consider when you're sharing DocBook documents with others.

Appendix G, DocBook V3.1 Quick Reference
: A Quick Reference to the elements in DocBook.

At the end of this book you'll find a Glossary and an Index.

Conventions Used in This Book

- **Garamond Book** is used for element and attribute names.
- `Constant Willison` is used for program examples, attribute value literals, start- and end-tags, and source code example text.
- *`Constant Willison Oblique`* is used for "replaceable" text or variables. Replaceable text is text that describes something you're supposed to type, like a *`filename`*, in which the word "filename" acts as a placeholder for the actual filename.
- *Garamond Italic* is used for filenames and (in the print version of the book) URLs.
- URLs (*http://docbook.org/*) are presented in parentheses after the name of the resource they describe in the print version of the book.

Getting This Book

If you want to hold this book in your hand and flip through its pages, you have to buy it as you would any other book. You can also get this book in electronic form, as a DocBook SGML document, and in HTML, either on the CD that accompanies the bound book or from this book's web site: *http://docbook.org/*.

Getting Examples from This Book

All of the examples are included on the CD-ROM and online at the book's web site. You can get the most up-to-date information about this book from the web site: *http://docbook.org/*.

Getting DocBook

The DocBook DTD, v3.1, is included on the CD-ROM. You can get the most up-to-date version and information about DocBook from the DocBook web page: *http://www.oasis-open.org/docbook/*.

Request for Comments

Please help us improve future editions of this book by reporting any errors, inaccuracies, bugs, misleading or confusing statements, and plain old typos that you find. An online errata list is maintained at *http://docbook.org/tdg/errata.html*. Email your bug reports and comments to us at *bookcomments@docbook.org*.

Acknowledgements from Norm

This book has been in the works for a long time. It could not have been completed without the help and encouragement of a lot of people, most especially my wife, Deborah, who supported me through the long hours and the late nights.

I also want to thank Lenny for collaborating with me and developing real prose out of my rough outlines, cryptic email messages, and scribbled notes.

A number of people contributed technical feedback as this book was being written, in particular Terry Allen and Eve Maler. I owe most of what I know about SGML to them, and to the other members of the Davenport Group who answered all my questions so many years ago, especially Jon Bosak, Eduardo Guttentag, and Murray Maloney. Paul Prescod, Mark Galassi, and Dave Pawson also provided invaluable feedback on the technical review draft. It's a better book because of them.

Acknowledgements from Lenny

My gratitude goes back to Dale Dougherty and Terry Allen, who long ago encouraged me and the production department at O'Reilly to learn SGML; and to Lar Kaufman, who also made large contributions to my knowledge and appreciation of SGML. But my greatest debt of thanks goes to Norm for all that he patiently taught me about DocBook, and for his supreme graciousness in keeping me a part of this project.

Acknowledgements from Norm and Lenny

Thanks finally to the great people at O'Reilly who encouraged us to write it (Frank Willison and Sheryl Avruch), agreed to edit it (Frank), helped design it (Alicia Cech, who worked on the interior design, and Edie Freeman, who designed the cover), proofed and produced it (Chris Maden, Madeline Newell, and David Futato), and indexed it (Ellen Troutman).

I

Introduction

1

Getting Started with SGML/XML

This chapter is intended to provide a quick introduction to structured markup (SGML and XML). If you're already familiar with SGML or XML, you only need to skim this chapter.

To work with DocBook, you need to understand a few basic concepts of structured editing in general, and DocBook, in particular. That's covered here. You also need some concrete experience with the way a DocBook document is structured. That's covered in the next chapter.

HTML and SGML vs. XML

This chapter doesn't assume that you know what HTML is, but if you do, you have a starting point for understanding structured markup. HTML (Hypertext Markup Language) is a way of marking up text and graphics so that the most popular web browsers can interpret them. HTML consists of a set of markup tags with specific meanings. Moreover, HTML is a very basic type of SGML markup that is easy to learn and easy for computer applications to generate. But the simplicity of HTML is both its virtue and its weakness. Because of HTML's limitations, web users and programmers have had to extend and enhance it by a series of customizations and revisions that still fall short of accommodating current, to say nothing of future, needs.

SGML, on the other hand, is an international standard that describes how markup languages are defined. SGML does not consist of particular tags or the rules for their usage. HTML is an example of a markup language defined in SGML.

XML promises an intelligent improvement over HTML, and compatibility with it is already being built into the most popular web browsers. XML is not a new markup language designed to compete with HTML, and it's not designed to create conversion headaches for people with tons of HTML documents. XML is intended to alleviate compatibility problems with browser software; it's a new, easier version of the standard rules that govern the markup itself, or, in other words, a new version of SGML. The rules of XML are designed to make it easier to write both applications that interpret its type of markup and applications that generate its markup. XML was developed by a team of SGML experts who understood and sought to correct the problems of learning and implementing SGML. XML is also *extensible* markup, which means that it is customizable. A browser or word processor that is XML-capable will be able to read any XML-based markup language that an individual user defines.

In this book, we tend to describe things in terms of SGML, but where there are differences between SGML and XML (and there are only a few), we point them out. For our purposes, it doesn't really matter whether you use SGML or XML.

During the coming months, we anticipate that XML-aware web browsers and other tools will become available. Nevertheless, it's not unreasonable to do your authoring in SGML and your online publishing in XML or HTML. By the same token, it's not unreasonable to do your authoring in XML.

Basic SGML/XML Concepts

Here are the basic SGML/XML concepts you need to grasp:

- structured, semantic markup
- elements
- attributes
- entities

Structured and Semantic Markup

An essential characteristic of structured markup is that it explicitly distinguishes (and accordingly "marks up" within a document) the structure and semantic content of a document. It does not mark up the way in which the document will appear to the reader, in print or otherwise.

In the days before word processors it was common for a typed manuscript to be submitted to a publisher. The manuscript identified the logical structures of the documents (chapters, section titles, and so on), but said nothing about its appearance. Working independently of the author, a designer then developed a specification for the appearance of the document, and a typesetter marked up and applied the designer's format to the document.

Because presentation or appearance is usually based on structure and content, SGML markup logically precedes and generally determines the way a document will look to a reader. If you are familiar with strict, simple HTML markup, you know that a given document that is structurally the same can also look different on different computers. That's because the markup does not specify many aspects of a document's appearance, although it does specify many aspects of a document's structure.

Many writers type their text into a word processor, line-by-line and word-for-word, italicizing technical terms, underlining words for emphasis, or setting section headers in a font complementary to the body text, and finally, setting the headers off with a few carriage returns fore and aft. The format such a writer imposes on the words on the screen imparts structure to the document by changing its appearance in ways that a reader can more or less reliably decode. The reliability depends on how consistently and unambiguously the changes in type and layout are made. By contrast, an SGML/XML markup of a section header explicitly specifies that a specific piece of text is a section header. This assertion does not specify the presentation or appearance of the section header, but it makes the fact that the text is a section header completely unambiguous.

SGML and XML use named elements, delimited by angle brackets ("<" and ">") to identify the markup in a document. In DocBook, a top-level section is `<sect1>`, so the title of a top-level section named *My First-Level Header* would be identified like this:

```
<sect1><title>My First-Level Header</title>
```

Note the following features of this markup:

Clarity

A title begins with `<title>` and ends with `</title>`. The **sect1** also has an ending `</sect1>`, but we haven't shown the whole section so it's not visible.

Hierarchy

"My First-Level Header" is the title of a top-level section because it occurs inside a title in a **sect1**. A **title** element occurring somewhere else, say in a **Chapter** element, would be the title of the chapter.

Plain text

SGML documents can have varying character sets, but most are ASCII. XML documents use the Unicode character set. This makes SGML and XML documents highly portable across systems and tools.

In an SGML document, there is no obligatory difference between the size or face of the type in a first-level section header and the title of a book in a footnote or the first sentence of a body paragraph. All SGML files are simple text files without font changes or special characters.* Similarly, an SGML document does not specify the words in a text that are to be set in italic, bold, or roman type. Instead, SGML marks certain kinds of texts for their semantic content. For example, if a particular word is the name of a file, then the tags around it should specify that it is a filename:

```
Many mail programs read configuration information from the
user's <filename>.mailrc</filename> file.
```

If the meaning of a phrase is particularly audacious, it might get tagged for boldness of thought instead of appearance. An SGML document contains all the information that a typesetter needs to lay out and typeset a printed page in the most effective and consistent way, but it does not specify the layout or the type.†

Not only is the structure of an SGML/XML document explicit, but it is also carefully controlled. An SGML document makes reference to a set of declarations—a document type definition (DTD)—that contains an inventory of tag names and specifies the combination rules for the various structural and semantic features that make up a document. What the distinctive features are and how they should be combined is "arbitrary" in the sense that almost any selection of features and rules of composition is theoretically possible. The DocBook DTD chooses a particular set of features and rules for its users.

Here is a specific example of how the DocBook DTD works. DocBook specifies that a third-level section can follow a second-level section but cannot follow a first-level section without an intervening second-level section.

This is valid:

```
<sect1><title>...</title>
  <sect2><title>...</title>
    <sect3><title>...</title>
      ...
    </sect3>
  </sect2>
</sect1>
```

This is not:

```
<sect1><title>...</title>
  <sect3><title>...</title>
    ...
  </sect3>
</sect1>
```

Because an SGML/XML document has an associated DTD that describes the valid, logical structures of the document, you can test the logical structure of any particular document against the DTD. This process is performed by a *parser*. An SGML processor must begin by parsing the document and determining if it is valid, that is, if it

* Some structured editors apply style to the document while it's being edited, using fonts and color to make the editing task easier, but this stylistic information is not stored in the actual SGML/XML document. Instead, it is provided by the editing application.

† The distinction between appearance or presentation and structure or content is essential to SGML, but there is a way to specify the appearance of an SGML document: attach a stylesheet to it. There are several standards for such stylesheets: CSS, XSL, FOSIs, and DSSSL. See Chapter 4, *Publishing DocBook Documents*.

conforms to the rules specified in the DTD. XML processors are not required to check for validity, but it's always a good idea to check for validity when authoring. Because you can test and validate the structure of an SGML/XML document with software, a DocBook document containing a first-level section followed immediately by a third-level section will be identified as invalid, meaning that it's not a valid *instance* or example of a document defined by the DocBook DTD. Presumably, a document with a logical structure won't normally jump from a first- to a third-level section, so the rule is a safeguard—but not a guarantee—of good writing, or at the very least, reasonable structure. A parser also verifies that the names of the tags are correct and that tags requiring an ending tag have them. This means that a valid document is also one that should format correctly, without runs of paragraphs incorrectly appearing in bold type or similar monstrosities that everyone has seen in print at one time or another. For more information about SGML/XML parsers, see Chapter 3, *Parsing DocBook Documents*.

In general, adherence to the explicit rules of structure and markup in a DTD is a useful and reassuring guarantee of consistency and reliability within documents, across document sets, and over time. This makes SGML/XML markup particularly desirable to corporations or governments that have large sets of documents to manage, but it is a boon to the individual writer as well.

How can this markup help you?

Semantic markup makes your documents more amenable to interpretation by software, especially publishing software. You can publish a white paper, authored as a DocBook **Article**, in the following formats:

- On the Web in HTML
- As a standalone document on $8\frac{1}{2} \times 11$ paper
- As part of a quarterly journal, in a 6×9 format
- In Braille
- In audio

You can produce each of these publications from exactly the same source document using the presentational techniques best suited to both the content of the document and the presentation medium. This versatility also frees the author to concentrate on the document content. For example, as we write this book, we don't know exactly how O'Reilly will choose to present chapter headings, bulleted lists, SGML terms, or any of the other semantic features. And we don't care. It's irrelevant; whatever presentation is chosen, the SGML sources will be transformed automatically into that style.

Semantic markup can relieve the author of other, more significant burdens as well (after all, careful use of paragraph and character styles in a word processor document theoretically allows us to change the presentation independently from the document). Using semantic markup opens up your documents to a world of possibilities. Documents become, in a loose sense, databases of information. Programs can compile, retrieve, and otherwise manipulate the documents in predictable, useful ways.

Consider the online version of this book: almost every element name (**Article**, **Book**, and so on) is a hyperlink to the reference page that describes that element. Maintaining these links by hand would be tedious and might be unreliable, as well. Instead, every element name is marked as an element using **SGMLTag**: a **Book** is tagged like `<sgmltag>Book</sgmltag>`.

Because each element name in this book is tagged semantically, the program that produces the online version can determine which occurrences of the word "book" in the text are actually references to the **Book** element. The program can then automatically generate the appropriate hyperlink when it should.

There's one last point to make about the versatility of SGML documents: how much you have depends on the DTD. If you take a good photo with a high resolution lens, you can print it and copy it and scan it and put it on the Web, and it will look good. If you start with a low-resolution picture it will not survive those transformations so well. DocBook SGML/XML has this advantage over, say, HTML: DocBook has specific and unambiguous semantic and structural markup, because you can convert its documents with ease into other presentational forms, and search them more precisely. If you start with HTML, whose markup is at a lower resolution than DocBook's, your versatility and searchability is substantially restricted and cannot be improved.

What are the shortcomings to structural authoring?

There are a few significant shortcomings to structured authoring:

- It requires a significant change in the authoring process. Writing structured documents is very different from writing with a typical word processor, and change is difficult. In particular, authors don't like giving up control over the appearance of their words especially now that they have acquired it with the advent of word processors. But many publishing companies need authors to relinquish that control, because book design and production remains their job, not their authors'.
- Because semantics are separate from appearance, in order to publish an SGML/XML document, a stylesheet or other tool must create the presentational form from the structural form. Writing stylesheets is a skill in its own right, and though not every author among a group of authors has to learn how to write them, someone has to.

- Authoring tools for SGML documents can generally be pretty expensive. While it's not entirely unreasonable to edit SGML/XML documents with a simple text editor, it's a bit tedious to do so. However, there are a few free tools that are SGML-aware. The widespread interest in XML may well produce new, clever, and less expensive XML editing tools.

Elements and Attributes

SGML/XML markup consists primarily of *elements*, *attributes*, and *entities*. Elements are the terms we have been speaking about most, like **sect1**, that describe a document's content and structure. Most elements come in pairs and mark the start and end of the construct they surround—for example, the SGML source for this particular paragraph begins with a `<para>` tag and ends with a `</para>` tag. Some elements are "empty" (such as DocBook's cross-reference element, `<xref>`) and require no end tag.*

Elements can, but don't necessarily, include one or more attributes, which are additional terms that extend the function or refine the content of a given element. For instance, in DocBook a `<sect1>` start tag can contain an identifier—an `id` attribute —that will ultimately allow the writer to cross-reference it or enable a reader to retrieve it. End tags cannot contain attributes. A `<sect1>` element with an `id` attribute looks like this:

```
<sect1 id="idvalue">
```

In SGML, the catalog of attributes that can occur on an element is predefined. You cannot add arbitrary attribute names to an element. Similarly, the values allowed for each attribute are predefined. In XML, the use of namespaces (*http://www.w3.org/TR/REC-xml-names/*) may allow you to add additional attributes to an element, but as of this writing, there's no way to perform validation on those attributes.

The `id` attribute is one half of a cross reference. An `idref` attribute on another element, for example `<xref linkend="idvalue">`, provides the other half. These attributes provide whatever application might process the SGML source with the data needed either to make a hypertext link or to substitute a named and/or numbered cross reference in place of the `<xref>`. Another use for attributes is to specify subclasses of certain elements. For instance, you can subdivide DocBook's `<systemitem>` into URLs and email addresses by making the content of the `role` attribute the distinction between them, as in `<systemitem role="URL">` versus `<systemitem role="emailaddr">`.

* In XML, this is written as `<xref/>`, as we'll see in the section "Typing an XML Document," in Chapter 2, *Creating DocBook Documents*.

Entities

Entities are a fundamental concept in SGML and XML, and can be somewhat daunting at first. They serve a number of related, but slightly different functions, and this makes them a little bit complicated.

In the most general terms, entities allow you to assign a name to some chunk of data, and use that name to refer to that data. The complexity arises because there are two different contexts in which you can use entities (in the DTD and in your documents), two types of entities (parsed and unparsed), and two or three different ways in which the entities can point to the chunk of data that they name.

In the rest of this section, we'll describe each of the commonly encountered entity types. If you find the material in this section confusing, feel free to skip over it now and come back to it later. We'll refer to the different types of entities as the need arises in our discussion of DocBook. Come back to this section when you're looking for more detail.

Entities can be divided into two broad categories, *general entities* and *parameter entities*. Parameter entities are most often used in the DTD, not in documents, so we'll describe them last. Before you can use any type of entity, it must be formally declared. This is typically done in the document prologue, as we'll explain in Chapter 2, *Creating DocBook Documents*, but we will show you how to declare each of the entities discussed here.

General Entities

In use, general entities are introduced with an ampersand (&) and end with a semicolon (;). Within the category of general entities, there are two types: *internal general entities* and *external general entities*.

Internal general entities

With internal entities, you can associate an essentially arbitrary piece of text (which may have other markup, including references to other entities) with a name. You can then include that text by referring to its name. For example, if your document frequently refers to, say, "O'Reilly & Associates," you might declare it as an entity:

```
<!ENTITY ora "O'Reilly &amp; Associates">
```

Then, instead of typing it out each time, you can insert it as needed in your document with the entity reference `&ora;`, simply to save time. Note that this entity declaration includes another entity reference within it. That's perfectly valid as long as the reference isn't directly or indirectly recursive.

If you find that you use a number of entities across many documents, you can add them directly to the DTD and avoid having to include the declarations in each document. See the discussion of *dbgenent.mod* in Chapter 5, *Customizing DocBook*.

External general entities

With external entities, you can reference other documents from within your document. If these entities contain document text (SGML or XML), then references to them cause the parser to insert the text of the external file directly into your document (these are called parsed entities). In this way, you can use entities to divide your single, logical document into physically distinct chunks. For example, you might break your document into four chapters and store them in separate files. At the top of your document, you would include entity declarations to reference the four files:

```
<!ENTITY ch01 SYSTEM "ch01.sgm">
<!ENTITY ch02 SYSTEM "ch02.sgm">
<!ENTITY ch03 SYSTEM "ch03.sgm">
<!ENTITY ch04 SYSTEM "ch04.sgm">
```

Your **Book** now consists simply of references to the entities:

```
<book>
&ch01;
&ch02;
&ch03;
&ch04;
</book>
```

Sometimes it's useful to reference external files that don't contain document text. For example, you might want to reference an external graphic. You can do this with entities by declaring the type of data that's in the entity using a notation (these are called unparsed entities). For example, the following declaration declares the entity `tree` as an encapsulated PostScript image:

```
<!ENTITY tree SYSTEM "tree.eps" NDATA EPS>
```

Entities declared this way cannot be inserted directly into your document. Instead, they must be used as entity attributes to elements:

```
<graphic entityref="tree"></graphic>
```

Conversely, you cannot use entities declared without a notation as the value of an entity attribute.

Special characters

In order for the parser to recognize markup in your document, it must be able to distinguish markup from content. It does this with two special characters: "<," which identifies the beginning of a start or end tag, and "&," which identifies the beginning of an entity reference.[*] If you want these characters to have their literal value, they must be encoded as entity references in your document. The entity reference < produces a left angle bracket; & produces the ampersand.[†]

If you do not encode each of these as their respective entity references, then an SGML parser or application is likely to interpret them as characters introducing elements or entities (an XML parser will always interpret them this way); consequently, they won't appear as you intended. If you wish to cite text that contains literal ampersands and less-than signs, you need to transform these two characters into entity references before they are included in a DocBook document. The only other alternative is to incorporate text that includes them in your document through some process that avoids the parser.

In SGML, character entities are frequently declared using a third entity category (one that we deliberately chose to overlook), called *data entities*. In XML, these are declared using numeric character references. Numeric character references resemble entity references, but technically aren't the same. They have the form &#*999*;, in which "999" is the numeric character number.

In XML, the numeric character number is always the Unicode character number. In addition, XML allows hexadecimal numeric character references of the form &#x*hhhh*;. In SGML, the numeric character number is a number from the document character set that's declared in the SGML declaration.

Character entities are also used to give a name to special characters that can't otherwise be typed or are not portable across applications and operating systems. You can then include these characters in your document by refering to their entity name. Instead of using the often obscure and inconsistent key combinations of your particular word processor to type, say, an uppercase letter U with an umlaut (Ü), you type in an entity for it instead. For instance, the entity for an uppercase letter U with an umlaut has been defined as the entity Uuml, so you would type in Ü to reference it instead of the actual character. The SGML application that eventually processes your document for presentation will match the entity to your platform's handling of special characters in order to render it appropriately.

* In XML, these characters are fixed. In SGML, it is possible to change the markup start characters, but we won't consider that case here. If you change the markup start characters, you know what you're doing. While we're on the subject, in SGML, these characters only have their special meaning if they are followed by a name character. It is, in fact, valid in an *SGML* (but not an XML) document to write "O'Reilly & Associates" because the ampersand is not followed by a name character. Don't do this, however.

† The sequence of characters that end a marked section (see "Marked sections"), such as]]> must also be encoded with at least one entity reference if it is not being used to end a marked section. For this purpose, you can use the entity reference > for the final right angle bracket.

Parameter Entities

Parameter entities are only recognized in markup declarations (in the DTD, for example). Instead of beginning with an ampersand, they begin with a percent sign. Parameter entities are most frequently used to customize the DTD. For a detailed discussion of this topic, see Chapter 5. Following are some other uses for them.

Marked sections

You might use a parameter entity reference in an SGML document in a marked section. Marking sections is a mechanism for indicating that special processing should apply to a particular block of text. Marked sections are introduced by the special sequence `<![`*`keyword`*`[` and end with `]]>`. In SGML, marked sections can appear in both DTDs and document instances. In XML, they're only allowed in the DTD.*

The most common keywords are `INCLUDE`, which indicates that the text in the marked section should be included in the document; `IGNORE`, which indicates that the text in the marked section should be ignored (it completely disappears from the parsed document); and `CDATA`, which indicates that all markup characters within that section should be ignored except for the closing characters `]]>`.

In SGML, these keywords can be parameter entities. For example, you might declare the following parameter entity in your document:

```
<!ENTITY % draft "INCLUDE">
```

Then you could put the sections of the document that are only applicable in a draft within marked sections:

```
<![%draft;[
<para>
This paragraph only appears in the draft version.
</para>
]]>
```

When you're ready to print the final version, simply change the `draft` parameter entity declaration:

```
<!ENTITY % draft "IGNORE">
```

and publish the document. None of the draft sections will appear.

How Does DocBook Fit In?

DocBook is a very popular set of tags for describing books, articles, and other prose documents, particularly technical documentation. DocBook is defined using the

* Actually, CDATA marked sections are allowed in an XML document, but the keyword cannot be a parameter entity, and it must be typed literally. See the examples on this page.

native DTD syntax of SGML and XML. Like HTML, DocBook is an example of a markup language defined in SGML/XML.

A Short DocBook History

DocBook is almost 10 years old. It began in 1991 as a joint project of HaL Computer Systems and O'Reilly. Its popularity grew, and eventually it spawned its own maintainance organization, the Davenport Group. In mid-1998, it became a Technical Committee (TC) of the Organization for the Advancement of Structured Information Standards (OASIS).

The HaL and O'Reilly era

The DocBook DTD was originally designed and implemented by HaL Computer Systems and O'Reilly & Associates around 1991. It was developed primarily to facilitate the exchange of UNIX documentation originally marked up in *troff*. Its design appears to have been based partly on input from SGML interchange projects conducted by the Unix International and Open Software Foundation consortia.

When DocBook V1.1 was published, discussion about its revision and maintenance began in earnest in the Davenport Group, a forum created by O'Reilly for computer documentation producers. V1.2 was influenced strongly by Novell and Digital.

In 1994, the Davenport Group became an officially chartered entity responsible for DocBook's maintenance. DocBook V1.2.2 was published simultaneously. The founding sponsors of this incarnation of Davenport include the following people:

- Jon Bosak, Novell
- Dale Dougherty, O'Reilly & Associates
- Ralph Ferris, Fujitsu OSSI
- Dave Hollander, Hewlett-Packard
- Eve Maler, Digital Equipment Corporation
- Murray Maloney, SCO
- Conleth O'Connell, HaL Computer Systems
- Nancy Paisner, Hitachi Computer Products
- Mike Rogers, SunSoft
- Jean Tappan, Unisys

The Davenport era

Under the auspices of the Davenport Group, the DocBook DTD began to widen its scope. It was now being used by a much wider audience, and for new purposes, such as direct authoring with SGML-aware tools, and publishing directly to paper. As the largest users of DocBook, Novell and Sun had a heavy influence on its design.

In order to help users manage change, the new Davenport charter established the following rules for DocBook releases:

- Minor versions ("point releases" such as V2.2) could add to the markup model, but could not change it in a backward-incompatible way. For example, a new kind of list element could be added, but it would not be acceptable for the existing itemized-list model to start requiring two list items inside it instead of only one. Thus, any document conforming to version *n*.0 would also conform to *n.m*.
- Major versions (such as V3.0) could both add to the markup model and make backward-incompatible changes. However, the changes would have to be announced in the last major release.
- Major-version introductions must be separated by at least a year.

V3.0 was released in January 1997. After that time, although DocBook's audience continued to grow, many of the Davenport Group stalwarts became involved in the XML effort, and development slowed dramatically. The idea of creating an official XML-compliant version of DocBook was discussed, but not implemented. (For more detailed information about DocBook V3.0 and plans for subsequent versions, see Appendix C, *DocBook Versions*.)

The sponsors wanted to close out Davenport in an orderly way to ensure that DocBook users would be supported. It was suggested that OASIS become DocBook's new home. An OASIS DocBook Technical Committee was formed in July, 1998, with Eduardo Gutentag of Sun Microsystems as chair.

The OASIS era

The DocBook Technical commitee is continuing the work started by the Davenport Group. The transition from Davenport to OASIS has been very smooth, in part because the core design team consists of essentially the same individuals (we all just changed hats).

DocBook V3.1, published in February 1999, was the first OASIS release. It integrated a number of changes that had been "in the wings" for some time.

The committee is undertaking new DocBook development to ensure that the DTD continues to meet the needs of its users, and that it has concrete plans to publish an XML-compliant version.

2

Creating DocBook Documents

This chapter explains in concrete, practical terms how to make DocBook documents. It's an overview of all the kinds of markup that are possible in DocBook documents. It explains how to create several kinds of DocBook documents: books, sets of books, chapters, articles, and reference manual entries. The idea is to give you enough basic information to actually start writing. The information here is intentionally skeletal; you can find "the details" in the reference section of this book.

Before we can examine DocBook markup, we have to take a look at what an SGML or XML system requires.

Making an SGML Document

SGML requires that your document have a specific prologue. The following sections describe the features of the prologue.

An SGML Declaration

SGML documents begin with an optional SGML Declaration. The declaration can precede the document instance, but generally it is stored in a separate file that is associated with the DTD. The SGML Declaration is a grab bag of SGML defaults. DocBook includes an SGML Declaration that is appropriate for most DocBook documents, so we won't go into a lot of detail here about the SGML Declaration.

In brief, the SGML Declaration describes, among other things, what characters are markup delimiters (the default is angle brackets), what characters can compose tag and attribute names (usually the alphabetical and numeric characters plus the dash and the period), what characters can legally occur within your document, how long SGML "names" and "numbers" can be, what sort of minimizations (abbreviation of markup) are allowed, and so on. Changing the SGML Declaration is rarely necessary, and because many tools only partially support changes to the declaration, changing it is best avoided, if possible.

Wayne Wholer has written an excellent tutorial on the SGML Declaration; if you're interested in more details, see *http://www.oasis-open.org/cover/wlw11.html*.

A Document Type Declaration

All SGML documents must begin with a document type declaration. This identifies the DTD that will be used by the document and what the root element of the document will be. A typical doctype declaration for a DocBook document looks like this:

```
<!DOCTYPE book PUBLIC "-//OASIS//DTD DocBook V3.1//EN">
```

This declaration indicates that the *root element*, which is the first element in the hierarchical structure of the document, will be **<book>** and that the DTD used will be the one identified by the public identifier `-//OASIS//DTD DocBook V3.1//EN`. See "Public Identifiers" later in this chapter.

An Internal Subset

It's also possible to provide additional declarations in a document by placing them in the document type declaration:

```
<!DOCTYPE book PUBLIC "-//OASIS//DTD DocBook V3.1//EN" [
<!ENTITY nwalsh "Norman Walsh">
<!ENTITY chap1 SYSTEM "chap1.sgm">
<!ENTITY chap2 SYSTEM "chap2.sgm">
]>
```

These declarations form what is known as the *internal subset*. The declarations stored in the file referenced by the public or system identifier in the `DOCTYPE` declaration is called the *external subset* and it is technically optional. It is legal to put the DTD in the internal subset and to have no external subset, but for a DTD as large as DocBook that wouldn't make much sense.

NOTE The internal subset is parsed *first* and, if multiple declarations for an entity occur, the first declaration is used. Declarations in the internal subset override declarations in the external subset.

The Document (or Root) Element

Although comments and processing instructions may occur between the document type declaration and the root element, the root element usually immediately follows the document type declaration:

```
<!DOCTYPE book PUBLIC "-//OASIS//DTD DocBook V3.1//EN" [
<!ENTITY nwalsh "Norman Walsh">
<!ENTITY chap1 SYSTEM "chap1.sgm">
<!ENTITY chap2 SYSTEM "chap2.sgm">
]>
<book>
&chap1;
&chap2;
</book>
```

You cannot place the root element of the document in an external entity.

Typing an SGML Document

If you are entering SGML using a text editor such as Emacs or vi, there are a few things to keep in mind.* Using a structured text editor designed for SGML hides most of these issues.

- DocBook element and attribute names are not case-sensitive. There's no difference between `<Para>` and `<pArA>`. Entity names are case-sensitive, however.

  If you are interested in future XML compatibility, input all element and attribute names strictly in lowercase.

- If attribute values contain spaces or punctuation characters, you must quote them. You are not required to quote attribute values if they consist of a single word or number, although it is not wrong to do so.

  When quoting attribute values, you can use either a straight single quote ('), or a straight double quote ("). Don't use the "curly" quotes (“ and ”) in your editing tool.

  If you are interested in future XML compatibility, always quote all attribute values.

- Several forms of markup minimization are allowed, including empty tags. Instead of typing the entire end tag for an element, you can type simply `</>`. For example:

  ```
  <para>
  This is <emphasis>important</>: never stick the tines of a fork
  ```

* Many of these things are influenced by the SGML declaration in use. For the purpose of this discussion, we assume you are using the standard DocBook declaration.

```
in an electrical outlet.
</para>
```

You can use this technique for any and every tag, but it will make your documents very hard to understand and difficult to debug if you introduce errors. It is best to use this technique only for inline elements containing a short string of text.

Empty start tags are also possible, but may be even more confusing. For the record, if you encounter an empty start tag, the SGML parser uses the element that ended last:

```
<para>
This is <emphasis>important</>.  So is <>this</>.
</para>
```

Both "important" and "this" are emphasized.

If you are interested in future XML compatibility, don't use any of these tricks.

- The null end tag (net) minimization feature allows constructions like this:

```
<para>
This is <emphasis/important/: never stick the tines of a fork
in an electrical outlet.
</para>
```

If, instead of ending a start tag with >, you end it with a slash, then the next occurrence of a slash ends the element.

If you are interested in future XML compatibility, don't use net tag minimization either.

If you are willing to modify both the declaration and the DTD, even more dramatic minimizations are possible, including completely omitted tags and "shortcut" markup.

Removing Minimizations

Although we've made a point of reminding you about which of these minimization features are not valid in XML, that's not really a sufficient reason to avoid using them. (The fact that many of the minimization features can lead to confusing, difficult-to-author documents might be.)

If you want to convert one of these documents to XML at some point in the future, you can run it through a program like *sgmlnorm*, which will remove all the minimizations and insert the correct, verbose markup. The *sgmlnorm* program is part of the SP and Jade distributions (*http://www.jclark.com/*), which are on the CD-ROM.

Making an XML Document

In order to create DocBook documents in XML, you'll need an XML version of DocBook. We've included one on the CD, but it hasn't been officially adopted by the OASIS DocBook Technical Committee yet. If you're interested in the technical details, Appendix B, *DocBook and XML*, describes the specific differences between SGML and XML versions of DocBook.

XML, like SGML, requires a specific prologue in your document. The following sections describe the features of the XML prologue.

An XML Declaration

XML documents should begin with an XML declaration. Unlike the SGML declaration, which is a grab bag of features, the XML declaration identifies a few simple aspects of the document:

```
<?xml version="1.0" standalone="no"?>
```

Identifying the version of XML ensures that future changes to the XML specification will not alter the semantics of this document. The standalone declaration simply makes explicit the fact that this document cannot "stand alone," and that it relies on an external DTD. The complete details of the XML declaration are described in the XML specification (*http://www.w3.org/TR/REC-xml*).

A Document Type Declaration

Strictly speaking, XML documents don't require a DTD. Realistically, DocBook XML documents will have one.

The document type declaration identifies the DTD that will be used by the document and what the root element of the document will be. A typical doctype declaration for a DocBook document looks like this:

```
<?xml version='1.0'?>
<!DOCTYPE book PUBLIC "-//Norman Walsh//DTD DocBk XML V3.1.4//EN"
                      "http://nwalsh.com/docbook/xml/3.1.4/db3xml.dtd">
```

This declaration indicates that the root element will be <book> and that the DTD used will be the one indentified by the public identifier `-//Norman Walsh//DTD DocBk XML V3.1.4//EN`. External declarations in XML must include a system identifier (the public identifier is optional). In this example, the DTD is stored on a web server.

System identifiers in XML must be URIs. Many systems may accept filenames and interpret them locally as `file:` URLs, but it's always correct to fully qualify them.

An Internal Subset

It's also possible to provide additional declarations in a document by placing them in the document type declaration:

```
<?xml version='1.0'?>
<!DOCTYPE book PUBLIC "-//Norman Walsh//DTD DocBk XML V3.1.4/EN"
                      "http://nwalsh.com/docbook/xml/3.1.4/db3xml.dtd" [
<!ENTITY nwalsh "Norman Walsh">
<!ENTITY chap1 SYSTEM "chap1.sgm">
<!ENTITY chap2 SYSTEM "chap2.sgm">
]>
```

These declarations form what is known as the internal subset. The declarations stored in the file referenced by the public or system identifier in the `DOCTYPE` declaration is called the external subset, which is technically optional. It is legal to put the DTD in the internal subset and to have no external subset, but for a DTD as large as DocBook, that would make very little sense.

NOTE The internal subset is parsed *first* in XML and, if multiple declarations for an entity occur, the first declaration is used. Declarations in the internal subset override declarations in the external subset.

The Document (or Root) Element

Although comments and processing instructions may occur between the document type declaration and the root element, the root element usually immediately follows the document type declaration:

```
<?xml version='1.0'?>
<!DOCTYPE book PUBLIC "-//Norman Walsh//DTD DocBk XML V3.1.4//EN"
                      "http://nwalsh.com/docbook/xml/3.1.4/db3xml.dtd" [
<!ENTITY nwalsh "Norman Walsh">
<!ENTITY chap1 SYSTEM "chap1.sgm">
<!ENTITY chap2 SYSTEM "chap2.sgm">
]>
<book>...</book>
```

The important point is that the root element must be physically present immediately after the document type declaration. You cannot place the root element of the document in an external entity.

Typing an XML Document

If you are entering SGML using a text editor such as Emacs or vi, there are a few things to keep in mind. Using a structured text editor designed for XML hides most of these issues.

- In XML, all markup is case-sensitive. In the XML version of DocBook, you must always type all element, attribute, and entity names in lowercase.
- You are required to quote all attribute values in XML.

  When quoting attribute values, you can use either a straight single quote ('), or a straight double quote ("). Don't use the "curly" quotes (" and ") in your editing tool.
- Empty elements in XML are marked with a distinctive syntax: `<xref/>`.
- Processing instructions in XML begin and end with a question mark: `<?pitarget data?>`.
- XML was designed to be served, received, and processed over the Web. Two of its most important design principles are ease of implementation and interoperability with both SGML and HTML.

  The markup minimization features in SGML documents make it more difficult to process, and harder to write a parser to interpret it; these minimization features also run counter to the XML design principles named above. As a result, XML does not support them.

  Luckily, a good authoring environment can offer all of the features of markup minimization without interfering with the interoperability of documents. And because XML tools are easier to write, it's likely that good, inexpensive XML authoring environments will be available eventually.

XML and SGML Markup Considerations in This Book

Conceptually, almost everything in this book applies equally to SGML and XML. But because DocBook V3.1 is an SGML DTD, we naturally tend to use SGML conventions in our writing. If you're primarily interested in XML, there are just a few small details to keep in mind.

- XML is case-sensitive, while the SGML version of DocBook is not. In this book, we've chosen to present the element names using mixed case (**Book**, **indexterm**, **XRef**, and so on), but in the DocBook XML DTD, all element, attribute, and entity names are strictly lowercase.
- Empty element start tags in XML are marked with a distinctive syntax: `<xref/>`. In SGML, the trailing slash is not present, so some of our examples need slight revisions to be valid XML elements.

- Processing instructions in XML begin and end with a question mark: `<?pitar-get data?>`. In SGML, the trailing question mark is not present, so some of our examples need slight revisions to be valid XML elements.
- Generally we use public identifiers in examples, but whenever system identifiers are used, don't forget that XML system identifiers must be Uniform Resource Indicators (URIs), in which SGML system identifiers are usually simple filenames.

For a more detailed discussion of DocBook and XML, see Appendix B.

Public Identifiers, System Identifiers, and Catalog Files

When a DTD or other external file is referenced from a document, the reference can be specified in three ways: using a *public identifier*, a *system identifier*, or both. In XML, the system identifier is *generally* required and the public identifier is optional. In SGML, neither is required, but at least one must be present.*

A public identifier is a globally unique, abstract name, such as the following, which is the official public identifier for DocBook V3.1:

```
-//OASIS//DTD DocBook V3.1//EN
```

The introduction of XML has added some small complications to system identifiers. In SGML, a system identifier generally points to a single, local version of a file using local system conventions. In XML, it must point with a Uniform Resource Indicator (URI). The most common URI today is the Uniform Resource Locator (URL), which is familiar to anyone who browses the Web. URLs are a lot like SGML system identifiers, because they generally point to a single version of a file on a particular machine. In the future, Uniform Resource Names (URN), another form of URI, will allow XML system identifiers to have the abstract characteristics of public identifiers.

The following filename is an example of an SGML system identifier:

```
/usr/local/sgml/docbook/3.1/docbook.dtd
```

An equivalent XML system identifier might be:

```
file:///usr/local/sgml/docbook/3.1/docbook.dtd
```

The advantage of using the public identifier is that it makes your documents more portable. For any system on which DocBook is installed, the public identifier will resolve to the appropriate local version of the DTD (if public identifiers can be resolved at all).

* This is not absolutely true. SGML allows for the possibility that the reference could be implied by the application, but this is very rarely the case.

Public identifiers have two disadvantages:

- Because XML does not require them, and because system identifiers are required, developing XML tools may not provide adequate support for public identifiers. To work with these systems you must use system identifiers.
- Public identifiers aren't magical. They're simply a method of indirection. For them to work, there must be a resolution mechanism for public identifiers. Luckily, several years ago, SGML Open (now OASIS (*http://www.oasis-open.org/*)) described a standard mechanism for mapping public identifiers to system identifers using catalog files.

  See OASIS Technical Resolution 9401:1997 (Amendment 2 to TR 9401). (*http://www.oasis-open.org/html/a401.htm*)

Public Identifiers

An important characteristic of public identifiers is that they are *globally unique.* Referring to a document with a public identifier should mean that the identifier will resolve to the same actual document on any system even though the location of that document on each system may vary. As a rule, you should never reuse public identifiers, and a published revision should have a new public identifier. Not following these rules defeats one purpose of the public identifier.

A public identifier can be any string of upper- and lowercase letters, digits, any of the following symbols: "'", "(", ")", "+", ",", "-", ".", "/", ":", "=", "?", and white space, including line breaks.

Formal public identifiers

Most public identifiers conform to the ISO 8879 standard that defines *formal public identifiers.* Formal public identifiers, frequently referred to as FPI, have a prescribed format that can ensure uniqueness:*

```
prefix//owner-identifier//text-class text-description//language//display-version
```

Here are descriptions of the identifiers in this string:

`prefix`
: The `prefix` is either a "+" or a "-" Registered public identifiers begin with "+"; unregistered identifiers begin with "-".

  (ISO standards sometimes use a third form beginning with `ISO` and the standard number, but this form is only available to ISO.)

* Essentially, it can ensure that two different owners won't accidentally tread on each other. Nothing can prevent a given owner from reusing public identifiers, except maybe common sense.

The purpose of registration is to guarantee a unique owner-identifier. There are few authorities with the power to issue registered public identifiers, so in practice unregistered identifiers are more common.

The Graphics Communication Association (*http://www.gca.org/*) (GCA) can assign registered public identifiers. They do this by issuing the applicant a unique string and declaring the format of the owner identifier. For example, the Davenport Group was issued the string "A00002" and could have published DocBook using an FPI of the following form:

```
+//ISO/IEC 9070/RA::A00002//...
```

Another way to use a registered public identifier is to use the format reserved for internet domain names. For example, O'Reilly can issue documents using an FPI of the following form:

```
+//IDN oreilly.com//...
```

As of DocBook V3.1, the OASIS Technical Committee responsible for DocBook has elected to use the unregistered owner identifier, `OASIS`, thus its prefix is `-`.

```
-//OASIS//...
```

`owner-identifier`

Identifies the person or organization that owns the identifier. Registration guarantees a unique owner identifier. Short of registration, some effort should be made to ensure that the owner identifier is globally unique. A company name, for example, is a reasonable choice as are Internet domain names. It's also not uncommon to see the names of individuals used as the owner-identifier, although clearly this may introduce collisions over time.

The owner-identifier for DocBook V3.1 is `OASIS`. Earlier versions used the owner-identifier `Davenport`.

`text-class`

The text class identifies the kind of document that is associated with this public identifier. Common text classes are

DOCUMENT

An SGML or XML document.

DTD

A DTD or part of a DTD.

ELEMENTS

A collection of element declarations.

ENTITIES

A collection of entity declarations.

NONSGML
Data that is not in SGML or XML.

DocBook is a DTD, thus its text class is DTD.

`text-description`
This field provides a description of the document. The text description is free-form, but cannot include the string //.

The text description of DocBook is `DocBook V3.1`.

In the uncommon case of unavailable public texts (FPIs for proprietary DTDs, for example), there are a few other options available (technically in front of or in place of the text description), but they're rarely used.*

`language`
Indicates the language in which the document is written. It is recommended that the ISO standard two-letter language codes be used if possible.

DocBook is an English-language DTD, thus its language is `EN`.

`display-version`
This field, which is not frequently used, distinguishes between public texts that are the same except for the display device or system to which they apply.

For example, the FPI for the ISO Latin 1 character set is:

```
-//ISO 8879-1986//ENTITIES Added Latin 1//EN
```

A reasonable FPI for an XML version of this character set is:

```
-//ISO 8879-1986//ENTITIES Added Latin 1//EN//XML
```

System Identifiers

System identifiers are usually filenames on the local system. In SGML, there's no constraint on what they can be. Anything that your SGML processing system recognizes is allowed. In XML, system identifiers must be URIs (Uniform Resource Identifiers).

The use of URIs as system identifiers introduces the possibility that a system identifier can be a URN. This allows the system identifier to benefit from the same global uniqueness benefit as the public identifier. It seems likely that XML system identifiers will eventually move in this direction.

Catalog Files

Catalog files are the standard mechanism for resolving public identifiers into system identifiers. Some resolution mechanism is necessary because DocBook refers to its

* See Appendix A of Maler and El Andaloussi, *Developing SGML DTDs*, for more details.

component modules with public identifiers, and those must be mapped to actual files on the system before any piece of software can actually load them.

The catalog file format was defined in 1994 by SGML Open (now OASIS). The formal specification is contained in OASIS Technical Resolution 9401:1997.

Informally, a catalog is a text file that contains a number of keyword/value pairs. The most frequently used keywords are `PUBLIC`, `SYSTEM`, `SGMLDECL`, `DTDDECL`, `CATALOG`, `OVERRIDE`, `DELEGATE`, and `DOCTYPE`.

`PUBLIC`
: The `PUBLIC` keyword maps public identifiers to system identifiers:

```
PUBLIC "-//OASIS//DTD DocBook V3.1//EN" "docbook/3.1/docbook.dtd"
```

`SYSTEM`
: The `SYSTEM` keyword maps system identifiers to system identifiers:

```
SYSTEM "http://nwalsh.com/docbook/xml/1.3/db3xml.dtd"
   "docbook/xml/1.3/dbo3xml.dtd"
```

`SGMLDECL`
: The `SGMLDECL` keyword identifies the system identifier of the SGML Declaration that should be used:

```
SGMLDECL "docbook/3.1/docbook.dcl"
```

`DTDDECL`
: Like `SGMLDECL`, `DTDDECL` identifies the SGML Declaration that should be used. `DTDDECL` associates a declaration with a particular public identifier for a DTD:

```
DTDDECL "-//OASIS//DTD DocBook V3.1//EN" "docbook/3.1/docbook.dcl"
```

Unfortunately, it is not supported by the free tools that are available. The practical benefit of `DTDDECL` can usually be achieved, albeit in a slightly cumbersome way, with multiple catalog files.

`CATALOG`
: The `CATALOG` keyword allows one catalog to include the content of another. This can make maintenance somewhat easier and allows a system to directly use the catalog files included in DTD distributions. For example, the DocBook distribution includes a catalog file. Rather than copying each of the declarations in that catalog into your system catalog, you can simply include the contents of the DocBook catalog:

```
CATALOG "docbook/3.1/catalog"
```

`OVERRIDE`
: The `OVERRIDE` keyword indicates whether or not public identifiers override system identifiers. If a given declaration includes both a system identifer and a

public identifier, most systems attempt to process the document referenced by the system identifier, and consequently ignore the public identifier. Specifying

```
OVERRIDE YES
```

in the catalog informs the processing system that resolution should be attempted first with the public identifier.

DELEGATE
: The DELEGATE keyword allows you to specify that some set of public identifiers should be resolved by another catalog. Unlike the CATALOG keyword, which loads the referenced catalog, DELEGATE does nothing until an attempt is made to resolve a public identifier.

The DELEGATE entry specifies a partial public identifier and an alternate catalog:

```
DELEGATE "-//OASIS" "/usr/sgml/oasis/catalog"
```

Partial public identifers are simply initial substring matches. Given the preceding entry, if an attempt is made to match any public identifier that begins with the string `-//OASIS`, the alternate catalog */usr/sgml/oasis/catalog* will be used instead of the current catalog.

DOCTYPE
: The DOCTYPE keyword allows you to specify a default system identifier. If an SGML document begins with a DOCTYPE declaration that specifies neither a public identifier nor a system identifier (or is missing a DOCTYPE declaration altogether), the DOCTYPE declaration may provide a default:

```
DOCTYPE BOOK n:/share/sgml/docbook/3.1/docbook.dtd
```

A small fragment of an actual catalog file is shown in Example 2-1.

Example 2-1. A Sample Catalog

```
-- Comments are delimited by pairs of double-hyphens,         ❶
   as in SGML and XML comments. --

OVERRIDE YES                                                  ❷

SGMLDECL "n:/share/sgml/docbook/3.1/docbook.dcl"              ❸

DOCTYPE  BOOK  n:/share/sgml/docbook/3.1/docbook.dtd          ❹

PUBLIC "-//OASIS//DTD DocBook V3.1//EN"                       ❺
  n:/share/sgml/docbook/3.1/docbook.dtd

SYSTEM "http://nwalsh.com/docbook/xml/1.3/db3xml.dtd"         ❻
  n:/share/sgml/Norman_Walsh/db3xml/db3xml.dtd
```

❶ Catalog files may also include comments.

❷ This catalog specifies that public identifiers should be used in favor of system identifiers, if both are present.

❸ The default declaration specified by this catalog is the DocBook declaration.

❹ Given an explicit (or implied) SGML `DOCTYPE` of

```
<!DOCTYPE BOOK SYSTEM>
```

use *n:/share/sgml/docbook/3.1/docbook.dtd* as the default system identifier. Note that this can only apply to SGML documents because the DOCTYPE declaration above is not a valid XML element.

❺ Map the OASIS public identifer to the local copy of the DocBook V3.1 DTD.

❻ Map a system identifer for the XML version of DocBook to a local version.

A few notes:

- It's not uncommon to have several catalog files. See below, "Locating catalog files".
- Like attributes on elements you can quote, the public identifier and system identifier are surrounded by either single or double quotes.
- White space in the catalog file is generally irrelevant. You can use spaces, tabs, or new lines between keywords and their arguments.
- When a relative system identifier is used, it is considered to be relative to the location of the catalog file, not the document being processed.

Locating catalog files

Catalog files go a long way towards making documents more portable by introducing a level of indirection. A problem still remains, however: how does a processor locate the appropriate catalog file(s)? OASIS outlines a complete interchange packaging scheme, but for most applications the answer is simply that the processor looks for a file called *catalog* or *CATALOG*.

Some applications allow you to specify a list of directories that should be examined for catalog files. Other tools allow you to specify the actual files.

Note that even if a list of directories or catalog files is provided, applications may still load catalog files that occur in directories in which other documents are found. For example, SP and Jade always load the catalog file that occurs in the directory in which a DTD or document resides, even if that directory is not on the catalog file list.

Physical Divisions: Breaking a Document into Physical Chunks

The rest of this chapter describes how you can break documents into logical chunks, such as books, chapters, sections, and so on. Before we begin, and while the subject of the internal subset is fresh in your mind, let's take a quick look at how to break documents into separate physical chunks.

Actually, we've already told you how to do it. If you recall, in the preceding sections we had declarations of the form:

```
<!ENTITY name SYSTEM "filename">
```

If you refer to the entity ***name*** in your document after this declaration, the system will insert the contents of the file ***filename*** into your document at that point. So, if you've got a book that consists of three chapters and two appendixes, you might create a file called *book.sgm*, which looks like this:

```
<!DOCTYPE book PUBLIC "-//OASIS//DTD DocBook V3.1//EN" [
<!ENTITY chap1 SYSTEM "chap1.sgm">
<!ENTITY chap2 SYSTEM "chap2.sgm">
<!ENTITY chap3 SYSTEM "chap3.sgm">
<!ENTITY appa SYSTEM "appa.sgm">
<!ENTITY appb SYSTEM "appb.sgm">
]>
<book><title>My First Book</title>
&chap1;
&chap2;
&chap3;
&appa;
&appb;
</book>
```

You can then write the chapters and appendixes conveniently in separate files. Note that these files do not and must not have document type declarations.

For example, Chapter 1 might begin like this:

```
<chapter id="ch1"><title>My First Chapter</title>
<para>My first paragraph.</para>
```

But it should not begin with its own document type declaration:

```
<!DOCTYPE chapter PUBLIC "-//OASIS//DTD DocBook V3.1//EN">
<chapter id="ch1"><title>My First Chapter</title>
<para>My first paragraph.</para>
```

Logical Divisions: The Categories of Elements in DocBook

DocBook elements can be divided broadly into these categories:

- Sets
- Books
- Divisions, which divide books into parts
- Components, which divide books or divisions into chapters
- Sections, which subdivide components
- Meta-information elements
- Block elements
- Inline elements

In the rest of this section, we'll describe briefly the elements that make up these categories. This section is designed to give you an overview. It is not an exhaustive list of every element in DocBook.

For more information about any specific element and the elements that it may contain, consult the reference page for the element in question.

Sets

A **Set** contains two or more **Books**. It's the hierarchical top of DocBook. You use the **Set** tag, for example, for a series of books on a single subject that you want to access and maintain as a single unit, such as the manuals for an airplane engine or the documentation for a programming language.

Books

A **Book** is probably the most common top-level element in a document. The DocBook definition of a book is very loose and general. Given the variety of books authored with DocBook and the number of different conventions for book organization used in countries around the world, attempting to impose a strict ordering of elements can make the content model extremely complex. But DocBook gives you free reign. It's very reasonable to use a local customization layer to impose a more strict ordering for your applications.

Books consist of a mixture of the following elements:

Dedication

Dedication pages almost always occur at the front of a book.

Navigational Components

There are a few component-level elements designed for navigation: **ToC**, for Tables of Contents; **LoT**, for Lists of Titles (for lists of figures, tables, examples, and so on); and **Index**, for indexes.

Divisions

Divisions are the first hierarchical level below **Book**. They contain **Parts** and **References**. **Parts**, in turn, contain components. **References** contain **RefEntrys**. These are discussed more thoroughly in "Making a Reference Page".

Books can contain components directly and are not required to contain divisions.

Components

These are the chapter-like elements of a **Book**.

Components

Components are the chapter-like elements of a **Book** or **Part**: **Preface**, **Chapter**, **Appendix**, **Glossary**, and **Bibliography**. **Articles** can also occur at the component level. We describe **Articles** in more detail in the section titled "Making an Article". Components generally contain block elements and/or sections, and some can contain navigational components and **RefEntrys**.

Sections

There are several flavors of sectioning elements in DocBook:

Sect1…Sect5 elements

The **Sect1**…**Sect5** elements are the most common sectioning elements. They can occur in most component-level elements. These numbered section elements must be properly nested (**Sect2**s can only occur inside **Sect1**s, **Sect3**s can only occur inside **Sect2**s, and so on). There are five levels of numbered sections.

Section element

The **Section** element, introduced in DocBook V3.1, is an alternative to numbered sections. **Sections** are recursive, meaning that you can nest them to any depth desired.

SimpleSect element

In addition to numbered sections, there's the **SimpleSect** element. It is a terminal section that can occur at any level, but it cannot have any other sectioning element nested within it.

BridgeHead

A **BridgeHead** provides a section title without any containing section.

RefSect1...RefSect3 elements
: These elements, which occur only in **RefEntrys**, are analogous to the numbered section elements in components. There are only three levels of numbered section elements in a **RefEntry**.

GlossDiv, BiblioDiv, and IndexDiv
: **Glossarys**, **Bibliographys**, and **Indexes** can be broken into top-level divisions, but not sections. Unlike sections, these elements do not nest.

Meta-Information

All of the elements at the section level and above include a wrapper for meta-information about the content. See, for example, **BookInfo**.

The meta-information wrapper is designed to contain bibliographic information about the content (**Author**, **Title**, **Publisher**, and so on) as well as other meta-information such as revision histories, keyword sets, and index terms.

Block Elements

The block elements occur immediately below the component and sectioning elements. These are the (roughly) paragraph-level elements in DocBook. They can be divided into a number of categories: lists, admonitions, line-specific environments, synopses of several sorts, tables, figures, examples, and a dozen or more miscellaneous elements.

Block vs. Inline Elements

At the paragraph-level, it's convenient to divide elements into two classes, *block* and *inline*. From a structural point of view, this distinction is based loosely on their relative size, but it's easiest to describe the difference in terms of their presentation.

Block elements are usually presented with a paragraph (or larger) break before and after them. Most can contain other block elements, and many can contain character data and inline elements. Paragraphs, lists, sidebars, tables, and block quotations are all common examples of block elements.

Inline elements are generally represented without any obvious breaks. The most common distinguishing mark of inline elements is a font change, but inline elements may present no visual distinction at all. Inline elements contain character data and possibly other inline elements, but they never contain block elements. Inline elements are used to mark up data such as cross references, filenames, commands, options, subscripts and superscripts, and glossary terms.

Lists

There are seven list elements in DocBook:

CalloutList
: A list of **CallOuts** and their descriptions. **CallOuts** are marks, frequently numbered and typically on a graphic or verbatim environment, that are described in a **CalloutList**, outside the element in which they occur.

GlossList
: A list of glossary terms and their definitions.

ItemizedList
: An unordered (bulleted) list. There are attributes to control the marks used.

OrderedList
: A numbered list. There are attributes to control the type of enumeration.

SegmentedList
: A repeating set of named items. For example, a list of states and their capitals might be represented as a **SegmentedList**.

SimpleList
: An unadorned list of items. **SimpleLists** can be inline or arranged in columns.

VariableList
: A list of terms and definitions or descriptions. (This list of list types is a **VariableList**.)

Admonitions

There are five types of admonitions in DocBook: **Caution**, **Important**, **Note**, **Tip**, and **Warning**.

All of the admonitions have the same structure: an optional **Title** followed by paragraph-level elements. The DocBook DTD does not impose any specific semantics on the individual admonitions. For example, DocBook does not mandate that **Warnings** be reserved for cases where bodily harm can result.

Line-specific environments

These environments preserve whitespace and line breaks in the source text. DocBook does not provide the equivalent of HTML's **BR** tag, so there's no way to interject a line break into normal running text.

Address
: The **Address** element is intended for postal addresses. In addition to being line-specific, **Address** contains additional elements suitable for marking up names and addresses.

LiteralLayout

A **LiteralLayout** does not have any semantic association beyond the preservation of whitespace and line breaks. In particular, while **ProgramListing** and **Screen** are frequently presented in a fixed-width font, a change of fonts is not necessarily implied by **LiteralLayout**.

ProgramListing

A **ProgramListing** is a verbatim environment, usually presented in Courier or some other fixed-width font, for program sources, code fragments, and similar listings.

Screen

A **Screen** is a verbatim or literal environment for text screen-captures, other fragments of an ASCII display, and similar things. **Screen** is also a frequent catch-all for any verbatim text.

ScreenShot

ScreenShot is actually a wrapper for a **Graphic** intended for screen shots of a GUI for example.

Synopsis

A **Synopsis** is a verbatim environment for command and function synopsis.

Examples, figures, and tables

Examples, Figures, and Tables are common block-level elements: **Example**, **InformalExample**, **Figure**, **InformalFigure**, **Table**, and **InformalTable**.

The distinction between formal and informal elements is that formal elements have titles while informal ones do not. The **InformalFigure** element was introduced in DocBook V3.1. In prior versions of DocBook, you could only achieve the effect of an informal figure by placing its content, unwrapped, at the location where the informal figure was desired.

Paragraphs

There are three paragraph elements: **Para**, **SimPara** (simple paragraphs may not contain other block-level elements), and **FormalPara** (formal paragraphs have titles).

Equations

There are two block-equation elements, **Equation** and **InformalEquation** (for inline equations, use **InlineEquation**).

Informal equations don't have titles. For reasons of backward-compatibility, **Equations** are not required to have titles. However, it may be more difficult for some stylesheet languages to properly enumerate **Equations** if they lack titles.

Graphics

Graphics occur most frequently in **Figures** and **ScreenShots**, but they can also occur without a wrapper. DocBook considers a **Graphic** a block element, even if it appears to occur inline. For graphics that you want to be represented inline, use **InlineGraphic**.

DocBook V3.1 introduced a new element to contain graphics and other media types: **MediaObject** and its inline cousin, **InlineMediaObject**. These elements may contain video, audio, image, and text data. A single media object can contain several alternative forms from which the presentation system can select the most appropriate object.

Questions and answers

DocBook V3.1 introduced the **QandASet** element, which is suitable for FAQs (Frequently Asked Questions) and other similar collections of **Questions** and **Answers**.

Miscellaneous block elements

The following block elements are also available:

BlockQuote
: A block quotation. Block quotations may have **Attributions**.

CmdSynopsis
: An environment for marking up all the parameters and options of a command.

Epigraph
: A short introduction, typically a quotation, at the beginning of a document. **Epigraphs** may have **Attributions**.

FuncSynopsis
: An environment for marking up the return value and arguments of a function.

Highlights
: A summary of the main points discussed in a book component (chapter, section, and so on).

MsgSet
: A set of related error messages.

Procedure
: A procedure. Procedures contain **Steps**, which may contain **SubSteps**.

Sidebar
: A sidebar.

Inline Elements

Users of DocBook are provided with a surfeit of inline elements. Inline elements are used to mark up running text. In published documents, inline elements often cause a font change or other small change, but they do not cause line or paragraph breaks.

In practice, writers generally settle on the tagging of inline elements that suits their time and subject matter. This may be a large number of elements or only a handful. What is important is that you choose to mark up not every possible item, but only those for which distinctive tagging will be useful in the production of the finished document for the readers who will search through it.

The following comprehensive list may be a useful tool for the process of narrowing down the elements that you will choose to mark up; it is not intended to overwhelm you by its sheer length. For convenience, we've divided the inlines into several subcategories.

The classification used here is not meant to be authoritative, only helpful in providing a feel for the nature of the inlines. Several elements appear in more than one category, and arguments could be made to support the placement of additional elements in other categories or entirely new categories.

Traditional publishing inlines

These inlines identify things that commonly occur in general writing:

Abbrev
: An abbreviation, especially one followed by a period.

Acronym
: An often pronounceable word made from the initial (or selected) letters of a name or phrase.

Emphasis
: Emphasized text.

Footnote
: A footnote. The location of the **Footnote** element identifies the location of the first reference to the footnote. Additional references to the same footnote can be inserted with **FootnoteRef**.

Phrase
: A span of text.

Quote
: An inline quotation.

Trademark
: A trademark.

Cross references

The cross reference inlines identify both explicit cross references, such as **Link**, and implicit cross references like **GlossTerm**. You can make the most of the implicit references explicit with a `LinkEnd` attribute.

Anchor
: A spot in the document.

Citation
: An inline bibliographic reference to another published work.

CiteRefEntry
: A citation to a reference page.

CiteTitle
: The title of a cited work.

FirstTerm
: The first occurrence of a term.

GlossTerm
: A glossary term.

Link
: A hypertext link.

OLink
: A link that addresses its target indirectly, through an entity.

ULink
: A link that addresses its target by means of a URL (Uniform Resource Locator).

XRef
: A cross reference to another part of the document.

Markup

These inlines are used to mark up text for special presentation:

ForeignPhrase
: A word or phrase in a language other than the primary language of the document.

WordAsWord
: A word meant specifically as a word and not representing anything else.

ComputerOutput
: Data, generally text, displayed or presented by a computer.

Literal
: Inline text that is some literal value.

Markup
: A string of formatting markup in text that is to be represented literally.

Prompt
: A character or string indicating the start of an input field in a computer display.

Replaceable
: Content that may or must be replaced by the user.

SGMLTag
: A component of SGML markup.

UserInput
: Data entered by the user.

Mathematics

DocBook does not define a complete set of elements for representing equations. No one has ever pressed the DocBook maintainers to add this functionality, and the prevailing opinion is that incorporating MathML (*http://www.w3.org/TR/REC-MathML/*) using a mechanism like namespaces (*http://www.w3.org/TR/REC-xml-names/*) is probably the best long-term solution.

InlineEquation
: A mathematical equation or expression occurring inline.

Subscript
: A subscript (as in H_2O, the molecular formula for water).

Superscript
: A superscript (as in x^2, the mathematical notation for x multiplied by itself).

User interfaces

These elements describe aspects of a user interface:

Accel
: A graphical user interface (GUI) keyboard shortcut.

GUIButton
: The text on a button in a GUI.

GUIIcon
: Graphic and/or text appearing as a icon in a GUI.

GUILabel
: The text of a label in a GUI.

GUIMenu
: The name of a menu in a GUI.

GUIMenuItem
: The name of a terminal menu item in a GUI.

GUISubmenu
: The name of a submenu in a GUI.

KeyCap
: The text printed on a key on a keyboard.

KeyCode
: The internal, frequently numeric, identifier for a key on a keyboard.

KeyCombo
: A combination of input actions.

KeySym
: The symbolic name of a key on a keyboard.

MenuChoice
: A selection or series of selections from a menu.

MouseButton
: The conventional name of a mouse button.

Shortcut
: A key combination for an action that is also accessible through a menu.

Programming languages and constructs

Many of the technical inlines in DocBook are related to programming.

Action
: A response to a user event.

ClassName
: The name of a class, in the object-oriented programming sense.

Constant
: A programming or system constant.

ErrorCode
: An error code.

ErrorName
: An error message.

ErrorType
: The classification of an error message.

Function
: The name of a function or subroutine, as in a programming language.

Interface
: An element of a GUI.

InterfaceDefinition
: The name of a formal specification of a GUI.

Literal
: Inline text that is some literal value.

MsgText
: The actual text of a message component in a message set.

Parameter
: A value or a symbolic reference to a value.

Property
: A unit of data associated with some part of a computer system.

Replaceable
: Content that may or must be replaced by the user.

ReturnValue
: The value returned by a function.

StructField
: A field in a structure (in the programming language sense).

StructName
: The name of a structure (in the programming language sense).

Symbol
: A name that is replaced by a value before processing.

Token
: A unit of information.

Type
: The classification of a value.

VarName
: The name of a variable.

Operating systems

These inlines identify parts of an operating system, or an operating environment:

Application
: The name of a software program.

Command
: The name of an executable program or other software command.

EnVar
: A software environment variable.

Filename
: The name of a file.

MediaLabel
: A name that identifies the physical medium on which some information resides.

MsgText
: The actual text of a message component in a message set.

Option
: An option for a software command.

Parameter
: A value or a symbolic reference to a value.

Prompt
: A character or string indicating the start of an input field in a computer display.

SystemItem
: A system-related item or term.

General purpose

There are also a number of general-purpose technical inlines.

Application
: The name of a software program.

Database
: The name of a database, or part of a database.

Email
: An email address.

Filename
: The name of a file.

Hardware
: A physical part of a computer system.

InlineGraphic
: An object containing or pointing to graphical data that will be rendered inline.

Literal
: Inline text that is some literal value.

MediaLabel
: A name that identifies the physical medium on which some information resides.

Option
: An option for a software command.

Optional
: Optional information.

Replaceable
: Content that may or must be replaced by the user.

Symbol
: A name that is replaced by a value before processing.

Token
: A unit of information.

Type
: The classification of a value.

Making a DocBook Book

A typical **Book**, in English at least, consists of some meta-information in a **BookInfo** (**Title**, **Author**, **Copyright**, and so on), one or more **Prefaces**, several **Chapters**, and perhaps a few **Appendixes**. A **Book** may also contain **Bibliographys**, **Glossarys**, **Indexes** and a **Colophon**.

Example 2-2 shows the structure of a typical book. Additional content is required where the ellipses occur.

Example 2-2. A Typical Book

```
<!DOCTYPE book PUBLIC "-//OASIS//DTD DocBook V3.1//EN">
<book>
<bookinfo>
  <title>My First Book</title>
  <author><firstname>Jane</firstname><surname>Doe</surname></author>
  <copyright><year>1998</year><holder>Jane Doe</holder></copyright>
</bookinfo>
<preface><title>Foreword</title> ... </preface>
<chapter> ... </chapter>
<chapter> ... </chapter>
<chapter> ... </chapter>
<appendix> ... </appendix>
<appendix> ... </appendix>
<index> ... </index>
</book>
```

Making a Chapter

Chapters, **Prefaces**, and **Appendixes** all have a similar structure. They consist of a **Title**, possibly some additional meta-information, and any number of block-level elements followed by any number of top-level sections. Each section may in turn contain any number of block-level elements followed by any number from the next section level, as shown in Example 2-3.

Example 2-3. A Typical Chapter

```
<!DOCTYPE chapter PUBLIC "-//OASIS//DTD DocBook V3.1//EN">
<chapter><title>My Chapter</title>
<para> ... </para>
<sect1><title>First Section</title>
<para> ... </para>
<example> ... </example>
</sect1>
</chapter>
```

Making an Article

For documents smaller than a book, such as: journal articles, white papers, or technical notes, **Article** is frequently the most logical starting point. The body of an **Article** is essentially the same as the body of a **Chapter** or any other component-level element, as shown in Example 2-4

Articles may include **Appendixes**, **Bibliographys**, **Indexes** and **Glossarys**.

Example 2-4. A Typical Article

```
<!DOCTYPE article PUBLIC "-//OASIS//DTD DocBook V3.1//EN">
<article>
<artheader>
  <title>My Article</title>
  <author><honorific>Dr</honorific><firstname>Emilio</firstname>
          <surname>Lizardo</surname></author>
</artheader>
<para> ... </para>
<sect1><title>On the Possibility of Going Home</title>
<para> ... </para>
</sect1>
<bibliography> ... </bibliography>
</article>
```

Making a Reference Page

The reference page or manual page in DocBook was inspired by, and in fact designed to reproduce, the common UNIX "manpage" concept. (We use the word "page" loosely here to mean a document of variable length containing reference material on a specific topic.) DocBook is rich in markup tailored for such documents, which often vary greatly in content, however well-structured they may be. To reflect both the structure and the variability of such texts, DocBook specifies that reference pages have a strict sequence of parts, even though several of them are actually optional.

Of the following sequence of elements that may appear in a **RefEntry**, only two are obligatory: **RefNameDiv** and **RefSect1**.

DocInfo

The **DocInfo** element contains meta-information about the reference page (which should not be confused with **RefMeta**, which it precedes). It marks up information about the author of the document, or the product to which it pertains, or the document's revision history, or other such information.

RefMeta

RefMeta contains a title for the reference page (which may be inferred if the **RefMeta** element is not present) and an indication of the volume number in which this reference page occurs. The **ManVolNum** is a very UNIX-centric concept. In traditional UNIX documentation, the subject of a reference page is typically identified by name and volume number; this allows you to distinguish between the *uname* command, "uname(1)" in volume 1 of the documentation and the *uname* function, "uname(3)" in volume 3.

Additional information of this sort such as conformance or vendor information specific to the particular environment you are working in, may be stored in **RefMiscInfo**.

RefNameDiv

The first obligatory element is **RefNameDiv**, which is a wrapper for information about whatever you're documenting, rather than the document itself. It can begin with a **RefDescriptor** if several items are being documented as a group and the group has a name. The **RefNameDiv** must contain at least one **RefName**, that is, the name of whatever you're documenting, and a single short statement that sums up the use or function of the item(s) at a glance: their **RefPurpose**. Also available is the **RefClass**, intended to detail the operating system configurations that the software element in question supports.

If no **RefEntryTitle** is given in the **RefMeta**, the title of the reference page is the **RefDescriptor**, if present, or the first **RefName**.

RefSynopsisDiv

A **RefSynopsisDiv** is intended to provide a quick synopsis of the topic covered by the reference page. For commands, this is generally a syntax summary of the command, and for functions, the function prototype, but other options are possible. A **Title** is allowed, but not required, presumably because the application that processes reference pages will generate the appropriate title if it is not given. In traditional UNIX documentation, its title is always "Synopsis".

RefSect1...RefSect3

Within **RefEntrys**, there are only three levels of sectioning elements: **RefSect1**, **RefSect2**, and **RefSect3**.

Example 2-5 shows the beginning of a **RefEntry** that illustrates one possible reference page:

Example 2-5. A Sample Reference Page

```
<refentry id="printf">

<refmeta>
<refentrytitle>printf</refentrytitle>
<manvolnum>3S</manvolnum>
</refmeta>

<refnamediv>
<refname>printf</refname>
<refname>fprintf</refname>
<refname>sprintf</refname>
<refpurpose>print formatted output</refpurpose>
</refnamediv>

<refsynopsisdiv>

<funcsynopsis>
<funcsynopsisinfo>
#include &lt;stdio.h&gt;
</funcsynopsisinfo>
<funcprototype>
  <funcdef>int <function>printf</function></funcdef>
  <paramdef>const char *<parameter>format</parameter></paramdef>
  <paramdef>...</paramdef>
</funcprototype>

<funcprototype>
  <funcdef>int <function>fprintf</function></funcdef>
  <paramdef>FILE *<parameter>strm</parameter></paramdef>
  <paramdef>const char *<parameter>format</parameter></paramdef>
  <paramdef>...</paramdef>
</funcprototype>

<funcprototype>
  <funcdef>int <function>sprintf</function></funcdef>
  <paramdef>char *<parameter>s</parameter></paramdef>
  <paramdef>const char *<parameter>format</parameter></paramdef>
  <paramdef>...</paramdef>
</funcprototype>
</funcsynopsis>

</refsynopsisdiv>
```

Example 2-5. A Sample Reference Page (continued)

```
<refsect1><title>Description</title>
<para>
<indexterm><primary>functions</primary>
  <secondary>printf</secondary></indexterm>
<indexterm><primary>printing function</primary></indexterm>

<function>printf</function> places output on the standard
output stream stdout.
&hellip;
</para>
```

Making Front- and Backmatter

DocBook contains markup for the usual variety of front- and backmatter necessary for books and articles: indexes, glossaries, bibliographies, and tables of contents. In many cases, these components are generated automatically, at least in part, from your document by an external processor, but you can create them by hand, and in either case, store them in DocBook.

Some forms of backmatter, like indexes and glossaries, usually require additional markup *in the document* to make generation by an application possible. Bibliographies are usually composed by hand like the rest of your text, unless you are automatically selecting bibliographic entries out of some larger database. Our principal concern here is to acquaint you with the kind of markup you need to include in your documents if you want to construct these components.

Frontmatter, like the table of contents, is almost always generated automatically from the text of a document by the processing application. If you need information about how to mark up a table of contents in DocBook, please consult the reference page for ToC.

Making an Index

In some highly-structured documents such as reference manuals, you can automate the whole process of generating an index successfully without altering or adding to the original source. You can design a processing application to select the information and compile it into an adequate index. But this is rare.

In most cases—and even in the case of some reference manuals—a useful index still requires human intervention to mark occurrences of words or concepts that will appear in the text of the index.

Marking index terms

Docbook distinguishes two kinds of index markers: those that are singular and result in a single page entry in the index itself, and those that are multiple and refer to a range of pages.

You put a singular index marker where the subject it refers to actually occurs in your text:

```
<para>
The tiger<indexterm>
<primary>Big Cats</primary>
<secondary>Tigers</secondary></indexterm>
is a very large cat indeed.
</para>
```

This index term has two levels, **primary** and **secondary**. They correspond to an increasing amount of indented text in the resultant index. DocBook allows for three levels of index terms, with the third labeled **tertiary**.

There are two ways that you can index a range of text. The first is to put index marks at both the beginning and end of the discussion. The mark at the beginning asserts that it is the start of a range, and the mark at the end refers back to the beginning. In this way, the processing application can determine what range of text is indexed. Here's the previous tiger example recast as starting and ending index terms:

```
<para>
The tiger<indexterm id="tiger-desc" class="startofrange">
<primary>Big Cats</primary>
<secondary>Tigers</secondary></indexterm>
is a very large cat indeed...
</para>
.
.
.
<para>
So much for tigers<indexterm startref="tiger-desc" class="endofrange">. Let's
talk about
leopards.
</para>
```

Note that the mark at the start of the range identifies itself as the start of a range with the `Class` attribute, and provides an `ID`. The mark at the end of the range points back to the start.

Another way to mark up a range of text is to specify that the entire content of an element, such as a chapter or section, is the complete range. In this case, all you need is for the index term to point to the `ID` of the element that contains the content in question. The `Zone` attribute of **indexterm** provides this functionality.

One of the interesting features of this method is that the actual index marks do not have to occur anywhere near the text being indexed. It is possible to collect all of them together, for example, in one file, but it is not invalid to have the index marker occur near the element it indexes.

Suppose the discussion of tigers in your document comprises a whole text object (like a **Sect1** or a **Chapter**) with an `ID` value of `tiger-desc`. You can put the following tag anywhere in your document to index that range of text:

```
<indexterm zone="tiger-desc">
<primary>Big Cats</primary>
<secondary>Tigers</secondary></indexterm>
```

DocBook also contains markup for index hits that point to other index hits (of the same type such as "See Cats, big" or "See also Lions"). See the reference pages for **See** and **SeeAlso**.

Printing an index

After you have added the appropriate markup to your document, an external application can use this information to build an index. The resulting index must have information about the page numbers on which the concepts appear. It's usually the document formatter that builds the index. In this case, it may never be instantiated in DocBook.

However, there are applications that can produce an index marked up in DocBook. The following example includes some one- and two-level **IndexEntry** elements (which correspond to the primary and secondary levels in the **indexterms** themselves) that begin with the letter D:

```
<!DOCTYPE index PUBLIC "-//OASIS//DTD DocBook V3.1//EN">
<index><title>Index</title>
<indexdiv><title>D</title>
<indexentry>
  <primaryie>database (bibliographic), 253, 255</primaryie>
     <secondaryie>structure, 255</secondaryie>
     <secondaryie>tools, 259</secondaryie>
</indexentry>
<indexentry>
  <primaryie>dates (language specific), 179</primaryie>
</indexentry>
<indexentry>
  <primaryie>DC fonts, <emphasis>172</emphasis>, 177</primaryie>
     <secondaryie>Math fonts, 177</secondaryie>
</indexentry>
</indexdiv>
</index>
```

Making a Glossary

Glossarys, like **Bibliographys**, are often constructed by hand. However, some applications are capable of building a skeletal index from glossary term markup in the document. If all of your terms are defined in some glossary database, it may even be possible to construct the complete glossary automatically.

To enable automatic glossary generation, or simply automatic linking from glossary terms in the text to glossary entries, you must add markup to your documents. In the text, you markup a term for compilation later with the inline **GlossTerm** tag. This tag can have a `LinkEnd` attribute whose value is the ID of the actual entry in the glossary.*

For instance, if you have this markup in your document:

```
<glossterm linkend="xml">Extensible Markup Language</glossterm> is a new
standard...
```

your glossary might look like this:

```
<!DOCTYPE glossary PUBLIC "-//OASIS//DTD DocBook V3.1//EN">
<glossary><title>Example Glossary</title>
.
.
.
<glossdiv><title>E</title>

<glossentry id="xml"><glossterm>Extensible Markup Language</glossterm>
  <acronym>XML</acronym>
<glossdef>
  <para>Some reasonable definition here.</para>
  <glossseealso otherterm="sgml">
</glossdef>
</glossentry>

</glossdiv>
```

Note that the **GlossTerm** tag reappears in the glossary to mark up the term and distinguish it from its definition within the **GlossEntry**. The `ID` that the **GlossEntry** referenced in the text is the ID of the **GlossEntry** in the **Glossary** itself. You can use the link between source and glossary to create a link in the online form of your document, as we have done with the online form of the glossary in this book.

* Some sophisticated formatters might even be able to establish the link simply by examining the content of the terms and the glossary. In that case, the author is not required to make explicit links.

Making a Bibliography

There are two ways to set up a bibliography in DocBook: you can have the data *raw* or *cooked*. Here's an example of a raw bibliographical item, wrapped in the **Biblioentry** element:

```
<biblioentry xreflabel="Kites75">
  <authorgroup>
    <author><firstname>Andrea</firstname><surname>Bahadur</surname></author>
    <author><firstname>Mark</><surname>Shwarek</></author>
  </authorgroup>
  <copyright><year>1974</year><year>1975</year>
     <holder>Product Development International Holding N. V.</holder>
     </copyright>
  <isbn>0-88459-021-6</isbn>
  <publisher>
    <publishername>Plenary Publications International, Inc.</publishername>
  </publisher>
  <title>Kites</title>
  <subtitle>Ancient Craft to Modern Sport</subtitle>
  <pagenums>988-999</pagenums>
  <seriesinfo>
    <title>The Family Creative Workshop</title>
    <seriesvolnums>1-22</seriesvolnums>
    <editor>
      <firstname>Allen</firstname>
      <othername role=middle>Davenport</othername>
      <surname>Bragdon</surname>
      <contrib>Editor in Chief</contrib>
    </editor>
  </seriesinfo>
</biblioentry>
```

The "raw" data in a **Biblioentry** is comprehensive to a fault—there are enough fields to suit a host of different bibliographical styles, and that is the point. An abundance of data requires processing applications to select, punctuate, order, and format the bibliographical data, and it is unlikely that all the information provided will actually be output.

All the "cooked" data in a **Bibliomixed** entry in a bibliography, on the other hand, is intended to be presented to the reader in the form and sequence in which it is provided. It even includes punctuation between the fields of data:

```
<bibliomixed>
  <bibliomset relation=article>
    <surname>Walsh</surname>, <firstname>Norman</firstname>.
    <title role=article>Introduction to Cascading Style Sheets</title>.
  </bibliomset>
  <bibliomset relation=journal>
    <title>The World Wide Web Journal</title>
    <volumenum>2</volumenum><issuenum>1</issuenum>.
    <publishername>O'Reilly & Associates, Inc.</publishername> and
```

```
    <corpname>The World Wide Web Consortium</corpname>.
    <pubdate>Winter, 1996</pubdate></bibliomset>.
</bibliomixed>
```

Clearly, these two ways of marking up bibliographical entries are suited to different circumstances. You should use one or the other for your bibliography, not both. Strictly speaking, mingling the raw and the cooked may be "kosher" as far as the DTD is concerned, but it will almost certainly cause problems for most processing applications.

3

Parsing DocBook Documents

A key feature of SGML and XML markup is that you *validate* it. The DocBook DTD is a precise description of valid nesting, the order of elements, and their content. All DocBook documents must conform to this description or they are not DocBook documents (by definition).

A *validating parser* is a program that can read the DTD and a particular document and determine whether the exact nesting and order of elements in the document is valid according to the DTD.

If you are not using a structured editor that can enforce the markup as you type, validation with an external parser is a particularly important step in the document creation process. You cannot expect to get rational results from subsequent processing (such as document publishing) if your documents are not valid.

The most popular free SGML parser is SP by James Clark, available at *http://www.jclark.com/*.

SP includes *nsgmls*, a fast command-line parser. In the world of free validating XML parsers, IBM AlphaWorks's *xml4j* and James Clark's *xp* are popular choices.

NOTE Not all XML parsers are validating, and although a non-validating parser may have many uses, it cannot ensure that your documents are valid according to the DTD.

Validating Your Documents

The exact way in which the parser is executed varies according to the parser in use, naturally. For information about your particular parser, consult the documentation that came with it.

Using nsgmls

The *nsgmls* command from SP is a validating SGML parser. The options used in the example below suppress the normal output (*-s*), except for error messages, print the version number (*-v*), and specify the catalog file that should be used to map public identifiers to system identifiers. Printing the version number guarantees that you always get *some* output, so that you know the command ran successfully:

```
[n:\dbtdg] nsgmls -sv -c \share\sgml\catalog test.sgm
m:\jade\nsgmls.exe:I: SP version "1.3.2"
```

Because no error messages were printed, we know our document is valid. If you're working with a document that you discover has many errors, the *-f* option offers a handy way to direct the errors to a file so they don't all scroll off your screen.

If you want to validate an XML document with SP, you must make sure that SP uses the correct declaration. An XML declaration called *xml.dcl* is included with SP.

The easiest way to make sure that SP uses *xml.dcl* is to include the declaration explicitly on the command line when you run *nsgmls* (or Jade, or other SP tools):

```
[n:\dbtdg] nsgmls -sv -c \share\sgml\catalog m:\jade\xml.dcl test.xml
m:\jade\nsgmls.exe:I: SP version "1.3.2"
```

Using xml4j

The xml4j distribution includes a sample program called *XJParse* that you can use to test the validity of XML documents:

```
[n:\dbtdg] java samples.XJParse.XJParse -d examples\simple.xml
❶ent/iso-lat2.ent: 49, 27: Warning: Entity name, "inodot", already defined.
This declaration will be ignored.
❷calstblx.dtd: 20, 22: Warning: Entity name, "bodyatt", already defined. This
declaration will be ignored.
calstblx.dtd: 22, 0: Warning: Entity name, "secur", already defined. This
declaration will be ignored.
calstblx.dtd: 44, 48: Warning: Entity name, "tbl.table.name", already defined.
This declaration will be ignored.
calstblx.dtd: 47, 78: Warning: Entity name, "tbl.table.mdl", already defined.
This declaration will be ignored.
calstblx.dtd: 64, 80: Warning: Entity name, "tbl.entry.mdl", already defined.
This declaration will be ignored.
❸<!DOCTYPE chapter PUBLIC "-//Norman Walsh//DTD DocBk XML V3.1.4//EN" "n:/
share/sgml/Norman_Walsh/db31xml/db3xml.dtd">
```

```
<chapter><title>Test Chapter</title>
<para>
This is a paragraph in the test chapter. It is unremarkable in
every regard. This is a paragraph in the test chapter. It is
unremarkable in every regard. This is a paragraph in the test
chapter. It is unremarkable in every regard.
</para>
```

❶ You can ignore the warning message about the duplicate character entity `inodot`. Both the ISO AMS Ordinary Math character entities and the ISO Latin 2 character entities define the `inodot` entity.

❷ Similarly, duplicate entities associated with the *calstblx.mod* module can be ignored. The CALS Table Model is customized by redefining parameter entities. It's part of the design of the DTD fragment.

❸ Finally, if there are no errors, *XJParse* prints the input document. This is an indication that the document is valid.

Using xp

The xp distribution includes several sample programs. One of these programs, *Time*, performs a validating parse of the document and prints the amount of time required to parse the DTD and the document. This program makes an excellent validity checker:

```
java com.jclark.xml.apps.Time examples\simple.xml
6.639
```

The result states that it took 6.639 seconds to parse the DTD and the document. This indicates that the document is valid. If the document is invalid, additional error messages are displayed.

Understanding Parse Errors

Every parser produces slightly different error messages, but most indicate exactly (at least technically)* what is wrong and where the error occurred. With a little experience, this information is all you'll need to quickly identify what's wrong.

In the rest of this section, we'll look at a number of common errors and the messages they produce in SP. We've chosen SP for the rest of these examples because that is the same parser used by Jade, which we'll be discussing further in Chapter 4, *Publishing DocBook Documents.*

* It is often the case that you can correct an error in the document in several ways. The parser suggests one possible fix, but this is not always the right fix. For example, the parser may suggest that you can correct out of context data by adding another element, when in fact it's "obvious" to human eyes that the problem is a missing end tag.

DTD Cannot Be Found

The telltale sign that SP could not find the DTD, or some module of the DTD, is the error message: "cannot generate system identifier for public text ...". Generally, the errors that occur after this are spurious; if SP couldn't find some part of the DTD, it's likely to think that *everything* is wrong.

Careful examination of the following document will show that we've introduced a simple typographic error into the public identifier (the word "DocBook" is misspelled with a lowercase "b"):

```
<!DOCTYPE chapter PUBLIC "-//OASIS//DTD Docbook V3.1//EN">
<chapter><title>Test Chapter</title>
<para>
This is a paragraph in the test chapter. It is unremarkable in
every regard. This is a paragraph in the test chapter. It is
unremarkable in every regard. This is a paragraph in the test
chapter. It is unremarkable in every regard.
</para>
<para>
<emphasis role=bold>This</emphasis> paragraph contains
<emphasis>some <emphasis>emphasized</emphasis> text</emphasis>
and a <superscript>super</superscript>script
and a <subscript>sub</subscript>script.
</para>
<para>
This is a paragraph in the test chapter. It is unremarkable in
every regard. This is a paragraph in the test chapter. It is
unremarkable in every regard. This is a paragraph in the test
chapter. It is unremarkable in every regard.
</para>
</chapter>
```

SP responds dramatically to this error:

```
[n:\dbtdg]nsgmls -sv -c examples\errs\cat1 examples\errs\nodtd.sgm
m:\jade\nsgmls.exe:I: SP version "1.3.2"
m:\jade\nsgmls.exe:examples\errs\nodtd.sgm:1:57:W: cannot generate system
identifier for public text "-//OASIS//DTD Docbook V3.1//EN"
m:\jade\nsgmls.exe:examples\errs\nodtd.sgm:1:57:E: reference to entity
"CHAPTER" for which no system identifier could be generated
m:\jade\nsgmls.exe:examples\errs\nodtd.sgm:1:0: entity was defined here
m:\jade\nsgmls.exe:examples\errs\nodtd.sgm:1:57:E: DTD did not contain element
declaration for document type name
m:\jade\nsgmls.exe:examples\errs\nodtd.sgm:2:8:E: element "CHAPTER" undefined
m:\jade\nsgmls.exe:examples\errs\nodtd.sgm:2:15:E: element "TITLE" undefined
m:\jade\nsgmls.exe:examples\errs\nodtd.sgm:3:5:E: element "PARA" undefined
m:\jade\nsgmls.exe:examples\errs\nodtd.sgm:9:5:E: element "PARA" undefined
m:\jade\nsgmls.exe:examples\errs\nodtd.sgm:10:15:E: there is no attribute
"ROLE"
m:\jade\nsgmls.exe:examples\errs\nodtd.sgm:10:19:E: element "EMPHASIS"
undefined
m:\jade\nsgmls.exe:examples\errs\nodtd.sgm:11:9:E: element "EMPHASIS"
```

```
undefined
m:\jade\nsgmls.exe:examples\errs\nodtd.sgm:11:24:E: element "EMPHASIS"
undefined
m:\jade\nsgmls.exe:examples\errs\nodtd.sgm:12:18:E: element "SUPERSCRIPT"
undefined
m:\jade\nsgmls.exe:examples\errs\nodtd.sgm:13:16:E: element "SUBSCRIPT"
undefined
m:\jade\nsgmls.exe:examples\errs\nodtd.sgm:15:5:E: element "PARA" undefined
```

Other things to look for, if you haven't misspelled the public identifier, are typos in the catalog or failure to specify a catalog that resolves the public identifier that can't be found.

ISO Entity Set Missing

A missing entity set is another example of either a misspelled public identifier, or a missing catalog or catalog entry.

In this case, there's nothing wrong with the document, but the catalog that's been specified is missing the public identifiers for the ISO entity sets:

```
[n:\dbtdg]nsgmls -sv -c examples\errs\cat2 examples\simple.sgm
m:\jade\nsgmls.exe:I: SP version "1.3.2"
m:\jade\nsgmls.exe:n:/share/sgml/docbook/3.1/dbcent.mod:53:65:W: cannot
generate system identifier for public text "ISO 8879:1986//ENTITIES Added Math
Symbols:Arrow Relations//EN"
m:\jade\nsgmls.exe:n:/share/sgml/docbook/3.1/dbcent.mod:54:8:E: reference to
entity "ISOamsa" for which no system identifier could be generated
m:\jade\nsgmls.exe:n:/share/sgml/docbook/3.1/dbcent.mod:52:0: entity was
defined here
m:\jade\nsgmls.exe:n:/share/sgml/docbook/3.1/dbcent.mod:60:66:W: cannot
generate system identifier for public text "ISO 8879:1986//ENTITIES Added Math
Symbols:Binary Operators//EN"
m:\jade\nsgmls.exe:n:/share/sgml/docbook/3.1/dbcent.mod:61:8:E: reference to
entity "ISOamsb" for which no system identifier could be generated
m:\jade\nsgmls.exe:n:/share/sgml/docbook/3.1/dbcent.mod:59:0: entity was
defined here
m:\jade\nsgmls.exe:n:/share/sgml/docbook/3.1/dbcent.mod:67:60:W: cannot
generate system identifier for public text "ISO 8879:1986//ENTITIES Added Math
Symbols:Delimiters//EN"
m:\jade\nsgmls.exe:n:/share/sgml/docbook/3.1/dbcent.mod:68:8:E: reference to
entity "ISOamsc" for which no system identifier could be generated
m:\jade\nsgmls.exe:n:/share/sgml/docbook/3.1/dbcent.mod:66:0: entity was
defined here
m:\jade\nsgmls.exe:n:/share/sgml/docbook/3.1/dbcent.mod:74:67:W: cannot
generate system identifier for public text "ISO 8879:1986//ENTITIES Added Math
Symbols:Negated Relations//EN"
```

The ISO entity sets are required by the DocBook DTD, but they are not distributed with it. That's because they aren't maintained by OASIS.*

* If you need to locate the entity sets, consult *http://www.oasis-open.org/cover/topics.html#entities.*

Character Data Not Allowed Here

Out of context character data is frequently caused by a missing start tag, but sometimes it's just the result of typing in the wrong place!

```
<!DOCTYPE chapter PUBLIC "-//Davenport//DTD DocBook V3.0//EN">
<chapter><title>Test Chapter</title>
<para>
This is a paragraph in the test chapter. It is unremarkable in
every regard. This is a paragraph in the test chapter. It is
unremarkable in every regard. This is a paragraph in the test
chapter. It is unremarkable in every regard.
</para>
You can't put character data here.
<para>
<emphasis role=bold>This</emphasis> paragraph contains
<emphasis>some <emphasis>emphasized</emphasis> text</emphasis>
and a <superscript>super</superscript>script
and a <subscript>sub</subscript>script.
</para>
<para>
This is a paragraph in the test chapter. It is unremarkable in
every regard. This is a paragraph in the test chapter. It is
unremarkable in every regard. This is a paragraph in the test
chapter. It is unremarkable in every regard.
</para>
</chapter>
```

```
[n:\dbtdg] nsgmls -sv -c \share\sgml\catalog examples\errs\badpcdata.sgm
m:\jade\nsgmls.exe:I: SP version "1.3.2"
m:\jade\nsgmls.exe:examples\errs\badpcdata.sgm:9:0:E: character data is not
allowed here
```

Chapters aren't allowed to contain character data directly. Here, a wrapper element, such as **Para**, is missing around the sentence between the first two paragraphs.

Misspelled Start Tag

If you spell it wrong, the parser gets confused.

```
<!DOCTYPE chapter PUBLIC "-//Davenport//DTD DocBook V3.0//EN">
<chapter><title>Test Chapter</title>
<para>
This is a paragraph in the test chapter. It is unremarkable in
every regard. This is a paragraph in the test chapter. It is
unremarkable in every regard. This is a paragraph in the test
chapter. It is unremarkable in every regard.
</para>
<paar>
<emphasis role=bold>This</emphasis> paragraph contains
<emphasis>some <emphasis>emphasized</emphasis> text</emphasis>
and a <superscript>super</superscript>script
and a <subscript>sub</subscript>script.
```

```
</para>
<para>
This is a paragraph in the test chapter. It is unremarkable in
every regard. This is a paragraph in the test chapter. It is
unremarkable in every regard. This is a paragraph in the test
chapter. It is unremarkable in every regard.
</para>
</chapter>


[n:\documents\books\dbtdg]nsgmls -sv -c \share\sgml\catalog examples\errs\
misspe
ll.sgm
m:\jade\nsgmls.exe:I: SP version "1.3.2"
m:\jade\nsgmls.exe:examples\errs\misspell.sgm:9:5:E: element "PAAR" undefined
m:\jade\nsgmls.exe:examples\errs\misspell.sgm:14:6:E: end tag for element
"PARA" which is not open
m:\jade\nsgmls.exe:examples\errs\misspell.sgm:21:9:E: end tag for "PAAR"
omitted, but OMITTAG NO was specified
m:\jade\nsgmls.exe:examples\errs\misspell.sgm:9:0: start tag was here
```

Luckily, these are pretty easy to spot, unless you accidentally spell the name of another element. In that case, your error might appear to be out of context.

Misspelled End Tag

Spelling the end tag wrong is just as confusing.

```
<!DOCTYPE chapter PUBLIC "-//Davenport//DTD DocBook V3.0//EN">
<chapter><title>Test Chapter</titel>
<para>
This is a paragraph in the test chapter. It is unremarkable in
every regard. This is a paragraph in the test chapter. It is
unremarkable in every regard. This is a paragraph in the test
chapter. It is unremarkable in every regard.
</para>
<para>
<emphasis role=bold>This</emphasis> paragraph contains
<emphasis>some <emphasis>emphasized</emphasis> text</emphasis>
and a <superscript>super</superscript>script
and a <subscript>sub</subscript>script.
</para>
<para>
This is a paragraph in the test chapter. It is unremarkable in
every regard. This is a paragraph in the test chapter. It is
unremarkable in every regard. This is a paragraph in the test
chapter. It is unremarkable in every regard.
</para>
</chapter>


[n:\dbtdg]nsgmls -sv -c \share\sgml\catalog examples\errs\misspell2.sgm
m:\jade\nsgmls.exe:I: SP version "1.3.2"
m:\jade\nsgmls.exe:examples\errs\misspell2.sgm:2:35:E: end tag for element
```

```
"TITEL" which is not open
m:\jade\nsgmls.exe:examples\errs\misspell2.sgm:3:5:E: document type does not
allow element "PARA" here; missing one of "FOOTNOTE", "MSGTEXT" start-tag
m:\jade\nsgmls.exe:examples\errs\misspell2.sgm:9:5:E: document type does not
allow element "PARA" here; missing one of "FOOTNOTE", "MSGTEXT" start-tag
m:\jade\nsgmls.exe:examples\errs\misspell2.sgm:15:5:E: document type does not
allow element "PARA" here; missing one of "FOOTNOTE", "MSGTEXT" start-tag
m:\jade\nsgmls.exe:examples\errs\misspell2.sgm:21:9:E: end tag for "TITLE"
omitted, but OMITTAG NO was specified
m:\jade\nsgmls.exe:examples\errs\misspell2.sgm:2:9: start tag was here
m:\jade\nsgmls.exe:examples\errs\misspell2.sgm:21:9:E: end tag for "CHAPTER"
which is not finished
```

These are pretty easy to spot as well, but look at how confused the parser became. From the parser's point of view, failure to close the open **Title** element means that all the following elements appear out of context.

Out of Context Start Tag

Sometimes the problem isn't spelling, but placing a tag in the wrong context. When this happens, the parser tries to figure out what it can add to your document to make it valid. Then it proceeds as if it had seen what was added in order to recover from the error seen, which can cause future errors.

```
<!DOCTYPE chapter PUBLIC "-//Davenport//DTD DocBook V3.0//EN">
<chapter><title>Test Chapter</title>
<para>
This is a paragraph in the test chapter. It is unremarkable in
every regard. This is a paragraph in the test chapter. It is
unremarkable in every regard. This is a paragraph in the test
chapter. It is unremarkable in every regard.
</para>
<para><title>Paragraph With Inlines</title>
<emphasis role=bold>This</emphasis> paragraph contains
<emphasis>some <emphasis>emphasized</emphasis> text</emphasis>
and a <superscript>super</superscript>script
and a <subscript>sub</subscript>script.
</para>
<para>
This is a paragraph in the test chapter. It is unremarkable in
every regard. This is a paragraph in the test chapter. It is
unremarkable in every regard. This is a paragraph in the test
chapter. It is unremarkable in every regard.
</para>
</chapter>
```

```
[n:\dbtdg]nsgmls -sv -c \share\sgml\catalog examples\errs\badstarttag.sgm
m:\jade\nsgmls.exe:I: SP version "1.3.2"
m:\jade\nsgmls.exe:examples\errs\badstarttag.sgm:9:12:E: document type does
not allow element "TITLE" here; missing one of "CALLOUTLIST", "SEGMENTEDLIST",
"VARIABLELIST", "CAUTION", "IMPORTANT", "NOTE", "TIP", "WARNING", "BLOCKQUOTE",
"EQUATION", "EXAMPLE", "FIGURE", "TABLE" start-tag
```

In this example, we probably wanted a **FormalPara**, so that we could have a title on the paragraph. But note that the parser didn't suggest this alternative. The parser only tries to add additional elements, rather than rename elements that it's already seen.

Missing End Tag

Leaving out an end tag is a lot like an out of context start tag. In fact, they're really the same error. The problem is never caused by the missing end tag per se, rather it's caused by the fact that something following it is now out of context.

```
<!DOCTYPE chapter PUBLIC "-//Davenport//DTD DocBook V3.0//EN">
<chapter><title>Test Chapter</title>
<para>
This is a paragraph in the test chapter. It is unremarkable in
every regard. This is a paragraph in the test chapter. It is
unremarkable in every regard. This is a paragraph in the test
chapter. It is unremarkable in every regard.
</para>
<para>
<emphasis role=bold>This</emphasis> paragraph contains
<emphasis>some <emphasis>emphasized</emphasis> text</emphasis>
and a <superscript>super</superscript>script
and a <subscript>sub</subscript>script.
<para>
This is a paragraph in the test chapter. It is unremarkable in
every regard. This is a paragraph in the test chapter. It is
unremarkable in every regard. This is a paragraph in the test
chapter. It is unremarkable in every regard.
</para>
</chapter>
```

```
[n:\dbtdg]nsgmls -sv -c \share\sgml\catalog examples\errs\noendtag.sgm
m:\jade\nsgmls.exe:I: SP version "1.3.2"
m:\jade\nsgmls.exe:examples\errs\noendtag.sgm:14:5:E: document type does not
allow element "PARA" here; missing one of "FOOTNOTE", "MSGTEXT", "CAUTION",
"IMPORTANT", "NOTE", "TIP", "WARNING", "BLOCKQUOTE", "INFORMALEXAMPLE" start-
tag
m:\jade\nsgmls.exe:examples\errs\noendtag.sgm:20:9:E: end tag for "PARA"
omitted, but OMITTAG NO was specified
m:\jade\nsgmls.exe:examples\errs\noendtag.sgm:9:0: start tag was here
```

In this case, the parser figured out that the best thing it could do is end the paragraph.

Bad Entity Reference

If you spell an entity name wrong, the parser will catch it.

```
<!DOCTYPE chapter PUBLIC "-//Davenport//DTD DocBook V3.0//EN">
<chapter><title>Test Chapter</title>
```

```
<para>
This is a paragraph in the test chapter. It is unremarkable in
every regard. This is a paragraph in the test chapter. It is
unremarkable in every regard. This is a paragraph in the test
chapter. It is unremarkable in every regard.
</para>
<para>
There's no entity called &xyzzy; defined in this document.
</para>
<para>
<emphasis role=bold>This</emphasis> paragraph contains
<emphasis>some <emphasis>emphasized</emphasis> text</emphasis>
and a <superscript>super</superscript>script
and a <subscript>sub</subscript>script.
</para>
<para>
This is a paragraph in the test chapter. It is unremarkable in
every regard. This is a paragraph in the test chapter. It is
unremarkable in every regard. This is a paragraph in the test
chapter. It is unremarkable in every regard.
</para>
</chapter>
```

```
[n:\dbtdg]nsgmls -sv -c \share\sgml\catalog examples\errs\badent.sgm
m:\jade\nsgmls.exe:I: SP version "1.3.2"
m:\jade\nsgmls.exe:examples\errs\badent.sgm:10:26:E: general entity "xyzzy"
not defined and no default entity
```

More often than not, you'll see this when you misspell a character entity name. For example, this happens when you type `&ldqou;` instead of `“`.

Invalid 8-Bit Character

In XML, the entire range of Unicode characters is available to you, but in SGML, the declaration indicates what characters are valid. The distributed DocBook declaration doesn't allow a bunch of fairly common 8-bit characters.

```
<!DOCTYPE chapter PUBLIC "-//Davenport//DTD DocBook V3.0//EN">
<chapter><title>Test Chapter</title>
<para>
This is a paragraph in the test chapter. It is unremarkable in
every regard. This is a paragraph in the test chapter. It is
unremarkable in every regard. This is a paragraph in the test
chapter. It is unremarkable in every regard.
</para>
<para>
The DocBook declaration in use doesn't allow 8-bit characters
like “this”.
</para>
<para>
<emphasis role=bold>This</emphasis> paragraph contains
<emphasis>some <emphasis>emphasized</emphasis> text</emphasis>
```

```
and a <superscript>super</superscript>script
and a <subscript>sub</subscript>script.
</para>
<para>
This is a paragraph in the test chapter. It is unremarkable in
every regard. This is a paragraph in the test chapter. It is
unremarkable in every regard. This is a paragraph in the test
chapter. It is unremarkable in every regard.
</para>
</chapter>
```

```
[n:\dbtdg]nsgmls -sv -c \share\sgml\catalog examples\errs\badchar.sgm
m:\jade\nsgmls.exe:I: SP version "1.3.2"
m:\jade\nsgmls.exe:examples\errs\badchar.sgm:11:0:E: non SGML character number
147
m:\jade\nsgmls.exe:examples\errs\badchar.sgm:11:5:E: non SGML character number
148
```

In this example, the Windows code page values for curly left and right quotes have been used, but they aren't in the declared character set. Fix this by converting them to character entities.

You can also fix them by changing the declaration, but if you do that, make sure all your interchange partners are aware of, and have a copy of, the modified declaration. See Appendix F, *Interchanging DocBook Documents*.

4

Publishing DocBook Documents

Creating and editing SGML/XML documents is usually only half the battle. After you've composed your document, you'll want to publish it. Publishing, for our purposes, means either print or web publishing. For SGML and XML documents, this is usually accomplished with some kind of *stylesheet*. In the (not too distant) future, you may be able to publish an XML document on the Web by simply putting it online with a stylesheet, but for now you'll probably have to translate your document into HTML.

There are many ways, using both free and commercial tools, to publish SGML documents. In this chapter, we're going to survey a number of possibilities, and then look at just one solution in detail: Jade (*http://www.jclark.com/jade/*) and the Modular DocBook Stylesheets. (*http://nwalsh.com/docbook/dsssl/*) We used jade to produce this book and to produce the online versions on the CD-ROM; it is also being deployed in other projects such as `<SGML>&tools;` (*http://www.sgmltools.org/*), which originated with the Linux Documentation Project.

For a brief survey of other tools, see Appendix D, *Resources*.

A Survey of Stylesheet Languages

Over the years, a number of attempts have been made to produce a standard stylesheet language and, failing that, a large number of proprietary languages have been developed.

FOSIs

First, the U.S. Department of Defense, in an attempt to standardize stylesheets across military branches, created the *Output Specification*, which is defined in

MIL-PRF-28001C, *Markup Requirements and Generic Style Specification for Electronic Printed Output and Exchange of Text.**

Commonly called FOSIs (for Formatting Output Specification Instances), they are supported by a few products including ADEPT Publisher by Arbortext (*http://www.arbortext.com/*) and DL Composer by Datalogics (*http://www.datalogics.com/*).

DSSSL

Next, the International Organization for Standardization (ISO) created DSSSL, the Document Style Semantics and Specification Language. Subsets of DSSSL are supported by Jade and a few other tools, but it never achieved widespread support.

CSS

The W3C CSS Working Group created CSS as a style attachment language for HTML, and, more recently, XML.

XSL

Most recently, the XML effort has identified a standard Extensible Style Language (XSL) as a requirement. The W3C XSL Working Group is currently pursuing that effort.

Stylesheet Examples

By way of comparison, here's an example of each of the standard style languages. In each case, the stylesheet fragment shown contains the rules that reasonably formatted the following paragraph:

```
<para>
This is an example paragraph. It should be presented in a
reasonable body font. <emphasis>Emphasized</emphasis> words
should be printed in italics. A single level of
<emphasis>Nested <emphasis>emphasis</emphasis> should also
be supported.</emphasis>
</para>
```

FOSI stylesheet

FOSIs are SGML documents. The element in the FOSI that controls the presentation of specific elements is the **e-i-c** (element in context) element. A sample FOSI fragment is shown in Example 4-1.

* See *Formally Published CALS Standards* (*http://www-cals.itsi.disa.mil/core/formal/fps.htm*) for more information.

Example 4-1. A Fragment of a FOSI Stylesheet

```
<e-i-c gi="para">
  <charlist>
    <textbrk startln="1" endln="1">
  </charlist>
</e-i-c>

<e-i-c gi="emphasis">
  <charlist inherit="1">
    <font posture="italic">
  </charlist>
</e-i-c>

<e-i-c gi="emphasis" context="emphasis">
  <charlist inherit="1">
    <font posture="upright">
  </charlist>
</e-i-c>
```

DSSSL stylesheet

DSSSL stylesheets are written in a Scheme-like language (see "Scheme" later in this chapter). It is the *element* function that controls the presentation of individual elements. See the example in Example 4-2.

Example 4-2. A Fragment of a DSSSL Stylesheet

```
(element para
  (make paragraph
    (process-children)))

(element emphasis
  (make sequence
    font-posture: 'italic
    (process-children)))

(element (emphasis emphasis)
  (make sequence
    font-posture: 'upright
    (process-children)))
```

CSS stylesheet

CSS stylesheets consist of selectors and formatting properties, as shown in Example 4-3.

Example 4-3. A Fragment of a CSS Stylesheet

```
para              { display: block }
emphasis          { display: inline;
                    font-style: italic; }
emphasis emphasis { display: inline;
                    font-style: upright; }
```

XSL stylesheet

XSL stylesheets are XML documents, as shown in Example 4-4. The element in the XSL stylesheet that controls the presentation of specific elements is the **xsl:template** element.

Example 4-4. A Fragment of an XSL Stylesheet

```
<?xml version='1.0'?>
<xsl:stylesheet xmlns:xsl="http://www.w3.org/1999/XSL/Transform"
                xmlns:fo="http://www.w3.org/1999/XSL/format">

<xsl:template match="para">
  <fo:block>
    <xsl:apply-templates/>
  </fo:block>
</xsl:template>

<xsl:template match="emphasis">
  <fo:sequence font-style="italic">
    <xsl:apply-templates/>
  </fo:sequence>
</xsl:template>

<xsl:template match="emphasis/emphasis">
  <fo:sequence font-style="upright">
    <xsl:apply-templates/>
  </fo:sequence>
</xsl:template>

</xsl:stylesheet>
```

Using Jade and DSSSL to Publish DocBook Documents

Jade is a free tool that applies DSSSL (*http://www.jclark.com/dsssl/*) stylesheets to SGML and XML documents. As distributed, Jade can output RTF, TeX, MIF, and SGML. The SGML backend can be used for SGML to SGML transformations (for example, DocBook to HTML).

A complete set of DSSSL stylesheets for creating print and HTML output from DocBook is included on the CD-ROM. More information about obtaining and installing Jade appears in Appendix A, *Installation*.

A Brief Introduction to DSSSL

DSSSL is a stylesheet language for both print and online rendering. The acronym stands for *Document Style Semantics and Specification Language*. It is defined by

ISO/IEC 10179:1996. For more general information about DSSSL, see the DSSSL Page (*http://www.jclark.com/dsssl/*).

Scheme

The DSSSL expression language is Scheme, a variant of Lisp. Lisp is a functional programming language with a remarkably regular syntax. Every expression looks like this:

```
(operator [arg1] [arg2] ... [argn] )
```

This is called "prefix" syntax because the operator comes before its arguments.

In Scheme, the expression that subtracts 2 from 3, is `(- 3 2)`. And `(+ (- 3 2) (* 2 4))` is 9. While the prefix syntax and the parentheses may take a bit of getting used to, Scheme is not hard to learn, in part because there are no exceptions to the syntax.

DSSSL Stylesheets

A complete DSSSL stylesheet is shown in Example 4-5. After only a brief examination of the stylesheet, you'll probably begin to have a feel for how it works. For each element in the document, there is an element rule that describes how you should format that element. The goal of the rest of this chapter is to make it possible for you to read, understand, and even write stylesheets at this level of complexity.

Example 4-5. A Complete DSSSL Stylesheet

```
<!DOCTYPE style-sheet PUBLIC "-//James Clark//DTD DSSSL Style Sheet//EN">

<style-sheet>
<style-specification>
<style-specification-body>

(element chapter
  (make simple-page-sequence
    top-margin: 1in
    bottom-margin: 1in
    left-margin: 1in
    right-margin: 1in
    font-size: 12pt
    line-spacing: 14pt
    min-leading: 0pt
    (process-children)))

(element title
  (make paragraph
    font-weight: 'bold
    font-size: 18pt
    (process-children)))
```

Example 4-5. A Complete DSSSL Stylesheet (continued)

```
(element para
  (make paragraph
    space-before: 8pt
    (process-children)))

(element emphasis
  (if (equal? (attribute-string "role") "strong")
      (make sequence
 font-weight: 'bold
 (process-children))
      (make sequence
 font-posture: 'italic
 (process-children))))

(element (emphasis emphasis)
  (make sequence
    font-posture: 'upright
    (process-children)))

(define (super-sub-script plus-or-minus
               #!optional (sosofo (process-children)))
  (make sequence
    font-size: (* (inherited-font-size) 0.8)
    position-point-shift: (plus-or-minus (* (inherited-font-size) 0.4))
    sosofo))

(element superscript (super-sub-script +))
(element subscript (super-sub-script -))

</style-specification-body>
</style-specification>
</style-sheet>
```

This stylesheet is capable of formatting simple DocBook documents like the one shown in Example 4-6.

Example 4-6. A Simple DocBook Document

```
<!DOCTYPE chapter PUBLIC "-//OASIS//DTD DocBook V3.1//EN">
<chapter><title>Test Chapter</title>
<para>
This is a paragraph in the test chapter. It is unremarkable in
every regard. This is a paragraph in the test chapter. It is
unremarkable in every regard. This is a paragraph in the test
chapter. It is unremarkable in every regard.
</para>
<para>
<emphasis role=strong>This</emphasis> paragraph contains
<emphasis>some <emphasis>emphasized</emphasis> text</emphasis>
and a <superscript>super</superscript>script
and a <subscript>sub</subscript>script.
</para>
```

Example 4-6. A Simple DocBook Document (continued)

```
<para>
This is a paragraph in the test chapter. It is unremarkable in
every regard. This is a paragraph in the test chapter. It is
unremarkable in every regard. This is a paragraph in the test
chapter. It is unremarkable in every regard.
</para>
</chapter>
```

The result of formatting a simple document with this stylesheet can be seen in Figure 4-1.

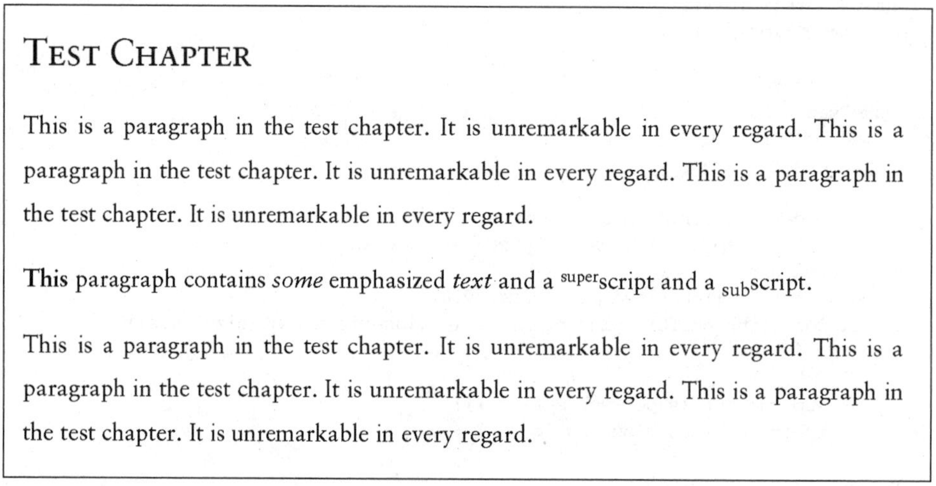

TEST CHAPTER

This is a paragraph in the test chapter. It is unremarkable in every regard. This is a paragraph in the test chapter. It is unremarkable in every regard. This is a paragraph in the test chapter. It is unremarkable in every regard.

This paragraph contains *some* emphasized ***text*** and a ^{super}script and a $_{\text{sub}}$script.

This is a paragraph in the test chapter. It is unremarkable in every regard. This is a paragraph in the test chapter. It is unremarkable in every regard. This is a paragraph in the test chapter. It is unremarkable in every regard.

Figure 4-1. The formatted simple document

We'll take a closer look at this stylesheet after you've learned a little more DSSSL.

DSSSL Stylesheets Are SGML Documents

One of the first things that may strike you about DSSSL stylesheets (aside from all the parentheses), is the fact that the stylesheet itself is an SGML document! This means that you have all the power of SGML documents at your disposal in DSSSL stylesheets. In particular, you can use entities and marked sections to build a modular stylesheet.

In fact, DSSSL stylesheets are defined so that they correspond to a particular*architecture*. This means that you can change the DTD used by stylesheets within the bounds of the architecture. A complete discussion of document architectures is beyond the scope of this book, but we'll show you one way to take advantage of them in your DSSSL stylesheets in "The DSSSL Architecture" later in the chapter.

DSSSL Processing Model

A DSSSL processor builds a tree out of the source document. Each element in the source document becomes a node in the tree (processing instructions and other constructs become nodes as well). Processing the source tree begins with the root rule and continues until there are no more nodes to process.

Global Variables and Side Effects

There aren't any global variables or side effects. It can be difficult to come to grips with this, especially if you're just starting out.

It is possible to define constants and functions and to create local variables with `let` expressions, but you can't create any global variables or change anything after you've defined it.

DSSSL Expressions

DSSSL has a rich vocabulary of expressions for dealing with all of the intricacies of formatting. Many, but by no means all of them, are supported by Jade. In this introduction, we'll cover only a few of the most common.

Element expressions

Element expressions, which define the rules for formatting particular elements, make up the bulk of most DSSSL stylesheets. A simple element rule can be seen in Example 4-7. This rule says that a **para** element should be formatted by making a paragraph (see "Make expressions").

Example 4-7. A Simple DSSSL Rule

```
(element para
  (make paragraph
    space-before: 8pt
    (process-children)))
```

An element expression can be made more specific by specifying an element and its ancestors instead of just specifying an element. The rule `(element title ...)` applies to all **Title** elements, but a rule that begins with `(element (figure title) ...)` applies only to **Title** elements that are immediate children of **Figure** elements.

If several rules apply, the most specific rule is used.

When a rule is used, the node in the source tree that was matched becomes the "current node" while that element expression is being processed.

Make expressions

A make expression specifies the characteristics of a "flow object." Flow objects are abstract representations of content (paragraphs, rules, tables, and so on). The expression:

```
(make paragraph
  font-size: 12pt
  line-spacing: 14pt ...)
```

specifies that the content that goes "here" is to be placed into a paragraph flow object with a font-size of 12pt and a line-spacing of 14pt (all of the unspecified characteristics of the flow object are defaulted in the appropriate way).

They're called flow objects because DSSSL, in its full generality, allows you to specify the characteristics of a sequence of flow objects and a set of areas on the physical page where you can place content. The content of the flow objects is then "poured on to" (or flows in to) the areas on the page(s).

In most cases, it's sufficient to think of the make expressions as constructing the flow objects, but they really only specify the *characteristics* of the flow objects. This detail is apparent in one of the most common and initially confusing pieces of DSSSL jargon: the *sosofo*. Sosofo stands for a "specification of a sequence of flow objects." All this means is that processing a document may result in a nested set of `make` expressions (in other words, the paragraph may contain a table that contains rows that contain cells that contain paragraphs, and so on).

The general form of a `make` expression is:

```
(make flow-object-name
  keyword1: value1
  keyword2: value2
  ...
  keywordn: valuen
  (content-expression))
```

Keyword arguments specify the characteristics of the flow object. The specific characteristics you use depends on the flow object. The *`content-expression`* can vary; it is usually another make expression or one of the processing expressions.

Some common flow objects in the print stylesheet are:

`simple-page-sequence`
: Contains a sequence of pages. The keyword arguments of this flow object let you specify margins, headers and footers, and other page-related characteristics. Print stylesheets should always produce one or more `simple-page-sequence` flow objects.

: Nesting `simple-page-sequence` does not work. Characteristics on the inner sequences are ignored.

`paragraph`
: A paragraph is used for any block of text. This may include not only paragraphs in the source document, but also titles, the terms in a definition list, glossary entries, and so on. Paragraphs in DSSSL can be nested.

`sequence`
: A sequence is a wrapper. It is most frequently used to change inherited characteristics (like font style) of a set of flow objects without introducing other semantics (such as line breaks).

`score`
: A score flow object creates underlining, strike-throughs, or overlining.

`table`
: A table flow object creates a table of rows and cells.

The HTML stylesheet uses the SGML backend, which has a different selection of flow objects.

`element`
: Creates an element. The content of this `make` expression will appear between the start and end tags. The expression:

```
(make element gi: "H1"
    (literal "Title"))
```

produces `<H1>Title</H1>`.

`empty-element`
: Creates an empty element that may not have content. The expression:

```
(make empty-element gi: "BR"
     attributes: '(("CLEAR" "ALL")))
```

produces `<BR CLEAR="ALL">`.

`sequence`
: Produces no output in of itself as a wrapper, but is still required in DSSSL contexts in which you want to output several flow objects but only one object top-level object may be returned.

`entity-ref`
: Inserts an entity reference. The expression:

```
(make entity-ref name: "nbsp")
```

produces ` `.

In both stylesheets, a completely empty flow object is constructed with `(empty-sosofo)`.

Selecting data

Extracting parts of the source document can be accomplished with these functions:

`(data nd)`
: Returns all of the character data from *nd* as a string.

`(attribute-string "attr" nd)`
: Returns the value of the *attr* attribute of *nd*.

`(inherited-attribute-string "attr" nd)`
: Returns the value of the *attr* attribute of *nd*. If that attribute is not specified on *nd*, it searches up the hierarchy for the first ancestor element that does set the attribute, and returns its value.

Selecting elements

A common requirement of formatting is the ability to reorder content. In order to do this, you must be able to select other elements in the tree for processing. DSSSL provides a number of functions that select other elements. These functions all return a list of nodes.

`(current-node)`
: Returns the current node.

`(children nd)`
: Returns the children of *nd*.

`(descendants nd)`
: Returns the descendants of *nd* (the children of *nd* and all their children's children, and so on).

`(parent nd)`
: Returns the parent of *nd*.

`(ancestor "name" nd)`
: Returns the first ancestor of *nd* named *name*.

`(element-with-id "id")`
: Returns the element in the document with the ID *id*, if such an element exists.

`(select-elements node-list "name")`
: Returns all of the elements of the *node-list* that have the name *name*. For example, `(select-elements (descendants (current-node)) "para")` returns a list of all the paragraphs that are descendants of the current node.

`(empty-node-list)`
: Returns a node list that contains no nodes.

Other functions allow you to manipulate node lists.

`(node-list-empty? nl)`
Returns true if (and only if) `nl` is an empty node list.

`(node-list-length nl)`
Returns the number of nodes in `nl`.

`(node-list-first nl)`
Returns a node list that consists of the single node that is the first node in `nl`.

`(node-list-rest nl)`
Returns a node list that contains all of the nodes in `nl` except the first node.

There are many other expressions for manipulating nodes and node lists.

Processing expressions

Processing expressions control which elements in the document will be processed and in what order. Processing an element is performed by finding a matching element rule and using that rule.

`(process-children)`
Processes all of the children of the current node. In most cases, if no process expression is given, processing the children is the default behavior.

`(process-node-list nl)`
Processes each of the elements in `nl`.

Define expressions

You can declare your own functions and constants in DSSSL. The general form of a function declaration is:

```
(define (function args)
  function-body)
```

A constant declaration is:

```
(define constant
  constant-function-body)
```

The distinction between constants and functions is that the body of a constant is evaluated when the definition occurs, while functions are evaluated when they are used.

Conditionals

In DSSSL, the constant `#t` represents true and `#f` false. There are several ways to test conditions and take action in DSSSL.

`if`

The form of an `if` expression is:

```
(if condition
  true-expression
  false-expression)
```

If the condition is true, the *`true-expression`* is evaluated, otherwise the *`false-expression`* is evaluated. You must always provide an expression to be evaulated when the condition is not met. If you want to produce nothing, use `(empty-sosofo)`.

`case`

`case` selects from among several alternatives:

```
(case expression
  ((constant1) (expression1))
  ((constant2) (expression2))
  ((constant3) (expression3))
  (else else-expression))
```

The value of the expression is compared against each of the constants in turn and the expression associated with the first matching constant is evaulated.

`cond`

`cond` also selects from among several alternatives, but the selection is performed by evaluating each expression:

```
(cond
  ((condition1) (expression1))
  ((condition2) (expression2))
  ((condition3) (expression3))
  (else else-expression))
```

The value of each conditional is calculated in turn. The expression associated with the first condition that is true is evaluated.

Any expression that returns `#f` is false; all other expressions are true. This can be somewhat counterintuitive. In many programming languages, it's common to assume that "empty" things are false (0 is false, a null pointer is false, an empty set is false, for example.) In DSSSL, this isn't the case; note, for example, that an empty node list is not `#f` and is therefore true. To avoid these difficulties, always use functions that return true or false in conditionals. To test for an empty node list, use `(node-list-empty?)`.

Let expressions

The way to create local variables in DSSSL is with `(let)`. The general form of a `let` expression is:

```
(let ((var1 expression1)
      (var2 expression2)
      ...
      (varn expressionn))
  let-body)
```

In a `let`; expression, all of the variables are defined "simultaneously." The expression that defines *var2* cannot contain any references to any other variables defined in the same `let` expression. A `let*` expression allows variables to refer to each other, but runs slightly slower.

Variables are available only within the *let-body*. A common use of `let` is within a `define` expression:

```
(define (cals-rule-default nd)
   (let* ((table (ancestor "table" nd))
          (frame (if (attribute-string "frame" table)
                     (attribute-string "frame" table)
                     "all")))
    (equal? frame "all")))
```

This function creates two local variables `table` and `frame`. `let` returns the value of the last expression in the body, so this function returns true if the `frame` attribute on the table is `all` or if no `frame` attribute is present.

Loops

DSSSL doesn't have any construct that resembles the "for loop" that occurs in most imperative languages like C and Java. Instead, DSSSL employs a common trick in functional languages for implementing a loop: tail recursion.

Loops in DSSSL use a special form of `let`. This loop counts from 1 to 10:

```
(let ❶loopvar ❷((count 1))
  ❸(if (> count 10)
    ❹#t
    (❺loopvar ❻(+ count 1))))
```

❶ This variable controls the loop. It is declared without an initial value, immediately after the `let` operand.

❷ Any number of additional local variables can be defined after the loop variable, just as they can in any other `let` expression.

❸ If you ever want the loop to end, you have to put some sort of a test in it.

❹ This is the value that will be returned.

❺ Note that you iterate the loop by using the loop variable as if it was a function name.

❻ The arguments to this "function" are the values that you want the local variables declared in ❷ to have in the next iteration.

A Closer Look at Example 4-5

Example 4-5 is a style sheet that contains a style specification. Stylesheets may consist of multiple specifications, as we'll see in "A Single Stylesheet for Both Print and HTML."

The actual DSSSL code goes in the style specification body, within the style specification. Each construction rule processes different elements from the source document.

Processing chapters

Chapters are processed by the `chapter` construction rule. Each **Chapter** is formatted as a `simple-page-sequence`. Every print stylesheet should format a document as one or more simple page sequences. Characteristics on the simple page sequence can specify headers and footers as well as margins and other page parameters.

One important note about simple page sequences: they cannot nest. This means that you cannot blindly process divisions (**Part**s, **Reference**) and the elements they contain (**Chapter**s, **RefEntry**s) as simple page sequences. This sometimes involves a little creativity.

Processing titles

The `make` expression in the `title` element rule ensures that **Title**s are formatted in large, bold print.

This construction rule applies equally to **Chapter** titles, **Figure** titles, and **Book** titles. It's unlikely that you'd want all of these titles to be presented in the same way, so a more robust stylesheet would have to arrange the processing of titles with more context. This might be achieved in the way that nested **Emphasis** elements are handled in "Processing emphasis."

Processing paragraphs

Para elements are simply formatted as paragraphs.

Processing emphasis

Processing **Emphasis** elements is made a little more interesting because we want to consider an attribute value and the possibility that **Emphasis** elements can be nested.

In the simple case, in which we're processing an **Emphasis** element that is not nested, we begin by testing the value of the `role` attribute. If the content of that attribute is the string `strong`, it is formatted in bold; otherwise, it is formatted in italic.

The nested case is handled by the `(emphasis emphasis)` rule. This rule simply formats the content using an upright (nonitalic) font. This rule, like the rule for **Titles**, is not robust. **Emphasis** nested inside `strong` **Emphasis** won't be distinguished, for example, and nestings more than two elements deep will be handled just as nestings that are two deep.

Processing subscripts and superscripts

Processing **Subscript** and **Superscript** elements is really handled by the `super-sub-script` function. There are several interesting things about this function:

The `plus-or-minus` *argument*

You might ordinarily think of passing a keyword or boolean argument to the *super-sub-script* function to indicate whether subscripts or superscripts are desired. But with Scheme, it's possible to pass the actual function as an argument!

Note that in the element construction rules for **Superscript** and **Subscript**, we pass the actual functions `+` and `-`. In the body of *super-sub-script*, we use the `plus-or-minus` argument as a function name (it appears immediately after an open parenthesis).

The optional argument

`optional` arguments are indicated by `#!optional` in the function declaration. Any number of `optional` arguments may be given, but each must specify a default value. This is accomplished by listing each argument and default value (an expression) as a pair.

In *super-sub-script*, the optional argument `sosofo` is initialized to `process-children`. This means that at the point where the function is *called*, `process-children` is evaluated and the resulting `sosofo` is passed to the function.

Use of inherited characteristics

It is possible to use the "current" value of an inherited characteristic to calculate a new value. Using this technique, superscripts and subscripts will be presented at 80 percent of the current font size.

Customizing the Stylesheets

The best way to customize the stylesheets is to write your own "driver" file; this is a stylesheet that contains your local modifications and then includes the appropriate stylesheet from the standard distribution by reference. This allows you to make local changes and extensions without modifying the distributed files, which makes upgrading to the next release much simpler.

Writing Your Own Driver

A basic driver file looks like this:

```
<!DOCTYPE style-sheet PUBLIC "-//James Clark//DTD DSSSL Style Sheet//EN" [
<!ENTITY dbstyle PUBLIC "-//Norman Walsh//DOCUMENT DocBook Print Stylesheet//
EN" CDATA DSSSL>
]>

<style-sheet>
<style-specification use="docbook">
<style-specification-body>

;; your changes go here...

</style-specification-body>
</style-specification>
<external-specification id="docbook" document="dbstyle">
</style-sheet>
```

There are two public identifiers associated with the Modular DocBook Stylesheets:

- `-//Norman Walsh//DOCUMENT DocBook Print Stylesheet//EN`
- `-//Norman Walsh//DOCUMENT DocBook HTML Stylesheet//EN`

The former selects the print stylesheet and the latter selects the HTML stylesheet. There is an SGML Open catalog file in the distribution that maps these public identifiers to the stylesheet files.

You can add your own definitions, or redefinitions, of stylesheet rules and parameters so that

```
;; your changes go here...
```

occurs in the previous example.

For a concrete example of a driver file, see *plain.dsl* in the *docbook/print* directory in the stylesheet distribution (or on the CD-ROM). This is a customization of the print stylesheet, which turns off title page and TOC generation.

Changing the Localization

As distributed, the stylesheets use English for all generated text, but other localization files are also provided. At the time of this writing, the stylesheets support Dutch, French, German, Italian, Norwegian, Polish, Portuguese, Russian, and Spanish. (If you can write a localization for another language, *please* contribute it.)

There are two ways to switch languages: by specifying a `lang` attribute, or by changing the default language in a customization.

Using the lang attribute

One of the DocBook common attributes is `lang`. If you specify a language, the DocBook stylesheets will use that language (and all its descendants, if no other language is specified) for generated text within that element.

Table 4-1 summarizes the language codes for the supported languages.* The following chapter uses text generated in French:

```
<chapter lang="fr"><title>Bêtises</title>
<para>Pierre qui roule n'amasse pas mousse.</para>
</chapter>
```

Table 4-1. DocBook Stylesheet Language Codes

Language Code	Language
da	Danish
de	German
en	English
es	Spanish
fi	Finnish
fr	French
it	Italian
nl	Dutch
no	Norwegian
pl	Polish
pt	Portuguese
ru	Russian
sv	Swedish

Changing the default language

If no `lang` attribute is specified, the default language is used. You can change the default language with a driver.

In the driver, define the default language. Table 4-1 summarizes the language codes for the supported languages. The following driver makes German the default language:

```
<!DOCTYPE style-sheet PUBLIC "-//James Clark//DTD DSSSL Style Sheet//EN" [
<!ENTITY dbstyle PUBLIC "-//Norman Walsh//DOCUMENT DocBook Print Stylesheet//
EN" CDATA DSSSL>
]>

<style-sheet>
```

* Language codes should conform to IETF RFC 1766.

```
<style-specification use="docbook">
<style-specification-body>

(define %default-language% "dege")

</style-specification-body>
</style-specification>
<external-specification id="docbook" document="dbstyle">
</style-sheet>
```

There are two other settings that can be changed only in a driver. Both of these settings are turned off in the distributed stylesheet:

`%gentext-language%`
: If a language code is specified in `%gentext-language%`, then that language will be used for all generated text, regardless of any `lang` attribute settings in the document.

`%gentext-use-xref-language%`
: If turned on (defined as `#t`), then the stylesheets will generate the text associated with a cross reference using the language of the target, not the current language. Consider the following book:

```
<book><title>A Test Book</title>
<preface>
<para>There are three chapters in this book: <xref linkend=c1>,
<xref linkend=c2>, and <xref linkend=c3>.
</para>
</preface>
<chapter lang=usen><title>English</title> ... </chapter>
<chapter lang=fr><title>French</title> ... </chapter>
<chapter lang=dege><title>Deutsch</title> ... </chapter>
</book>
```

The standard stylesheets render the Preface as something like this:

> There are three chapters in this book: Chapter 1, Chapter 2, and Chapter 3.

With `%gentext-use-xref-language%` turned on, it would render like this:

> There are are three chapters in this book: Chapter 1, Chapitre 2, and Kapitel 3.

A Single Stylesheet for Both Print and HTML

A DSSSL stylesheet consists of one or more "style specifications." Using more than one style specification allows you to build a single stylesheet file that can format with either the print or SGML backends. Example 4-8 shows a stylesheet with two style specifications.

Example 4-8. both.dsl: A Stylesheet with Two Style Specifications

```
<!DOCTYPE style-sheet PUBLIC "-//James Clark//DTD DSSSL Style Sheet//EN" [
<!ENTITY html-ss
  PUBLIC "-//Norman Walsh//DOCUMENT DocBook HTML Stylesheet//EN" CDATA dsssl>
<!ENTITY print-ss
  PUBLIC "-//Norman Walsh//DOCUMENT DocBook Print Stylesheet//EN" CDATA dsssl>
]>
<style-sheet>
<style-specification id="print" use="print-stylesheet">
<style-specification-body>

;; customize the print stylesheet

</style-specification-body>
</style-specification>
<style-specification id="html" use="html-stylesheet">
<style-specification-body>

;; customize the html stylesheet

</style-specification-body>
</style-specification>
<external-specification id="print-stylesheet" document="print-ss">
<external-specification id="html-stylesheet"  document="html-ss">
</style-sheet>
```

Once you have stylesheets with more than one style specification, you have to be able to indicate which style specification you want to use. In Jade, you indicate this by providing the ID of the style specification after the stylesheet filename, separated with a hash mark: #.

Using the code from Example 4-8, you can format a document using the print stylesheet by running:

```
jade -t rtf -d both.dsl#print file.sgm
```

and using the HTML stylesheet by running:

```
jade -t sgml -d both.dsl#html file.sgm
```

Dealing with Multiple Declarations

The DocBook SGML DTD and the DocBook DSSSL Stylesheets happen to use the same SGML declaration. This makes it very easy to run Jade with DocBook. However, you may sometimes wish to use Jade with other document types, for example the DocBook XML DTD, which has a different declaration. There are a couple of ways to do this.

Pass the Declaration Explicitly

If your stylesheets parse fine with the default declaration, but you want to use an alternate declaration with a particular document, just pass the declaration on the command line:

```
jade options the-declaration the-document
```

Note that there's no option required before the declaration; it simply occurs before the first filename. Jade concatenates all of the files that you give it together, and parses them as if they were one document.

Use the Catalogs

The other way to fix this is with a little catalog trickery.

First, note that Jade always looks in the file called *catalog* in the same directory as the document that it is loading, and uses settings in that file in preference to settings in other catalogs.

With this fact, we can employ the following trick:

- Put a *catalog* file in the directory that contains your stylesheets, which contain an `SGMLDECL` directive. Jade understands the directive, which points to the SGML declaration that you should use when parsing the stylesheets. For the DocBook stylesheets, the DocBook declaration works fine.
- In the directory that contains the document you want to process, create a *catalog* file that contains an `SGMLDECL` directive that points to the SGML declaration that should be used when parsing the document.

There's no easy way to have both the stylesheet and the document in the same directory if they must be processed with different declarations. But this is usually not too inconvenient.

The DSSSL Architecture

The concept of an architecture was promoted by HyTime. In some ways, it takes the standard SGML/XML notions of the role of elements and attributes and inverts them. Instead of relying on the name of an element to assign its primary semantics, it uses the values of a small set of fixed attributes.

While this may be counterintuitive initially, it has an interesting benefit. An architecture-aware processor can work transparently with many different DTDs. A small example will help illustrate this point.

NOTE The following example demonstrates the concept behind architectures, but for the sake of simplicity, it does not properly implement an architecture as defined in HyTime.

Imagine that you wrote an application that can read an SGML/XML document containing a letter (conforming to some letter DTD), and automatically print an envelope for the letter. It's easy to envision how this works. The application reads the content of the letter, extracts the address and return address elements from the source, and uses them to generate an envelope:

```
<?xml version='1.0'>
<!DOCTYPE letter "/share/sgml/letter/letter.dtd" [
<!ENTITY myaddress "/share/sgml/entities/myaddress.xml">
]>
<letter>
<returnaddress>&myaddress;</returnaddress>
<address>
<name>Leonard Muellner</name>
<company>O'Reilly &amp; Associates</company>
<street>90 Sherman Street</street>
<city>Cambridge</city><state>MA</state><zip>02140</zip>
</address>
<body>
<salutation>Hi Lenny</salutation>
...
</body>
```

The processor extracts the **Returnaddress** and **Address** elements and their children and prints the envelope accordingly.

Now suppose that a colleague from payroll comes by and asks you to adapt the application to print envelopes for mailing checks, using the information in the payroll database, which has a different DTD. And a week later, someone from sales comes by and asks if you can modify the application to use the contact information DTD. After a while, you would have 11 versions of this program to maintain.

Suppose that instead of using the actual element names to locate the addresses in the documents, you asked each person to add a few attributes to their DTD. By forcing the attributes to have fixed values, they'd automatically be present in each document, but authors would never have to worry about them.

For example, the address part of the letter DTD might look like this:

```
<!ELEMENT address (name, company? street*, city, state, zip)>
<!ATTLIST address
 ADDRESS CDATA #FIXED "START"
>
```

```
<!ELEMENT name (#PCDATA)*>
<!ATTLIST name
 ADDRESS CDATA #FIXED "NAME"
>

<!ELEMENT company (#PCDATA)*>
<!ATTLIST company
 ADDRESS CDATA #FIXED "COMPANY"
>

<!ELEMENT street (#PCDATA)*>
<!ATTLIST street
 ADDRESS CDATA #FIXED "STREET"
>

<!ELEMENT city (#PCDATA)*>
<!ATTLIST city
 ADDRESS CDATA #FIXED "CITY"
>

<!ELEMENT state (#PCDATA)*>
<!ATTLIST state
 ADDRESS CDATA #FIXED "STATE"
>

<!ELEMENT zip (#PCDATA)*>
<!ATTLIST zip
 ADDRESS CDATA #FIXED "ZIP"
>
```

Effectively, each address in a letter would look like this:

```
<address ADDRESS="START">
<name ADDRESS="NAME">Leonard Muellner</name>
<company ADDRESS="COMPANY">O'Reilly &amp;amp; Associates</company>
<street> ADDRESS="STREET">90 Sherman Street</street>
<city ADDRESS="CITY">Cambridge</city><state ADDRESS="STATE">MA</state>
<zip ADDRESS="ZIP">02140</zip>
</address>
```

In practice, the author would not include the `ADDRESS` attributes; they are automatically provided by the DTD because they are **`#FIXED`**.*

Now the address portion of the payroll DTD might look like this:

```
<!ELEMENT employee (name, mailingaddress)>

<!ELEMENT name (#PCDATA)*>
<!ATTLIST name
 ADDRESS CDATA #FIXED "NAME"
```

* The use of uppercase names here is intentional. These are not attributes that an author is ever expected to type. In XML, which is case-sensitive, using uppercase for things like this reduces the likelihood of collision with "real" attribute names in the DTD.

```
>

<!ELEMENT mailingaddress (addrline1, addrline2,
                          city, state.or.province, postcode)>
<!ATTLIST mailingaddress
 ADDRESS CDATA #FIXED "START"
>

<!ELEMENT addrline1 (#PCDATA)*>
<!ATTLIST addrline1
 ADDRESS CDATA #FIXED "STREET"
>

<!ELEMENT addrline2 (#PCDATA)*>
<!ATTLIST addrline2
 ADDRESS CDATA #FIXED "STREET"
>

<!ELEMENT city (#PCDATA)*>
<!ATTLIST city
 ADDRESS CDATA #FIXED "CITY"
>

<!ELEMENT state.or.province (#PCDATA)*>
<!ATTLIST state.or.province
 ADDRESS CDATA #FIXED "STATE"
>

<!ELEMENT postcode (#PCDATA)*>
<!ATTLIST postcode
 ADDRESS CDATA #FIXED "ZIP"
>
```

The employee records will look like this:

```
<employee><name ADDRESS="NAME">Leonard Muellner</name>
<mailingaddress ADDRESS="START">
<addrline1 ADDRESS="STREET">90 Sherman Street</addrline1>
<city ADDRESS="CITY">Cambridge</city>
<state.or.province ADDRESS="STATE">MA</state.or.province>
<postcode ADDRESS="ZIP">02140</postcode>
</mailingaddress>
</employee>
```

Your application no longer cares about the actual element names. It simply looks for the elements with the correct attributes and uses them. This is the power of an architecture: it provides a level of abstraction that processing applications can use to their advantage. In practice, architectural forms are a bit more complex to set up because they have facilities for dealing with attribute name conflicts, among other things.

Why have we told you all this? Because DSSSL is an architecture. This means you can modify the stylesheet DTD and still run your stylesheets through Jade.

Consider the case presented earlier in Example 4-8. In order to use this stylesheet, you must specify three things: the backend you want to use, the stylesheet you want to use, and the style specification you want to use. If you mismatch any of the parameters, you'll get the wrong results. In practice, the problem is compounded further:

- Some stylesheets support several backends (RTF, TeX, and SGML).
- Some stylesheets support only some backends (RTF and SGML, but not TeX or MIF).
- Some stylesheets support multiple outputs using the same backend (several kinds of HTML output, for example, using the SGML backend: HTML, HTMLHelp, JavaHelp, and so on).
- If you have complex stylesheets, some backends may require additional options to define parameter entities or stylesheet options.

None of this complexity is really necessary, after all, the options don't change—you just have to use the correct combinations. The mental model is really something like this: "I want a certain kind of output, TeX say, so I have to use this combination of parameters."

You can summarize this information in a table to help keep track of it:

Desired Output	Backend	Style specification	Options	Supported?
rtf	rtf	print	-V rtf-backend	yes
tex	tex	print	-V tex-backend -i tex	yes
html	sgml	htmlweb	-i html	yes
javahelp	sgml	help	-i help	yes
htmlhelp				no

Putting this information in a table will help you keep track of it, but it's not the best solution. The ideal solution is to keep this information on your system, and let the software figure it all out. You'd like to be able to run a command, tell it what output you want from what stylesheet, what file you want to process, and then let it figure everything else out. For example:

```
format html mybook.dsl mydoc.sgm
```

One way to do this is to put the configuration data in a separate file, and have the *format* command load it out of this other file. The disadvantage of this solution is that it introduces another file that you have to maintain and it's independent from the stylesheet so it isn't easy to keep it up-to-date.

In the DSSSL case, a better alternative is to modify the stylesheet DTD so you can store the configuration data *in the stylesheet*. Using this alternate DTD, your *mybook.dsl* stylesheets might look like this:

```
<!DOCTYPE style-sheet
  PUBLIC "-//Norman Walsh//DTD Annotated DSSSL Style Sheet V1.2//EN" [
<!-- perhaps additional declarations here -->
]>
<style-sheet>
<title>DocBook Stylesheet</title>
<doctype pubid="-//OASIS//DTD DocBook V3.1//EN">
<doctype pubid="-//Davenport//DTD DocBook V3.0//EN">
<doctype pubid="-//Norman Walsh//DTD Website V1.4//EN">
<backend name="rtf" backend="rtf" fragid="print"
         options="-V rtf-backend" default="true">
<backend name="tex" backend="tex" fragid="print"
         options="-V tex-backend -i tex">
<backend name="html" backend="sgml" fragid="htmlweb" options="-i html">
<backend name="javahelp" backend="sgml" fragid="help" options="-i help">
<backend name="htmlhelp" supported="no">
<style-specification id="print" use="docbook">
<style-specification-body>
```

In this example, the stylesheet has been annotated with a title, a list of the public IDs to which it is applicable, and a table that provides information about the output formats that it supports.

Using this information, the *format* command can get all the information it needs to construct the appropriate call to Jade. To make HTML from *myfile.sgm*, *format* would run the following:

```
jade -t sgml -d mybook.dsl#htmlweb -i html myfile.sgm
```

The additional information, titles and public IDs, can be used as part of a GUI interface to simplify the selection of stylesheets for an author.

The complete annotated stylesheet DTD, and an example of the *format* command script, are provided on the CD-ROM.

5

Customizing DocBook

For the applications you have in mind, DocBook "out of the box" may not be exactly what you need. Perhaps you need additional inline elements or perhaps you want to remove elements that you never want your authors to use. By design, DocBook makes this sort of customization easy.

This chapter explains how to make your own *customization layer*. You might do this in order to:

- Add new elements
- Remove elements
- Change the structure of existing elements
- Add new attributes
- Remove attributes
- Broaden the range of values allowed in an attribute
- Narrow the range of values in an attribute to a specific list or a fixed value

You can use customization layers to extend DocBook or subset it. Creating a DTD that is a strict subset of DocBook means that all of your instances are still completely valid DocBook instances, which may be important to your tools and stylesheets, and to other people with whom you share documents. An *extension* adds new structures, or changes the DTD in a way that is not compatible with DocBook. Extensions can be very useful, but might have a great impact on your environment.

Customization layers can be as small as restricting an attribute value or as large as adding an entirely different hierarchy on top of the inline elements.

Should You Do This?

Changing a DTD can have a wide-ranging impact on the tools and stylesheets that you use. It can have an impact on your authors and on your legacy documents. This is especially true if you make an extension. If you rely on your support staff to install and maintain your authoring and publishing tools, check with them before you invest a lot of time modifying the DTD. There may be additional issues that are outside your immediate control. Proceed with caution.

That said, DocBook is designed to be easy to modify. This chapter assumes that you are comfortable with SGML/XML DTD syntax, but the examples presented should be a good springboard to learning the syntax if it's not already familiar to you.

If You Change DocBook, It's Not DocBook Anymore!

The DocBook DTD is usually referenced by its public identifier:

```
-//OASIS//DTD DocBook V3.1//EN
```

Previous versions of DocBook, V3.0 and the V2 variants, used the owner identifier Davenport, rather than OASIS.

If you make any changes to the structure of the DTD, it is imperative that you alter the public identifier that you use for the DTD and the modules you changed. The license agreement under which DocBook is distributed gives you complete freedom to change, modify, reuse, and generally hack the DTD in any way you want, except that you must not call your alterations "DocBook."

You should change both the owner identifier and the description. The original DocBook formal public identifiers use the following syntax:

```
-//OASIS//text-class DocBook description Vversion//EN
```

Your own formal public identifiers should use the following syntax in order to record their DocBook derivation:

```
-//your-owner-ID//text-class DocBook Vversion-Based [Subset|Extension|Variant]
your-descrip-and-version//lang
```

For example:

```
-//O'Reilly//DTD DocBook V3.0-Based Subset V1.1//EN
```

If your DTD is a proper subset, you can advertise this status by using the `Subset` keyword in the description. If your DTD contains any markup model extensions, you can advertise this status by using the `Extension` keyword. If you'd rather not characterize your variant specifically as a subset or an extension, you can leave out this field entirely, or, if you prefer, use the `Variant` keyword.

There is only one file that you may change without changing the public identifier: *dbgenent.mod*. And you can add only entity and notation declarations to that file. (You can add anything you want, naturally, but if you add anything other than entity and notation declarations, you must change the public identifier!)

Customization Layers

SGML and XML DTDs are really just collections of declarations. These declarations are stored in one or more files. A complete DTD is formed by combining these files together logically. Parameter entities are used for this purpose. Consider the following fragment:

```
<!ENTITY % dbpool SYSTEM "dbpool.mod"> ❶
<!ENTITY % dbhier SYSTEM "dbhier.mod"> ❷
%dbpool;                               ❸
%dbhier;                               ❹
```

❶ This line declares the parameter entity `dbpool` and associates it with the file *dbpool.mod*.

❷ This line declares the parameter entity `dbhier` and associates it with the file *dbhier.mod*.

❸ This line references `dbpool`, which loads the file *dbpool.mod* and inserts its content here.

❹ Similarly, this line loads *dbhier.mod*.

It is an important feature of DTD parsing that entity declarations can be repeated. If an entity is declared more than once, then the *first* declaration is used. Given this fragment:

```
<!ENTITY foo "Lenny">
<!ENTITY foo "Norm">
```

The replacement text for `&foo;` is "Lenny."

These two notions, that you can break a DTD into modules referenced with parameter entities and that the first entity declaration is the one that counts, are used to build "customization layers." With customization layers you can write a DTD that references some or all of DocBook, but adds your own modifications. Modifying the DTD this way means that you never have to edit the DocBook modules directly, which is a tremendous boon to maintaining your modules. When the next release of DocBook comes out, you usually only have to make changes to your customization layer and your modification will be back in sync with the new version.

Customization layers work particularly well in DocBook because the base DTD makes extensive use of parameter entities that can be redefined.

Understanding DocBook Structure

DocBook is a large and, at first glance, fairly complex DTD. Much of the apparent complexity is caused by the prolific use of parameter entities. This was an intentional choice on the part of the maintainers, who traded "raw readability" for customizability. This section provides a general overview of the structure of the DTD. After you understand it, DocBook will probably seem much less complicated.

DocBook Modules

DocBook is composed of seven primary modules. These modules decompose the DTD into large, related chunks. Most modifications are restricted to a single chunk. Figure 5-1 shows the module structure of DocBook as a flowchart.

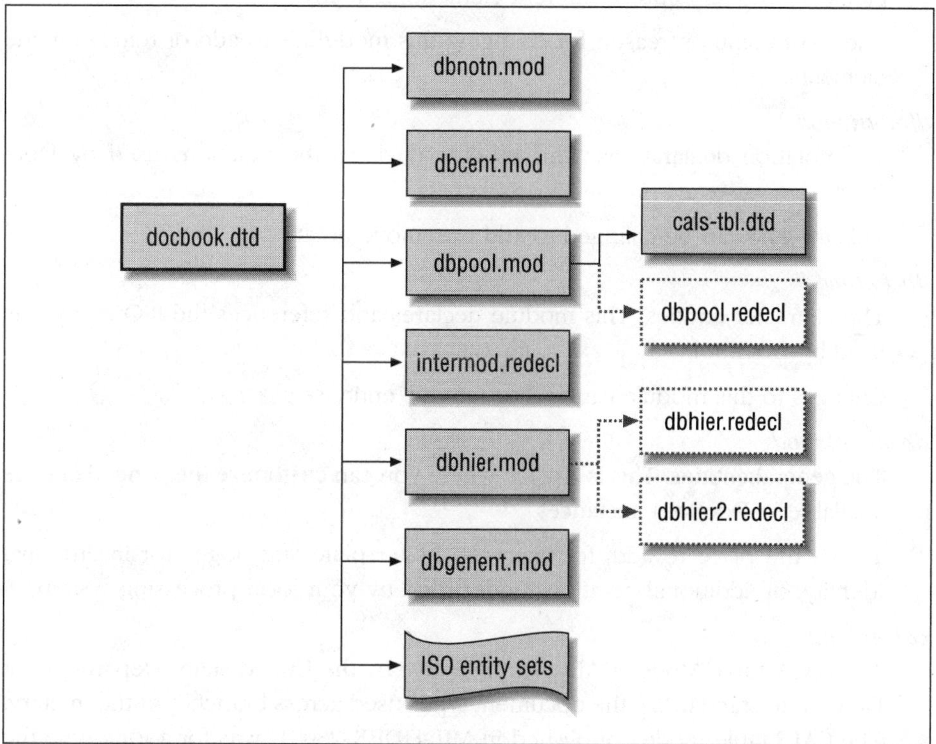

Figure 5-1. Structure of the DocBook DTD

The modules are:

docbook.dtd
: The main driver file. This module declares and references the other top-level modules.

dbhier.mod
: The hierarchy. This module declares the elements that provide the hierarchical structure of DocBook (sets, books, chapters, articles, and so on).

  Changes to this module alter the top-level structure of the DTD. If you want to write a DocBook-derived DTD with a different structure (something other than a book), but with the same paragraph and inline-level elements, you make most of your changes in this module.

dbpool.mod
: The information pool. This module declares the elements that describe content (inline elements, bibliographic data, block quotes, sidebars, and so on) but are not part of the large-scale hierarchy of a document. You can incorporate these elements into an entirely different element hierarchy.

  The most common reason for changing this module is to add or remove inline elements.

dbnotn.mod
: The notation declarations. This module declares the notations used by DocBook.

  This module can be changed to add or remove notations.

dbcent.mod
: The character entities. This module declares and references the ISO entity sets used by DocBook.

  Changes to this module can add or remove entity sets.

dbgenent.mod
: The general entities. This is a place where you can customize the general entities available in DocBook instances.

  This is the place to add, for example, boiler plate text, logos for institutional identity, or additional notations understood by your local processing system.

cals-tbl.dtd
: The CALS Table Model. CALS is an initiative by the United States Department of Defense to standardize the document types used across branches of the military. The CALS table model, published in MIL-HDBK-28001, was for a long time the most widely supported SGML table model (one might now argue that the HTML table model is more widely supported by some definitions of "widely supported"). In any event, it is the table model used by DocBook.

DocBook predates the publication of the OASIS Technical Resolution TR 9503:1995 (*http://www.oasis-open.org/html/a503.htm*), which defines an industry standard exchange table model and thus incorporates the *full* CALS Table Model.

Most changes to the CALS table model can be accomplished by modifying parameter entities in *dbpool.mod*; changing this DTD fragment is strongly discouraged. If you want to use a different table model, remove this one and add your own.

**.gml*

The ISO standard character entity sets. These entity sets are not actually part of the official DocBook distribution, but are referenced by default.

There are some additional modules, initially undefined, that can be inserted at several places for "redeclaration." This is described in more detail in "Removing Admonitions from Table Entries."

DocBook Parameterization

Customization layers are possible because DocBook has been extensively parameterized so that it is possible to make any changes that might be desired without ever editing the actual distributed modules. The parameter entities come in several flavors:

`%*.class;`

Classes group elements of a similar type: for example all the lists are in the `%list.class;`.

If you want to add a new kind of something (a new kind of list or a new kind of verbatim environment, for example), you generally want to add the name of the new element to the appropriate class.

`%*.mix;`

Mixtures are collections of classes that appear in content models. For example, the content model of the **Example** element includes `%example.mix;`. Not every element's content model is a single mixture, but elements in the same class tend to have the same mixture in their content model.

If you want to change the content model of some class of elements (lists or admonitions, perhaps), you generally want to change the definition of the appropriate mixture.

`%*.module;`

The `%*.module;` parameter entities control marked sections around individual elements and their attribute lists. For example, the element and attribute declarations for **Abbrev** occur within a marked section delimited by `%abbrev.module;`.

If you want to remove or redefine an element or its attribute list, you generally want to change its module marked section to `IGNORE` and possibly add a new definition for it in your customization layer.

`%*.element;`
: The `%*.element;` parameter entities were introduced in DocBook V3.1; they control marked sections around individual element declarations.

`%*.attlist;`
: The `%*.attlist;` parameter entities were introduced in DocBook V3.1; they control marked sections around individual attribute list declarations.

`%*.inclusion;`
`%*.exclusion;`
: These parameter entities control the inclusion and exclusion markup in element declarations.

Changing these declarations allows you to make global changes to the inclusions and exclusions in the DTD.

`%local.*;`
: The `%local.*;` parameter entities are a local extension mechanism. You can add markup to most entity declarations simply by declaring the appropriate local parameter entity.

The General Structure of Customization Layers

Although customization layers vary in complexity, most of them have the same general structure as other customization layers of similar complexity.

In the most common case, you probably want to include the entire DTD, but you want to make some small changes. These customization layers tend to look like this:

```
❶ Overrides of Entity Declarations Here

❷ <!ENTITY % orig-docbook "-//OASIS//DTD DocBook V3.1//EN">
  %orig-docbook;

❸ New/Modified Element and Attribute Declarations Here
```

❶ Declare new values for parameter entities (`%local.*;`, `%*.element;`, `%*.attlist;`) that you wish to modify.

❷ Include the entire DocBook DTD by parameter entity reference.

❸ Add new element and attribute declarations for any elements that you added to the DTD.

In slightly more complex customization layers, the changes that you want to make are influenced by the interactions between modules. In these cases, rather than including the whole DTD at once, you include each of the modules separately, perhaps with entity or element declarations between them:

```
Overrides of Most Entity Declarations Here

<!ENTITY % orig-pool "-//OASIS//ELEMENTS DocBook Information Pool V3.1//EN">
%orig-pool;

Overrides of Document Hierarchy Entities Here

<!ENTITY % orig-hier "-//OASIS//ELEMENTS DocBook Document Hierarchy V3.1//EN">
%orig-hier;

New/Modified Element and Attribute Declarations Here

<!ENTITY % orig-notn "-//OASIS//ENTITIES DocBook Notations V3.1//EN">
%orig-notn;

<!ENTITY % orig-cent "-//OASIS//ENTITIES DocBook Character Entities V3.1//EN">
%orig-cent;

<!ENTITY % orig-gen  "-//OASIS//ENTITIES DocBook Additional General Entities
V3.1//EN">
%orig-gen;
```

Finally, it's worth noting that in the rare case in which you need certain kinds of very simple, "one-off" customizations, you can do them in the document subset:

```
<!DOCTYPE book PUBLIC "-//OASIS//DTD DocBook V3.1//EN" [
Overrides of Entity Declarations Here
New/Modified Element and Attribute Declarations Here
]>
<book>...</book>
```

Writing, Testing, and Using a Customization Layer

The procedure for creating, testing, and using a customization layer is always about the same. In this section, we'll go through the process in some detail. The rest of the sections in this chapter describe a range of useful customization layers.

Deciding What to Change

If you're considering writing a customization layer, there must be something that you want to change. Perhaps you want to add an element or attribute, remove one, or change some other aspect of the DTD.

Adding an element, particularly an inline element, is one possibility. If you're writing documentation about an object-oriented system, you may have noticed that DocBook provides **ClassName** but not **MethodName**. Suppose you want to add **MethodName**?

Deciding How to Change a Customization Layer

Figuring out what to change may be the hardest part of the process. The organization of the parameter entities is quite logical, and, bearing in mind the organization described in "Understanding DocBook Structure," finding something similar usually provides a good model for new changes.

Two online resources may be useful. First, the parameter entity reference section of the online book provides more detail than the print version. Second, there is an alternate version of the book online that shows all of the element content models in terms of the parameter entities that define them, rather than the "flattened" versions shown here.

MethodName is similar to **ClassName**, so **ClassName** is probably a good model. **ClassName** is an inline element, not a hierarchy element, so it's in *dbpool.mod*. Searching for "classname" in *dbpool.mod* reveals:

```
<!ENTITY % local.tech.char.class "">
<!ENTITY % tech.char.class
        "Action|Application|ClassName|Command|ComputerOutput
        |Database|Email|EnVar|ErrorCode|ErrorName|ErrorType|Filename
        |Function|GUIButton|GUIIcon|GUILabel|GUIMenu|GUIMenuItem
        |GUISubmenu|Hardware|Interface|InterfaceDefinition|KeyCap
        |KeyCode|KeyCombo|KeySym|Literal|Constant|Markup|MediaLabel
        |MenuChoice|MouseButton|MsgText|Option|Optional|Parameter
        |Prompt|Property|Replaceable|ReturnValue|SGMLTag|StructField
        |StructName|Symbol|SystemItem|Token|Type|UserInput|VarName
        %local.tech.char.class;">
```

Searching further reveals the element and attribute declarations for **ClassName**.

It would seem (and, in fact, it is the case) that adding **MethodName** can be accomplished by adding it to the local extension mechanism for `%tech.char.class;`, namely `%local.tech.char.class;`, and adding element and attribute declarations for it. A customization layer that does this can be seen in Example 5-1.

Example 5-1. Adding MethodName with a Customization Layer

```
<!ENTITY % local.tech.char.class "|MethodName">      ❶

<!-- load DocBook -->                                ❷
<!ENTITY % DocBookDTD PUBLIC "-//OASIS//DTD DocBook V3.1//EN">
%DocBookDTD;

<!ELEMENT MethodName - - ((%smallcptr.char.mix;)+)  ❸>
<!ATTLIST MethodName                                 ❹
        %common.attrib;
        %classname.role.attrib;
        %local.classname.attrib;
>
```

❶ Declare the appropriate parameter entity (these are described in "DocBook Parameterization"). The declaration in your customization layer is encountered first, so it overrides the definition in the DocBook DTD (all the local classes are defined as empty in the DTD).

❷ Use a parameter entity to load the entire DocBook DTD.

❸ Add an element declaration for the new element. The content model for this element is taken directly from the content model of **ClassName**.

❹ Add an attribute list declaration for the new element. These are the same attributes as **ClassName**.

Using Your Customization Layer

In order to use the new customization layer, you must save it in a file, for example *mydocbk.dtd*, and then you must use the new DTD in your document.

The simplest way to use the new DTD is to point to it with a system identifier:

```
<!DOCTYPE chapter SYSTEM "/path/to/mydocbk.dtd">
<chapter><title>My Chapter</title>
<para>
The Java <classname>Math</classname> class provides a
<methodname>abs</methodname> method to compute absolute value of a number.
</para>
</chapter>
```

If you plan to use your customization layer in many documents, or exchange it with interchange partners, consider giving your DTD its own public identifier, as described in "If You Change DocBook, It's Not DocBook Anymore!"

In order to use the new public identifier, you must add it to your catalog:

```
PUBLIC "-//Your Organization//DTD DocBook V3.1-Based Extension V1.0//EN"
       "/share/sgml/mydocbk.dtd"
```

and use that public identifier in your documents:

```
<!DOCTYPE chapter
  PUBLIC "-//Your Organization//DTD DocBook V3.1-Based Extension V1.0//EN">
```

```
<chapter><title>My Chapter</title>
<para>
The Java <classname>Math</classname> class provides a
<methodname>abs</methodname> method to compute absolute value of a number.
</para>
</chapter>
```

If you're using XML, remember that you must provide a system identifier that satisfies the requirements of a Uniform Resource Identifier (URI).

Testing Your Work

DTDs, by their nature, contain many complex, interrelated elements. Whenever you make a change to the DTD, it's always wise to use a validating parser to double-check your work. A parser like *nsgmls* from James Clark's SP can identify elements (attributes, parameter entities) that are declared but unused, as well as ones that are used but undeclared.

A comprehensive test can be accomplished with *nsgmls* using the *-wall* option. Create a simple test document and run:

```
nsgmls ❶-sv ❷-wall test.sgm
```

❶ The *-s* option tells *nsgmls* to suppress its normal output (it will still show errors, if there are any). The *-v* option tells *nsgmls* to print its version number; this ensures that you always get *some* output, even if there are no errors.

❷ The *-wall* option tells *nsgmls* to provide a comprehensive list of all errors and warnings. You can use less verbose, and more specific options instead; for example, *-wundefined* to flag undefined elements or *-wunused-param* to warn you about unused parameter entities. The *nsgmls* documentation provides a complete list of warning types.

DocBook V3.1 Warnings

If you run the preceding command over DocBook V3.1, you'll discover one warning generated by the DTD:

```
nsgmls:I: SP version "1.3"
nsgmls:cals-tbl.dtd:314:37:W: content model is mixed but does not allow #PCDATA
everywhere
```

This is not truly an error in the DTD, and can safely be ignored. The warning is caused by "pernicious mixed content" in the content model of DocBook's **Entry** element. See the **Entry** reference page for a complete discussion.

Removing Elements

DocBook has a large number of elements. In some authoring environments, it may be useful or necessary to remove some of these elements.

Removing MsgSet

MsgSet is a favorite target. It has a complex internal structure designed for describing interrelated error messages, especially on systems that may exhibit messages from several different components. Many technical documents can do without it, and removing it leaves one less complexity to explain to your authors.

Example 5-2 shows a customization layer that removes the **MsgSet** element from DocBook:

Example 5-2. Removing MsgSet

```
<!ENTITY % compound.class "Procedure|SideBar"> ❶
<!ENTITY % msgset.content.module "IGNORE">     ❷
<!-- load DocBook -->
<!ENTITY % DocBookDTD PUBLIC "-//OASIS//DTD DocBook V3.1//EN">
%DocBookDTD;
```

❶ Remove **MsgSet** from the `%compound.class;`. This is the only place in the DTD where **MsgSet** is referenced.

❷ Exclude the definition of **MsgSet** and all of its subelements from the DTD.

Removing Computer Inlines

DocBook contains a large number of computer inlines. The DocBook inlines define a domain-specific vocabulary. If you're working in another domain, many of them may be unnecessary. You can remove a bunch of them by redefining the `%tech.char.class;` parameter entity and then excluding the declarations for the elements removed. The initial definition of `%tech.char.class;` is:

```
<!ENTITY % tech.char.class
     "Action|Application|ClassName|Command|ComputerOutput
     |Database|Email|EnVar|ErrorCode|ErrorName|ErrorType|Filename
     |Function|GUIButton|GUIIcon|GUILabel|GUIMenu|GUIMenuItem
     |GUISubmenu|Hardware|Interface|InterfaceDefinition|KeyCap
     |KeyCode|KeyCombo|KeySym|Literal|Markup|MediaLabel|MenuChoice
     |MouseButton|MsgText|Option|Optional|Parameter|Prompt|Property
     |Replaceable|ReturnValue|SGMLTag|StructField|StructName
     |Symbol|SystemItem|Token|Type|UserInput
     %local.tech.char.class;">
```

When examining this list, it seems that you can delete all of the inlines except, perhaps, **Application**, **Command**, **Email**, **Filename**, **Literal**, **Replaceable**, **Symbol**, and **SystemItem**. The following customization layer removes them.

Example 5-3. Removing Computer Inlines

```
<!ENTITY % tech.char.class
        "Application|Command|Email|Filename|Literal
        |Replaceable|Symbol|SystemItem">
<!ENTITY % action.module "IGNORE">
<!ENTITY % classname.module "IGNORE">
<!ENTITY % computeroutput.module "IGNORE">
<!ENTITY % database.module "IGNORE">
<!ENTITY % envar.module "IGNORE">
<!ENTITY % errorcode.module "IGNORE">
<!ENTITY % errorname.module "IGNORE">
<!ENTITY % errortype.module "IGNORE">
<!--<!ENTITY % function.module "IGNORE">-->
<!ENTITY % guibutton.module "IGNORE">
<!ENTITY % guiicon.module "IGNORE">
<!ENTITY % guilabel.module "IGNORE">
<!ENTITY % guimenu.module "IGNORE">
<!ENTITY % guimenuitem.module "IGNORE">
<!ENTITY % guisubmenu.module "IGNORE">
<!ENTITY % hardware.module "IGNORE">
<!ENTITY % interface.module "IGNORE">
<!ENTITY % interfacedefinition.module "IGNORE">
<!--<!ENTITY % keycap.module "IGNORE">-->
<!ENTITY % keycode.module "IGNORE">
<!--<!ENTITY % keycombo.module "IGNORE">-->
<!--<!ENTITY % keysym.module "IGNORE">-->
<!ENTITY % markup.module "IGNORE">
<!ENTITY % medialabel.module "IGNORE">
<!ENTITY % menuchoice.module "IGNORE">
<!--<!ENTITY % mousebutton.module "IGNORE">-->
<!--<!ENTITY % msgtext.module "IGNORE">-->
<!--<!ENTITY % option.module "IGNORE">-->
<!--<!ENTITY % optional.module "IGNORE">-->
<!--<!ENTITY % parameter.module "IGNORE">-->
<!ENTITY % prompt.module "IGNORE">
<!ENTITY % property.module "IGNORE">
<!ENTITY % returnvalue.module "IGNORE">
<!ENTITY % sgmltag.module "IGNORE">
<!ENTITY % structfield.module "IGNORE">
<!ENTITY % structname.module "IGNORE">
<!ENTITY % token.module "IGNORE">
<!ENTITY % type.module "IGNORE">
<!ENTITY % userinput.module "IGNORE">
<!-- load DocBook -->
<!ENTITY % DocBookDTD PUBLIC "-//OASIS//DTD DocBook V3.1//EN">
%DocBookDTD;
```

Initially we removed several more elements from `%tech.char.class;` (`%function.module;`, `%keycap.module;`), but using the testing procedure described in "Testing Your Work," we discovered that these elements are used in other content models. Because they are used in other content modules, they cannot simply be removed from the DTD by deleting them from `%tech.char.class;`. Even though they can't be deleted outright, we've taken them out of most inline contexts.

It's likely that a customization layer that removed this many technical inlines would also remove some larger technical structures (**MsgSet**, **FuncSynopsis**), which allows you to remove additional elements from the DTD.

Removing Synopsis Elements

Another possibility is removing the complex Synopsis elements. The customization layer in Example 5-4 removes **CmdSynopsis** and **FuncSynopsis**.

Example 5-4. Removing CmdSynopsis and FuncSynopsis

```
<!ENTITY % synop.class "Synopsis">
<!-- Instead of "Synopsis|CmdSynopsis|FuncSynopsis %local.synop.class;" -->

<!ENTITY % funcsynopsis.content.module "IGNORE">
<!ENTITY % cmdsynsynopsis.content.module "IGNORE">

<!-- load DocBook -->
<!ENTITY % DocBookDTD PUBLIC "-//OASIS//DTD DocBook V3.1//EN">
%DocBookDTD;
```

Completely removing all Synopsis elements would require a more extensive customization. You can't make any of the `%*.class;` parameter entities completely empty without changing all of the parameter entities that use them. See "Removing an Entire Class."

Removing Sectioning Elements

Perhaps you want to restrict your authors to only three levels of sectioning. To do that, you must remove the **Sect4** and **Sect5** elements, as shown in Example 5-5.

Example 5-5. Removing Sect4 and Sect5 Elements

```
<!ENTITY % sect3.module "IGNORE">
<!ENTITY % sect4.module "IGNORE">
<!ENTITY % sect5.module "IGNORE">

<!ENTITY % DocBookDTD PUBLIC "-//OASIS//DTD DocBook V3.1//EN">
%DocBookDTD;

<!ENTITY % local.sect3.attrib "">
<!ENTITY % sect3.role.attrib "%role.attrib;">
<!ELEMENT Sect3 - O (Sect3Info?, (%sect.title.content;), (%nav.class;)*,
(((%divcomponent.mix;)+,
((%refentry.class;)* | SimpleSect*))
| (%refentry.class;)+ | SimpleSect+), (%nav.class;)*)>
<!ATTLIST Sect3
--
Renderas: Indicates the format in which the heading should
appear
--
```

Example 5-5. Removing Sect4 and Sect5 Elements (continued)

```
Renderas(Sect1
|Sect2
|Sect4
|Sect5)#IMPLIED
%label.attrib;
%status.attrib;
%common.attrib;
%sect3.role.attrib;
%local.sect3.attrib;
>
```

In order to completely remove an element that isn't in the information pool, it is usually necessary to redefine the elements that include it. In this case, because we're removing the **Sect4** element, we must redefine the **Sect3** element that uses it.

Removing Admonitions from Table Entries

All of the customization layers that we've examined so far have been fairly straightforward. This section describes a much more complex customization layer. Back in "DocBook Modules" we mentioned that several additional modules existed for "redeclaration." The customization layer developed in this section cannot be written without them.

The goal is to remove admonitions (**Warning**, **Caution**, **Note**) from table entries.

Example 5-6 is a straightforward, and incorrect, attempt.

Example 5-6. Removing Admonitions (First Attempt: Incorrect)

```
<!-- THIS CUSTOMIZATION LAYER CONTAINS ERRORS -->
<!ENTITY % tabentry.mix
        "%list.class;
        |%linespecific.class;
        |%para.class;           |Graphic
        %local.tabentry.mix;">
<!-- load DocBook -->
<!ENTITY % DocBookDTD PUBLIC "-//OASIS//DTD DocBook V3.1//EN">
%DocBookDTD;
```

Because the parameter entity `%tabentry.mix;` defines the mixture of elements allowed in table entries, you should remove admonitions.

If you attempt to parse this DTD, you'll find that the declaration of `%tabentry.mix;` contains errors. While you can redefine parameter entities, you cannot make reference to entities that have not been defined yet, so the use of `%list.class;`, `%linespecific.class;`, and so on, aren't allowed.

Your second attempt might look like Example 5-7.

Example 5-7. Removing Admonitions (Second Attempt: Incorrect)

```
<!-- THIS CUSTOMIZATION LAYER DOESN'T WORK -->
<!-- load DocBook -->
<!ENTITY % DocBookDTD PUBLIC "-//OASIS//DTD DocBook V3.1//EN">
%DocBookDTD;
<!ENTITY % tabentry.mix
        "%list.class;
        |%linespecific.class;
        |%para.class;          |Graphic
        %local.tabentry.mix;">
```

Declaring `%tabentry.mix;` after the DTD has been loaded removes the errors.

This example contains no errors, but it also doesn't have any effect. Remember, only the first entity declaration counts, so the declaration of `%tabentry.mix;` in *dbpool.mod* is the one used, not your redeclaration.

The only way to fix this problem is to make use of one of the redeclaration placeholders in DocBook.

Redeclaration placeholders are spots in which you can insert definitions into the middle of the DTD. There are four redeclaration placeholders in DocBook:

`%rdbmods;`
: Inserted in *docbook.dtd*, between *dbpool.mod* and *dbhier.mod*. This placeholder is controlled by the `%intermod.redecl.module;` marked section.

`%rdbpool;`
: Inserted in the middle of *dbpool.mod*, between the `%*.class;` and `%*.mix;` entity declarations. This placeholder is controlled by the `%dbpool.redecl.module;` marked section.

`%rdbhier;`
: Inserted in the middle of *dbhier.mod*, between the `%*.class;` and `%*.mix;` entity declarations. This placeholder is controlled by the `%dbhier.redecl.module;` marked section.

`%rdbhier2;`
: Also inserted into *dbhier.mod*, after the `%*.mix;` entity declarations. This placeholder is controlled by the `%dbhier.redecl2.module;` marked section.

Use the redeclaration placeholder that it occurs nearest to, but before the entity that you want to redeclare. In our case, this is `%rdbpool;`, as seen in Example 5-8.

Example 5-8. Removing Admonitions (Third Attempt: Correct, if confusing)

```
<!ENTITY % dbpool.redecl.module "INCLUDE">
<!ENTITY % rdbpool
'<!ENTITY % local.tabentry.mix "">
<!ENTITY % tabentry.mix
        "&#37;list.class;
        |&#37;linespecific.class;
        |&#37;para.class;          |Graphic
        &#37;local.tabentry.mix;">'>

<!-- load DocBook -->
<!ENTITY % DocBookDTD PUBLIC "-//OASIS//DTD DocBook V3.1//EN">
%DocBookDTD;
```

Example 5-8 uses numeric character entity references to escape the `%` signs in the entity declarations and nests an entity declaration in another parameter entity. All of this is perfectly legal, but a bit confusing. A clearer solution, and the only practical solution if you're doing anything more than a single redeclaration, is to place the new declarations in another file and include them in your customization layer by reference, like in Example 5-9.

Example 5-9. Removing Admonitions (Fourth Attempt: Correct)

In your customization layer:

```
<!ENTITY % dbpool.redecl.module "INCLUDE">
<!ENTITY % rdbpool SYSTEM "rdbpool.mod">

<!-- load DocBook -->
<!ENTITY % DocBookDTD PUBLIC "-//OASIS//DTD DocBook V3.1//EN">
%DocBookDTD;
```

In *rdbpool.mod*:

```
<!ENTITY % local.tabentry.mix "">
<!ENTITY % tabentry.mix
        "%list.class;
        |%linespecific.class;
        |%para.class;          |Graphic
        %local.tabentry.mix;">
```

Removing an Entire Class

Perhaps the modification that you want to make is to completely remove an entire class of elements. (If you have no need for synopsis elements of any sort, why not remove them?) In order to remove an entire class of elements, you must not only redefine the class as empty, but you must also redefine all of the parameter entities that use that class. The customization layer below completely removes the `% synop.class;` from DocBook. It requires a customization layer, shown in Example 5-10, that includes both a redeclaration module in *dbpool.mod* and a redeclaration module in *dbhier.mod*.

Example 5-10. Removing %synop.class;

In the customization layer:

```
<!ENTITY % synop.class "">

<!ENTITY % dbpool.redecl.module "INCLUDE">
<!ENTITY % rdbpool SYSTEM "remv.synop.class.rdbpool.mod">

<!ENTITY % dbhier.redecl.module "INCLUDE">
<!ENTITY % rdbhier SYSTEM "remv.synop.class.rdbhier.mod">

<!-- load DocBook -->
<!ENTITY % DocBookDTD PUBLIC "-//OASIS//DTD DocBook V3.1//EN">
%DocBookDTD;
```

In *remv.synop.class.rdbpool.mod*:

```
<!ENTITY % local.component.mix "">
<!ENTITY % component.mix
  "%list.class;   |%admon.class;
  |%linespecific.class;
  |%para.class;   |%informal.class;
  |%formal.class;   |%compound.class;
  |%genobj.class;   |%descobj.class;
  %local.component.mix;">

<!ENTITY % local.sidebar.mix "">
<!ENTITY % sidebar.mix
  "%list.class;   |%admon.class;
  |%linespecific.class;
  |%para.class;   |%informal.class;
  |%formal.class;   |Procedure
  |%genobj.class;
  %local.sidebar.mix;">

<!ENTITY % local.footnote.mix "">
<!ENTITY % footnote.mix
  "%list.class;
  |%linespecific.class;
  |%para.class;   |%informal.class;
  %local.footnote.mix;">

<!ENTITY % local.example.mix "">
<!ENTITY % example.mix
  "%list.class;
  |%linespecific.class;
  |%para.class;   |%informal.class;
  %local.example.mix;">

<!ENTITY % local.admon.mix "">
<!ENTITY % admon.mix
  "%list.class;
  |%linespecific.class;
  |%para.class;   |%informal.class;
```

Example 5-10. Removing %synop.class; (continued)

```
  |%formal.class;  |Procedure|Sidebar
  |Anchor|BridgeHead|Comment
  %local.admon.mix;">

<!ENTITY % local.figure.mix "">
<!ENTITY % figure.mix
  "%linespecific.class;
     |%informal.class;
  %local.figure.mix;">

<!ENTITY % local.glossdef.mix "">
<!ENTITY % glossdef.mix
  "%list.class;
  |%linespecific.class;
  |%para.class;  |%informal.class;
  |%formal.class;
  |Comment
  %local.glossdef.mix;">

<!ENTITY % local.para.char.mix "">
<!ENTITY % para.char.mix
  "#PCDATA
  |%xref.char.class; |%gen.char.class;
  |%link.char.class; |%tech.char.class;
  |%base.char.class; |%docinfo.char.class;
  |%other.char.class; |%inlineobj.char.class;
  %local.para.char.mix;">
```

In *remv.synop.class.rdbhier.mod*:

```
<!ENTITY % local.divcomponent.mix "">
<!ENTITY % divcomponent.mix
  "%list.class;  |%admon.class;
  |%linespecific.class;
  |%para.class;  |%informal.class;
  |%formal.class;  |%compound.class;
  |%genobj.class;  |%descobj.class;
  %local.divcomponent.mix;">

<!ENTITY % local.refcomponent.mix "">
<!ENTITY % refcomponent.mix
  "%list.class;  |%admon.class;
  |%linespecific.class;
  |%para.class;  |%informal.class;
  |%formal.class;  |%compound.class;
  |%genobj.class;  |%descobj.class;
  %local.refcomponent.mix;">

<!ENTITY % local.indexdivcomponent.mix "">
<!ENTITY % indexdivcomponent.mix
  "ItemizedList|OrderedList|VariableList|SimpleList
  |%linespecific.class;
  |%para.class;  |%informal.class;
```

Example 5-10. Removing %synop.class; (continued)

```
  |Anchor|Comment
  |%link.char.class;
  %local.indexdivcomponent.mix;">
```

Removing Attributes

Just as there may be more elements than you need, there may be more attributes.

Removing an Attribute

Suppose you want to remove the **RenderAs** attribute from the **Sect1** element. **RenderAs** allows the author to "cheat" in the presentation of hierarchy by specifying that the stylesheet should render a **Sect1** as something else: a **Sect3**, perhaps. Example 5-11 details the removal of **RenderAs**.

Example 5-11. Removing RenderAs from Sect1

```
<!ENTITY % sect1.module "IGNORE">                    ❶

<!-- load DocBook -->                                ❷
<!ENTITY % DocBookDTD PUBLIC "-//OASIS//DTD DocBook V3.1//EN">
%DocBookDTD;

<!ENTITY % local.sect1.attrib "">                    ❸
<!ENTITY % sect1.role.attrib "%role.attrib;">        ❹
<!ELEMENT Sect1 - O (Sect1Info?, (%sect.title.content;), (%nav.class;)*,   ❺
        (((%divcomponent.mix;)+,
        ((%refentry.class;)* | Sect2* | SimpleSect*))
        | (%refentry.class;)+ | Sect2+ | SimpleSect+), (%nav.class;)*)
        +(%ubiq.mix;)>
<!ATTLIST Sect1                                      ❻
        %label.attrib;
        %status.attrib;
        %common.attrib;
        %sect1.role.attrib;
        %local.sect1.attrib;
>
```

❶ Turn off the **Sect1** module so that the element and attribute declarations in the DTD will be ignored.

❷ Include the DocBook DTD.

❸ By keeping the local attribute declaration, we leave open the possibility of a simple customization layer on top of our customization layer.

❹ Similarly, we keep the parameterized definition of the `Role` attribute.

❺ We're changing the attribute list, not the element, so we've simply copied the **Sect1** element declaration from the DocBook DTD.

❻ Finally, we declare the attribute list, leaving out the `RenderAs`.

Subsetting the Common Attributes

DocBook defines eleven common attributes; these attributes appear on *every* element. Depending on how you're processing your documents, removing some of them can both simplify the authoring task and improve processing speed.

Some obvious candidates are:

Effectivity attributes (`Arch`, `OS`,...)
: If you're not using all of the effectivity attributes in your documents, you can get rid of up to seven attributes in one fell swoop.

`Lang`
: If you're not producing multilingual documents, you can remove `Lang`.

`Remap`
: The `Remap` attribute is designed to hold the name of a semantically equivalent construct from a previous markup scheme (for example, a Microsoft Word style template name, if you're converting from Word). If you're authoring from scratch, or not preserving previous constructs with `Remap`, you can get rid of it.

`XrefLabel`
: If your processing system isn't using `XrefLabel`, it's a candidate as well.

The customization layer in Example 5-12 reduces the common attributes to just `ID` and `Lang`.

Example 5-12. Removing Common Attributes

```
<!ENTITY % common.attrib
"ID   ID    #IMPLIED
 Lang CDATA #IMPLIED"
>
<!ENTITY % idreq.common.attrib
"ID   ID    #REQUIRED
 Lang CDATA #IMPLIED"
>
<!-- load DocBook -->
<!ENTITY % DocBookDTD PUBLIC "-//OASIS//DTD DocBook V3.1//EN">
%DocBookDTD;
```

By definition, whatever attributes you define in the `%common.attrib;` and `%idreq.common.attrib;` parameter entities are the common attributes. In *dbpool.mod*, these parameter entities are defined in terms of other parameter entities, but there's no way to preserve that structure in your customization layer.

Adding Elements: Adding a Sect6

Adding a structural (as opposed to information pool) element generally requires adding its name to a class and then providing the appropriate definitions. Example 5-13 extends DocBook by adding a **Sect6** element.

Example 5-13. Adding a Sect6 Element

```
<!ENTITY % sect5.module "IGNORE">
<!ENTITY % DocBookDTD PUBLIC "-//OASIS//DTD DocBook V3.1//EN">
%DocBookDTD;
<!-- Add Sect6 to content model of Sect5 -->
<!ENTITY % sect5.role.attrib "%role.attrib;">
<!ELEMENT Sect5 - O (Sect5Info?, (%sect.title.content;), (%nav.class;)*,
        (((%divcomponent.mix;)+,
                ((%refentry.class;)* | Sect6* | SimpleSect*))
        | (%refentry.class;)+ | Sect6+ | SimpleSect+), (%nav.class;)*)>
<!ATTLIST Sect5
        %label.attrib;
        %status.attrib;
        %common.attrib;
        %sect5.role.attrib;
>
<!ENTITY % sect6.role.attrib "%role.attrib;">
<!ELEMENT Sect6 - O (Sect6Info?, (%sect.title.content;), (%nav.class;)*,
        (((%divcomponent.mix;)+, ((%refentry.class;)* | SimpleSect*))
        | (%refentry.class;)+ | SimpleSect+), (%nav.class;)*)>
<!ATTLIST Sect6
        %label.attrib;
        %status.attrib;
        %common.attrib;
        %sect6.role.attrib;
>
```

Here we've redefined **Sect5** to include **Sect6** and provided a declaration for **Sect6**. Note that we didn't bother to provide `RenderAs` attributes in our redefinitions. To properly support **Sect6**, you might want to redefine all of the sectioning elements so that `Sect6` is a legal attribute value for `RenderAs`.

Other Modifications: Classifying a Role

The `Role` attribute, found on almost all of the elements in DocBook, is a `CDATA` attribute that can be used to subclass an element. In some applications, it may be useful to modify the definition of `Role` so that authors must choose one of a specific set of possible values.

In Example 5-14, `Role` on the **Procedure** element is constrained to the values `Required` or `Optional`.

Example 5-14. Changing Role on Procedure

```
<!ENTITY % procedure.role.attrib "Role (Required|Optional) #IMPLIED">
<!-- load DocBook -->
<!ENTITY % DocBookDTD PUBLIC "-//OASIS//DTD DocBook V3.1//EN">
%DocBookDTD;>>
```

II

Reference

DocBook Element Reference

This reference describes every element in the DocBook DTD. Elements marked **3.1** are new in DocBook V3.1, which was released in February, 1999.

Organization of Reference Pages

The description of each element in this reference is divided into the following sections:

Synopsis

Provides a quick synopsis of the element. The content of the synopsis table varies according to the nature of the element described, but may include any or all of the following sections:

Content Model or Declared Content

Describes the content model of the element in SGML/XML DTD terms. See "Understanding Content Models."

Inclusions

Lists "inclusions." Inclusions are an SGML feature. Included elements can appear anywhere inside the element that includes them, even in places that aren't ordinarily valid. For example, **Chapter** includes **IndexTerm**. This means that within a **Chapter**, **IndexTerm** can appear inside **Emphasis**, for instance, even though the content model of **Emphasis** does not explicitly allow **IndexTerms**.

Exclusions

Lists "exclusions." Exclusions are an SGML feature. Excluded elements cannot appear anywhere inside the element that excludes them, even in places that are ordinarily valid. For example, **Footnote** excludes **Fotnote**. This means that a **Footnote** cannot appear inside a **Para** inside a **Footnote**, even though **Footnote** appears in the content model of **Para**.

Lists elements that are excluded from appearing at any level below the element described.

Attributes

Provides a synopsis of the attributes on the element. For brevity, common attributes are described only once, in this introduction.

Parameter Entities

Lists the parameter entities in which the element described appears. Parameter entities are important when you are customizing the DTD.

Description

Describes the semantics of the element in detail.

Processing expectations

Summarizes specific formatting expectations of the element. Many processing expectations are influenced by attribute values. Be sure to consult the description of element attributes as well.

Future changes

Identifies changes that are scheduled for future versions of the DTD. These changes are highlighted because they involve some backward-incompatability that may make currently valid DocBook documents no longer valid under the new version.

Attributes

Describes the semantics of each attribute in detail.

See Also

Lists similar or related elements.

Examples

Provides examples of proper usage for the element. Generally, the smallest example required to reasonably demonstrate the element is used. In many cases, a formatted version of the example is also shown.

All of the examples printed in the book use the SGML version of DocBook. The CD-ROM includes the full text of all of the examples.

Formatted examples are indicated using a vertical bar.

Understanding Content Models

Each element synopsis begins with a concise description of the elements it can contain. This description is in DTD "content model" syntax, with all parameter entities expanded.

Content models are the way that DTDs describe the name, number, and order of other elements that may be used inside an element. The primary feature of content model syntax is that it is concise, but this conciseness comes at the cost of legibility until you are familiar with the syntax.

There are six components to content model syntax: *element names, keywords, repetitions, sequences, alternatives*, and *groups*.

Element names

An element name in a content model indicates that an element of that type may (or must) occur at that position.

A content model of `Para` indicates that the element must contain a single paragraph.

Keywords

There are two keywords that occur in the content models of DocBook elements: `EMPTY`, and `#PCDATA`.

A content model that consists of the single keyword `EMPTY` identifes an element as an empty element. Empty elements are not allowed to have any content. In order for the word "EMPTY" to have this special meaning, it must be the first and only word in the content model. The word "EMPTY" at any other place is treated as an element name.

The `#PCDATA` keyword indicates that text may occur at that position. The text may consist of entity references and any characters that are legal in the document character set. For XML documents, the document character set is always Unicode. In SGML the declaration can identify character sets and ranges that are allowed. DocBook SGML documents use the ISO Latin 1 character set.

Repetitions

An unadorned element name indicates that an element must occur exactly once at that position. A content model can also specify that an element may occur zero or more times, one or more times, or exactly zero or one time. This is accomplished by following the element name with one of the following characters: `*` for zero or more times, `+` for one or more times, or `?` for exactly zero or one times.

A content model of `Para+` indicates that the element must contain at least one paragraph and may contain many.

Sequences

If element names in a content model are separated by commas, then they must occur in sequence.

A content model of `Title, Para` indicates that the element must contain a single title followed by a single paragraph.

Alternatives

If element names in a content model are separated by vertical bars (|), then they are alternatives. These are sometimes called "or groups" because they require the selection of one or another element.

A content model of `Phrase | Para` indicates that the element must contain either a single phrase or a single paragraph.

In SGML, there is another connector: the ampersand (&). The ampersand is a kind of combination of alternative and sequence, which means that all of the elements must occur, but they can occur in any order. DocBook does not have any content models that use the ampersand connector. XML does not allow it.

Groups

Finally, parenthesis may be used around part of a content model. A group formed this way can have repetition indicators and may occur as part of a sequence.

A content model of `(Literal | Replaceable)+` indicates that either **Literal** or **Replaceable** must occur and they can be repeated (and mixed) any number of times.

Content models and validity

A parser uses the content models to determine if a given document is valid. In order for a document to be valid, the content of every element in the document must "match" the content model for that element.

In practical terms, match means that it must be possible to expand the content model until it exactly matches the sequence of elements in the document.

For example, consider the content model of the **Epigraph** element: `Attribution?, (FormalPara | Para | SimPara)+`. This indicates that the following document fragment is valid:

```
<epigraph>
<para>Some text</para>
</epigraph>
```

It is valid because the following expansion of the content model exactly matches the actual content: choose zero occurances of **Attribution**, choose the alternative **Para** from the group, and choose to let the "+" match once.

By the same token, this example is not valid because there is no expansion of the content model that can match it:

```
<epigraph>
<para>Some text</para>
<attribution>John Doe</attribution>
</epigraph>
```

There is one additional restriction on the matching ability of the parser: it is not allowed to "look ahead." This means that there are many useful content models that are ambiguous.

Ambiguity

Ambiguity is not allowed. The parser must always be able to choose exactly what to match based upon the next input token. Consider the following content model: `Meta*, Title?, Meta*`.

The intent is clear: to allow some meta-information and a single, optional **Title**. But this content model is ambiguous for the following reason: if the document content begins with a **Meta** element, it is impossible to tell if it matches the **Meta** before the **Title** or after without looking ahead.

Ambiguous content models are detected by the parser when it reads the DTD. It is not sufficient that your document simply be unambiguous; it must not be possible to construct any ambiguous document.

#PCDATA and repetition

The `#PCDATA` keyword can always match the empty string. This makes it impossible to force an element that may contain characters not to be empty. In other words, the following content model *does not* guarantee that the element is not empty: `(#PCDATA)+`.

In XML, the `#PCDATA` keyword is only allowed in optional, repeatable "or groups", and it must be the first member of the group.

Common Attributes

The following attributes occur on all elements. They are summarized here once for brevity and to make the additional attributes that occur on many elements stand out.

Name	Type	Default
`Arch`	CDATA	*None*
`Conformance`	NMTOKENS	*None*
`ID`	ID	*None/Required*[a]
`Lang`	CDATA	*None*
`OS`	CDATA	*None*
`Remap`	CDATA	*None*
`Role`	CDATA	*None*
`Revision`	CDATA	*None*

Name	Type	Default
RevisionFlag	*Enumerated:* Changed Added Deleted Off	*None*
UserLevel	CDATA	*None*
Vendor	CDATA	*None*
XrefLabel	CDATA	*None*

[a] On a few elements, the ID is required, but on most it is not.

Arch

Arch designates the computer or chip architecture to which the element applies.

Conformance

Conformance indicates standards conformance characteristics of the item contained in the element. These characteristics are application-specific. DocBook provides no defaults.

ID

ID is an identifying string for the element. It must be unique at least within the document and must begin with a letter.

Lang

Lang should be a language code drawn from ISO 639 (perhaps extended with a country code drawn from ISO 3166, as en_US). Use it when you need to signal your application to change hyphenation and other display characteristics.

OS

OS indicates the operating system to which the element is applicable.

Remap

Remap contains an element name or similar semantic identifier assigned to the content in a previous markup scheme.

Role

Role contains a string used to classify or subclassify an element.

While Role is a common attribute in the sense that it occurs on almost all elements, it is not part of either of the common attributes parameter entities (%common.attrib; or %idreq.common.attrib;). It is parameterized differently because it is useful to be able to subclass Role independently on different elements.

Revision

Revision indicates the editorial revision to which the element belongs.

`RevisionFlag`
: `RevisionFlag` indicates the revision status of element; the default is that the element hasn't been revised. `RevisionFlag` is intended only for simple revision management: to track the entire history of a document use a proper revision control system. Use `RevisionFlag` for indicating changes from one version to the next, no more.

`UserLevel`
: `UserLevel` indicates the level of user experience to which element applies.

`Vendor`
: `Vendor` indicates the computer vendor to which the element applies.

`XrefLabel`
: `XrefLabel` holds text to be used when a cross reference (**XRef**) is made to the element.

Attribute Types

SGML offers a small selection of attribute types. (XML offers a subset of these.) For convenience, a brief description of each of these types is provided here:

`CDATA`
: A string of characters.

`NUMBER`
: A number. Numbers must begin with a hyphen or digit and can include the decimal point.

`NMTOKEN`
: A sequence of name characters (letters, digits, hyphens, and periods). This differs from a `CDATA` attribute because it cannot contain spaces, punctuation, or other non-name characters.

`NMTOKENS`
: A sequence of one or more space-delimited `NMTOKEN` values.

`NUTOKEN`
: A sequence of number characters (digits, hyphens, and periods). This differs from a `NUMBER` field because it is not required to begin with a digit or a hyphen.

`ENTITY`
: An entity name. The value of an `ENTITY` attribute must be the name of a declared entity.

`NAME`
: A name. A name must begin with a letter and can consist of letters, digits, hyphens, and periods.

NAMES

A sequence of one or more space-delimited NAME values.

ID

An ID. IDs are names that must be globally unique within the document. The ID attribute declares the ID.

IDREF

An single ID. IDs are names that must be globally unique within the document. The value of an IDREF attribute must be the name of an ID attribute defined in the document.

IDREFS

A sequence of one or more space-delimited ID values.

Abbrev—An abbreviation, especially one followed by a period

Synopsis

Mixed Content Model

```
Abbrev ::=
((#PCDATA|Acronym|Emphasis|Trademark|Link|OLink|ULink|Anchor|
  Comment|Subscript|Superscript|InlineGraphic|InlineMediaObject|
  IndexTerm)+)
```

Attributes	Common attributes	
Parameter Entities		
%bibliocomponent.mix;	%gen.char.class;	%ndxterm.char.mix;
%para.char.mix;	%programlisting.content;	%refinline.char.mix;
%screen.content;	%tbl.entry.mdl;	%title.char.mix;

Description

An abbreviation, especially one followed by a period.

Processing expectations

Formatted inline.

See Also

Acronym, **Emphasis**, **ForeignPhrase**, **Phrase**, **Quote**, **WordAsWord**

Examples

```
<!DOCTYPE para PUBLIC "-//OASIS//DTD DocBook V3.1//EN">
<para>
The <abbrev>Assn.</> of Computing Machinery would probably never
abbreviate &ldquo;Association&rdquo; like this.
</para>
```

The Assn. of Computing Machinery would probably never abbreviate "Association" like this.

For additional examples, see also **Bibliography**, **BiblioSet**, **Footnote**, **Glossary**.

Abstract—A summary

Synopsis

Content Model
`Abstract ::=`
`(Title?,`
` (FormalPara|Para|SimPara)+)`		

Attributes	Common attributes	
Parameter Entities		
`%bibliocomponent.mix;`	`%bookcomponent.content;`	`%component.mix;`
`%descobj.class;`	`%divcomponent.mix;`	`%refcomponent.mix;`

Description

An abstract can occur in most components of DocBook. It is expected to contain some sort of summary of the content with which it is associated (by containment).

Processing expectations

Formatted as a displayed block. Sometimes suppressed. Often presented in alternate outputs.

See Also

BlockQuote, **Epigraph**, **Highlights**, **Sidebar**

Examples

```
<!DOCTYPE chapter PUBLIC "-//OASIS//DTD DocBook V3.1//EN">
<chapter><title>Some Chapter</title>
<abstract>
<para>
In brief, &hellip;
</para>
</abstract>
<para>
In this chapter, &hellip;
</para>
</chapter>
```

For additional examples, see also **Section**.

Accel—A graphical user interface (GUI) keyboard shortcut

Synopsis

Mixed Content Model
`Accel ::=`
`((#PCDATA|Replaceable|InlineGraphic|InlineMediaObject|IndexTerm)+)`	

Attributes	Common attributes

Description

An accelerator is usually a letter used with a meta key (such as control or alt) to activate some element of a GUI without using the mouse to point and click at it.

Processing expectations

Formatted inline. Often underlined.

See Also

GUIButton, **GUIIcon**, **GUILabel**, **GUIMenu**, **GUIMenuItem**, **GUISubmenu**, **KeyCap**, **KeyCode**, **KeyCombo**, **KeySym**, **MenuChoice**, **MouseButton**, **Shortcut**

Examples

```
<!DOCTYPE para PUBLIC "-//OASIS//DTD DocBook V3.1//EN">
<para OS="windows">
You can exit most Windows applications by selecting
<guimenuitem><accel>Q</accel>uit</guimenuitem> or
<guimenuitem>E<accel>x</accel>it</guimenuitem> from
the <guimenu><accel>F</>ile</guimenu> menu.
</para>
```

You can exit most Windows applications by selecting *Quit* or *Exit* from the *File* menu.

For additional examples, see also **GUIMenu**.

Ackno—Acknowledgements in an **Article**

Synopsis

Mixed Content Model
`Ackno ::=`
`((#PCDATA|Link|OLink|ULink|Emphasis|Trademark|Replaceable|Comment|`
`Subscript|Superscript|InlineGraphic|InlineMediaObject|IndexTerm)+)`	

Attributes	Common attributes

Description

Acknowledgements in an **Article**.

Processing expectations

Formatted as a displayed block.

Examples

```
<!DOCTYPE article PUBLIC "-//OASIS//DTD DocBook V3.1//EN">
<article>
<artheader>
<author><firstname>Norman</firstname><surname>Walsh</surname></author>
</artheader>
<para>
This is an odd, minimalist sort of article example.
</para>
<ackno>
First, I'd like to thank the members of the academy, &hellip;
</ackno>
</article>
```

Acronym—An often pronounceable word made from the initial (or selected) letters of a name or phrase

Synopsis

Mixed Content Model
`Acronym ::=`
`((#PCDATA|Acronym|Emphasis|Trademark|Link|OLink|ULink|Anchor|`
`Comment|Subscript|Superscript|InlineGraphic|InlineMediaObject|`
`IndexTerm)+)`		

Attributes	Common attributes	
Parameter Entities		
`%acronym.exclusion;`	`%gen.char.class;`	`%ndxterm.char.mix;`
`%para.char.mix;`	`%programlisting.con-tent;`	`%refinline.char.mix;`
`%screen.content;`	`%tbl.entry.mdl;`	`%title.char.mix;`
`%word.char.mix;`		

Description

A pronounceable contraction of initials. An acronym is often printed in all capitals or small capitals, although this is sometimes incorrect (consider dpi or bps).

Processing expectations

Formatted inline. The `MoreInfo` attribute can help generate a link or query to retrieve additional information.

See Also

Abbrev, **Emphasis**, **ForeignPhrase**, **Phrase**, **Quote**, **WordAsWord**

Examples

```
<!DOCTYPE para PUBLIC "-//OASIS//DTD DocBook V3.1//EN">
<para>
In the United States, <acronym>NASA</> stands for the
National Aeronautics and Space Administration.
</para>
```

In the United States, NASA stands for the National Aeronautics and Space Administration.

For additional examples, see also **Application**, **Command**, **Glossary**, **Hardware**, **Option**, **RefEntry**, **VariableList**.

Action—A response to a user event

Synopsis

Mixed Content Model

```
Action ::=
((#PCDATA|Link|OLink|ULink|Action|Application|ClassName|Command|
  ComputerOutput|Database|Email|EnVar|ErrorCode|ErrorName|
  ErrorType|Filename|Function|GUIButton|GUIIcon|GUILabel|GUIMenu|
  GUIMenuItem|GUISubmenu|Hardware|Interface|InterfaceDefinition|
  KeyCap|KeyCode|KeyCombo|KeySym|Literal|Constant|Markup|
  MediaLabel|MenuChoice|MouseButton|MsgText|Option|Optional|
  Parameter|Prompt|Property|Replaceable|ReturnValue|SGMLTag|
  StructField|StructName|Symbol|SystemItem|Token|Type|UserInput|
  VarName|Anchor|Comment|Subscript|Superscript|InlineGraphic|
  InlineMediaObject|IndexTerm)+)
```

Attributes **Name**	Common attributes **Type**	**Default**
MoreInfo	*Enumeration:* None RefEntry	"None"

Parameter Entities

%cptr.char.mix;	%ndxterm.char.mix;	%para.char.mix;
%programlisting.content;	%refinline.char.mix;	%refname.char.mix;
%screen.content;	%tbl.entry.mdl;	%tech.char.class;
%title.char.mix;		

Description

Actions are usually associated with GUIs. An event might be movement or clicking of the mouse, a change in focus, or any number of other occurrences.

Processing expectations

Formatted inline. The `MoreInfo` attribute can help generate a link or query to retrieve additional information.

4.0 *Future Changes*

The content model of **Action** will be constrained to `(#PCDATA | Replaceable | InlineGraphic)` in DocBook V4.0.

Attributes

MoreInfo

If `MoreInfo` is set to `RefEntry`, it implies that a **RefEntry** exists which further describes the **Action**.

Examples

```
<!DOCTYPE para PUBLIC "-//OASIS//DTD DocBook V3.1//EN">
<para>
Selecting <guimenuitem>Close</> closes the file and automatically
runs <action>end of job cleanup</>.
</para>
```

Selecting *Close* closes the file and automatically runs end of job cleanup.

Address—A real-world address, generally a postal address

Synopsis

Mixed Content Model
`Address ::=`
`(#PCDATA|Honorific|FirstName|Surname|Lineage|OtherName|`
`Affiliation|AuthorBlurb|Contrib|Street|POB|Postcode|City|State|`
`Country|Phone|Fax|Email|OtherAddr)*`		

Attributes **Name**	Common attributes **Type**	**Default**
Format	*Enumerated notation:* linespecific	"linespecific"
Parameter Entities		
`%admon.mix;`	`%bibliocomponent.mix;`	`%bookcomponent.content;`
`%component.mix;`	`%divcomponent.mix;`	`%example.mix;`
`%figure.mix;`	`%footnote.mix;`	`%glossdef.mix;`
`%indexdivcomponent.mix;`	`%informal.class;`	`%para.mix;`
`%qandaset.mix;`	`%refcomponent.mix;`	`%sidebar.mix;`

Description

An address is generally a postal address, although it does contain elements for **FAX** and **Email** addresses as well as the catch-all **OtherAddr**.

The `linespecific` notation on the `Format` attribute makes line breaks and other spaces significant in an **Address**.

Processing expectations

Formatted as a displayed block. This element is displayed "verbatim"; whitespace and linebreaks within this element are significant.

Attributes

Format

The `Format` attribute applies the `linespecific` notation to all **Address**es. All white space and line breaks must be preserved.

See Also

City, **Country**, **Email**, **Fax**, **OtherAddr**, **Phone**, **POB**, **Postcode**, **State**, **Street**

Examples

```
<!DOCTYPE para PUBLIC "-//OASIS//DTD DocBook V3.1//EN">
<para>
An example of a postal mail address in the United States is:
<address>
John and Jane Doe
<street>100 Main Street</street>
<city>Anytown</city>, <state>NY</state> <postcode>12345</postcode>
<country>USA</country>
</address>
</para>
```

An example of a postal mail address in the United States is:

> John and Jane Doe
100 Main Street
Anytown, NY 12345
USA

For additional examples, see also **BookInfo**, **ConfGroup**, **Publisher**.

Affiliation—The institutional affiliation of an individual

Synopsis

Content Model
`Affiliation ::=`
`(ShortAffil?,JobTitle*,OrgName?,OrgDiv*,Address*)`	

Attributes	Common attributes
Parameter Entities `%bibliocomponent.mix;`	`%person.ident.mix;`

Description

The institutional affiliation of an author, contributor, or other individual.

Processing expectations

May be formatted inline or as a displayed block, depending on context. Sometimes suppressed.

4.0 *Future Changes*

In DocBook V4.0, **Affiliation** will be removed from some of the places in which it now occurs. Instead of appearing inside **Author**, for example, a new wrapper element will be created to hold **Author**, **AuthorBlurb**, and **Affiliation**.

See Also

CorpName, **FirstName**, **Honorific**, **JobTitle**, **Lineage**, **OrgDiv**, **OrgName**, **OtherName**, **ShortAffil**, **Surname**

Examples

For examples, see **Author**, **AuthorGroup**, **BookInfo**, **ContractSponsor**.

Alt—Text representation for a graphical element

Synopsis

Mixed Content Model	
`Alt ::=` `(#PCDATA)`	
Attributes	Common attributes

Description

A text (or other nonvisual) description of a graphical element. This is intended to be an alternative to the graphical presentation.

Processing expectations

May be formatted inline or as a displayed block, depending on context. Sometimes suppressed.

See Also

AudioObject, **Caption**, **Graphic**, **ImageObject**, **InlineGraphic**, **InlineMediaObject**, **MediaObject**, **TextObject**, **VideoObject**

Examples

For examples, see **Equation**, **InformalEquation**, **InlineEquation**.

Anchor—A spot in the document

Synopsis

Content Model

```
Anchor ::=
EMPTY
```

Attributes

Name	Type	Default
Role	CDATA	*None*
OS	CDATA	*None*
XRefLabel	CDATA	*None*
Remap	CDATA	*None*
UserLevel	CDATA	*None*
RevisionFlag	*Enumeration:* Added Changed Deleted Off	*None*
Conformance	NMTOKENS	*None*
Id	ID	*Required*
Pagenum	CDATA	*None*
Vendor	CDATA	*None*
Arch	CDATA	*None*
Revision	CDATA	*None*

Parameter Entities

`%admon.mix;`	`%base.char.class;`	`%bookcomponent.content;`
`%component.mix;`	`%cptr.char.mix;`	`%divcomponent.mix;`
`%genobj.class;`	`%indexdivcomponent.mix;`	`%ndxterm.char.mix;`
`%para.char.mix;`	`%programlisting.con-tent;`	`%qandaset.mix;`
`%refcomponent.mix;`	`%refinline.char.mix;`	`%screen.content;`
`%sidebar.mix;`	`%tbl.entry.mdl;`	`%title.char.mix;`
`%word.char.mix;`		

Description

An anchor identifies a single spot in the content. This may serve as the target for a cross reference, for example, from a **Link**. The **Anchor** element may occur almost anywhere.

Anchor has the `Role` attribute and all of the common attributes except `Lang`.

Processing expectations

Anchor has no content and generally produces no output. It is a link target.

Attributes

Pagenum

`PageNum` indicates the page on which the anchor occurs in some printed version of the document.

The `PageNum` attribute does not influence the pagination or page numbering of an SGML application processing the document; it is informative, not declarative.

See Also

Link, **OLink**, **ULink**, **XRef**

Examples

```
<!DOCTYPE para PUBLIC "-//OASIS//DTD DocBook V3.1//EN">
<para>
The anchor element<anchor id="example.anchor.1"> is empty and contributes
nothing to the flow of the content in which it occurs.  It is only useful
as a target.
</para>
```

The anchor element is empty and contributes nothing to the flow of the content in which it occurs. It is only useful as a target.

Answer—An answer to a question posed in a QandASet

Synopsis

Content Model

```
Answer ::=
(Label?,
 (CalloutList|GlossList|ItemizedList|OrderedList|SegmentedList|
  SimpleList|VariableList|LiteralLayout|ProgramListing|
  ProgramListingCO|Screen|ScreenCO|ScreenShot|Synopsis|
  CmdSynopsis|FuncSynopsis|FormalPara|Para|SimPara|Address|
  BlockQuote|Graphic|GraphicCO|MediaObject|MediaObjectCO|
  InformalEquation|InformalExample|InformalFigure|InformalTable|
  Equation|Example|Figure|Table|Procedure|Anchor|BridgeHead|
  Comment|Highlights|IndexTerm)*,
 QandAEntry*)
```

Attributes	Common attributes

Description

Within a **QandAEntry**, a **Question** may have an **Answer**. An **Answer** is optional (some questions have no answers) and may be repeated (some questions have more than one answer).

Processing expectations

Answers are frequently introduced with a label, such as "A:". Several attributes control the generation of the label text.

If the `DefaultLabel` attribute on the nearest ancestor **QandASet** is not `Label`, then the **Label** element on **Answer** is ignored. Otherwise, the content of the **Label** element is used as the label for the **Answer**.

Examples

For examples, see **QandASet**.

Appendix—An appendix in a **Book** or **Article**

Synopsis

Content Model

```
Appendix ::=
((DocInfo?,Title,Subtitle?,TitleAbbrev?),
 ToCchap?,
 (((CalloutList|GlossList|ItemizedList|OrderedList|SegmentedList|
    SimpleList|VariableList|Caution|Important|Note|Tip|Warning|
    LiteralLayout|ProgramListing|ProgramListingCO|Screen|ScreenCO|
    ScreenShot|Synopsis|CmdSynopsis|FuncSynopsis|FormalPara|Para|
    SimPara|Address|BlockQuote|Graphic|GraphicCO|MediaObject|
    MediaObjectCO|InformalEquation|InformalExample|InformalFigure|
    InformalTable|Equation|Example|Figure|Table|MsgSet|Procedure|
    Sidebar|QandASet|Anchor|BridgeHead|Comment|Highlights|
    Abstract|AuthorBlurb|Epigraph|IndexTerm)+,
   (Sect1*|
    (RefEntry)*|
    SimpleSect*|Section*))|
  (Sect1+|
   (RefEntry)+|
   SimpleSect+|Section+)))
```

Attributes	Common attributes	
Name	**Type**	**Default**
Label	CDATA	*None*
Status	CDATA	*None*

Parameter Entities

`%appendix.class;` `%partcontent.mix;`

Description

Appendixes usually occur at the end of a document.

Processing expectations

Formatted as a displayed block. Usually introduces a forced page break and often starts on the next recto page. Sometimes restarts page numbering. Typically, appendixes are lettered rather than numbered, and appear in the table of contents.

Attributes

Label

`Label` specifies an identifying string for presentation purposes. The second **Appendix** might be labeled "B", for example.

Generally, an explicit `Label` attribute is used only if the processing system is incapable of generating the label automatically. If present, the `Label` is normative; it will used even if the processing system is capable of automatic labelling.

Status

`Status` identifies the editorial or publication status of the **Appendix**.

Publication status might be used to control formatting (for example, printing a "draft" watermark on drafts) or processing (perhaps a document with a status of "final" should not include any components that are not final).

See Also

Article, **Book**, **Chapter**, **Colophon**, **Dedication**, **Part**, **PartIntro**, **Preface**, **Set**

Examples

```
<!DOCTYPE book PUBLIC "-//OASIS//DTD DocBook V3.1//EN">
<book>
<chapter><title>Required Chapter</title>
<para>
At least one chapter, reference, part, or article is required in a book.
</para>
</chapter>
<appendix><title>Demonstration Appendix</title>
<para>
This appendix demonstrates an appendix in a book.  It has the
same broad content model as a chapter.
</para>
</appendix>
</book>
```

For additional examples, see also **Book**.

Application—The name of a software program

Synopsis

Mixed Content Model

```
Application ::=
((#PCDATA|FootnoteRef|XRef|Abbrev|Acronym|Citation|CiteRefEntry|
  CiteTitle|Emphasis|FirstTerm|ForeignPhrase|GlossTerm|Footnote|
  Phrase|Quote|Trademark|WordAsWord|Link|OLink|ULink|Action|
  Application|ClassName|Command|ComputerOutput|Database|Email|
  EnVar|ErrorCode|ErrorName|ErrorType|Filename|Function|GUIButton|
  GUIIcon|GUILabel|GUIMenu|GUIMenuItem|GUISubmenu|Hardware|
  Interface|InterfaceDefinition|KeyCap|KeyCode|KeyCombo|KeySym|
  Literal|Constant|Markup|MediaLabel|MenuChoice|MouseButton|
  MsgText|Option|Optional|Parameter|Prompt|Property|Replaceable|
  ReturnValue|SGMLTag|StructField|StructName|Symbol|SystemItem|
  Token|Type|UserInput|VarName|Anchor|Author|AuthorInitials|
  CorpAuthor|ModeSpec|OtherCredit|ProductName|ProductNumber|
  RevHistory|Comment|Subscript|Superscript|InlineGraphic|
  InlineMediaObject|InlineEquation|Synopsis|CmdSynopsis|
  FuncSynopsis|IndexTerm)+)
```

Attributes	Common attributes	
Name	**Type**	**Default**
Class	*Enumeration:* Hardware Software	*None*
MoreInfo	*Enumeration:* None RefEntry	"None"

Parameter Entities

`%cptr.char.mix;`	`%ndxterm.char.mix;`	`%para.char.mix;`
`%programlisting.content;`	`%refclass.char.mix;`	`%refinline.char.mix;`
`%refname.char.mix;`	`%screen.content;`	`%tbl.entry.mdl;`
`%tech.char.class;`	`%title.char.mix;`	

Description

The appelation "application" is usually reserved for larger software packages—WordPerfect, for example, but not *grep*. In some domains, **Application** may also apply to a piece of hardware.

Processing expectations

Formatted inline. The `MoreInfo` attribute can help generate a link or query to retrieve additional information.

4.0 *Future Changes*

The **InterfaceDefinition** element will be discarded in DocBook V4.0. It will no longer be available in the content model of this element.

Attributes

Class

Class identifies an application as either a hardware application or a software application.

MoreInfo

If MoreInfo is set to RefEntry, it implies that a **RefEntry** exists which further describes the **Application**.

See Also

Database, **Filename**, **Hardware**, **MediaLabel**, **ProductName**

Examples

```
<!DOCTYPE para PUBLIC "-//OASIS//DTD DocBook V3.1//EN">
<para>
<application>Word Perfect</application> is one of several word
processors to claim support for <acronym>SGML</>.
</para>
```

Word Perfect is one of several word processors to claim support for SGML.

For additional examples, see also **EnVar**, **MediaLabel**, **SystemItem**.

Area—A region defined for a **Callout** in a graphic or code example

Synopsis

Content Model Area ::= EMPTY		
Attributes	Common attributes	
Name	**Type**	**Default**
Label	CDATA	*None*
Units	*Enumeration:* CALSPair LineColumn LineColumnPair LineRange Other	*None*
OtherUnits	NAME	*None*
Linkends	IDREFS	*None*
Coords	CDATA	*Required*

Description

An **Area** is an empty element holding information about a region in a graphic, program listing, or screen.

The region is generally decorated with a number, symbol, or other distinctive mark. The mark is usually used as the label for the **Callout** in a **CalloutList**, which allows the reader to identify which callouts are associated with which regions. The marks may be generated by the processing application from the **Areas**, or it may be added by some other process. (This is an interchange issue. See Appendix F, *Interchanging DocBook Documents.*)

For a complete description of callouts, see **Callout**.

Processing expectations

Suppressed. This element provides data for processing but it is not expected to be rendered directly.

The processing expectations of **Callouts** are likely to deserve special consideration for interchange. See Appendix F.

The `Coords`, which are required, identify the location of the region. The coordinates are CDATA; how they are interpreted depends on the `Units` specified:

`CALSPair`
: The coordinates are expressed using the semantics of the CALS graphic attributes. The format of the coordinates is "x1,y1 x2,y2". This identifies a rectangle with the lower-left corner at (x1,y1) and the upper-right corner at (x2,y2). The X and Y coordinates are integers in the range 0 to 10000; they express a percentage of the total distance from 0.00 to 100.00%.

`LineColumn`
: The coordinates are expressed using lines and columns. The format of the coordinates is "line column." In a graphic context, the meaning of this unit is unspecified.

`LineRange`
: The coordinates are expressed using lines. The format of the coordinates is "startingline endingline." In a graphic context, the meaning of this unit is unspecified.

`LineColumnPair`
: The coordinates are expressed as a continuous flow of characters. The format of the coordinates is "line1 col1 line2 col2". This identifies a flow of characters that begins at col1 of line1 and extends to col2 of line2. If line1 and line2 are different, then the region includes all of the intervening lines (including text that occurs before col1 and after col2). In other words, this unit does not specify a rectangle. In a graphic context, the meaning of this unit is unspecified.

`OtherUnits`
: If specified, then the `OtherUnits` attribute is expected to identify the units in some implementation-specific way.

The `Units` attribute is not required, if it is not specified, the semantics of the coordinates must be inherited from the surrounding **AreaSpec** or **AreaSet** element or implied in some implementation-specific manner.

In processing systems in which the mark is inserted automatically, the `Label` attribute is provided as a mechanism for specifying what the mark should be.

The author may point to any relevant information with `Linkends`. DocBook does not specify a semantic for these links. One possible use would be for providing a link back to the appropriate **Callout** in an online environment.

Attributes

Coords

`Coords` provides the coordinates of the **Area**. The coordinates should be interpreted using the `Units` (or `OtherUnits`) specified.

Label

`Label` specifies an identifying number or string that may be used in presentation. The **Area** label might be drawn on top of the figure, for example, at the position indicated by `Coords`.

Linkends

`Linkends` points to the **Callout**(s) which refer to this **Area**. (This provides bidirectional linking, which may be useful in online presentation.)

OtherUnits

If none of the `Units` are applicable, set `Units` to `Other` and set `OtherUnits` to some application-specific description of the desired units.

Units

`Units` indicate how the specified `Coords` are to be interpreted. The default units vary according to the type of callout specified; `CALSPair` for graphics and `LineColumn` for line-oriented elements.

Examples

For examples, see **GraphicCO**, **MediaObjectCO**, **ProgramListingCO**.

AreaSet—A set of related areas in a graphic or code example

Synopsis

Content Model

```
AreaSet ::=
(Area+)
```

Attributes	Common attributes	
Name	**Type**	**Default**

Label	CDATA	*None*
Units	*Enumeration:* CALSPair LineColumn LineColumnPair LineRange Other	*None*
OtherUnits	NAME	*None*
Coords	CDATA	*Required*

Description

An **AreaSet** contains one or more **Areas**. These areas are bound in a set in order to associate them with a single **Callout** description. See **Area** for a more complete description of the areas.

For a complete description of callouts, see **Callout**.

Processing expectations

Suppressed.

4.0 *Future Changes*

The `Coords` attribute will be removed in DocBook V4.0.

Attributes

Coords

`Coords` provides the coordinates of the **AreaSet**. The coordinates should be interpreted using the `Units` (or `OtherUnits`) specified. *This attribute is erroneous since the enclosed* ***Areas*** *must also provide* `Coords`. *It will go away in DocBook 4.0.*

Label

`Label` specifies an identifying number or string that may be used in presentation.

OtherUnits

If none of the `Units` are applicable, set `Units` to `Other` and set `OtherUnits` to some application-specific description of the desired units.

Units

`Units` indicate how `Coords` are to be interpreted.

Examples

For examples, see **GraphicCO**, **MediaObjectCO**, **ProgramListingCO**.

AreaSpec—A collection of regions in a graphic or code example

Synopsis

Content Model

```
AreaSpec ::=
((Area|AreaSet)+)
```

Attributes Name	Common attributes **Type**	**Default**
Units	*Enumeration:* CALSPair LineColumn LineColumnPair LineRange Other	*None*
OtherUnits	NAME	*None*

Description

An **AreaSpec** holds a collection of regions and/or region sets in a graphic, program listing, or screen that are associated with **Callout** descriptions. See **Area** for a description of the attributes.

Processing expectations

Suppressed. This element provides data for processing but it is not expected to be rendered directly.

Attributes

OtherUnits

If none of the `Units` are applicable, set `Units` to `Other` and set `OtherUnits` to some application-specific description of the desired units.

Units

`Units` indicate how the specified `Coords` are to be interpreted. The default units vary according to the type of callout specified; `CALSPair` for graphics and `LineColumn` for line-oriented elements.

See Also

CalloutList, **CO**, **GraphicCO**, **ImageObjectCO**, **MediaObjectCO**, **ProgramListingCO**, **ScreenCO**

Examples

For examples, see **GraphicCO**, **MediaObjectCO**, **ProgramListingCO**.

Arg—An argument in a **CmdSynopsis**

Synopsis

Mixed Content Model		
`Arg ::=` `((#PCDATA|Arg|Group|Option|SynopFragmentRef|Replaceable|SBR)+)`		
Attributes **Name**	Common attributes **Type**	**Default**
Rep	*Enumeration:* Norepeat Repeat	"Norepeat"
Choice	*Enumeration:* Opt Plain Req	"Opt"

Description

See **CmdSynopsis** for more information.

Processing expectations

May be formatted inline or as a displayed block, depending on context.

Attributes

Choice

`Choice` indicates whether the **Arg** is required (`Req` or `Plain`) or optional (`Opt`). Arguments identified as `Plain` are required, but are shown without additional decoration.

Rep

A `Rep` value of `Repeat` indicates that the **Arg** is reapeatable. This is frequently rendered with an ellipsis.

See Also

CmdSynopsis, **Group**, **RefSynopsisDiv**, **SBR**, **SynopFragment**, **SynopFragmentRef**

Examples

For examples, see **CmdSynopsis**, **SynopFragment**.

ArtHeader—Meta-information for an **Article**

Synopsis

Content Model	

`ArtHeader ::=`
`((Graphic|MediaObject|LegalNotice|ModeSpec|SubjectSet|KeywordSet|`
`ITermSet|Abbrev|Abstract|Address|ArtPageNums|Author|AuthorGroup|`
`AuthorInitials|BiblioMisc|BiblioSet|Collab|ConfGroup|`
`ContractNum|ContractSponsor|Copyright|CorpAuthor|CorpName|Date|`
`Edition|Editor|InvPartNumber|ISBN|ISSN|IssueNum|OrgName|`
`OtherCredit|PageNums|PrintHistory|ProductName|ProductNumber|`
`PubDate|Publisher|PublisherName|PubsNumber|ReleaseInfo|`
`RevHistory|SeriesVolNums|Subtitle|Title|TitleAbbrev|VolumeNum|`
`CiteTitle|Honorific|FirstName|Surname|Lineage|OtherName|`
`Affiliation|AuthorBlurb|Contrib|IndexTerm|BookBiblio)+)`	

Attributes	Common attributes

Description

Like the other "info" elements, **Sect1Info** contains meta-information about the section of the document in which it occurs.

Processing expectations

Suppressed. Many of the elements in this wrapper may be used in presentation, but they are not generally printed as part of the formatting of the wrapper; it merely serves to identify where they occur.

4.0 *Future Changes*

ArtHeader will be renamed to **ArticleInfo** in DocBook V4.0.

AuthorBlurb and **Affiliation** will be removed from the inline content of this element. A new wrapper element will be created to associate this information with authors, editors, and other contributors.

BookBiblio will be discarded.

See Also

BookBiblio, **BookInfo**, **DocInfo**, **ObjectInfo**, **RefSynopsisDivInfo**, **ScreenInfo**, **Sect1Info**, **Sect2Info**, **Sect3Info**, **Sect4Info**, **Sect5Info**, **SectionInfo**, **SetInfo**

Examples

For examples, see **Ackno**, **Article**, **ContractSponsor**, **OtherCredit**.

Article—An article

Synopsis

Content Model

```
Article ::=
((Title,Subtitle?,TitleAbbrev?)?,
 ArtHeader?,ToCchap?,LoT*,
 (((CalloutList|GlossList|ItemizedList|OrderedList|SegmentedList|
    SimpleList|VariableList|Caution|Important|Note|Tip|Warning|
    LiteralLayout|ProgramListing|ProgramListingCO|Screen|ScreenCO|
    ScreenShot|Synopsis|CmdSynopsis|FuncSynopsis|FormalPara|Para|
    SimPara|Address|BlockQuote|Graphic|GraphicCO|MediaObject|
    MediaObjectCO|InformalEquation|InformalExample|InformalFigure|
    InformalTable|Equation|Example|Figure|Table|MsgSet|Procedure|
    Sidebar|QandASet|Anchor|BridgeHead|Comment|Highlights|
    Abstract|AuthorBlurb|Epigraph|IndexTerm)+,
   (Sect1*|
    (RefEntry)*|
    SimpleSect*|Section*))|
  (Sect1+|
   (RefEntry)+|
   SimpleSect+|Section+)),
 ((ToC|LoT|Index|Glossary|Bibliography)|
  (Appendix)|
  Ackno)*)
```

Attributes — Common attributes

Name	Type	Default
Status	CDATA	*None*
ParentBook	IDREF	*None*
Class	*Enumeration:* FAQ JournalArticle ProductSheet TechReport WhitePaper	*None*

Parameter Entities

`%article.class;` `%partcontent.mix;`

Description

The **Article** element is a general-purpose container for articles. The content model is both quite complex and rather loose in order to accommodate the wide range of possible **Article** structures. Although changes to the **Article** element have been discussed on several occasions, no better model has been presented.

An **Article** is composed of a header and a body. The body may include a table of contents and multiple lists of tables, figures, and so on, before the main text of the article and may include a number of common end-matter components at the end.

Processing expectations

Formatted as a displayed block. Frequently causes a forced page break in print media. May be numbered separately and presented in the table of contents.

4.0 *Future Changes*

The **ToC** element in the content model may be replaced by **TocChap**. This change may be delayed if the DocBook technical committee decides to review the whole **ToC/LoT** apparatus.

Attributes

Class

`Class` identifies the type of article.

ParentBook

`ParentBook` holds the ID of an enclosing **Book**, if applicable.

Status

`Status` identifies the editorial or publication status of the **Article**.

Publication status might be used to control formatting (for example, printing a "draft" watermark on drafts) or processing (perhaps a document with a status of "final" should not include any components that are not final).

See Also

Appendix, **Book**, **Chapter**, **Colophon**, **Dedication**, **Part**, **PartIntro**, **Preface**, **Set**

Examples

```
<!DOCTYPE article PUBLIC "-//OASIS//DTD DocBook V3.1//EN">
<article>
<artheader>
  <author><firstname>Norman</><surname>Walsh</></author>
  <authorinitials>ndw</authorinitials>
  <artpagenums>339-343</artpagenums>
  <volumenum>15</volumenum>
  <issuenum>3</issuenum>
  <publisher><publishername>The TeX User's Group</publishername></publisher>
  <pubdate>1994</pubdate>
  <title>A World Wide Web Interface to CTAN</title>
  <titleabbrev>CTAN-Web</titleabbrev>
  <revhistory>
     <revision>
        <revnumber>1.0</revnumber>
        <date>28 Mar 1994</date>
        <revremark>Submitted.</revremark>
     </revision>
     <revision>
        <revnumber>0.5</revnumber>
```

```
        <date>15 Feb 1994</date>
        <revremark>First draft for review.</revremark>
    </revision>
  </revhistory>
</artheader>
<para>
The body of the article &hellip;
</para>
</article>
```

For additional examples, see also **Ackno**, **ContractSponsor**, **QandASet**.

ArtPageNums—The page numbers of an article as published

Synopsis

Mixed Content Model

```
ArtPageNums ::=
((#PCDATA|Link|OLink|ULink|Emphasis|Trademark|Replaceable|Comment|
  Subscript|Superscript|InlineGraphic|InlineMediaObject|IndexTerm)+)
```

Attributes	Common attributes

Parameter Entities

```
%bibliocomponent.mix;
```

Description

This element holds the page numbers of an article as published. Its content is not intended to influence the page numbers used by a presentation system formatting the parent **Article**.

Processing expectations

Formatted inline. Sometimes suppressed. Although it appears at the beginning of the content model for **BlockQuote** and **Epigraph**, it is often output at the end.

Examples

For examples, see **Article**.

Attribution—The source of a block quote or epigraph

Synopsis

Mixed Content Model

```
Attribution ::=
((#PCDATA|FootnoteRef|XRef|Abbrev|Acronym|Citation|CiteRefEntry|
  CiteTitle|Emphasis|FirstTerm|ForeignPhrase|GlossTerm|Footnote|
  Phrase|Quote|Trademark|WordAsWord|Link|OLink|ULink|Action|
  Application|ClassName|Command|ComputerOutput|Database|Email|
  EnVar|ErrorCode|ErrorName|ErrorType|Filename|Function|GUIButton|
  GUIIcon|GUILabel|GUIMenu|GUIMenuItem|GUISubmenu|Hardware|
```

`Interface|InterfaceDefinition|KeyCap|KeyCode|KeyCombo|KeySym|Literal|Constant|Markup|MediaLabel|MenuChoice|MouseButton|MsgText|Option|Optional|Parameter|Prompt|Property|Replaceable|ReturnValue|SGMLTag|StructField|StructName|Symbol|SystemItem|Token|Type|UserInput|VarName|Anchor|Author|AuthorInitials|CorpAuthor|ModeSpec|OtherCredit|ProductName|ProductNumber|RevHistory|Comment|Subscript|Superscript|InlineGraphic|InlineMediaObject|InlineEquation|Synopsis|CmdSynopsis|FuncSynopsis|IndexTerm)+)`	
Attributes	Common attributes

Description

An **Attribution** identifies the source to whom a **BlockQuote** or **Epigraph** is ascribed.

Processing expectations

May be formatted inline or as a displayed block, depending on context. Sometimes suppressed.

4.0 *Future Changes*

The **InterfaceDefinition** element will be discarded in DocBook V4.0. It will no longer be available in the content model of this element.

See Also

BlockQuote, **Epigraph**

Examples

```
<!DOCTYPE blockquote PUBLIC "-//OASIS//DTD DocBook V3.1//EN">
<blockquote>
<attribution>William Shakespeare</>
<literallayout>
What say you?  Will you yield, and this avoid?
Or, guilty in defense, be thus destroyed?
</literallayout>
</blockquote>
```

> What say you? Will you yield, and this avoid?
> Or, guilty in defense, be thus destroyed?
>
> —William Shakespeare

For additional examples, see also **BlockQuote**, **Chapter**, **LiteralLayout**.

AudioData—Pointer to external audio data

Synopsis

Content Model

```
AudioData ::=
EMPTY
```

Attributes	Common attributes	
Name	**Type**	**Default**
SrcCredit	CDATA	*None*
Format	*Enumeration:* BMP CGM-BINARY CGM-CHAR CGM-CLEAR DITROFF DVI EPS EQN FAX GIF GIF87a GIF89a IGES JPEG JPG linespecific PCX PIC PS SGML TBL TEX TIFF WMF WPG	*None*
EntityRef	ENTITY	*None*
FileRef	CDATA	*None*

Description

This empty element points to external audio data.

Processing expectations

There are two ways to provide content for **AudioData**: `EntityRef` or `FileRef`. It is best to use only one of these methods. However, if multiple sources are provided, `EntityRef` will be used in favor of `FileRef`.

Attributes

EntityRef

`EntityRef` identifies the general entity which points to the content of the audio data.

FileRef

`FileRef` specifies the name of the file which contains the content of the audio data.

Format

`Format` identifies the format of the audio data. The `Format` must be a defined notation.

SrcCredit

`SrcCredit` contains details about the source of the audio data.

Examples

For examples, see **AudioObject**.

AudioObject—A wrapper for audio data and its associated meta-information

Synopsis

Content Model
`AudioObject ::=`
`(ObjectInfo?,AudioData)`	

Attributes	Common attributes
Parameter Entities `%mediaobject.mix;`	

Description

AudioObject is a wrapper for **AudioData**.

Processing expectations

Its content is rendered aurally or not at all. It might not be rendered, depending on its placement within a **MediaObject** or **InlineMediaObject** and the constraints on the publishing system. For a more detailed description of the semantics involved, see **MediaObject**.

See Also

Alt, **Caption**, **Graphic**, **ImageObject**, **InlineGraphic**, **InlineMediaObject**, **MediaObject**, **TextObject**, **VideoObject**

Examples

```
<!DOCTYPE mediaobject PUBLIC "-//OASIS//DTD DocBook V3.1//EN">
<mediaobject>
<audioobject>
  <objectinfo>
    <title>Phaser sound effect</title>
  </objectinfo>
  <audiodata fileref="phaser.wav">
</audioobject>
<textobject>
<phrase>A <trademark>Star Trek</trademark> phaser sound effect</phrase>
</textobject>
</mediaobject>
```

A Star Trek™ phaser sound effect

Author—The name of an individual author

Synopsis

Content Model		
Author ::= ((Honorific|FirstName|Surname|Lineage|OtherName|Affiliation| AuthorBlurb|Contrib)+)		
Attributes	Common attributes	
Parameter Entities		
%bibliocomponent.mix;	%docinfo.char.class;	%ndxterm.char.mix;
%para.char.mix;	%programlisting.content;	%refinline.char.mix;
%screen.content;	%tbl.entry.mdl;	%title.char.mix;

Description

The **Author** element holds information about the author of the document in which it occurs; it is meta-information about the current document or document section, not a reference to the author of an external document.

Processing expectations

May be formatted inline or as a displayed block, depending on context. Sometimes suppressed.

4.0 Future Changes

AuthorBlurb and **Affiliation** will be removed from the inline content of **Author** in DocBook V4.0. A new wrapper element will be created to hold **Author**, **AuthorBlurb**, and **Affiliation**.

See Also

AuthorBlurb, **AuthorGroup**, **Collab**, **CollabName**, **Contrib**, **CorpAuthor**, **Editor**, **OtherCredit**

Examples

```
<!DOCTYPE author PUBLIC "-//OASIS//DTD DocBook V3.1//EN">
<author>
  <honorific>Mr</honorific>
  <firstname>Norman</firstname>
  <surname>Walsh</surname>
  <othername role=mi>D</othername>
  <affiliation>
    <shortaffil>ATI</shortaffil>
    <jobtitle>Senior Application Analyst</jobtitle>
    <orgname>ArborText, Inc.</orgname>
    <orgdiv>Application Developement</orgdiv>
  </affiliation>
</author>
```

For additional examples, see also **Ackno**, **Article**, **AuthorGroup**, **Bibliography**, **BiblioSet**, **Book**, **BookInfo**, **OtherCredit**.

AuthorBlurb—A short description or note about an author

Synopsis

Content Model		
`AuthorBlurb ::= (Title?, (FormalPara|Para|SimPara)+)`		
Attributes	Common attributes	
Parameter Entities		
`%bibliocomponent.mix;`	`%bookcomponent.content;`	`%component.mix;`
`%descobj.class;`	`%divcomponent.mix;`	`%person.ident.mix;`
`%refcomponent.mix;`		

Description

A short description of an author.

Processing expectations

Formatted as a displayed block. Sometimes suppressed.

4.0 Future Changes

In DocBook V4.0, **AuthorBlurb** will be removed from some of the places in which it now occurs. Instead of appearing inside **Author**, for example, a new wrapper element will be created to hold **Author**, **AuthorBlurb**, and **Affiliation**.

See Also

Author, **AuthorGroup**, **Collab**, **CollabName**, **Contrib**, **CorpAuthor**, **Editor**, **OtherCredit**

Examples

For examples, see **AuthorGroup**.

AuthorGroup—Wrapper for author information when a document has multiple authors or collabarators

Synopsis

Content Model
`AuthorGroup ::=`
`((Author|Editor|Collab|CorpAuthor|OtherCredit)+)`	

Attributes	Common attributes
Parameter Entities `%bibliocomponent.mix;`	

Description

The **AuthorGroup** element is a wrapper around multiple authors or other collaborators.

Processing expectations

May be formatted inline or as a displayed block, depending on context. Sometimes given very special treatment, especially on title pages or other displayed areas. Sometimes suppressed.

See Also

Author, **AuthorBlurb**, **Collab**, **CollabName**, **Contrib**, **CorpAuthor**, **Editor**, **OtherCredit**

Examples

The example below demonstrates **AuthorGroup** and many of the elements of **Author**.

```
<!DOCTYPE authorgroup PUBLIC "-//OASIS//DTD DocBook V3.1//EN">
<authorgroup>
  <author>
    <honorific>Dr.</honorific>
    <firstname>Lois</firstname>
    <surname>Common-Demoninator</surname>
    <affiliation>
      <shortaffil>Director, M. Behn School of Coop. Eng.</shortaffil>
      <jobtitle>Director of Cooperative Efforts</jobtitle>
```

```
    <orgname>The Marguerite Behn International School of
             Cooperative Engineering</orgname>
  </affiliation>
</author>

<editor>
  <firstname>Peter</firstname>
  <surname>Parker</surname>
  <lineage>Sr.</lineage>
  <othername>Spiderman</othername>
  <authorblurb>
    <para>
    Peter's a super hero in his spare time.
    </para>
  </authorblurb>
</editor>
</authorgroup>
```

For additional examples, see also **Bibliography**, **BookInfo**, **Collab**.

AuthorInitials—The initials or other short identifier for an author

Synopsis

Mixed Content Model
`AuthorInitials ::=`
`((#PCDATA|Link|OLink|ULink|Emphasis|Trademark|Replaceable|Comment|`
`  Subscript|Superscript|InlineGraphic|InlineMediaObject|IndexTerm)+)`		

Attributes	Common attributes	
Parameter Entities		
`%bibliocomponent.mix;`	`%docinfo.char.class;`	`%ndxterm.char.mix;`
`%para.char.mix;`	`%programlisting.con-tent;`	`%refinline.char.mix;`
`%screen.content;`	`%tbl.entry.mdl;`	`%title.char.mix;`

Description

Author initials occur most frequently in a **Revision** or **Comment**.

Processing expectations

Formatted inline. Sometimes suppressed.

Examples

For examples, see **Article**, **RevHistory**.

BeginPage—The location of a page break in a print version of the document

Synopsis

Content Model
`BeginPage ::=`
`EMPTY`		

Attributes **Name**	Common attributes **Type**	 **Default**
Pagenum	CDATA	*None*

Parameter Entities
`%beginpage.exclusion;`
`%ubiq.inclusion;`
	
	`%highlights.exclusion;`
	`%ubiq.mix;`
		
		`%ubiq.exclusion;`

Description

The **BeginPage** element marks the location of an actual page break in a print version of the document, as opposed to where a page break might appear in a further rendition of the document. This information may be used, for example, to allow support staff using an online system to coordinate with a user referring to a page number in a printed manual.

Processing expectations

The break identified by **BeginPage** may be displayed in an online version of the document or used for legacy purposes, but it is not expected to cause a page break when the document is processed by an SGML system.

Attributes

Pagenum

`PageNum` contains the page number of the page in the printed document which begins at the location of the **BeginPage** element.

Examples

For examples, see **Chapter**.

BiblioDiv—A section of a Bibliography

Synopsis

```
Content Model
BiblioDiv ::=
((Title,Subtitle?,TitleAbbrev?)?,
 (CalloutList|GlossList|ItemizedList|OrderedList|SegmentedList|
  SimpleList|VariableList|Caution|Important|Note|Tip|Warning|
  LiteralLayout|ProgramListing|ProgramListingCO|Screen|ScreenCO|
  ScreenShot|Synopsis|CmdSynopsis|FuncSynopsis|FormalPara|Para|
```

```
  SimPara|Address|BlockQuote|Graphic|GraphicCO|MediaObject|
  MediaObjectCO|InformalEquation|InformalExample|InformalFigure|
  InformalTable|Equation|Example|Figure|Table|MsgSet|Procedure|
  Sidebar|QandASet|Anchor|BridgeHead|Comment|Highlights|Abstract|
  AuthorBlurb|Epigraph|IndexTerm)*,
 (BiblioEntry|BiblioMixed)+)
```

Attributes Name	Common attributes Type	Default
Status	CDATA	*None*

Description

BiblioDiv is a section of a **Bibliography**. A bibliography might be divided into sections in order to group different types of sources together, like books, journal articles, web sites, and so on.

A bibliography may contain any number of **BiblioEntry** or **BiblioMixed** elements or any number of **BiblioDivs**, but it cannot contain a mixture of both at the same level.

Processing expectations

Formatted as a displayed block. Some systems may display only those entries within a **BiblioDiv** that are cited in the containing document. This may be an interchange issue. See Appendix F.

Attributes

Status

Status identifies the editorial or publication status of the **BiblioDiv**.

Publication status might be used to control formatting (for example, printing a "draft" watermark on drafts) or processing (perhaps a document with a status of "final" should not include any components that are not final).

Examples

For examples, see **Bibliography**.

BiblioEntry—An entry in a **Bibliography**

Synopsis

Content Model

```
BiblioEntry ::=
((ArtHeader|BookBiblio|SeriesInfo|
  (Abbrev|Abstract|Address|ArtPageNums|Author|AuthorGroup|
   AuthorInitials|BiblioMisc|BiblioSet|Collab|ConfGroup|
   ContractNum|ContractSponsor|Copyright|CorpAuthor|CorpName|Date|
   Edition|Editor|InvPartNumber|ISBN|ISSN|IssueNum|OrgName|
   OtherCredit|PageNums|PrintHistory|ProductName|ProductNumber|
```

```
PubDate|Publisher|PublisherName|PubsNumber|ReleaseInfo|
RevHistory|SeriesVolNums|Subtitle|Title|TitleAbbrev|VolumeNum|
CiteTitle|Honorific|FirstName|Surname|Lineage|OtherName|
Affiliation|AuthorBlurb|Contrib|IndexTerm))+)
```

Attributes	Common attributes

Description

A **BiblioEntry** is an entry in a **Bibliography**. The contents of **BiblioEntry** is a "database" of named fields. Presentation systems frequently suppress some elements in a **BiblioEntry**.

Processing expectations

Formatted as a displayed block.

BiblioEntrys are "raw." They contain a database-like collection of named fields. It is the responsibility of the processing system to select elements from within a **BiblioEntry**, present them in the correct order, and add all punctuation.

There is no expectation that a system will present all of the fields in a **BiblioEntry** or that they will be displayed in the order in which they occur.

Correct formatting of **BiblioEntry**s is an interchange issue. See Appendix F.

4.0 *Future Changes*

AuthorBlurb and **Affiliation** will be removed from the inline content of **BiblioEntry** in DocBook V4.0. A new wrapper element will be created to associate this information with authors, editors, and other contributors.

BookBiblio will be discarded.

See Also

BiblioMisc, **BiblioMixed**, **BiblioMSet**, **BiblioSet**, **BookBiblio**

Examples

For examples, see **Bibliography**, **BiblioSet**.

Bibliography—A bibliography

Synopsis

Content Model

```
Bibliography ::=
((DocInfo?,Title,Subtitle?,TitleAbbrev?)?,
 (CalloutList|GlossList|ItemizedList|OrderedList|SegmentedList|
  SimpleList|VariableList|Caution|Important|Note|Tip|Warning|
  LiteralLayout|ProgramListing|ProgramListingCO|Screen|ScreenCO|
```

<table>
<tr><td colspan="3"><pre> ScreenShot|Synopsis|CmdSynopsis|FuncSynopsis|FormalPara|Para|
  SimPara|Address|BlockQuote|Graphic|GraphicCO|MediaObject|
  MediaObjectCO|InformalEquation|InformalExample|InformalFigure|
  InformalTable|Equation|Example|Figure|Table|MsgSet|Procedure|
  Sidebar|QandASet|Anchor|BridgeHead|Comment|Highlights|Abstract|
  AuthorBlurb|Epigraph|IndexTerm)*,
 (BiblioDiv+|
  (BiblioEntry|BiblioMixed)+))</pre></td></tr>
<tr><td>Attributes
Name</td><td>Common attributes
Type</td><td>Default</td></tr>
<tr><td>Status</td><td>CDATA</td><td>None</td></tr>
<tr><td>Parameter Entities
<code>%nav.class;</code></td><td><code>%partcontent.mix;</code></td><td></td></tr>
</table>

Description

A bibliography. A DocBook bibliography may contain some preferatory matter, but its main content is a set of bibliography entries (either **BiblioEntry** or **BiblioMixed**). These may occur inside **BiblioDivs**, instead of appearing directly in the **Bibliograpy**.

Processing expectations

Formatted as a displayed block. A **Bibliography** in a **Book** frequently causes a forced page break in print media.

Some systems may display only those entries within a **Bibliography** that are cited in the containing document. This may be an interchange issue. See Appendix F.

The two styles of bibliography entry have quite different processing expectations. **BiblioEntry**s are "raw;" they contain a database-like collection of named fields. **BiblioMixed** entries are "cooked;" the fields occur in the order in which they will be presented and additional punctuation may be sprinkled between the fields.

See **BiblioEntry** and **BiblioMixed** for further discussion.

Attributes

Status

`Status` identifies the editorial or publication status of the **Bibliography**.

Publication status might be used to control formatting (for example, printing a "draft" watermark on drafts) or processing (perhaps a document with a status of "final" should not include any components that are not final).

Examples

The entries in a **Bibliography** come in two general forms, "raw" and "cooked". A raw entry is a database-like collection of named fields:

```
<!DOCTYPE bibliography PUBLIC "-//OASIS//DTD DocBook V3.1//EN">
<bibliography>
<title>A Test Bibliography</title>

<bibliodiv><title>Books</title>

<biblioentry>
  <abbrev>AhoSethiUllman96</abbrev>
  <authorgroup>
    <author><firstname>Alfred V.</firstname><surname>Aho</surname></author>
    <author><firstname>Ravi</firstname><surname>Sethi</surname></author>
    <author><firstname>Jeffrey D.</firstname><surname>Ullman</surname></author>
  </authorgroup>
  <copyright><year>1996</year>
          <holder>Bell Telephone Laboratories, Inc.</holder></copyright>
  <editor><firstname>James T.</firstname><surname>DeWolf</surname></editor>
  <isbn>0-201-10088-6</isbn>
  <publisher>
    <publishername>Addison-Wesley Publishing Company</publishername>
  </publisher>
  <title>Compilers, Principles, Techniques, and Tools</title>
  <seriesinfo>
    <title>Computer Science</title>
    <editor>
      <firstname>Michael A.</firstname>
      <surname>Harrison</surname>
    </editor>
    <publisher>
      <publishername>Addison-Wesley Publishing Company</publishername>
    </publisher>
  </seriesinfo>
</biblioentry>

<biblioentry xreflabel="Kites75">
  <authorgroup>
    <author><firstname>Andrea</firstname><surname>Bahadur</surname></author>
    <author><firstname>Mark</firstname><surname>Shwarek</surname></author>
  </authorgroup>
  <copyright><year>1974</year><year>1975</year>
     <holder>Product Development International Holding N. V.</holder>
     </copyright>
  <isbn>0-88459-021-6</isbn>
  <publisher>
    <publishername>Plenary Publications International, Inc.</publishername>
  </publisher>
  <title>Kites</title>
  <subtitle>Ancient Craft to Modern Sport</subtitle>
  <pagenums>988-999</pagenums>
  <seriesinfo>
    <title>The Family Creative Workshop</title>
    <seriesvolnums>1-22</seriesvolnums>
    <editor>
      <firstname>Allen</firstname>
      <othername role=middle>Davenport</othername>
```

```
      <surname>Bragdon</surname>
      <contrib>Editor in Chief</contrib>
    </editor>
  </seriesinfo>
</biblioentry>

</bibliodiv>
<bibliodiv><title>Periodicals</title>

<biblioentry>
  <abbrev>Walsh97</abbrev>
  <biblioset relation=journal>
    <title>XML: Principles, Tools, and Techniques</title>
    <publisher>
      <publishername>O'Reilly &amp; Associates, Inc.</publishername>
    </publisher>
    <issn>1085-2301</issn>
    <editor><firstname>Dan</firstname><surname>Connolly</surname></editor>
  </biblioset>
  <biblioset relation=article>
    <title>A Guide to XML</title>
    <author><surname>Walsh</surname><firstname>Norman</firstname></author>
    <copyright><year>1997</year><holder>ArborText, Inc.</holder></copyright>
    <pagenums>97-108</pagenums>
  </biblioset>
</biblioentry>

</bibliodiv>

</bibliography>
```

A cooked entry is formatted, including additional#PCDATA, so that it is easy to render.

```
<!DOCTYPE bibliography PUBLIC "-//OASIS//DTD DocBook V3.1//EN">
<bibliography><title>References</title>

<bibliomixed>
  <bibliomset relation=article>
    <surname>Walsh</surname>, <firstname>Norman</firstname>.
    <title role=article>Introduction to Cascading Style Sheets</title>.
  </bibliomset>
  <bibliomset relation=journal>
    <title>The World Wide Web Journal</title>
    <volumenum>2</volumenum><issuenum>1</issuenum>.
    <publishername>O'Reilly &amp; Associates, Inc.</publishername> and
    <corpname>The World Wide Web Consortium</corpname>.
    <pubdate>Winter, 1996</pubdate></bibliomset>.
</bibliomixed>

</bibliography>
```

BiblioMisc—Untyped bibliographic information

Synopsis

Mixed Content Model

```
BiblioMisc ::=
((#PCDATA|FootnoteRef|XRef|Abbrev|Acronym|Citation|CiteRefEntry|
  CiteTitle|Emphasis|FirstTerm|ForeignPhrase|GlossTerm|Footnote|
  Phrase|Quote|Trademark|WordAsWord|Link|OLink|ULink|Action|
  Application|ClassName|Command|ComputerOutput|Database|Email|
  EnVar|ErrorCode|ErrorName|ErrorType|Filename|Function|GUIButton|
  GUIIcon|GUILabel|GUIMenu|GUIMenuItem|GUISubmenu|Hardware|
  Interface|InterfaceDefinition|KeyCap|KeyCode|KeyCombo|KeySym|
  Literal|Constant|Markup|MediaLabel|MenuChoice|MouseButton|
  MsgText|Option|Optional|Parameter|Prompt|Property|Replaceable|
  ReturnValue|SGMLTag|StructField|StructName|Symbol|SystemItem|
  Token|Type|UserInput|VarName|Anchor|Author|AuthorInitials|
  CorpAuthor|ModeSpec|OtherCredit|ProductName|ProductNumber|
  RevHistory|Comment|Subscript|Superscript|InlineGraphic|
  InlineMediaObject|InlineEquation|Synopsis|CmdSynopsis|
  FuncSynopsis|IndexTerm)+)
```

Attributes	Common attributes

Parameter Entities

`%bibliocomponent.mix;`

Description

The **BiblioMisc** element is a wrapper for bibliographic information that does not fit neatly into the other bibliographic fields (such as **Author** and **Publisher**).

Processing expectations

Formatted inline. It is recommended that the `Role` attribute be used to identify the kind of information that this element contains.

4.0 *Future Changes*

The **InterfaceDefinition** element will be discarded in DocBook V4.0. It will no longer be available in the content model of this element.

See Also

BiblioEntry, **BiblioMixed**, **BiblioMSet**, **BiblioSet**, **BookBiblio**

Examples

For examples, see **Bibliography**.

BiblioMixed—An entry in a bibliography

Synopsis

Mixed Content Model

```
BiblioMixed ::=
((Abbrev|Abstract|Address|ArtPageNums|Author|AuthorGroup|
  AuthorInitials|BiblioMisc|BiblioSet|Collab|ConfGroup|
  ContractNum|ContractSponsor|Copyright|CorpAuthor|CorpName|Date|
  Edition|Editor|InvPartNumber|ISBN|ISSN|IssueNum|OrgName|
  OtherCredit|PageNums|PrintHistory|ProductName|ProductNumber|
  PubDate|Publisher|PublisherName|PubsNumber|ReleaseInfo|
  RevHistory|SeriesVolNums|Subtitle|Title|TitleAbbrev|VolumeNum|
  CiteTitle|Honorific|FirstName|Surname|Lineage|OtherName|
  Affiliation|AuthorBlurb|Contrib|IndexTerm|BiblioMSet|#PCDATA)+)
```

Attributes	Common attributes

Description

BiblioMixed is an entry in a **Bibliography**. The contents of **BiblioMixed** includes all necessary punctuation for formatting. Presentation systems usually display all of the elements in a **BiblioMixed**.

Processing expectations

Formatted as a displayed block.

BiblioMixed entries are "cooked." In addition to named fields, they can contain interspersed #PCDATA to provide punctuation and other formatting information.

The processing system is generally expected to present each and every element in the entry, and all interspersed #PCDATA, in the order in which it occurs.

4.0 *Future Changes*

AuthorBlurb and **Affiliation** will be removed from the inline content of **BiblioEntry** in DocBook V4.0. A new wrapper element will be created to associate this information with authors, editors, and other contributors.

5.0 *Future Changes*

BiblioSet will be removed from the content model of **BiblioMixed**. Allowing a "raw" container inside a "cooked" one confuses processing expectations.

See Also

BiblioEntry, **BiblioMisc**, **BiblioMSet**, **BiblioSet**, **BookBiblio**

Examples

For examples, see **Bibliography**, **BiblioMSet**.

BiblioMSet—A "cooked" container for related bibliographic information

Synopsis

Mixed Content Model

```
BiblioMSet ::=
((Abbrev|Abstract|Address|ArtPageNums|Author|AuthorGroup|
  AuthorInitials|BiblioMisc|BiblioSet|Collab|ConfGroup|
  ContractNum|ContractSponsor|Copyright|CorpAuthor|CorpName|Date|
  Edition|Editor|InvPartNumber|ISBN|ISSN|IssueNum|OrgName|
  OtherCredit|PageNums|PrintHistory|ProductName|ProductNumber|
  PubDate|Publisher|PublisherName|PubsNumber|ReleaseInfo|
  RevHistory|SeriesVolNums|Subtitle|Title|TitleAbbrev|VolumeNum|
  CiteTitle|Honorific|FirstName|Surname|Lineage|OtherName|
  Affiliation|AuthorBlurb|Contrib|IndexTerm|BiblioMSet|#PCDATA)+)
```

Attributes	Common attributes	
Name	**Type**	**Default**
Relation	CDATA	*None*

Description

BiblioMSet is a "cooked" wrapper for a collection of bibliographic information.

The purpose of this wrapper is to assert the relationship that binds the collection. For example, in a **BiblioMixed** entry for an article in a journal, you might use two **BiblioMSet**s to wrap the fields related to the article and the fields related to the journal.

Processing expectations

Formatted as a displayed block.

BiblioMSets are "cooked." In addition to named fields, they can contain interspersed #PCDATA to provide punctuation and other formatting information.

The processing system is generally expected to present each and every element in the set, all interspersed #PCDATA, in the order in which it occurs.

4.0 *Future Changes*

AuthorBlurb and **Affiliation** will be removed from the inline content of **BiblioMSet** in DocBook V4.0. A new wrapper element will be created to associate this information with authors, editors, and other contributors.

5.0 *Future Changes*

BiblioSet will be removed from the content model of **BiblioMSet**. Allowing a "raw" container inside a "cooked" one confuses processing expectations.

Attributes

Relation

`Relation` identifies the relationship between the various elements in the **BiblioMSet**.

See Also

BiblioEntry, **BiblioMisc**, **BiblioMixed**, **BiblioSet**, **BookBiblio**

Examples

```
<!DOCTYPE bibliomixed PUBLIC "-//OASIS//DTD DocBook V3.1//EN">
<bibliomixed>
  <bibliomset relation=article>
    <surname>Walsh</surname>, <firstname>Norman</firstname>.
    <title role=article>Introduction to Cascading Style Sheets</title>.
  </bibliomset>
  <bibliomset relation=journal>
    <title>The World Wide Web Journal</title>
    <volumenum>2</volumenum><issuenum>1</issuenum>.
    <publishername>O'Reilly &amp; Associates, Inc.</publishername> and
    <corpname>The World Wide Web Consortium</corpname>.
    <pubdate>Winter, 1996</pubdate></bibliomset>.
</bibliomixed>
```

For additional examples, see also **Bibliography**.

BiblioSet—A "raw" container for related bibliographic information

Synopsis

Content Model

```
BiblioSet ::=
((Abbrev|Abstract|Address|ArtPageNums|Author|AuthorGroup|
  AuthorInitials|BiblioMisc|BiblioSet|Collab|ConfGroup|
  ContractNum|ContractSponsor|Copyright|CorpAuthor|CorpName|Date|
  Edition|Editor|InvPartNumber|ISBN|ISSN|IssueNum|OrgName|
  OtherCredit|PageNums|PrintHistory|ProductName|ProductNumber|
  PubDate|Publisher|PublisherName|PubsNumber|ReleaseInfo|
  RevHistory|SeriesVolNums|Subtitle|Title|TitleAbbrev|VolumeNum|
  CiteTitle|Honorific|FirstName|Surname|Lineage|OtherName|
  Affiliation|AuthorBlurb|Contrib|IndexTerm)+)
```

Attributes	Common attributes	
Name	**Type**	**Default**
Relation	CDATA	*None*

Parameter Entities

`%bibliocomponent.mix;`

Description

BiblioSet is a "raw" wrapper for a collection of bibliographic information.

The purpose of this wrapper is to assert the relationship that binds the collection. For example, in a **BiblioEntry** for an article in a journal, you might use two **BiblioSets** to wrap the fields related to the article and the fields related to the journal.

Processing expectations

Formatted as a displayed block.

BiblioSets are "raw." They contain a database-like collection of named fields. It is the responsibility of the processing system to select elements from within a **BiblioSet**, present them in the correct order, and add all punctuation.

There is no expectation that a system will present all of the fields in a **BiblioSet** or that they will be displayed in the order in which they occur.

Correct formatting of **BiblioSets** is an interchange issue. See Appendix F.

4.0 *Future Changes*

AuthorBlurb and **Affiliation** will be removed from the inline content of **BiblioSet** in DocBook V4.0. A new wrapper element will be created to associate this information with authors, editors, and other contributors.

Attributes

Relation

`Relation` identifies the relationship between the of the contents of the **BiblioSet**.

See Also

BiblioEntry, **BiblioMisc**, **BiblioMixed**, **BiblioMSet**, **BookBiblio**

Examples

```
<!DOCTYPE biblioentry PUBLIC "-//OASIS//DTD DocBook V3.1//EN">
<biblioentry>
  <abbrev>Walsh97</abbrev>
  <biblioset relation=journal>
    <title>XML: Principles, Tools, and Techniques</title>
    <publisher>
      <publishername>O'Reilly &amp; Associates, Inc.</publishername>
    </publisher>
    <issn>1085-2301</issn>
    <editor><firstname>Dan</firstname><surname>Connolly</surname></editor>
  </biblioset>
  <biblioset relation=article>
```

```
    <title>A Guide to XML</title>
    <author><surname>Walsh</surname><firstname>Norman</firstname></author>
    <copyright><year>1997</year><holder>ArborText, Inc.</holder></copyright>
    <pagenums>97-108</pagenums>
  </biblioset>
</biblioentry>
```

For additional examples, see also **Bibliography**.

BlockQuote—A quotation set off from the main text

Synopsis

Content Model		
`BlockQuote ::= (Title?,Attribution?, (CalloutList|GlossList|ItemizedList|OrderedList|SegmentedList| SimpleList|VariableList|Caution|Important|Note|Tip|Warning| LiteralLayout|ProgramListing|ProgramListingCO|Screen|ScreenCO| ScreenShot|Synopsis|CmdSynopsis|FuncSynopsis|FormalPara|Para| SimPara|Address|BlockQuote|Graphic|GraphicCO|MediaObject| MediaObjectCO|InformalEquation|InformalExample|InformalFigure| InformalTable|Equation|Example|Figure|Table|MsgSet|Procedure| Sidebar|QandASet|Anchor|BridgeHead|Comment|Highlights|Abstract| AuthorBlurb|Epigraph|IndexTerm)+)`		
Attributes	Common attributes	
Parameter Entities		
%admon.mix;	%bookcomponent.content;	%component.mix;
%divcomponent.mix;	%example.mix;	%figure.mix;
%footnote.mix;	%glossdef.mix;	%indexdivcomponent.mix;
%informal.class;	%legalnotice.mix;	%para.mix;
%qandaset.mix;	%refcomponent.mix;	%sidebar.mix;
%textobject.mix;		

Description

Block quotations are set off from the main text, as opposed to occurring inline.

Processing expectations

Formatted as a displayed block.

[4.0] *Future Changes*

Epigraph will not be allowed in **BlockQuote** in DocBook V4.0.

See Also

Abstract, **Attribution**, **Epigraph**, **Highlights**, **Sidebar**

Examples

```
<!DOCTYPE blockquote PUBLIC "-//OASIS//DTD DocBook V3.1//EN">
<blockquote><attribution>Richard Dawkins</attribution>
<para>
The universe that we observe has precisely the properties we should
expect if there is, at bottom, no design, no purpose, no evil and
no good, nothing but pitiless indifference.
</para>
</blockquote>
```

> The universe that we observe has precisely the properties we should expect if there is, at bottom, no design, no purpose, no evil and no good, nothing but pitiless indifference.
>
> —Richard Dawkins

For additional examples, see also **Attribution**, **LiteralLayout**.

Book—A book

Synopsis

Content Model

```
Book ::=
((Title,Subtitle?,TitleAbbrev?)?,
 BookInfo?,
 (Dedication|ToC|LoT|Glossary|Bibliography|Preface|Chapter|
  Reference|Part|Article|Appendix|Index|SetIndex|Colophon)*)
```

Attributes Common attributes

Name	Type	Default
Label	CDATA	*None*
Status	CDATA	*None*
FPI	CDATA	*None*

Parameter Entities

`%book.class;`

Description

A complete book. This is probably the most common document starting point in DocBook documents. The content model of **Book** was made dramatically less restrictive in DocBook V3.1.

Processing expectations

Formatted as a displayed block. Generally causes a forced page break, restarts page numbering, and may generate additional front and back matter (tables of contents and indexes, for example) automatically. In a **Set**, **Book** almost always begins on the next available recto page.

The input order of major components is taken to be the desired output order.

Attributes

FPI

`FPI` holds the Formal Public Identifier for the **Book**.

Label

`Label` specifies an identifying string for presentation purposes. The third **Book** in a **Set** might be labeled "Volume III", for example.

Generally, an explicit `Label` attribute is used only if the processing system is incapable of generating the label automatically. If present, the `Label` is normative; it will used even if the processing system is capable of automatic labelling.

Status

`Status` identifies the editorial or publication status of the **Book**.

Publication status might be used to control formatting (for example, printing a "draft" watermark on drafts) or processing (perhaps a document with a status of "final" should not include any components that are not final).

See Also

Appendix, **Article**, **Chapter**, **Colophon**, **Dedication**, **Part**, **PartIntro**, **Preface**, **Set**

Examples

```
<!DOCTYPE book PUBLIC "-//OASIS//DTD DocBook V3.1//EN">
<book>
<title>An Example Book</title>
<titleabbrev>Example</titleabbrev>
<bookinfo>
  <legalnotice><para>No notice is required.</para></legalnotice>
  <author><firstname>Norman</><surname>Walsh</></author>
</bookinfo>
<dedication>
<para>
This book is dedicated to you.
</para>
</dedication>
<preface><title>Forword</title>
<para>
Some content is always required.
</para>
</preface>
<chapter><title>Required Chapter</title>
<para>
At least one chapter, reference, part, or article is required in a book.
</para>
</chapter>
<appendix><title>Optional Appendix</title>
<para>
Appendixes are optional.
```

```
</para>
</appendix>
</book>
```

For additional examples, see also **Appendix**, **Collab**, **Set**, **XRef**.

BookBiblio—Meta-information about a book used in a bibliographical citation

Synopsis

Content Model

```
BookBiblio ::=
((Abbrev|Abstract|Address|ArtPageNums|Author|AuthorGroup|
  AuthorInitials|BiblioMisc|BiblioSet|Collab|ConfGroup|
  ContractNum|ContractSponsor|Copyright|CorpAuthor|CorpName|Date|
  Edition|Editor|InvPartNumber|ISBN|ISSN|IssueNum|OrgName|
  OtherCredit|PageNums|PrintHistory|ProductName|ProductNumber|
  PubDate|Publisher|PublisherName|PubsNumber|ReleaseInfo|
  RevHistory|SeriesVolNums|Subtitle|Title|TitleAbbrev|VolumeNum|
  CiteTitle|Honorific|FirstName|Surname|Lineage|OtherName|
  Affiliation|AuthorBlurb|Contrib|IndexTerm|SeriesInfo)+)
```

Attributes	Common attributes

Description

This was one of the original wrapper elements for bibliographic data. Over time, the structure of bibliographies has become broad enough to make this wrapper seem redundant.

Processing expectations

Formatted as a displayed block.

4.0 *Future Changes*

BookBiblio will be discarded in DocBook V4.0.

See Also

ArtHeader, **BiblioEntry**, **BiblioMisc**, **BiblioMixed**, **BiblioMSet**, **BiblioSet**, **BookInfo**, **DocInfo**, **ObjectInfo**, **RefSynopsisDivInfo**, **ScreenInfo**, **Sect1Info**, **Sect2Info**, **Sect3Info**, **Sect4Info**, **Sect5Info**, **SectionInfo**, **SetInfo**

BookInfo—Meta-information for a Book

Synopsis

Content Model

```
BookInfo ::=
((Graphic|MediaObject|LegalNotice|ModeSpec|SubjectSet|KeywordSet|
```

ITermSet|Abbrev|Abstract|Address|ArtPageNums|Author|AuthorGroup| AuthorInitials|BiblioMisc|BiblioSet|Collab|ConfGroup| ContractNum|ContractSponsor|Copyright|CorpAuthor|CorpName|Date| Edition|Editor|InvPartNumber|ISBN|ISSN|IssueNum|OrgName| OtherCredit|PageNums|PrintHistory|ProductName|ProductNumber| PubDate|Publisher|PublisherName|PubsNumber|ReleaseInfo| RevHistory|SeriesVolNums|Subtitle|Title|TitleAbbrev|VolumeNum| CiteTitle|Honorific|FirstName|Surname|Lineage|OtherName| Affiliation|AuthorBlurb|Contrib|IndexTerm|BookBiblio)+)		
Attributes **Name**	Common attributes **Type**	**Default**
Contents	IDREFS	*None*

Description

Meta-information for a Book.

Processing expectations

Suppressed. Many of the elements in this wrapper may be used in presentation, but they are not generally printed as part of the formatting of the wrapper. It merely serves to identify where they occur.

4.0 *Future Changes*

AuthorBlurb and **Affiliation** will be removed from the inline content of **BookInfo** in DocBook V4.0. A new wrapper element will be created to associate this information with authors, editors, and other contributors.

BookBiblio will be discarded.

Attributes

Contents

`Contents`, if specified, should contain a list of all the IDs of the chapter-level subelements of the **Book**, in their natural order.

See Also

ArtHeader, **BookBiblio**, **DocInfo**, **ObjectInfo**, **RefSynopsisDivInfo**, **ScreenInfo**, **Sect1Info**, **Sect2Info**, **Sect3Info**, **Sect4Info**, **Sect5Info**, **SectionInfo**, **SetInfo**

Examples

```
<!DOCTYPE bookinfo PUBLIC "-//OASIS//DTD DocBook V3.1//EN">
<bookinfo>
  <title>User's Guide for the DocBook DTD</title>
  <authorgroup>
    <author><firstname>Terry</firstname><surname>Allen</surname></author>
    <author><firstname>Eve</firstname><surname>Maler</surname>
      <affiliation><orgname>Arbortext, Inc.</orgname></affiliation>
```

```
    </author>
    <author><firstname>Norman</firstname><surname>Walsh</surname>
      <affiliation><orgname>Arbortext, Inc.</orgname></affiliation>
    </author>
  </authorgroup>
  <edition>User's Guide version 1.0 for DocBook V3.0</edition>
  <pubdate>1997</pubdate>
  <copyright><year>1992</year>
    <year>1993</year>
    <year>1994</year>
    <year>1995</year>
    <year>1996</year>
    <year>1997</year>
<holder>Arbortext, Inc.,
HaL Computer Systems, Inc.,
Fujitsu Software Corp., and
O'Reilly &amp; Associates, Inc.
</holder>
</copyright>

<legalnotice>
<para>Permission to use, copy, modify and distribute
the DocBook DTD and its accompanying documentation for any purpose and
without fee is hereby granted in perpetuity, provided that the above
copyright notice and this paragraph appear in all copies.</para>
</legalnotice>

<legalnotice>
<para>The copyright holders make no representation about the suitability of
this DTD for any purpose. It is provided <quote>as is</quote> without expressed
or implied warranty.  If you modify the DocBook DTD in any way, except for
declaring and referencing additional general entities and declaring additional
notations, identify your DTD as a variant of DocBook.</para>
</legalnotice>

</bookinfo>
```

For additional examples, see also **Book**, **Collab**.

BridgeHead—A free-floating heading

Synopsis

Mixed Content Model

```
BridgeHead ::=
((#PCDATA|FootnoteRef|XRef|Abbrev|Acronym|Citation|CiteRefEntry|
  CiteTitle|Emphasis|FirstTerm|ForeignPhrase|GlossTerm|Footnote|
  Phrase|Quote|Trademark|WordAsWord|Link|OLink|ULink|Action|
  Application|ClassName|Command|ComputerOutput|Database|Email|
  EnVar|ErrorCode|ErrorName|ErrorType|Filename|Function|GUIButton|
  GUIIcon|GUILabel|GUIMenu|GUIMenuItem|GUISubmenu|Hardware|
  Interface|InterfaceDefinition|KeyCap|KeyCode|KeyCombo|KeySym|
  Literal|Constant|Markup|MediaLabel|MenuChoice|MouseButton|
  MsgText|Option|Optional|Parameter|Prompt|Property|Replaceable|
  ReturnValue|SGMLTag|StructField|StructName|Symbol|SystemItem|
```

```
Token|Type|UserInput|VarName|Anchor|Author|AuthorInitials|
CorpAuthor|ModeSpec|OtherCredit|ProductName|ProductNumber|
RevHistory|Comment|Subscript|Superscript|InlineGraphic|
InlineMediaObject|InlineEquation|IndexTerm)+)
```

Attributes Name	Common attributes Type	**Default**
Renderas	*Enumeration:* Other, Sect1, Sect2, Sect3, Sect4, Sect5	*None*

Parameter Entities

`%admon.mix;`	`%bookcomponent.content;`	`%component.mix;`
`%divcomponent.mix;`	`%genobj.class;`	`%qandaset.mix;`
`%refcomponent.mix;`	`%sidebar.mix;`	

Description

Some documents, usually legacy documents, use headings that are not tied to the normal sectional hieararchy. These headings may be represented in DocBook with the **BridgeHead** element.

BridgeHeads may also be useful in fiction or journalistic works that don't have a nested hierarchy.

Processing expectations

A **BridgeHead** is formatted as a block, using the same display properties as the section heading which it masquerades as. The `RenderAs` attribute controls which heading it mimics.

4.0 *Future Changes*

The **InterfaceDefinition** element will be discarded in DocBook V4.0. It will no longer be available in the content model of this element.

Attributes

Renderas

The `RenderAs` attribute identifies how the **BridgeHead** should be rendered. In this way, a **BridgeHead** can be made to appear as a **Sect1**, for example.

See Also

Sect1, **Sect2**, **Sect3**, **Sect4**, **Sect5**, **Section**, **SimpleSect**

Examples

For examples, see **Chapter**.

Callout—A "called out" description of a marked **Area**

Synopsis

Content Model

```
Callout ::=
((CalloutList|GlossList|ItemizedList|OrderedList|SegmentedList|
  SimpleList|VariableList|Caution|Important|Note|Tip|Warning|
  LiteralLayout|ProgramListing|ProgramListingCO|Screen|ScreenCO|
  ScreenShot|Synopsis|CmdSynopsis|FuncSynopsis|FormalPara|Para|
  SimPara|Address|BlockQuote|Graphic|GraphicCO|MediaObject|
  MediaObjectCO|InformalEquation|InformalExample|InformalFigure|
  InformalTable|Equation|Example|Figure|Table|MsgSet|Procedure|
  Sidebar|QandASet|Anchor|BridgeHead|Comment|Highlights|Abstract|
  AuthorBlurb|Epigraph|IndexTerm)+)
```

Attributes	Common attributes	
Name	**Type**	**Default**
AreaRefs	IDREFS	*Required*

Description

A "callout" is a visual device for associating annotations with an image, program listing, or similar figure. Each location is identified with a mark, and the annotation is identified with the same mark. This is somewhat analagous to the notion of footnotes in print.

An example will help illustrate the concept. In the following example, the synopsis for the *mv* command is annotated with two marks. Note the location of the old and new filenames.

```
mv ❶oldfile ❷newfile
```

Somewhere else in the document, usually close by, a **CalloutList** provides a description for each of the callouts:

❶ The old filename. The *mv* command renames the file currently called `oldfile`, which must exist when *mv* is executed.

❷ The new filename. The *mv* command changes the name of the old file to `newfile`. If `newfile` exists when *mv* is executed, it will be replaced by the old file.

Each **Callout** contains an annotation for an individual callout or a group of callouts. The **Callout** points to the areas that it annotates with ID references. The areas are identified by coordinates in an an **Area** or **AreaSet**, or by an explicit **CO** element.

Processing expectations

Formatted as a displayed block.

CallOuts usually generate text that points the reader to the appropriate area on the object being augmented. Often, these are numbered bullets or other distinct visual icons. The same icons should be used in both places. In other words, whatever identifies the callouts on the object should generate the same icons on the respective callouts.

In online environments, it may also be possible to establish a linking relationship between the two elements.

The processing expectations of **Callouts** are likely to deserve special consideration for interchange. See Appendix F. This is especially true if your interchange partners are producing documentation in a medium that has restricted visual presentation features, such as aural media or Braille.

Attributes

AreaRefs

`AreaRefs` must point to one or more **Areas** or **AreaSets**. These, in turn, identify the portions of the object described by this **Callout**.

Examples

For examples, see **ProgramListingCO**, **ScreenCO**.

CalloutList—A list of **Callouts**

Synopsis

Content Model
`CalloutList ::=`
`((Title,TitleAbbrev?)?,`
`Callout+)`		

Attributes	Common attributes	
Parameter Entities		
`%admon.mix;`	`%bookcomponent.content;`	`%component.mix;`
`%divcomponent.mix;`	`%example.mix;`	`%footnote.mix;`
`%glossdef.mix;`	`%highlights.mix;`	`%legalnotice.mix;`
`%list.class;`	`%para.mix;`	`%qandaset.mix;`
`%refcomponent.mix;`	`%sidebar.mix;`	`%tabentry.mix;`
`%tbl.entry.mdl;`	`%textobject.mix;`	

Description

A **CalloutList** is a list of annotations or descriptions. Each **Callout** points to the area on a **Graphic**, **ProgramListing**, or **Screen** that it augments.

The areas are identified by coordinates in an an **Area** or **AreaSet**, or by an explicit **CO** element.

Processing expectations

Formatted as a displayed block.

See Also

AreaSpec, **CO**, **GraphicCO**, **ImageObjectCO**, **ItemizedList**, **ListItem**, **MediaObjectCO**, **OrderedList**, **ProgramListingCO**, **ScreenCO**, **SegmentedList**, **SimpleList**, **VariableList**

Examples

For examples, see **ProgramListingCO**, **ScreenCO**.

Caption—A caption

Synopsis

Content Model	
`Caption ::= (CalloutList|GlossList|ItemizedList|OrderedList|SegmentedList| SimpleList|VariableList|Caution|Important|Note|Tip|Warning| LiteralLayout|ProgramListing|ProgramListingCO|Screen|ScreenCO| ScreenShot|FormalPara|Para|SimPara|BlockQuote)*`	
Attributes	Common attributes

Description

A **Caption** is an extended description of a **MediaObject**. Unlike a **TextObject**, which is an alternative to the other elements in the **MediaObject**, the **Caption** augments the object.

Processing expectations

Formatted as a displayed block.

See Also

Alt, **AudioObject**, **Graphic**, **ImageObject**, **InlineGraphic**, **InlineMediaObject**, **MediaObject**, **TextObject**, **VideoObject**

Examples

For examples, see **ImageObject**, **InformalFigure**.

Caution—A note of caution

Synopsis

Content Model

```
Caution ::=
(Title?,
 (CalloutList|GlossList|ItemizedList|OrderedList|SegmentedList|
  SimpleList|VariableList|LiteralLayout|ProgramListing|
  ProgramListingCO|Screen|ScreenCO|ScreenShot|Synopsis|
  CmdSynopsis|FuncSynopsis|FormalPara|Para|SimPara|Address|
  BlockQuote|Graphic|GraphicCO|MediaObject|MediaObjectCO|
  InformalEquation|InformalExample|InformalFigure|InformalTable|
  Equation|Example|Figure|Table|Procedure|Sidebar|Anchor|
  BridgeHead|Comment|IndexTerm)+)
```

Attributes	Common attributes	
Parameter Entities		
%admon.class;	%admon.exclusion;	%bookcomponent.content;
%component.mix;	%divcomponent.mix;	%highlights.mix;
%legalnotice.mix;	%para.mix;	%refcomponent.mix;
%sidebar.mix;	%tabentry.mix;	%tbl.entry.mdl;
%textobject.mix;		

Description

A **Caution** is an admonition, usually set off from the main text.

In some types of documentation, the semantics of admonitions are clearly defined (**Caution** might imply the possibility of harm to equipment whereas **Warning** might imply harm to a person) However, DocBook makes no such assertions.

Processing expectations

Formatted as a displayed block. Often outputs the generated text “Caution” or some other visible indication of the type of admonition, especially if a **Title** is not present. Sometimes outputs a graphical icon or other symbol as well.

See Also

Important, **Note**, **Tip**, **Warning**

Examples

```
<!DOCTYPE caution PUBLIC "-//OASIS//DTD DocBook V3.1//EN">
<caution><title>No User Servicable Parts Inside</title>
<para>Breaking this seal voids all warranties.</para>
</caution>
```

No User Servicable Parts Inside

Breaking this seal voids all warranties.

Chapter—A chapter, as of a book

Synopsis

Content Model

```
Chapter ::=
((DocInfo?,Title,Subtitle?,TitleAbbrev?),
 ToCchap?,
 (((CalloutList|GlossList|ItemizedList|OrderedList|SegmentedList|
    SimpleList|VariableList|Caution|Important|Note|Tip|Warning|
    LiteralLayout|ProgramListing|ProgramListingCO|Screen|ScreenCO|
    ScreenShot|Synopsis|CmdSynopsis|FuncSynopsis|FormalPara|Para|
    SimPara|Address|BlockQuote|Graphic|GraphicCO|MediaObject|
    MediaObjectCO|InformalEquation|InformalExample|InformalFigure|
    InformalTable|Equation|Example|Figure|Table|MsgSet|Procedure|
    Sidebar|QandASet|Anchor|BridgeHead|Comment|Highlights|
    Abstract|AuthorBlurb|Epigraph|IndexTerm)+,
   (Sect1*|
    (RefEntry)*|
    SimpleSect*|Section*))|
  (Sect1+|
   (RefEntry)+|
   SimpleSect+|Section+)),
 (Index|Glossary|Bibliography)*)
```

Attributes	Common attributes	
Name	**Type**	**Default**
Label	CDATA	*None*
Status	CDATA	*None*

Parameter Entities

`%chapter.class;`	`%partcontent.mix;`

Description

Chapter is a chapter of a **Book**.

Processing expectations

Formatted as a displayed block. Usually introduces a forced page break and often starts on the next recto page. The first chapter of a document usually restarts page numbering. Typically, chapters are numbered and presented in the table of contents.

Attributes

Label

`Label` specifies an identifying string for presentation purposes. The fourth **Chapter** in a **Book** might be labeled "4", for example.

Generally, an explicit `Label` attribute is used only if the processing system is incapable of generating the label automatically. If present, the `Label` is normative; it will used even if the processing system is capable of automatic labelling.

Status

`Status` identifies the editorial or publication status of the **Chapter**.

Publication status might be used to control formatting (for example, printing a "draft" watermark on drafts) or processing (perhaps a document with a status of "final" should not include any components that are not final).

See Also

Appendix, **Article**, **Book**, **Colophon**, **Dedication**, **Part**, **PartIntro**, **Preface**, **Set**

Examples

```
<!DOCTYPE chapter PUBLIC "-//OASIS//DTD DocBook V3.1//EN">
<chapter label="6" id="figures"><beginpage pagenum=129>
<docinfo>
<keywordset>
  <keyword>images</keyword>
  <keyword>illustrations</keyword>
</keywordset>
<itermset>
  <indexterm zone="figures"><primary>Figures</primary></indexterm>
  <indexterm zone="figures"><primary>Pictures</primary></indexterm>
  <indexterm zone="notreal">
    <primary>Sections</primary><secondary>Not Real</secondary>
  </indexterm>
</itermset>
</docinfo>
<title>Pictures and Figures</title>
<epigraph>
<attribution>William Safire</attribution>
<para>
Knowing how things work is the basis for appreciation, and is
thus a source of civilized delight.
</para>
</epigraph>
<para>
Pictures and figures &hellip;
</para>
<sect1><title>Top Level Section</title>
<para>
&hellip;
</para>
<bridgehead id="notreal" renderas=sect3>Not a Real Section</bridgehead>
<para>
This paragraph appears to be under a Sect3 heading, but it's really
in the same Sect1 as the preceding paragraph.
</para>
</sect1>
</chapter>
```

For additional examples, see also **Abstract**, **Appendix**, **Book**, **Collab**, **Highlights**, **IndexTerm**, **OLink**, **Part**, **Section**, **TitleAbbrev**, **XRef**.

Citation—An inline bibliographic reference to another published work

Synopsis

Mixed Content Model

```
Citation ::=
((#PCDATA|FootnoteRef|XRef|Abbrev|Acronym|Citation|CiteRefEntry|
  CiteTitle|Emphasis|FirstTerm|ForeignPhrase|GlossTerm|Footnote|
  Phrase|Quote|Trademark|WordAsWord|Link|OLink|ULink|Action|
  Application|ClassName|Command|ComputerOutput|Database|Email|
  EnVar|ErrorCode|ErrorName|ErrorType|Filename|Function|GUIButton|
  GUIIcon|GUILabel|GUIMenu|GUIMenuItem|GUISubmenu|Hardware|
  Interface|InterfaceDefinition|KeyCap|KeyCode|KeyCombo|KeySym|
  Literal|Constant|Markup|MediaLabel|MenuChoice|MouseButton|
  MsgText|Option|Optional|Parameter|Prompt|Property|Replaceable|
  ReturnValue|SGMLTag|StructField|StructName|Symbol|SystemItem|
  Token|Type|UserInput|VarName|Anchor|Author|AuthorInitials|
  CorpAuthor|ModeSpec|OtherCredit|ProductName|ProductNumber|
  RevHistory|Comment|Subscript|Superscript|InlineGraphic|
  InlineMediaObject|InlineEquation|Synopsis|CmdSynopsis|
  FuncSynopsis|IndexTerm)+)
```

Attributes	Common attributes	
Parameter Entities		
%gen.char.class;	%ndxterm.char.mix;	%para.char.mix;
%programlisting.content;	%refinline.char.mix;	%screen.content;
%tbl.entry.mdl;	%title.char.mix;	

Description

The content of a **Citation** is assumed to be a reference string, perhaps identical to an abbreviation in an entry in a **Bibliography**.

Processing expectations

Formatted inline.

4.0 *Future Changes*

The **InterfaceDefinition** element will be discarded in DocBook V4.0. It will no longer be available in the content model of this element.

See Also

CiteRefEntry, **CiteTitle**

Examples

```
<!DOCTYPE para PUBLIC "-//OASIS//DTD DocBook V3.1//EN">
<para>
Consult <citation>AhoSethiUllman96</citation> for more details on
abstract syntax tree construction.
</para>
```

Consult [AhoSethiUllman96] for more details on abstract syntax tree construction.

CiteRefEntry—A citation to a reference page

Synopsis

Content Model CiteRefEntry ::= (RefEntryTitle,ManVolNum?)		
Attributes	Common attributes	
Parameter Entities		
%gen.char.class;	%ndxterm.char.mix;	%para.char.mix;
%programlisting.content;	%refinline.char.mix;	%screen.content;
%tbl.entry.mdl;	%title.char.mix;	

Description

This element is a citation to a **RefEntry**. It must include a **RefEntryTitle** that should exactly match the title of a **RefEntry**.

Processing expectations

This element implicitly links to the **RefEntry** with the same **RefEntryTitle** (in the same volume, as defined by **ManVolNum**).

Formatted inline. Usually the **ManVolNum** is put in parentheses.

See Also

Citation, **CiteTitle**

Examples

```
<!DOCTYPE para PUBLIC "-//OASIS//DTD DocBook V3.1//EN">
<para>
For a further description of print formats, consult the
<citerefentry><refentrytitle>printf</refentrytitle>
<manvolnum>3S</manvolnum></citerefentry> manual page.
</para>
```

For a further description of print formats, consult the printf(3S) manual page.

For additional examples, see also **ManVolNum**.

CiteTitle—The title of a cited work

Synopsis

```
Mixed Content Model
CiteTitle ::=
((#PCDATA|FootnoteRef|XRef|Abbrev|Acronym|Citation|CiteRefEntry|
  CiteTitle|Emphasis|FirstTerm|ForeignPhrase|GlossTerm|Footnote|
  Phrase|Quote|Trademark|WordAsWord|Link|OLink|ULink|Action|
```

```
Application|ClassName|Command|ComputerOutput|Database|Email|
EnVar|ErrorCode|ErrorName|ErrorType|Filename|Function|GUIButton|
GUIIcon|GUILabel|GUIMenu|GUIMenuItem|GUISubmenu|Hardware|
Interface|InterfaceDefinition|KeyCap|KeyCode|KeyCombo|KeySym|
Literal|Constant|Markup|MediaLabel|MenuChoice|MouseButton|
MsgText|Option|Optional|Parameter|Prompt|Property|Replaceable|
ReturnValue|SGMLTag|StructField|StructName|Symbol|SystemItem|
Token|Type|UserInput|VarName|Anchor|Author|AuthorInitials|
CorpAuthor|ModeSpec|OtherCredit|ProductName|ProductNumber|
RevHistory|Comment|Subscript|Superscript|InlineGraphic|
InlineMediaObject|InlineEquation|Synopsis|CmdSynopsis|
FuncSynopsis|IndexTerm)+)
```

Attributes Name	Common attributes **Type**	**Default**
Pubwork	*Enumeration:* Article Book Chapter Journal Manuscript Part RefEntry Section Series Set	*None*

Parameter Entities		
`%bibliocomponent.mix;`	`%gen.char.class;`	`%ndxterm.char.mix;`
`%para.char.mix;`	`%programlisting.content;`	`%refinline.char.mix;`
`%screen.content;`	`%tbl.entry.mdl;`	`%title.char.mix;`

Description

CiteTitle provides inline markup for the title of a cited work.

Processing expectations

Formatted inline. Often italicized for **Books** and quoted for **Articles**.

4.0 *Future Changes*

The **InterfaceDefinition** element will be discarded in DocBook V4.0. It will no longer be available in the content model of this element.

Attributes

Pubwork

`Pubwork` identifies the genre of the cited publication.

See Also

Citation, **CiteRefEntry**

Examples

```
<!DOCTYPE para PUBLIC "-//OASIS//DTD DocBook V3.1//EN">
<para>
For a complete methodology for DTD creation, see
<citetitle pubwork="book">Developing SGML DTDs: From Text to Model
to Markup</citetitle> by Eve Maler and Jeanne El Andaloussi.
</para>
```

For a complete methodology for DTD creation, see *Developing SGML DTDs: From Text to Model to Markup* by Eve Maler and Jeanne El Andaloussi.

For additional examples, see also **Emphasis**, **Footnote**, **LiteralLayout**, **ProductNumber**, **ULink**.

City—The name of a city in an address

Synopsis

Mixed Content Model
`City ::=`
`((#PCDATA|Link|OLink|ULink|Emphasis|Trademark|Replaceable|Comment|Subscript|Superscript|InlineGraphic|InlineMediaObject|IndexTerm)+)`	

Attributes	Common attributes

Description

The name of a city in an **Address**.

Processing expectations

Formatted inline. In an **Address**, this element may inherit the verbatim qualities of an address.

See Also

Address, **Country**, **Email**, **Fax**, **OtherAddr**, **Phone**, **POB**, **Postcode**, **State**, **Street**

Examples

For examples, see **Address**.

ClassName—The name of a class, in the object-oriented programming sense

Synopsis

Mixed Content Model
`ClassName ::=`
`((#PCDATA|Replaceable|InlineGraphic|InlineMediaObject|IndexTerm)+)`	

Attributes	Common attributes

Parameter Entities		
%cptr.char.mix;	%ndxterm.char.mix;	%para.char.mix;
%programlisting.content;	%refinline.char.mix;	%refname.char.mix;
%screen.content;	%tbl.entry.mdl;	%tech.char.class;
%title.char.mix;		

Description

The **ClassName** tag is used to identify the name of a class. This is likely to occur only in documentation about object-oriented programming systems, languages, and architectures.

DocBook does not contain a complete set of inlines appropriate for describing object-oriented programming environments. (While it has **ClassName**, for example, it has nothing suitable for methods.) This will be addressed in a future version of DocBook.

Processing expectations

Formatted inline.

See Also

Interface, **InterfaceDefinition**, **Property**, **StructField**, **StructName**, **Symbol**, **Token**, **Type**

Examples

```
<!DOCTYPE para PUBLIC "-//OASIS//DTD DocBook V3.1//EN">
<para>
All user-interface components must be descendants of the
<classname>Widget</classname> class.
</para>
```

All user-interface components must be descendants of the Widget class.

CmdSynopsis—A syntax summary for a software command

Synopsis

Content Model

```
CmdSynopsis ::=
((Command|Arg|Group|SBR)+,
 SynopFragment*)
```

Attributes Name	Common attributes Type	Default
Label	CDATA	*None*
CmdLength	CDATA	*None*
Sepchar	CDATA	" "

Parameter Entities		
%admon.mix;	%bookcomponent.content;	%component.mix;
%divcomponent.mix;	%example.mix;	%figure.mix;
%footnote.mix;	%glossdef.mix;	%indexdivcomponent.mix;
%para.char.mix;	%programlisting.content;	%qandaset.mix;
%refcomponent.mix;	%screen.content;	%sidebar.mix;
%synop.class;	%tbl.entry.mdl;	

Description

A **CmdSynopsis** summarizes the options and parameters of a command started from a text prompt. This is usually a program started from the DOS, Windows, or UNIX shell prompt.

CmdSynopsis operates under the following general model: commands have arguments, that may be grouped; arguments and groups may be required or optional and may be repeated.

Processing expectations

The processing expectations of **CmdSynopsis** are fairly complex.

- Arguments are generally identified with a prefix character.

  In the UNIX world, this character is almost universally the dash or hyphen although plus signs and double dashes have become more common in recent years.

  In the DOS/Windows world, forward slashes are somewhat more common than dashes.

  The DocBook processing expectations on this point are intentionally vague. In some environments it may be most convenient to generate these characters automatically, in other environments it may be more convenient to insert them literally in the content.

  Whichever processing model you choose, note that this will be an interchange issue if you share documents with other users (see Appendix F).
- Brackets are used to distinguish between optional, required, or plain arguments. Usually square brackets are placed around optional arguments, `[-g]`, and curly brackets are placed around required arguments, `{-g}`. Plain arguments are required, but are not decorated with brackets.
- Repeatable arguments are followed by an ellipsis.
- Multiple arguments within a group are considered exclusive and are separated by vertical bars.

- Groups, like arguments, may be optional, required, or plain and may or may not repeat. The same brackets and ellipses that are used to indicate these characteristics on arguments are used on groups.
- Arguments and groups may nest more-or-less arbitrarily.
- Formatted as a displayed block. The processing system is free to introduce line breaks where required, but the **SBR** element may be introduced by the author to provide an explicit break location.

Attributes

CmdLength

`CmdLength` indicates displayed length of the command; this information may be used to intelligently indent command synopses which extend beyond one line.

Label

`Label` specifies an identifying number or string that may be used in presentation.

Sepchar

`SepChar` specifies the character (a space by default) that should separate the **Command** and its top-level arguments.

See Also

Arg, **FuncSynopsis**, **Group**, **RefSynopsisDiv**, **SBR**, **SynopFragment**, **SynopFragmentRef**, **Synopsis**

Examples

```
<!DOCTYPE cmdsynopsis PUBLIC "-//OASIS//DTD DocBook V3.1//EN">
<cmdsynopsis>
  <command>cd</command>
  <arg choice=req><replaceable>directory</replaceable></arg>
</cmdsynopsis>
```

```
cd {directory}
```

```
<!DOCTYPE cmdsynopsis PUBLIC "-//OASIS//DTD DocBook V3.1//EN">
<cmdsynopsis>
  <command>cal</command>
  <arg>-j</arg>
  <arg>-y</arg>
  <arg>month <arg>year</arg></arg>
</cmdsynopsis>
```

```
cal [-j] [-y] [month [year]]
```

```
<!DOCTYPE cmdsynopsis PUBLIC "-//OASIS//DTD DocBook V3.1//EN">
<cmdsynopsis>
  <command>chgrp</command>
  <arg>-R
    <group>
      <arg>-H</arg>
      <arg>-L</arg>
      <arg>-P</arg>
    </group>
  </arg>
  <arg>-f</arg>
  <arg choice=plain><replaceable>group</replaceable></arg>
  <arg rep=repeat choice=plain><replaceable>file</replaceable></arg>
</cmdsynopsis>
```

`chgrp [-R  [-H | -L | -P] ] [-f]` *`group file...`*

```
<!DOCTYPE cmdsynopsis PUBLIC "-//OASIS//DTD DocBook V3.1//EN">
<cmdsynopsis>
  <command>emacs</command>
  <arg>-t <replaceable>file</replaceable></arg>
  <arg>-q</arg>
  <arg>-u <replaceable>user</replaceable></arg>
  <arg>+<replaceable>number</replaceable></arg>
  <arg rep=repeat>-f <replaceable>function</replaceable></arg>
  <sbr>
  <arg rep=repeat>-l <replaceable>file</replaceable></arg>
  <arg rep=repeat choice=plain><replaceable>file</replaceable></arg>
</cmdsynopsis>
```

```
emacs [-t file] [-q] [-u user] [+number] [-f function...]
  [-l file...] file...
```

Note the use of **SBR** in this example to force line breaks at reasonable places in the synopsis.

For additional examples, see also **SynopFragment**.

CO—The location of a callout embedded in text

Synopsis

Content Model
`CO ::=`
`EMPTY`		

Attributes **Name**	Common attributes **Type**	**Default**
Label Linkends	CDATA IDREFS	*None* *None*
Parameter Entities `%programlisting.content;`	`%screen.content;`	

Description

A **CO** identifies (by its location) a point of reference for a callout. See **Callout**.

Processing expectations

Formatted inline. This element provides data for processing, but is not expected to be rendered directly.

Attributes

Label

`Label` specifies an identifying number or string that may be used in presentation.

Linkends

`Linkends` points to the **Callout**(s) which refer to this **CO**. (This provides bidirectional linking, which may be useful in online presentation, for example.)

See Also

AreaSpec, **CalloutList**, **GraphicCO**, **ImageObjectCO**, **MediaObjectCO**, **ProgramListingCO**, **ScreenCO**

Examples

For examples, see **ScreenCO**.

Collab—Identifies a collaborator

Synopsis

Content Model
`Collab ::=`
`(CollabName,Affiliation*)`	

Attributes	Common attributes
Parameter Entities `%bibliocomponent.mix;`	

Description

This element identifies a collaborative partner in a document. It associates the name of a collaborator with his or her **Affiliation**.

Processing expectations

May be formatted inline or as a displayed block, depending on context. Sometimes suppressed.

See Also

Author, **AuthorBlurb**, **AuthorGroup**, **CollabName**, **Contrib**, **CorpAuthor**, **Editor**, **OtherCredit**

Examples

```
<!DOCTYPE book PUBLIC "-//OASIS//DTD DocBook V3.1//EN">
<book>
<bookinfo>
  <title>DocBook: The Definitive Guide</title>
  <authorgroup>
    <collab><collabname>Lenny Muellner</collabname></collab>
    <collab><collabname>Norman Walsh</collabname></collab>
  </authorgroup>
</bookinfo>
<chapter><title>Just an Example</title>
<para>
This is just an example, in real life, Lenny and Norm are both
<sgmltag>Author</>s.
</para>
</chapter>
</book>
```

For additional examples, see also **ContractSponsor**.

CollabName—The name of a collaborator

Synopsis

Mixed Content Model
`CollabName ::=`
`((#PCDATA|Link|OLink|ULink|Emphasis|Trademark|Replaceable|Comment|`
`  Subscript|Superscript|InlineGraphic|InlineMediaObject|IndexTerm)+)`	

Attributes	Common attributes

Description

The name of a collaborator.

Processing expectations

May be formatted inline or as a displayed block, depending on context. Sometimes suppressed.

See Also

Author, **AuthorBlurb**, **AuthorGroup**, **Collab**, **Contrib**, **CorpAuthor**, **Editor**, **OtherCredit**

Examples

For examples, see **Collab**, **ContractSponsor**.

Colophon—Text at the back of a book describing facts about its production

Synopsis

Content Model

```
Colophon ::=
((Title,Subtitle?,TitleAbbrev?)?,
 (CalloutList|GlossList|ItemizedList|OrderedList|SegmentedList|
  SimpleList|VariableList|Caution|Important|Note|Tip|Warning|
  LiteralLayout|ProgramListing|ProgramListingCO|Screen|ScreenCO|
  ScreenShot|FormalPara|Para|SimPara|BlockQuote)+)
```

Attributes	Common attributes	
Name	**Type**	**Default**
Status	CDATA	*None*

Description

A **Colophon**, if present, almost always occurs at the very end of a book. It contains factual information about the book, especially about its production, and includes details about typographic style, the fonts used, the paper used, and perhaps the binding method of the book.

Font geeks like Norm think every book should have one.

Processing expectations

Formatted as a displayed block.

Attributes

Status

`Status` identifies the editorial or publication status of the **Colophon**.

Publication status might be used to control formatting (for example, printing a "draft" watermark on drafts) or processing (perhaps a document with a status of "final" should not include any components that are not final).

See Also

Appendix, **Article**, **Book**, **Chapter**, **Dedication**, **Part**, **PartIntro**, **Preface**, **Set**

Examples

```
<!DOCTYPE colophon PUBLIC "-//OASIS//DTD DocBook V3.1//EN">
<colophon>
<para>
Draft versions of this book were produced with the
DocBook DSSSL Stylesheets. Final production was
performed with Troff.
</para>
</colophon>
```

colspec—Specifications for a column in a table

Synopsis

Content Model

```
colspec ::=
EMPTY
```

Attributes

Name	Type	Default
rowsep	NUMBER	*None*
colsep	NUMBER	*None*
charoff	NUTOKEN	*None*
align	*Enumeration:* center char justify left right	*None*
colnum	NUMBER	*None*
colwidth	CDATA	*None*
char	CDATA	*None*
colname	NMTOKEN	*None*

Parameter Entities

`%tbl.entrytbl.mdl;`	`%tbl.hdft.mdl;`	`%tbl.tgroup.mdl;`

Description

The attributes of this empty element specify the presentation characteristics of entries in a column of a table.

Each **ColSpec** refers to a single column. Columns are numbered sequentially from left to right in the table. If the `ColNum` attribute is not specified, the **ColSpec** is for the next column after the preceeding **ColSpec** or column 1 if it is the first **ColSpec**.

Processing expectations

Suppressed. This element is expected to obey the semantics of the *CALS Table Model Document Type Definition*, as specified by *OASIS Technical Memorandum TM 9502:1995* (*http://www.oasis-open.org/html/a502.htm*).

Attributes

align

`Align` specifies the horizontal alignment of **Entrys** (or **EntryTbls**) in the column. The default alignment is inherited from the enclosing **TGroup**. If `Char` is specified, see also `Char` and `CharOff`. Individual **Entrys** and **EntryTbls** can specify an alternate alignment.

char

`Char` specifies the alignment character when the `Align` attribute is set to `Char`.

charoff

`CharOff` specifies the percentage of the column's total width that should appear to the left of the first occurance of the character identified in `Char` when the `Align` attribute is set to `Char`. This attribute is inherited from the enclosing **TGroup**.

colname

`ColName` gives a symbolic name to a column. The symbolic name can then be used in subsequent **Entrys** and **SpanSpecs** to identify the column.

colnum

`ColNum` gives the number of the column defined by this **ColSpec**. If not specified, this **ColSpec** describes the next column to the right of the column defined by the previous **ColSpec** or the first column (column 1) if this is the first **ColSpec**.

colsep

If `ColSep` has the value 1 (true), then a rule will be drawn to the right of the column described by this **ColSpec**. A value of 0 (false) suppresses the rule. The rule to the right of the last column in the table is controlled by the `Frame` attribute of the enclosing **Table** or **InformalTable** and the `ColSep` of the last column in the table is ignored. If unspecified, this attribute is inherited from enclosing elements. Individual **Entrys** or **EntryTbls** can override the **ColSpec** setting of this attribute.

colwidth

`ColWidth` specifies the desired width of the relevant column. It can be either a fixed measure using one of the CALS units (36pt, 10pc, etc.) or a proportional measure. Proportional measures have the form "*number**", meaning this column should be *number* times wider than a column with the measure "`1*`" (or just "`*`"). These two forms can be mixed, as in "`3*+1pc`".

rowsep

If `RowSep` has the value 1 (true), then a rule will be drawn below the cells in the specified column. A value of 0 (false) suppresses the rule. The rule below the last row in the table is controlled by the `Frame` attribute of the enclosing **Table** or **InformalTable** and the `RowSep` of the last row is ignored. If unspecified, this attribute is inherited from enclosing elements. Individual **Entrys** or **EntryTbls** can override the **ColSpec** setting of this attribute.

See Also

entry, **entrytbl**, **InformalTable**, **row**, **spanspec**, **Table**, **tbody**, **tfoot**, **tgroup**, **thead**

Examples

For examples, see **InformalTable**, **RefEntry**, **Table**.

Command—The name of an executable program or other software command

Synopsis

Mixed Content Model

```
Command ::=
((#PCDATA|Link|OLink|ULink|Action|Application|ClassName|Command|
  ComputerOutput|Database|Email|EnVar|ErrorCode|ErrorName|
  ErrorType|Filename|Function|GUIButton|GUIIcon|GUILabel|GUIMenu|
  GUIMenuItem|GUISubmenu|Hardware|Interface|InterfaceDefinition|
  KeyCap|KeyCode|KeyCombo|KeySym|Literal|Constant|Markup|
  MediaLabel|MenuChoice|MouseButton|MsgText|Option|Optional|
  Parameter|Prompt|Property|Replaceable|ReturnValue|SGMLTag|
  StructField|StructName|Symbol|SystemItem|Token|Type|UserInput|
  VarName|Anchor|Comment|Subscript|Superscript|InlineGraphic|
  InlineMediaObject|IndexTerm)+)
```

Attributes	Common attributes	
Name	**Type**	**Default**
MoreInfo	*Enumeration:* None RefEntry	"None"

Parameter Entities		
`%cptr.char.mix;`	`%ndxterm.char.mix;`	`%para.char.mix;`
`%programlisting.content;`	`%refinline.char.mix;`	`%refname.char.mix;`
`%screen.content;`	`%tbl.entry.mdl;`	`%tech.char.class;`
`%title.char.mix;`		

Description

This element holds the name of an executable program or the text of a command that a user enters to execute a program.

Command is an integral part of the **CmdSynopsis** environment as well as being a common inline.

Processing expectations

Formatted inline. The `MoreInfo` attribute can help generate a link or query to retrieve additional information.

4.0 *Future Changes*

The content model of **Command** will be constrained to `(#PCDATA | Replaceable | InlineGraphic)` in DocBook V4.0.

Attributes

MoreInfo

If `MoreInfo` is set to `RefEntry`, it implies that a **RefEntry** exists which further describes the **Command**.

See Also

Constant, **Literal**, **Replaceable**, **VarName**

Examples

```
<!DOCTYPE para PUBLIC "-//OASIS//DTD DocBook V3.1//EN">
<para>
In <acronym>UNIX</acronym>,
<command>ls</command> is used to get a directory listing.
</para>
```

In UNIX, *ls* is used to get a directory listing.

For additional examples, see also **CmdSynopsis**, **MediaLabel**, **Option**, **Parameter**, **SynopFragment**.

Comment—A comment intended for presentation in a draft manuscript

Synopsis

Mixed Content Model

```
Comment ::=
((#PCDATA|FootnoteRef|XRef|Abbrev|Acronym|Citation|CiteRefEntry|
  CiteTitle|Emphasis|FirstTerm|ForeignPhrase|GlossTerm|Footnote|
  Phrase|Quote|Trademark|WordAsWord|Link|OLink|ULink|Action|
  Application|ClassName|Command|ComputerOutput|Database|Email|
  EnVar|ErrorCode|ErrorName|ErrorType|Filename|Function|GUIButton|
  GUIIcon|GUILabel|GUIMenu|GUIMenuItem|GUISubmenu|Hardware|
  Interface|InterfaceDefinition|KeyCap|KeyCode|KeyCombo|KeySym|
  Literal|Constant|Markup|MediaLabel|MenuChoice|MouseButton|
  MsgText|Option|Optional|Parameter|Prompt|Property|Replaceable|
  ReturnValue|SGMLTag|StructField|StructName|Symbol|SystemItem|
  Token|Type|UserInput|VarName|Anchor|Author|AuthorInitials|
  CorpAuthor|ModeSpec|OtherCredit|ProductName|ProductNumber|
  RevHistory|Comment|Subscript|Superscript|InlineGraphic|
  InlineMediaObject|InlineEquation|Synopsis|CmdSynopsis|
  FuncSynopsis|IndexTerm)+)
```

Attributes	Common attributes	
Parameter Entities		
%admon.mix;	%bookcomponent.content;	%component.mix;
%cptr.char.mix;	%divcomponent.mix;	%docinfo.char.mix;
%genobj.class;	%glossdef.mix;	%indexdivcomponent.mix;
%ndxterm.char.mix;	%other.char.class;	%para.char.mix;
%programlisting.content;	%qandaset.mix;	%refcomponent.mix;
%refinline.char.mix;	%screen.content;	%sidebar.mix;
%tbl.entry.mdl;	%title.char.mix;	%word.char.mix;

Description

The **Comment** element is designed to hold remarks, for example, editorial comments, that are useful while the document is in the draft stage, but are not intended for final publication.

NOTE The **Comment** element is unrelated to the `<!--comment-->` declaration. SGML comments are not (usually) available to the processing system whereas the contents of DocBook **Comments** are available for presentation (as marginal notes, for example).

Comments are available almost anywhere and have a particularly broad content model. Your processing system may or may not support either the use of comments everywhere they are allowed or the full generality of the **Comment** content model.

Processing expectations

May be formatted inline or as a displayed block, depending on context. Comments are often printed only in draft versions of a document and suppressed otherwise. This may be controlled by the `Status` attribute of an ancestor element (for example, **Chapter**), or by external processes, such as selecting an alternate stylesheet when publishing.

Comments must not be nested within other **Comments**. Because DocBook is harmonizing towards XML, this restriction cannot be enforced by the DTD. The processing of nested comments is undefined.

4.0 *Future Changes*

Comment will be renamed to **Remark** in DocBook V4.0.

The **InterfaceDefinition** element will be discarded in DocBook V4.0. It will no longer be available in the content model of this element.

Examples

```
<!DOCTYPE example PUBLIC "-//OASIS//DTD DocBook V3.1//EN">
<example><title>The Grand Unified Theory</title>
<para>
<comment>Some details are still a bit shaky</comment>
&hellip;
Q.E.D.
</para>
</example>
```

Example 1. The Grand Unified Theory

Some details are still a bit shaky ...Q.E.D.

ComputerOutput—Data, generally text, displayed or presented by a computer

Synopsis

Mixed Content Model

```
ComputerOutput ::=
((#PCDATA|Link|OLink|ULink|Action|Application|ClassName|Command|
  ComputerOutput|Database|Email|EnVar|ErrorCode|ErrorName|
  ErrorType|Filename|Function|GUIButton|GUIIcon|GUILabel|GUIMenu|
  GUIMenuItem|GUISubmenu|Hardware|Interface|InterfaceDefinition|
  KeyCap|KeyCode|KeyCombo|KeySym|Literal|Constant|Markup|
  MediaLabel|MenuChoice|MouseButton|MsgText|Option|Optional|
  Parameter|Prompt|Property|Replaceable|ReturnValue|SGMLTag|
  StructField|StructName|Symbol|SystemItem|Token|Type|UserInput|
  VarName|Anchor|Comment|Subscript|Superscript|InlineGraphic|
  InlineMediaObject|IndexTerm)+)
```

Attributes	Common attributes	
Name	**Type**	**Default**
MoreInfo	*Enumeration:* None RefEntry	"None"

Parameter Entities		
`%cptr.char.mix;`	`%ndxterm.char.mix;`	`%para.char.mix;`
`%programlisting.content;`	`%refinline.char.mix;`	`%refname.char.mix;`
`%screen.content;`	`%tbl.entry.mdl;`	`%tech.char.class;`
`%title.char.mix;`		

Description

ComputerOutput identifies lines of text generated by a computer program (messages, results, or other output).

Note that **ComputerOutput** is not a verbatim environment, but an inline.

Processing expectations

Formatted inline. The `MoreInfo` attribute can help generate a link or query to retrieve additional information. It's often presented in a fixed width font.

4.0 *Future Changes*

The **InterfaceDefinition** element will be discarded in DocBook V4.0. It will no longer be available in the content model of this element.

Attributes

MoreInfo

If `MoreInfo` is set to `RefEntry`, it implies that a **RefEntry** exists which further describes the **ComputerOutput**.

See Also

Constant, **EnVar**, **Filename**, **LineAnnotation**, **Literal**, **LiteralLayout**, **Markup**, **Option**, **Optional**, **Parameter**, **ProgramListing**, **Prompt**, **Replaceable**, **Screen**, **ScreenShot**, **SGMLTag**, **Synopsis**, **SystemItem**, **UserInput**, **VarName**

Examples

```
<!DOCTYPE para PUBLIC "-//OASIS//DTD DocBook V3.1//EN">
<para>
The output from the date command,
<computeroutput>Sun  Nov 16, 1997  21:03:29</computeroutput>,
uses fixed-width fields so that it can easily be parsed.
</para>
```

The output from the date command, `Sun  Nov 16, 1997  21:03:29`, uses fixed-width fields so that it can easily be parsed.

ConfDates—The dates of a conference for which a document was written

Synopsis

Mixed Content Model	
`ConfDates ::= ((#PCDATA|Link|OLink|ULink|Emphasis|Trademark|Replaceable|Comment|Subscript|Superscript|InlineGraphic|InlineMediaObject|IndexTerm)+)`	
Attributes	Common attributes

Description

ConfDates holds the dates of a conference for which a document was written or at which it was presented.

Processing expectations

May be formatted inline or as a displayed block, depending on context. Sometimes suppressed.

See Also

ConfGroup, **ConfNum**, **ConfSponsor**, **ConfTitle**, **ContractNum**, **ContractSponsor**

Examples

For examples, see **ConfGroup**.

ConfGroup—A wrapper for document meta-information about a conference

Synopsis

Content Model ConfGroup ::= ((ConfDates|ConfTitle|ConfNum|Address|ConfSponsor)*)	
Attributes	Common attributes
Parameter Entities %bibliocomponent.mix;	

Description

If a document, for example an **Article**, is written in connection with a conference, the elements in this wrapper are used to hold information about the conference: titles, sponsors, addresses, dates, etc.

Processing Expectations

May be formatted inline or as a displayed block, depending on context. Sometimes suppressed.

See Also

ConfDates, **ConfNum**, **ConfSponsor**, **ConfTitle**, **ContractNum**, **ContractSponsor**

Examples

```
<!DOCTYPE confgroup PUBLIC "-//OASIS//DTD DocBook V3.1//EN">
<confgroup>
<confdates>April, 1998</confdates>
<conftitle>The World Wide Web Conference</conftitle>
<confnum>7</confnum>
<address>Brisbane, Australia</address>
<confsponsor>World Wide Web Conference Committee (W3C3)</confsponsor>
</confgroup>
```

ConfNum—An identifier, frequently numerical, associated with a conference for which a document was written

Synopsis

Mixed Content Model ConfNum ::= ((#PCDATA|Link|OLink|ULink|Emphasis|Trademark|Replaceable|Comment| Subscript|Superscript|InlineGraphic|InlineMediaObject|IndexTerm)+)	
Attributes	Common attributes

Description

See **ConfGroup**.

Processing expectations

May be formatted inline or as a displayed block, depending on context. Sometimes suppressed.

See Also

ConfDates, **ConfGroup**, **ConfSponsor**, **ConfTitle**, **ContractNum**, **ContractSponsor**

Examples

For examples, see **ConfGroup**.

ConfSponsor—The sponsor of a conference for which a document was written

Synopsis

Mixed Content Model	

`ConfSponsor ::=`
`((#PCDATA|Link|OLink|ULink|Emphasis|Trademark|Replaceable|Comment|`
`  Subscript|Superscript|InlineGraphic|InlineMediaObject|IndexTerm)+)`	

Attributes	Common attributes

Description

See **ConfGroup**.

Processing expectations

May be formatted inline or as a displayed block, depending on context. Sometimes suppressed.

See Also

ConfDates, **ConfGroup**, **ConfNum**, **ConfTitle**, **ContractNum**, **ContractSponsor**

Examples

For examples, see **ConfGroup**.

ConfTitle—The title of a conference for which a document was written

Synopsis

Mixed Content Model
`ConfTitle ::=`
`((#PCDATA|Link|OLink|ULink|Emphasis|Trademark|Replaceable|Comment|`
`  Subscript|Superscript|InlineGraphic|InlineMediaObject|IndexTerm)+)`	

Attributes	Common attributes

Description

See **ConfGroup**.

Processing expectations

May be formatted inline or as a displayed block, depending on context. Sometimes suppressed.

See Also

ConfDates, **ConfGroup**, **ConfNum**, **ConfSponsor**, **ContractNum**, **ContractSponsor**

Examples

For examples, see **ConfGroup**.

Constant—A programming or system constant

Synopsis

Mixed Content Model
`Constant ::=`
`(#PCDATA|Replaceable|InlineGraphic|InlineMediaObject|IndexTerm)*`		

Attributes **Name**	Common attributes **Type**	 **Default**
Class	*Enumeration:* Limit	*None*
Parameter Entities		
`%cptr.char.mix;`	`%ndxterm.char.mix;`	`%para.char.mix;`
`%programlisting.content;`	`%refinline.char.mix;`	`%refname.char.mix;`
`%screen.content;`	`%tbl.entry.mdl;`	`%tech.char.class;`
`%title.char.mix;`		

Description

A **Constant** identifies a value as immutable. It is most often used to identify system limitations or other defined constants.

Processing expectations

Formatted inline.

Attributes

Class

`Class` identifies constants that are system or application limits (for example, the maximum length of a filename).

See Also

Command, **ComputerOutput**, **Literal**, **Markup**, **Option**, **Optional**, **Parameter**, **Prompt**, **Replaceable**, **SGMLTag**, **UserInput**, **VarName**

Examples

```
<!DOCTYPE para PUBLIC "-//OASIS//DTD DocBook V3.1//EN">
<para>
In ACL, <constant>main::PCS</constant> contains the path component
separator character.
</para>
```

In ACL, `main::PCS` contains the path component separator character.

```
<!DOCTYPE para PUBLIC "-//OASIS//DTD DocBook V3.1//EN">
<para>
The maximum legal length for a path name is
<constant class=limit>PATH_MAX</constant>, defined in
<filename class=headerfile>limits.h</filename>.
</para>
```

The maximum legal length for a path name is `PATH_MAX`, defined in *limits.h*.

ContractNum—The contract number of a document

Synopsis

Mixed Content Model
`ContractNum ::=`
`((#PCDATA|Link|OLink|ULink|Emphasis|Trademark|Replaceable|Comment|`
`Subscript|Superscript|InlineGraphic|InlineMediaObject|IndexTerm)+)`	

Attributes	Common attributes
Parameter Entities `%bibliocomponent.mix;`	

Description

The **ContractNum** element that occurs in bibliographic metadata contains information about the contract number of a contract under which a document was written.

Processing expectations

May be formatted inline or as a displayed block, depending on context. Sometimes suppressed.

See Also

ConfDates, **ConfGroup**, **ConfNum**, **ConfSponsor**, **ConfTitle**, **ContractSponsor**

Examples

For examples, see **ContractSponsor**.

ContractSponsor—The sponsor of a contract

Synopsis

Mixed Content Model
`ContractSponsor ::=`
`((#PCDATA|Link|OLink|ULink|Emphasis|Trademark|Replaceable|Comment|`
`  Subscript|Superscript|InlineGraphic|InlineMediaObject|IndexTerm)+)`	

Attributes	Common attributes
Parameter Entities `%bibliocomponent.mix;`	

Description

The **ContractSponsor** element that occurs in bibliographic metadata contains information about the sponser of a contract under which a document was written.

Processing expectations

May be formatted inline or as a displayed block, depending on context. Sometimes suppressed.

See Also

ConfDates, **ConfGroup**, **ConfNum**, **ConfSponsor**, **ConfTitle**, **ContractNum**

Examples

```
<!DOCTYPE article PUBLIC "-//OASIS//DTD DocBook V3.1//EN">
<article>
<artheader>
  <title>Retrofitting Class A Widgets</title>
  <contractsponsor>Xyzzy Engineering Resources</contractsponsor>
  <contractnum>314-592-7</contractnum>
  <pubsnumber>XER-314-7A</pubsnumber>
  <corpauthor>Technical Documentation Consultants, Inc.</corpauthor>
  <collab><collabname>John Whorfin</collabname>
```

```
    <affiliation><orgname>Yoyodyne Industries</orgname></affiliation>
  </collab>
</artheader>
<para>&hellip;</para>
</article>
```

Contrib—A summary of the contributions made to a document by a credited source

Synopsis

Mixed Content Model
`Contrib ::=`
`((#PCDATA|Link|OLink|ULink|Emphasis|Trademark|Replaceable|Comment|`
`  Subscript|Superscript|InlineGraphic|InlineMediaObject|IndexTerm)+)`	

Attributes	Common attributes
Parameter Entities `%bibliocomponent.mix;`	`%person.ident.mix;`

Description

The **Contrib** element contains a summary or description of the contributions made by an author, editor, or other credited source.

Processing expectations

May be formatted inline or as a displayed block, depending on context. Sometimes suppressed.

See Also

Author, **AuthorBlurb**, **AuthorGroup**, **Collab**, **CollabName**, **CorpAuthor**, **Editor**, **Other-Credit**

Examples

For examples, see **Bibliography**, **OtherCredit**.

Copyright—Copyright information about a document

Synopsis

Content Model
`Copyright ::=`
`(Year+,Holder*)`	

Attributes	Common attributes
Parameter Entities `%bibliocomponent.mix;`	

Description

The **Copyright** element holds information about the date(s) and holder(s) of a document copyright. If an extended block of text describing the copyright or other legal status is required, use **LegalNotice**.

The **Copyright** element is confined to meta-information. For copyright statements in running text, see **Trademark**.

Processing expectations

May be formatted inline or as a displayed block, depending on context. Sometimes suppressed.

A displayed copyright notice usually includes the copyright symbol, ©, as generated text and is formatted with commas separating multiple years. Additional generated text, such as the legend "All rights reserved," may also be generated.

See Also

LegalNotice, **ProductName**, **Trademark**

Examples

```
<!DOCTYPE copyright PUBLIC "-//OASIS//DTD DocBook V3.1//EN">
<copyright>
  <year>1996</year>
  <year>1997</year>
  <holder>O'Reilly &amp; Associates, Inc.</holder>
</copyright>
```

For additional examples, see also **Bibliography**, **BiblioSet**, **BookInfo**.

CorpAuthor—A corporate author, as opposed to an individual

Synopsis

<table>
<tr><td colspan="3">Mixed Content Model
<code>CorpAuthor ::=</code>
<code>((#PCDATA|Link|OLink|ULink|Emphasis|Trademark|Replaceable|Comment|</code>
<code> Subscript|Superscript|InlineGraphic|InlineMediaObject|IndexTerm)+)</code></td></tr>
<tr><td>Attributes</td><td colspan="2">Common attributes</td></tr>
<tr><td colspan="3">Parameter Entities</td></tr>
<tr><td><code>%bibliocomponent.mix;</code></td><td><code>%docinfo.char.class;</code></td><td><code>%ndxterm.char.mix;</code></td></tr>
<tr><td><code>%para.char.mix;</code></td><td><code>%programlisting.content;</code></td><td><code>%refinline.char.mix;</code></td></tr>
<tr><td><code>%screen.content;</code></td><td><code>%tbl.entry.mdl;</code></td><td><code>%title.char.mix;</code></td></tr>
</table>

Description

In documents that have no specific authors, but are credited as authored by a corporation, the **CorpAuthor** tag can be used in place of the **Author** tag to indicate authorship. This element is used in bibliographic metadata.

Processing expectations

May be formatted inline or as a displayed block, depending on context. Sometimes suppressed.

See Also

Author, **AuthorBlurb**, **AuthorGroup**, **Collab**, **CollabName**, **Contrib**, **Editor**, **OtherCredit**

Examples

For examples, see **ContractSponsor**, **Set**.

CorpName—The name of a corporation

Synopsis

Mixed Content Model

```
CorpName ::=
((#PCDATA|Link|OLink|ULink|Emphasis|Trademark|Replaceable|Comment|
  Subscript|Superscript|InlineGraphic|InlineMediaObject|IndexTerm)+)
```

Attributes	Common attributes

Parameter Entities

```
%bibliocomponent.mix;
```

Description

The name of a corporation.

Processing expectations

May be formatted inline or as a displayed block, depending on context. Sometimes suppressed.

See Also

Affiliation, **JobTitle**, **OrgDiv**, **OrgName**, **PublisherName**, **ShortAffil**

Examples

For examples, see **Bibliography**, **BiblioMSet**.

Country—The name of a country

Synopsis

Mixed Content Model

`Country ::=`
 `((#PCDATA|Link|OLink|ULink|Emphasis|Trademark|Replaceable|Comment|`
 `Subscript|Superscript|InlineGraphic|InlineMediaObject|IndexTerm)+)`

Attributes	Common attributes

Description

The name of a country, typically in an address.

Processing expectations

Formatted inline. In an **Address**, this element may inherit the verbatim qualities of an address.

See Also

Address, **City**, **Email**, **Fax**, **OtherAddr**, **Phone**, **POB**, **Postcode**, **State**, **Street**

Examples

For examples, see **Address**.

Database—The name of a database, or part of a database

Synopsis

Mixed Content Model

`Database ::=`
 `((#PCDATA|Link|OLink|ULink|Action|Application|ClassName|Command|`
 `ComputerOutput|Database|Email|EnVar|ErrorCode|ErrorName|`
 `ErrorType|Filename|Function|GUIButton|GUIIcon|GUILabel|GUIMenu|`
 `GUIMenuItem|GUISubmenu|Hardware|Interface|InterfaceDefinition|`
 `KeyCap|KeyCode|KeyCombo|KeySym|Literal|Constant|Markup|`
 `MediaLabel|MenuChoice|MouseButton|MsgText|Option|Optional|`
 `Parameter|Prompt|Property|Replaceable|ReturnValue|SGMLTag|`
 `StructField|StructName|Symbol|SystemItem|Token|Type|UserInput|`
 `VarName|Anchor|Comment|Subscript|Superscript|InlineGraphic|`
 `InlineMediaObject|IndexTerm)+)`

Attributes **Name**	Common attributes **Type**	**Default**
Class	*Enumeration:* Field Key1 Key2 Name Record Table	*None*

MoreInfo	*Enumeration:* None RefEntry	"None"
Parameter Entities		
`%cptr.char.mix;`	`%ndxterm.char.mix;`	`%para.char.mix;`
`%programlisting.content;`	`%refinline.char.mix;`	`%refname.char.mix;`
`%screen.content;`	`%tbl.entry.mdl;`	`%tech.char.class;`
`%title.char.mix;`		

Description

The name of a database, or part of a database.

Processing expectations

Formatted inline. The `MoreInfo` attribute can help generate a link or query to retrieve additional information.

4.0 *Future Changes*

The content model of **Database** will be constrained to `(#PCDATA | Replaceable | InlineGraphic)` in DocBook V4.0.

Attributes

Class

`Class` allows the author to identify particular elements of a database.

MoreInfo

If `MoreInfo` is set to `RefEntry`, it implies that a **RefEntry** exists which further describes the **Database**.

See Also

Application, **Filename**, **Hardware**, **MediaLabel**, **ProductName**

Examples

```
<!DOCTYPE para PUBLIC "-//OASIS//DTD DocBook V3.1//EN">
<para>
The <database>ProjectStatus</database> database has been updated.
Please note that <database class=field>Year</database> has been
extended to four digits.
</para>
```

The *ProjectStatus* database has been updated. Please note that *Year* has been extended to four digits.

Date—The date of publication or revision of a document

Synopsis

Mixed Content Model
```
Date ::=
((#PCDATA|Link|OLink|ULink|Emphasis|Trademark|Replaceable|Comment|
  Subscript|Superscript|InlineGraphic|InlineMediaObject|IndexTerm)+)
```

Attributes	Common attributes

Parameter Entities
```
%bibliocomponent.mix;
```

Description

The **Date** element identifies a date.

Processing expectations

Formatted inline.

DocBook does not specify the format of the date.

See Also

Edition, **PrintHistory**, **PubDate**, **ReleaseInfo**, **RevHistory**

Examples

For examples, see **Article**, **RevHistory**.

Dedication—A wrapper for the dedication section of a book

Synopsis

Content Model
```
Dedication ::=
((Title,Subtitle?,TitleAbbrev?)?,
 (CalloutList|GlossList|ItemizedList|OrderedList|SegmentedList|
  SimpleList|VariableList|Caution|Important|Note|Tip|Warning|
  LiteralLayout|ProgramListing|ProgramListingCO|Screen|ScreenCO|
  ScreenShot|FormalPara|Para|SimPara|BlockQuote|IndexTerm)+)
```

Attributes	Common attributes	
Name	**Type**	**Default**
Status	CDATA	*None*

Description

A **Dedication** is a section at the very beginning of a book (before any other body matter) containing a tribute to something (frequently someone) in connection with the writing or publication of the **Book**.

Processing expectations

Formatted as a displayed block. Frequently appears on a page by itself at the beginning of a book.

Attributes

Status

`Status` identifies the editorial or publication status of the **Dedication**.

Publication status might be used to control formatting (for example, printing a "draft" watermark on drafts) or processing (perhaps a document with a status of "final" should not include any components that are not final).

See Also

Appendix, **Article**, **Book**, **Chapter**, **Colophon**, **Part**, **PartIntro**, **Preface**, **Set**

Examples

For examples, see **Book**.

DocInfo—Meta-data for a book component

Synopsis

Content Model

```
DocInfo ::=
((Graphic|MediaObject|LegalNotice|ModeSpec|SubjectSet|KeywordSet|
  ITermSet|Abbrev|Abstract|Address|ArtPageNums|Author|AuthorGroup|
  AuthorInitials|BiblioMisc|BiblioSet|Collab|ConfGroup|
  ContractNum|ContractSponsor|Copyright|CorpAuthor|CorpName|Date|
  Edition|Editor|InvPartNumber|ISBN|ISSN|IssueNum|OrgName|
  OtherCredit|PageNums|PrintHistory|ProductName|ProductNumber|
  PubDate|Publisher|PublisherName|PubsNumber|ReleaseInfo|
  RevHistory|SeriesVolNums|Subtitle|Title|TitleAbbrev|VolumeNum|
  CiteTitle|Honorific|FirstName|Surname|Lineage|OtherName|
  Affiliation|AuthorBlurb|Contrib|IndexTerm)+)
```

Attributes	Common attributes
Parameter Entities	
`%bookcomponent.title.content;`	`%otherinfo.class;`

Description

The **DocInfo** element is a wrapper for a large collection of meta-information about a component. Much of this data is bibliographic in nature.

Processing expectations

Suppressed. Many of the elements in this wrapper may be used in presentation, but they are not generally printed as part of the formatting of the wrapper. It merely serves to identify where they occur.

4.0 *Future Changes*

In DocBook V4.0, the **DocInfo** element will be split into **ChapterInfo**, **AppendixInfo**, and so on.

AuthorBlurb and **Affiliation** will be removed from the inline content of these elements. A new wrapper element will be created to associate this information with authors, editors, and other contributors.

See Also

ArtHeader, **BookBiblio**, **BookInfo**, **ObjectInfo**, **RefSynopsisDivInfo**, **ScreenInfo**, **Sect1Info**, **Sect2Info**, **Sect3Info**, **Sect4Info**, **Sect5Info**, **SectionInfo**, **SetInfo**

Examples

For examples, see **Chapter**, **OLink**, **RefEntry**.

Edition—The name or number of an edition of a document

Synopsis

Mixed Content Model

```
Edition ::=
((#PCDATA|Link|OLink|ULink|Emphasis|Trademark|Replaceable|Comment|
  Subscript|Superscript|InlineGraphic|InlineMediaObject|IndexTerm)+)
```

Attributes	Common attributes

Parameter Entities

```
%bibliocomponent.mix;
```

Description

The **Edition** contains the name or number of the edition of the document.

Processing expectations

May be formatted inline or as a displayed block, depending on context. Sometimes suppressed.

See Also

Date, **PrintHistory**, **PubDate**, **ReleaseInfo**, **RevHistory**

Examples

For examples, see **BookInfo**.

Editor—The name of the editor of a document

Synopsis

Content Model
`Editor ::=`
`((Honorific|FirstName|Surname|Lineage|OtherName|Affiliation|`
`  AuthorBlurb|Contrib)+)`	

Attributes	Common attributes
Parameter Entities `%bibliocomponent.mix;`	

Description

The name of the editor of a document.

Processing expectations

May be formatted inline or as a displayed block, depending on context. Sometimes suppressed.

4.0 *Future Changes*

AuthorBlurb and **Affiliation** will be removed from the inline content of **Editor** in DocBook V4.0. A new wrapper element will be created to hold **Editor**, **AuthorBlurb**, and **Affiliation**.

See Also

Author, **AuthorBlurb**, **AuthorGroup**, **Collab**, **CollabName**, **Contrib**, **CorpAuthor**, **OtherCredit**

Examples

For examples, see **AuthorGroup**, **Bibliography**, **BiblioSet**.

Email—An email address

Synopsis

Mixed Content Model
`Email ::=`
`((#PCDATA|Link|OLink|ULink|Emphasis|Trademark|Replaceable|Comment|`
`  Subscript|Superscript|InlineGraphic|InlineMediaObject|IndexTerm)+)`	

Attributes	Common attributes

Parameter Entities		
`%cptr.char.mix;`	`%ndxterm.char.mix;`	`%para.char.mix;`
`%programlisting.con-tent;`	`%refinline.char.mix;`	`%refname.char.mix;`
`%screen.content;`	`%tbl.entry.mdl;`	`%tech.char.class;`
`%title.char.mix;`		

Description

Inline markup identifying an email address.

Processing expectations

Formatted inline. **Email** may generate surrounding punctuation, such as angle brackets. This is an interchange issue. See Appendix F.

In some processing environments, **Email** may automatically generate a hypertext link (a `mailto:` URL).

In an **Address**, this element may inherit the verbatim qualities of an address.

See Also

Address, **City**, **Country**, **Fax**, **OtherAddr**, **Phone**, **POB**, **Postcode**, **State**, **Street**

Examples

For examples, see **Address**, **BookInfo**.

Emphasis—Emphasized text

Synopsis

Mixed Content Model

```
Emphasis ::=
((#PCDATA|FootnoteRef|XRef|Abbrev|Acronym|Citation|CiteRefEntry|
  CiteTitle|Emphasis|FirstTerm|ForeignPhrase|GlossTerm|Footnote|
  Phrase|Quote|Trademark|WordAsWord|Link|OLink|ULink|Action|
  Application|ClassName|Command|ComputerOutput|Database|Email|
  EnVar|ErrorCode|ErrorName|ErrorType|Filename|Function|GUIButton|
  GUIIcon|GUILabel|GUIMenu|GUIMenuItem|GUISubmenu|Hardware|
  Interface|InterfaceDefinition|KeyCap|KeyCode|KeyCombo|KeySym|
  Literal|Constant|Markup|MediaLabel|MenuChoice|MouseButton|
  MsgText|Option|Optional|Parameter|Prompt|Property|Replaceable|
  ReturnValue|SGMLTag|StructField|StructName|Symbol|SystemItem|
  Token|Type|UserInput|VarName|Anchor|Author|AuthorInitials|
  CorpAuthor|ModeSpec|OtherCredit|ProductName|ProductNumber|
  RevHistory|Comment|Subscript|Superscript|InlineGraphic|
  InlineMediaObject|InlineEquation|Synopsis|CmdSynopsis|
  FuncSynopsis|IndexTerm)+)
```

Attributes	Common attributes

Parameter Entities		
%docinfo.char.mix;	%gen.char.class;	%ndxterm.char.mix;
%para.char.mix;	%programlisting.con-tent;	%refinline.char.mix;
%screen.content;	%tbl.entry.mdl;	%title.char.mix;
%word.char.mix;		

Description

Emphasis provides a method for indicating that certain text should be stressed in some way.

Processing expectations

Formatted inline. Emphasized text is traditionally presented in italics or boldface. A `Role` attribute of `bold` or `strong` is often used to generate boldface, if italics is the default presentation.

Emphasis is often used wherever its typographic presentation is desired, even when other markup might theoretically be more appropriate.

4.0 *Future Changes*

The **InterfaceDefinition** element will be discarded in DocBook V4.0. It will no longer be available in the content model of this element.

See Also

Abbrev, **Acronym**, **ForeignPhrase**, **Phrase**, **Quote**, **WordAsWord**

Examples

```
<!DOCTYPE para PUBLIC "-//OASIS//DTD DocBook V3.1//EN">
<para>
The <emphasis>most</emphasis> important example of this
phenomenon occurs in A. Nonymous's book
<citetitle>Power Snacking</citetitle>.
</para>
```

The *most* important example of this phenomenon occurs in A. Nonymous's book *Power Snacking*.

For additional examples, see also **Index**, **ProgramListingCO**, **Type**.

---

entry—A cell in a table

Synopsis

Content Model

```
entry ::=
(((CalloutList|GlossList|ItemizedList|OrderedList|SegmentedList|
   SimpleList|VariableList|Caution|Important|Note|Tip|Warning|
```

```
LiteralLayout|ProgramListing|ProgramListingCO|Screen|ScreenCO|
ScreenShot|FormalPara|Para|SimPara|Graphic|MediaObject)+|
(#PCDATA|FootnoteRef|XRef|Abbrev|Acronym|Citation|CiteRefEntry|
CiteTitle|Emphasis|FirstTerm|ForeignPhrase|GlossTerm|Footnote|
Phrase|Quote|Trademark|WordAsWord|Link|OLink|ULink|Action|
Application|ClassName|Command|ComputerOutput|Database|Email|
EnVar|ErrorCode|ErrorName|ErrorType|Filename|Function|
GUIButton|GUIIcon|GUILabel|GUIMenu|GUIMenuItem|GUISubmenu|
Hardware|Interface|InterfaceDefinition|KeyCap|KeyCode|KeyCombo|
KeySym|Literal|Constant|Markup|MediaLabel|MenuChoice|
MouseButton|MsgText|Option|Optional|Parameter|Prompt|Property|
Replaceable|ReturnValue|SGMLTag|StructField|StructName|Symbol|
SystemItem|Token|Type|UserInput|VarName|Anchor|Author|
AuthorInitials|CorpAuthor|ModeSpec|OtherCredit|ProductName|
ProductNumber|RevHistory|Comment|Subscript|Superscript|
InlineGraphic|InlineMediaObject|InlineEquation|Synopsis|
CmdSynopsis|FuncSynopsis|IndexTerm)+))
```

Attributes Common attributes

Name	**Type**	**Default**
rowsep	NUMBER	*None*
valign	*Enumeration:* bottom middle top	*None*
colsep	NUMBER	*None*
namest	NMTOKEN	*None*
align	*Enumeration:* center char justify left right	*None*
rotate	NUMBER	*None*
spanname	NMTOKEN	*None*
nameend	NMTOKEN	*None*
charoff	NUTOKEN	*None*
char	CDATA	*None*
morerows	NUMBER	*None*
colname	NMTOKEN	*None*

Parameter Entities
`%tbl.row.mdl;`

Description

Entry is a cell in a table.

Each **Entry** may specify its starting column. Entries that do not explicitly specify a starting column begin implicitly in the column that is immediately adjacent to the preceding cell. Note that **Entry**s with the `MoreRows` attribute from preceding rows implicitly occupy cells in the succeeding **Rows**.

Rows are not required to be full. It is legal for some entries to be completely absent (at the beginning, middle, or end of a row).

Pernicious Mixed Content

The content model of the **Entry** element exhibits a nasty peculiarity that we call "pernicious mixed content".[a]

Every other element in DocBook contains either block elements or inline elements (including #PCDATA) unambiguously. In these cases, the meaning of line breaks and spaces are well understood; they are insignificant between block elements and significant (to the SGML parser, anyway) where inline markup can occur.

Table entries are different; they can contain either block or inline elements, but not both at the same time. In other words, one **Entry** in a table might contain a paragraph or a list while another contains simply #PCDATA or another inline markup, but no single **Entry** can contain both.

Because the content model of an **Entry** allows both kinds of markup, each time the SGML parser encounters an **Entry**, it has to decide what variety of markup it contains. SGML parsers are forbidden to use more than a single token of lookahead to reach this decision. In practical terms, what this means is that a line feed or space after an **Entry** start tag causes the parser to decide that the cell contains inline markup. Subsequent discovery of a paragraph or another block element causes a parsing error.

All of these are legal:

```
<entry>3.1415927</entry>
<entry>General <emphasis>#PCDATA</emphasis></entry>
<entry><para>
A paragraph of text
</para></entry>
```

However, each of these is an error:

```
<entry>                 Error, cannot have a line break before a block element
<para>
A paragraph of text.
</para></entry>

<entry><para>
A paragraph of text.
</para>                 Error, cannot have a line break between block elements
<para>
A paragraph of text.
</para></entry>
```

—Continued—

a. A term coined by Terry Allen.

```
<entry><para>
A paragraph of text.
</para>                    Error, cannot have a line break after a block element
</entry>
```

When designing a DTD, it is wise to avoid pernicious mixed content. Unfortunately, the only way to correct the pernicious mixed content problem that already exists in DocBook is to require some sort of wrapper (a block element, or an inline like **Phrase**) around #PCDATA within table **Entrys**. This is annoying and inconvenient in a great many tables in which #PCDATA cells predominate and, in addition, differ from CALS.

Processing expectations

This element is expected to obey the semantics of the *CALS Table Model Document Type Definition*, as specified by *OASIS Technical Memorandum TM 9502:1995* (*http://www.oasis-open.org/html/a502.htm*).

The content of **Entry** is formatted to fit within the table cell that it occupies. Horizontal and vertical spanning may allow the content of an **Entry** to occupy several physical cells.

4.0 *Future Changes*

The **InterfaceDefinition** element will be discarded in DocBook V4.0. It will no longer be available in the content model of this element.

Attributes

align

`Align` specifies the horizontal alignment of text (and other elements) within the **Entry**. If no alignment is specified, it is inherited from the **ColSpec** for the current column, or the **SpanSpec** if this entry occurs in a span. If `Char` is specified, see also `Char` and `CharOff`.

char

`Char` specifies the alignment character when the `Align` attribute is set to `Char`.

charoff

`CharOff` specifies the percentage of the column's total width that should appear to the left of the first occurance of the character identified in `Char` when the `Align` attribute is set to `Char`. This attribute is inherited from the relevant **ColSpec** or **SpanSpec**.

colname

`ColName` identifies the column in which this entry should appear; it must have been previously defined in a **ColSpec**. **Entrys** cannot be given out of order, the column referenced must be to the right of the last **Entry** or **EntryTbl** placed in the current row. It is an error to specify both a `ColName` and a `SpanName`.

colsep

If `ColSep` has the value 1 (true), then a rule will be drawn to the right of this **Entry**. A value of 0 (false) suppresses the rule. The rule to the right of the last column in the table is controlled by the `Frame` attribute of the enclosing **Table** or **InformalTable** and the `ColSep` of an entry in the last column in the table is ignored. If unspecified, this attribute is inherited from the the corresponding **ColSpec** or **SpanSpec** and enclosing elements.

morerows

`MoreRows` indicates how many more rows, in addition to the current row, this **Entry** is to occupy. It creates a vertical span. The default of `0` indicates that the **Entry** occupies only a single row.

nameend

`NameEnd` is the name (defined in a **ColSpec**) of the rightmost column of a span. On **Entry**, specifying both `NameSt` and `NameEnd` defines a horizontal span for the current **Entry**. (See also `SpanName`.)

namest

`NameSt` ("name start") is the name (defined in a **ColSpec**) of the leftmost column of a span. On **Entry**, specifying both `NameSt` and `NameEnd` defines a horizontal span for the current **Entry**. (See also `SpanName`.)

rotate

If `Rotate` has the value 1 (true), the **Entry** is to be rotated 90 degrees counterclockwise in the table cell. A value of 0 (false) indicates that no rotation is to occur. If the stylesheet also specifies rotation, the value of `Rotate` is ignored; they are not additive. Only the values 0 and 1 are legal.

rowsep

If `RowSep` has the value 1 (true), then a rule will be drawn below the **Entry**. A value of 0 (false) suppresses the rule. The rule below the last row in the table is controlled by the `Frame` attribute of the enclosing **Table** or **InformalTable** and the `RowSep` of the last row is ignored. If unspecified, this attribute is inherited from enclosing elements.

spanname

`SpanName` is the name (defined in a **SpanSpec**) of a span. This cell will be rendered with the specified horizontal span.

valign

`VAlign` specifies the vertical alignment of text (and other elements) within the **Entry**. If no alignment is specified, it is inherited from enclosing elements.

See Also

colspec, **entrytbl**, **InformalTable**, **row**, **spanspec**, **Table**, **tbody**, **tfoot**, **tgroup**, **thead**

Examples

For examples, see **entrytbl**, **FootnoteRef**, **InformalTable**, **RefEntry**, **Table**.

---

entrytbl—A subtable appearing in place of an Entry in a table

Synopsis

Content Model

```
entrytbl ::=
(colspec*,spanspec*,thead?,tbody)
```

Attributes Name	Common attributes Type	Default
rowsep	NUMBER	*None*
colsep	NUMBER	*None*
namest	NMTOKEN	*None*
align	*Enumeration:* center char justify left right	*None*
cols	NUMBER	*Required*
tgroupstyle	NMTOKEN	*None*
spanname	NMTOKEN	*None*
nameend	NMTOKEN	*None*
charoff	NUTOKEN	*None*
char	CDATA	*None*
colname	NMTOKEN	*None*

Parameter Entities

`%tbl.entrytbl.excep;` `%tbl.hdft.excep;` `%tbl.row.mdl;`

Description

The **EntryTbl** element allows for a single level of nesting within tables. This element is expected to obey the semantics of the *CALS Table Model Document Type Definition*, as specified by *OASIS Technical Memorandum TM 9502:1995* (*http://www.oasis-open.org/html/a502.htm*).

An entry table may occur in a row instead of an **Entry**. **EntryTbls** have most of the elements of a table but may not include themselves, thus limiting nesting to a single level.

Processing expectations

The content of **EntryTbl** is formatted, *as a table*, to fit within the table cell that it occupies. Horizontal and vertical spanning may allow an **EntryTbl** to occupy several physical cells in the table that contains it.

If multiple **EntryTbls** occur in a single row, formatters that support **EntryTbl** are not required to ensure that subrows within the various tables are vertically aligned.

Many formatters are incapable of supporting **EntryTbls**. This is an interchange issue. See Appendix F.

Attributes

align

`Align` specifies the horizontal alignment of the **EntryTbl** in the cell in which it occurs. If no alignment is specified, it is inherited from the **ColSpec** for the current column, or the **SpanSpec** if this entry occurs in a span.

char

`Char` specifies the alignment character when the `Align` attribute is set to `Char`.

charoff

`CharOff` specifies the percentage of the column's total width that should appear to the left of the first occurance of the character identified in `Char` when the `Align` attribute is set to `Char`. This attribute is inherited from the relevant **ColSpec** or **SpanSpec**.

colname

`ColName` identifies the column in which this entry table should appear; it must have been previously defined in a **ColSpec**. **EntryTbls** cannot be given out of order, the column referenced must be to the right of the last **Entry** or **EntryTbl** placed in the current row. It is an error to specify both a `ColName` and a `SpanName`.

cols

`Cols` specifies the number of columns in the **EntryTbl**.

colsep

If `ColSep` has the value 1 (true), then a rule will be drawn to the right of this **EntryTbl**. A value of 0 (false) suppresses the rule. The rule to the right of the last column in the table is controlled by the `Frame` attribute of the enclosing **Table** or **InformalTable** and the `ColSep` of an entry in the last column in the table is ignored. If unspecified, this attribute is inherited from the the corresponding **ColSpec** or **SpanSpec** and enclosing elements.

nameend

NameEnd is the name (defined in a **ColSpec**) of the rightmost column of a span. On **EntryTbl**, specifying both NameSt and NameEnd defines a horizontal span for the current **EntryTbl**. (See also SpanName.)

namest

NameSt ("name start") is the name (defined in a **ColSpec**) of the leftmost column of a span. On **EntryTbl**, specifying both NameSt and NameEnd defines a horizontal span for the current **EntryTbl**. (See also SpanName.)

rowsep

If RowSep has the value 1 (true), then a rule will be drawn below the **EntryTbl**. A value of 0 (false) suppresses the rule. The rule below the last row in the table is controlled by the Frame attribute of the enclosing **Table** or **InformalTable** and the RowSep of the last row is ignored. If unspecified, this attribute is inherited from enclosing elements.

spanname

SpanName is the name (defined in a **SpanSpec**) of a span. This cell will be rendered with the specified horizontal span.

tgroupstyle

TGroupstyle holds the name of a table group style defined in a stylesheet that will be used to process this document.

See Also

colspec, **entry**, **InformalTable**, **row**, **spanspec**, **Table**, **tbody**, **tfoot**, **tgroup**, **thead**

Examples

```
<!DOCTYPE informaltable PUBLIC "-//OASIS//DTD DocBook V3.1//EN">
<!-- entrytbl not supported, fake it in descrip.1 -->
<informaltable frame=all>
<tgroup cols=3>
<tbody>
<row>
  <entry>a1</entry>
  <entry>b1</entry>
  <entry>c1</entry>
</row>
<row>
  <entry>a2</entry>
  <entrytbl cols=3>
    <tbody>
      <row>
        <entry>b2a1</entry>
        <entry>b2b1</entry>
        <entry>b2c1</entry>
      </row>
```

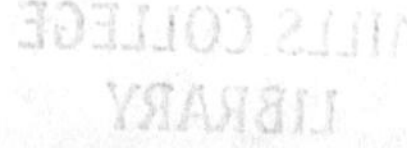

```
      <row>
        <entry>b2a2</entry>
        <entry>b2b2</entry>
        <entry>b2c2</entry>
      </row>
      <row>
        <entry>b2a3</entry>
        <entry>b2b3</entry>
        <entry>b2c3</entry>
      </row>
    </tbody>
  </entrytbl>
  <entry>c2</entry>
</row>
<row>
  <entry>a3</entry>
  <entry>b3</entry>
  <entry>c3</entry>
</row>
</tbody>
</tgroup>
</informaltable>
```

The preceding table would look something like this when formatted:

<table>
<tr><td>a1</td><td colspan="3">b1</td><td>c1</td></tr>
<tr><td rowspan="3">a2</td><td>b2a1</td><td>b2b1</td><td>b2c1</td><td rowspan="3">c2</td></tr>
<tr><td>b2a2</td><td>b2b2</td><td>b2c2</td></tr>
<tr><td>b2a3</td><td>b2b3</td><td>b2c3</td></tr>
<tr><td>a3</td><td colspan="3">b3</td><td>c3</td></tr>
</table>

EnVar—A software environment variable

Synopsis

Mixed Content Model

```
EnVar ::=
((#PCDATA|Replaceable|InlineGraphic|InlineMediaObject|IndexTerm)+)
```

Attributes Common attributes

Parameter Entities

`%cptr.char.mix;`	`%ndxterm.char.mix;`	`%para.char.mix;`
`%programlisting.content;`	`%refinline.char.mix;`	`%refname.char.mix;`
`%screen.content;`	`%tbl.entry.mdl;`	`%tech.char.class;`
`%title.char.mix;`		

Description

EnVar is an environment variable used most often for the UNIX, DOS, or Windows environments.

Processing expectations

Formatted inline.

See Also

ComputerOutput, **Filename**, **Prompt**, **SystemItem**, **UserInput**

Examples

```
<!DOCTYPE para PUBLIC "-//OASIS//DTD DocBook V3.1//EN">
<para>
In order to translate public identifiers into local system identifiers,
<application>Jade</> and <application>SP</> read the catalog files
pointed to by <envar>SGML_CATALOG_FILES</envar>.
</para>
```

In order to translate public identifiers into local system identifiers, Jade and SP read the catalog files pointed to by *SGML_CATALOG_FILES*.

Epigraph—A short inscription at the beginning of a document or component

Synopsis

Content Model
`Epigraph ::=`
`(Attribution?,`
` (FormalPara|Para|SimPara)+)`		

Attributes	Common attributes	

Parameter Entities
`%bookcomponent.content;`
`%divcomponent.mix;`
	
	`%component.mix;`
	`%refcomponent.mix;`
		
		`%descobj.class;`

Description

An **Epigraph** is a short inscription, often a quotation or poem, set at the beginning of a document or component. Epigraphs are usually related somehow to the content that follows them and may help set the tone for the component.

Processing expectations

Formatted as a displayed block.

4.0 Future Changes

Epigraph will not be allowed in **BlockQuote** in DocBook V4.0.

See Also

Abstract, **Attribution**, **BlockQuote**, **Highlights**, **Sidebar**

Examples

For examples, see **Chapter**.

Equation—A displayed mathematical equation

Synopsis

Content Model

```
Equation ::=
((Title,TitleAbbrev?)?,
 (InformalEquation|
  (Alt?,
   (Graphic+|MediaObject+))))
```

Attributes	Common attributes	
Name	**Type**	**Default**
Label	CDATA	*None*

Parameter Entities

%admon.mix;	%bookcomponent.content;	%component.mix;
%divcomponent.mix;	%footnote.exclusion;	%formal.class;
%formal.exclusion;	%glossdef.mix;	%highlights.exclusion;
%para.mix;	%qandaset.mix;	%refcomponent.mix;
%sidebar.mix;	%tbl.table.excep;	

Description

An **Equation** is a formal mathematical equation (with an optional rather than required title).

Processing expectations

Formatted as a displayed block. For an inline equation, use **InlineEquation**.

Processing systems that number equations or build a table of equations at the beginning of a document may have difficulty correctly formatting documents that contain both **Equations** with **Titles** and **Equations** without **Titles**. You are advised to use **InformalEquation** for equations without titles.

[5.0] *Future Changes*

In some future version of DocBook, probably V5.0, even though the change has not yet been announced, the **Title** on **Equation** will be required. For equations without titles, use **InformalEquation**.

Attributes

Label

Label specifies an identifying string for presentation purposes.

Generally, an explicit Label attribute is used only if the processing system is incapable of generating the label automatically. If present, the Label is normative; it will used even if the processing system is capable of automatic labelling.

See Also

Example, **Figure**, **InformalEquation**, **InformalExample**, **InformalFigure**, **InformalTable**, **InlineEquation**, **Subscript**, **Superscript**, **Table**

Examples

```
<!DOCTYPE equation PUBLIC "-//OASIS//DTD DocBook V3.1//EN">
<equation><title>Fermat's Last Theorum</title>
  <alt>x^n + y^n &ne; z^n &forall; n &ne; 2</alt>
  <graphic fileref="figures/fermat"></graphic>
</equation>
```

Fermat's Last Theorum

$$x^n + y^n \neq z^n \forall n \neq 2$$

For additional examples, see also **InlineMediaObject**.

ErrorCode—An error code

Synopsis

Mixed Content Model ErrorCode ::= ((#PCDATA|Replaceable|InlineGraphic|InlineMediaObject|IndexTerm)+)		
Attributes **Name**	Common attributes **Type**	**Default**
MoreInfo	*Enumeration:* None RefEntry	"None"
Parameter Entities		
%cptr.char.mix;	%ndxterm.char.mix;	%para.char.mix;
%programlisting.content;	%refinline.char.mix;	%refname.char.mix;
%screen.content;	%tbl.entry.mdl;	%tech.char.class;
%title.char.mix;		

Description

An error code. Error codes are often numeric, but in some environments they may be symbolic constants.

Processing expectations

Formatted inline. The `MoreInfo` attribute can help generate a link or query to retrieve additional information.

Attributes

MoreInfo

If `MoreInfo` is set to `RefEntry`, it implies that a **RefEntry** exists which further describes the **ErrorCode**.

See Also

ErrorName, **ErrorType**, **MsgSet**

Examples

```
<!DOCTYPE para PUBLIC "-//OASIS//DTD DocBook V3.1//EN">
<para>
On most DOS-derived systems, functions signal a <errorname>File
Not Found</errorname> error by returning
<errorcode>2</errorcode>.  This is usually a
<errortype>recoverable</errortype> (non-fatal) error.
</para>
```

On most DOS-derived systems, functions signal a "File Not Found" error by returning 2. This is usually a recoverable (non-fatal) error.

```
<!DOCTYPE para PUBLIC "-//OASIS//DTD DocBook V3.1//EN">
<para>
On most UNIX systems, functions signal a <errorname>File
Not Found</errorname> error by returning
<errorcode>ENOENT</errorcode>, defined in
<filename>errno.h</filename>.  This is usually a
<errortype>recoverable</errortype> (non-fatal) error.
</para>
```

On most UNIX systems, functions signal a "File Not Found" error by returning ENOENT, defined in *errno.h*. This is usually a recoverable (non-fatal) error.

ErrorName—An error message

Synopsis

Mixed Content Model
`ErrorName ::=`
`((#PCDATA|Replaceable|InlineGraphic|InlineMediaObject|IndexTerm)+)`	

Attributes	Common attributes

Parameter Entities		
%cptr.char.mix;	%ndxterm.char.mix;	%para.char.mix;
%programlisting.content;	%refinline.char.mix;	%refname.char.mix;
%screen.content;	%tbl.entry.mdl;	%tech.char.class;
%title.char.mix;		

Description

ErrorName holds the text of an error message. Usually this is a short message associated with an **ErrorCode** that is intended to be understood by the user.

Processing expectations

Formatted inline.

See Also

ErrorCode, **ErrorType**, **MsgSet**

Examples

For examples, see **ErrorCode**, **ReturnValue**.

ErrorType—The classification of an error message

Synopsis

Mixed Content Model		
`ErrorType ::= ((#PCDATA|Replaceable|InlineGraphic|InlineMediaObject|IndexTerm)+)`		
Attributes	Common attributes	
Parameter Entities		
%cptr.char.mix;	%ndxterm.char.mix;	%para.char.mix;
%programlisting.content;	%refinline.char.mix;	%refname.char.mix;
%screen.content;	%tbl.entry.mdl;	%tech.char.class;
%title.char.mix;		

Description

The **ErrorType** element identifies a class of error. The exact classifications are naturally going to vary by system, but "recoverable" and "fatal" are two possibilities.

Processing expectations

Formatted inline.

See Also

ErrorCode, **ErrorName**, **MsgSet**

Examples

For examples, see **ErrorCode**.

Example—A formal example, with a title

Synopsis

Content Model

```
Example ::=
((Title,TitleAbbrev?),
 (CalloutList|GlossList|ItemizedList|OrderedList|SegmentedList|
  SimpleList|VariableList|LiteralLayout|ProgramListing|
  ProgramListingCO|Screen|ScreenCO|ScreenShot|Synopsis|
  CmdSynopsis|FuncSynopsis|FormalPara|Para|SimPara|Address|
  BlockQuote|Graphic|GraphicCO|MediaObject|MediaObjectCO|
  InformalEquation|InformalExample|InformalFigure|InformalTable|
  IndexTerm)+)
```

Attributes	Common attributes	
Name	**Type**	**Default**
Width	NUMBER	*None*
Label	CDATA	*None*

Parameter Entities

`%admon.mix;`	`%bookcomponent.content;`	`%component.mix;`
`%divcomponent.mix;`	`%footnote.exclusion;`	`%formal.class;`
`%formal.exclusion;`	`%glossdef.mix;`	`%highlights.exclusion;`
`%para.mix;`	`%qandaset.mix;`	`%refcomponent.mix;`
`%sidebar.mix;`	`%tbl.table.excep;`	

Description

Example is a formal example with a title. Examples often contain **ProgramListing**s or other large, block elements. Frequently they are given IDs and referenced from the text with **XRef** or **Link**.

Processing expectations

Formatted as a displayed block. DocBook does not specify the location of the example within the final displayed flow of text; it may float or remain where it is located.

A list of examples may be generated at the beginning of a document.

Attributes

Label

Label specifies an identifying string for presentation purposes.

Generally, an explicit Label attribute is used only if the processing system is incapable of generating the label automatically. If present, the Label is normative; it will used even if the processing system is capable of automatic labelling.

Width

Width specifies the width (in characters) of the longest line in this **Example** (formatters may use this value to determine scaling or rotation).

See Also

Equation, **Figure**, **InformalEquation**, **InformalExample**, **InformalFigure**, **InformalTable**, **Table**

Examples

```
<!DOCTYPE example PUBLIC "-//OASIS//DTD DocBook V3.1//EN">
<example><title>A DSSSL Function</title>
<programlisting>
(define (node-list-filter-by-gi nodelist gilist)
  ;; Returns the node-list that contains every element of the original
  ;; nodelist whose gi is in gilist
  (let loop ((result (empty-node-list)) (nl nodelist))
    (if (node-list-empty? nl)
result
(if (member (gi (node-list-first nl)) gilist)
    (loop (node-list result (node-list-first nl))
  (node-list-rest nl))
    (loop result (node-list-rest nl))))))
</programlisting>
</example>
```

Example 1. A DSSSL Function

```
(define (node-list-filter-by-gi nodelist gilist)
  ;; Returns the node-list that contains every element of the original
  ;; nodelist whose gi is in gilist
  (let loop ((result (empty-node-list)) (nl nodelist))
    (if (node-list-empty? nl)
result
(if (member (gi (node-list-first nl)) gilist)
    (loop (node-list result (node-list-first nl))
  (node-list-rest nl))
    (loop result (node-list-rest nl))))))
```

For additional examples, see also **Comment**.

Fax—A fax number

Synopsis

Mixed Content Model
`Fax ::=`
`((#PCDATA|Link|OLink|ULink|Emphasis|Trademark|Replaceable|Comment|`
`  Subscript|Superscript|InlineGraphic|InlineMediaObject|IndexTerm)+)`	

Attributes	Common attributes
Parameter Entities `%notation.class;`	

Description

Fax is a fax number in an address.

Processing expectations

Formatted inline. Sometimes suppressed. In an **Address**, this element may inherit the verbatim qualities of an address.

See Also

Address, **City**, **Country**, **Email**, **OtherAddr**, **Phone**, **POB**, **Postcode**, **State**, **Street**

Examples

For examples, see **Address**.

Figure—A formal figure, generally an illustration, with a title

Synopsis

Content Model

```
Figure ::=
((Title,TitleAbbrev?),
 (LiteralLayout|ProgramListing|ProgramListingCO|Screen|ScreenCO|
  ScreenShot|Synopsis|CmdSynopsis|FuncSynopsis|Address|BlockQuote|
  Graphic|GraphicCO|MediaObject|MediaObjectCO|InformalEquation|
  InformalExample|InformalFigure|InformalTable|IndexTerm|Link|
  OLink|ULink)+)
```

Attributes	Common attributes	
Name	**Type**	**Default**
Label	CDATA	*None*
PgWide	NUMBER	*None*
Float	NUMBER	“0”

Parameter Entities

`%admon.mix;`	`%bookcomponent.content;`	`%component.mix;`
`%divcomponent.mix;`	`%footnote.exclusion;`	`%formal.class;`
`%formal.exclusion;`	`%glossdef.mix;`	`%highlights.exclusion;`
`%para.mix;`	`%qandaset.mix;`	`%refcomponent.mix;`
`%sidebar.mix;`	`%tbl.table.excep;`	

Description

Figure is a formal example with a title. Figures often contain **Graphics**, or other large, display elements. Frequently they are given IDs and referenced from the text with **XRef** or **Link**.

Processing expectations

Formatted as a displayed block.

Figures may contain multiple display elements. DocBook does not specify how these elements are to be presented with respect to one another.

DocBook does not specify the location of the figure within the final displayed flow of text; it may float or remain where it is located.

A list of figures may be generated at the beginning of a document.

Attributes

Float

If `Float` has the value 1 (true), then the processing system is free to move the figure to a convenient location. (Where convenient location may be described in the style sheet or may be application dependent.) A value of 0 (false) indicates that the figure should be placed precisely where it occurs in the flow.

Label

`Label` specifies an identifying string for presentation purposes.

Generally, an explicit `Label` attribute is used only if the processing system is incapable of generating the label automatically. If present, the `Label` is normative; it will used even if the processing system is capable of automatic labelling.

PgWide

If `Pgwide` has the value 0 (false), then the **Figure** is rendered in the current text flow (with flow column width). A value of 1 (true) specifies that the figure should be rendered across the full text page.

See Also

Equation, **Example**, **InformalEquation**, **InformalExample**, **InformalFigure**, **InformalTable**, **Table**

Examples

```
<!DOCTYPE figure PUBLIC "-//OASIS//DTD DocBook V3.1//EN">
<figure><title>The Pythagorean Theorum Illustrated</title>
<graphic fileref="figures/pythag"></graphic>
</figure>
```

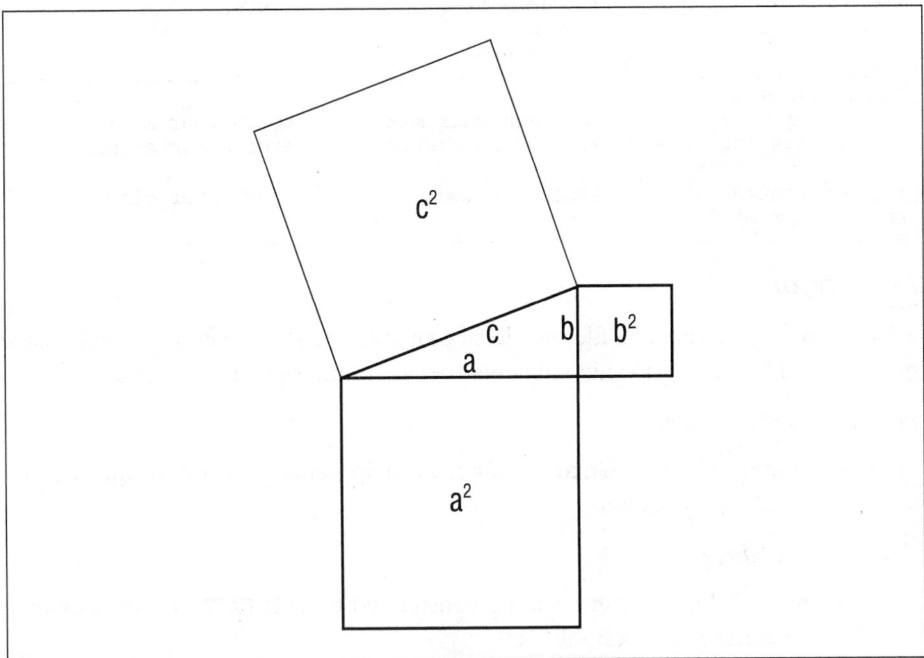

Figure 1. The Pythagorean Theorum Illustrated

For additional examples, see also **Graphic**.

Filename—The name of a file

Synopsis

Mixed Content Model

```
Filename ::=
((#PCDATA|Link|OLink|ULink|Action|Application|ClassName|Command|
  ComputerOutput|Database|Email|EnVar|ErrorCode|ErrorName|
  ErrorType|Filename|Function|GUIButton|GUIIcon|GUILabel|GUIMenu|
  GUIMenuItem|GUISubmenu|Hardware|Interface|InterfaceDefinition|
  KeyCap|KeyCode|KeyCombo|KeySym|Literal|Constant|Markup|
  MediaLabel|MenuChoice|MouseButton|MsgText|Option|Optional|
  Parameter|Prompt|Property|Replaceable|ReturnValue|SGMLTag|
  StructField|StructName|Symbol|SystemItem|Token|Type|UserInput|
  VarName|Anchor|Comment|Subscript|Superscript|InlineGraphic|
  InlineMediaObject|IndexTerm)+)
```

Attributes **Name**	Common attributes **Type**	**Default**
Class	*Enumeration:* Directory HeaderFile SymLink	*None*
Path	CDATA	*None*

MoreInfo	*Enumeration:* None RefEntry	"None"
Parameter Entities		
%cptr.char.mix;	%ndxterm.char.mix;	%para.char.mix;
%programlisting.content;	%refinline.char.mix;	%refname.char.mix;
%screen.content;	%tbl.entry.mdl;	%tech.char.class;
%title.char.mix;		

Description

A **Filename** is the name of a file on a local or network disk. It may be a simple name or may include a path or other elements specific to the operating system.

Processing expectations

Formatted inline. The `MoreInfo` attribute can help generate a link or query to retrieve additional information.

4.0 Future Changes

The content model of **Filename** will be constrained to `(#PCDATA | Replaceable | InlineGraphic)` in DocBook V4.0.

Attributes

Class

`Class` allows the author to identify particular kinds of files.

MoreInfo

If `MoreInfo` is set to `RefEntry`, it implies that a **RefEntry** exists which further describes the **Filename**.

Path

`Path` contains the *search* path, possibly in a system or application specific form, on which the file can be found.

See Also

Application, **ComputerOutput**, **Database**, **EnVar**, **Hardware**, **MediaLabel**, **ProductName**, **Prompt**, **SystemItem**, **UserInput**

Examples

```
<!DOCTYPE para PUBLIC "-//OASIS//DTD DocBook V3.1//EN">
<para>
The symbolic constants for error numbers are defined in
<filename class=headerfile>errno.h</filename> in
<filename class=directory>/usr/include/sys</filename>.
</para>
```

| The symbolic constants for error numbers are defined in *errno.h* in */usr/include/sys.*

For additional examples, see also **Constant**, **ErrorCode**, **KeyCap**, **KeyCode**, **KeySym**, **VariableList**.

FirstName—The first name of a person

Synopsis

Mixed Content Model

```
FirstName ::=
((#PCDATA|Link|OLink|ULink|Emphasis|Trademark|Replaceable|Comment|
  Subscript|Superscript|InlineGraphic|InlineMediaObject|IndexTerm)+)
```

Attributes	Common attributes

Parameter Entities

%biblicomponent.mix;	%person.ident.mix;

Description

The Western-style first name of an author, editor, or other individual.

Processing expectations

Formatted inline. In an **Address**, this element may inherit the verbatim qualities of an address.

See Also

Affiliation, **Honorific**, **Lineage**, **OtherName**, **Surname**

Examples

For examples, see **Ackno**, **Article**, **Author**, **AuthorGroup**, **Bibliography**, **BiblioMSet**, **BiblioSet**, **Book**, **BookInfo**, **OtherCredit**.

FirstTerm—The first occurrence of a term

Synopsis

Mixed Content Model

```
FirstTerm ::=
((#PCDATA|Acronym|Emphasis|Trademark|Link|OLink|ULink|Anchor|
  Comment|Subscript|Superscript|InlineGraphic|InlineMediaObject|
  IndexTerm)+)
```

Attributes — Common attributes

Name	**Type**	**Default**
Linkend	IDREF	*None*

Parameter Entities		
%gen.char.class;	%ndxterm.char.mix;	%para.char.mix;
%programlisting.content;	%refinline.char.mix;	%screen.content;
%tbl.entry.mdl;	%title.char.mix;	

Description

This element marks the first occurrence of a word or term in a given context.

Processing expectations

Formatted inline. **FirstTerms** are often given special typographic treatment, such as italics.

Attributes

Linkend

Linkend points to a related element, perhaps the **Glossary** definition of the term.

See Also

GlossTerm

Examples

```
<!DOCTYPE para PUBLIC "-//OASIS//DTD DocBook V3.1//EN">
<para>
In an <firstterm>Object Oriented</firstterm> programming language,
data and procedures (called <glossterm>methods</glossterm>) are
bound together.
</para>
```

In an *Object Oriented* programming language, data and procedures (called*methods*) are bound together.

Footnote—A footnote

Synopsis

Content Model

```
Footnote ::=
((CalloutList|GlossList|ItemizedList|OrderedList|SegmentedList|
  SimpleList|VariableList|LiteralLayout|ProgramListing|
  ProgramListingCO|Screen|ScreenCO|ScreenShot|Synopsis|
  CmdSynopsis|FuncSynopsis|FormalPara|Para|SimPara|Address|
  BlockQuote|Graphic|GraphicCO|MediaObject|MediaObjectCO|
  InformalEquation|InformalExample|InformalFigure|InformalTable)+)
```

Attributes Name	Common attributes Type	Default
Label	CDATA	*None*

Parameter Entities		
%footnote.exclusion;	%gen.char.class;	%ndxterm.char.mix;
%para.char.mix;	%programlisting.con-tent;	%refinline.char.mix;
%screen.content;	%tbl.entry.mdl;	%title.char.mix;

Description

This element is a wrapper around the contents of a footnote.

Additional references to the same footnote may be generated with **FootnoteRef**.

Processing expectations

The **Footnote** element usually generates a mark (a superscript symbol or number) at the place in the flow of the document in which it occurs. The body of the footnote is then presented elsewhere, typically at the bottom of the page.

Alternative presentations are also possible. In print environments that do not support footnotes at the bottom of the page, they may be presented as end notes occurring at the end of the component that contains the **Footnote**. Online systems may choose to present them inline or as "pop-ups," or links, or any combination thereof.

Attributes

Label

`Label` identifies the desired footnote mark.

Examples

```
<!DOCTYPE para PUBLIC "-//OASIS//DTD DocBook V3.1//EN">
<para>
An annual percentage rate (<abbrev>APR</>) of 13.9%<footnote>
<para>
The prime rate, as published in the <citetitle>Wall Street
Journal</citetitle> on the first business day of the month,
plus 7.0%.
</para>
</footnote>
will be charged on all balances carried forward.
</para>
```

An annual percentage rate (APR) of 13.9%* will be charged on all balances carried forward.

* The prime rate, as published in the *Wall Street Journal* on the first business day of the month, plus 7.0%.

For additional examples, see also **FootnoteRef**, **RefEntry**.

FootnoteRef—A cross reference to a footnote (a footnote mark)

Synopsis

Content Model		
`FootnoteRef ::=` `EMPTY`		
Attributes	Common attributes	
Name	**Type**	**Default**
Label	CDATA	*None*
Linkend	IDREF	*Required*
Parameter Entities		
`%ndxterm.char.mix;`	`%para.char.mix;`	`%programlisting.content;`
`%refinline.char.mix;`	`%screen.content;`	`%tbl.entry.mdl;`
`%title.char.mix;`	`%xref.char.class;`	

Description

This element forms an IDREF link to a **Footnote**. It generates the same mark or link as the **Footnote** to which it points.

In technical documentation, **FootnoteRef** occurs most frequently in tables.

Processing expectations

The **FootnoteRef** element usually generates the same mark as the **Footnote** to which it points, although its mark can be influenced by the `Label` attribute.

Neither SGML nor XML provide a mechnism (at this time) for asserting that some IDREF links must point to specific classes of elements. If a **FootnoteRef** points to something other than a **Footnote**, the parser will not report it as an error. It is an error nonetheless. Processing is undefined.

Attributes

Label

`Label` identifies the desired footnote mark.

Linkend

`Linkend` points to the **Footnote** referenced.

Examples

```
<!DOCTYPE informaltable PUBLIC "-//OASIS//DTD DocBook V3.1//EN">
<informaltable>
<tgroup cols=2>
<tbody>
<row>
<entry>foo<footnote id=fnrex1a><para>A meaningless
word</para></footnote></entry>
```

```
<entry>3<footnote id=fnrex1b><para>A meaningless
number</para></footnote></entry>
</row>
<row>
<entry>bar<footnoteref linkend=fnrex1a></entry>
<entry>5<footnoteref linkend=fnrex1b></entry>
</row>
</tbody>
</tgroup>
</informaltable>
```

foo[a]	3[b]
bar[a]	5[b]

[a] A meaningless word
[b] A meaningless number

ForeignPhrase—A word or phrase in a language other than the primary language of the document

Synopsis

Mixed Content Model

```
ForeignPhrase ::=
((#PCDATA|FootnoteRef|XRef|Abbrev|Acronym|Citation|CiteRefEntry|
  CiteTitle|Emphasis|FirstTerm|ForeignPhrase|GlossTerm|Footnote|
  Phrase|Quote|Trademark|WordAsWord|Link|OLink|ULink|Action|
  Application|ClassName|Command|ComputerOutput|Database|Email|
  EnVar|ErrorCode|ErrorName|ErrorType|Filename|Function|GUIButton|
  GUIIcon|GUILabel|GUIMenu|GUIMenuItem|GUISubmenu|Hardware|
  Interface|InterfaceDefinition|KeyCap|KeyCode|KeyCombo|KeySym|
  Literal|Constant|Markup|MediaLabel|MenuChoice|MouseButton|
  MsgText|Option|Optional|Parameter|Prompt|Property|Replaceable|
  ReturnValue|SGMLTag|StructField|StructName|Symbol|SystemItem|
  Token|Type|UserInput|VarName|Anchor|Author|AuthorInitials|
  CorpAuthor|ModeSpec|OtherCredit|ProductName|ProductNumber|
  RevHistory|Comment|Subscript|Superscript|InlineGraphic|
  InlineMediaObject|InlineEquation|Synopsis|CmdSynopsis|
  FuncSynopsis|IndexTerm)+)
```

Attributes Common attributes

Parameter Entities

%gen.char.class;	%ndxterm.char.mix;	%para.char.mix;
%programlisting.content;	%refinline.char.mix;	%screen.content;
%tbl.entry.mdl;	%title.char.mix;	

Description

The **ForeignPhrase** element can be used to markup the text of a foreign word or phrase. "Foreign" in this context means that it is a language other than the primary language of the document and is not intended to be pejorative in any way.

Processing expectations

ForeignPhrases are often given special typographic treatment, such as italics.

4.0 *Future Changes*

The **InterfaceDefinition** element will be discarded in DocBook V4.0. It will no longer be available in the content model of this element.

See Also

Abbrev, **Acronym**, **Emphasis**, **Phrase**, **Quote**, **WordAsWord**

Examples

```
<!DOCTYPE para PUBLIC "-//OASIS//DTD DocBook V3.1//EN">
<para>
Like so many others, it became a <foreignphrase>de facto</foreignphrase>
standard.
</para>
```

Like so many others, it became a *de facto* standard.

FormalPara—A paragraph with a title

Synopsis

Content Model

```
FormalPara ::=
(Title,
 (IndexTerm)*,
 Para)
```

Attributes	Common attributes	
Parameter Entities		
%admon.mix;	%bookcomponent.content;	%component.mix;
%divcomponent.mix;	%example.mix;	%footnote.mix;
%glossdef.mix;	%highlights.mix;	%indexdivcomponent.mix;
%legalnotice.mix;	%para.class;	%qandaset.mix;
%refcomponent.mix;	%sidebar.mix;	%tabentry.mix;
%tbl.entry.mdl;	%textobject.mix;	

Description

Formal paragraphs have a title.

Processing expectations

Formatted as a displayed block. The **Title** of a **FormalPara** is often rendered as a run-in head.

See Also

Para, SimPara

Examples

```
<!DOCTYPE formalpara PUBLIC "-//OASIS//DTD DocBook V3.1//EN">
<formalpara><title>This Paragraph Has a Title</title>
<para>
This is a test.  This is only a test.  Had this been a real
example, it would have made more sense.  Or less.
</para>
</formalpara>
```

This Paragraph Has a Title. This is a test. This is only a test. Had this been a real example, it would have made more sense. Or less.

For additional examples, see also **Para**.

FuncDef—A function (subroutine) name and its return type

Synopsis

Mixed Content Model
`FuncDef ::=`
`((#PCDATA|Replaceable|Function)*)`	

Attributes	Common attributes

Description

A **FuncDef** contains the name of a programming language function, and its return type.

Within the **FuncDef**, the function name is identified with **Function**, and the rest of the content is assumed to be the return type.

In the following definition, *max* is the name of the function and *int* is the return type:

```
<funcdef>int <function>max</function></funcdef>
```

Processing expectations

Formatted inline. For a complete description of the processing expecations, see **FuncSynopsis**.

See Also

FuncParams, **FuncPrototype**, **FuncSynopsisInfo**, **Function**, **ParamDef**, **Parameter**, **ReturnValue**, **VarArgs**, **Void**

Examples

```
<!DOCTYPE funcsynopsis PUBLIC "-//OASIS//DTD DocBook V3.1//EN">
<funcsynopsis>
<funcprototype>
<funcdef>int <function>rand</function></funcdef>
  <void>
</funcprototype>
</funcsynopsis>
```

```
int rand(void);
```

For additional examples, see also **FuncSynopsis**, **ParamDef**, **VarArgs**.

FuncParams—Parameters for a function referenced through a function pointer in a synopsis

Synopsis

Mixed Content Model

```
FuncParams ::=
((#PCDATA|Link|OLink|ULink|Action|Application|ClassName|Command|
  ComputerOutput|Database|Email|EnVar|ErrorCode|ErrorName|
  ErrorType|Filename|Function|GUIButton|GUIIcon|GUILabel|GUIMenu|
  GUIMenuItem|GUISubmenu|Hardware|Interface|InterfaceDefinition|
  KeyCap|KeyCode|KeyCombo|KeySym|Literal|Constant|Markup|
  MediaLabel|MenuChoice|MouseButton|MsgText|Option|Optional|
  Parameter|Prompt|Property|Replaceable|ReturnValue|SGMLTag|
  StructField|StructName|Symbol|SystemItem|Token|Type|UserInput|
  VarName|Anchor|Comment|Subscript|Superscript|InlineGraphic|
  InlineMediaObject|IndexTerm)*)
```

Attributes	Common attributes

Description

In some programming languages (like C), it is possible for a function to have a pointer to another function as one of its parameters. In the syntax summary for such a function, the **FuncParams** element provides a wrapper for the function pointer.

For example, the following prototype describes the function *sort*, which takes two parameters. The first parameter, *arr*, is an array of integers. The second parameter is a pointer to a function, *comp* that returns an *int*. The *comp* function takes two parameters, both of type *int **:

```
<funcprototype>
  <funcdef>void <function>sort</function></funcdef>
    <paramdef>int *<parameter>arr</parameter>[]</paramdef>
    <paramdef>int <parameter>(* comp)</parameter>
      <funcparams>int *, int *</funcparams></paramdef>
</funcprototype>
```

Processing expectations

Formatted inline. For a complete description of the processing expecations, see **FuncSynopsis**.

4.0 *Future Changes*

The **InterfaceDefinition** element will be discarded in DocBook V4.0. It will no longer be available in the content model of this element.

See Also

FuncDef, **FuncPrototype**, **FuncSynopsisInfo**, **Function**, **ParamDef**, **Parameter**, **ReturnValue**, **VarArgs**, **Void**

Examples

```
<!DOCTYPE funcsynopsis PUBLIC "-//OASIS//DTD DocBook V3.1//EN">
<funcsynopsis>
<funcprototype>
  <funcdef>void <function>qsort</function></funcdef>
    <paramdef>void *<parameter>dataptr</parameter>[]</paramdef>
    <paramdef>int <parameter>left</parameter></paramdef>
    <paramdef>int <parameter>right</parameter></paramdef>
    <paramdef>int <parameter>(* comp)</parameter>
      <funcparams>void *, void *</funcparams></paramdef>
</funcprototype>
</funcsynopsis>
```

```
void qsort(void *dataptr[], int left, int right, int (* comp)
(void *, void *));
```

For additional examples, see also **FuncSynopsis**.

FuncPrototype—The prototype of a function

Synopsis

Content Model
`FuncPrototype ::=`
`(FuncDef,`
`  (Void|VarArgs|ParamDef+))`	

Attributes	Common attributes

Description

A wrapper for a function prototype in a **FuncSynopsis**.

Processing expectations

See **FuncSynopsis**.

See Also

FuncDef, **FuncParams**, **FuncSynopsisInfo**, **Function**, **ParamDef**, **Parameter**, **ReturnValue**, **VarArgs**, **Void**

Examples

For examples, see **FuncDef**, **FuncSynopsis**, **ParamDef**, **VarArgs**.

FuncSynopsis—The syntax summary for a function definition

Synopsis

Content Model

```
FuncSynopsis ::=
(FuncSynopsisInfo?,
 (FuncPrototype+|
  (FuncDef,
   (Void|VarArgs|ParamDef+))+),
 FuncSynopsisInfo?)
```

Attributes	Common attributes	
Name	**Type**	**Default**
Label	CDATA	*None*

Parameter Entities

`%admon.mix;`	`%bookcomponent.content;`	`%component.mix;`
`%divcomponent.mix;`	`%example.mix;`	`%figure.mix;`
`%footnote.mix;`	`%glossdef.mix;`	`%indexdivcomponent.mix;`
`%para.char.mix;`	`%programlisting.content;`	`%qandaset.mix;`
`%refcomponent.mix;`	`%screen.content;`	`%sidebar.mix;`
`%synop.class;`	`%tbl.entry.mdl;`	

Description

A **FuncSynopsis** contains the syntax summary of a function prototype or a set of function prototypes. The content model of this element was designed specifically to capture the semantics of most C-language function prototypes (for use in UNIX reference pages).

This is one of the few places where DocBook attempts to model as well as describe. Using **FuncSynopsis** for languages that are unrelated to C may prove difficult.

Processing expectations

For the most part, the processing application is expected to generate all of the parenthesis, semicolons, commas, and so on. required in the rendered synopsis. The exception to this rule is that the spacing and other punctuation inside a parameter that is a pointer to a function must be provided in the source markup.

With sufficient author cooperation, it should be possible to markup a function synopsis with enough clarity so that a processing system can generate either K&R-style or ANSI-style renderings.

A Note on the Use of VarArgs

The content model of **FuncPrototype** is such that you cannot use **VarArgs** in a function prototype in which the first few parameters to the function are given explicitly before the variable arguments (generally rendered as an ellipsis).

In other words, the following synopsis cannot be rendered with **VarArgs**:

```
int printf(char *format, ...)
```

Instead, you can enclose the ellipsis in a final **Parameter**, like this:

```
<funcsynopsis>
<funcprototype><funcdef>int <function>printf</function></funcdef>
<paramdef>
  <parameter>char *format</parameter>
  <parameter>...</parameter>
</paramdef>
</funcprototype>
</funcsynopsis>
```

4.0 ***Future Changes***

In DocBook V4.0, the content model fragment beginning with **FuncDef** will be removed from the content model of **FuncSynopsis**. Instead **FuncSynopsis** will become a mixture of **FuncSynopsisInfo**s and **FuncPrototype**s.

Future Changes

Future versions of DocBook may provide additional environments for describing the syntax summaries of functions in other programming languages.

Attributes

Label

`Label` specifies an identifying number or string that may be used in presentation.

See Also

CmdSynopsis, **Synopsis**

Examples

The function *max* returns the larger of two integers:

```
<!DOCTYPE funcsynopsis PUBLIC "-//OASIS//DTD DocBook V3.1//EN">
<funcsynopsis>
```

```
<funcprototype>
  <funcdef>int <function>max</function></funcdef>
  <paramdef>int <parameter>int1</parameter></paramdef>
  <paramdef>int <parameter>int2</parameter></paramdef>
</funcprototype>
</funcsynopsis>
```

```
int max(int int1, int int2);
```

One can imagine a more flexible *max* function that takes any number of integer arguments and returns the largest integer in the list:

```
<!DOCTYPE funcsynopsis PUBLIC "-//OASIS//DTD DocBook V3.1//EN">
<funcsynopsis>
<funcsynopsisinfo>
#include &lt;varargs.h&gt;
</funcsynopsisinfo>
<funcprototype>
  <funcdef>int <function>max</function></funcdef>
  <varargs>
</funcprototype>
</funcsynopsis>
```

```
#include <varargs.h>

int max(...);
```

The *rand* function takes no arguments and returns a psuedorandom integer between 0 and 2^{31}-1:

```
<!DOCTYPE funcsynopsis PUBLIC "-//OASIS//DTD DocBook V3.1//EN">
<funcsynopsis>
<funcprototype>
<funcdef>int <function>rand</function></funcdef>
  <void>
</funcprototype>
</funcsynopsis>
```

```
int rand(void);
```

The *qsort* function takes several arguments, including a pointer to a function (the function that should perform the comparison between two elements in order to sort them).

```
<!DOCTYPE funcsynopsis PUBLIC "-//OASIS//DTD DocBook V3.1//EN">
<funcsynopsis>
<funcprototype>
  <funcdef>void <function>qsort</function></funcdef>
    <paramdef>void *<parameter>dataptr</parameter>[]</paramdef>
    <paramdef>int <parameter>left</parameter></paramdef>
    <paramdef>int <parameter>right</parameter></paramdef>
    <paramdef>int <parameter>(* comp)</parameter>
      <funcparams>void *, void *</funcparams></paramdef>
</funcprototype>
</funcsynopsis>
```

```
void qsort(void *dataptr[], int left, int right, int (* comp)
(void *, void *));
```

For additional examples, see also **FuncDef**, **ParamDef**, **VarArgs**.

FuncSynopsisInfo—Information supplementing the **FuncDefs** of a **FuncSynopsis**

Synopsis

Mixed Content Model		
`FuncSynopsisInfo ::= ((LineAnnotation|#PCDATA|Link|OLink|ULink|Action|Application| ClassName|Command|ComputerOutput|Database|Email|EnVar|ErrorCode| ErrorName|ErrorType|Filename|Function|GUIButton|GUIIcon| GUILabel|GUIMenu|GUIMenuItem|GUISubmenu|Hardware|Interface| InterfaceDefinition|KeyCap|KeyCode|KeyCombo|KeySym|Literal| Constant|Markup|MediaLabel|MenuChoice|MouseButton|MsgText| Option|Optional|Parameter|Prompt|Property|Replaceable| ReturnValue|SGMLTag|StructField|StructName|Symbol|SystemItem| Token|Type|UserInput|VarName|Anchor|Comment|Subscript| Superscript|InlineGraphic|InlineMediaObject|IndexTerm)*)`		
Attributes	Common attributes	
Name	**Type**	**Default**
Format	*Enumerated notation:* linespecific	"linespecific"

Description

Supplementary information in a **FuncSynopsis**. See **FuncSynopsis**.

Unlike the otherinfo elements, **FuncSynopsisInfo** is not a container for meta-information. Instead **FuncSynopsisInfo** is a verbatim environment for adding additional information to a function synopsis.

Processing expectations

This element is displayed "verbatim"; whitespace and linebreaks within this element are significant.

4.0 *Future Changes*

The **InterfaceDefinition** element will be discarded in DocBook V4.0. It will no longer be available in the content model of this element.

Attributes

Format

The `Format` attribute applies the `linespecific` notation to all **FuncSynopsisInfos**. All white space and line breaks must be preserved.

See Also

FuncDef, **FuncParams**, **FuncProtoype**, **Function**, **ParamDef**, **Parameter**, **ReturnValue**, **VarArgs**, **Void**

Examples

For examples, see **FuncSynopsis**, **VarArgs**.

Function—The name of a function or subroutine, as in a programming language

Synopsis

Mixed Content Model

```
Function ::=
((#PCDATA|Link|OLink|ULink|Action|Application|ClassName|Command|
  ComputerOutput|Database|Email|EnVar|ErrorCode|ErrorName|
  ErrorType|Filename|Function|GUIButton|GUIIcon|GUILabel|GUIMenu|
  GUIMenuItem|GUISubmenu|Hardware|Interface|InterfaceDefinition|
  KeyCap|KeyCode|KeyCombo|KeySym|Literal|Constant|Markup|
  MediaLabel|MenuChoice|MouseButton|MsgText|Option|Optional|
  Parameter|Prompt|Property|Replaceable|ReturnValue|SGMLTag|
  StructField|StructName|Symbol|SystemItem|Token|Type|UserInput|
  VarName|Anchor|Comment|Subscript|Superscript|InlineGraphic|
  InlineMediaObject|IndexTerm)+)
```

Attributes Name	Common attributes Type	**Default**
MoreInfo	*Enumeration:* None RefEntry	"None"

Parameter Entities

`%cptr.char.mix;`	`%ndxterm.char.mix;`	`%para.char.mix;`
`%programlisting.content;`	`%refinline.char.mix;`	`%refname.char.mix;`
`%screen.content;`	`%tbl.entry.mdl;`	`%tech.char.class;`
`%title.char.mix;`		

Description

This element marks up the name of a function. To markup the parts of a function definition, see **FuncSynopsis**.

Processing expectations

Formatted inline. The `MoreInfo` attribute can help generate a link or query to retrieve additional information.

In some environments, the **Function** element generates additional punctuation, such as a set of trailing parenthesis.

4.0 *Future Changes*

The **InterfaceDefinition** element will be discarded in DocBook V4.0. It will no longer be available in the content model of this element.

Attributes

MoreInfo

If `MoreInfo` is set to `RefEntry`, it implies that a **RefEntry** exists which further describes the **Function**.

See Also

FuncDef, **FuncParams**, **FuncPrototype**, **FuncSynopsisInfo**, **ParamDef**, **Parameter**, **ReturnValue**, **VarArgs**, **Void**

Examples

For examples, see **FuncDef**, **FuncSynopsis**, **ParamDef**, **ProgramListingCO**, **ReturnValue**, **StructName**, **Type**, **VarArgs**.

Glossary—A glossary

Synopsis

Content Model

```
Glossary ::=
((DocInfo?,Title,Subtitle?,TitleAbbrev?)?,
 (CalloutList|GlossList|ItemizedList|OrderedList|SegmentedList|
  SimpleList|VariableList|Caution|Important|Note|Tip|Warning|
  LiteralLayout|ProgramListing|ProgramListingCO|Screen|ScreenCO|
  ScreenShot|Synopsis|CmdSynopsis|FuncSynopsis|FormalPara|Para|
  SimPara|Address|BlockQuote|Graphic|GraphicCO|MediaObject|
  MediaObjectCO|InformalEquation|InformalExample|InformalFigure|
  InformalTable|Equation|Example|Figure|Table|MsgSet|Procedure|
  Sidebar|QandASet|Anchor|BridgeHead|Comment|Highlights|Abstract|
  AuthorBlurb|Epigraph|IndexTerm)*,
 (GlossDiv+|GlossEntry+),
 Bibliography?)
```

Attributes	Common attributes	
Name	**Type**	**Default**
Status	CDATA	*None*

Parameter Entities

`%nav.class;` `%partcontent.mix;`

Description

A **Glossary** contains a collection of terms and brief descriptions or definitions of those terms.

Processing expectations

Formatted as a displayed block. A **Glossary** in a **Book** frequently causes a forced page break in print media.

Attributes

Status

`Status` identifies the editorial or publication status of the **Glossary**.

Publication status might be used to control formatting (for example, printing a "draft" watermark on drafts) or processing (perhaps a document with a status of "final" should not include any components that are not final).

Examples

```
<!DOCTYPE glossary PUBLIC "-//OASIS//DTD DocBook V3.1//EN">
<glossary><title>Example Glossary</title>
<para>
This is not a real glossary, it's just an example.
</para>

<!-- ... -->

<glossdiv><title>E</title>

<glossentry id="xml"><glossterm>Extensible Markup Language</glossterm>
  <acronym>XML</acronym>
<glossdef>
  <para>Some reasonable definition here.</para>
  <glossseealso otherterm="sgml">
</glossdef>
</glossentry>

</glossdiv>

<!-- ... -->

<glossdiv><title>S</title>

<glossentry><glossterm>SGML</glossterm>
<glosssee otherterm=sgml>
</glossentry>

<glossentry id=sgml><glossterm>Standard Generalized
  Markup Language</glossterm><acronym>SGML</acronym>
  <abbrev>ISO 8879:1986</abbrev>
<glossdef>
  <para>Some reasonable definition here.</para>
  <glossseealso otherterm="xml">
</glossdef>
</glossentry>
```

```
</glossdiv>
</glossary>
```

GlossDef—A definition in a GlossEntry

Synopsis

Content Model

```
GlossDef ::=
((CalloutList|GlossList|ItemizedList|OrderedList|SegmentedList|
  SimpleList|VariableList|LiteralLayout|ProgramListing|
  ProgramListingCO|Screen|ScreenCO|ScreenShot|Synopsis|
  CmdSynopsis|FuncSynopsis|FormalPara|Para|SimPara|Address|
  BlockQuote|Graphic|GraphicCO|MediaObject|MediaObjectCO|
  InformalEquation|InformalExample|InformalFigure|InformalTable|
  Equation|Example|Figure|Table|Comment|IndexTerm)+,
 GlossSeeAlso*)
```

Attributes	Common attributes	
Name	**Type**	**Default**
Subject	CDATA	*None*

Description

A **GlossDef** contains the description or definition of a **GlossTerm**.

Processing expectations

Formatted as a displayed block.

4.0 *Future Changes*

The `Subject` attribute will be renamed `Keywords` in DocBook V4.0.

Attributes

Subject

`Subject` holds a list of keywords for the **GlossDef**'s definition.

See Also

GlossSee, **GlossSeeAlso**

Examples

For examples, see **Glossary**, **GlossList**.

GlossDiv—A division in a **Glossary**

Synopsis

Content Model

```
GlossDiv ::=
((Title,Subtitle?,TitleAbbrev?),
 (CalloutList|GlossList|ItemizedList|OrderedList|SegmentedList|
  SimpleList|VariableList|Caution|Important|Note|Tip|Warning|
  LiteralLayout|ProgramListing|ProgramListingCO|Screen|ScreenCO|
  ScreenShot|Synopsis|CmdSynopsis|FuncSynopsis|FormalPara|Para|
  SimPara|Address|BlockQuote|Graphic|GraphicCO|MediaObject|
  MediaObjectCO|InformalEquation|InformalExample|InformalFigure|
  InformalTable|Equation|Example|Figure|Table|MsgSet|Procedure|
  Sidebar|QandASet|Anchor|BridgeHead|Comment|Highlights|Abstract|
  AuthorBlurb|Epigraph|IndexTerm)*,
 GlossEntry+)
```

Attributes	Common attributes	
Name	**Type**	**Default**
Status	CDATA	*None*

Description

A **GlossDiv** is a section of a **Glossary**. A Glossary might be divided into sections in order to group terms, perhaps alphabetically.

A Glossary may contain any number of **GlossEntry** or **GlossDiv** elements, but it cannot contain a mixture of both at the same level.

Processing expectations

Formatted as a displayed block.

Attributes

Status

`Status` identifies the editorial or publication status of the **GlossDiv**.

Publication status might be used to control formatting (for example, printing a "draft" watermark on drafts) or processing (perhaps a document with a status of "final" should not include any components that are not final).

Examples

For examples, see **Glossary**.

GlossEntry—An entry in a **Glossary** or **GlossList**

Synopsis

Content Model		
`GlossEntry ::= (GlossTerm,Acronym?,Abbrev?, (IndexTerm)*, RevHistory?, (GlossSee|GlossDef+))`		
Attributes	Common attributes	
Name	**Type**	**Default**
SortAs	CDATA	*None*

Description

GlossEntry is a wrapper around a glossary term and its definition.

Processing expectations

Formatted as a displayed block. Glossary entries are usually formatted to highlight the terms and definitions, frequently in a style similar to **VarListEntry**s.

Attributes

SortAs

`SortAs` specifies the string by which the element's content is to be sorted. If unspecified, the proper content is used.

Examples

For examples, see **Glossary**, **GlossList**.

GlossList—A wrapper for a set of **GlossEntry**s

Synopsis

Content Model		
`GlossList ::= (GlossEntry+)`		
Attributes	Common attributes	
Parameter Entities		
`%admon.mix;`	`%bookcomponent.content;`	`%component.mix;`
`%divcomponent.mix;`	`%example.mix;`	`%footnote.mix;`
`%glossdef.mix;`	`%highlights.mix;`	`%legalnotice.mix;`
`%list.class;`	`%para.mix;`	`%qandaset.mix;`
`%refcomponent.mix;`	`%sidebar.mix;`	`%tabentry.mix;`
`%tbl.entry.mdl;`	`%textobject.mix;`	

Description

While **Glossarys** are usually limited to component or section boundaries, appearing at the end of a **Book** or **Chapter**, for instance, **GlossLists** can appear anywhere that the other list types are allowed.

Using a **GlossList** in running text, instead of a **VariableList**, for example, maintains the semantic distinction of a Glossary. This distinction may be necessary if you want to automatically point to the members of the list with **GlossTerms** in the body of the text.

Processing expectations

Formatted as a displayed block.

Examples

```
<!DOCTYPE glosslist PUBLIC "-//OASIS//DTD DocBook V3.1//EN">
<glosslist>
<glossentry><glossterm>C</glossterm>
<glossdef>
<para>
A procedural programming language invented by K&amp;R.
</para>
</glossdef>
</glossentry>
<glossentry><glossterm>Pascal</glossterm>
<glossdef>
<para>
A procedural programming language invented by Niklaus Wirth.
</para>
</glossdef>
</glossentry>
</glosslist>
```

C
    A procedural programming language invented by K&R.

Pascal
    A procedural programming language invented by Niklaus Wirth.

GlossSee—A cross-reference from one **GlossEntry** to another

Synopsis

Mixed Content Model

```
GlossSee ::=
((#PCDATA|FootnoteRef|XRef|Abbrev|Acronym|Citation|CiteRefEntry|
  CiteTitle|Emphasis|FirstTerm|ForeignPhrase|GlossTerm|Footnote|
  Phrase|Quote|Trademark|WordAsWord|Link|OLink|ULink|Action|
  Application|ClassName|Command|ComputerOutput|Database|Email|
  EnVar|ErrorCode|ErrorName|ErrorType|Filename|Function|GUIButton|
```

```
GUIIcon|GUILabel|GUIMenu|GUIMenuItem|GUISubmenu|Hardware|
Interface|InterfaceDefinition|KeyCap|KeyCode|KeyCombo|KeySym|
Literal|Constant|Markup|MediaLabel|MenuChoice|MouseButton|
MsgText|Option|Optional|Parameter|Prompt|Property|Replaceable|
ReturnValue|SGMLTag|StructField|StructName|Symbol|SystemItem|
Token|Type|UserInput|VarName|Anchor|Author|AuthorInitials|
CorpAuthor|ModeSpec|OtherCredit|ProductName|ProductNumber|
RevHistory|Comment|Subscript|Superscript|InlineGraphic|
InlineMediaObject|InlineEquation|Synopsis|CmdSynopsis|
FuncSynopsis|IndexTerm)+)
```

Attributes **Name**	Common attributes **Type**	**Default**
OtherTerm	IDREF	*Content reference*

Description

GlossSee directs the reader to another **GlossEntry** instead of this one. A "See" cross-reference occurs in place of the definition.

Processing Expectations

Formatted as a displayed block, in the same style as a **GlossDef**.

GlossSee elements are expected to generate the necessary cross-reference text, usually "See" in English, as well as any necessary punctuation.

4.0 *Future Changes*

The **InterfaceDefinition** element will be discarded in DocBook V4.0. It will no longer be available in the content model of this element.

Attributes

OtherTerm

`OtherTerm` points to the **GlossEntry** being cross-referenced. (Go see *that* one.)

See Also

GlossDef, **GlossSeeAlso**

Examples

For examples, see **Glossary**.

GlossSeeAlso—A cross-reference from one **GlossEntry** to another

Synopsis

Mixed Content Model

```
GlossSeeAlso ::=
((#PCDATA|FootnoteRef|XRef|Abbrev|Acronym|Citation|CiteRefEntry|
```

```
CiteTitle|Emphasis|FirstTerm|ForeignPhrase|GlossTerm|Footnote|
Phrase|Quote|Trademark|WordAsWord|Link|OLink|ULink|Action|
Application|ClassName|Command|ComputerOutput|Database|Email|
EnVar|ErrorCode|ErrorName|ErrorType|Filename|Function|GUIButton|
GUIIcon|GUILabel|GUIMenu|GUIMenuItem|GUISubmenu|Hardware|
Interface|InterfaceDefinition|KeyCap|KeyCode|KeyCombo|KeySym|
Literal|Constant|Markup|MediaLabel|MenuChoice|MouseButton|
MsgText|Option|Optional|Parameter|Prompt|Property|Replaceable|
ReturnValue|SGMLTag|StructField|StructName|Symbol|SystemItem|
Token|Type|UserInput|VarName|Anchor|Author|AuthorInitials|
CorpAuthor|ModeSpec|OtherCredit|ProductName|ProductNumber|
RevHistory|Comment|Subscript|Superscript|InlineGraphic|
InlineMediaObject|InlineEquation|Synopsis|CmdSynopsis|
FuncSynopsis|IndexTerm)+)
```

Attributes	Common attributes	
Name	**Type**	**Default**
OtherTerm	IDREF	*Content reference*

Description

GlossSeeAlso directs the reader to another **GlossEntry** for additional information. It is presented in addition to the **GlossDef**.

Processing expectations

Formatted as a displayed block, in the same style as the **GlossDef**.

GlossSeeAlso elements are expected to generate the necessary cross-reference text, usually "See also" in English, as well as any necessary punctuation.

4.0 *Future Changes*

The **InterfaceDefinition** element will be discarded in DocBook V4.0. It will no longer be available in the content model of this element.

Attributes

OtherTerm

`OtherTerm` points to the **GlossEntry** being cross-referenced. (Go see *that* one, too.)

See Also

GlossDef, **GlossSee**

Examples

For examples, see **Glossary**.

GlossTerm—A glossary term

Synopsis

Mixed Content Model

```
GlossTerm ::=
((#PCDATA|FootnoteRef|XRef|Abbrev|Acronym|Citation|CiteRefEntry|
  CiteTitle|Emphasis|FirstTerm|ForeignPhrase|GlossTerm|Footnote|
  Phrase|Quote|Trademark|WordAsWord|Link|OLink|ULink|Action|
  Application|ClassName|Command|ComputerOutput|Database|Email|
  EnVar|ErrorCode|ErrorName|ErrorType|Filename|Function|GUIButton|
  GUIIcon|GUILabel|GUIMenu|GUIMenuItem|GUISubmenu|Hardware|
  Interface|InterfaceDefinition|KeyCap|KeyCode|KeyCombo|KeySym|
  Literal|Constant|Markup|MediaLabel|MenuChoice|MouseButton|
  MsgText|Option|Optional|Parameter|Prompt|Property|Replaceable|
  ReturnValue|SGMLTag|StructField|StructName|Symbol|SystemItem|
  Token|Type|UserInput|VarName|Anchor|Author|AuthorInitials|
  CorpAuthor|ModeSpec|OtherCredit|ProductName|ProductNumber|
  RevHistory|Comment|Subscript|Superscript|InlineGraphic|
  InlineMediaObject|InlineEquation|Synopsis|CmdSynopsis|
  FuncSynopsis|IndexTerm)+)
```

Attributes	Common attributes	
Name	**Type**	**Default**
Linkend	IDREF	*None*
BaseForm	CDATA	*None*

Parameter Entities		
`%gen.char.class;`	`%ndxterm.char.mix;`	`%para.char.mix;`
`%programlisting.content;`	`%refinline.char.mix;`	`%screen.content;`
`%tbl.entry.mdl;`	`%title.char.mix;`	

Description

GlossTerm identifies a term that appears in a **Glossary** or **GlossList**. This element occurs in two very different places: it is both an inline, and a structure element of a **GlossEntry**. As an inline, it identifies a term defined in a glossary, and may point to it. Within a **GlossEntry**, it identifies the term defined by that particular entry.

Processing expectations

As an inline, **GlossTerms** frequently get special typographic treatment, such as italics. In an online environment, they may also form a link (explicitly or implicitly) to the corresponding definition in a glossary.

GlossTerms must not be nested within other **GlossTerms**. Because DocBook is harmonizing towards XML, this restriction is difficult to enforce with the DTD. The processing of nested **GlossTerms** is undefined.

As part of a **GlossEntry**, **GlossTerms** are usually set as block and separated from the definition.

4.0 *Future Changes*

The **InterfaceDefinition** element will be discarded in DocBook V4.0. It will no longer be available in the content model of this element.

Attributes

BaseForm

`BaseForm`, if specified, contains the root form of the word identified as a **GlossTerm**. If unspecified, the content of **GlossTerm** element should be used. `BaseForm` allows sorting, collating, and indexing to work properly even when different parts of speech are identifed as **GlossTerms**. For example, `<glossterm>sort</glossterm>` and `<glossterm baseform="sort">sorting</glossterm>`.

Linkend

`Linkend` points to a related element, generally the **GlossEntry** that defines it.

See Also

FirstTerm

Examples

For examples, see **FirstTerm**, **Glossary**, **GlossList**.

Graphic—A displayed graphical object (not an inline)

Synopsis

Declared Content

```
Graphic ::=
CDATA
```

Attributes Name	Common attributes **Type**	**Default**
Width	NUTOKEN	*None*
SrcCredit	CDATA	*None*
Scale	NUMBER	*None*
Format	*Enumerated notation:*	*None*
	BMP	
	CGM-BINARY	
	CGM-CHAR	
	CGM-CLEAR	
	DITROFF	
	DVI	
	EPS	
	EQN	
	FAX	
	GIF	
	GIF87a	

Name	Type	Default
Format (cont.)	GIF89a IGES JPEG JPG linespecific PCX PIC PS SGML TBL TEX TIFF WMF WPG	
Align	*Enumeration:* Center Left Right	*None*
Scalefit	NUMBER	*None*
Depth	NUTOKEN	*None*
EntityRef	ENTITY	*None*
FileRef	CDATA	*None*
Parameter Entities		
`%admon.mix;`	`%bookcomponent.content;`	`%component.mix;`
`%divcomponent.mix;`	`%equation.content;`	`%example.mix;`
`%figure.mix;`	`%footnote.mix;`	`%glossdef.mix;`
`%indexdivcomponent.mix;`	`%informal.class;`	`%inlineequation.content;`
`%para.mix;`	`%qandaset.mix;`	`%refcomponent.mix;`
`%sidebar.mix;`	`%tabentry.mix;`	`%tbl.entry.mdl;`
`%tbl.table-main.mdl;`	`%tbl.table.mdl;`	

Description

This element contains graphical data, or a pointer to an external entity containing graphical data. One of the deficiencies of the DocBook **Graphic** element is that there is no way to specify an alternate text description of the graphic. This has been rectified by the introduction of **MediaObject**.

Processing expectations

Formatted as a displayed block.

There are several ways to provide content for a **Graphic**. It is best to use only one of these methods. However, if multiple graphic sources are provided, the processing expectations are as follows: element content should be used in favor of either `EntityRef` or `FileRef` and `EntityRef` should be used in favor of `FileRef`.

4.0 *Future Changes*

In DocBook V4.0, **Graphic** will be declared `EMPTY`. This change will require that any embedded graphic content be stored outside the SGML source and pointed to with an `EntityRef` or `FileRef` attribute.

5.0 *Future Changes*

In DocBook V5.0, **Graphic** will be discarded. At that time, graphics will have to be incorporated using **MediaObject** or **InlineMediaObject**.

Attributes

Align

`Align` specifies the horizontal alignment of the graphic on the page or within the element that frames it.

Depth

`Depth` specifies the desired depth (vertical distance, at least in horizontal writing systems) of the image.

EntityRef

`EntityRef` identifies the general entity which contains (or points to) the content of the graphic.

FileRef

`FileRef` specifies the name of the file which contains the content of the graphic.

Format

`Format` identifies the format of the graphic content. The `Format` must be a defined notation.

Scale

`Scale` specifies integer representing a percentage scaling factor (retaining the relative dimensions of the original graphic). If unspecified, the value 100 (100%) is assumed.

Scalefit

If `ScaleFit` has the value 1 (true), then the graphic is to be scaled (uniformly) to the specified width or depth. The default value of 0 (false) indicates that the image will not be scaled to fit (although it may still be scaled by the `Scale` attribute).

SrcCredit

`SrcCredit` contains details about the source of the **Graphic**.

Width

`Width` indicates the width of the graphic.

See Also

Alt, **AudioObject**, **Caption**, **ImageObject**, **InlineGraphic**, **InlineMediaObject**, **MediaObject**, **TextObject**, **VideoObject**

Examples

```
<!DOCTYPE figure PUBLIC "-//OASIS//DTD DocBook V3.1//EN">
<figure><title>Notre Dame Cathedral</title>
<graphic srccredit="Norman Walsh, 1998" fileref="figures/notredame">
</graphic>
</figure>
```

Figure 1. Notre Dame Cathedral

For additional examples, see also **Equation**, **Figure**, **GraphicCO**, **InformalEquation**, **InlineEquation**, **ScreenShot**.

GraphicCO—A graphic that contains callout areas

Synopsis

<table>
<tr><td colspan="3">Content Model
<code>GraphicCO ::=</code>
<code>(AreaSpec,Graphic,CalloutList*)</code></td></tr>
<tr><td>Attributes</td><td colspan="2">Common attributes</td></tr>
<tr><td colspan="3">Parameter Entities</td></tr>
<tr><td><code>%admon.mix;</code></td><td><code>%bookcomponent.content;</code></td><td><code>%component.mix;</code></td></tr>
<tr><td><code>%divcomponent.mix;</code></td><td><code>%example.mix;</code></td><td><code>%figure.mix;</code></td></tr>
<tr><td><code>%footnote.mix;</code></td><td><code>%glossdef.mix;</code></td><td><code>%indexdivcomponent.mix;</code></td></tr>
<tr><td><code>%informal.class;</code></td><td><code>%para.mix;</code></td><td><code>%qandaset.mix;</code></td></tr>
<tr><td><code>%refcomponent.mix;</code></td><td><code>%sidebar.mix;</code></td><td></td></tr>
</table>

Description

Callouts, such as numbered bullets, are an annotation mechanism. In an online system, these bullets are frequently "hot," and clicking on them sends you to the corresponding annotation.

A **GraphicCO** is a wrapper around an **AreaSpec** and a **Graphic**. An **AreaSpec** identifies the locations (coordinates) on the **Graphic** in which the callouts occur. The **GraphicCO** may also contain the list of annotations in a **CalloutList**, although the **CalloutList** may also occur outside of the wrapper, elsewhere in the document.

Processing expectations

Formatted as a displayed block.

The mandatory processing expectations of a **GraphicCO** are minimal: a system is expected to render the graphic, if possible, and the callout list, if present.

In online environments, the processing system may be able to instantiate the linking relationships between the callout marks on the graphic and the annotations. For example, an HTML presentation system might use the coordinate information to construct a client-side image map. Some processing systems may even be able to go a step further and generate the callout marks automatically from the coordinate information. But this level of sophistication is not mandatory.

5.0 *Future Changes*

In DocBook V5.0, **GraphicCO** will be discarded. In its place, use **MediaObjectCO**.

See Also

AreaSpec, **CalloutList**, **CO**, **ImageObjectCO**, **MediaObjectCO**, **ProgramListingCO**, **ScreenCO**

Examples

```
<!DOCTYPE graphicco PUBLIC "-//OASIS//DTD DocBook V3.1//EN">
<graphicco>
<areaspec units="calspair">
  <areaset id="oneway" coords="">
    <area id="oneway1" coords="300 400">
    <area id="oneway2" coords="325 340">
  </areaset>
  <area id="myhouse" coords="425 590">
</areaspec>
<graphic fileref="http://somemap.site.com/EARTH?USA?MA?AMHERST"></graphic>
</graphicco>
```

Group—A group of elements in a **CmdSynopsis**

Synopsis

Content Model
`Group ::=`
`((Arg|Group|Option|SynopFragmentRef|Replaceable|SBR)+)`		

Attributes **Name**	Common attributes **Type**	**Default**
Rep	*Enumeration:* Norepeat Repeat	"Norepeat"
Choice	*Enumeration:* Opt Optmult Plain Req Reqmult	"Opt"

Description

A **Group** surrounds several related items. Usually, they are grouped because they are mutually exclusive. The user is expected to select one of the items.

Processing expectations

Formatted inline. The additional processing expectations of a **Group** are significant. For a complete discussion, see **CmdSynopsis**.

- Multiple arguments within a group are considered exclusive and are separated by vertical bars.
- Brackets are used to distinguish between optional, required, or plain arguments. Usually square brackets are placed around optional arguments, *[-f | -g]*, and curly brackets are placed around required arguments, *{-f | -g}*. Plain arguments are required, but are not decorated with brackets.
- Repeatable arguments are followed by an ellipsis.

4.0 *Future Changes*

The `OptMult` and `ReqMult` values for the `Choice` attribute will be removed in DocBook V4.0. Use the `Rep` attribute instead to indicate that the choice is repeatable.

Attributes

Choice

`Choice` indicates whether the **Arg** is required (`Req` or `Plain`) or optional (`Opt`). Arguments identified as `Plain` are required, but are shown without additional decoration. The `OptMult` and `ReqMult` choices will be removed in DocBook V4.0; use the `Rep` attribute instead.

Rep

A `Rep` value of `Repeat` indicates that the **Group** is reapeatable. This is frequently rendered with an ellipsis.

See Also

Arg, **CmdSynopsis**, **RefSynopsisDiv**, **SBR**, **SynopFragment**, **SynopFragmentRef**

Examples

For examples, see **CmdSynopsis**, **SynopFragment**.

GUIButton—The text on a button in a GUI

Synopsis

Mixed Content Model

```
GUIButton ::=
((#PCDATA|Replaceable|InlineGraphic|InlineMediaObject|IndexTerm|
  Accel)+)
```

Attributes	Common attributes	
Name	**Type**	**Default**
MoreInfo	*Enumeration:* None RefEntry	"None"

Parameter Entities		
`%cptr.char.mix;`	`%ndxterm.char.mix;`	`%para.char.mix;`
`%programlisting.content;`	`%refinline.char.mix;`	`%refname.char.mix;`
`%screen.content;`	`%tbl.entry.mdl;`	`%tech.char.class;`
`%title.char.mix;`		

Description

GUIButton identifies the text that appears on a button in a graphical user interface.

Processing expectations

Formatted inline. The `MoreInfo` attribute can help generate a link or query to retrieve additional information.

Attributes

MoreInfo

If `MoreInfo` is set to `RefEntry`, it implies that a **RefEntry** exists which further describes the **GUIButton**.

See Also

Accel, **GUIIcon**, **GUILabel**, **GUIMenu**, **GUIMenuItem**, **GUISubmenu**, **KeyCap**, **KeyCode**, **KeyCombo**, **KeySym**, **MenuChoice**, **MouseButton**, **Shortcut**

Examples

```
<!DOCTYPE para PUBLIC "-//OASIS//DTD DocBook V3.1//EN">
<para>
The exact text of the <guilabel>Legend</> and other labels on the
graph is dependent upon the language of the current locale.  Likewise,
the text of the <guibutton>OK</> button and other buttons may vary.
The <guiicon><inlinegraphic fileref="figures/legend"></inlinegraphic></guiicon>
icon and the other icons on the left side of the display may be
configured by the local administrator, but they are not
generally expected to vary from locale to locale.
</para>
```

The exact text of the *Legend* and other labels on the graph is dependent upon the language of the current locale. Likewise, the text of the *OK* button and other buttons may vary. The icon and the other icons on the left side of the display may be configured by the local administrator, but they are not generally expected to vary from locale to locale.

For additional examples, see also **GUIIcon**, **GUILabel**.

GUIIcon—Graphic and/or text appearing as a icon in a GUI

Synopsis

Mixed Content Model

```
GUIIcon ::=
((#PCDATA|Replaceable|InlineGraphic|InlineMediaObject|IndexTerm|
  Accel)+)
```

Attributes **Name**	Common attributes **Type**	**Default**
MoreInfo	*Enumeration:* None RefEntry	"None"

Parameter Entities		
`%cptr.char.mix;`	`%ndxterm.char.mix;`	`%para.char.mix;`
`%programlisting.content;`	`%refinline.char.mix;`	`%refname.char.mix;`
`%screen.content;`	`%tbl.entry.mdl;`	`%tech.char.class;`
`%title.char.mix;`		

Description

GUIIcon identifies a graphic or text icon that appears in a graphical user interface.

Processing expectations

Formatted inline. The `MoreInfo` attribute can help generate a link or query to retrieve additional information.

Attributes

MoreInfo

If `MoreInfo` is set to `RefEntry`, it implies that a **RefEntry** exists which further describes the **GUIIcon**.

See Also

Accel, **GUIButton**, **GUILabel**, **GUIMenu**, **GUIMenuItem**, **GUISubmenu**, **KeyCap**, **KeyCode**, **KeyCombo**, **KeySym**, **MenuChoice**, **MouseButton**, **Shortcut**

Examples

```
<!DOCTYPE para PUBLIC "-//OASIS//DTD DocBook V3.1//EN">
<para>
The exact text of the <guilabel>Legend</> and other labels on the
graph is dependent upon the language of the current locale.  Likewise,
the text of the <guibutton>OK</> button and other buttons may vary.
The <guiicon><inlinegraphic fileref="figures/legend"></inlinegraphic></guiicon>
icon and the other icons on the left side of the display may be
configured by the local administrator, but they are not
generally expected to vary from locale to locale.
</para>
```

The exact text of the *Legend* and other labels on the graph is dependent upon the language of the current locale. Likewise, the text of the *OK* button and other buttons may vary. The icon and the other icons on the left side of the display may be configured by the local administrator, but they are not generally expected to vary from locale to locale.

For additional examples, see also **GUIButton**, **GUILabel**.

GUILabel—The text of a label in a GUI

Synopsis

Mixed Content Model

```
GUILabel ::=
((#PCDATA|Replaceable|InlineGraphic|InlineMediaObject|IndexTerm|
  Accel)+)
```

Attributes **Name**	Common attributes **Type**	 **Default**
MoreInfo	*Enumeration:* None RefEntry	"None"

Parameter Entities		
%cptr.char.mix;	%ndxterm.char.mix;	%para.char.mix;
%programlisting.content;	%refinline.char.mix;	%refname.char.mix;
%screen.content;	%tbl.entry.mdl;	%tech.char.class;
%title.char.mix;		

Description

GUILabel identifies text that appears as a label in a graphical user interface.

What constitutes a label may vary from application to application. In general, any text that appears in a GUI may be considered a label, for example a message in a dialog box or a window title.

Processing expectations

Formatted inline. The `MoreInfo` attribute can help generate a link or query to retrieve additional information.

Attributes

MoreInfo

If `MoreInfo` is set to `RefEntry`, it implies that a **RefEntry** exists which further describes the **GUILabel**.

See Also

Accel, **GUIButton**, **GUIIcon**, **GUIMenu**, **GUIMenuItem**, **GUISubmenu**, **KeyCap**, **KeyCode**, **KeyCombo**, **KeySym**, **MenuChoice**, **MouseButton**, **Shortcut**

Examples

```
<!DOCTYPE para PUBLIC "-//OASIS//DTD DocBook V3.1//EN">
<para>
The exact text of the <guilabel>Legend</> and other labels on the
graph is dependent upon the language of the current locale.  Likewise,
the text of the <guibutton>OK</> button and other buttons may vary.
The <guiicon><inlinegraphic fileref="figures/legend"></inlinegraphic></guiicon>
icon and the other icons on the left side of the display may be
configured by the local administrator, but they are not
generally expected to vary from locale to locale.
</para>
```

The exact text of the *Legend* and other labels on the graph is dependent upon the language of the current locale. Likewise, the text of the *OK* button and other buttons may vary. The icon and the other icons on the left side of the display may be configured by the local administrator, but they are not generally expected to vary from locale to locale.

For additional examples, see also **GUIButton**, **GUIIcon**.

GUIMenu—The name of a menu in a GUI

Synopsis

Mixed Content Model GUIMenu ::= ((#PCDATA|Replaceable|InlineGraphic|InlineMediaObject|IndexTerm| Accel)+)		
Attributes	Common attributes	
Name	**Type**	**Default**
MoreInfo	*Enumeration:* None RefEntry	"None"
Parameter Entities		
%cptr.char.mix;	%ndxterm.char.mix;	%para.char.mix;
%programlisting.con- tent;	%refinline.char.mix;	%refname.char.mix;
%screen.content;	%tbl.entry.mdl;	%tech.char.class;
%title.char.mix;		

Description

GUIMenu identifies a menu name in a graphical user interface. In particular, this is distinct from a menu item (**GUIMenuItem**), which is terminal, and a submenu (**GUISubmenu**), which occurs as a selection from a menu.

Processing expectations

Formatted inline. The `MoreInfo` attribute can help generate a link or query to retrieve additional information.

Attributes

MoreInfo

If `MoreInfo` is set to `RefEntry`, it implies that a **RefEntry** exists which further describes the **GUIMenu**.

See Also

Accel, **GUIButton**, **GUIIcon**, **GUILabel**, **GUIMenuItem**, **GUISubmenu**, **KeyCap**, **KeyCode**, **KeyCombo**, **KeySym**, **MenuChoice**, **MouseButton**, **Shortcut**

Examples

```
<!DOCTYPE para PUBLIC "-//OASIS//DTD DocBook V3.1//EN">
<para>
You can exit from GNU Emacs with the keyboard shortcut
<keycombo><keysym>C-x</keysym><keysym>C-c</keysym></keycombo>
or by selecting <guimenuitem>Exit Emacs</> from the <guimenu>Files</> menu.
</para>
```

You can exit from GNU Emacs with the keyboard shortcut `C-c+C-x` or by selecting *Exit Emacs* from the *Files* menu.

For additional examples, see also **Accel**, **GUIMenuItem**, **GUISubmenu**, **MenuChoice**, **Shortcut**.

GUIMenuItem—The name of a terminal menu item in a GUI

Synopsis

Mixed Content Model

```
GUIMenuItem ::=
((#PCDATA|Replaceable|InlineGraphic|InlineMediaObject|IndexTerm|
  Accel)+)
```

Attributes	Common attributes	
Name	**Type**	**Default**
MoreInfo	*Enumeration:* None RefEntry	"None"

Parameter Entities

%cptr.char.mix;	%ndxterm.char.mix;	%para.char.mix;
%programlisting.con-tent;	%refinline.char.mix;	%refname.char.mix;
%screen.content;	%tbl.entry.mdl;	%tech.char.class;
%title.char.mix;		

Description

GUIMenuItem identifies a terminal selection from a menu in a graphical user interface. In particular, this is distinct from a menu (**GUIMenu**) and a submenu (**GUISubmenu**). The distinction between a **GUIMenuItem** and a **GUISubmenu** is simply whether or not the selection is terminal or leads to an additional submenu.

Processing expectations

Formatted inline. The `MoreInfo` attribute can help generate a link or query to retrieve additional information.

Attributes

MoreInfo

If `MoreInfo` is set to `RefEntry`, it implies that a **RefEntry** exists which further describes the **GUIMenuItem**.

See Also

Accel, **GUIButton**, **GUIIcon**, **GUILabel**, **GUIMenu**, **GUISubmenu**, **KeyCap**, **KeyCode**, **KeyCombo**, **KeySym**, **MenuChoice**, **MouseButton**, **Shortcut**

Examples

```
<!DOCTYPE para PUBLIC "-//OASIS//DTD DocBook V3.1//EN">
<para>
You can exit from GNU Emacs with the keyboard shortcut
<keycombo><keysym>C-c</keysym><keysym>C-x</keysym></keycombo>
or by selecting <guimenuitem>Exit Emacs</> from
the <guimenu>Files</> menu.
</para>
```

You can exit from GNU Emacs with the keyboard shortcut `C-c+C-x` or by selecting *Exit Emacs* from the *Files* menu.

For additional examples, see also **Accel**, **Action**, **GUIMenu**, **GUISubmenu**, **MenuChoice**, **Shortcut**.

GUISubmenu—The name of a submenu in a GUI

Synopsis

Mixed Content Model
`GUISubmenu ::=`
`((#PCDATA|Replaceable|InlineGraphic|InlineMediaObject|IndexTerm|Accel)+)`		

Attributes **Name**	Common attributes **Type**	**Default**
MoreInfo	*Enumeration:* None RefEntry	"None"

Parameter Entities
`%cptr.char.mix;`
`%programlisting.content;`
`%screen.content;`
`%title.char.mix;`
	
	`%ndxterm.char.mix;`
	`%refinline.char.mix;`
	`%tbl.entry.mdl;`
		
		`%para.char.mix;`
		`%refname.char.mix;`
		`%tech.char.class;`

Description

The name of a submenu in a graphical user interface is identified by the **GUISubmenu** element. A submenu is a menu invoked from another menu that leads either to terminal items (**GUIMenuItems**) or additional submenus.

Processing expectations

Formatted inline. The `MoreInfo` attribute can help generate a link or query to retrieve additional information.

Attributes

MoreInfo

If `MoreInfo` is set to `RefEntry`, it implies that a **RefEntry** exists which further describes the **GUISubMenu**.

See Also

Accel, **GUIButton**, **GUIIcon**, **GUILabel**, **GUIMenu**, **GUIMenuItem**, **KeyCap**, **KeyCode**, **KeyCombo**, **KeySym**, **MenuChoice**, **MouseButton**, **Shortcut**

Examples

```
<!DOCTYPE para PUBLIC "-//OASIS//DTD DocBook V3.1//EN">
<para>
In GNU Emacs, the <guimenuitem>Print Buffer</guimenuitem> command is
located off of the <guisubmenu>Print</guisubmenu> submenu of the
<guimenu>Tools</guimenu> menu.
</para>
```

In GNU Emacs, the *Print Buffer* command is located off of the *Print* submenu of the *Tools* menu.

Hardware—A physical part of a computer system

Synopsis

Mixed Content Model

```
Hardware ::=
((#PCDATA|Link|OLink|ULink|Action|Application|ClassName|Command|
  ComputerOutput|Database|Email|EnVar|ErrorCode|ErrorName|
  ErrorType|Filename|Function|GUIButton|GUIIcon|GUILabel|GUIMenu|
  GUIMenuItem|GUISubmenu|Hardware|Interface|InterfaceDefinition|
  KeyCap|KeyCode|KeyCombo|KeySym|Literal|Constant|Markup|
  MediaLabel|MenuChoice|MouseButton|MsgText|Option|Optional|
  Parameter|Prompt|Property|Replaceable|ReturnValue|SGMLTag|
  StructField|StructName|Symbol|SystemItem|Token|Type|UserInput|
  VarName|Anchor|Comment|Subscript|Superscript|InlineGraphic|
  InlineMediaObject|IndexTerm)+)
```

Attributes	Common attributes	
Name	**Type**	**Default**
MoreInfo	*Enumeration:* None RefEntry	"None"

Parameter Entities

`%cptr.char.mix;`	`%ndxterm.char.mix;`	`%para.char.mix;`
`%programlisting.content;`	`%refinline.char.mix;`	`%refname.char.mix;`
`%screen.content;`	`%tbl.entry.mdl;`	`%tech.char.class;`
`%title.char.mix;`		

Description

Hardware identifies some physical component of a computer system. Even though DocBook provides a broad range of inlines for describing the various software components of a system, it provides relatively few for describing hardware.

If you need to identify a number of different hardware components, you may wish to consider extending DocBook, or at least using the `Role` attribute to further classify **Hardware**.

Processing expectations

Formatted inline. The `MoreInfo` attribute can help generate a link or query to retrieve additional information.

4.0 *Future Changes*

In DocBook V4.0, the content model of **Hardware** will be constrained to `(#PCDATA | Replaceable | InlineGraphic)`.

Attributes

MoreInfo

If `MoreInfo` is set to `RefEntry`, it implies that a **RefEntry** exists which further describes the **Hardware**.

See Also

Application, **Database**, **Filename**, **MediaLabel**, **ProductName**

Examples

```
<!DOCTYPE para PUBLIC "-//OASIS//DTD DocBook V3.1//EN">
<para>
The <acronym>IRQ</acronym> of the <hardware>SCSI Controller</hardware>
can be set to 7, 11, or 15.  The factory default setting is 7.
</para>
```

The IRQ of the SCSI Controller can be set to 7, 11, or 15. The factory default setting is 7.

Highlights—A summary of the main points of the discussed component

Synopsis

Content Model

```
Highlights ::=
((CalloutList|GlossList|ItemizedList|OrderedList|SegmentedList|
  SimpleList|VariableList|Caution|Important|Note|Tip|Warning|
  FormalPara|Para|SimPara|IndexTerm)+)
```

Attributes	Common attributes	
Parameter Entities		
%bookcomponent.content;	%component.mix;	%divcomponent.mix;
%genobj.class;	%qandaset.mix;	%refcomponent.mix;
%sidebar.mix;		

Description

Highlights are generally presented at the beginning of a component and offer some sort of summary of the main points that will be discussed.

Processing expectations

Formatted as a displayed block. Highlights often contain some sort of list.

See Also

Abstract, **BlockQuote**, **Epigraph**, **Sidebar**

Examples

```
<!DOCTYPE chapter PUBLIC "-//OASIS//DTD DocBook V3.1//EN">
<chapter><title>Example Chapter</title>
<highlights>
<para>
This chapter will teach you
<itemizedlist>
<listitem>
<para>
How to disassemble an automobile.
</para>
</listitem>
<listitem>
<para>
How to properly carry the component pieces.
</para>
</listitem>
<listitem>
<para>
How to reassemble an automobile in a standard telephone booth.
</para>
</listitem>
</itemizedlist>
</para>
</highlights>
<para>&hellip</para>
</chapter>
```

Holder—The name of the individual or organization that holds a copyright

Synopsis

Mixed Content Model
`Holder ::=`
`((#PCDATA|Link|OLink|ULink|Emphasis|Trademark|Replaceable|Comment|`
`  Subscript|Superscript|InlineGraphic|InlineMediaObject|IndexTerm)+)`	

Attributes	Common attributes

Description

Holder in **Copyright** identifies an individual or organization that asserts a copyright on the document.

Processing expectations

The formatting of **Holder** depends on the formatting of its parent **Copyright**. In the case of a **Copyright** with multiple holders, additional punctuation may need to be generated when **Holder** is processed.

Examples

For examples, see **Bibliography**, **BiblioSet**, **BookInfo**, **Copyright**.

Honorific—The title of a person

Synopsis

Mixed Content Model
`Honorific ::=`
`((#PCDATA|Link|OLink|ULink|Emphasis|Trademark|Replaceable|Comment|`
`  Subscript|Superscript|InlineGraphic|InlineMediaObject|IndexTerm)+)`	

Attributes	Common attributes
Parameter Entities `%bibliocomponent.mix;`	 `%person.ident.mix;`

Description

An **Honorific** occurs in the name of an individual. It is the honorific title of the individual, such as "Dr.," "Mr.," or "Ms."

Processing expectations

Formatted inline. In an **Address**, this element may inherit the verbatim qualities of an address.

On some systems, **Honorific** may generate the trailing period automatically.

See Also

Affiliation, **FirstName**, **Lineage**, **OtherName**, **Surname**

Examples

For examples, see **Author**, **AuthorGroup**.

ImageData—Pointer to external image data

Synopsis

Content Model
```
ImageData ::=
EMPTY
```

Attributes	Common attributes	
Name	**Type**	**Default**
Width	NUTOKEN	*None*
SrcCredit	CDATA	*None*
Scale	NUMBER	*None*
Format	*Enumeration:* BMP CGM-BINARY CGM-CHAR CGM-CLEAR DITROFF DVI EPS EQN FAX GIF GIF87a GIF89a IGES JPEG JPG linespecific PCX PIC PS SGML TBL TEX TIFF WMF WPG	*None*
Scalefit	NUMBER	*None*
Align	*Enumeration:* Center Left Right	*None*
Depth	NUTOKEN	*None*
EntityRef	ENTITY	*None*
FileRef	CDATA	*None*

Description

This element points to an external entity containing graphical image data.

Processing expectations

May be formatted inline or as a displayed block, depending on context. Render the image.

There are two ways to provide content for **ImageData**: `EntityRef` or `FileRef`. It is best to use only one of these methods, however, if multiple sources are provided, `EntityRef` will be used in favor of `FileRef`.

Attributes

Align

`Align` specifies the horizontal alignment of the image data on the page or within the element that frames it.

Depth

`Depth` specifies the desired depth (vertical distance, at least in horizontal writing systems) of the image data.

EntityRef

`EntityRef` identifies the general entity which points to the content of the image data.

FileRef

`FileRef` specifies the name of the file which contains the content of the image data.

Format

`Format` identifies the format of the image data. The `Format` must be a defined notation.

Scale

`Scale` specifies integer representing a percentage scaling factor (retaining the relative dimensions of the original image data). If unspecified, the value 100 (100%) is assumed.

Scalefit

If `ScaleFit` has the value 1 (true), then the image data is to be scaled (uniformly) to the specified width or depth. The default value of 0 (false) indicates that the image will not be scaled to fit (although it may still be scaled by the `Scale` attribute).

SrcCredit

`SrcCredit` contains details about the source of the image data.

Width

Width indicates the width of the graphic.

Examples

For examples, see **ImageObject**, **InformalFigure**, **InlineMediaObject**, **MediaObject-CO**, **VideoObject**.

ImageObject—A wrapper for image data and its associated meta-information

Synopsis

Content Model
`ImageObject ::=`
`(ObjectInfo?,ImageData)`	

Attributes	Common attributes
Parameter Entities `%mediaobject.mix;`	

Description

An **ImageObject** is a wrapper containing **ImageData** and its associated meta-information.

Processing expectations

May be formatted inline or as a displayed block, depending on context. It might not be rendered at all, depending on its placement within a **MediaObject** or **InlineMediaObject** and the constraints on the publishing system. For a more detailed description of the semantics involved, see **MediaObject**.

See Also

Alt, **AudioObject**, **Caption**, **Graphic**, **InlineGraphic**, **InlineMediaObject**, **MediaObject**, **TextObject**, **VideoObject**

Examples

```
<!DOCTYPE mediaobject PUBLIC "-//OASIS//DTD DocBook V3.1//EN">
<mediaobject>
<imageobject>
<imagedata fileref="figures/eiffeltower.eps" format="eps">
</imageobject>
<imageobject>
<imagedata fileref="figures/eiffeltower.gif" format="gif">
</imageobject>
```

```
<textobject>
<phrase>The Eiffel Tower</phrase>
</textobject>
<caption>
<para>Designed by Gustave Eiffel in 1889, The Eiffel Tower is one of the
most widely recognized buildings in the world.
</para>
</caption>
</mediaobject>
```

Designed by Gustave Eiffel in 1889, The Eiffel Tower is one of the most widely recognized buildings in the world.

For additional examples, see also **InformalFigure**, **InlineMediaObject**, **MediaObject-CO**, **VideoObject**.

ImageObjectCO—A wrapper for an image object with callouts

Synopsis

Content Model
`ImageObjectCO ::=`
`(AreaSpec,ImageObject,CalloutList*)`	

Attributes	Common attributes

Description

Callouts, such as numbered bullets, are an annotation mechanism. In an online system, these bullets are frequently "hot," and clicking on them navigates to the corresponding annotation.

A **ImageObjectCO** is a wrapper around an **AreaSpec** and an **ImageObject**. An **AreaSpec** identifies the locations (coordinates) on the image where the **Callouts** occur. The **ImageObjectCO** may also contain the list of annotations in a **CalloutList**, although the **CalloutList** may also occur outside of the wrapper, elsewhere in the document.

Processing expectations

Formatted as a displayed block. It may not be rendered at all, depending on its placement within the **MediaObject** that contains it and the constraints on the publishing system. For a more detailed description of the semantics involved, see **MediaObject**.

The mandatory processing expectations of a **ImageObjectCO** are minimal: a system is expected to render the image, if possible, and the callout list, if present.

In online environments, the processing system may be able to instantiate the linking relationships between the callout marks on the image and the annotations. For example, an HTML presentation system might use the coordinate information to construct a client-side image map. Some processing systems may even be able to go a step further and generate the callout marks automatically from the coordinate information. But this level of sophistication is not mandatory.

5.0 *Future Changes*

In DocBook V5.0, **ImageObjectCO** will be discarded. In its place, use **MediaObjectCO**.

See Also

AreaSpec, **CalloutList**, **CO**, **GraphicCO**, **MediaObjectCO**, **ProgramListingCO**, **ScreenCO**

Examples

For examples, see **MediaObjectCO**.

Important—An admonition set off from the text

Synopsis

Content Model

```
Important ::=
(Title?,
 (CalloutList|GlossList|ItemizedList|OrderedList|SegmentedList|
  SimpleList|VariableList|LiteralLayout|ProgramListing|
  ProgramListingCO|Screen|ScreenCO|ScreenShot|Synopsis|
  CmdSynopsis|FuncSynopsis|FormalPara|Para|SimPara|Address|
  BlockQuote|Graphic|GraphicCO|MediaObject|MediaObjectCO|
  InformalEquation|InformalExample|InformalFigure|InformalTable|
  Equation|Example|Figure|Table|Procedure|Sidebar|Anchor|
  BridgeHead|Comment|IndexTerm)+)
```

Attributes	Common attributes	
Parameter Entities		
%admon.class;	%admon.exclusion;	%bookcomponent.content;
%component.mix;	%divcomponent.mix;	%highlights.mix;
%legalnotice.mix;	%para.mix;	%refcomponent.mix;
%sidebar.mix;	%tabentry.mix;	%tbl.entry.mdl;
%textobject.mix;		

Description

Important is an admonition set off from the main text.

In some types of documentation, the semantics of admonitions are clearly defined (**Caution** might imply the possibility of harm to equipment whereas **Warning** might imply harm to a person), but DocBook makes no such assertions.

Processing expectations

Formatted as a displayed block. It often outputs the generated text "Important" or some other visible indication of the type of admonition, especially if a **Title** is not present. Sometimes outputs a graphical icon or other symbol as well.

See Also

Caution, **Note**, **Tip**, **Warning**

Examples

```
<!DOCTYPE important PUBLIC "-//OASIS//DTD DocBook V3.1//EN">
<important>
<para>
No user-servicable parts inside. Breaking this seal voids all warranties.
```

```
</para>
</important>
```

IMPORTANT No user-servicable parts inside. Breaking this seal voids all warranties.

Index—An index

Synopsis

Content Model
`Index ::=`
`((DocInfo?,Title,Subtitle?,TitleAbbrev?)?,`
` (CalloutList|GlossList|ItemizedList|OrderedList|SegmentedList|`
`  SimpleList|VariableList|Caution|Important|Note|Tip|Warning|`
`  LiteralLayout|ProgramListing|ProgramListingCO|Screen|ScreenCO|`
`  ScreenShot|Synopsis|CmdSynopsis|FuncSynopsis|FormalPara|Para|`
`  SimPara|Address|BlockQuote|Graphic|GraphicCO|MediaObject|`
`  MediaObjectCO|InformalEquation|InformalExample|InformalFigure|`
`  InformalTable|Equation|Example|Figure|Table|MsgSet|Procedure|`
`  Sidebar|QandASet|Anchor|BridgeHead|Comment|Highlights|Abstract|`
`  AuthorBlurb|Epigraph|IndexTerm)*,`
` (IndexDiv*|IndexEntry*))`		

Attributes	Common attributes	
Parameter Entities `%index.class;`	`%nav.class;`	`%partcontent.mix;`

Description

An **Index** contains the formatted index of a document. An index may begin with introductory material, followed by any number of **IndexEntry**s or **IndexDiv**s.

Processing expectations

Formatted as a displayed block. An **Index** in a **Book** frequently causes a forced page break in print media.

In many processing systems, indexes are generated automatically or semiautomatically and never appear instantiated as DocBook markup.

Examples

```
<!DOCTYPE index PUBLIC "-//OASIS//DTD DocBook V3.1//EN">
<index><title>Index</title>
<indexdiv><title>D</title>
<indexentry>
  <primaryie>database (bibliographic), 253, 255</primaryie>
  <secondaryie>structure, 255</secondaryie>
  <secondaryie>tools, 259</secondaryie>
</indexentry>
<indexentry>
```

```
  <primaryie>dates (language specific), 179</primaryie>
</indexentry>
<indexentry>
  <primaryie>DC fonts, <emphasis>172</emphasis>, 177</primaryie>
  <secondaryie>Math fonts, 177</secondaryie>
</indexentry>
</indexdiv>
</index>

<!DOCTYPE index PUBLIC "-//OASIS//DTD DocBook V3.1//EN">
<index>
<indexentry>
  <primaryie>Example</primaryie>
  <secondaryie>Chapter</secondaryie>
  <seeie>Example Chapter</seeie>
</indexentry>

<indexentry>
  <primaryie>Example Chapter, 35-48</primaryie>
  <seealsoie>Examples</seealsoie>
</indexentry>

<indexentry>
  <primaryie>Examples, 18, 36, 72-133</primaryie>
</indexentry>

</index>
```

IndexDiv—A division in an index

Synopsis

Content Model

```
IndexDiv ::=
((Title,Subtitle?,TitleAbbrev?)?,
 ((ItemizedList|OrderedList|VariableList|SimpleList|LiteralLayout|
   ProgramListing|ProgramListingCO|Screen|ScreenCO|ScreenShot|
   Synopsis|CmdSynopsis|FuncSynopsis|FormalPara|Para|SimPara|
   Address|BlockQuote|Graphic|GraphicCO|MediaObject|MediaObjectCO|
   InformalEquation|InformalExample|InformalFigure|InformalTable|
   Anchor|Comment|Link|OLink|ULink)*,
  (IndexEntry+|SegmentedList)))
```

Attributes	Common attributes

Description

An **IndexDiv** identifies a section of an **Index**. An index might be divided into sections in order to group entries, usually alphabetically.

An index may contain any number of **IndexEntry** or **IndexDiv** elements, but it cannot contain a mixture of both at the same level.

Processing expectations

Formatted as a displayed block.

Examples

For examples, see **Index**.

IndexEntry—An entry in an index

Synopsis

Content Model	
`IndexEntry ::= (PrimaryIE, (SeeIE|SeeAlsoIE)*, (SecondaryIE, (SeeIE|SeeAlsoIE|TertiaryIE)*)*)`	
Attributes	Common attributes

```
IndexEntry ::=
(PrimaryIE,
 (SeeIE|SeeAlsoIE)*,
 (SecondaryIE,
  (SeeIE|SeeAlsoIE|TertiaryIE)*)*)
```

Description

An **IndexEntry** wraps all of the index terms associated with a particular primary index term. This includes an arbitrary list of secondary and tertiary elements as well as See and SeeAlso elements.

Processing expectations

Formatted as a displayed block. A rendered index usually places secondary items under primary items and tertiary items under secondary.

See Also

IndexTerm, **Primary**, **PrimaryIE**, **Secondary**, **SecondaryIE**, **See**, **SeeAlso**, **SeeAlsoIE**, **SeeIE**, **Tertiary**, **TertiaryIE**

Examples

For examples, see **Index**.

IndexTerm—A wrapper for terms to be indexed

Synopsis

Content Model

```
IndexTerm ::=
(Primary,
 ((Secondary,
   ((Tertiary,
     (See|SeeAlso+)?)|
    See|SeeAlso+)?)|
  See|SeeAlso+)?)
```

Attributes	Common attributes	
Name	**Type**	**Default**
Significance	*Enumeration:* Normal Preferred	"Normal"
StartRef	IDREF	*Content reference*
Pagenum	CDATA	*None*
Class	*Enumeration:* EndOfRange Singular StartOfRange	*None*
Scope	*Enumeration:* All Global Local	*None*
Zone	IDREFS	*None*

Parameter Entities		
`%admon.mix;`	`%bibliocomponent.mix;`	`%bookcomponent.content;`
`%component.mix;`	`%cptr.char.mix;`	`%divcomponent.mix;`
`%docinfo.char.mix;`	`%example.mix;`	`%figure.mix;`
`%glossdef.mix;`	`%highlights.exclusion;`	`%highlights.mix;`
`%legalnotice.mix;`	`%ndxterm.class;`	`%ndxterm.exclusion;`
`%para.char.mix;`	`%programlisting.content;`	`%qandaset.mix;`
`%refcomponent.mix;`	`%refinline.char.mix;`	`%screen.content;`
`%sidebar.mix;`	`%smallcptr.char.mix;`	`%tbl.entry.mdl;`
`%tbl.table.mdl;`	`%title.char.mix;`	`%ubiq.exclusion;`
`%ubiq.inclusion;`	`%ubiq.mix;`	`%word.char.mix;`

Description

IndexTerms identify text that is to be placed in the index. In the simplest case, the placement of the **IndexTerm** in the document identifies the location of the term in the text. In other words, the **IndexTerm** is placed in the flow of the document at the point where the **IndexEntry** in the **Index** should point. In other cases, attributes on **IndexTerm** are used to identify the location of the term in the text.

IndexTerms mark either a single point in the document or a range. A single point is marked with an **IndexTerm** placed in the text at the point of reference. There are two ways to identify a range of text:

- Place an **IndexTerm** at the beginning of the range with `Class` set to `StartOfRange` and give this term an `ID`. Place another **IndexTerm** at the end of the range with `StartRef` pointing to the `ID` of the starting **IndexTerm**. This second **IndexTerm** must be empty.

  The advantage of this method is that the range can span unbalanced element boundries.

- Place the **IndexTerm** anywhere you like and point to the element that contains the range of text you wish to index with the `Zone` attribute on the **IndexTerm**.

Note that `Zone` is defined as `IDREFS` so a single **IndexTerm** can point to multiple ranges.

The advantage of this method is that **IndexTerms** can be collected together or even stored totally outside the flow of the document (in the meta for example).

Processing expectations

IndexTerms are suppressed in the primary text flow, although they contribute to the population of an index and serve as anchors for cross references. Under no circumstances is the actual content of **IndexTerm** rendered in the primary flow.

It is possible to construct index terms that are difficult to parse at best and totally illogical at worst. Consider the following:

```
<indexterm class=startofrange zone="id1 id2">...</indexterm>
```

There is no way that this can fit into the semantics of an **IndexTerm**. Although it claims to be the start of a range, it does not have an `ID` for the end-of-range **IndexTerm** to point back to. In addition, it includes zoned terms, and mixing the two different methods for indicating a range in the same **IndexTerm** is probably a bad idea.

Attributes

Class

`Class` identifies the type of **IndexTerm**. If `StartRef` is supplied, the default for `Class` is `EndOfRange`, otherwise it is `Singular`.

Pagenum

`PageNum` indicates the page on which this index term occurs in some version of the printed document.

Scope

`Scope` identifies in which indexes the **IndexTerm** should appear. `Global` means the index for the whole collection of documents, `Local` means the index for this document only, and `All` means both indexes.

Significance

`Significance` specifies whether or not this **IndexTerm** is considered the most important location for information about the terms being indexed. Generally, `Preferred` **IndexTerms** get special typographic treatment in the **Index**.

StartRef

The use of `StartRef` implies a spanning index entry. `StartRef` is used on the term that defines the end of the span and points to the term which defines the beginning.

Zone

The use of `Zone` implies a spanning index entry. `Zone` holds the IDs of the elements to which it applies. The **IndexTerm** applies to the contents of the entire element(s) to which it points. If **Zone** is used, the phyiscal placement of the **IndexTerm** in the flow of the document *is irrelavant.*

See Also

IndexEntry, **Primary**, **PrimaryIE**, **Secondary**, **SecondaryIE**, **See**, **SeeAlso**, **SeeAlsoIE**, **SeeIE**, **Tertiary**, **TertiaryIE**

Examples

```
<!DOCTYPE para PUBLIC "-//OASIS//DTD DocBook V3.1//EN">
<para>
The Tiger<indexterm>
<primary>Big Cats</primary>
<secondary>Tigers</secondary></indexterm>
is a very large cat indeed.
</para>
```

The Tiger is a very large cat indeed.

```
<!DOCTYPE chapter PUBLIC "-//OASIS//DTD DocBook V3.1//EN">
<chapter><title>Example Chapter</title>

<!-- index term for "Example Chapter" is a span -->
<indexterm id="idxexchap" class=startofrange>
  <primary>Example Chapter</primary></indexterm>

<!-- index term for "Example Chapter" also cross references the
     "Examples" entry in the index -->
<indexterm><primary>Example Chapter</primary>
  <seealso>Examples</seealso></indexterm>

<!-- index term for "Chapter, Example" refers the reader to the entry
     under which the index term is actually listed, "Example Chapter" -->
<indexterm><primary>Chapter</primary><secondary>Example</secondary>
  <see>Example Chapter</see></indexterm>

<!-- other content -->

<!-- index term, end of "Example Chapter" span -->
<indexterm startref="idxexchap" class=endofrange>

<para>some content</para>
</chapter>
```

```
<!DOCTYPE chapter PUBLIC "-//OASIS//DTD DocBook V3.1//EN">
<chapter><title>Example Chapter</title>
<indexterm zone="a1"><primary>Network Configuration</primary></indexterm>
<!-- other content here -->
<sect1 id=a1><title>Configuring Your Network</title>
<para>&hellip;</para>
</sect1>
</chapter>
```

For additional examples, see also **Chapter**.

InformalEquation—A displayed mathematical equation without a title

Synopsis

Content Model		

`InformalEquation ::=`
`(Alt?,`
`(Graphic+|MediaObject+))`		

Attributes	Common attributes	
Parameter Entities		
`%admon.mix;`	`%bookcomponent.content;`	`%component.mix;`
`%divcomponent.mix;`	`%example.mix;`	`%figure.mix;`
`%footnote.mix;`	`%glossdef.mix;`	`%indexdivcomponent.mix;`
`%informal.class;`	`%para.mix;`	`%qandaset.mix;`
`%refcomponent.mix;`	`%sidebar.mix;`	

Description

An **InformalEquation** is usually a mathematical equation or a group of related mathematical equations.

Processing expectations

Formatted as a displayed block.

See Also

Equation, **Example**, **Figure**, **InformalExample**, **InformalFigure**, **InformalTable**, **InlineEquation**, **Subscript**, **Superscript**, **Table**

Examples

```
<!DOCTYPE para PUBLIC "-//OASIS//DTD DocBook V3.1//EN">
<para>
The equation
<informalequation>
  <alt>e^(pi*i) + 1 = 0</alt>
  <graphic fileref="figures/epi10"></graphic>
</informalequation>
is delightful because it joins together five of the most
important mathematical constants.
</para>
```

The equation

$$e^{\pi i} + 1 = 0$$

is delightful because it joins together five of the most important mathematical constants.

InformalExample—A displayed example without a title

Synopsis

Content Model

```
InformalExample ::=
((CalloutList|GlossList|ItemizedList|OrderedList|SegmentedList|
  SimpleList|VariableList|LiteralLayout|ProgramListing|
  ProgramListingCO|Screen|ScreenCO|ScreenShot|Synopsis|
  CmdSynopsis|FuncSynopsis|FormalPara|Para|SimPara|Address|
  BlockQuote|Graphic|GraphicCO|MediaObject|MediaObjectCO|
  InformalEquation|InformalExample|InformalFigure|InformalTable|
  IndexTerm)+)
```

Attributes Name	Common attributes Type	Default
Width	NUMBER	*None*

Parameter Entities

%admon.mix;	%bookcomponent.content;	%component.mix;
%divcomponent.mix;	%example.mix;	%figure.mix;
%footnote.mix;	%glossdef.mix;	%indexdivcomponent.mix;
%informal.class;	%para.mix;	%qandaset.mix;
%refcomponent.mix;	%sidebar.mix;	

Description

InformalExample is a wrapper for an example without a title. Examples often contain **ProgramListing**s or other large block elements.

Processing expectations

Formatted as a displayed block.

Attributes

Width

`Width` specifies the width (in characters) of the longest line in this **InformalExample** (formatters may use this value to determine scaling or rotation).

See Also

Equation, **Example**, **Figure**, **InformalEquation**, **InformalFigure**, **InformalTable**, **Table**

Examples

```
<!DOCTYPE informalexample PUBLIC "-//OASIS//DTD DocBook V3.1//EN">
<informalexample>
<programlisting>
sub print_content_model {
    my($self) = shift;
    local($_) = shift;
    local(*FILE) = shift;
```

```
    my(@cm) = $self->format_content_model2($_);
    foreach $_ (@cm) {
        print FILE $self->make_links($_, 1, 1), "\n";
    }
}
</programlisting>
</informalexample>
```

```
sub print_content_model {
    my($self) = shift;
    local($_) = shift;
    local(*FILE) = shift;

    my(@cm) = $self->format_content_model2($_);
    foreach $_ (@cm) {
        print FILE $self->make_links($_, 1, 1), "\n";
    }
}
```

For additional examples, see also **ScreenCO**.

InformalFigure—A untitled figure

Synopsis

Content Model

```
InformalFigure ::=
((LiteralLayout|ProgramListing|ProgramListingCO|Screen|ScreenCO|
  ScreenShot|Synopsis|CmdSynopsis|FuncSynopsis|Address|BlockQuote|
  Graphic|GraphicCO|MediaObject|MediaObjectCO|InformalEquation|
  InformalExample|InformalFigure|InformalTable|IndexTerm|Link|
  OLink|ULink)+)
```

Attributes **Name**	Common attributes **Type**	**Default**
Label	CDATA	*None*
PgWide	NUMBER	*None*
Float	NUMBER	"0"

Parameter Entities

%admon.mix;	%bookcomponent.content;	%component.mix;
%divcomponent.mix;	%example.mix;	%figure.mix;
%footnote.mix;	%glossdef.mix;	%indexdivcomponent.mix;
%informal.class;	%para.mix;	%qandaset.mix;
%refcomponent.mix;	%sidebar.mix;	

Description

An **InformalFigure** is a figure without a title. Figures often contain **Graphics**, or other large display elements.

Processing expectations

Formatted as a displayed block.

Attributes

Float

If `Float` has the value 1 (true), then the processing system is free to move the figure to a convenient location. (Where convenient location may be described in the style sheet or may be application dependent.) A value of 0 (false) indicates that the figure should be placed precisely where it occurs in the flow.

Label

`Label` specifies an identifying string for presentation purposes.

Generally, an explicit `Label` attribute is used only if the processing system is incapable of generating the label automatically. If present, the `Label` is normative; it will used even if the processing system is capable of automatic labelling.

PgWide

If `Pgwide` has the value 0 (false), then the **InformalFigure** is rendered in the current text flow (with flow column width). A value of 1 (true) specifies that the figure should be rendered across the full text page.

See Also

Equation, **Example**, **Figure**, **InformalEquation**, **InformalExample**, **InformalTable**, **Table**

Examples

```
<!DOCTYPE informalfigure PUBLIC "-//OASIS//DTD DocBook V3.1//EN">
<informalfigure>
<mediaobject>
<imageobject>
<imagedata fileref="watarun.eps" srccredit="Norman Walsh, 1998">
</imageobject>
<textobject><phrase>Wat Arun</phrase></textobject>
<caption><para>Wat Arun, Temple of the Dawn, on the Chao Phraya River
in Bangkok,
Thailand. In April, 1998, Wat Arun was in the midst of renovation.</para>
</caption>
</mediaobject>
</informalfigure>
```

Wat Arun, Temple of the Dawn, on the Chao Phraya River in Bangkok, Thailand. In April, 1998, Wat Arun was in the midst of renovation.

InformalTable—A table without a title

Synopsis

Content Model

```
InformalTable ::=
(Graphic+|MediaObject+|TGroup+)
```

Attributes	Common attributes	
Name	**Type**	**Default**
Label	CDATA	*None*
pgwide	NUMBER	*None*
Rowsep	NUMBER	*None*
shortentry	NUMBER	*None*
Colsep	NUMBER	*None*
tabstyle	NMTOKEN	*None*
Frame	*Enumeration:* All Bottom None Sides Top Topbot	*None*

Name	Type	Default
orient	*Enumeration:* land port	*None*
tocentry	NUMBER	*None*
Parameter Entities		
`%admon.mix;`	`%bookcomponent.content;`	`%component.mix;`
`%divcomponent.mix;`	`%example.mix;`	`%figure.mix;`
`%footnote.mix;`	`%glossdef.mix;`	`%indexdivcomponent.mix;`
`%informal.class;`	`%para.mix;`	`%qandaset.mix;`
`%refcomponent.mix;`	`%sidebar.mix;`	`%tbl.table.excep;`

Description

An **InformalTable** element identifies an informal table (one without a **Title**). DocBook uses the CALS table model, which describes tables geometrically using rows, columns, and cells.

Tables may include column headers and footers, but there is no provision for row headers.

Processing expectations

Formatted as a displayed block. This element is expected to obey the semantics of the *CALS Table Model Document Type Definition*, as specified by *OASIS Technical Memorandum TM 9502:1995* (*http://www.oasis-open.org/html/a502.htm*).

Attributes

Colsep

If `ColSep` has the value 1 (true), then a rule will be drawn to the right of all columns in this table. A value of 0 (false) suppresses the rule. The rule to the right of the last column in the table is controlled by the `Frame` attribute, not the `ColSep`.

Frame

`Frame` specifies how the table is to be framed.

Label

`Label` specifies an identifying string for presentation purposes.

Generally, an explicit `Label` attribute is used only if the processing system is incapable of generating the label automatically. If present, the `Label` is normative; it will used even if the processing system is capable of automatic labelling.

Rowsep

If `RowSep` has the value 1 (true), then a rule will be drawn below all the rows in the **InformalTable** (unless other, interior elements, suppress some or all of the rules). A value of 0 (false) suppresses the rule. The rule below the last row in the table is controlled by the `Frame` attribute and the `RowSep` of the last row is ignored.

orient

`Orient` specifies the orientation of the **InformalTable**. An orientation of `Port` is the "upright", the same orientation as the rest of the text flow. An orientation of `Land` is 90 degrees counterclockwise from the upright orientation.

pgwide

If `Pgwide` has the value 0 (false), then the **InformalTable** is rendered in the current text flow (with flow column width). A value of 1 (true) specifies that the table should be rendered across the full text page.

shortentry

This attribute is meaningless on **InformalTable**..

tabstyle

`TabStyle` holds the name of a table style defined in a stylesheet (e.g., a FOSI) that will be used to process this document.

tocentry

This attribute is meaningless on **InformalTable**.

See Also

colspec, **entry**, **entrytbl**, **Equation**, **Example**, **Figure**, **InformalEquation**, **InformalExample**, **InformalFigure**, **row**, **spanspec**, **Table**, **tbody**, **tfoot**, **tgroup**, **thead**

Examples

```
<!DOCTYPE informaltable PUBLIC "-//OASIS//DTD DocBook V3.1//EN">
<informaltable frame=none>
<tgroup cols=2>
<colspec colwidth=0.5in>
<colspec colwidth=0.5in>
<tbody>
<row><entry>1</entry><entry>1</entry></row>
<row><entry>2</entry><entry>4</entry></row>
<row><entry>3</entry><entry>9</entry></row>
</tbody>
</tgroup>
</informaltable>
```

1	1
2	4
3	9

For additional examples, see also **entrytbl**, **FootnoteRef**, **RefEntry**.

InlineEquation—A mathematical equation or expression occurring inline

Synopsis

Content Model
`InlineEquation ::=`
`(Alt?,`
` (Graphic+|InlineMediaObject+))`		

Attributes	Common attributes	
Parameter Entities `%inlineobj.char.class;`	`%para.char.mix;`	`%programlisting.con-tent;`
`%screen.content;`	`%tbl.entry.mdl;`	`%title.char.mix;`

Description

InlineEquations are expressions (usually mathematical) that occur in the text flow.

Processing expectations

Formatted inline.

InlineEquation should not contain **Graphic**. Instead, it should contain **InlineGraphic**. Within an **InlineEquation**, **Graphic** should be rendered inline.

5.0 *Future Changes*

In DocBook V5.0, **InlineGraphic** and **Graphic** will be discarded.

See Also

Equation, **InformalEquation**, **Subscript**, **Superscript**

Examples

```
<!DOCTYPE para PUBLIC "-//OASIS//DTD DocBook V3.1//EN">
<para>
Einstein's theory of relativity includes one of the most
widely recognized formulas in the world:
<inlineequation>
  <alt>e=mc^2</alt>
  <graphic fileref="figures/emc2"></graphic>
</inlineequation>
</para>
```

Einstein's theory of relativity includes one of the most widely recognized formulas in the world: $e = mc^2$

For additional examples, see also **InlineMediaObject**.

InlineGraphic—An object containing or pointing to graphical data that will be rendered inline

Synopsis

Declared Content

```
InlineGraphic ::=
CDATA
```

Attributes Common attributes

Name	Type	Default
Width	NUTOKEN	*None*
SrcCredit	CDATA	*None*
Scale	NUMBER	*None*
Format	*Enumerated notation:* BMP CGM-BINARY CGM-CHAR CGM-CLEAR DITROFF DVI EPS EQN FAX GIF GIF87a GIF89a IGES JPEG JPG linespecific PCX PIC PS SGML TBL TEX TIFF WMF WPG	*None*
Align	*Enumeration:* Center Left Right	*None*
Scalefit	NUMBER	*None*
Depth	NUTOKEN	*None*
EntityRef	ENTITY	*None*
FileRef	CDATA	*None*

Parameter Entities

`%cptr.char.mix;`	`%docinfo.char.mix;`	`%inlineobj.char.class;`
`%ndxterm.char.mix;`	`%para.char.mix;`	`%programlisting.content;`
`%screen.content;`	`%smallcptr.char.mix;`	`%tbl.entry.mdl;`
`%title.char.mix;`	`%word.char.mix;`	

Description

This element contains graphical data, or a pointer to an external entity containing graphical data. One of the deficiencies of the DocBook **Graphic** element is that there is no way to specify an alternate text description of the graphic. This has been rectified by the introduction of **InlineMediaObject**.

Processing expectations

Formatted inline.

There are several ways to provide content for a **Graphic**. It is best to use only one of these methods. However, if multiple graphic sources are provided, the processing expectations are as follows: element content should be used in favor of either `EntityRef` or `FileRef` and `EntityRef` should be used in favor of `FileRef`.

4.0 *Future Changes*

In DocBook V4.0, **InlineGraphic** will be declared `EMPTY`. This change will require that any embedded graphic content be stored outside the SGML source and pointed to with an `EntityRef` or `FileRef` attribute.

5.0 *Future Changes*

In DocBook V5.0, **InlineGraphic** will be discarded. At that time, graphics will have to be incorporated using **MediaObject** or **InlineMediaObject**.

Attributes

Align

`Align` specifies the horizontal alignment of the graphic within the element that frames it.

Depth

`Depth` specifies the desired depth (vertical distance, at least in horizontal writing systems) of the image.

EntityRef

`EntityRef` identifies the general entity which contains (or points to) the content of the graphic.

FileRef

`FileRef` specifies the name of the file which contains the content of the graphic.

Format

`Format` identifies the format of the graphic content. The `Format` must be a defined notation.

Scale

`Scale` specifies integer representing a percentage scaling factor (retaining the relative dimensions of the original graphic). If unspecified, the value 100 (100%) is assumed.

Scalefit

If `ScaleFit` has the value 1 (true), then the graphic is to be scaled (uniformly) to the specified width or depth. The default value of 0 (false) indicates that the image will not be scaled to fit (although it may still be scaled by the `Scale` attribute).

SrcCredit

`SrcCredit` contains details about the source of the **InlineGraphic**.

Width

`Width` indicates the width of the graphic.

See Also

Alt, **AudioObject**, **Caption**, **Graphic**, **ImageObject**, **InlineMediaObject**, **MediaObject**, **TextObject**, **VideoObject**

Examples

For examples, see **GUIButton**, **GUIIcon**, **GUILabel**.

InlineMediaObject—An inline media object (video, audio, image, and so on)

Synopsis

Content Model

```
InlineMediaObject ::=
(ObjectInfo?,
 (VideoObject|AudioObject|ImageObject),
 (VideoObject|AudioObject|ImageObject|TextObject)*)
```

Attributes	Common attributes	
Parameter Entities		
`%cptr.char.mix;`	`%docinfo.char.mix;`	`%inlineequation.content;`
`%inlineobj.char.class;`	`%ndxterm.char.mix;`	`%para.char.mix;`
`%programlisting.content;`	`%screen.content;`	`%smallcptr.char.mix;`
`%tbl.entry.mdl;`	`%title.char.mix;`	`%word.char.mix;`

Description

InlineMediaObject contains a set of alternative "graphical objects." In DocBook V3.1, three types of external graphical objects are defined: **VideoObjects**, **AudioOb-**

jects, and **ImageObjects**. Additional textual descriptions may be provided with **TextObjects**.

Processing expectations

Formatted inline.

The primary purpose of the **InlineMediaObject** is to provide a wrapper around a set of alternative presentations of the same information.

If possible, the processing system should use the content of the first object within the **InlineMediaObject**. If the first object cannot be used, the remaining objects should be considered in the order that they occur. A processor should use the first object that it can, although it is free to choose any of the remaining objects if the primary one cannot be used.

Under no circumstances should more than one object in an **InlineMediaObject** be used or presented at the same time.

For example, an **InlineMediaObject** might contain a high resolution image, a low resolution image, and a text description. For print publishing, the high resolution image is used; for online systems, either the high or low resolution image is used, possibly including the text description as an online alternative. In a text-only environment, the text description is used.

5.0 *Future Changes*

In DocBook V5.0, **InlineMediaObject** will replace **InlineGraphic**.

See Also

Alt, **AudioObject**, **Caption**, **Graphic**, **ImageObject**, **InlineGraphic**, **MediaObject**, **TextObject**, **VideoObject**

Examples

In the following example, the **InlineEquation** uses **InlineMediaObject** to provide to alternate renderings for the equation. One is a graphic, the other is a text representation.

For display purposes, both in print and in the online presentation, the graphic is selected. If you were generating content for some other medium, a text only browser or a cell phone, for example, only the text representation might be selected.

```
<!DOCTYPE para PUBLIC "-//OASIS//DTD DocBook V3.1//EN">
<para>
Einstein's most famous equation,
<inlineequation>
<inlinemediaobject>
<imageobject>
```

```
<imagedata fileref="figures/emc2.gif">
</imageobject>
<textobject>
<phrase>E=mc<superscript>2</superscript></phrase>
</textobject>
</inlinemediaobject>
</inlineequation>, expresses the relationship between matter
and energy.
</para>
```

Einstein's most famous equation, $e = mc^2$, expresses the relationship between matter and energy.

Interface—An element of a GUI

Synopsis

Mixed Content Model

```
Interface ::=
((#PCDATA|Link|OLink|ULink|Action|Application|ClassName|Command|
  ComputerOutput|Database|Email|EnVar|ErrorCode|ErrorName|
  ErrorType|Filename|Function|GUIButton|GUIIcon|GUILabel|GUIMenu|
  GUIMenuItem|GUISubmenu|Hardware|Interface|InterfaceDefinition|
  KeyCap|KeyCode|KeyCombo|KeySym|Literal|Constant|Markup|
  MediaLabel|MenuChoice|MouseButton|MsgText|Option|Optional|
  Parameter|Prompt|Property|Replaceable|ReturnValue|SGMLTag|
  StructField|StructName|Symbol|SystemItem|Token|Type|UserInput|
  VarName|Anchor|Comment|Subscript|Superscript|InlineGraphic|
  InlineMediaObject|IndexTerm|Accel)+)
```

Attributes — Common attributes

Name	Type	Default
Class	*Enumeration:* Button Icon Menu MenuItem	*None*
MoreInfo	*Enumeration:* None RefEntry	"None"

Parameter Entities

`%cptr.char.mix;`	`%ndxterm.char.mix;`	`%para.char.mix;`
`%programlisting.content;`	`%refinline.char.mix;`	`%refname.char.mix;`
`%screen.content;`	`%tbl.entry.mdl;`	`%tech.char.class;`
`%title.char.mix;`		

Description

An **Interface** identifies some part of a graphical user interface. This element became obsolete in DocBook V3.0 with the introduction of **GUIButton**, **GUIIcon**, **GUILabel**, **GUIMenu**, **GUIMenuItem**, and **GUISubMenu**.

Processing expectations

Formatted inline. The `MoreInfo` attribute can help generate a link or query to retrieve additional information.

4.0 *Future Changes*

In DocBook V4.0, the `Class` attribute will be dropped from **Interface**. Use one of the GUI* tags instead or subclass locally with the `Role` attribute.

The content model of **Interface** will also be constrained to `(#PCDATA | Replaceable | InlineGraphic)`.

Attributes

Class
: `Class` indicates the type of the **Interface**.

MoreInfo
: If `MoreInfo` is set to `RefEntry`, it implies that a **RefEntry** exists which further describes the **Interface**.

See Also

ClassName, **InterfaceDefinition**, **Property**, **StructField**, **StructName**, **Symbol**, **Token**, **Type**

InterfaceDefinition—The name of a formal specification of a GUI

Synopsis

Mixed Content Model

```
InterfaceDefinition ::=
((#PCDATA|Link|OLink|ULink|Action|Application|ClassName|Command|
  ComputerOutput|Database|Email|EnVar|ErrorCode|ErrorName|
  ErrorType|Filename|Function|GUIButton|GUIIcon|GUILabel|GUIMenu|
  GUIMenuItem|GUISubmenu|Hardware|Interface|InterfaceDefinition|
  KeyCap|KeyCode|KeyCombo|KeySym|Literal|Constant|Markup|
  MediaLabel|MenuChoice|MouseButton|MsgText|Option|Optional|
  Parameter|Prompt|Property|Replaceable|ReturnValue|SGMLTag|
  StructField|StructName|Symbol|SystemItem|Token|Type|UserInput|
  VarName|Anchor|Comment|Subscript|Superscript|InlineGraphic|
  InlineMediaObject|IndexTerm)+)
```

Attributes	Common attributes	
Name	**Type**	**Default**
MoreInfo	*Enumeration:* None RefEntry	"None"

Parameter Entities		
`%cptr.char.mix;`	`%ndxterm.char.mix;`	`%para.char.mix;`
`%programlisting.content;`	`%refinline.char.mix;`	`%refname.char.mix;`
`%screen.content;`	`%tbl.entry.mdl;`	`%tech.char.class;`
`%title.char.mix;`		

Description

An **InterfaceDefinition** was intended to hold the name of the specification for a graphical user interface. Exactly what this meant has never been clear.

Processing expectations

Formatted inline. The `MoreInfo` attribute can help generate a link or query to retrieve additional information.

4.0 *Future Changes*

The **InterfaceDefinition** element will be discarded in DocBook V4.0.

Attributes

MoreInfo

If `MoreInfo` is set to `RefEntry`, it implies that a **RefEntry** exists which further describes the **InterfaceDefinition**.

See Also

ClassName, **Interface**, **Property**, **StructField**, **StructName**, **Symbol**, **Token**, **Type**

InvPartNumber—An inventory part number

Synopsis

Mixed Content Model

```
InvPartNumber ::=
((#PCDATA|Link|OLink|ULink|Emphasis|Trademark|Replaceable|Comment|
  Subscript|Superscript|InlineGraphic|InlineMediaObject|IndexTerm)+)
```

Attributes	Common attributes

Parameter Entities

`%bibliocomponent.mix;`

Description

An **InvPartNumber** identifies a number (an "inventory part number") in some organization-specific numbering scheme.

Processing expectations

Formatted inline. Sometimes suppressed.

DocBook does not control, or specify, the numbering scheme used by an **InvPartNumber**. It is likely that this number uniquely identifies the document within the organization that assigns the numbers.

See Also

ISBN, **ISSN**, **IssueNum**, **ProductNumber**, **PubsNumber**, **SeriesVolNums**, **VolumeNum**

ISBN—The International Standard Book Number of a document

Synopsis

Mixed Content Model
`ISBN ::=`
`((#PCDATA|Link|OLink|ULink|Emphasis|Trademark|Replaceable|Comment|`
`  Subscript|Superscript|InlineGraphic|InlineMediaObject|IndexTerm)+)`	

Attributes	Common attributes
Parameter Entities `%bibliocomponent.mix;`	

Description

An **ISBN** is the International Standard Book Number of a document.

Processing expectations

Formatted inline. Sometimes suppressed.

See Also

InvPartNumber, **ISSN**, **IssueNum**, **ProductNumber**, **PubsNumber**, **SeriesVolNums**, **VolumeNum**

Examples

For examples, see **Bibliography**.

ISSN—The International Standard Serial Number of a periodical

Synopsis

Mixed Content Model
`ISSN ::=`
`((#PCDATA|Link|OLink|ULink|Emphasis|Trademark|Replaceable|Comment|`
`  Subscript|Superscript|InlineGraphic|InlineMediaObject|IndexTerm)+)`

Attributes	Common attributes
Parameter Entities `%bibliocomponent.mix;`	

Description

An ISSN is the International Standard Serial Number of a periodical.

Processing expectations

Formatted inline. Sometimes suppressed.

See Also

InvPartNumber, **ISBN**, **IssueNum**, **ProductNumber**, **PubsNumber**, **SeriesVolNums**, **VolumeNum**

Examples

For examples, see **Bibliography**, **BiblioSet**.

IssueNum—The number of an issue of a journal

Synopsis

Mixed Content Model

```
IssueNum ::=
((#PCDATA|Link|OLink|ULink|Emphasis|Trademark|Replaceable|Comment|
  Subscript|Superscript|InlineGraphic|InlineMediaObject|IndexTerm)+)
```

Attributes	Common attributes
Parameter Entities `%bibliocomponent.mix;`	

Description

The **IssueNum** contains the issue number of a periodical.

Processing expectations

May be formatted inline or as a displayed block, depending on context. Sometimes suppressed.

See Also

InvPartNumber, **ISBN**, **ISSN**, **ProductNumber**, **PubsNumber**, **SeriesVolNums**, **VolumeNum**

Examples

For examples, see **Article**, **Bibliography**, **BiblioMSet**.

ItemizedList—A list in which each entry is marked with a bullet or other dingbat

Synopsis

Content Model		
`ItemizedList ::=`		
`(ListItem+)`		
Attributes	Common attributes	
Name	**Type**	**Default**
Spacing	*Enumeration:* Compact Normal	*None*
Mark	CDATA	*None*
Parameter Entities		
`%admon.mix;`	`%bookcomponent.content;`	`%component.mix;`
`%divcomponent.mix;`	`%example.mix;`	`%footnote.mix;`
`%glossdef.mix;`	`%highlights.mix;`	`%indexdivcomponent.mix;`
`%legalnotice.mix;`	`%list.class;`	`%para.mix;`
`%qandaset.mix;`	`%refcomponent.mix;`	`%sidebar.mix;`
`%tabentry.mix;`	`%tbl.entry.mdl;`	`%textobject.mix;`

Description

In an **ItemizedList**, each member of the list is marked with a bullet, dash, or other symbol.

Processing expectations

Formatted as a displayed block.

DocBook specifies neither the initial mark nor the sequence of marks to be used in nested lists. If explicit control is desired, the `Mark` attribute should be used. The values of the `Mark` attribute are expected to be keywords, not representations (numerical character references, entities, and so on.) of the actual mark.

In order to enforce a standard set of marks at your organization, it may be useful to construct a customization layer that limits the values of the `Mark` attribute to an enumerated list. See Chapter 5, *Customizing DocBook*.

Attributes

Mark

`Mark` contains a keyword indicating the type of mark to be used on items in this **ItemizedList**. DocBook does not provide a fixed list of appropriate keywords.

Spacing

Spacing indicates whether or not the vertical space in the list should be minimized.

See Also

CalloutList, **ListItem**, **OrderedList**, **SegmentedList**, **SimpleList**, **VariableList**

Examples

```
<!DOCTYPE itemizedlist PUBLIC "-//OASIS//DTD DocBook V3.1//EN">
<itemizedlist mark=opencircle>
<listitem>
<para>
TeX and LaTeX
</para>
</listitem>
<listitem override=bullet>
<para>
Troff
</para>
</listitem>
<listitem>
<para>
Lout
</para>
</listitem>
</itemizedlist>
```

- ❍ TeX and LaTeX
- • Troff
- ❍ Lout

For additional examples, see also **Highlights**, **Para**, **XRef**.

ITermSet—A set of index terms in the meta-information of a document

Synopsis

Content Model
`ITermSet ::=`
`(IndexTerm+)`	

Attributes	Common attributes

Description

When **IndexTerms** use the Zone attribute to point to index ranges, it may be handy to hoist them out of the flow and put them in the document meta-information.

The **ITermSet** element, which occurs in the DocBook containers for meta-information, is one place to put them. **ITermSet** is simply a wrapper around a group of **IndexTerms**.

Processing expectations

Suppressed.

Although more than one **ITermSet** may appear in the meta-information for a document, neither a relationship nor a specific facility for constructing a relationship is defined.

Examples

For examples, see **Chapter**.

JobTitle—The title of an individual in an organization

Synopsis

Mixed Content Model

```
JobTitle ::=
((#PCDATA|Link|OLink|ULink|Emphasis|Trademark|Replaceable|Comment|
  Subscript|Superscript|InlineGraphic|InlineMediaObject|IndexTerm)+)
```

Attributes	Common attributes

Description

A **JobTitle** describes the position of an individual within an organization. This tag is generally reserved for the name of the title for which an individual is paid.

Processing expectations

May be formatted inline or as a displayed block, depending on context. Sometimes suppressed.

See Also

Affiliation, **CorpName**, **OrgDiv**, **OrgName**, **ShortAffil**

Examples

For examples, see **Author**, **AuthorGroup**.

KeyCap—The text printed on a key on a keyboard

Synopsis

Mixed Content Model

```
KeyCap ::=
((#PCDATA|Link|OLink|ULink|Action|Application|ClassName|Command|
  ComputerOutput|Database|Email|EnVar|ErrorCode|ErrorName|
  ErrorType|Filename|Function|GUIButton|GUIIcon|GUILabel|GUIMenu|
  GUIMenuItem|GUISubmenu|Hardware|Interface|InterfaceDefinition|
  KeyCap|KeyCode|KeyCombo|KeySym|Literal|Constant|Markup|
  MediaLabel|MenuChoice|MouseButton|MsgText|Option|Optional|
  Parameter|Prompt|Property|Replaceable|ReturnValue|SGMLTag|
  StructField|StructName|Symbol|SystemItem|Token|Type|UserInput|
  VarName|Anchor|Comment|Subscript|Superscript|InlineGraphic|
  InlineMediaObject|IndexTerm)+)
```

Attributes	Common attributes	
Name	**Type**	**Default**
MoreInfo	*Enumeration:* None RefEntry	"None"

Parameter Entities

`%cptr.char.mix;`	`%ndxterm.char.mix;`	`%para.char.mix;`
`%programlisting.content;`	`%refinline.char.mix;`	`%refname.char.mix;`
`%screen.content;`	`%tbl.entry.mdl;`	`%tech.char.class;`
`%title.char.mix;`		

Description

The **KeyCap** identifies the text printed on a physical key on a computer keyboard. This is distinct from any scan code that it may generate (**KeyCode**), or any symbolic name (**KeySym**) that might exist for the key.

Processing expectations

Formatted inline. The `MoreInfo` attribute can help generate a link or query to retrieve additional information.

4.0 *Future Changes*

In DocBook V4.0, the content model of **KeyCap** will be constrained to `(#PCDATA | Replaceable | InlineGraphic)`.

Attributes

MoreInfo

If `MoreInfo` is set to `RefEntry`, it implies that a **RefEntry** exists which further describes the **Keycap**.

See Also

Accel, **GUIButton**, **GUIIcon**, **GUILabel**, **GUIMenu**, **GUIMenuItem**, **GUISubmenu**, **KeyCode**, **KeyCombo**, **KeySym**, **MenuChoice**, **MouseButton**, **Shortcut**

Examples

```
<!DOCTYPE para PUBLIC "-//OASIS//DTD DocBook V3.1//EN">
<para>
The <keycap>F1</keycap> key on an IBM PC keyboard generates the
scan code <keycode>0x3B</keycode> when pressed.  This value
is defined as <keysym>KEY_F1</keysym> in
<filename class="headerfile">keyboard.h</filename>.
</para>
```

The `F1` key on an IBM PC keyboard generates the scan code 0x3B when pressed. This value is defined as `KEY_F1` in *keyboard.h*.

For additional examples, see also **KeyCode**, **KeyCombo**, **KeySym**.

KeyCode—The internal, frequently numeric, identifier for a key on a keyboard

Synopsis

Mixed Content Model
`KeyCode ::=`
`((#PCDATA|Replaceable|InlineGraphic|InlineMediaObject|IndexTerm)+)`		

Attributes	Common attributes	
Parameter Entities		
`%cptr.char.mix;`	`%ndxterm.char.mix;`	`%para.char.mix;`
`%programlisting.content;`	`%refinline.char.mix;`	`%refname.char.mix;`
`%screen.content;`	`%tbl.entry.mdl;`	`%tech.char.class;`
`%title.char.mix;`		

Description

The **KeyCode** identifies the numeric value associated with a key on a computer keyboard. This is distinct from any scan code that it may generate (**KeyCode**), or any symbolic name (**KeySym**) that might exist for the key.

Processing expectations

Formatted inline.

See Also

Accel, **GUIButton**, **GUIIcon**, **GUILabel**, **GUIMenu**, **GUIMenuItem**, **GUISubmenu**, **KeyCap**, **KeyCombo**, **KeySym**, **MenuChoice**, **MouseButton**, **Shortcut**

Examples

```
<!DOCTYPE para PUBLIC "-//OASIS//DTD DocBook V3.1//EN">
<para>
The <keycap>F1</keycap> key on an IBM PC keyboard generates the
scan code <keycode>0x3B</keycode> when pressed.  This value
is defined as <keysym>KEY_F1</keysym> in
<filename class="headerfile">keyboard.h</filename>.
</para>
```

The `F1` key on an IBM PC keyboard generates the scan code 0x3B when pressed. This value is defined as `KEY_F1` in *keyboard.h*.

For additional examples, see also **KeyCap**, **KeySym**.

KeyCombo—A combination of input actions

Synopsis

<table>
<tr><td colspan="3">Content Model
KeyCombo ::=
((KeyCap|KeyCombo|KeySym|MouseButton)+)</td></tr>
<tr><td>Attributes
Name</td><td>Common attributes
Type</td><td>
Default</td></tr>
<tr><td>OtherAction
Action

MoreInfo</td><td>CDATA
Enumeration:
Click
Double-Click
Other
Press
Seq
Simul
Enumeration:
None
RefEntry</td><td>None
None

“None”</td></tr>
<tr><td>Parameter Entities
%cptr.char.mix;
%programlisting.content;
%screen.content;
%title.char.mix;</td><td>
%ndxterm.char.mix;
%refinline.char.mix;
%tbl.entry.mdl;</td><td>
%para.char.mix;
%refname.char.mix;
%tech.char.class;</td></tr>
</table>

Description

For actions that require multiple keystrokes, mouse actions, or other physical input selections, the **KeyCombo** element provides a wrapper for the entire set of events.

Processing expectations

Formatted inline. The `MoreInfo` attribute can help generate a link or query to retrieve additional information.

Attributes

Action

Action identifies the nature of the action taken. If **KeyCombo** contains more than one action element, Simul is the default value for Action, otherwise there is no default.

If Other is specified, OtherAction should be used to identify the nature of the action.

MoreInfo

If MoreInfo is set to RefEntry, it implies that a **RefEntry** exists which further describes the **Keycombo**.

OtherAction

OtherAction should be used when Action is set to Other. It identifes the nature of the action in some application-specific way.

See Also

Accel, **GUIButton**, **GUIIcon**, **GUILabel**, **GUIMenu**, **GUIMenuItem**, **GUISubmenu**, **KeyCap**, **KeyCode**, **KeySym**, **MenuChoice**, **MouseButton**, **Shortcut**

Examples

```
<!DOCTYPE para PUBLIC "-//OASIS//DTD DocBook V3.1//EN">
<para>
To move a highlighted region, use
<keycombo action=simul>
  <keycap>Shift</keycap>
  <mousebutton>Button1</mousebutton>
</keycombo>
and drag the text to the new location.
</para>
```

To move a highlighted region, use Shift+Button1 and drag the text to the new location.

For additional examples, see also **GUIMenu**, **GUIMenuItem**, **MenuChoice**, **Shortcut**.

KeySym—The symbolic name of a key on a keyboard

Synopsis

Mixed Content Model KeySym ::= ((#PCDATA|Replaceable|InlineGraphic|InlineMediaObject|IndexTerm)+)	
Attributes	Common attributes

Parameter Entities		
%cptr.char.mix;	%ndxterm.char.mix;	%para.char.mix;
%programlisting.content;	%refinline.char.mix;	%refname.char.mix;
%screen.content;	%tbl.entry.mdl;	%tech.char.class;
%title.char.mix;		

Description

The **KeySym** identifies the symbolic name of a key on a computer keyboard. This is distinct from any scan code that it may generate (**KeyCode**), or any symbolic name (**KeySym**) that might exist for the key.

Processing expectations

Formatted inline.

See Also

Accel, **GUIButton**, **GUIIcon**, **GUILabel**, **GUIMenu**, **GUIMenuItem**, **GUISubmenu**, **KeyCap**, **KeyCode**, **KeyCombo**, **MenuChoice**, **MouseButton**, **Shortcut**

Examples

```
<!DOCTYPE para PUBLIC "-//OASIS//DTD DocBook V3.1//EN">
<para>
The <keycap>F1</keycap> key on an IBM PC keyboard generates the
scan code <keycode>0x3B</keycode> when pressed.  This value
is defined as <keysym>KEY_F1</keysym> in
<filename class="headerfile">keyboard.h</filename>.
</para>
```

The `F1` key on an IBM PC keyboard generates the scan code 0x3B when pressed. This value is defined as `KEY_F1` in *keyboard.h*.

For additional examples, see also **GUIMenu**, **GUIMenuItem**, **KeyCap**, **KeyCode**, **MenuChoice**, **Shortcut**.

Keyword—One of a set of keywords describing the content of a document

Synopsis

Mixed Content Model Keyword ::= (#PCDATA)	
Attributes	Common attributes

Description

A **Keyword** is a term describing the content of a document. The keyword applies to the document component that contains it.

Processing expectations

Keywords are rarely displayed to a reader. Usually, they are reserved for searching and retrieval purposes. If they are displayed, they may be displayed either inline or as a displayed block, depending on context.

Unlike **SubjectTerms**, which should be drawn from a controlled vocabulary, keywords may be chosen freely.

See Also

KeywordSet, **Subject**, **SubjectSet**, **SubjectTerm**

Examples

For examples, see **Chapter**, **RefEntry**.

KeywordSet—A set of keywords describing the content of a document

Synopsis

Content Model
`KeywordSet ::=`
`(Keyword+)`	

Attributes	Common attributes

Description

A set of keywords, provided by the author, editor, publisher, and so on, can be stored in the document meta-information in a **KeywordSet**.

Keywords can form an important part of an automated indexing or searching strategy for a collection of documents.

Processing expectations

May be formatted inline or as a displayed block, depending on context. Keywords are rarely displayed to a reader. Usually, they are reserved for searching and retrieval purposes.

Unlike **SubjectTerms**, which should be drawn from a controlled vocabulary, keywords may be chosen freely.

Although more than one **KeywordSet** may appear in the meta-information for a document, neither a relationship nor a specific facility for constructing a relationship is defined by DocBook.

Additionally, no relationship is defined between the **KeywordSets** of a document component and the **KeywordSets** of its parents or children.

See Also

Keyword, **Subject**, **SubjectSet**, **SubjectTerm**

Examples

For examples, see **Chapter**, **RefEntry**.

Label—A label on a **Question** or **Answer**

Synopsis

Mixed Content Model

```
Label ::=
(#PCDATA|Acronym|Emphasis|Trademark|Link|OLink|ULink|Anchor|
 Comment|Subscript|Superscript|InlineGraphic|InlineMediaObject|
 IndexTerm)*
```

Attributes	Common attributes

Description

The **Label** on a **Question** or **Answer** identifies the label that is to be used when formatting the question or answer.

Processing expectations

If the `DefaultLabel` attribute on the nearest ancestor **QandASet** is not `Label`, then the `Label` attribute is ignored.

Otherwise, the value of the `Label` attribute is used as the label for the **Question** or **Answer**.

LegalNotice—A statement of legal obligations or requirements

Synopsis

Content Model

```
LegalNotice ::=
(Title?,
 (CalloutList|GlossList|ItemizedList|OrderedList|SegmentedList|
  SimpleList|VariableList|Caution|Important|Note|Tip|Warning|
  LiteralLayout|ProgramListing|ProgramListingCO|Screen|ScreenCO|
  ScreenShot|FormalPara|Para|SimPara|BlockQuote|IndexTerm)+)
```

Attributes	Common attributes

Description

LegalNotice identifies a statement of legal obligation, requirement, or warranty. It occurs in the meta-information for a document in which it frequently explains copyright, trademark, and other legal formalities of a document.

Processing expectations

Formatted as a displayed block.

LegalNotices may be presented in a number of ways. In printed documents, they often occur on the verso of the title page, sometimes in a reduced font size. Online, they may occur on the title page or in a separate document behind a hypertext link.

See Also

Copyright, **Trademark**

Examples

For examples, see **Book**, **BookInfo**, **Sect1Info**.

Lineage—The portion of a person's name indicating a relationship to ancestors

Synopsis

Mixed Content Model

```
Lineage ::=
((#PCDATA|Link|OLink|ULink|Emphasis|Trademark|Replaceable|Comment|
  Subscript|Superscript|InlineGraphic|InlineMediaObject|IndexTerm)+)
```

Attributes	Common attributes

Parameter Entities

`%bibliocomponent.mix;`	`%person.ident.mix;`

Description

Lineage is a portion of a person's name, typically "Jr." or "Sr."

Processing expectations

Formatted inline. In an **Address**, this element may inherit the verbatim qualities of an address.

See Also

Affiliation, **FirstName**, **Honorific**, **OtherName**, **Surname**

Examples

For examples, see **AuthorGroup**.

LineAnnotation—A comment on a line in a verbatim listing

Synopsis

Mixed Content Model

```
LineAnnotation ::=
((#PCDATA|FootnoteRef|XRef|Abbrev|Acronym|Citation|CiteRefEntry|
  CiteTitle|Emphasis|FirstTerm|ForeignPhrase|GlossTerm|Footnote|
  Phrase|Quote|Trademark|WordAsWord|Link|OLink|ULink|Action|
  Application|ClassName|Command|ComputerOutput|Database|Email|
  EnVar|ErrorCode|ErrorName|ErrorType|Filename|Function|GUIButton|
  GUIIcon|GUILabel|GUIMenu|GUIMenuItem|GUISubmenu|Hardware|
  Interface|InterfaceDefinition|KeyCap|KeyCode|KeyCombo|KeySym|
  Literal|Constant|Markup|MediaLabel|MenuChoice|MouseButton|
  MsgText|Option|Optional|Parameter|Prompt|Property|Replaceable|
  ReturnValue|SGMLTag|StructField|StructName|Symbol|SystemItem|
  Token|Type|UserInput|VarName|Anchor|Author|AuthorInitials|
  CorpAuthor|ModeSpec|OtherCredit|ProductName|ProductNumber|
  RevHistory|Comment|Subscript|Superscript|InlineGraphic|
  InlineMediaObject|InlineEquation|Synopsis|CmdSynopsis|
  FuncSynopsis|IndexTerm)+)
```

Attributes	Common attributes
Parameter Entities	
`%programlisting.content;`	`%screen.content;`

Description

A **LineAnnotation** is an author or editor's comment on a line in one of the verbatim environments. These are annotations added by the documentor, not part of the original listing.

Processing expectations

Formatted inline. In verbatim environments like **ProgramListing**, which are often presented in a fixed width font, they may get special typographic treatment, such as italics.

If several **LineAnnotations** occur in the same listing, they may be aligned horizontally.

4.0 *Future Changes*

The **InterfaceDefinition** element will be discarded in DocBook V4.0. It will no longer be available in the content model of this element.

See Also

ComputerOutput, **LiteralLayout**, **ProgramListing**, **Screen**, **ScreenShot**, **Synopsis**, **UserInput**

Examples

The following example, from the description of **Entry**, shows how **LineAnnotation** can be used to annotate a **Screen** listing:

```
<!DOCTYPE screen PUBLIC "-//OASIS//DTD DocBook V3.1//EN">
<screen>
&lt;entry>              <lineannotation>Error, cannot have a line break before a
block element</lineannotation>
&lt;para>
A paragraph of text.
&lt;/para>&lt;/entry>
</screen>
```

```
<entry>              Error, cannot have a line break before a block element
<para>
A paragraph of text.
</para></entry>
```

Link—A hypertext link

Synopsis

Mixed Content Model

```
Link ::=
((#PCDATA|FootnoteRef|XRef|Abbrev|Acronym|Citation|CiteRefEntry|
  CiteTitle|Emphasis|FirstTerm|ForeignPhrase|GlossTerm|Footnote|
  Phrase|Quote|Trademark|WordAsWord|Link|OLink|ULink|Action|
  Application|ClassName|Command|ComputerOutput|Database|Email|
  EnVar|ErrorCode|ErrorName|ErrorType|Filename|Function|GUIButton|
  GUIIcon|GUILabel|GUIMenu|GUIMenuItem|GUISubmenu|Hardware|
  Interface|InterfaceDefinition|KeyCap|KeyCode|KeyCombo|KeySym|
  Literal|Constant|Markup|MediaLabel|MenuChoice|MouseButton|
  MsgText|Option|Optional|Parameter|Prompt|Property|Replaceable|
  ReturnValue|SGMLTag|StructField|StructName|Symbol|SystemItem|
  Token|Type|UserInput|VarName|Anchor|Author|AuthorInitials|
  CorpAuthor|ModeSpec|OtherCredit|ProductName|ProductNumber|
  RevHistory|Comment|Subscript|Superscript|InlineGraphic|
  InlineMediaObject|InlineEquation|Synopsis|CmdSynopsis|
  FuncSynopsis|IndexTerm)+)
```

Attributes	Common attributes	
Name	**Type**	**Default**
Type	CDATA	*None*
Linkend	IDREF	*Required*
Endterm	IDREF	*None*

Parameter Entities		
%cptr.char.mix;	%docinfo.char.mix;	%indexdivcomponent.mix;
%link.char.class;	%ndxterm.char.mix;	%para.char.mix;
%programlisting.content;	%refinline.char.mix;	%screen.content;
%tbl.entry.mdl;	%title.char.mix;	%word.char.mix;

Description

Link is a general purpose hypertext element. Usually, **Link** surrounds the text that should be made "hot," (unlike **XRef** which must generate the text) but the **EndTerm** attribute can be used to copy text from another element.

Processing expectations

Formatted inline.

If the **Link** element specifies an **EndTerm**, and then the content of the element pointed to by **EndTerm** should be repeated at the location of the **Link** and used as the "hot" text *instead* of the **Link** content, which should be suppressed.

Linking elements must not be nested within other linking elements (including themselves). Because DocBook is harmonizing towards XML, this restriction cannot easily be enforced by the DTD. The processing of nested linking elements is undefined.

4.0 Future Changes

The **InterfaceDefinition** element will be discarded in DocBook V4.0. It will no longer be available in the content model of this element.

Attributes

Endterm

Endterm points to the element whose content is to be used as the text of the link. If **Endterm** is supplied on a **Link** which has content, the value of **Endterm** should be ignored.

Linkend

Linkend points to the target of the link.

Type

Type is available for application-specific customization of the linking behavior.

See Also

Anchor, **OLink**, **ULink**, **XRef**

Examples

```
<!DOCTYPE sect1 PUBLIC "-//OASIS//DTD DocBook V3.1//EN">
<sect1><title>Examples of <sgmltag>Link</sgmltag></title>

<para>
In this sentence <link linkend=nextsect>this</link> word is
hot and points to the following section.
</para>
```

```
<para>
There is also a link to the section called
<quote><link linkend=nextsect endterm="nextsect.title"></link></quote>
in this sentence.
</para>

<sect2 id=nextsect><title id=nextsect.title>A Subsection</title>

<para>
This section only exists to be the target of a couple of links.
</para>

</sect2>
</sect1>
```

ListItem—A wrapper for the elements of a list item

Synopsis

Content Model

```
ListItem ::=
((CalloutList|GlossList|ItemizedList|OrderedList|SegmentedList|
  SimpleList|VariableList|Caution|Important|Note|Tip|Warning|
  LiteralLayout|ProgramListing|ProgramListingCO|Screen|ScreenCO|
  ScreenShot|Synopsis|CmdSynopsis|FuncSynopsis|FormalPara|Para|
  SimPara|Address|BlockQuote|Graphic|GraphicCO|MediaObject|
  MediaObjectCO|InformalEquation|InformalExample|InformalFigure|
  InformalTable|Equation|Example|Figure|Table|MsgSet|Procedure|
  Sidebar|QandASet|Anchor|BridgeHead|Comment|Highlights|Abstract|
  AuthorBlurb|Epigraph|IndexTerm)+)
```

Attributes	Common attributes	
Name	**Type**	**Default**
Override	CDATA	*None*

Description

The **ListItem** element is a wrapper around an item in a list. In an **ItemizedList** or an **OrderedList**, the **ListItem** surrounds the entire list item. In a **VariableList**, **ListItem** surrounds the "definition" part of the list item.

Processing expectations

Formatted as a displayed block. List items usually generate the appropriate mark (a number or bullet) and appear indented, next to the mark. In a **VariableList**, the presentation may be influenced by the length of the **Term** or **Terms** that precede the list item and by attributes on the list itself.

Attributes

Override

`Override` specifies the keyword for the type of mark to be used on *this* **ListItem** instead of the mark currently in use for the list.

See Also

CalloutList, **ItemizedList**, **OrderedList**, **SegmentedList**, **SimpleList**, **VariableList**

Examples

For examples, see **Highlights**, **ItemizedList**, **OrderedList**, **Para**, **RefEntry**, **VariableList**, **XRef**.

Literal—Inline text that is some literal value

Synopsis

Mixed Content Model

```
Literal ::=
((#PCDATA|Link|OLink|ULink|Action|Application|ClassName|Command|
  ComputerOutput|Database|Email|EnVar|ErrorCode|ErrorName|
  ErrorType|Filename|Function|GUIButton|GUIIcon|GUILabel|GUIMenu|
  GUIMenuItem|GUISubmenu|Hardware|Interface|InterfaceDefinition|
  KeyCap|KeyCode|KeyCombo|KeySym|Literal|Constant|Markup|
  MediaLabel|MenuChoice|MouseButton|MsgText|Option|Optional|
  Parameter|Prompt|Property|Replaceable|ReturnValue|SGMLTag|
  StructField|StructName|Symbol|SystemItem|Token|Type|UserInput|
  VarName|Anchor|Comment|Subscript|Superscript|InlineGraphic|
  InlineMediaObject|IndexTerm)+)
```

Attributes	Common attributes	
Name	**Type**	**Default**
MoreInfo	*Enumeration:* None RefEntry	"None"

Parameter Entities		
`%cptr.char.mix;`	`%ndxterm.char.mix;`	`%para.char.mix;`
`%programlisting.content;`	`%refinline.char.mix;`	`%refname.char.mix;`
`%screen.content;`	`%tbl.entry.mdl;`	`%tech.char.class;`
`%title.char.mix;`		

Description

A **Literal** is some specific piece of data, taken literally, from a computer system. It is similar in some ways to **UserInput** and **ComputerOutput**, but is somewhat more of a general classification. The sorts of things that constitute literals varies by domain.

Processing expectations

Formatted inline. A literal is frequently distinguished typographically and **Literal** is often used wherever that typographic presentation is desired.

The `MoreInfo` attribute can help generate a link or query to retrieve additional information.

4.0 *Future Changes*

The content model of **Literal** will be constrained to `(#PCDATA | Replaceable | InlineGraphic)` in DocBook V4.0.

Attributes

MoreInfo

If `MoreInfo` is set to `RefEntry`, it implies that a **RefEntry** exists which further describes the **Literal**.

See Also

Command, **ComputerOutput**, **Constant**, **Markup**, **Option**, **Optional**, **Parameter**, **Prompt**, **Replaceable**, **SGMLTag**, **UserInput**, **VarName**

Examples

```
<!DOCTYPE para PUBLIC "-//OASIS//DTD DocBook V3.1//EN">
<para>There are several undocumented settings for <varname>debug</varname>,
among them <literal>3.27</literal> to enable a complete trace and
<literal>3.8</literal> to debug the spell checker. For a complete
list of the possible settings,
see <filename class="headerfile">edit/debug.h</filename>.</para>
```

There are several undocumented settings for debug, among them `3.27` to enable a complete trace and `3.8` to debug the spell checker. For a complete list of the possible settings, see *edit/debug.h*.

For additional examples, see also **BookInfo**, **ProgramListingCO**.

LiteralLayout—A block of text in which line breaks and white space are to be reproduced faithfully

Synopsis

Mixed Content Model

```
LiteralLayout ::=
((LineAnnotation|#PCDATA|FootnoteRef|XRef|Abbrev|Acronym|Citation|
  CiteRefEntry|CiteTitle|Emphasis|FirstTerm|ForeignPhrase|
  GlossTerm|Footnote|Phrase|Quote|Trademark|WordAsWord|Link|OLink|
  ULink|Action|Application|ClassName|Command|ComputerOutput|
  Database|Email|EnVar|ErrorCode|ErrorName|ErrorType|Filename|
```

```
Function|GUIButton|GUIIcon|GUILabel|GUIMenu|GUIMenuItem|
GUISubmenu|Hardware|Interface|InterfaceDefinition|KeyCap|
KeyCode|KeyCombo|KeySym|Literal|Constant|Markup|MediaLabel|
MenuChoice|MouseButton|MsgText|Option|Optional|Parameter|Prompt|
Property|Replaceable|ReturnValue|SGMLTag|StructField|StructName|
Symbol|SystemItem|Token|Type|UserInput|VarName|Anchor|Author|
AuthorInitials|CorpAuthor|ModeSpec|OtherCredit|ProductName|
ProductNumber|RevHistory|Comment|Subscript|Superscript|
InlineGraphic|InlineMediaObject|InlineEquation|Synopsis|
CmdSynopsis|FuncSynopsis|IndexTerm)+)
```

Attributes **Name**	Common attributes **Type**	**Default**
Width	NUMBER	*None*
Class	*Enumeration:* Monospaced Normal	"Normal"
Format	*Enumerated notation:* linespecific	"linespecific"

Parameter Entities		
`%admon.mix;`	`%bookcomponent.content;`	`%component.mix;`
`%divcomponent.mix;`	`%example.mix;`	`%figure.mix;`
`%footnote.mix;`	`%glossdef.mix;`	`%indexdivcomponent.mix;`
`%legalnotice.mix;`	`%linespecific.class;`	`%para.mix;`
`%qandaset.mix;`	`%refcomponent.mix;`	`%sidebar.mix;`
`%tabentry.mix;`	`%tbl.entry.mdl;`	`%textobject.mix;`

Description

LiteralLayout is a verbatim environment. Unlike the other verbatim environments, it does not have strong semantic overtones and may not imply a font change.

Processing expectations

This element is displayed "verbatim"; whitespace and linebreaks within this element are significant.

Unlike **ProgramListing** and **Screen**, which usually imply a font change, **LiteralLayout** does not. How spaces are to be represented faithfully in a proportional font is not addressed by DocBook.

In DocBook V3.1, the `Class` attribute was added to give users control over the font used in **LiteralLayouts**. If the `Class` attribute is specified and its value is **`Monospaced`**, then the **LiteralLayout** will be presented in a monospaced font, probably the same one used for other verbatim environments. The default value for `Class` is `Normal`, meaning that no font change will occur.

4.0 *Future Changes*

The **InterfaceDefinition** element will be discarded in DocBook V4.0. It will no longer be available in the content model of this element.

Attributes

Class

Class distinguishes between literal layout environments that are presented in a monospaced font and literal layout environments that have no implicit font change.

Format

The Format attribute applies the linespecific notation to all **LiteralLayouts**. All white space and line breaks must be preserved.

Width

Width specifies the width (in characters) of the longest line in this **LiteralLayout** (formatters may use this value to determine scaling or rotation).

See Also

ComputerOutput, **LineAnnotation**, **ProgramListing**, **Screen**, **ScreenShot**, **Synopsis**, **UserInput**

Examples

```
<!DOCTYPE blockquote PUBLIC "-//OASIS//DTD DocBook V3.1//EN">
<blockquote>
<attribution>William Shakespeare, <citetitle>Henry V</citetitle></attribution>
<literallayout>
  O, for a muse of fire, that would ascend
The brightest heaven of invention!
A kingdom for a stage, princes to act,
And monarchs to behold the swelling scene!
</literallayout>
</blockquote>
```

> O, for a muse of fire, that would ascend
> The brightest heaven of invention!
> A kingdom for a stage, princes to act,
> And monarchs to behold the swelling scene!
>
> —William Shakespeare, *Henry V*

For additional examples, see also **Part**.

LoT—A list of the titles of formal objects (as tables or figures) in a document

Synopsis

Content Model

```
LoT ::=
((DocInfo?,Title,Subtitle?,TitleAbbrev?)?,
 LoTentry*)
```

Attributes	Common attributes	
Name	**Type**	**Default**
Label	CDATA	*None*
Parameter Entities		
`%nav.class;`	`%partcontent.mix;`	

Description

A **LoT** is a *list of titles.* It can be used to generate lists of **Figures**, **Tables**, **Examples**, or **Equations**.

Processing expectations

Formatted as a displayed block. A list of titles in a **Book** usually introduces a forced page break.

Most often, lists of titles are generated automatically by the presentation system and never have to be represented explicitly in the document source.

Attributes

Label

`Label` specifies an identifying number or string that may be used in presentation.

Examples

```
<!DOCTYPE lot PUBLIC "-//OASIS//DTD DocBook V3.1//EN">
<lot><title>List of Figures</title>
<lotentry pagenum=5>The Letters &ldquo;g&rdquo; and &ldquo;h&rdquo;
   inside their boxes</lotentry>
<lotentry pagenum=15>Example figure produced by both TeX and
   troff</lotentry>
<!-- ... -->
</lot>
```

LoTentry—An entry in a list of titles

Synopsis

Mixed Content Model

```
LoTentry ::=
((#PCDATA|FootnoteRef|XRef|Abbrev|Acronym|Citation|CiteRefEntry|
  CiteTitle|Emphasis|FirstTerm|ForeignPhrase|GlossTerm|Footnote|
  Phrase|Quote|Trademark|WordAsWord|Link|OLink|ULink|Action|
  Application|ClassName|Command|ComputerOutput|Database|Email|
  EnVar|ErrorCode|ErrorName|ErrorType|Filename|Function|GUIButton|
  GUIIcon|GUILabel|GUIMenu|GUIMenuItem|GUISubmenu|Hardware|
  Interface|InterfaceDefinition|KeyCap|KeyCode|KeyCombo|KeySym|
  Literal|Constant|Markup|MediaLabel|MenuChoice|MouseButton|
  MsgText|Option|Optional|Parameter|Prompt|Property|Replaceable|
```

```
ReturnValue|SGMLTag|StructField|StructName|Symbol|SystemItem|
Token|Type|UserInput|VarName|Anchor|Author|AuthorInitials|
CorpAuthor|ModeSpec|OtherCredit|ProductName|ProductNumber|
RevHistory|Comment|Subscript|Superscript|InlineGraphic|
InlineMediaObject|InlineEquation|Synopsis|CmdSynopsis|
FuncSynopsis|IndexTerm)+)
```

Attributes	Common attributes	
Name	**Type**	**Default**
SrcCredit	CDATA	*None*
Linkend	IDREF	*None*
Pagenum	CDATA	*None*

Description

A **LoTentry** identifies an individual title in a **LoT**. For example, in a *list of figures*, each individual figure title would be repeated in a **LoTentry** in the **LoT** for the list of figures.

Processing expectations

Formatted as a displayed block.

4.0 *Future Changes*

The **InterfaceDefinition** element will be discarded in DocBook V4.0. It will no longer be available in the content model of this element.

Attributes

Linkend

`Linkend` points to the element which is represented in this **LoTEntry**.

Pagenum

`PageNum` indicates the page on which this entry occurs in some version of the printed document.

SrcCredit

`SrcCredit` contains details about the source of the element referenced by this entry.

Examples

For examples, see **LoT**.

ManVolNum—A reference volume number

Synopsis

Mixed Content Model
`ManVolNum ::=`
`((#PCDATA|Acronym|Emphasis|Trademark|Link|OLink|ULink|Anchor|`
`Comment|Subscript|Superscript|InlineGraphic|InlineMediaObject|`
`IndexTerm)+)`	

Attributes	Common attributes

Description

In a DocBook reference page, the **ManVolNum** holds the number of the volume in which the **RefEntry** belongs.

The notion of a volume number is historical. UNIX manual pages ("man pages"), for which **RefEntry** was devised, were typically stored in three ring binders. Each bound manual was a volume in a set and contained information about a particular class of things. For example, volume 1 was for user commands, and volume 8 was for administrator commands.

Volume numbers need not be strictly numerical; volume "l" frequently held manual pages for local additions to the system, and the X Window System manual pages had an "x" in the volume number: for example, 1x.

Processing expectations

The content of **ManVolNum** is usually printed in parentheses after the element title or citation.

Examples

```
<!DOCTYPE para PUBLIC "-//OASIS//DTD DocBook V3.1//EN">
<para>
For a further description of print formats, consult the
<citerefentry><refentrytitle>printf</refentrytitle>
<manvolnum>3S</manvolnum></citerefentry> manual page.
</para>
```

For a further description of print formats, consult the printf(3S) manual page.

For additional examples, see also **CiteRefEntry**.

Markup—A string of formatting markup in text that is to be represented literally

Synopsis

Mixed Content Model
`Markup ::=`
`((#PCDATA|Replaceable|InlineGraphic|InlineMediaObject|IndexTerm)+)`		

Attributes	Common attributes	
Parameter Entities		
`%cptr.char.mix;`	`%ndxterm.char.mix;`	`%para.char.mix;`
`%programlisting.content;`	`%refinline.char.mix;`	`%refname.char.mix;`
`%screen.content;`	`%tbl.entry.mdl;`	`%tech.char.class;`
`%title.char.mix;`		

Description

Markup contains a string of formatting markup that is to be represented literally in the text. The utility of this element is almost wholly constrained to books about document formatting tools.

Processing expectations

Formatted inline.

See Also

ComputerOutput, **Constant**, **Literal**, **Option**, **Optional**, **Parameter**, **Prompt**, **Replaceable**, **SGMLTag**, **UserInput**, **VarName**

Examples

```
<!DOCTYPE para PUBLIC "-//OASIS//DTD DocBook V3.1//EN">
<para>
A presentation system using TeX as a back end might allow you
to insert inline markup, such as <markup role="tex">$x^2$</markup>,
using TeX syntax directly.
</para>
```

A presentation system using TeX as a back end might allow you to insert inline markup, such as `$x^2$`, using TeX syntax directly.

MediaLabel—A name that identifies the physical medium on which some information resides

Synopsis

Mixed Content Model
`MediaLabel ::=`
`((#PCDATA|Replaceable|InlineGraphic|InlineMediaObject|IndexTerm)+)`		

Attributes **Name**	Common attributes **Type**	**Default**
Class	*Enumeration:* Cartridge CDRom Disk Tape	*None*

Parameter Entities
`%cptr.char.mix;`
`%programlisting.content;`
`%screen.content;`
`%title.char.mix;`
	
	`%ndxterm.char.mix;`
	`%refinline.char.mix;`
	`%tbl.entry.mdl;`
		
		`%para.char.mix;`
		`%refname.char.mix;`
		`%tech.char.class;`

Description

The **MediaLabel** element identifies the name of a specific piece of physical media, such as a tape or disk label. Usually, a media label is something external, written by hand on the media itself, for example, but it may also refer to digital labels.

Processing expectations

Formatted inline.

Attributes

Class

`Class` indicates the type of media labeled.

See Also

Application, **Database**, **Filename**, **Hardware**, **ProductName**

Examples

```
<!DOCTYPE para PUBLIC "-//OASIS//DTD DocBook V3.1//EN">
<para>
To install <application>The Great Foo</application>, insert the disk
labelled <medialabel>TGF Setup 1</medialabel> and run
<command>setup</command>.
</para>
```

To install The Great Foo, insert the disk labelled *TGF Setup 1* and run *setup*.

```
<!DOCTYPE para PUBLIC "-//OASIS//DTD DocBook V3.1//EN">
<para>
The weekly incremental backup tape is labelled
<medialabel>Backup <replaceable>nn</replaceable></medialabel>, where
<replaceable>nn</replaceable> is the week number.
</para>
```

The weekly incremental backup tape is labelled *Backup nn*, where *nn* is the week number.

MediaObject—A displayed media object (video, audio, image, etc.)

Synopsis

Content Model

```
MediaObject ::=
(ObjectInfo?,
 (VideoObject|AudioObject|ImageObject),
 (VideoObject|AudioObject|ImageObject|TextObject)*,
 Caption?)
```

Attributes	Common attributes	
Parameter Entities		
%admon.mix;	%bookcomponent.content;	%component.mix;
%divcomponent.mix;	%equation.content;	%example.mix;
%figure.mix;	%footnote.mix;	%glossdef.mix;
%indexdivcomponent.mix;	%informal.class;	%para.mix;
%qandaset.mix;	%refcomponent.mix;	%sidebar.mix;
%tabentry.mix;	%tbl.entry.mdl;	%tbl.table.mdl;

Description

This element contains a set of alternative "media objects." In DocBook V3.1, three types of external objects are defined: **VideoObjects**, **AudioObjects**, and **ImageObjects**. Additional textual descriptions may be provided with **TextObjects**.

Processing expectations

Formatted as a displayed block.

The primary purpose of the **MediaObject** is to provide a wrapper around a set of alternative presentations of the same information.

If possible, the processing system should use the content of the first object within the **MediaObject**. If the first object cannot be used, the remaining objects should be considered in the order that they occur. A processor should use the first object that it can, although it is free to choose any of the remaining objects if the primary one cannot be used.

Under no circumstances should more than one object in a **MediaObject** be used or presented at the same time.

For example, a **MediaObject** might contain a video, a high resolution image, a low resolution image, a long text description, and a short text description. In a "high end" online system, the video is used. For print publishing, the high resolution image is used. For other online systems, either the high or low resolution image is used, possibly including the short text description as the online alternative. In a text-only environment, either the long or short text descriptions are used.

5.0 ***Future Changes***

In DocBook V5.0, **MediaObject** will replace **Graphic**.

See Also

Alt, **AudioObject**, **Caption**, **Graphic**, **ImageObject**, **InlineGraphic**, **InlineMediaObject**, **TextObject**, **VideoObject**

Examples

For examples, see **AudioObject**, **ImageObject**, **InformalFigure**, **VideoObject**.

MediaObjectCO—A media object that contains callouts

Synopsis

Content Model

```
MediaObjectCO ::=
(ObjectInfo?,ImageObjectCO,
 (ImageObjectCO|TextObject)*)
```

Attributes	Common attributes	

Parameter Entities

%admon.mix;	%bookcomponent.content;	%component.mix;
%divcomponent.mix;	%example.mix;	%figure.mix;
%footnote.mix;	%glossdef.mix;	%indexdivcomponent.mix;
%informal.class;	%para.mix;	%qandaset.mix;
%refcomponent.mix;	%sidebar.mix;	

Description

A **MediaObjectCO** is a wrapper around a set of alternative, annotated media objects.

Processing expectations

Formatted as a displayed block.

See also **MediaObject**.

See Also

AreaSpec, **CalloutList**, **CO**, **GraphicCO**, **ImageObjectCO**, **ProgramListingCO**, **ScreenCO**

Examples

```
<!DOCTYPE mediaobjectco PUBLIC "-//OASIS//DTD DocBook V3.1//EN">
<mediaobjectco>
<imageobjectco>
<areaspec units="calspair">
  <areaset id="oneway" coords="">
    <area id="oneway1" coords="300 400">
    <area id="oneway2" coords="325 340">
  </areaset>
  <area id="myhouse" coords="425 590">
</areaspec>
<imageobject>
<imagedata fileref="http://somemap.site.com/EARTH?USA?MA?01007">
</imageobject>
</imageobjectco>
</mediaobjectco>
```

Member—An element of a simple list

Synopsis

Mixed Content Model

```
Member ::=
((#PCDATA|FootnoteRef|XRef|Abbrev|Acronym|Citation|CiteRefEntry|
  CiteTitle|Emphasis|FirstTerm|ForeignPhrase|GlossTerm|Footnote|
  Phrase|Quote|Trademark|WordAsWord|Link|OLink|ULink|Action|
  Application|ClassName|Command|ComputerOutput|Database|Email|
  EnVar|ErrorCode|ErrorName|ErrorType|Filename|Function|GUIButton|
  GUIIcon|GUILabel|GUIMenu|GUIMenuItem|GUISubmenu|Hardware|
  Interface|InterfaceDefinition|KeyCap|KeyCode|KeyCombo|KeySym|
  Literal|Constant|Markup|MediaLabel|MenuChoice|MouseButton|
  MsgText|Option|Optional|Parameter|Prompt|Property|Replaceable|
  ReturnValue|SGMLTag|StructField|StructName|Symbol|SystemItem|
  Token|Type|UserInput|VarName|Anchor|Author|AuthorInitials|
  CorpAuthor|ModeSpec|OtherCredit|ProductName|ProductNumber|
  RevHistory|Comment|Subscript|Superscript|InlineGraphic|
  InlineMediaObject|InlineEquation|Synopsis|CmdSynopsis|
  FuncSynopsis|IndexTerm)+)
```

Attributes	Common attributes

Description

A **Member** is an element of a **SimpleList**. Unlike the other lists, items in a **SimpleList** are constrained to character data and inline elements.

Processing expectations

Formatted inline. How the inline **Members** are formatted with respect to each other is controlled by the containing **SimpleList**.

4.0 *Future Changes*

The **InterfaceDefinition** element will be discarded in DocBook V4.0. It will no longer be available in the content model of this element.

Examples

For examples, see **SimpleList**.

MenuChoice—A selection or series of selections from a menu

Synopsis

Content Model

```
MenuChoice ::=
(Shortcut?,
  (GUIButton|GUIIcon|GUILabel|GUIMenu|GUIMenuItem|GUISubmenu|
   Interface)+)
```

Attributes	Common attributes	
Name	**Type**	**Default**
MoreInfo	*Enumeration:* None RefEntry	"None"

Parameter Entities

`%cptr.char.mix;`	`%ndxterm.char.mix;`	`%para.char.mix;`
`%programlisting.content;`	`%refinline.char.mix;`	`%refname.char.mix;`
`%screen.content;`	`%tbl.entry.mdl;`	`%tech.char.class;`
`%title.char.mix;`		

Description

In applications that present graphical user interfaces, it is often necessary to select an item, or a series of items, from a menu in order to accomplish some action. The **MenuChoice** element provides a wrapper to contain the complete combination of selections.

Processing expectations

Formatted inline. The `MoreInfo` attribute can help generate a link or query to retrieve additional information.

MenuChoice may generate arrows or other punctuation between multiple GUI elements. The **ShortCut** may be suppressed, or sometimes it is presented in parentheses after the rest of the items.

Attributes

MoreInfo

If `MoreInfo` is set to `RefEntry`, it implies that a **RefEntry** exists which further describes the **MenuChoice**.

See Also

Accel, GUIButton, GUIIcon, GUILabel, GUIMenu, GUIMenuItem, GUISubmenu, KeyCap, KeyCode, KeyCombo, KeySym, MouseButton, Shortcut

Examples

```
<!DOCTYPE para PUBLIC "-//OASIS//DTD DocBook V3.1//EN">
<para>
You can exit from GNU Emacs with
<menuchoice>
  <shortcut>
    <keycombo><keysym>C-x</keysym><keysym>C-c</keysym></keycombo>
  </shortcut>
  <guimenu>Files</guimenu>
  <guimenuitem>Exit Emacs</guimenuitem>
</menuchoice>.
</para>
```

You can exit from GNU Emacs with *Files* → *Exit Emacs* (`C-x`+`C-c`).

Compare this example with the similar example in **GUIMenu**. Here the **KeyCombo** and **MenuChoice** elements are required to process thier content in some intelligent way in order to produce useful output.

For additional examples, see also **Shortcut**.

ModeSpec—Application-specific information necessary for the completion of an OLink

Synopsis

Mixed Content Model

```
ModeSpec ::=
((#PCDATA|Link|OLink|ULink|Emphasis|Trademark|Replaceable|Comment|
  Subscript|Superscript|InlineGraphic|InlineMediaObject|IndexTerm)+)
```

Attributes	Common attributes	
Name	**Type**	**Default**
Application	*Enumerated notation:* BMP CGM-BINARY CGM-CHAR CGM-CLEAR DITROFF DVI EPS EQN FAX GIF GIF87a GIF89a	*None*

Name	Type	Default
Application (cont.)	IGES JPEG JPG linespecific PCX PIC PS SGML TBL TEX TIFF WMF WPG	
Parameter Entities		
`%docinfo.char.class;`	`%ndxterm.char.mix;`	`%para.char.mix;`
`%programlisting.content;`	`%refinline.char.mix;`	`%screen.content;`
`%tbl.entry.mdl;`	`%title.char.mix;`	

Description

ModeSpec contains application-specific instructions required to process an **OLink**. See **OLink**.

Processing expectations

Suppressed. This element provides data for processing but is not expected to be rendered directly.

Attributes

Application

`Application` indicates the nature of the action required to complete the **OLink**. `Application` must be a notation declared in the DTD.

Examples

For examples, see **OLink**.

MouseButton—The conventional name of a mouse button

Synopsis

Mixed Content Model

```
MouseButton ::=
((#PCDATA|Replaceable|InlineGraphic|InlineMediaObject|IndexTerm)+)
```

Attributes Name	Common attributes Type	Default
MoreInfo	*Enumeration:* None RefEntry	"None"
Parameter Entities		
`%cptr.char.mix;`	`%ndxterm.char.mix;`	`%para.char.mix;`
`%programlisting.content;`	`%refinline.char.mix;`	`%refname.char.mix;`
`%screen.content;`	`%tbl.entry.mdl;`	`%tech.char.class;`
`%title.char.mix;`		

Description

The **MouseButton** element identifies the conventional name of a mouse button. Because mouse buttons are not physically labelled, the name is just that, a convention. Adding explicit markup for the naming of mouse buttons allow easier translation from one convention to another and might allow an online system to adapt to right- or left-handed usage.

Processing expectations

Formatted inline. The `MoreInfo` attribute can help generate a link or query to retrieve additional information.

Attributes

MoreInfo

If `MoreInfo` is set to `RefEntry`, it implies that a **RefEntry** exists which further describes the **MouseButton**.

See Also

Accel, **GUIButton**, **GUIIcon**, **GUILabel**, **GUIMenu**, **GUIMenuItem**, **GUISubmenu**, **KeyCap**, **KeyCode**, **KeyCombo**, **KeySym**, **MenuChoice**, **Shortcut**

Examples

```
<!DOCTYPE para PUBLIC "-//OASIS//DTD DocBook V3.1//EN">
<para>
Select a region of text by dragging the mouse pointer with the
<mousebutton>left</mousebutton> mouse button depressed.  Copy the
selected text to a new location by placing the mouse pointer at the
desired position and pressing the <mousebutton>middle</mousebutton>
button.
</para>
```

Select a region of text by dragging the mouse pointer with the left mouse button depressed. Copy the selected text to a new location by placing the mouse pointer at the desired position and pressing the middle button.

For additional examples, see also **KeyCombo**.

Msg—A message in a message set

Synopsis

Content Model
`Msg ::=`
`(Title?,MsgMain,`
` (MsgSub|MsgRel)*)`	

Attributes	Common attributes

Description

In a **MsgSet**, each **MsgEntry** contains at least one **Msg**. A **Msg** consists of a main message (**MsgMain**), and optionally one or more submessages (**MsgSub**) or related messages (**MsgRel**).

Additional information or explanation for the message is contained in the siblings of **Msg** within the **MsgEntry**.

See **MsgSet**.

Processing expectations

Formatted as a displayed block. Sometimes suppressed.

On the whole, the semantics of **MsgSet** are not clearly defined.

Examples

For examples, see **MsgSet**.

MsgAud—The audience to which a message in a message set is relevant

Synopsis

Mixed Content Model

```
MsgAud ::=
((#PCDATA|FootnoteRef|XRef|Abbrev|Acronym|Citation|CiteRefEntry|
  CiteTitle|Emphasis|FirstTerm|ForeignPhrase|GlossTerm|Footnote|
  Phrase|Quote|Trademark|WordAsWord|Link|OLink|ULink|Action|
  Application|ClassName|Command|ComputerOutput|Database|Email|
  EnVar|ErrorCode|ErrorName|ErrorType|Filename|Function|GUIButton|
  GUIIcon|GUILabel|GUIMenu|GUIMenuItem|GUISubmenu|Hardware|
  Interface|InterfaceDefinition|KeyCap|KeyCode|KeyCombo|KeySym|
  Literal|Constant|Markup|MediaLabel|MenuChoice|MouseButton|
```

```
MsgText|Option|Optional|Parameter|Prompt|Property|Replaceable|
ReturnValue|SGMLTag|StructField|StructName|Symbol|SystemItem|
Token|Type|UserInput|VarName|Anchor|Author|AuthorInitials|
CorpAuthor|ModeSpec|OtherCredit|ProductName|ProductNumber|
RevHistory|Comment|Subscript|Superscript|InlineGraphic|
InlineMediaObject|InlineEquation|Synopsis|CmdSynopsis|
FuncSynopsis|IndexTerm)+)
```

Attributes	Common attributes

Description

MsgAud is part of the additional information associated with a message in a **MsgSet**. It identifies the audience to which a particular **Msg** is relevant.

Processing expectations

May be formatted inline or as a displayed block, depending on context. Sometimes suppressed.

DocBook doesn't specify anything about how a particular audience might be identified, or how different audiences are distinguished.

On the whole, the semantics of **MsgSet** are not clearly defined.

4.0 Future Changes

The **InterfaceDefinition** element will be discarded in DocBook V4.0. It will no longer be available in the content model of this element.

Examples

For examples, see **MsgSet**.

MsgEntry—A wrapper for an entry in a message set

Synopsis

Content Model
`MsgEntry ::=`
`(Msg+,MsgInfo?,MsgExplan*)`	

Attributes	Common attributes

Description

In a **MsgSet**, each **MsgEntry** contains some number of messages (**Msgs**) and additional informative and explanatory material about them.

Processing expectations

Formatted as a displayed block.

On the whole, the semantics of **MsgSet** are not clearly defined.

Examples

For examples, see **MsgSet**.

MsgExplan—Explanatory material relating to a message in a message set

Synopsis

Content Model

```
MsgExplan ::=
(Title?,
 (CalloutList|GlossList|ItemizedList|OrderedList|SegmentedList|
  SimpleList|VariableList|Caution|Important|Note|Tip|Warning|
  LiteralLayout|ProgramListing|ProgramListingCO|Screen|ScreenCO|
  ScreenShot|Synopsis|CmdSynopsis|FuncSynopsis|FormalPara|Para|
  SimPara|Address|BlockQuote|Graphic|GraphicCO|MediaObject|
  MediaObjectCO|InformalEquation|InformalExample|InformalFigure|
  InformalTable|Equation|Example|Figure|Table|MsgSet|Procedure|
  Sidebar|QandASet|Anchor|BridgeHead|Comment|Highlights|Abstract|
  AuthorBlurb|Epigraph|IndexTerm)+)
```

Attributes	Common attributes

Description

A **MsgExplan** contains some sort of explanatory information about a **Msg** or a set of **Msg**s in a **MsgEntry**.

Processing expectations

Formatted as a displayed block. Sometimes suppressed.

If a **MsgEntry** contains multiple **Msg**s and multiple **MsgExplan**s, DocBook makes no assertions about how they are related.

On the whole, the semantics of **MsgSet** are not clearly defined.

Examples

For examples, see **MsgSet**.

MsgInfo—Information about a message in a message set

Synopsis

Content Model

```
MsgInfo ::=
((MsgLevel|MsgOrig|MsgAud)*)
```

Attributes	Common attributes

Description

MsgInfo provides additional information about a **Msg** in a **MsgEntry**.

Processing expectations

May be formatted inline or as a displayed block, depending on context. Sometimes suppressed.

On the whole, the semantics of **MsgSet** are not clearly defined.

Examples

For examples, see **MsgSet**.

MsgLevel—The level of importance or severity of a message in a message set

Synopsis

Mixed Content Model
`MsgLevel ::=`
`((#PCDATA|Replaceable|InlineGraphic|InlineMediaObject|IndexTerm)+)`	

Attributes	Common attributes

Description

MsgLevel is part of the additional information associated with a message in a **MsgSet**. It identifies the relative importance or severity of a message.

Processing expectations

May be formatted inline or as a displayed block, depending on context. Sometimes suppressed.

On the whole, the semantics of **MsgSet** are not clearly defined.

Examples

For examples, see **MsgSet**.

MsgMain—The primary component of a message in a message set

Synopsis

Content Model
`MsgMain ::=`
`(Title?,MsgText)`	

Attributes	Common attributes

Description

Every **Msg** must have one primary message. This is stored in the **MsgMain**. The primary message is distinguished from any number of submessages (**MsgSub**) or related messages (**MsgRel**) that a **Msg** might have.

Processing expectations

Formatted as a displayed block.

On the whole, the semantics of **MsgSet** are not clearly defined.

Examples

For examples, see **MsgSet**.

MsgOrig—The origin of a message in a message set

Synopsis

Mixed Content Model
`MsgOrig ::=`
`((#PCDATA|Replaceable|InlineGraphic|InlineMediaObject|IndexTerm)+)`	

Attributes	Common attributes

Description

MsgOrig is part of the additional information associated with a message in a **MsgSet**. It identifies the origin or source of a particular **Msg**, for example, a piece of hardware, the operating system, or an application.

Processing expectations

May be formatted inline or as a displayed block, depending on context. Sometimes suppressed.

On the whole, the semantics of **MsgSet** are not clearly defined.

Examples

For examples, see **MsgSet**.

MsgRel—A related component of a message in a message set

Synopsis

Content Model
`MsgRel ::=`
`(Title?,MsgText)`	

Attributes	Common attributes

Description

Every **Msg** has one primary message (**MsgMain**). It may also have any number of related messages, stored in **MsgRel** elements within the same **Msg**.

Related messages are usually messages that appear elsewhere in response to the same event (or set of events) that triggered the main message. For example, if a network client produces a failure or warning message, a related message might appear on the server console.

Processing expectations

May be formatted inline or as a displayed block, depending on context. Sometimes suppressed.

On the whole, the semantics of **MsgSet** are not clearly defined.

Examples

For examples, see **MsgSet**.

MsgSet—A detailed set of messages, usually error messages

Synopsis

Content Model		

`MsgSet ::=`
`((Title,TitleAbbrev?)?,`
` MsgEntry+)`		

Attributes	Common attributes	
Parameter Entities		
`%bookcomponent.content;`	`%component.mix;`	`%compound.class;`
`%divcomponent.mix;`	`%refcomponent.mix;`	

Description

MsgSet is a complex structure designed to hold a detailed set of messages, usually error messages. In addition to the actual text of each message, it can contain additional information about each message and the messages related to it.

Processing expectations

Formatted as a displayed block.

On the whole, the semantics of **MsgSet** are not clearly defined.

See Also

ErrorCode, **ErrorName**, **ErrorType**

Examples

```
<!DOCTYPE msgset PUBLIC "-//OASIS//DTD DocBook V3.1//EN">
<msgset>
  <msgentry>
    <msg>
      <msgmain>
        <msgtext><para>Record failed CRC</para></msgtext>
      </msgmain>
      <msgsub>
        <msgtext><para>Record <replaceable>n</replaceable>
                  in <replaceable>database</replaceable></para></msgtext>
      </msgsub>
      <msgrel>
        <msgtext><para>File read error on
                 <replaceable>database</replaceable></para></msgtext>
      </msgrel>
      <msgrel>
        <msgtext><para>Panic! Corrupt record!</para></msgtext>
      </msgrel>
    </msg>
    <msginfo>
      <msglevel>severe</msglevel>
      <msgorig>server</msgorig>
      <msgaud>all</msgaud>
    </msginfo>
    <msgexplan>
      <para>
      Indicates that some sort of error occurred while attempting to load
      a record from the database.  Retry.  If failure persists,
      contact the database administrator.
      </para>
    </msgexplan>
  </msgentry>
  <!-- more entries -->
</msgset>
```

Record failed CRC

Record *n* in *database*

File read error on *database*

Panic! Corrupt record!

Level: severe
Origin: server
Audience: all

Indicates that some sort of error occurred while attempting to load a record from the database. Retry. If failure persists, contact the database administrator.

MsgSub—A subcomponent of a message in a message set

Synopsis

Content Model
`MsgSub ::=`
`(Title?,MsgText)`	

Attributes	Common attributes

Description

A **MsgSub** represents some subpart of a message. Different **MsgSub**s might arise in different contexts.

Processing expectations

May be formatted inline or as a displayed block, depending on context. Sometimes suppressed.

On the whole, the semantics of **MsgSet** are not clearly defined.

Examples

For examples, see **MsgSet**.

MsgText—The actual text of a message component in a message set

Synopsis

Content Model

```
MsgText ::=
((CalloutList|GlossList|ItemizedList|OrderedList|SegmentedList|
  SimpleList|VariableList|Caution|Important|Note|Tip|Warning|
  LiteralLayout|ProgramListing|ProgramListingCO|Screen|ScreenCO|
  ScreenShot|Synopsis|CmdSynopsis|FuncSynopsis|FormalPara|Para|
  SimPara|Address|BlockQuote|Graphic|GraphicCO|MediaObject|
  MediaObjectCO|InformalEquation|InformalExample|InformalFigure|
  InformalTable|Equation|Example|Figure|Table|MsgSet|Procedure|
  Sidebar|QandASet|Anchor|BridgeHead|Comment|Highlights|Abstract|
  AuthorBlurb|Epigraph|IndexTerm)+)
```

Attributes	Common attributes	
Parameter Entities		
`%cptr.char.mix;`	`%ndxterm.char.mix;`	`%para.char.mix;`
`%programlisting.content;`	`%refinline.char.mix;`	`%refname.char.mix;`
`%screen.content;`	`%tbl.entry.mdl;`	`%tech.char.class;`
`%title.char.mix;`		

Description

The **MsgText** is the actual content of the message in a **MsgMain**, **MsgSub**, or **MsgRel**.

Processing expectations

May be formatted inline or as a displayed block, depending on context.

On the whole, the semantics of **MsgSet** are not clearly defined.

4.0 Future Changes

MsgText is currently one of the general, technical inlines by accident. In DocBook V4.0, it will be limited to use within a **MsgSet**.

Examples

For examples, see **MsgSet**.

Note—A message set off from the text

Synopsis

Content Model

```
Note ::=
(Title?,
 (CalloutList|GlossList|ItemizedList|OrderedList|SegmentedList|
  SimpleList|VariableList|LiteralLayout|ProgramListing|
  ProgramListingCO|Screen|ScreenCO|ScreenShot|Synopsis|
  CmdSynopsis|FuncSynopsis|FormalPara|Para|SimPara|Address|
  BlockQuote|Graphic|GraphicCO|MediaObject|MediaObjectCO|
  InformalEquation|InformalExample|InformalFigure|InformalTable|
  Equation|Example|Figure|Table|Procedure|Sidebar|Anchor|
  BridgeHead|Comment|IndexTerm)+)
```

Attributes	Common attributes	

Parameter Entities

%admon.class;	%admon.exclusion;	%bookcomponent.content;
%component.mix;	%divcomponent.mix;	%highlights.mix;
%legalnotice.mix;	%para.mix;	%refcomponent.mix;
%sidebar.mix;	%tabentry.mix;	%tbl.entry.mdl;
%textobject.mix;		

Description

A **Note** is an admonition set off from the main text.

In some types of documentation, the semantics of admonitions are clearly defined (**Caution** might imply the possibility of harm to equipement whereas **Warning** might imply harm to a person), but DocBook makes no such assertions.

Processing expectations

Formatted as a displayed block. Often outputs the generated text "Note" or some other visible indication of the type of admonition, especially if a **Title** is not present. Sometimes outputs a graphical icon or another symbol as well.

See Also

Caution, **Important**, **Tip**, **Warning**

Examples

```
<!DOCTYPE note PUBLIC "-//OASIS//DTD DocBook V3.1//EN">
<note><title>Upcoming Changes</title>
<para>
Future versions of this feature may not be backward-compatible.
Consider implementing the revised interface now.
</para>
</note>
```

Upcoming Changes

Future versions of this feature may not be backward-compatible. Consider implementing the revised interface now.

For additional examples, see also **ProgramListingCO**.

ObjectInfo—Meta-information for an object

Synopsis

Content Model

```
ObjectInfo ::=
((Graphic|MediaObject|LegalNotice|ModeSpec|SubjectSet|KeywordSet|
  ITermSet|Abbrev|Abstract|Address|ArtPageNums|Author|AuthorGroup|
  AuthorInitials|BiblioMisc|BiblioSet|Collab|ConfGroup|
  ContractNum|ContractSponsor|Copyright|CorpAuthor|CorpName|Date|
  Edition|Editor|InvPartNumber|ISBN|ISSN|IssueNum|OrgName|
  OtherCredit|PageNums|PrintHistory|ProductName|ProductNumber|
  PubDate|Publisher|PublisherName|PubsNumber|ReleaseInfo|
  RevHistory|SeriesVolNums|Subtitle|Title|TitleAbbrev|VolumeNum|
  CiteTitle|Honorific|FirstName|Surname|Lineage|OtherName|
  Affiliation|AuthorBlurb|Contrib|IndexTerm)+)
```

Attributes	Common attributes

Description

The **ObjectInfo** element is a wrapper for the meta-information about a video, audio, image, or text object.

Processing expectations

Suppressed. Many of the elements in this wrapper may be used in presentation, but they are not generally printed as part of the formatting of the wrapper. The wrapper merely serves to identify where they occur.

4.0 *Future Changes*

AuthorBlurb and **Affiliation** will be removed from the inline content of **DivisionInfo** in DocBook V4.0. A new wrapper element will be created to associate this information with authors, editors, and other contributors.

See Also

ArtHeader, **BookBiblio**, **BookInfo**, **DocInfo**, **RefSynopsisDivInfo**, **ScreenInfo**, **Sect1Info**, **Sect2Info**, **Sect3Info**, **Sect4Info**, **Sect5Info**, **SectionInfo**, **SetInfo**

Examples

For examples, see **AudioObject**.

OLink—A link that addresses its target indirectly, through an entity

Synopsis

Mixed Content Model

```
OLink ::=
((#PCDATA|FootnoteRef|XRef|Abbrev|Acronym|Citation|CiteRefEntry|
  CiteTitle|Emphasis|FirstTerm|ForeignPhrase|GlossTerm|Footnote|
  Phrase|Quote|Trademark|WordAsWord|Link|OLink|ULink|Action|
  Application|ClassName|Command|ComputerOutput|Database|Email|
  EnVar|ErrorCode|ErrorName|ErrorType|Filename|Function|GUIButton|
  GUIIcon|GUILabel|GUIMenu|GUIMenuItem|GUISubmenu|Hardware|
  Interface|InterfaceDefinition|KeyCap|KeyCode|KeyCombo|KeySym|
  Literal|Constant|Markup|MediaLabel|MenuChoice|MouseButton|
  MsgText|Option|Optional|Parameter|Prompt|Property|Replaceable|
  ReturnValue|SGMLTag|StructField|StructName|Symbol|SystemItem|
  Token|Type|UserInput|VarName|Anchor|Author|AuthorInitials|
  CorpAuthor|ModeSpec|OtherCredit|ProductName|ProductNumber|
  RevHistory|Comment|Subscript|Superscript|InlineGraphic|
  InlineMediaObject|InlineEquation|Synopsis|CmdSynopsis|
  FuncSynopsis|IndexTerm)+)
```

Attributes	Common attributes	
Name	**Type**	**Default**
Type	CDATA	*None*
LinkMode	IDREF	*None*
TargetDocEnt	ENTITY	*None*
LocalInfo	CDATA	*None*

Parameter Entities

`%cptr.char.mix;`	`%docinfo.char.mix;`	`%indexdivcomponent.mix;`
`%link.char.class;`	`%ndxterm.char.mix;`	`%para.char.mix;`
`%programlisting.content;`	`%refinline.char.mix;`	`%screen.content;`
`%tbl.entry.mdl;`	`%title.char.mix;`	`%word.char.mix;`

Description

Unlike **Link** and **ULink**, the semantics of **OLink** are application-specific. **OLink** provides a mechanism for establishing links across documents, where ID/IDREF linking is not possible and **ULink** is inappropriate.

In general terms, the strategy employed by **OLink** is to point to the target document via an external general entity, and point into that document in some application-specific way.

Processing expectations

Formatted inline.

OLink points to its target primarily with the `TargetDocEnt` attribute. `TargetDocEnt` must be the name of an entity (previously declared in the DTD or in the*document subset*).

Because `TargetDocEnt` is an entity attribute, the entity used as its value must be declared with a notation. Because the target is usually another SGML or XML document, the notation `SGML` is most often used:

```
<!ENTITY myotherdoc SYSTEM "myotherdoc.sgm" NDATA SGML>
```

The semantics of the link are controlled by three other attributes: `LinkMode`, `LocalInfo`, and `Type`. The `LinkMode` attribute points to a **ModeSpec**. The content of **ModeSpec** describes the semantic of the link in an entirely application-specific way.

The values of `LocalInfo` and `Type` may also influence the application. For example, if the **ModeSpec** describes some sort of query, `LocalInfo` might hold the query text (allowing multiple **OLinks** to use the same **ModeSpec** to achieve different queries with the same query engine).

Linking elements must not be nested within other linking elements (including themselves). Because DocBook is harmonizing towards XML, this restriction cannot easily be enforced by the DTD. The processing of nested linking elements is undefined.

4.0 *Future Changes*

The **InterfaceDefinition** element will be discarded in DocBook V4.0. It will no longer be available in the content model of this element.

Attributes

LinkMode

`LinkMode` points to the **ModeSpec** which provides additional application-specific information for resolving this **OLink**.

LocalInfo

`LocalInfo` hold additional information that may be used with the **ModeSpec** (pointed to by `LinkMode`) by the application when resolving this **OLink**.

TargetDocEnt

`TargetDocEnt` specifies the name of an entity that is to be used as part of the **OLink**. Exactly how the link is resolved is application dependent and may be influenced by the `MoreInfo` and `LocalInfo` attributes.

Type

`Type` is available for application-specific customization of the linking behavior.

See Also

Anchor, **Link**, **ULink**, **XRef**

Examples

In this example, we see how an **OLink** might be used for searching. Here the **ModeSpec** describes the search query (in a fictitious and entirely concocted syntax): "look in the titles of sections and return links using the title as the text of the link". When the user selects the link, the application is expected to perform the query and then might display the list of titles as a pop-up window in the user interface.

```
<!DOCTYPE chapter PUBLIC "-//OASIS//DTD DocBook V3.1//EN" [
<!ENTITY refbook SYSTEM "refbook.sgm" CDATA SGML>
]>
<chapter>
<docinfo>
  <modespec id=s1query>query in sect*, title return link text title</modespec>
</docinfo>
<title>Printing</title>

<para>
Blah, blah, blah.
</para>

<sect1><title>See Also</title>

<para>
For more information <olink targetdocent=refbook linkmode=s1query
localinfo="print or printing">about printing</olink>, consult
the <ulink url="refbook.sgm">reference manual</ulink>.
</para>
</chapter>
```

Option—An option for a software command

Synopsis

Mixed Content Model

```
Option ::=
((#PCDATA|Link|OLink|ULink|Action|Application|ClassName|Command|
  ComputerOutput|Database|Email|EnVar|ErrorCode|ErrorName|
  ErrorType|Filename|Function|GUIButton|GUIIcon|GUILabel|GUIMenu|
  GUIMenuItem|GUISubmenu|Hardware|Interface|InterfaceDefinition|
  KeyCap|KeyCode|KeyCombo|KeySym|Literal|Constant|Markup|
  MediaLabel|MenuChoice|MouseButton|MsgText|Option|Optional|
  Parameter|Prompt|Property|Replaceable|ReturnValue|SGMLTag|
  StructField|StructName|Symbol|SystemItem|Token|Type|UserInput|
  VarName|Anchor|Comment|Subscript|Superscript|InlineGraphic|
  InlineMediaObject|IndexTerm)+)
```

Attributes	Common attributes	
Parameter Entities		
%cptr.char.mix;	%ndxterm.char.mix;	%para.char.mix;
%programlisting.content;	%refinline.char.mix;	%refname.char.mix;
%screen.content;	%tbl.entry.mdl;	%tech.char.class;
%title.char.mix;		

Description

Option identifies an optional argument to a software command.

Processing expectations

Formatted inline.

DocBook does not specify whether or not a symbol (such as - or /) is generated before the content of **Option**, or what that symbol might be. Generating the text may or may not be desirable, but in either case, it is an interchange issue. See Appendix F.

4.0 *Future Changes*

The content model of **Option** will be constrained to `(#PCDATA | Replaceable | InlineGraphic)` in DocBook V4.0.

See Also

ComputerOutput, **Constant**, **Literal**, **Markup**, **Optional**, **Parameter**, **Prompt**, **Replaceable**, **SGMLTag**, **UserInput**, **VarName**

Examples

```
<!DOCTYPE para PUBLIC "-//OASIS//DTD DocBook V3.1//EN">
<para>
The <option>-a</option> option on the <acronym>UNIX</acronym>
<command>ls</command> command or the <option>/r</option> option on the
```

```
<acronym>DOS</acronym> <command>attrib</command>
command, for example.
</para>
```

The *-a* option on the UNIX *ls* command or the */r* option on the DOS *attrib* command, for example.

For additional examples, see also **Optional**.

Optional—Optional information

Synopsis

Mixed Content Model

```
Optional ::=
((#PCDATA|Link|OLink|ULink|Action|Application|ClassName|Command|
  ComputerOutput|Database|Email|EnVar|ErrorCode|ErrorName|
  ErrorType|Filename|Function|GUIButton|GUIIcon|GUILabel|GUIMenu|
  GUIMenuItem|GUISubmenu|Hardware|Interface|InterfaceDefinition|
  KeyCap|KeyCode|KeyCombo|KeySym|Literal|Constant|Markup|
  MediaLabel|MenuChoice|MouseButton|MsgText|Option|Optional|
  Parameter|Prompt|Property|Replaceable|ReturnValue|SGMLTag|
  StructField|StructName|Symbol|SystemItem|Token|Type|UserInput|
  VarName|Anchor|Comment|Subscript|Superscript|InlineGraphic|
  InlineMediaObject|IndexTerm)+)
```

Attributes	Common attributes	
Parameter Entities		
%cptr.char.mix;	%ndxterm.char.mix;	%para.char.mix;
%programlisting.content;	%refinline.char.mix;	%refname.char.mix;
%screen.content;	%tbl.entry.mdl;	%tech.char.class;
%title.char.mix;		

Description

The **Optional** element indicates that a specified argument, option, or other text is optional. The precise meaning of "optional" varies according to the application or process begin documented.

Processing expectations

Formatted inline.

Optional arguments in a **Synopsis** are usually given special typographic treatment, often they are surrounded by square brackets. The **Optional** tag is expected to *generate* the brackets.

Outside a **Synopsis**, the typographic treatment of **Optional** is application-specific.

4.0 *Future Changes*

The **InterfaceDefinition** element will be discarded in DocBook V4.0. It will no longer be available in the content model of this element.

See Also

ComputerOutput, Constant, Literal, Markup, Option, Parameter, Prompt, Replaceable, SGMLTag, UserInput, VarName

Examples

The UNIX *ls* command could be documented as follows:

```
<!DOCTYPE synopsis PUBLIC "-//OASIS//DTD DocBook V3.1//EN">
<synopsis>
ls <optional><option>-abcCdfFgilLmnopqrRstux1</option></optional>
   <optional>names</optional>
</synopsis>
```

which might generate the following output:

```
    ls [ -abcCdfFgilLmnopqrRstux1 ]
       [names]
```

OrderedList—A list in which each entry is marked with a sequentially incremented label

Synopsis

Content Model
`OrderedList ::=`
`(ListItem+)`

Attributes Name	Common attributes Type	Default
Numeration	*Enumeration:* Arabic Loweralpha Lowerroman Upperalpha Upperroman	*None*
InheritNum	*Enumeration:* Ignore Inherit	"Ignore"
Spacing	*Enumeration:* Compact Normal	*None*
Continuation	*Enumeration:* Continues Restarts	"Restarts"

Parameter Entities

%admon.mix;	%bookcomponent.content;	%component.mix;
%divcomponent.mix;	%example.mix;	%footnote.mix;
%glossdef.mix;	%highlights.mix;	%indexdivcomponent.mix;
%legalnotice.mix;	%list.class;	%para.mix;
%qandaset.mix;	%refcomponent.mix;	%sidebar.mix;
%tabentry.mix;	%tbl.entry.mdl;	%textobject.mix;

Description

In an **OrderedList**, each member of the list is marked with a numeral, letter, or other sequential symbol (such as roman numerals).

Processing expectations

Formatted as a displayed block.

If no value is specified for `Numeration`, Arabic numerals (1, 2, 3, ...) are to be used.

In nested lists, DocBook does not specify the sequence of numerations.

Note that the attributes of **OrderedList** have a significant influence on the processing expectations.

Attributes

Continuation

If `Continuation` is specified, it indicates how list numbering should begin relative to the immediately preceding list. `Restarts`, the default, indicates that numbering should begin again at 1. `Continues` indicates that numbering should begin where the preceding list left off.

InheritNum

In a nested list, `InheritNum` indicates whether or not the enumeration of interior lists should include the numbers of containing list items. If `InheritNum` is `Inherit` then the third item of a list inside the second item of a list inside the fourth item of a list might be enumerated as "4.2.3". If it is `Ignore`, the default, then it would be simply "3". (The `Numeration` attribute controls the actual format of the item numbers, of course.)

Numeration

`Numeration` specifies the style of numbering to be used for items in the current **OrderedList**.

Spacing

`Spacing` indicates whether or not the vertical space in the list should be minimized.

See Also

CalloutList, **ItemizedList**, **ListItem**, **SegmentedList**, **SimpleList**, **VariableList**

Examples

```
<!DOCTYPE orderedlist PUBLIC "-//OASIS//DTD DocBook V3.1//EN">
<orderedlist numeration="lowerroman">
<listitem>
```

```
<para>One</para>
</listitem>
<listitem>
<para>Two</para>
</listitem>
<listitem>
<para>Three</para>
</listitem>
<listitem>
<para>Four</para>
</listitem>
</orderedlist>
```

i. One

ii. Two

iii. Three

iv. Four

OrgDiv—A division of an organization

Synopsis

Mixed Content Model
`OrgDiv ::=`
`((#PCDATA|Link|OLink|ULink|Emphasis|Trademark|Replaceable|Comment|`
`Subscript|Superscript|InlineGraphic|InlineMediaObject|IndexTerm)+)`	

Attributes	Common attributes

Description

OrgDiv identifies a division in an organization, such as "Chrysler" in "General Motors."

Processing expectations

Formatted inline. Sometimes suppressed.

See Also

Affiliation, **CorpName**, **JobTitle**, **OrgName**, **ShortAffil**

Examples

For examples, see **Author**.

OrgName—The name of an organization other than a corporation

Synopsis

Mixed Content Model
`OrgName ::=`
`((#PCDATA|Link|OLink|ULink|Emphasis|Trademark|Replaceable|Comment|`
`  Subscript|Superscript|InlineGraphic|InlineMediaObject|IndexTerm)+)`	

Attributes	Common attributes
Parameter Entities `%bibliocomponent.mix;`	

Description

An **OrgName** identifies the name of an organization or corporation. Outside of an **Affiliation**, **CorpName** is a more appropriate element for the name of a corporation.

Processing expectations

Formatted inline. Sometimes suppressed.

See Also

Affiliation, **CorpName**, **JobTitle**, **OrgDiv**, **PublisherName**, **ShortAffil**

Examples

For examples, see **Author**, **AuthorGroup**, **BookInfo**, **ContractSponsor**.

OtherAddr—Uncategorized information in address

Synopsis

Mixed Content Model
`OtherAddr ::=`
`((#PCDATA|Link|OLink|ULink|Emphasis|Trademark|Replaceable|Comment|`
`  Subscript|Superscript|InlineGraphic|InlineMediaObject|IndexTerm)+)`	

Attributes	Common attributes

Description

Within an **Address**, **OtherAddr** is a wrapper for parts of an address other than **Street**, **POB**, **Postcode**, **City**, **State**, **Country**, **Phone**, **Fax**, and **Email**, all of which have elements specific to their content.

In early versions of DocBook, **Address** was not allowed to contain character data (it was a database-like collection of fields). In that context, a wrapper was necessary for any random pieces of information that might be required for an address. With the introduction of character data directly in the **Address** element, **OtherAddr** may have lost most of its *raison d'être.*

Processing expectations

Formatted inline. This element may inherit the verbatim qualities of an **Address**.

See Also

Address, **City**, **Country**, **Email**, **Fax**, **Phone**, **POB**, **Postcode**, **State**, **Street**

Examples

For examples, see **Address**.

OtherCredit—A person or entity, other than an author or editor, credited in a document

Synopsis

Content Model

```
OtherCredit ::=
((Honorific|FirstName|Surname|Lineage|OtherName|Affiliation|
  AuthorBlurb|Contrib)+)
```

Attributes	Common attributes	
Parameter Entities		
%bibliocomponent.mix;	%docinfo.char.class;	%ndxterm.char.mix;
%para.char.mix;	%programlisting.con-tent;	%refinline.char.mix;
%screen.content;	%tbl.entry.mdl;	%title.char.mix;

Description

DocBook allows you to directly identify **Authors** and **Editors**. **OtherCredit** provides a mechanism for identifying other individuals, for example, contributors or production editors, in a similar context.

Processing expectations

May be formatted inline or as a displayed block, depending on context. Sometimes suppressed.

4.0 *Future Changes*

AuthorBlurb and **Affiliation** will be removed from the inline content of **OtherCredit** in DocBook V4.0. A new wrapper element will be created to hold **OtherCredit**, **AuthorBlurb**, and **Affiliation**.

See Also

Author, **AuthorBlurb**, **AuthorGroup**, **Collab**, **CollabName**, **Contrib**, **CorpAuthor**, **Editor**

Examples

```
<!DOCTYPE artheader PUBLIC "-//OASIS//DTD DocBook V3.1//EN">
<artheader>
  <title>Something Snappy</title>
  <author>
    <firstname>Norman</firstname>
    <surname>Walsh</surname>
  </author>
  <othercredit>
    <firstname>John</firstname>
    <surname>Doe</surname>
    <contrib>Extensive review and rough drafts of Section 1.3, 1.4, and 1.5
      </contrib>
  </othercredit>
  <pubsnumber>5</pubsnumber>
</artheader>
```

OtherName—A component of a persons name that is not a first name, surname, or lineage

Synopsis

Mixed Content Model	

`OtherName ::=`
`((#PCDATA|Link|OLink|ULink|Emphasis|Trademark|Replaceable|Comment|`
`  Subscript|Superscript|InlineGraphic|InlineMediaObject|IndexTerm)+)`	

Attributes	Common attributes
Parameter Entities `%bibliocomponent.mix;`	`%person.ident.mix;`

Description

OtherName is a generic wrapper for parts of an individual's name other than **Honorific**, **FirstName**, **Surname** and **Lineage**. One common use is to identify an individual's middle name or initial. Use `Role` to classify the type of other name.

Processing expectations

Formatted inline. In an **Address**, this element may inherit the verbatim qualities of an address.

See Also

Affiliation, **FirstName**, **Honorific**, **Lineage**, **Surname**

Examples

For examples, see **Author**, **AuthorGroup**, **Bibliography**.

PageNums—The numbers of the pages in a book, for use in a bibliographic entry

Synopsis

Mixed Content Model

```
PageNums ::=
((#PCDATA|Link|OLink|ULink|Emphasis|Trademark|Replaceable|Comment|
  Subscript|Superscript|InlineGraphic|InlineMediaObject|IndexTerm)+)
```

Attributes	Common attributes

Parameter Entities

```
%bibliocomponent.mix;
```

Description

PageNums identifies a page or range of pages. This may be useful in the bibliography of a book, to indicate the number of pages, or in a citation to a journal article.

Processing expectations

Formatted inline. Sometimes suppressed.

Examples

For examples, see **Bibliography**, **BiblioSet**.

Para—A paragraph

Synopsis

Mixed Content Model

```
Para ::=
((#PCDATA|FootnoteRef|XRef|Abbrev|Acronym|Citation|CiteRefEntry|
  CiteTitle|Emphasis|FirstTerm|ForeignPhrase|GlossTerm|Footnote|
  Phrase|Quote|Trademark|WordAsWord|Link|OLink|ULink|Action|
  Application|ClassName|Command|ComputerOutput|Database|Email|
  EnVar|ErrorCode|ErrorName|ErrorType|Filename|Function|GUIButton|
  GUIIcon|GUILabel|GUIMenu|GUIMenuItem|GUISubmenu|Hardware|
  Interface|InterfaceDefinition|KeyCap|KeyCode|KeyCombo|KeySym|
```

```
Literal|Constant|Markup|MediaLabel|MenuChoice|MouseButton|
MsgText|Option|Optional|Parameter|Prompt|Property|Replaceable|
ReturnValue|SGMLTag|StructField|StructName|Symbol|SystemItem|
Token|Type|UserInput|VarName|Anchor|Author|AuthorInitials|
CorpAuthor|ModeSpec|OtherCredit|ProductName|ProductNumber|
RevHistory|Comment|Subscript|Superscript|InlineGraphic|
InlineMediaObject|InlineEquation|Synopsis|CmdSynopsis|
FuncSynopsis|IndexTerm|CalloutList|GlossList|ItemizedList|
OrderedList|SegmentedList|SimpleList|VariableList|Caution|
Important|Note|Tip|Warning|LiteralLayout|ProgramListing|
ProgramListingCO|Screen|ScreenCO|ScreenShot|Address|BlockQuote|
Graphic|GraphicCO|MediaObject|MediaObjectCO|InformalEquation|
InformalExample|InformalFigure|InformalTable|Equation|Example|
Figure|Table)+)
```

Attributes	Common attributes	
Parameter Entities		
%admon.mix;	%bookcomponent.content;	%component.mix;
%divcomponent.mix;	%example.mix;	%footnote.mix;
%glossdef.mix;	%highlights.mix;	%indexdivcomponent.mix;
%legalnotice.mix;	%para.class;	%qandaset.mix;
%refcomponent.mix;	%sidebar.mix;	%tabentry.mix;
%tbl.entry.mdl;	%textobject.mix;	

Description

A **Para** is a paragraph. Paragraphs in DocBook may contain almost all inlines and most block elements. Sectioning and higher-level structural elements are excluded. DocBook offers two variants of paragraph: **SimPara**, which cannot contain block elements, and **FormalPara**, which has a title.

Some processing systems may find the presence of block elements in a paragraph difficult to handle. On the other hand, it is frequently most logical, from a structural point of view, to include block elements, especially informal block elements, in the paragraphs that describe their content. There is no easy answer to this problem.

Processing expectations

Formatted as a displayed block.

4.0 *Future Changes*

The **InterfaceDefinition** element will be discarded in DocBook V4.0. It will no longer be available in the content model of this element.

See Also

FormalPara, **SimPara**

Examples

Ordinary paragraphs can contain most block elements:

```
<!DOCTYPE para PUBLIC "-//OASIS//DTD DocBook V3.1//EN">
<para>
The component suffered from three failings:
<itemizedlist>
<listitem><para>It was slow</para></listitem>
<listitem><para>It ran hot</para></listitem>
<listitem><para>It didn't actually work</para></listitem>
</itemizedlist>
Of these three, the last was probably the most important.
</para>
```

The component suffered from three failings:

- It was slow
- It ran hot
- It didn't actually work

Of these three, the last was probably the most important.

```
<!DOCTYPE formalpara PUBLIC "-//OASIS//DTD DocBook V3.1//EN">
<formalpara><title>A Test</title>
<para>
This is a test.  This is only a test.  Had this been a real
example, it would have made more sense.
</para>
</formalpara>
```

A Test. This is a test. This is only a test. Had this been a real example, it would have made more sense.

```
<!DOCTYPE simpara PUBLIC "-//OASIS//DTD DocBook V3.1//EN">
<simpara>
Just the text, ma'am.
</simpara>
```

Just the text, ma'am.

ParamDef—Information about a function parameter in a programming language

Synopsis

Mixed Content Model
`ParamDef ::=`
`((#PCDATA|Replaceable|Parameter|FuncParams)*)`	

Attributes	Common attributes

Description

In the syntax summary for a function in a programming language, **ParamDef** provides the description of a parameter to the function. Typically, this includes the data type of the parameter and its name. For parameters that are pointers to functions, it also includes a summary of the nested parameters.

Within the **ParamDef**, the parameter name is identified with **Parameter**, and the rest of the content is assumed to be the data type.

In the following definition, *str* is the name of the parameter and *char ** is its type:

```
<paramdef>char *<parameter>str</parameter></paramdef>
```

Sometimes a data type requires punctuation on both sides of the parameter. For example, the *a* parameter in this definition is an array of *char **:

```
<paramdef>char *<parameter>a</parameter>[]</paramdef>
```

Processing expectations

Formatted inline. For a complete description of the processing expectations, see **FuncSynopsis**.

See Also

FuncDef, **FuncParams**, **FuncPrototype**, **FuncSynopsisInfo**, **Function**, **Parameter**, **ReturnValue**, **VarArgs**, **Void**

Examples

```
<!DOCTYPE funcsynopsis PUBLIC "-//OASIS//DTD DocBook V3.1//EN">
<funcsynopsis>
<funcprototype>
  <funcdef>int <function>max</function></funcdef>
  <paramdef>int <parameter>int1</parameter></paramdef>
  <paramdef>int <parameter>int2</parameter></paramdef>
</funcprototype>
</funcsynopsis>
```

```
int max(int int1, int int2);
```

For additional examples, see also **FuncDef**, **FuncSynopsis**.

Parameter—A value or a symbolic reference to a value

Synopsis

Mixed Content Model

```
Parameter ::=
((#PCDATA|Link|OLink|ULink|Action|Application|ClassName|Command|
  ComputerOutput|Database|Email|EnVar|ErrorCode|ErrorName|
```

```
ErrorType|Filename|Function|GUIButton|GUIIcon|GUILabel|GUIMenu|
GUIMenuItem|GUISubmenu|Hardware|Interface|InterfaceDefinition|
KeyCap|KeyCode|KeyCombo|KeySym|Literal|Constant|Markup|
MediaLabel|MenuChoice|MouseButton|MsgText|Option|Optional|
Parameter|Prompt|Property|Replaceable|ReturnValue|SGMLTag|
StructField|StructName|Symbol|SystemItem|Token|Type|UserInput|
VarName|Anchor|Comment|Subscript|Superscript|InlineGraphic|
InlineMediaObject|IndexTerm)+)
```

Attributes	Common attributes	
Name	**Type**	**Default**
Class	*Enumeration:* Command Function Option	*None*
MoreInfo	*Enumeration:* None RefEntry	"None"

Parameter Entities		
`%cptr.char.mix;`	`%ndxterm.char.mix;`	`%para.char.mix;`
`%programlisting.content;`	`%refinline.char.mix;`	`%refname.char.mix;`
`%screen.content;`	`%tbl.entry.mdl;`	`%tech.char.class;`
`%title.char.mix;`		

Description

A **Parameter** identifies something passed from one part of a computer system to another. In this regard **Parameter** is fairly generic, but it may have a more constrained semantic in some contexts (for example in a **ParamDef**).

In an document that describes more than one kind of parameter, for example, parameters to functions and commands, the `Class` attribute can be used to distinguish between them, if necessary.

Processing expectations

Formatted inline. The `MoreInfo` attribute can help generate a link or query to retrieve additional information.

4.0 *Future Changes*

In DocBook V4.0, the content model of **Parameter** will be constrained to `(#PCDATA | Replaceable | InlineGraphic)`.

Attributes

Class

`Class` indicates the type of **Parameter**.

MoreInfo

If `MoreInfo` is set to `RefEntry`, it implies that a **RefEntry** exists which further describes the **Parameter**.

See Also

ComputerOutput, **Constant**, **FuncDef**, **FuncParams**, **FuncPrototype**, **FuncSynopsisInfo**, **Function**, **Literal**, **Markup**, **Option**, **Optional**, **ParamDef**, **Prompt**, **Replaceable**, **ReturnValue**, **SGMLTag**, **UserInput**, **VarArgs**, **VarName**, **Void**

Examples

```
<!DOCTYPE para PUBLIC "-//OASIS//DTD DocBook V3.1//EN">
<para>
Using the <parameter class=command>/w</parameter> parameter on the
DOS <command>dir</command> command prints a wide directory listing.
</para>
```

Using the `/w` parameter on the DOS *dir* command prints a wide directory listing.

For additional examples, see also **FuncDef**, **FuncSynopsis**, **ParamDef**.

Part—A division in a book

Synopsis

Content Model

```
Part ::=
((DocInfo?,Title,Subtitle?,TitleAbbrev?),
 PartIntro?,
 (Appendix|Chapter|ToC|LoT|Index|Glossary|Bibliography|Article|
  Preface|RefEntry|Reference)+)
```

Attributes	Common attributes	
Name	**Type**	**Default**
Label	CDATA	*None*
Status	CDATA	*None*

Description

Parts segment a book into divisions. Each division can contain a number of component-level elements, such as **Chapters**.

Processing expectations

Formatted as a displayed block. **Parts** almost always introduce a forced page break. Sometimes starts on the next recto page. Frequently, they also produce a part separator page, on which may be printed the content of the **PartIntro**.

4.0 *Future Changes*

In DocBook V4.0, the **ToC** element in the content model will be replaced by **TocChap**.

Attributes

Label

`Label` specifies an identifying string for presentation purposes. The first **Part** in a **Book** might be labeled "Part I", for example.

Generally, an explicit `Label` attribute is used only if the processing system is incapable of generating the label automatically. If present, the `Label` is normative; it will used even if the processing system is capable of automatic labelling.

Status

`Status` identifies the editorial or publication status of the **Part**.

Publication status might be used to control formatting (for example, printing a "draft" watermark on drafts) or processing (perhaps a document with a status of "final" should not include any components that are not final).

See Also

Appendix, **Article**, **Book**, **Chapter**, **Colophon**, **Dedication**, **PartIntro**, **Preface**, **Set**

Examples

The following example comes from *Java in a Nutshell*:

```
<!DOCTYPE part PUBLIC "-//OASIS//DTD DocBook V3.1//EN">
<part label="II">
<title>Programming with the Java API</title>
<partintro>
<para>
The sections in Part II present real-world examples of
programming with Java.  You can study and learn from the
examples, and you can adapt them for use in your own programs.
</para>

<para>
The example code in these chapters is available for downloading.
See <systemitem role=url>http://www.ora.com/catalog/books/javanut</>.
</para>

<literallayout>
<xref linkend="jnut-ch-04">
<xref linkend="jnut-ch-05">
<xref linkend="jnut-ch-06">
<xref linkend="jnut-ch-07">
<xref linkend="jnut-ch-08">
<xref linkend="jnut-ch-09">
```

```
</literallayout>
</partintro>
<chapter id="jnut-ch-04"><para>...content...</para></chapter>
<chapter id="jnut-ch-05"><para>...content...</para></chapter>
<chapter id="jnut-ch-06"><para>...content...</para></chapter>
<chapter id="jnut-ch-07"><para>...content...</para></chapter>
<chapter id="jnut-ch-08"><para>...content...</para></chapter>
<chapter id="jnut-ch-09"><para>...content...</para></chapter>
</part>
```

PartIntro—An introduction to the contents of a part

Synopsis

Content Model

```
PartIntro ::=
((Title,Subtitle?,TitleAbbrev?)?,
 (((CalloutList|GlossList|ItemizedList|OrderedList|SegmentedList|
    SimpleList|VariableList|Caution|Important|Note|Tip|Warning|
    LiteralLayout|ProgramListing|ProgramListingCO|Screen|ScreenCO|
    ScreenShot|Synopsis|CmdSynopsis|FuncSynopsis|FormalPara|Para|
    SimPara|Address|BlockQuote|Graphic|GraphicCO|MediaObject|
    MediaObjectCO|InformalEquation|InformalExample|InformalFigure|
    InformalTable|Equation|Example|Figure|Table|MsgSet|Procedure|
    Sidebar|QandASet|Anchor|BridgeHead|Comment|Highlights|
    Abstract|AuthorBlurb|Epigraph|IndexTerm)+,
   (Sect1*|
    (RefEntry)*|
    SimpleSect*|Section*))|
  (Sect1+|
   (RefEntry)+|
   SimpleSect+|Section+)))
```

Attributes Name	Common attributes Type	Default
Label	CDATA	*None*

Description

PartIntro contains introductory text, often an overview of the content of the **Part**.

Processing expectations

Formatted as a displayed block. Sometimes suppressed.

PartIntro content is often printed on a part separator page.

Attributes

Label

`Label` specifies an identifying string for presentation purposes.

Generally, an explicit `Label` attribute is used only if the processing system is incapable of generating the label automatically. If present, the `Label` is normative; it will used even if the processing system is capable of automatic labelling.

See Also

Appendix, **Article**, **Book**, **Chapter**, **Colophon**, **Dedication**, **Part**, **Preface**, **Set**

Examples

For examples, see **Part**.

Phone—A telephone number

Synopsis

Mixed Content Model

```
Phone ::=
((#PCDATA|Link|OLink|ULink|Emphasis|Trademark|Replaceable|Comment|
  Subscript|Superscript|InlineGraphic|InlineMediaObject|IndexTerm)+)
```

Attributes	Common attributes

Description

Phone identifies a telephone number in an **Address**.

Processing expectations

Formatted inline. Sometimes suppressed. In an **Address**, this element may inherit the verbatim qualities of an address.

See Also

Address, **City**, **Country**, **Email**, **Fax**, **OtherAddr**, **POB**, **Postcode**, **State**, **Street**

Examples

For examples, see **Address**.

Phrase—A span of text

Synopsis

Mixed Content Model

```
Phrase ::=
((#PCDATA|FootnoteRef|XRef|Abbrev|Acronym|Citation|CiteRefEntry|
  CiteTitle|Emphasis|FirstTerm|ForeignPhrase|GlossTerm|Footnote|
  Phrase|Quote|Trademark|WordAsWord|Link|OLink|ULink|Action|
  Application|ClassName|Command|ComputerOutput|Database|Email|
```

EnVar|ErrorCode|ErrorName|ErrorType|Filename|Function|GUIButton|GUIIcon|GUILabel|GUIMenu|GUIMenuItem|GUISubmenu|Hardware|Interface|InterfaceDefinition|KeyCap|KeyCode|KeyCombo|KeySym|Literal|Constant|Markup|MediaLabel|MenuChoice|MouseButton|MsgText|Option|Optional|Parameter|Prompt|Property|Replaceable|ReturnValue|SGMLTag|StructField|StructName|Symbol|SystemItem|Token|Type|UserInput|VarName|Anchor|Author|AuthorInitials|CorpAuthor|ModeSpec|OtherCredit|ProductName|ProductNumber|RevHistory|Comment|Subscript|Superscript|InlineGraphic|InlineMediaObject|InlineEquation|Synopsis|CmdSynopsis|FuncSynopsis|IndexTerm)+)		
Attributes	Common attributes	
Parameter Entities		
%gen.char.class;	%ndxterm.char.mix;	%para.char.mix;
%programlisting.content;	%refinline.char.mix;	%screen.content;
%tbl.entry.mdl;	%title.char.mix;	

Description

The **Phrase** element in DocBook has no specific semantic. It is provided as a wrapper around a selection of words smaller than a paragraph so that it is possible to provide an ID or other attributes for them.

For example, if you are making note of changes to a document using one of the effectivity attributes, you might use **Phrase** to mark up specific sentences with revisions.

Processing expectations

Formatted inline.

4.0 *Future Changes*

The **InterfaceDefinition** element will be discarded in DocBook V4.0. It will no longer be available in the content model of this element.

See Also

Abbrev, **Acronym**, **Emphasis**, **ForeignPhrase**, **Quote**, **WordAsWord**

Examples

```
<!DOCTYPE para PUBLIC "-//OASIS//DTD DocBook V3.1//EN">
<para>
Effectivity attributes can be used to keep track of modifications
to a document <phrase revisionflag="deleted">at the word or
sentence level</phrase><phrase revisionflag="added"> as long as the number
and complexity of changes is not too high</phrase>.
</para>
```

Effectivity attributes can be used to keep track of modifications to a document at the word or sentence levelas long as the number and complexity of changes is not too high.

For additional examples, see also **AudioObject**, **ImageObject**, **InformalFigure**, **InlineMediaObject**.

POB—A post office box in an address

Synopsis

Mixed Content Model

```
POB ::=
((#PCDATA|Link|OLink|ULink|Emphasis|Trademark|Replaceable|Comment|
  Subscript|Superscript|InlineGraphic|InlineMediaObject|IndexTerm)+)
```

Attributes	Common attributes

Description

POB is a post office box number in an **Address**.

Processing expectations

Formatted inline. In an **Address**, this element may inherit the verbatim qualities of an address.

See Also

Address, **City**, **Country**, **Email**, **Fax**, **OtherAddr**, **Phone**, **Postcode**, **State**, **Street**

Examples

For examples, see **Address**.

Postcode—A postal code in an address

Synopsis

Mixed Content Model

```
Postcode ::=
((#PCDATA|Link|OLink|ULink|Emphasis|Trademark|Replaceable|Comment|
  Subscript|Superscript|InlineGraphic|InlineMediaObject|IndexTerm)+)
```

Attributes	Common attributes

Description

PostCode is a postal code (in the United States, a ZIP code) in an **Address**.

Processing expectations

Formatted inline. In an **Address**, this element may inherit the verbatim qualities of an address.

See Also

Address, **City**, **Country**, **Email**, **Fax**, **OtherAddr**, **Phone**, **POB**, **State**, **Street**

Examples

For examples, see **Address**.

Preface—Introductory matter preceding the first chapter of a book

Synopsis

Content Model

```
Preface ::=
((DocInfo?,Title,Subtitle?,TitleAbbrev?),
 (((CalloutList|GlossList|ItemizedList|OrderedList|SegmentedList|
    SimpleList|VariableList|Caution|Important|Note|Tip|Warning|
    LiteralLayout|ProgramListing|ProgramListingCO|Screen|ScreenCO|
    ScreenShot|Synopsis|CmdSynopsis|FuncSynopsis|FormalPara|Para|
    SimPara|Address|BlockQuote|Graphic|GraphicCO|MediaObject|
    MediaObjectCO|InformalEquation|InformalExample|InformalFigure|
    InformalTable|Equation|Example|Figure|Table|MsgSet|Procedure|
    Sidebar|QandASet|Anchor|BridgeHead|Comment|Highlights|
    Abstract|AuthorBlurb|Epigraph|IndexTerm)+,
   (Sect1*|
    (RefEntry)*|
    SimpleSect*|Section*))|
  (Sect1+|
   (RefEntry)+|
   SimpleSect+|Section+)))
```

Attributes — Common attributes

Name	Type	Default
Status	CDATA	*None*

Parameter Entities

```
%partcontent.mix;
```

Description

Preface is a preface or forward in a **Book**. The **Preface** element may appear more than once and should be used for all introductory chapter-like material. For example, a **Book** might have both a *Foreward* and an *Introduction*. Both should be tagged as **Prefaces** in DocBook.

Processing expectations

Formatted as a displayed block. Usually introduces a forced page break and often starts on the next recto page. It is common for the page numbers in prefaces to be displayed as roman numerals rather than arabic numerals. **Preface**s are usually listed in the Table of Contents.

Attributes

Status

`Status` identifies the editorial or publication status of the **Preface**.

Publication status might be used to control formatting (for example, printing a "draft" watermark on drafts) or processing (perhaps a document with a status of "final" should not include any components that are not final).

See Also

Appendix, **Article**, **Book**, **Chapter**, **Colophon**, **Dedication**, **Part**, **PartIntro**, **Set**

Examples

For examples, see **Book**.

Primary—The primary word or phrase under which an index term should be sorted

Synopsis

Mixed Content Model

```
Primary ::=
((#PCDATA|FootnoteRef|XRef|Abbrev|Acronym|Citation|CiteRefEntry|
  CiteTitle|Emphasis|FirstTerm|ForeignPhrase|GlossTerm|Footnote|
  Phrase|Quote|Trademark|WordAsWord|Link|OLink|ULink|Action|
  Application|ClassName|Command|ComputerOutput|Database|Email|
  EnVar|ErrorCode|ErrorName|ErrorType|Filename|Function|GUIButton|
  GUIIcon|GUILabel|GUIMenu|GUIMenuItem|GUISubmenu|Hardware|
  Interface|InterfaceDefinition|KeyCap|KeyCode|KeyCombo|KeySym|
  Literal|Constant|Markup|MediaLabel|MenuChoice|MouseButton|
  MsgText|Option|Optional|Parameter|Prompt|Property|Replaceable|
  ReturnValue|SGMLTag|StructField|StructName|Symbol|SystemItem|
  Token|Type|UserInput|VarName|Anchor|Author|AuthorInitials|
  CorpAuthor|ModeSpec|OtherCredit|ProductName|ProductNumber|
  RevHistory|Comment|Subscript|Superscript|InlineGraphic|
  InlineMediaObject)+)
```

Attributes	Common attributes	
Name	**Type**	**Default**
SortAs	CDATA	*None*

Description

In an **IndexTerm**, **Primary** identifies the most significant word or words in the entry. All **IndexTerms** must have a **Primary**.

Processing expectations

Suppressed. This element provides data for processing but it is not rendered in the primary flow of text.

4.0 *Future Changes*

The **InterfaceDefinition** element will be discarded in DocBook V4.0. It will no longer be available in the content model of this element.

Attributes

SortAs

`SortAs` specifies the string by which the element's content is to be sorted. If unspecified, the proper content is used.

See Also

IndexEntry, **IndexTerm**, **PrimaryIE**, **Secondary**, **SecondaryIE**, **See**, **SeeAlso**, **SeeAlsoIE**, **SeeIE**, **Tertiary**, **TertiaryIE**

Examples

For examples, see **Chapter**, **IndexTerm**.

PrimaryIE—A primary term in an index entry, not in the text

Synopsis

Mixed Content Model

```
PrimaryIE ::=
((#PCDATA|FootnoteRef|XRef|Abbrev|Acronym|Citation|CiteRefEntry|
  CiteTitle|Emphasis|FirstTerm|ForeignPhrase|GlossTerm|Footnote|
  Phrase|Quote|Trademark|WordAsWord|Link|OLink|ULink|Action|
  Application|ClassName|Command|ComputerOutput|Database|Email|
  EnVar|ErrorCode|ErrorName|ErrorType|Filename|Function|GUIButton|
  GUIIcon|GUILabel|GUIMenu|GUIMenuItem|GUISubmenu|Hardware|
  Interface|InterfaceDefinition|KeyCap|KeyCode|KeyCombo|KeySym|
  Literal|Constant|Markup|MediaLabel|MenuChoice|MouseButton|
  MsgText|Option|Optional|Parameter|Prompt|Property|Replaceable|
  ReturnValue|SGMLTag|StructField|StructName|Symbol|SystemItem|
  Token|Type|UserInput|VarName|Anchor|Author|AuthorInitials|
  CorpAuthor|ModeSpec|OtherCredit|ProductName|ProductNumber|
  RevHistory|Comment|Subscript|Superscript|InlineGraphic|
  InlineMediaObject)+)
```

Attributes Name	Common attributes Type	Default
Linkends	IDREFS	*None*

Description

PrimaryIE identifies the most significant word or words in an **IndexEntry**. **IndexEntrys** occur in an **Index**, not in the flow of the text. They are part of a formatted index, not markers for indexing.

If a document includes both **IndexTerms** and **IndexEntrys**, the **IndexEntrys** are usually constructed from the **IndexTerms** by some external process.

Processing expectations

Formatted as a displayed block. The **PrimaryIE** starts a new entry in the **Index**.

4.0 *Future Changes*

The **InterfaceDefinition** element will be discarded in DocBook V4.0. It will no longer be available in the content model of this element.

Attributes

Linkends

`Linkends`, if used, points to the **IndexTerms** indexed by this entry.

See Also

IndexEntry, **IndexTerm**, **Primary**, **Secondary**, **SecondaryIE**, **See**, **SeeAlso**, **SeeAlsoIE**, **SeeIE**, **Tertiary**, **TertiaryIE**

Examples

For examples, see **Index**.

PrintHistory—The printing history of a document

Synopsis

Content Model	
`PrintHistory ::=` `((FormalPara|Para|SimPara)+)`	
Attributes	Common attributes
Parameter Entities `%bibliocomponent.mix;`	

Description

The **PrintHistory** of a document identifies when various editions and revisions were printed.

Processing expectations

Formatted as a displayed block. Sometimes suppressed.

See Also

Date, **Edition**, **PubDate**, **ReleaseInfo**, **RevHistory**

Examples

```
<!DOCTYPE printhistory PUBLIC "-//OASIS//DTD DocBook V3.1//EN">
<printhistory>
<para>
September, 1996    First Printing
</para>
</printhistory>
```

For a printed example of **PrintHistory**, consult the reverse of the full title page of this book (if you're holding the print version from O'Reilly).

Procedure—A list of operations to be performed in a well-defined sequence

Synopsis

Content Model

```
Procedure ::=
((Title,TitleAbbrev?)?,
 (CalloutList|GlossList|ItemizedList|OrderedList|SegmentedList|
  SimpleList|VariableList|Caution|Important|Note|Tip|Warning|
  LiteralLayout|ProgramListing|ProgramListingCO|Screen|ScreenCO|
  ScreenShot|Synopsis|CmdSynopsis|FuncSynopsis|FormalPara|Para|
  SimPara|Address|BlockQuote|Graphic|GraphicCO|MediaObject|
  MediaObjectCO|InformalEquation|InformalExample|InformalFigure|
  InformalTable|Equation|Example|Figure|Table|MsgSet|Procedure|
  Sidebar|QandASet|Anchor|BridgeHead|Comment|Highlights|Abstract|
  AuthorBlurb|Epigraph|IndexTerm)*,
 Step+)
```

Attributes	Common attributes	
Parameter Entities		
%admon.mix;	%bookcomponent.content;	%component.mix;
%compound.class;	%divcomponent.mix;	%qandaset.mix;
%refcomponent.mix;	%sidebar.mix;	

Description

A **Procedure** encapsulates a task composed of **Steps** (and possibly, **SubSteps**). Procedures are usually performed sequentially, unless individual **Steps** direct the reader explicitly.

Often it is important to assure that certain conditions exist before a procedure is performed, and that the outcome of the procedure matches the expected results. DocBook does not provide explicit semantic markup for these pre- and post-conditions. Instead, they must be described as steps (check the pre-conditions in the first step and the results in the last step), or described outside the body of the procedure.

Processing expectations

Formatted as a displayed block.

Examples

```
<!DOCTYPE procedure PUBLIC "-//OASIS//DTD DocBook V3.1//EN">
<procedure><title>An Example Procedure</title>
<step>
  <para>
    A Step
  </para>
</step>
<step>
  <para>
    Another Step
  </para>
  <substeps>
    <step>
      <para>
        Substeps can be nested indefinitely deep.
      </para>
    </step>
  </substeps>
</step>
<step>
  <para>
    A Final Step
  </para>
</step>
</procedure>
```

An Example Procedure

1. A Step
2. Another Step
    a. Substeps can be nested indefinitely deep.
3. A Final Step

ProductName—The formal name of a product

Synopsis

Mixed Content Model

```
ProductName ::=
((#PCDATA|FootnoteRef|XRef|Abbrev|Acronym|Citation|CiteRefEntry|
  CiteTitle|Emphasis|FirstTerm|ForeignPhrase|GlossTerm|Footnote|
  Phrase|Quote|Trademark|WordAsWord|Link|OLink|ULink|Action|
  Application|ClassName|Command|ComputerOutput|Database|Email|
  EnVar|ErrorCode|ErrorName|ErrorType|Filename|Function|GUIButton|
  GUIIcon|GUILabel|GUIMenu|GUIMenuItem|GUISubmenu|Hardware|
  Interface|InterfaceDefinition|KeyCap|KeyCode|KeyCombo|KeySym|
  Literal|Constant|Markup|MediaLabel|MenuChoice|MouseButton|
  MsgText|Option|Optional|Parameter|Prompt|Property|Replaceable|
  ReturnValue|SGMLTag|StructField|StructName|Symbol|SystemItem|
  Token|Type|UserInput|VarName|Anchor|Author|AuthorInitials|
  CorpAuthor|ModeSpec|OtherCredit|ProductName|ProductNumber|
  RevHistory|Comment|Subscript|Superscript|InlineGraphic|
  InlineMediaObject|InlineEquation|Synopsis|CmdSynopsis|
  FuncSynopsis|IndexTerm)+)
```

Attributes Name	Common attributes **Type**	**Default**
Class	*Enumeration:* Copyright Registered Service Trade	"Trade"

Parameter Entities

%bibliocomponent.mix;	%docinfo.char.class;	%ndxterm.char.mix;
%para.char.mix;	%programlisting.content;	%refinline.char.mix;
%screen.content;	%tbl.entry.mdl;	%title.char.mix;

Description

A **ProductName** is the formal name of any product. Identifying a product this way may be useful if you need to provide explicit disclaimers about product names or information.

For example, the copyright statement on this book includes the following general notice:

> Some of the designations used by manufacturers and sellers to distinguish their products are claimed as trademarks. Where those designations appear in this book, and O'Reilly &Associates, Inc., was aware of the trademark claim, the designations have been printed in caps or initial caps.

or words to that effect. If every product name in this book had been diligently coded as a **ProductName**, we could have automatically generated a complete list of all the product names and mentioned them explicitly in the notice.

In running prose, the distinction between an **Application** and a **ProductName** may be very subjective.

Processing expectations

Formatted inline.

Two of the values of the `Class` attribute on **ProductName**, `Trade` and `Registered`, make assertions about trademarks. DocBook also has a **TradeMark** element; presumably the same markup is intended regardless of which one is used.

The `Service` and **`Copyright`** values should also generate the anticipated marks, if appropriate.

4.0 *Future Changes*

The **InterfaceDefinition** element will be discarded in DocBook V4.0. It will no longer be available in the content model of this element.

Attributes

Class

`Class` indicates the type of **ProductName**.

See Also

Application, **Copyright**, **Database**, **Filename**, **Hardware**, **MediaLabel**, **Trademark**

Examples

```
<!DOCTYPE para PUBLIC "-//OASIS//DTD DocBook V3.1//EN">
<para>
<productname class=trade>Frobozz</productname>: it's not
just for breakfast anymore.
</para>
```

Frobozz™: it's not just for breakfast anymore.

As noted above, the **TradeMark** element could also be used:

```
<!DOCTYPE para PUBLIC "-//OASIS//DTD DocBook V3.1//EN">
<para>
<trademark>Frobozz</trademark>: it's not
just for breakfast anymore.
</para>
```

Frobozz™: it's not just for breakfast anymore.

ProductNumber—A number assigned to a product

Synopsis

Mixed Content Model
`ProductNumber ::=`
`((#PCDATA|Link|OLink|ULink|Emphasis|Trademark|Replaceable|Comment|`
`Subscript|Superscript|InlineGraphic|InlineMediaObject|IndexTerm)+)`		

Attributes	Common attributes	
Parameter Entities		
`%bibliocomponent.mix;`	`%docinfo.char.class;`	`%ndxterm.char.mix;`
`%para.char.mix;`	`%programlisting.content;`	`%refinline.char.mix;`
`%screen.content;`	`%tbl.entry.mdl;`	`%title.char.mix;`

Description

An **ProductNumber** identifies a "product number" in some unspecified numbering scheme. It's possible that product numbers for different products might not even come from the same scheme.

Processing expectations

Formatted inline. Sometimes suppressed.

DocBook does not control, or specify, the numbering scheme used for products.

See Also

InvPartNumber, **ISBN**, **ISSN**, **IssueNum**, **PubsNumber**, **SeriesVolNums**, **VolumeNum**

Examples

```
<!DOCTYPE para PUBLIC "-//OASIS//DTD DocBook V3.1//EN">
<para>
You can order <citetitle>DocBook: The Definitive Guide</citetitle> directly
from O'Reilly &amp Associates.  Order product number
<productnumber>5807</productnumber> by phone or
<ulink url="http://www.oreilly.com/">over the web</ulink>.
</para>
```

You can order *DocBook: The Definitive Guide* directly from O'Reilly &Associates. Order product number 5807 by phone or over the web (*http://www.oreilly.com/*).

ProgramListing—A literal listing of all or part of a program

Synopsis

Mixed Content Model
`ProgramListing ::=`
`((CO|LineAnnotation|#PCDATA|FootnoteRef|XRef|Abbrev|Acronym|`
`Citation|CiteRefEntry|CiteTitle|Emphasis|FirstTerm|`

```
ForeignPhrase|GlossTerm|Footnote|Phrase|Quote|Trademark|
WordAsWord|Link|OLink|ULink|Action|Application|ClassName|
Command|ComputerOutput|Database|Email|EnVar|ErrorCode|ErrorName|
ErrorType|Filename|Function|GUIButton|GUIIcon|GUILabel|GUIMenu|
GUIMenuItem|GUISubmenu|Hardware|Interface|InterfaceDefinition|
KeyCap|KeyCode|KeyCombo|KeySym|Literal|Constant|Markup|
MediaLabel|MenuChoice|MouseButton|MsgText|Option|Optional|
Parameter|Prompt|Property|Replaceable|ReturnValue|SGMLTag|
StructField|StructName|Symbol|SystemItem|Token|Type|UserInput|
VarName|Anchor|Author|AuthorInitials|CorpAuthor|ModeSpec|
OtherCredit|ProductName|ProductNumber|RevHistory|Comment|
Subscript|Superscript|InlineGraphic|InlineMediaObject|
InlineEquation|Synopsis|CmdSynopsis|FuncSynopsis|IndexTerm)+)
```

Attributes	Common attributes	
Name	**Type**	**Default**
Width	NUMBER	*None*
Format	*Enumerated notation:* linespecific	"linespecific"

Parameter Entities

`%admon.mix;`	`%bookcomponent.content;`	`%component.mix;`
`%divcomponent.mix;`	`%example.mix;`	`%figure.mix;`
`%footnote.mix;`	`%glossdef.mix;`	`%indexdivcomponent.mix;`
`%legalnotice.mix;`	`%linespecific.class;`	`%para.mix;`
`%qandaset.mix;`	`%refcomponent.mix;`	`%sidebar.mix;`
`%tabentry.mix;`	`%tbl.entry.mdl;`	`%textobject.mix;`

Description

A **ProgramListing** is a verbatim environment for program source or source fragment listings. **ProgramListing**s are often placed in **Example**s or **Figure**s so that they can be cross-referenced from the text.

Processing Expectations

Formatted as a displayed block. This element is displayed "verbatim"; whitespace and linebreaks within this element are significant. **ProgramListing**s are usually displayed in a fixed width font.

Other markup within a **ProgramListing** is recognized. Contrast this with systems like LaTeX, in which verbatim environments disable markup recognition. If you want to disable markup recognition, you must use a *CDATA section*:

```
<programlisting>
<![CDATA[
This is a programlisting so white       space and line
breaks are significant.  But it is also a CDATA
section so <emphasis>tags</emphasis> and &entities;
are not recognized.  The only markup that is recognized
is the end-of-section marker, which is two
"]"'s in a row followed by a >.
]]>
</programlisting>
```

Two markup tags have special significance in **ProgramListings**: **CO** and **LineAnnotation**. A **CO** identifies the location of a **Callout**. A **LineAnnotation** is a comment, added by the *documentor*—not the programmer.

Processing expectations

This element is displayed "verbatim"; whitespace and linebreaks within this element are significant.

4.0 *Future Changes*

The **InterfaceDefinition** element will be discarded in DocBook V4.0. It will no longer be available in the content model of this element.

Attributes

Format

The `Format` attribute applies the `linespecific` notation to all **ProgramListings**. All white space and line breaks must be preserved.

Width

`Width` specifies the width (in characters) of the longest line in this **ProgramListing** (formatters may use this value to determine scaling or rotation).

See Also

ComputerOutput, **LineAnnotation**, **LiteralLayout**, **Screen**, **ScreenShot**, **Synopsis**, **UserInput**

Examples

For examples, see **Example**, **InformalExample**, **ProgramListingCO**.

ProgramListingCO—A program listing with associated areas used in callouts

Synopsis

Content Model
`ProgramListingCO ::=`
`(AreaSpec,ProgramListing,CalloutList*)`		

Attributes	Common attributes	
Parameter Entities		
`%admon.mix;`	`%bookcomponent.content;`	`%component.mix;`
`%divcomponent.mix;`	`%example.mix;`	`%figure.mix;`
`%footnote.mix;`	`%glossdef.mix;`	`%indexdivcomponent.mix;`
`%legalnotice.mix;`	`%linespecific.class;`	`%para.mix;`
`%qandaset.mix;`	`%refcomponent.mix;`	`%sidebar.mix;`
`%tabentry.mix;`	`%tbl.entry.mdl;`	`%textobject.mix;`

Description

Callouts, such as numbered bullets, are an annotation mechanism. In an online system, these bullets are frequently "hot," and clicking on them sends you to the corresponding annotation.

A **ProgramListingCO** is a wrapper around an **AreaSpec** and a **ProgramListing**. An **AreaSpec** identifies the locations (coordinates) in the **ProgramListing** where the callouts occur. The **ProgramListingCO** may also contain the list of annotations in a **CalloutList**, although the **CalloutList** may also occur outside of the wrapper, elsewhere in the document.

It is also possible to embed **CO** elements directly in the verbatim text, in order to avoid having to calculate the correct coordinates. If you decided to go this route, use a **ProgramListing** and a **CalloutList** without the **ProgramListingCO** wrapper. A **ProgramListingCO** must specify at least one coordinate.

For a complete description of callouts, see **Callout**.

Processing expectations

Formatted as a displayed block. This element is displayed "verbatim"; whitespace and linebreaks within this element are significant.

The mandatory processing expectations of a **ProgramListingCO** are minimal: a system is expected to render the program listing and the callout list, if present.

If explicit **CO** elements are embedded in a **ProgramListing**, they must generate appropriate callout marks.

In online environments, the processing system may be able to instantiate the linking relationships between the callout marks in the program listing and the annotations. Some systems may even be able to go a step further and generate the callout marks automatically from the coordinate information, but this level of sophistication is not mandatory.

See Also

AreaSpec, **CalloutList**, **CO**, **GraphicCO**, **ImageObjectCO**, **MediaObjectCO**, **ScreenCO**

Examples

```
<!DOCTYPE programlistingco PUBLIC "-//OASIS//DTD DocBook V3.1//EN">
<programlistingco>
<areaspec>
<areaset id="ex.plco.const" coords="">
  <area id="ex.plco.c1" coords=4>
  <area id="ex.plco.c2" coords=8>
</areaset>
```

```
<area id="ex.plco.ret" coords=12>
<area id="ex.plco.dest" coords=12>
</areaspec>
<programlisting>
sub do_nothing_useful {
    my($a, $b, $c);

    $a = new A;

    $a->does_nothing_either();

    $b = new B;

    $c = "frog";

    return ($a, $c);
}
</programlisting>
<calloutlist>
<callout arearefs="ex.plco.const">
<para>
These are calls to the constructor <function>new</function> in the object
classes.
</para>
</callout>
<callout arearefs="ex.plco.ret">
<para>
This function returns a two-element list.
</para>
</callout>
<callout arearefs="ex.plco.dest">
<para>
The <emphasis>destructor</emphasis> (<function>DESTROY</function>) for
the object <literal>$b</literal> will be called automatically for this
object since there can be no other references to it outside this function.
</para>
</callout>
</calloutlist>
</programlistingco>
```

```
sub do_nothing_useful {
    my($a, $b, $c);

    $a = new A;                                   ❶

    $a->does_nothing_either();

    $b = new B;                                   ❶

    $c = "frog";

    return ($a, $c);                              ❷❸
}
```

❶ These are calls to the constructor *new* in the object classes.

❷ This function returns a two-element list.

❸ The *destructor* (*DESTROY*) for the object `$b` will be called automatically for this object since there can be no other references to it outside this function.

Prompt—A character or string indicating the start of an input field in a computer display

Synopsis

Mixed Content Model		
`Prompt ::=` `((#PCDATA|Replaceable|InlineGraphic|InlineMediaObject|IndexTerm)+)`		
Attributes	Common attributes	
Name	**Type**	**Default**
MoreInfo	*Enumeration:* None RefEntry	"None"
Parameter Entities		
`%cptr.char.mix;`	`%ndxterm.char.mix;`	`%para.char.mix;`
`%programlisting.content;`	`%refinline.char.mix;`	`%refname.char.mix;`
`%screen.content;`	`%tbl.entry.mdl;`	`%tech.char.class;`
`%title.char.mix;`		

Description

A **Prompt** is a character or character string marking the beginning of an input field. **Prompts** are generally associated with command-line interfaces and not graphical user interfaces (GUIs). In GUIs, **GUILabel** is usually more appropriate.

Processing expectations

Formatted inline. The `MoreInfo` attribute can help generate a link or query to retrieve additional information.

4.0 *Future Changes*

Prompt was added in DocBook V3.0. It duplicates the semantics of `<systemitem class="prompt">`. The `prompt` attribute will be removed from **SystemItem** in the future.

Attributes

MoreInfo

If `MoreInfo` is set to `RefEntry`, it implies that a **RefEntry** exists which further describes the **Prompt**.

See Also

ComputerOutput, Constant, EnVar, Filename, Literal, Markup, Option, Optional, Parameter, Replaceable, SGMLTag, SystemItem, UserInput, VarName

Examples

```
<!DOCTYPE para PUBLIC "-//OASIS//DTD DocBook V3.1//EN">
<para>
Enter your user name when the system presents the
<prompt>login:</prompt> prompt.
</para>
```

Enter your user name when the system presents the `login:` prompt.

Property—A unit of data associated with some part of a computer system

Synopsis

Mixed Content Model

```
Property ::=
((#PCDATA|Link|OLink|ULink|Action|Application|ClassName|Command|
  ComputerOutput|Database|Email|EnVar|ErrorCode|ErrorName|
  ErrorType|Filename|Function|GUIButton|GUIIcon|GUILabel|GUIMenu|
  GUIMenuItem|GUISubmenu|Hardware|Interface|InterfaceDefinition|
  KeyCap|KeyCode|KeyCombo|KeySym|Literal|Constant|Markup|
  MediaLabel|MenuChoice|MouseButton|MsgText|Option|Optional|
  Parameter|Prompt|Property|Replaceable|ReturnValue|SGMLTag|
  StructField|StructName|Symbol|SystemItem|Token|Type|UserInput|
  VarName|Anchor|Comment|Subscript|Superscript|InlineGraphic|
  InlineMediaObject|IndexTerm)+)
```

Attributes	Common attributes	
Name	**Type**	**Default**
MoreInfo	*Enumeration:* None RefEntry	"None"

Parameter Entities		
`%cptr.char.mix;`	`%ndxterm.char.mix;`	`%para.char.mix;`
`%programlisting.content;`	`%refinline.char.mix;`	`%refname.char.mix;`
`%screen.content;`	`%tbl.entry.mdl;`	`%tech.char.class;`
`%title.char.mix;`		

Description

The notion of a **Property** is very domain-dependent in computer documentation. Some object-oriented systems speak of properties; the components from which GUIs are constructed have properties; and one can speak of properties in very general terms; "the properties of a relational database."

You might use **Property** for any of these in your documentation.

Processing expectations

Formatted inline. The `MoreInfo` attribute can help generate a link or query to retrieve additional information.

4.0 *Future Changes*

The content model of **Property** will be constrained to `(#PCDATA | Replaceable | InlineGraphic)` in DocBook V4.0.

Attributes

MoreInfo

If `MoreInfo` is set to `RefEntry`, it implies that a **RefEntry** exists which further describes the **Property**.

See Also

ClassName, **Interface**, **InterfaceDefinition**, **StructField**, **StructName**, **Symbol**, **Token**, **Type**

Examples

```
<!DOCTYPE para PUBLIC "-//OASIS//DTD DocBook V3.1//EN">
<para>
When Emacs is running under X Windows, the <property>borderWidth</property>
resource controls the width of the external border.
</para>
```

When Emacs is running under X Windows, the borderWidth resource controls the width of the external border.

PubDate—The date of publication of a document

Synopsis

Mixed Content Model
`PubDate ::=`
`((#PCDATA|Link|OLink|ULink|Emphasis|Trademark|Replaceable|Comment|`
`Subscript|Superscript|InlineGraphic|InlineMediaObject|IndexTerm)+)`	

Attributes	Common attributes
Parameter Entities `%bibliocomponent.mix;`	

Description

The **PubDate** is the date of publication of a document.

Processing expectations

Formatted inline. Sometimes suppressed.

See Also

Date, **Edition**, **PrintHistory**, **ReleaseInfo**, **RevHistory**

Examples

For examples, see **Article**, **Bibliography**, **BiblioMSet**, **BookInfo**.

Publisher—The publisher of a document

Synopsis

Content Model
`Publisher ::=`
`(PublisherName,Address*)`	

Attributes	Common attributes
Parameter Entities `%bibliocomponent.mix;`	

Description

Publisher associates a **PublisherName** and an **Address**. Many publishers have offices in more than one city. **Publisher** can be used to list or distinguish between the multiple offices.

Processing expectations

May be formatted inline or as a displayed block, depending on context. Sometimes suppressed.

Examples

```
<!DOCTYPE publisher PUBLIC "-//OASIS//DTD DocBook V3.1//EN">
<publisher>
  <publishername>O'Reilly &amp; Associates, Inc.</publishername>
  <address><street>101 ...</street>
  ...
  </address>
</publisher>
```

For additional examples, see also **Article**, **Bibliography**, **BiblioSet**.

PublisherName—The name of the publisher of a document

Synopsis

Mixed Content Model
`PublisherName ::=`
`((#PCDATA|Link|OLink|ULink|Emphasis|Trademark|Replaceable|Comment|`
`Subscript|Superscript|InlineGraphic|InlineMediaObject|IndexTerm)+)`	

Attributes	Common attributes
Parameter Entities `%bibliocomponent.mix;`	

Description

A **PublisherName** is the name of a publisher. Historically, this has been used in bibliographic meta-information to identify the publisher of a book or other document. It is also reasonable to identify the publisher of an electronic publication in this way.

Processing expectations

May be formatted inline or as a displayed block, depending on context. Sometimes suppressed.

See Also

CorpName, **OrgName**

Examples

For examples, see **Article**, **Bibliography**, **BiblioMSet**, **BiblioSet**, **Publisher**.

PubsNumber—A number assigned to a publication other than an ISBN or ISSN or inventory part number

Synopsis

Mixed Content Model
`PubsNumber ::=`
`((#PCDATA|Link|OLink|ULink|Emphasis|Trademark|Replaceable|Comment|`
`Subscript|Superscript|InlineGraphic|InlineMediaObject|IndexTerm)+)`	

Attributes	Common attributes
Parameter Entities `%bibliocomponent.mix;`	

Description

A **PubsNumber** identifies a document in some unspecified numbering scheme. This number may exist instead of, or in addition to, an **ISBN** or **ISSN** number.

Processing expectations

Formatted inline. Sometimes suppressed.

DocBook does not control, or specify, the numbering scheme used for documents.

See Also

InvPartNumber, **ISBN**, **ISSN**, **IssueNum**, **ProductNumber**, **SeriesVolNums**, **VolumeNum**

Examples

For examples, see **ContractSponsor**, **OtherCredit**.

QandADiv—A titled division in a **QandASet**

Synopsis

Content Model

```
QandADiv ::=
((Title,TitleAbbrev?)?,
 (CalloutList|GlossList|ItemizedList|OrderedList|SegmentedList|
  SimpleList|VariableList|LiteralLayout|ProgramListing|
  ProgramListingCO|Screen|ScreenCO|ScreenShot|Synopsis|
  CmdSynopsis|FuncSynopsis|FormalPara|Para|SimPara|Address|
  BlockQuote|Graphic|GraphicCO|MediaObject|MediaObjectCO|
  InformalEquation|InformalExample|InformalFigure|InformalTable|
  Equation|Example|Figure|Table|Procedure|Anchor|BridgeHead|
  Comment|Highlights|IndexTerm)*,
 (QandADiv+|QandAEntry+))
```

Attributes	Common attributes

Description

QandADiv is a section of a **QandASet**. A question and answer set might be divided into sections in order to group different sets of questions together, perhaps by topic.

A **QandASet** may contain any number of **QandADiv** or **QandAEntry** elements, but it cannot contain a mixture of both at the same level.

Processing expectations

Formatted as a displayed block.

A table of contents for the question and answer set is sometimes generated, especially in online environments.

Examples

For examples, see **QandASet**.

QandAEntry—A question/answer set within a **QandASet**

Synopsis

Content Model
`QandAEntry ::=`
`(Question,Answer*)`	

Attributes	Common attributes

Description

A **QandAEntry** is an entry in a **QandASet**. Each **QandAEntry** defines a **Question** and (possibly) its **Answer** or **Answers**.

Processing expectations

Formatted as a displayed block. **Questions** are usually presented before the **Answers**, and often the **Answers** are indented to make the questions stand out.

Examples

For examples, see **QandASet**.

QandASet—A question-and-answer set

Synopsis

Content Model

```
QandASet ::=
((Title,TitleAbbrev?)?,
 (CalloutList|GlossList|ItemizedList|OrderedList|SegmentedList|
  SimpleList|VariableList|LiteralLayout|ProgramListing|
  ProgramListingCO|Screen|ScreenCO|ScreenShot|Synopsis|
  CmdSynopsis|FuncSynopsis|FormalPara|Para|SimPara|Address|
  BlockQuote|Graphic|GraphicCO|MediaObject|MediaObjectCO|
  InformalEquation|InformalExample|InformalFigure|InformalTable|
  Equation|Example|Figure|Table|Procedure|Anchor|BridgeHead|
  Comment|Highlights|IndexTerm)*,
 (QandADiv+|QandAEntry+))
```

Attributes **Name**	Common attributes **Type**	**Default**
DefaultLabel	*Enumeration:* none number qanda	*None*

Parameter Entities		
`%bookcomponent.content;`	`%component.mix;`	`%compound.class;`
`%divcomponent.mix;`	`%refcomponent.mix;`	

Description

A **QandASet** is a list consisting of **Questions** and **Answers**. **QandASets** can be divided into sections.

Every entry in a **QandASet** must contain a **Question**, but **Answers** are optional (some questions have no answers), and may be repeated (some questions have more than one answer).

Common uses for **QandASets** include reader questionnaires and lists of "Frequently Asked Questions" (FAQs). For the purpose of an FAQ, DocBook V3.1 added the `FAQ` class to **Article**.

Processing expectations

Formatted as a displayed block. The `DefaultLabel` attribute has a significant influence on the presentation of **Questions** and **Answers**.

Attributes

DefaultLabel

`DefaultLabel`Identifies the default label that should be used for **Questions** and **Answers**:

`qanda`
: **Questions** are labeled "Q:" and **Answers** are labeled "A:". Other similar labels may be substituted, for example, the words might be spelled out, "Question:" and "Answer:", and the actual characters or words used are dependent on the language.

`number`
: The entries are enumerated.

`label`
: The content of the `Label` attribute on each **Question** and **Answer** is used.

`none`
: No distinguishing label precedes **Questions** or **Answers**.

If no value is specified, the implied presentation may be any one of these, as defined by the stylesheet.

Examples

```
<!DOCTYPE qandaset PUBLIC "-//OASIS//DTD DocBook V3.1//EN">
<qandaset defaultlabel='qanda'>
<qandaentry>
<question>
<para>
To be, or not to be?
</para>
```

```
</question>
<answer>
<para>
That is the question.
</para>
</answer>
</qandaentry>
</qandaset>
```

Q: To be, or not to be?

A: That is the question.

```
<!DOCTYPE article PUBLIC "-//OASIS//DTD DocBook V3.1//EN">
<article class=faq>
<title>Frequently Asked Questions About Fonts</title>

<para>...</para>

<qandaset>
<qandadiv><title>General Information</title>

<para>...</para>

<qandadiv><title>Font Houses</title>

<qandaentry><question><para>Adobe Systems, Inc.</para></question>
<answer><para>...</para></answer>

<qandaentry><question><para>Agfa, Inc.</para></question>
<answer><para>...</para></answer>

</qandadiv>
</qandadiv>
</qandaset>
</article>
```

Question—A question in a **QandASet**

Synopsis

Content Model

```
Question ::=
(Label?,
 (CalloutList|GlossList|ItemizedList|OrderedList|SegmentedList|
  SimpleList|VariableList|LiteralLayout|ProgramListing|
  ProgramListingCO|Screen|ScreenCO|ScreenShot|Synopsis|
  CmdSynopsis|FuncSynopsis|FormalPara|Para|SimPara|Address|
  BlockQuote|Graphic|GraphicCO|MediaObject|MediaObjectCO|
  InformalEquation|InformalExample|InformalFigure|InformalTable|
  Equation|Example|Figure|Table|Procedure|Anchor|BridgeHead|
  Comment|Highlights|IndexTerm)+)
```

Attributes	Common attributes

Description

A **Question** in a **QandAEntry** poses a question or states a problem that is addressed by the following **Answer**(s). **Answers** are optional (some questions have no answers) and may be repeated (some questions have more than one answer).

Processing expectations

Questions are frequently introduced with a label, such as "Q:". Several attributes control the generation of the label text.

If the `DefaultLabel` attribute on the nearest ancestor **QandASet** is not "`label`," then the `Label` attribute on **Question** is ignored. Otherwise, the value of the `Label` attribute is used as the label for the **Question**.

Examples

For examples, see **QandASet**.

Quote—An inline quotation

Synopsis

Mixed Content Model

```
Quote ::=
((#PCDATA|FootnoteRef|XRef|Abbrev|Acronym|Citation|CiteRefEntry|
  CiteTitle|Emphasis|FirstTerm|ForeignPhrase|GlossTerm|Footnote|
  Phrase|Quote|Trademark|WordAsWord|Link|OLink|ULink|Action|
  Application|ClassName|Command|ComputerOutput|Database|Email|
  EnVar|ErrorCode|ErrorName|ErrorType|Filename|Function|GUIButton|
  GUIIcon|GUILabel|GUIMenu|GUIMenuItem|GUISubmenu|Hardware|
  Interface|InterfaceDefinition|KeyCap|KeyCode|KeyCombo|KeySym|
  Literal|Constant|Markup|MediaLabel|MenuChoice|MouseButton|
  MsgText|Option|Optional|Parameter|Prompt|Property|Replaceable|
  ReturnValue|SGMLTag|StructField|StructName|Symbol|SystemItem|
  Token|Type|UserInput|VarName|Anchor|Author|AuthorInitials|
  CorpAuthor|ModeSpec|OtherCredit|ProductName|ProductNumber|
  RevHistory|Comment|Subscript|Superscript|InlineGraphic|
  InlineMediaObject|InlineEquation|Synopsis|CmdSynopsis|
  FuncSynopsis|IndexTerm)+)
```

Attributes	Common attributes	
Parameter Entities		
`%gen.char.class;`	`%ndxterm.char.mix;`	`%para.char.mix;`
`%programlisting.content;`	`%refinline.char.mix;`	`%screen.content;`
`%tbl.entry.mdl;`	`%title.char.mix;`	

Description

Quote surrounds an inline quotation. Using an element for quotations is frequently more convenient than entering the character entities for the quotation marks by hand, and makes it possible for a presentation system to alter the format of the quotation marks.

Block quotations are properly identified as **BlockQuotes**.

Processing expectations

Formatted inline. The **Quote** element is expected to generate the proper quotation marks. These may be influenced by the `Lang` attribute on an ancestor element. For example, a quote in French might use «guillments» instead of English "quote marks."

4.0 *Future Changes*

The **InterfaceDefinition** element will be discarded in DocBook V4.0. It will no longer be available in the content model of this element.

See Also

Abbrev, **Acronym**, **Emphasis**, **ForeignPhrase**, **Phrase**, **WordAsWord**

Examples

```
<!DOCTYPE para PUBLIC "-//OASIS//DTD DocBook V3.1//EN">
<para>
This software is provided <quote>as is</quote>, without expressed
or implied warranty.
</para>
```

This software is provided "as is", without expressed or implied warranty.

For additional examples, see also **BookInfo**, **Link**.

RefClass—The scope or other indication of applicability of a reference entry

Synopsis

Mixed Content Model
`RefClass ::=`
`((#PCDATA|Application)+)`	

Attributes	Common attributes

Description

The **RefClass** element describes the applicability or scope of a **RefEntry**. A **RefClass** might indicate that the entry was only applicable to a particular application, for example, or only to a particular vendor's operating system.

Processing expectations

May be formatted inline or as a displayed block, depending on context. Sometimes suppressed.

Formatting reference pages may require a fairly sophisticated processing system. Much of the meta-information about a reference page (its name, type, purpose, title, and classification) is stored in wrappers near the beginning of the **RefEntry**.

Common presentational features, such as titles and running heads, may require data from several of these wrappers plus some generated text. Other formatting often requires that these elements be reordered.

Examples

For examples, see **RefEntry**.

RefDescriptor—A description of the topic of a reference page

Synopsis

Mixed Content Model

```
RefDescriptor ::=
((#PCDATA|Action|Application|ClassName|Command|ComputerOutput|
  Database|Email|EnVar|ErrorCode|ErrorName|ErrorType|Filename|
  Function|GUIButton|GUIIcon|GUILabel|GUIMenu|GUIMenuItem|
  GUISubmenu|Hardware|Interface|InterfaceDefinition|KeyCap|
  KeyCode|KeyCombo|KeySym|Literal|Constant|Markup|MediaLabel|
  MenuChoice|MouseButton|MsgText|Option|Optional|Parameter|Prompt|
  Property|Replaceable|ReturnValue|SGMLTag|StructField|StructName|
  Symbol|SystemItem|Token|Type|UserInput|VarName)+)
```

Attributes	Common attributes

Description

Reference pages (**RefEntrys**) are usually identified by a short, succinct topic name, such as the name of a function or command. The **RefName** (or one of the **RefNames**, in the case of a reference page that has several) is generally used as the topic name. When none of the **RefNames** is appropriate, **RefDescriptor** is used to specify the topic name.

RefDescriptor is unnecessary when an appropriate **RefName** can be selected automatically. At least one **RefName** is required, so **RefDescriptor** cannot be used in place of a name, only in addition to it.

Processing expectations

May be formatted inline or as a displayed block, depending on context.

Formatting reference pages may require a fairly sophisticated processing system. Much of the meta-information about a reference page (its name, type, purpose, title, and classification) is stored in wrappers near the beginning of the **RefEntry**.

Common presentational features, such as titles and running heads, may require data from several of these wrappers plus some generated text. Other formatting often requires that these elements be reordered.

If a **RefDescriptor** is present, it should be used for the short topic name. This name usually appears in the running header along with the **ManVolNum** in print media. It may also appear in tables of contents and the index.

4.0 *Future Changes*

The **InterfaceDefinition** element will be discarded in DocBook V4.0. It will no longer be available in the content model of this element.

See Also

RefEntryTitle, **RefName**

Examples

For examples, see **RefEntry**.

RefEntry—A reference page (originally a UNIX man-style reference page)

Synopsis

Content Model

```
RefEntry ::=
(DocInfo?,RefMeta?,
 (Comment|Link|OLink|ULink)*,
 RefNameDiv,RefSynopsisDiv?,RefSect1+)
```

Attributes	Common attributes	
Name	**Type**	**Default**
Status	CDATA	*None*

Parameter Entities

```
%bookcomponent.content; %moreinfo.attrib;    %partcontent.mix;
%refentry.class;
```

Description

A **RefEntry** is a reference page. In UNIX parlance this has historically been called a "man page" (short for manual page).

RefEntry is an appropriate wrapper for any small unit of reference documentation describing a single topic. Canonical examples are programming language functions and user commands (one **RefEntry** per function or command).*

On some projects, the structure of reference pages may be rigorously defined right down to the number, order, and title of individual sections (some or all of which may be required).

Processing expectations

Formatted as a displayed block. It is not uncommon for **RefEntrys** to introduce a forced page break in print media.

Formatting reference pages may require a fairly sophisticated processing system. Much of the meta-information about a reference page (its name, type, purpose, title, and classification) is stored in wrappers near the beginning of the **RefEntry**.

Common presentational features, such as titles and running heads, may require data from several of these wrappers plus some generated text. Other formatting often requires that these elements be reordered.

Attributes

Status

`Status` identifies the editorial or publication status of the **RefEntry**.

Publication status might be used to control formatting (for example, printing a "draft" watermark on drafts) or processing (perhaps a document with a status of "final" should not include any components that are not final).

Examples

A typical reference page for a command:

```
<!DOCTYPE refentry PUBLIC "-//OASIS//DTD DocBook V3.1//EN">
<refentry id="ls">

<refmeta>
<refentrytitle>ls</refentrytitle>
<manvolnum>1</manvolnum>
</refmeta>

<refnamediv>
<refname>ls</refname>
<refpurpose>list contents of a directory</refpurpose>
</refnamediv>
```

* You're reading a **RefEntry** right now.

```
<refsynopsisdiv>
<cmdsynopsis>
<command>/usr/bin/ls</command>
<arg choice="opt">
  <option>aAbcCdfFgilLmnopqrRstux1</option>
</arg>
<arg choice="opt" rep="repeat">file</arg>
</cmdsynopsis>

<refsect1><title>Description</title>
<para>
For each file that is a directory, <command>ls</> lists the contents of
the directory; for each file that is an ordinary file, <command>ls</>
repeats its name and any other information requested.
</para>
<para>&hellip;</para>
</refsect1>
</refentry>
```

A typical reference page for a function:

```
<!DOCTYPE refentry PUBLIC "-//OASIS//DTD DocBook V3.1//EN">
<refentry id="printf">

<refmeta>
<refentrytitle>printf</refentrytitle>
<manvolnum>3S</manvolnum>
</refmeta>

<refnamediv>
<refname>printf</refname>
<refname>fprintf</refname>
<refname>sprintf</refname>
<refpurpose>print formatted output</refpurpose>
</refnamediv>

<refsynopsisdiv>

<funcsynopsis>
<funcsynopsisinfo>
#include &lt;stdio.h&gt;
</funcsynopsisinfo>
<funcprototype>
  <funcdef>int <function>printf</function></funcdef>
  <paramdef>const char *<parameter>format</parameter></paramdef>
  <paramdef>...</paramdef>
</funcprototype>

<funcprototype>
  <funcdef>int <function>fprintf</function></funcdef>
  <paramdef>FILE *<parameter>strm</parameter></paramdef>
  <paramdef>const char *<parameter>format</parameter></paramdef>
  <paramdef>...</paramdef>
</funcprototype>
```

```
<funcprototype>
  <funcdef>int <function>sprintf</function></funcdef>
  <paramdef>char *<parameter>s</parameter></paramdef>
  <paramdef>const char *<parameter>format</parameter></paramdef>
  <paramdef>...</paramdef>
</funcprototype>
</funcsynopsis>

</refsynopsisdiv>

<refsect1><title>Description</title>
<para>
<function>printf</function> places output on the standard
output stream stdout.
</para>
<para>&hellip;</para>
</refsect1>
</refentry>
```

A reference page for a data structure:

```
<!DOCTYPE refentry PUBLIC "-//OASIS//DTD DocBook V3.1//EN">
<refentry id="iovec">

<refmeta>
<refentrytitle>iovec</refentrytitle>
<manvolnum>9S</manvolnum>
</refmeta>

<refnamediv>
<refname>iovec</refname>
<refpurpose>data storage structure for I/O using uio</refpurpose>
</refnamediv>

<refsynopsisdiv>
<synopsis>
#include &lt;sys/uio.h&gt;
</synopsis>
</refsynopsisdiv>

<refsect1><title>Interface Level</title>
<para>
Architecture independent level 1 (DDI/DKI).
</para>
</refsect1>

<refsect1><title>Description</title>

<para>
An <structname>iovec</structname> structure describes a data
storage area for transfer in a
<citerefentry><refentrytitle>uio</refentrytitle>
  <manvolnum>9S</manvolnum>
</citerefentry>
structure. Conceptually,
```

```
it may be thought of as a base address and length specification.
</para>

</refsect1>
<refsect1><title>Structure Members</title>

<programlisting>
     caddr_t  iov_base;   /* base address of the data storage area */
                          /* represented by the iovec structure */
     int      iov_len;    /* size of the data storage area in bytes */
</programlisting>

<para>&hellip;</para>
</refsect1>
</refentry>
```

For additional examples, see also **Reference**.

RefEntryTitle—The title of a reference page

Synopsis

Mixed Content Model	
RefEntryTitle ::= ((#PCDATA|FootnoteRef|XRef|Abbrev|Acronym|Citation|CiteRefEntry|CiteTitle|Emphasis|FirstTerm|ForeignPhrase|GlossTerm|Footnote|Phrase|Quote|Trademark|WordAsWord|Link|OLink|ULink|Action|Application|ClassName|Command|ComputerOutput|Database|Email|EnVar|ErrorCode|ErrorName|ErrorType|Filename|Function|GUIButton|GUIIcon|GUILabel|GUIMenu|GUIMenuItem|GUISubmenu|Hardware|Interface|InterfaceDefinition|KeyCap|KeyCode|KeyCombo|KeySym|Literal|Constant|Markup|MediaLabel|MenuChoice|MouseButton|MsgText|Option|Optional|Parameter|Prompt|Property|Replaceable|ReturnValue|SGMLTag|StructField|StructName|Symbol|SystemItem|Token|Type|UserInput|VarName|Anchor|Author|AuthorInitials|CorpAuthor|ModeSpec|OtherCredit|ProductName|ProductNumber|RevHistory|Comment|Subscript|Superscript|InlineGraphic|InlineMediaObject|InlineEquation|Synopsis|CmdSynopsis|FuncSynopsis|IndexTerm)+)	
Attributes	Common attributes

Description

A **RefEntryTitle** is the title of a reference page. It is frequently the same as the first **RefName** or the **RefDescriptor**, although it may also be a longer, more general title.

Processing expectations

Formatted as a displayed block.

Formatting reference pages may require a fairly sophisticated processing system. Much of the meta-information about a reference page (its name, type, purpose, title, and classification) is stored in wrappers near the beginning of the **RefEntry**.

Common presentational features, such as titles and running heads, may require data from several of these wrappers plus some generated text. Other formatting often requires that these elements be reordered.

4.0 *Future Changes*

The **InterfaceDefinition** element will be discarded in DocBook V4.0. It will no longer be available in the content model of this element.

See Also

RefDescriptor, **RefName**

Examples

For examples, see **CiteRefEntry**, **ManVolNum**, **RefEntry**.

Reference—A collection of reference entries

Synopsis

Content Model

```
Reference ::=
((DocInfo?,Title,Subtitle?,TitleAbbrev?),
 PartIntro?,
 (RefEntry)+)
```

Attributes	Common attributes	
Name	**Type**	**Default**
Label	CDATA	*None*
Status	CDATA	*None*

Parameter Entities

```
%partcontent.mix;
```

Description

A **Reference** is a collection of **RefEntrys**. In a **Book**, a **Reference** can occur at either the **Part** or **Chapter** level.

Reference pages are usually bound together by topic; in traditional UNIX documentation they are most frequently bound into volumes. See **ManVolNum**.

Processing expectations

Formatted as a displayed block. **Referencess** often introduce a forced page break and may start on the next recto page. Frequently, they also produce a separator page, on which may be printed the content of the **PartIntro**.

Attributes

Label

`Label` specifies an identifying string for presentation purposes.

Generally, an explicit `Label` attribute is used only if the processing system is incapable of generating the label automatically. If present, the `Label` is normative; it will used even if the processing system is capable of automatic labelling.

Status

`Status` identifies the editorial or publication status of the **Reference**.

Publication status might be used to control formatting (for example, printing a "draft" watermark on drafts) or processing (perhaps a document with a status of "final" should not include any components that are not final).

Examples

```
<!DOCTYPE reference PUBLIC "-//OASIS//DTD DocBook V3.1//EN">

<reference><title>Reference Pages</title>
<refentry>...</refentry>
<refentry>...</refentry>
...
</reference>
```

RefMeta—Meta-information for a reference entry

Synopsis

Content Model
`RefMeta ::=`
`(RefEntryTitle,ManVolNum?,RefMiscInfo*)`	

Attributes	Common attributes

Description

RefMeta holds the title of the reference page, the number of the volume in which this reference page occurs, and possibly other miscellaneous information (typically used in printing the reference page).

Processing expectations

Suppressed. Most of the elements contained in **RefMeta** are used in presentation, but they are not generally printed as part of the formatting of the **RefMeta** wrapper--it merely serves to identify where they occur.

Examples

For examples, see **RefEntry**.

RefMiscInfo—Meta-information for a reference entry other than the title and volume number

Synopsis

Mixed Content Model

```
RefMiscInfo ::=
((#PCDATA|Link|OLink|ULink|Emphasis|Trademark|Replaceable|Comment|
  Subscript|Superscript|InlineGraphic|InlineMediaObject|IndexTerm)+)
```

Attributes	Common attributes	
Name	**Type**	**Default**
Class	CDATA	*None*

Description

RefMiscInfo is an escape hatch for additional meta-information about a reference page. It may hold copyright information, release or revision information, descriptive text for use in a print header or footer, or any other information not explicitly provided for in **RefMeta**.

Processing expectations

May be formatted inline or as a displayed block, depending on context.

Attributes

Class

`Class` on **RefMiscInfo** can be used to indicate the nature of the miscellaneous information being added to **RefMeta**. Naming this attribute "class" is a violation of DocBook semantics (where `Class` attributes have delimited value sets), it should really be called `Type`.

Examples

For examples, see **RefEntry**.

RefName—The name of (one of) the subject(s) of a reference page

Synopsis

Mixed Content Model

```
RefName ::=
((#PCDATA|Action|Application|ClassName|Command|ComputerOutput|
  Database|Email|EnVar|ErrorCode|ErrorName|ErrorType|Filename|
  Function|GUIButton|GUIIcon|GUILabel|GUIMenu|GUIMenuItem|
  GUISubmenu|Hardware|Interface|InterfaceDefinition|KeyCap|
  KeyCode|KeyCombo|KeySym|Literal|Constant|Markup|MediaLabel|
  MenuChoice|MouseButton|MsgText|Option|Optional|Parameter|Prompt|
  Property|Replaceable|ReturnValue|SGMLTag|StructField|StructName|
  Symbol|SystemItem|Token|Type|UserInput|VarName)+)
```

Attributes	Common attributes

Description

RefEntrys are small units of reference documentation describing a single topic. The **RefName** identifies the topic. Often this is the name of the command or function that the reference page describes.

Some reference pages describe a whole family of very closely related commands or functions. In this case, a **RefEntry** will have multiple **RefName**s, one for each command or function. When a **RefEntry** has several **RefName**s, it is likely to have a **RefDescriptor** that identifies the whole family of functions.

Processing expectations

May be formatted inline or as a displayed block, depending on context.

Formatting reference pages may require a fairly sophisticated processing system. Much of the meta-information about a reference page (its name, type, purpose, title, and classification) is stored in wrappers near the beginning of the **RefEntry**.

Common presentational features, such as titles and running headers, may require data from several of these wrappers plus some generated text. Other formatting often requires that these elements be reordered.

4.0 *Future Changes*

The **InterfaceDefinition** element will be discarded in DocBook V4.0. It will no longer be available in the content model of this element.

See Also

RefDescriptor, **RefEntryTitle**

Examples

For examples, see **RefEntry**.

RefNameDiv—The name, purpose, and classification of a reference page

Synopsis

Content Model	
`RefNameDiv ::= (RefDescriptor?,RefName+,RefPurpose,RefClass*, (Comment|Link|OLink|ULink)*)`	
Attributes	Common attributes

Description

RefNameDiv is the first mandatory section in a **RefEntry**. It is a peer to **RefSynopsis-Div** and **RefSect1**.

The elements in **RefNameDiv** identify the topic of the reference page (**RefDescriptor** or **RefName**), provide a concise summary (**RefPurpose**), and classify the page (**Ref-Class**).

Processing expectations

Formatted as a displayed block. **RefNameDiv** usually generates a section heading, in the same typographic style as a **RefSect1 Title**, called "Name."

The content of this section is traditionally the **RefDescriptor** or **RefName**, and the **RefPurpose**, separated by an em dash.

The **RefClass** may be presented, or it may be suppressed and used only to select a group of reference pages to process. You might use the value of **RefClass** to print all the reference pages appropriate to Solaris™ UNIX, for example.

Formatting reference pages may require a fairly sophisticated processing system. Much of the meta-information about a reference page (its name, type, purpose, title, and classification) is stored in wrappers near the beginning of the **RefEntry**.

Common presentational features, such as titles and running headers, may require data from several of these wrappers plus some generated text. Other formatting often requires that these elements be reordered.

See Also

RefSect1, **RefSynopsisDiv**

Examples

For examples, see **RefEntry**.

RefPurpose—A short (one sentence) synopsis of the topic of a reference page

Synopsis

Mixed Content Model

```
RefPurpose ::=
((#PCDATA|FootnoteRef|XRef|Abbrev|Acronym|Citation|CiteRefEntry|
  CiteTitle|Emphasis|FirstTerm|ForeignPhrase|GlossTerm|Footnote|
  Phrase|Quote|Trademark|WordAsWord|Link|OLink|ULink|Action|
  Application|ClassName|Command|ComputerOutput|Database|Email|
  EnVar|ErrorCode|ErrorName|ErrorType|Filename|Function|GUIButton|
  GUIIcon|GUILabel|GUIMenu|GUIMenuItem|GUISubmenu|Hardware|
```

```
Interface|InterfaceDefinition|KeyCap|KeyCode|KeyCombo|KeySym|
Literal|Constant|Markup|MediaLabel|MenuChoice|MouseButton|
MsgText|Option|Optional|Parameter|Prompt|Property|Replaceable|
ReturnValue|SGMLTag|StructField|StructName|Symbol|SystemItem|
Token|Type|UserInput|VarName|Anchor|Author|AuthorInitials|
CorpAuthor|ModeSpec|OtherCredit|ProductName|ProductNumber|
RevHistory|Comment|Subscript|Superscript|IndexTerm)+)
```

Attributes	Common attributes

Description

The **RefPurpose** is a concise summary of the topic of the reference page. A **RefPurpose** is usually limited to a single, short sentence.

Processing expectations

Formatted inline. See **RefNameDiv**.

In a large **Reference**, **RefNames** and **RefPurposes** are sometimes used to construct a permuted index. A permuted index is a keyword-in-context concordance of lines, like the short definitions in this element reference; the keyword cycles alphabetically through the words of the (definition) lines.

Formatting reference pages may require a fairly sophisticated processing system. Much of the meta-information about a reference page (its name, type, purpose, title, and classification) is stored in wrappers near the beginning of the **RefEntry**.

Common presentational features, such as titles and running headers, may require data from several of these wrappers plus some generated text. Other formatting often requires that these elements be reordered.

4.0 *Future Changes*

The **InterfaceDefinition** element will be discarded in DocBook V4.0. It will no longer be available in the content model of this element.

Examples

For examples, see **RefEntry**.

RefSect1—A major subsection of a reference entry

Synopsis

Content Model

```
RefSect1 ::=
(RefSect1Info?,
 (Title,Subtitle?,TitleAbbrev?),
 (((CalloutList|GlossList|ItemizedList|OrderedList|SegmentedList|
   SimpleList|VariableList|Caution|Important|Note|Tip|Warning|
   LiteralLayout|ProgramListing|ProgramListingCO|Screen|ScreenCO|
```

```
    ScreenShot|Synopsis|CmdSynopsis|FuncSynopsis|FormalPara|Para|
    SimPara|Address|BlockQuote|Graphic|GraphicCO|MediaObject|
    MediaObjectCO|InformalEquation|InformalExample|InformalFigure|
    InformalTable|Equation|Example|Figure|Table|MsgSet|Procedure|
    Sidebar|QandASet|Anchor|BridgeHead|Comment|Highlights|
    Abstract|AuthorBlurb|Epigraph|IndexTerm)+,
   RefSect2*)|
  RefSect2+))
```

Attributes	Common attributes	
Name	**Type**	**Default**
Status	CDATA	*None*

Description

Reference pages have their own hierarchical structure. A **RefSect1** is a major division in a **RefEntry**, analagous to a **Sect1** elsewhere in the document.

The value of a separate hierarchical structure is that it allows the content model of sections in reference pages to be customized differently than the content model of sections outside. For example, because of this split, it was easy to add a recursive sectioning element (**Section**) as a peer to **Sect1** in DocBook V3.1 without introducing it to **RefEntrys**, in which it would not be desirable.

Processing expectations

Formatted as a displayed block.

In some environments, the name, number, and order of major divisions in a reference page is strictly defined by house style. For example, one style requires that the first major section after the synopsis be the "Description," which it must have as its title.

In those cases, it may be useful to replace **RefSect1** in the content model with a set of named sections (following the pattern of **RefNameDiv** and **RefSynopsisDiv**).

Formatting reference pages may require a fairly sophisticated processing system. Much of the meta-information about a reference page (its name, type, purpose, title, and classification) is stored in wrappers near the beginning of the **RefEntry**.

Common presentational features, such as titles and running headers, may require data from several of these wrappers plus some generated text. Other formatting often requires that these elements be reordered.

Attributes

Status

`Status` identifies the editorial or publication status of the **RefSect1**.

Publication status might be used to control formatting (for example, printing a "draft" watermark on drafts) or processing (perhaps a document with a status of "final" should not include any components that are not final).

See Also

RefNameDiv, **RefSynopsisDiv**

Examples

For examples, see **RefEntry**.

RefSect1Info—Meta-information for a RefSect1

Synopsis

Content Model

```
RefSect1Info ::=
((Graphic|MediaObject|LegalNotice|ModeSpec|SubjectSet|KeywordSet|
  ITermSet|Abbrev|Abstract|Address|ArtPageNums|Author|AuthorGroup|
  AuthorInitials|BiblioMisc|BiblioSet|Collab|ConfGroup|
  ContractNum|ContractSponsor|Copyright|CorpAuthor|CorpName|Date|
  Edition|Editor|InvPartNumber|ISBN|ISSN|IssueNum|OrgName|
  OtherCredit|PageNums|PrintHistory|ProductName|ProductNumber|
  PubDate|Publisher|PublisherName|PubsNumber|ReleaseInfo|
  RevHistory|SeriesVolNums|Subtitle|Title|TitleAbbrev|VolumeNum|
  CiteTitle|Honorific|FirstName|Surname|Lineage|OtherName|
  Affiliation|AuthorBlurb|Contrib|IndexTerm)+)
```

Attributes	Common attributes

Parameter Entities

```
%otherinfo.class;
```

Description

Like the other "info" elements, **RefSect1Info** contains meta-information about the section of the document in which it occurs.

Processing expectations

Suppressed. Many of the elements in this wrapper may be used in presentation, but they are not generally printed as part of the formatting of the wrapper. The wrapper merely serves to identify where they occur.

4.0 *Future Changes*

AuthorBlurb and **Affiliation** will be removed from the inline content of **RefSect1Info** in DocBook V4.0. A new wrapper element will be created to associate this information with authors, editors, and other contributors.

Examples

For examples, see **RefEntry**.

RefSect2—A subsection of a RefSect1

Synopsis

Content Model
```
RefSect2 ::=
(RefSect2Info?,
 (Title,Subtitle?,TitleAbbrev?),
 (((CalloutList|GlossList|ItemizedList|OrderedList|SegmentedList|
   SimpleList|VariableList|Caution|Important|Note|Tip|Warning|
   LiteralLayout|ProgramListing|ProgramListingCO|Screen|ScreenCO|
   ScreenShot|Synopsis|CmdSynopsis|FuncSynopsis|FormalPara|Para|
   SimPara|Address|BlockQuote|Graphic|GraphicCO|MediaObject|
   MediaObjectCO|InformalEquation|InformalExample|InformalFigure|
   InformalTable|Equation|Example|Figure|Table|MsgSet|Procedure|
   Sidebar|QandASet|Anchor|BridgeHead|Comment|Highlights|
   Abstract|AuthorBlurb|Epigraph|IndexTerm)+,
  RefSect3*)|
 RefSect3+))
```

Attributes	Common attributes	
Name	**Type**	**Default**
Status	CDATA	*None*

Description

A **RefSect2** is a second level section in a **RefEntry**, analogous to a **Sect2** elsewhere in the document. See **RefSect1**.

Processing expectations

Formatted as a displayed block.

Attributes

Status

`Status` identifies the editorial or publication status of the **RefSect2**.

Publication status might be used to control formatting (for example, printing a "draft" watermark on drafts) or processing (perhaps a document with a status of "final" should not include any components that are not final).

Examples

For examples, see **RefEntry**.

RefSect2Info—Meta-information for a RefSect2

Synopsis

Content Model

```
RefSect2Info ::=
((Graphic|MediaObject|LegalNotice|ModeSpec|SubjectSet|KeywordSet|
  ITermSet|Abbrev|Abstract|Address|ArtPageNums|Author|AuthorGroup|
  AuthorInitials|BiblioMisc|BiblioSet|Collab|ConfGroup|
  ContractNum|ContractSponsor|Copyright|CorpAuthor|CorpName|Date|
  Edition|Editor|InvPartNumber|ISBN|ISSN|IssueNum|OrgName|
  OtherCredit|PageNums|PrintHistory|ProductName|ProductNumber|
  PubDate|Publisher|PublisherName|PubsNumber|ReleaseInfo|
  RevHistory|SeriesVolNums|Subtitle|Title|TitleAbbrev|VolumeNum|
  CiteTitle|Honorific|FirstName|Surname|Lineage|OtherName|
  Affiliation|AuthorBlurb|Contrib|IndexTerm)+)
```

Attributes Common attributes

Parameter Entities

```
%otherinfo.class;
```

Description

Like the other "info" elements, **RefSect2Info** contains meta-information about the section of the document in which it occurs.

Processing expectations

Suppressed. Many of the elements in this wrapper may be used in presentation, but they are not generally printed as part of the formatting of the wrapper. The wrapper merely serves to identify where they occur.

4.0 *Future Changes*

AuthorBlurb and **Affiliation** will be removed from the inline content of **RefSect2Info** in DocBook V4.0. A new wrapper element will be created to associate this information with authors, editors, and other contributors.

Examples

See **RefSect1Info** in **RefEntry** for an analogous example.

RefSect3—A subsection of a RefSect2

Synopsis

Content Model

```
RefSect3 ::=
(RefSect3Info?,
 (Title,Subtitle?,TitleAbbrev?),
 (CalloutList|GlossList|ItemizedList|OrderedList|SegmentedList|
  SimpleList|VariableList|Caution|Important|Note|Tip|Warning|
  LiteralLayout|ProgramListing|ProgramListingCO|Screen|ScreenCO|
```

```
  ScreenShot|Synopsis|CmdSynopsis|FuncSynopsis|FormalPara|Para|
  SimPara|Address|BlockQuote|Graphic|GraphicCO|MediaObject|
  MediaObjectCO|InformalEquation|InformalExample|InformalFigure|
  InformalTable|Equation|Example|Figure|Table|MsgSet|Procedure|
  Sidebar|QandASet|Anchor|BridgeHead|Comment|Highlights|Abstract|
  AuthorBlurb|Epigraph|IndexTerm)+)
```

Attributes	Common attributes	
Name	**Type**	**Default**
Status	CDATA	*None*

Description

A **RefSect3** is a third level section in a **RefEntry**, analogous to a **Sect3** elsewhere in the document. See **RefSect1**.

In DocBook, **RefSect3** is the lowest-level section allowed in a **RefEntry**. There is no element analogous to a **Sect4**.

Processing expectations

Formatted as a displayed block.

Attributes

Status

`Status` identifies the editorial or publication status of the **RefSect3**.

Publication status might be used to control formatting (for example, printing a "draft" watermark on drafts) or processing (perhaps a document with a status of "final" should not include any components that are not final).

Examples

See **RefSect1** and **RefSect2** in **RefEntry** for analogous examples.

RefSect3Info—Meta-information for a RefSect3

Synopsis

Content Model

```
RefSect3Info ::=
((Graphic|MediaObject|LegalNotice|ModeSpec|SubjectSet|KeywordSet|
  ITermSet|Abbrev|Abstract|Address|ArtPageNums|Author|AuthorGroup|
  AuthorInitials|BiblioMisc|BiblioSet|Collab|ConfGroup|
  ContractNum|ContractSponsor|Copyright|CorpAuthor|CorpName|Date|
  Edition|Editor|InvPartNumber|ISBN|ISSN|IssueNum|OrgName|
  OtherCredit|PageNums|PrintHistory|ProductName|ProductNumber|
  PubDate|Publisher|PublisherName|PubsNumber|ReleaseInfo|
  RevHistory|SeriesVolNums|Subtitle|Title|TitleAbbrev|VolumeNum|
  CiteTitle|Honorific|FirstName|Surname|Lineage|OtherName|
  Affiliation|AuthorBlurb|Contrib|IndexTerm)+)
```

Attributes	Common attributes
Parameter Entities `%otherinfo.class;`	

Description

Like the other "info" elements, **RefSect3Info** contains meta-information about the section of the document in which it occurs.

Processing expectations

Suppressed. Many of the elements in this wrapper may be used in presentation, but they are not generally printed as part of the formatting of the wrapper. The wrapper merely serves to identify where they occur.

4.0 Future Changes

AuthorBlurb and **Affiliation** will be removed from the inline content of **RefSect3Info** in DocBook V4.0. A new wrapper element will be created to associate this information with authors, editors, and other contributors.

Examples

See **RefSect1Info** in **RefEntry** for an analogous example.

RefSynopsisDiv—A syntactic synopsis of the subject of the reference page

Synopsis

Content Model

```
RefSynopsisDiv ::=
(RefSynopsisDivInfo?,
 (Title,Subtitle?,TitleAbbrev?)?,
 (((CalloutList|GlossList|ItemizedList|OrderedList|SegmentedList|
    SimpleList|VariableList|Caution|Important|Note|Tip|Warning|
    LiteralLayout|ProgramListing|ProgramListingCO|Screen|ScreenCO|
    ScreenShot|Synopsis|CmdSynopsis|FuncSynopsis|FormalPara|Para|
    SimPara|Address|BlockQuote|Graphic|GraphicCO|MediaObject|
    MediaObjectCO|InformalEquation|InformalExample|InformalFigure|
    InformalTable|Equation|Example|Figure|Table|MsgSet|Procedure|
    Sidebar|QandASet|Anchor|BridgeHead|Comment|Highlights|
    Abstract|AuthorBlurb|Epigraph|IndexTerm)+,
   RefSect2*)|
  (RefSect2+)))
```

Attributes	Common attributes

Description

RefSynopsisDiv contains a syntactic synopsis of the function or command described by the **RefEntry**. When **RefEntrys** are used to describe other sorts of things, **RefSyn-**

opsisDiv should be used for whatever succinct, synopsis information seems appropriate.[*]

Processing expectations

Formatted as a displayed block. **RefSynopsisDiv** usually generates a section heading, in the same typographic style as a **RefSect1 Title**, called "Synopsis."

Formatting reference pages may require a fairly sophisticated processing system. Much of the meta-information about a reference page (its name, type, purpose, title, and classification) is stored in wrappers near the beginning of the **RefEntry**.

Common presentational features, such as titles and running headers, may require data from several of these wrappers plus some generated text. Other formatting often requires that these elements be reordered.

See Also

Arg, **CmdSynopsis**, **Group**, **RefNameDiv**, **RefSect1**, **SBR**, **SynopFragment**, **SynopFragmentRef**

Examples

For examples, see **RefEntry**.

RefSynopsisDivInfo—Meta-information for a RefSynopsisDiv

Synopsis

Content Model

```
RefSynopsisDivInfo ::=
((Graphic|MediaObject|LegalNotice|ModeSpec|SubjectSet|KeywordSet|
  ITermSet|Abbrev|Abstract|Address|ArtPageNums|Author|AuthorGroup|
  AuthorInitials|BiblioMisc|BiblioSet|Collab|ConfGroup|
  ContractNum|ContractSponsor|Copyright|CorpAuthor|CorpName|Date|
  Edition|Editor|InvPartNumber|ISBN|ISSN|IssueNum|OrgName|
  OtherCredit|PageNums|PrintHistory|ProductName|ProductNumber|
  PubDate|Publisher|PublisherName|PubsNumber|ReleaseInfo|
  RevHistory|SeriesVolNums|Subtitle|Title|TitleAbbrev|VolumeNum|
  CiteTitle|Honorific|FirstName|Surname|Lineage|OtherName|
  Affiliation|AuthorBlurb|Contrib|IndexTerm)+)
```

Attributes	Common attributes

Parameter Entities

```
%otherinfo.class;
```

---

[*] In this book, each element of the DTD is described on a reference page, and the **RefSynopsisDiv** is used for the synopsis at the beginning of each entry.

Description

Like the other "info" elements, **RefSynopsisDivInfo** contains meta-information about the section of the document in which it occurs.

Processing expectations

Suppressed. Many of the elements in this wrapper may be used in presentation, but they are not generally printed as part of the formatting of the wrapper. The wrapper merely serves to identify where they occur.

4.0 Future Changes

AuthorBlurb and **Affiliation** will be removed from the inline content of **RefSynopsisDivInfo** in DocBook V4.0. A new wrapper element will be created to associate this information with authors, editors, and other contributors.

See Also

ArtHeader, **BookBiblio**, **BookInfo**, **DocInfo**, **ObjectInfo**, **ScreenInfo**, **Sect1Info**, **Sect2Info**, **Sect3Info**, **Sect4Info**, **Sect5Info**, **SectionInfo**, **SetInfo**

Examples

For examples, see **RefEntry**.

ReleaseInfo—Information about a particular release of a document

Synopsis

Mixed Content Model	

`ReleaseInfo ::=`
`((#PCDATA|Link|OLink|ULink|Emphasis|Trademark|Replaceable|Comment|`
`  Subscript|Superscript|InlineGraphic|InlineMediaObject|IndexTerm)+)`	

Attributes	Common attributes
Parameter Entities `%bibliocomponent.mix;`	

Description

ReleaseInfo contains a brief description of the release or published version of a document or part of a document.

For example, the release information may state that the document is in beta, or that the software it describes is a beta version. It may also contain more specific information, such as the version number from a revision control system.

Processing expectations

May be formatted inline or as a displayed block, depending on context. Sometimes suppressed.

See Also

Date, **Edition**, **PrintHistory**, **PubDate**, **RevHistory**

Examples

For examples, see **RefEntry**.

Replaceable—Content that may or must be replaced by the user

Synopsis

Mixed Content Model

```
Replaceable ::=
((#PCDATA|Link|OLink|ULink|Optional|Anchor|Comment|Subscript|
  Superscript|InlineGraphic|InlineMediaObject)+)
```

Attributes **Name**	Common attributes **Type**	**Default**
Class	*Enumeration:* Command Function Option Parameter	*None*

Parameter Entities

%cptr.char.mix;	%docinfo.char.mix;	%ndxterm.char.mix;
%para.char.mix;	%programlisting.content;	%refinline.char.mix;
%refname.char.mix;	%screen.content;	%smallcptr.char.mix;
%tbl.entry.mdl;	%tech.char.class;	%title.char.mix;

Description

Replaceable is used to mark text that describes *what* a user is supposed to enter, but not the *actual text* that they are supposed to enter.

It is used to identify a class of object in the document, in which the user is expected to replace the text that identifies the class with some specific instance of that class. A canonical example is

```
<replaceable>filename</replaceable>
```

in which the user is expected to provide the name of some specific file to replace the text "filename."

Processing expectations

Formatted inline. Usually, the text is given special typographic treatment, such as italics, as a clue to the user that this is replaceable text. Often the font used is described in a "conventions" section at the beginning of the document.

Attributes

Class

`Class` identifies the type of the replaceable information.

See Also

Command, **ComputerOutput**, **Constant**, **Literal**, **Markup**, **Option**, **Optional**, **Parameter**, **Prompt**, **SGMLTag**, **UserInput**, **VarName**

Examples

For examples, see **CmdSynopsis**, **MediaLabel**, **MsgSet**, **SynopFragment**.

ReturnValue—The value returned by a function

Synopsis

Mixed Content Model
`ReturnValue ::=`
`((#PCDATA|Replaceable|InlineGraphic|InlineMediaObject|IndexTerm)+)`		

Attributes	Common attributes	
Parameter Entities		
`%cptr.char.mix;`	`%ndxterm.char.mix;`	`%para.char.mix;`
`%programlisting.content;`	`%refinline.char.mix;`	`%refname.char.mix;`
`%screen.content;`	`%tbl.entry.mdl;`	`%tech.char.class;`
`%title.char.mix;`		

Description

ReturnValue identifies the value returned by a function or command.

Processing expectations

Formatted inline.

See Also

FuncDef, **FuncParams**, **FuncPrototype**, **FuncSynopsisInfo**, **Function**, **ParamDef**, **Parameter**, **VarArgs**, **Void**

Examples

```
<!DOCTYPE para PUBLIC "-//OASIS//DTD DocBook V3.1//EN">
<para>
The <function>open</function> function returns <returnvalue>2</returnvalue>
(<errorname>ENOFILE</errorname>) if the file does not exist.
</para>
```

The *open* function returns 2 ("ENOFILE") if the file does not exist.

RevHistory—A history of the revisions to a document

Synopsis

Content Model
`RevHistory ::=`
`(Revision+)`		

Attributes	Common attributes	
Parameter Entities		
`%bibliocomponent.mix;`	`%docinfo.char.class;`	`%ndxterm.char.mix;`
`%para.char.mix;`	`%programlisting.content;`	`%refinline.char.mix;`
`%screen.content;`	`%tbl.entry.mdl;`	`%title.char.mix;`

Description

RevHistory is a structure for documenting a history of changes, specifically, a history of changes to the document or section in which it occurs.

Processing expectations

Formatted as a displayed block. A tabular or list presentation is most common.

5.0 *Future Changes*

Due to a parameterization oversight in the DTD, **RevHistory** is allowed in some outlandish places. Still, it is not an inline, so it should not be used inside **LineAnnotations**, **Links**, or **Quotes**. (Not to mention the truly outlandish places like **Title** and **SeeAlso**!)

In a future version of DocBook, **RevHistory** will be removed from these inline contexts.

The original intent for **RevHistory** was simply to document the history of changes to the document that contains it. In keeping with this meaning, you are advised to limit its use to places where bibliographic meta-information is allowed (the "info" elements).

One can argue that **RevHistory** has broader applicability for documenting changes to other systems as well, and in light of this, it may become available in more contexts, but that has not yet been decided.

See Also

Date, **Edition**, **PrintHistory**, **PubDate**, **ReleaseInfo**

Examples

```
<!DOCTYPE revhistory PUBLIC "-//OASIS//DTD DocBook V3.1//EN">
<revhistory>

<revision>
  <revnumber>0.91</revnumber>
  <date>11 Dec 1996</date>
  <authorinitials>ndw</authorinitials>
  <revremark>Bug fixes</revremark>
</revision>

<revision>
  <revnumber>0.90</revnumber>
  <date>30 Nov 1996</date>
  <authorinitials>ndw</authorinitials>
  <revremark>First beta release</revremark>
</revision>

</revhistory>
```

For additional examples, see also **Article**.

Revision—An entry describing a single revision in the history of the revisions to a document

Synopsis

Content Model	
Revision ::= (RevNumber,Date,AuthorInitials*,RevRemark?)	
Attributes	Common attributes

Description

Revision contains information about a single revision to a document. Revisions are identified by a number and a date. They may also include the initials of the author, and additional remarks.

Processing expectations

Revisions are often presented in a list or table. In a tabular presentation, each revision most likely forms a row in the table.

Examples

For examples, see **Article**, **RevHistory**.

RevNumber—A document revision number

Synopsis

Mixed Content Model	

`RevNumber ::=`
`((#PCDATA|Link|OLink|ULink|Emphasis|Trademark|Replaceable|Comment|`
`Subscript|Superscript|InlineGraphic|InlineMediaObject|IndexTerm)+)`	

Attributes	Common attributes

Description

A **RevNumber** identifies the revision number of a document. The revision number should uniquely identify a particular revision of a document.

Processing expectations

Formatted inline. DocBook does not require that **RevNumber**s be sequential or make any demands on their format. They can be numeric, alphanumeric, or whatever suits your needs.

Examples

For examples, see **Article**, **RevHistory**.

RevRemark—A description of a revision to a document

Synopsis

Mixed Content Model	

`RevRemark ::=`
`((#PCDATA|Link|OLink|ULink|Emphasis|Trademark|Replaceable|Comment|`
`Subscript|Superscript|InlineGraphic|InlineMediaObject|IndexTerm)+)`	

Attributes	Common attributes

Description

The **RevRemark** associated with a revision is a short summary of the changes made in that revision. There's no provision in a **RevHistory** for an extended description of the changes made.

Processing expectations

May be formatted inline or as a displayed block, depending on context. Sometimes suppressed.

Examples

For examples, see **Article**, **RevHistory**.

---

row—A row in a table

Synopsis

Content Model

```
row ::=
((entry|entrytbl)+)
```

Attributes	Common attributes	
Name	**Type**	**Default**
rowsep	NUMBER	*None*
valign	*Enumeration:* bottom middle top	*None*

Parameter Entities

`%tbl.hdft.mdl;`

Description

A **Row** is a row in a table. It contains all of the cells (**Entrys** or **EntryTbls**) that appear in that row.

Processing expectations

This element is expected to obey the semantics of the *CALS Table Model Document Type Definition*, as specified by *OASIS Technical Memorandum TM 9502:1995* (*http://www.oasis-open.org/html/a502.htm*).

Within a **Row**, cells are arranged horizontally from the start of the row to the end. Cells can, but are not required to, specify the column in which they occur, so it is possible for a row to contain fewer cells than there are columns in the table. This introduces missing cells, which are assumed to be empty. These missing cells can occur anywhere in the row.

Once a cell has been allocated to a column, subsequent cells may not fill preceding columns. In other words, while three cells can specify that they occur in columns 1, 3, and 5, they cannot specify that they occur in columns 1, 5, and 3. Once a column is passed, you can never go back.

If cells do not specify the column in which they occur, they are placed in the next available column. Calculation of the next available column is complicated by horizontal and vertical spanning. Cells from preceding rows can have a vertical span that causes them to extend into the current row, thus occupying space in the current row. These logically occupied cells are skipped when looking for the next available column. Similarly, if a cell has a horizontal span, it logically occupies the columns that follow it. Cells can simultaneously span rows and columns.

Each of the following conditions is an error:

- A cell spans beyond the boundries of the table.
- A row contains more cells than there are columns in the table.
- The arrangement of cells in a row forces one or more cells past the last column of the table.

Attributes

rowsep

If `RowSep` has the value 1 (true), then a rule will be drawn below all the cells in this **Row** (unless other, interior elements, suppress some or all of the rules). A value of 0 (false) suppresses the rule. The rule below the last row in the table is controlled by the `Frame` attribute of the enclosing **Table** or **InformalTable** and the `RowSep` of the last row is ignored. If unspecified, this attribute is inherited from enclosing elements.

valign

`VAlign` specifies the vertical alignment of text (and other elements) within the cells of this **Row**. If no alignment is specified, it is inherited from enclosing elements.

See Also

colspec, **entry**, **entrytbl**, **InformalTable**, **spanspec**, **Table**, **tbody**, **tfoot**, **tgroup**, **thead**

Examples

For examples, see **entrytbl**, **FootnoteRef**, **InformalTable**, **RefEntry**, **Table**.

SBR—An explicit line break in a command synopsis

Synopsis

Content Model
`SBR ::=`
`EMPTY`	

Attributes	Common attributes

Description

For the most part, DocBook attempts to describe document structure rather than presentation. However, in some complex environments, it is possible to demonstrate that there is no reasonable set of processing expectations that can guarantee correct formatting.

CmdSynopsis is one of those environments. Within a long synopsis, it may be necessary to specify the location of a line break explicitly.

The **SBR** element indicates the position of such a line break in a **CmdSynopsis**. It is purely presentational.

Processing expectations

SBR causes a line break.

See Also

Arg, **CmdSynopsis**, **Group**, **RefSynopsisDiv**, **SynopFragment**, **SynopFragmentRef**

Examples

For examples, see **SynopFragment**.

Screen—Text that a user sees or might see on a computer screen

Synopsis

Mixed Content Model

```
Screen ::=
((CO|LineAnnotation|#PCDATA|FootnoteRef|XRef|Abbrev|Acronym|
  Citation|CiteRefEntry|CiteTitle|Emphasis|FirstTerm|
  ForeignPhrase|GlossTerm|Footnote|Phrase|Quote|Trademark|
  WordAsWord|Link|OLink|ULink|Action|Application|ClassName|
  Command|ComputerOutput|Database|Email|EnVar|ErrorCode|ErrorName|
  ErrorType|Filename|Function|GUIButton|GUIIcon|GUILabel|GUIMenu|
  GUIMenuItem|GUISubmenu|Hardware|Interface|InterfaceDefinition|
  KeyCap|KeyCode|KeyCombo|KeySym|Literal|Constant|Markup|
  MediaLabel|MenuChoice|MouseButton|MsgText|Option|Optional|
  Parameter|Prompt|Property|Replaceable|ReturnValue|SGMLTag|
  StructField|StructName|Symbol|SystemItem|Token|Type|UserInput|
```

```
VarName|Anchor|Author|AuthorInitials|CorpAuthor|ModeSpec|
OtherCredit|ProductName|ProductNumber|RevHistory|Comment|
Subscript|Superscript|InlineGraphic|InlineMediaObject|
InlineEquation|Synopsis|CmdSynopsis|FuncSynopsis|IndexTerm)+)
```

Attributes	Common attributes	
Name	**Type**	**Default**
Width	NUMBER	*None*
Format	*Enumerated notation:* linespecific	"linespecific"

Parameter Entities		
`%admon.mix;`	`%bookcomponent.content;`	`%component.mix;`
`%divcomponent.mix;`	`%example.mix;`	`%figure.mix;`
`%footnote.mix;`	`%glossdef.mix;`	`%indexdivcomponent.mix;`
`%legalnotice.mix;`	`%linespecific.class;`	`%para.mix;`
`%qandaset.mix;`	`%refcomponent.mix;`	`%sidebar.mix;`
`%tabentry.mix;`	`%tbl.entry.mdl;`	`%textobject.mix;`

Description

A **Screen** is a verbatim environment for displaying text that the user might see on a computer terminal. It is often used to display the results of a command.

Having less specific semantic overtones, **Screen** is often used wherever a verbatim presentation is desired, but the semantic of **ProgramListing** is inappropriate.

Processing expectations

This element is displayed "verbatim"; whitespace and linebreaks within this element are significant. **Screens** are usually displayed in a fixed width font.

[4.0] *Future Changes*

The **InterfaceDefinition** element will be discarded in DocBook V4.0. It will no longer be available in the content model of this element.

Attributes

Format

The `Format` attribute applies the `linespecific` notation to all **Screens**. All white space and line breaks must be preserved.

Width

`Width` specifies the width (in characters) of the longest line in this **Screen** (formatters may use this value to determine scaling or rotation).

See Also

ComputerOutput, **LineAnnotation**, **LiteralLayout**, **ProgramListing**, **ScreenShot**, **Synopsis**, **UserInput**

Examples

```
<!DOCTYPE screen PUBLIC "-//OASIS//DTD DocBook V3.1//EN">
<screen>
 Volume in drive C is SYSTEM         Serial number is 2350:717C
 Directory of  C:\

10/17/97   9:04         &lt;DIR&gt;    bin
10/16/97  14:11         &lt;DIR&gt;    DOS
10/16/97  14:40         &lt;DIR&gt;    Program Files
10/16/97  14:46         &lt;DIR&gt;    TEMP
10/17/97   9:04         &lt;DIR&gt;    tmp
10/16/97  14:37         &lt;DIR&gt;    WINNT
10/16/97  14:25             119  AUTOEXEC.BAT
 2/13/94   6:21          54,619  COMMAND.COM
10/16/97  14:25             115  CONFIG.SYS
11/16/97  17:17      61,865,984  pagefile.sys
 2/13/94   6:21           9,349  WINA20.386
</screen>
```

```
 Volume in drive C is SYSTEM         Serial number is 2350:717C
 Directory of  C:\

10/17/97   9:04         <DIR>    bin
10/16/97  14:11         <DIR>    DOS
10/16/97  14:40         <DIR>    Program Files
10/16/97  14:46         <DIR>    TEMP
10/17/97   9:04         <DIR>    tmp
10/16/97  14:37         <DIR>    WINNT
10/16/97  14:25             119  AUTOEXEC.BAT
 2/13/94   6:21          54,619  COMMAND.COM
10/16/97  14:25             115  CONFIG.SYS
11/16/97  17:17      61,865,984  pagefile.sys
 2/13/94   6:21           9,349  WINA20.386
```

For additional examples, see also **LineAnnotation**, **ScreenCO**.

ScreenCO—A screen with associated areas used in callouts

Synopsis

Content Model
`ScreenCO ::=`
`(AreaSpec,Screen,CalloutList*)`		

Attributes	Common attributes	
Parameter Entities		
`%admon.mix;`	`%bookcomponent.content;`	`%component.mix;`
`%divcomponent.mix;`	`%example.mix;`	`%figure.mix;`
`%footnote.mix;`	`%glossdef.mix;`	`%indexdivcomponent.mix;`
`%legalnotice.mix;`	`%linespecific.class;`	`%para.mix;`
`%qandaset.mix;`	`%refcomponent.mix;`	`%sidebar.mix;`
`%tabentry.mix;`	`%tbl.entry.mdl;`	`%textobject.mix;`

Description

Callouts, such as numbered bullets, are an annotation mechanism. In an online system, these bullets are frequently "hot," and clicking on them navigates to the corresponding annotation.

A **ScreenCO** is a wrapper around an **AreaSpec** and a **Screen**. An **AreaSpec** identifies the locations (coordinates) in the **Screen** where the callouts occur. The **ScreenCO** may also contain the list of annotations in a **CalloutList**, although the **CalloutList** may also occur outside of the wrapper, elsewhere in the document.

It is also possible to embed **CO** elements directly in the verbatim text, in order to avoid the overhead of calculating the correct coordinates. If you decide to follow this route, use a **Screen** and a **CalloutList** without the **ScreenCO** wrapper. A **ScreenCO** must specify at least one coordinate.

For a complete description of callouts, see **Callout**.

Processing expectations

Formatted as a displayed block. This element is displayed "verbatim"; whitespace and linebreaks within this element are significant.

The mandatory processing expectations of a **ScreenCO** are minimal: a system is expected to render the program listing and the callout list, if present.

If explicit **CO** elements are embedded in a **Screen**, they must generate appropriate callout marks.

In online environments, the processing system may be able to instantiate the linking relationships between the callout marks in the program listing and the annotations. Some systems may even be able to go a step further and generate the callout marks automatically from the coordinate information, but this level of sophistication is not mandatory.

See Also

AreaSpec, **CalloutList**, **CO**, **GraphicCO**, **ImageObjectCO**, **MediaObjectCO**, **ProgramListingCO**

Examples

```
<!DOCTYPE informalexample PUBLIC "-//OASIS//DTD DocBook V3.1//EN">
<informalexample>
<screen>
 Volume in drive C is SYSTEM         Serial number is 2350:717C
 Directory of  C:\
```

```
10/17/97   9:04          &lt;DIR>    bin
10/16/97  14:11          &lt;DIR>    DOS            <co id="dos">
10/16/97  14:40          &lt;DIR>    Program Files
10/16/97  14:46          &lt;DIR>    TEMP
10/17/97   9:04          &lt;DIR>    tmp
10/16/97  14:37          &lt;DIR>    WINNT
10/16/97  14:25              119  AUTOEXEC.BAT   <co id="autoexec.bat">
 2/13/94   6:21           54,619  COMMAND.COM    <co id="command.com">
10/16/97  14:25              115  CONFIG.SYS     <co id="config.sys">
11/16/97  17:17       61,865,984  pagefile.sys
 2/13/94   6:21            9,349  WINA20.386     <co id="wina20.386">
</screen>
<calloutlist>
<callout arearefs="dos">
<para>
This directory holds <trademark>MS-DOS</trademark>, the
operating system that was installed before <trademark>Windows
NT</trademark>.
</para>
</callout>

<callout arearefs="autoexec.bat command.com config.sys">
<para>
System startup code for DOS.
</para>
</callout>

<callout arearefs="wina20.386">
<para>
Some sort of <trademark>Windows 3.1</trademark> hack for some 386 processors,
as I recall.
</para>
</callout>
</calloutlist>
</informalexample>
```

```
 Volume in drive C is SYSTEM          Serial number is 2350:717C
 Directory of  C:\

10/17/97   9:04          <DIR>    bin
10/16/97  14:11          <DIR>    DOS            ❶
10/16/97  14:40          <DIR>    Program Files
10/16/97  14:46          <DIR>    TEMP
10/17/97   9:04          <DIR>    tmp
10/16/97  14:37          <DIR>    WINNT
10/16/97  14:25              119  AUTOEXEC.BAT   ❷
 2/13/94   6:21           54,619  COMMAND.COM    ❸
10/16/97  14:25              115  CONFIG.SYS     ❹
11/16/97  17:17       61,865,984  pagefile.sys
 2/13/94   6:21            9,349  WINA20.386     ❺
```

❶ This directory holds MS-DOS™, the operating system that was installed before Windows NT™.

❷❸❹ System startup code for DOS.

❺ Some sort of Windows 3.1™ hack for some 386 processors, as I recall.

For additional examples, see also **Screen**.

ScreenInfo—Information about how a screen shot was produced

Synopsis

Mixed Content Model

```
ScreenInfo ::=
((#PCDATA|FootnoteRef|XRef|Abbrev|Acronym|Citation|CiteRefEntry|
  CiteTitle|Emphasis|FirstTerm|ForeignPhrase|GlossTerm|Footnote|
  Phrase|Quote|Trademark|WordAsWord|Link|OLink|ULink|Action|
  Application|ClassName|Command|ComputerOutput|Database|Email|
  EnVar|ErrorCode|ErrorName|ErrorType|Filename|Function|GUIButton|
  GUIIcon|GUILabel|GUIMenu|GUIMenuItem|GUISubmenu|Hardware|
  Interface|InterfaceDefinition|KeyCap|KeyCode|KeyCombo|KeySym|
  Literal|Constant|Markup|MediaLabel|MenuChoice|MouseButton|
  MsgText|Option|Optional|Parameter|Prompt|Property|Replaceable|
  ReturnValue|SGMLTag|StructField|StructName|Symbol|SystemItem|
  Token|Type|UserInput|VarName|Anchor|Author|AuthorInitials|
  CorpAuthor|ModeSpec|OtherCredit|ProductName|ProductNumber|
  RevHistory|Comment|Subscript|Superscript|InlineGraphic|
  InlineMediaObject|InlineEquation|Synopsis|CmdSynopsis|
  FuncSynopsis|IndexTerm)+)
```

Attributes	Common attributes

Description

ScreenInfo contains meta-information about how a **ScreenShot** was produced. Note that the content model of **ScreenShot** is radically different from the other “info” elements, to which it bears little or no resemblance.

ScreenInfo is a good place to store information about how and at what resolution a screen shot was produced, when it was produced, and by whom.

Processing expectations

Suppressed.

[4.0] *Future Changes*

The **InterfaceDefinition** element will be discarded in DocBook V4.0. It will no longer be available in the content model of this element.

See Also

ArtHeader, **BookBiblio**, **BookInfo**, **DocInfo**, **ObjectInfo**, **RefSynopsisDivInfo**, **Sect1Info**, **Sect2Info**, **Sect3Info**, **Sect4Info**, **Sect5Info**, **SectionInfo**, **SetInfo**

Examples

For examples, see **ScreenShot**.

ScreenShot—A representation of what the user sees or might see on a computer screen

Synopsis

Content Model

```
ScreenShot ::=
(ScreenInfo?,
  (Graphic|GraphicCO|MediaObject|MediaObjectCO))
```

Attributes	Common attributes	

Parameter Entities

%admon.mix;	%bookcomponent.content;	%component.mix;
%divcomponent.mix;	%example.mix;	%figure.mix;
%footnote.mix;	%glossdef.mix;	%indexdivcomponent.mix;
%legalnotice.mix;	%linespecific.class;	%para.mix;
%qandaset.mix;	%refcomponent.mix;	%sidebar.mix;
%tabentry.mix;	%tbl.entry.mdl;	%textobject.mix;

Description

A **ScreenShot** is a graphical environment for displaying an image of what the user might see on a computer screen. It is often used to display application screen shots, dialog boxes, and other components of a graphical user interface.

Processing expectations

Formatted as a displayed block.

See Also

ComputerOutput, **LineAnnotation**, **LiteralLayout**, **ProgramListing**, **Screen**, **Synopsis**, **UserInput**

Examples

```
<!DOCTYPE screenshot PUBLIC "-//OASIS//DTD DocBook V3.1//EN">

<screenshot>
<screeninfo>640x480x256</screeninfo>
<graphic fileref="copilot.gif"></graphic>
</screenshot>
```

Secondary—A secondary word or phrase in an index term

Synopsis

Mixed Content Model

```
Secondary ::=
((#PCDATA|FootnoteRef|XRef|Abbrev|Acronym|Citation|CiteRefEntry|
  CiteTitle|Emphasis|FirstTerm|ForeignPhrase|GlossTerm|Footnote|
  Phrase|Quote|Trademark|WordAsWord|Link|OLink|ULink|Action|
  Application|ClassName|Command|ComputerOutput|Database|Email|
  EnVar|ErrorCode|ErrorName|ErrorType|Filename|Function|GUIButton|
  GUIIcon|GUILabel|GUIMenu|GUIMenuItem|GUISubmenu|Hardware|
  Interface|InterfaceDefinition|KeyCap|KeyCode|KeyCombo|KeySym|
  Literal|Constant|Markup|MediaLabel|MenuChoice|MouseButton|
  MsgText|Option|Optional|Parameter|Prompt|Property|Replaceable|
  ReturnValue|SGMLTag|StructField|StructName|Symbol|SystemItem|
  Token|Type|UserInput|VarName|Anchor|Author|AuthorInitials|
  CorpAuthor|ModeSpec|OtherCredit|ProductName|ProductNumber|
  RevHistory|Comment|Subscript|Superscript|InlineGraphic|
  InlineMediaObject)+)
```

Attributes	Common attributes	
Name	**Type**	**Default**
SortAs	CDATA	*None*

Description

Secondary contains a secondary word or phrase in an **IndexTerm**. The text of a **Secondary** term is less significant than the **Primary** term, but more significant than the **Tertiary** term for sorting and display purposes.

In **IndexTerms**, you can only have one primary, secondary, and tertiary term. If you want to index multiple secondary terms for the same primary, you must repeat the primary in another **IndexTerm**. You cannot place several **Secondarys** in the same primary.

Processing expectations

Suppressed. This element provides data for processing but is not rendered in the primary flow of text.

4.0 *Future Changes*

The **InterfaceDefinition** element will be discarded in DocBook V4.0. It will no longer be available in the content model of this element.

Attributes

SortAs

`SortAs` specifies the string by which the element's content is to be sorted. If unspecified, the proper content is used.

See Also

IndexEntry, **IndexTerm**, **Primary**, **PrimaryIE**, **SecondaryIE**, **See**, **SeeAlso**, **SeeAlsoIE**, **SeeIE**, **Tertiary**, **TertiaryIE**

Examples

For examples, see **Chapter**, **IndexTerm**.

SecondaryIE—A secondary term in an index entry, rather than in the text

Synopsis

Mixed Content Model

```
SecondaryIE ::=
((#PCDATA|FootnoteRef|XRef|Abbrev|Acronym|Citation|CiteRefEntry|
  CiteTitle|Emphasis|FirstTerm|ForeignPhrase|GlossTerm|Footnote|
  Phrase|Quote|Trademark|WordAsWord|Link|OLink|ULink|Action|
  Application|ClassName|Command|ComputerOutput|Database|Email|
  EnVar|ErrorCode|ErrorName|ErrorType|Filename|Function|GUIButton|
  GUIIcon|GUILabel|GUIMenu|GUIMenuItem|GUISubmenu|Hardware|
  Interface|InterfaceDefinition|KeyCap|KeyCode|KeyCombo|KeySym|
  Literal|Constant|Markup|MediaLabel|MenuChoice|MouseButton|
  MsgText|Option|Optional|Parameter|Prompt|Property|Replaceable|
  ReturnValue|SGMLTag|StructField|StructName|Symbol|SystemItem|
  Token|Type|UserInput|VarName|Anchor|Author|AuthorInitials|
  CorpAuthor|ModeSpec|OtherCredit|ProductName|ProductNumber|
  RevHistory|Comment|Subscript|Superscript|InlineGraphic|
  InlineMediaObject)+)
```

Attributes	Common attributes	
Name	**Type**	**Default**
Linkends	IDREFS	*None*

Description

SecondaryIE identifies a secondary word or words in an **IndexEntry**.

In **IndexEntrys**, you can specify as many secondary terms that are necessary. Secondary and tertiary terms can be mixed, following the primary.

Processing expectations

Formatted as a displayed block. **SecondaryIEs** occur below the **PrimaryIE**, usually aligned with each other and indented from the primary.

[4.0] Future Changes

The **InterfaceDefinition** element will be discarded in DocBook V4.0. It will no longer be available in the content model of this element.

Attributes

Linkends

Linkends, if used, points to the **IndexTerms** indexed by this entry.

See Also

IndexEntry, **IndexTerm**, **Primary**, **PrimaryIE**, **Secondary**, **See**, **SeeAlso**, **SeeAlsoIE**, **SeeIE**, **Tertiary**, **TertiaryIE**

Examples

For examples, see **Index**.

Sect1—A top-level section of document

Synopsis

Content Model

```
Sect1 ::=
(Sect1Info?,
 (Title,Subtitle?,TitleAbbrev?),
 (ToC|LoT|Index|Glossary|Bibliography)*,
 (((CalloutList|GlossList|ItemizedList|OrderedList|SegmentedList|
    SimpleList|VariableList|Caution|Important|Note|Tip|Warning|
    LiteralLayout|ProgramListing|ProgramListingCO|Screen|ScreenCO|
    ScreenShot|Synopsis|CmdSynopsis|FuncSynopsis|FormalPara|Para|
    SimPara|Address|BlockQuote|Graphic|GraphicCO|MediaObject|
    MediaObjectCO|InformalEquation|InformalExample|InformalFigure|
    InformalTable|Equation|Example|Figure|Table|MsgSet|Procedure|
    Sidebar|QandASet|Anchor|BridgeHead|Comment|Highlights|
    Abstract|AuthorBlurb|Epigraph|IndexTerm)+,
   ((RefEntry)*|
    Sect2*|SimpleSect*))|
  (RefEntry)+|
  Sect2+|SimpleSect+),
 (ToC|LoT|Index|Glossary|Bibliography)*)
```

Attributes	Common attributes	
Name	**Type**	**Default**
Label	CDATA	*None*
Status	CDATA	*None*
Renderas	*Enumeration:* Sect2 Sect3 Sect4 Sect5	*None*

Parameter Entities

```
%bookcomponent.content;
```

Description

Sect1 is one of the top-level sectioning elements in a component. There are three types of sectioning elements in DocBook:

- Explicitly numbered sections, **Sect1**...**Sect5**, which must be properly nested and can only be five levels deep.
- Recursive **Sections**, which are alternative to the numbered sections and have unbounded depth.
- **SimpleSects**, which are terminal. **SimpleSects** can occur as the "leaf" sections in either recursive sections or any of the numbered sections, or directly in components.

None of the sectioning elements is allowed to "float" in a component. You can place paragraphs and other block elements before a section, but you cannot place anything after it.

This means that you cannot have content in the **Sect1** after the end of a **Sect2**. This is consistent with the DocBook book model, because in a printed book it is usually impossible for a reader to detect the end of the enclosed second level section and, therefore, all content after a second level section appears in that section.

Processing Expectations

Formatted as a displayed block. Sometimes sections are numbered.

4.0 *Future Changes*

In DocBook V4.0, the **ToC** element in the content model will be replaced by **TocChap**.

Attributes

Label

`Label` specifies an identifying string for presentation purposes.

Generally, an explicit `Label` attribute is used only if the processing system is incapable of generating the label automatically. If present, the `Label` is normative; it will used even if the processing system is capable of automatic labelling.

Renderas

The `RenderAs` attribute identifies how the section should be rendered. In this way, a section at one level of the structural hierarchy can be made to appear to be at another level.

Status

`Status` identifies the editorial or publication status of the **Sect1**.

Publication status might be used to control formatting (for example, printing a "draft" watermark on drafts) or processing (perhaps a document with a status of "final" should not include any components that are not final).

See Also

BridgeHead, **Sect2**, **Sect3**, **Sect4**, **Sect5**, **Section**, **SimpleSect**

Examples

For examples, see **Chapter**, **IndexTerm**, **OLink**.

Sect1Info—Meta-information for a Sect1

Synopsis

Content Model

```
Sect1Info ::=
((Graphic|MediaObject|LegalNotice|ModeSpec|SubjectSet|KeywordSet|
  ITermSet|Abbrev|Abstract|Address|ArtPageNums|Author|AuthorGroup|
  AuthorInitials|BiblioMisc|BiblioSet|Collab|ConfGroup|
  ContractNum|ContractSponsor|Copyright|CorpAuthor|CorpName|Date|
  Edition|Editor|InvPartNumber|ISBN|ISSN|IssueNum|OrgName|
  OtherCredit|PageNums|PrintHistory|ProductName|ProductNumber|
  PubDate|Publisher|PublisherName|PubsNumber|ReleaseInfo|
  RevHistory|SeriesVolNums|Subtitle|Title|TitleAbbrev|VolumeNum|
  CiteTitle|Honorific|FirstName|Surname|Lineage|OtherName|
  Affiliation|AuthorBlurb|Contrib|IndexTerm)+)
```

Attributes	Common attributes

Parameter Entities

```
%otherinfo.class;
```

Description

Like the other "info" elements, **Sect1Info** contains meta-information about the section of the document in which it occurs.

Processing expectations

Suppressed. Many of the elements in this wrapper may be used in presentation, but they are not generally printed as part of the formatting of the wrapper. The wrapper merely serves to identify where they occur.

4.0 *Future Changes*

AuthorBlurb and **Affiliation** will be removed from the inline content of **Sect1Info** in DocBook V4.0. A new wrapper element will be created to associate this information with authors, editors, and other contributors.

See Also

ArtHeader, BookBiblio, BookInfo, DocInfo, ObjectInfo, RefSynopsisDivInfo, ScreenInfo, Sect2Info, Sect3Info, Sect4Info, Sect5Info, SectionInfo, SetInfo

Examples

```
<!DOCTYPE sect1 PUBLIC "-//OASIS//DTD DocBook V3.1//EN">
<sect1>
  <sect1info>
    <legalnotice><para>In the public domain.</para></legalnotice>
    <title>Something Pithy</title>
    <subtitle>How I Made Up a Silly Example</subtitle>
  </sect1info>
<title>Something Pithy</title>
<para>
Content.
</para>
</sect1>
```

Sect2—A subsection within a Sect1

Synopsis

Content Model

```
Sect2 ::=
(Sect2Info?,
 (Title,Subtitle?,TitleAbbrev?),
 (ToC|LoT|Index|Glossary|Bibliography)*,
 (((CalloutList|GlossList|ItemizedList|OrderedList|SegmentedList|
    SimpleList|VariableList|Caution|Important|Note|Tip|Warning|
    LiteralLayout|ProgramListing|ProgramListingCO|Screen|ScreenCO|
    ScreenShot|Synopsis|CmdSynopsis|FuncSynopsis|FormalPara|Para|
    SimPara|Address|BlockQuote|Graphic|GraphicCO|MediaObject|
    MediaObjectCO|InformalEquation|InformalExample|InformalFigure|
    InformalTable|Equation|Example|Figure|Table|MsgSet|Procedure|
    Sidebar|QandASet|Anchor|BridgeHead|Comment|Highlights|
    Abstract|AuthorBlurb|Epigraph|IndexTerm)+,
   ((RefEntry)*|
    Sect3*|SimpleSect*))|
  (RefEntry)+|
  Sect3+|SimpleSect+),
 (ToC|LoT|Index|Glossary|Bibliography)*)
```

Attributes	Common attributes	
Name	**Type**	**Default**
Label	CDATA	*None*
Status	CDATA	*None*
Renderas	*Enumeration:* Sect1 Sect3 Sect4 Sect5	*None*

Description

A **Sect2** is a second-level section in a document.

Processing expectations

Formatted as a displayed block. Sometimes sections are numbered.

4.0 *Future Changes*

In DocBook V4.0, the **ToC** element in the content model will be replaced by **TocChap**.

Attributes

Label

`Label` specifies an identifying string for presentation purposes.

Generally, an explicit `Label` attribute is used only if the processing system is incapable of generating the label automatically. If present, the `Label` is normative; it will used even if the processing system is capable of automatic labelling.

Renderas

The `RenderAs` attribute identifies how the section should be rendered. In this way, a section at one level of the structural hierarchy can be made to appear to be at another level.

Status

`Status` identifies the editorial or publication status of the **Sect2**.

Publication status might be used to control formatting (for example, printing a "draft" watermark on drafts) or processing (perhaps a document with a status of "final" should not include any components that are not final).

See Also

BridgeHead, **Sect1**, **Sect3**, **Sect4**, **Sect5**, **Section**, **SimpleSect**

Examples

For examples, see **Link**.

Sect2Info—Meta-information for a Sect2

Synopsis

Content Model

```
Sect2Info ::=
((Graphic|MediaObject|LegalNotice|ModeSpec|SubjectSet|KeywordSet|
  ITermSet|Abbrev|Abstract|Address|ArtPageNums|Author|AuthorGroup|
  AuthorInitials|BiblioMisc|BiblioSet|Collab|ConfGroup|
```

ContractNum|ContractSponsor|Copyright|CorpAuthor|CorpName|Date| Edition|Editor|InvPartNumber|ISBN|ISSN|IssueNum|OrgName| OtherCredit|PageNums|PrintHistory|ProductName|ProductNumber| PubDate|Publisher|PublisherName|PubsNumber|ReleaseInfo| RevHistory|SeriesVolNums|Subtitle|Title|TitleAbbrev|VolumeNum| CiteTitle|Honorific|FirstName|Surname|Lineage|OtherName| Affiliation|AuthorBlurb|Contrib|IndexTerm)+)	
Attributes	Common attributes
Parameter Entities %otherinfo.class;	

Description

Like the other "info" elements, **Sect2Info** contains meta-information about the section of the document in which it occurs.

Processing expectations

Suppressed. Many of the elements in this wrapper may be used in presentation, but they are not generally printed as part of the formatting of the wrapper. The wrapper merely serves to identify where they occur.

4.0 Future Changes

AuthorBlurb and **Affiliation** will be removed from the inline content of **Sect2Info** in DocBook V4.0. A new wrapper element will be created to associate this information with authors, editors, and other contributors.

See Also

ArtHeader, **BookBiblio**, **BookInfo**, **DocInfo**, **ObjectInfo**, **RefSynopsisDivInfo**, **ScreenInfo**, **Sect1Info**, **Sect3Info**, **Sect4Info**, **Sect5Info**, **SectionInfo**, **SetInfo**

Examples

See **Sect1Info** for an analogous example.

Sect3—A subsection within a Sect2

Synopsis

Content Model

```
Sect3 ::=
(Sect3Info?,
 (Title,Subtitle?,TitleAbbrev?),
 (ToC|LoT|Index|Glossary|Bibliography)*,
 (((CalloutList|GlossList|ItemizedList|OrderedList|SegmentedList|
    SimpleList|VariableList|Caution|Important|Note|Tip|Warning|
    LiteralLayout|ProgramListing|ProgramListingCO|Screen|ScreenCO|
    ScreenShot|Synopsis|CmdSynopsis|FuncSynopsis|FormalPara|Para|
    SimPara|Address|BlockQuote|Graphic|GraphicCO|MediaObject|
```

```
    MediaObjectCO|InformalEquation|InformalExample|InformalFigure|
    InformalTable|Equation|Example|Figure|Table|MsgSet|Procedure|
    Sidebar|QandASet|Anchor|BridgeHead|Comment|Highlights|
    Abstract|AuthorBlurb|Epigraph|IndexTerm)+,
   ((RefEntry)*|
    Sect4*|SimpleSect*))|
  (RefEntry)+|
  Sect4+|SimpleSect+),
 (ToC|LoT|Index|Glossary|Bibliography)*)
```

Attributes	Common attributes	
Name	**Type**	**Default**
Label	CDATA	*None*
Status	CDATA	*None*
Renderas	*Enumeration:* Sect1 Sect2 Sect4 Sect5	*None*

Description

A **Sect3** is a third-level section in a document.

Processing expectations

Formatted as a displayed block. Sometimes sections are numbered.

4.0 *Future Changes*

In DocBook V4.0, the **ToC** element in the content model will be replaced by **TocChap**.

Attributes

Label

`Label` specifies an identifying string for presentation purposes.

Generally, an explicit `Label` attribute is used only if the processing system is incapable of generating the label automatically. If present, the `Label` is normative; it will used even if the processing system is capable of automatic labelling.

Renderas

The `RenderAs` attribute identifies how the section should be rendered. In this way, a section at one level of the structural hierarchy can be made to appear to be at another level.

Status

`Status` identifies the editorial or publication status of the **Sect3**.

Publication status might be used to control formatting (for example, printing a "draft" watermark on drafts) or processing (perhaps a document with a status of "final" should not include any components that are not final).

See Also

BridgeHead, **Sect1**, **Sect2**, **Sect4**, **Sect5**, **Section**, **SimpleSect**

Sect3Info—Meta-information for a Sect3

Synopsis

Content Model

```
Sect3Info ::=
((Graphic|MediaObject|LegalNotice|ModeSpec|SubjectSet|KeywordSet|
  ITermSet|Abbrev|Abstract|Address|ArtPageNums|Author|AuthorGroup|
  AuthorInitials|BiblioMisc|BiblioSet|Collab|ConfGroup|
  ContractNum|ContractSponsor|Copyright|CorpAuthor|CorpName|Date|
  Edition|Editor|InvPartNumber|ISBN|ISSN|IssueNum|OrgName|
  OtherCredit|PageNums|PrintHistory|ProductName|ProductNumber|
  PubDate|Publisher|PublisherName|PubsNumber|ReleaseInfo|
  RevHistory|SeriesVolNums|Subtitle|Title|TitleAbbrev|VolumeNum|
  CiteTitle|Honorific|FirstName|Surname|Lineage|OtherName|
  Affiliation|AuthorBlurb|Contrib|IndexTerm)+)
```

Attributes Common attributes

Parameter Entities

```
%otherinfo.class;
```

Description

Like the other "info" elements, **Sect3Info** contains meta-information about the section of the document in which it occurs.

Processing expectations

Suppressed. Many of the elements in this wrapper may be used in presentation, but they are not generally printed as part of the formatting of the wrapper. The wrapper merely serves to identify where they occur.

4.0 Future Changes

AuthorBlurb and **Affiliation** will be removed from the inline content of **Sect3Info** in DocBook V4.0. A new wrapper element will be created to associate this information with authors, editors, and other contributors.

See Also

ArtHeader, **BookBiblio**, **BookInfo**, **DocInfo**, **ObjectInfo**, **RefSynopsisDivInfo**, **ScreenInfo**, **Sect1Info**, **Sect2Info**, **Sect4Info**, **Sect5Info**, **SectionInfo**, **SetInfo**

Examples

See **Sect1Info** for an analogous example.

Sect4—A subsection within a Sect3

Synopsis

Content Model

```
Sect4 ::=
(Sect4Info?,
 (Title,Subtitle?,TitleAbbrev?),
 (ToC|LoT|Index|Glossary|Bibliography)*,
 (((CalloutList|GlossList|ItemizedList|OrderedList|SegmentedList|
    SimpleList|VariableList|Caution|Important|Note|Tip|Warning|
    LiteralLayout|ProgramListing|ProgramListingCO|Screen|ScreenCO|
    ScreenShot|Synopsis|CmdSynopsis|FuncSynopsis|FormalPara|Para|
    SimPara|Address|BlockQuote|Graphic|GraphicCO|MediaObject|
    MediaObjectCO|InformalEquation|InformalExample|InformalFigure|
    InformalTable|Equation|Example|Figure|Table|MsgSet|Procedure|
    Sidebar|QandASet|Anchor|BridgeHead|Comment|Highlights|
    Abstract|AuthorBlurb|Epigraph|IndexTerm)+,
   ((RefEntry)*|
    Sect5*|SimpleSect*))|
  (RefEntry)+|
  Sect5+|SimpleSect+),
 (ToC|LoT|Index|Glossary|Bibliography)*)
```

Attributes	Common attributes	
Name	**Type**	**Default**
Label	CDATA	*None*
Status	CDATA	*None*
Renderas	*Enumeration:* Sect1 Sect2 Sect3 Sect5	*None*

Description

A **Sect4** is a fourth-level section in a document.

Processing expectations

Formatted as a displayed block. Sometimes sections are numbered.

[4.0] *Future Changes*

In DocBook V4.0, the **ToC** element in the content model will be replaced by **TocChap**.

Attributes

Label

`Label` specifies an identifying string for presentation purposes.

Generally, an explicit `Label` attribute is used only if the processing system is incapable of generating the label automatically. If present, the `Label` is normative; it will used even if the processing system is capable of automatic labelling.

Renderas

The **RenderAs** attribute identifies how the section should be rendered. In this way, a section at one level of the structural hierarchy can be made to appear to be at another level.

Status

`Status` identifies the editorial or publication status of the **Sect4**.

Publication status might be used to control formatting (for example, printing a "draft" watermark on drafts) or processing (perhaps a document with a status of "final" should not include any components that are not final).

See Also

BridgeHead, **Sect1**, **Sect2**, **Sect3**, **Sect5**, **Section**, **SimpleSect**

Sect4Info—Meta-information for a Sect4

Synopsis

Content Model

```
Sect4Info ::=
((Graphic|MediaObject|LegalNotice|ModeSpec|SubjectSet|KeywordSet|
  ITermSet|Abbrev|Abstract|Address|ArtPageNums|Author|AuthorGroup|
  AuthorInitials|BiblioMisc|BiblioSet|Collab|ConfGroup|
  ContractNum|ContractSponsor|Copyright|CorpAuthor|CorpName|Date|
  Edition|Editor|InvPartNumber|ISBN|ISSN|IssueNum|OrgName|
  OtherCredit|PageNums|PrintHistory|ProductName|ProductNumber|
  PubDate|Publisher|PublisherName|PubsNumber|ReleaseInfo|
  RevHistory|SeriesVolNums|Subtitle|Title|TitleAbbrev|VolumeNum|
  CiteTitle|Honorific|FirstName|Surname|Lineage|OtherName|
  Affiliation|AuthorBlurb|Contrib|IndexTerm)+)
```

Attributes	Common attributes

Parameter Entities

`%otherinfo.class;`

Description

Like the other "info" elements, **Sect4Info** contains meta-information about the section of the document in which it occurs.

Processing expectations

Suppressed. Many of the elements in this wrapper may be used in presentation, but they are not generally printed as part of the formatting of the wrapper. The wrapper merely serves to identify where they occur.

4.0 *Future Changes*

AuthorBlurb and **Affiliation** will be removed from the inline content of **Sect4Info** in DocBook V4.0. A new wrapper element will be created to associate this information with authors, editors, and other contributors.

See Also

ArtHeader, **BookBiblio**, **BookInfo**, **DocInfo**, **ObjectInfo**, **RefSynopsisDivInfo**, **ScreenInfo**, **Sect1Info**, **Sect2Info**, **Sect3Info**, **Sect5Info**, **SectionInfo**, **SetInfo**

Examples

See **Sect1Info** for an analogous example.

Sect5—A subsection within a Sect4

Synopsis

Content Model

```
Sect5 ::=
(Sect5Info?,
 (Title,Subtitle?,TitleAbbrev?),
 (ToC|LoT|Index|Glossary|Bibliography)*,
 (((CalloutList|GlossList|ItemizedList|OrderedList|SegmentedList|
    SimpleList|VariableList|Caution|Important|Note|Tip|Warning|
    LiteralLayout|ProgramListing|ProgramListingCO|Screen|ScreenCO|
    ScreenShot|Synopsis|CmdSynopsis|FuncSynopsis|FormalPara|Para|
    SimPara|Address|BlockQuote|Graphic|GraphicCO|MediaObject|
    MediaObjectCO|InformalEquation|InformalExample|InformalFigure|
    InformalTable|Equation|Example|Figure|Table|MsgSet|Procedure|
    Sidebar|QandASet|Anchor|BridgeHead|Comment|Highlights|
    Abstract|AuthorBlurb|Epigraph|IndexTerm)+,
   ((RefEntry)*|
    SimpleSect*))|
  (RefEntry)+|
  SimpleSect+),
 (ToC|LoT|Index|Glossary|Bibliography)*)
```

Attributes Common attributes

Name	**Type**	**Default**
Label	CDATA	*None*
Status	CDATA	*None*
Renderas	*Enumeration:* Sect1 Sect2 Sect3 Sect4	*None*

Description

A **Sect5** is a fifth-level section in a document. This is the lowest-level numbered sectioning element. There is no **Sect6**.

Processing expectations

Formatted as a displayed block. Sometimes sections are numbered.

4.0 Future Changes

In DocBook V4.0, the **ToC** element in the content model will be replaced by **TocChap**.

Attributes

Label

`Label` specifies an identifying string for presentation purposes.

Generally, an explicit `Label` attribute is used only if the processing system is incapable of generating the label automatically. If present, the `Label` is normative; it will used even if the processing system is capable of automatic labelling.

Renderas

The `RenderAs` attribute identifies how the section should be rendered. In this way, a section at one level of the structural hierarchy can be made to appear to be at another level.

Status

`Status` identifies the editorial or publication status of the **Sect5**.

Publication status might be used to control formatting (for example, printing a "draft" watermark on drafts) or processing (perhaps a document with a status of "final" should not include any components that are not final).

See Also

BridgeHead, **Sect1**, **Sect2**, **Sect3**, **Sect4**, **Section**, **SimpleSect**

Sect5Info—Meta-information for a Sect5

Synopsis

Content Model

```
Sect5Info ::=
((Graphic|MediaObject|LegalNotice|ModeSpec|SubjectSet|KeywordSet|
  ITermSet|Abbrev|Abstract|Address|ArtPageNums|Author|AuthorGroup|
  AuthorInitials|BiblioMisc|BiblioSet|Collab|ConfGroup|
  ContractNum|ContractSponsor|Copyright|CorpAuthor|CorpName|Date|
  Edition|Editor|InvPartNumber|ISBN|ISSN|IssueNum|OrgName|
  OtherCredit|PageNums|PrintHistory|ProductName|ProductNumber|
  PubDate|Publisher|PublisherName|PubsNumber|ReleaseInfo|
```

```
  RevHistory|SeriesVolNums|Subtitle|Title|TitleAbbrev|VolumeNum|
  CiteTitle|Honorific|FirstName|Surname|Lineage|OtherName|
  Affiliation|AuthorBlurb|Contrib|IndexTerm)+)
```

Attributes	Common attributes

Parameter Entities
`%otherinfo.class;`

Description

Like the other "info" elements, **Sect5Info** contains meta-information about the section of the document in which it occurs.

Processing expectations

Suppressed. Many of the elements in this wrapper may be used in presentation, but they are not generally printed as part of the formatting of the wrapper. The wrapper merely serves to identify where they occur.

4.0 *Future Changes*

AuthorBlurb and **Affiliation** will be removed from the inline content of **Sect5Info** in DocBook V4.0. A new wrapper element will be created to associate this information with authors, editors, and other contributors.

See Also

ArtHeader, **BookBiblio**, **BookInfo**, **DocInfo**, **ObjectInfo**, **RefSynopsisDivInfo**, **ScreenInfo**, **Sect1Info**, **Sect2Info**, **Sect3Info**, **Sect4Info**, **SectionInfo**, **SetInfo**

Examples

See **Sect1Info** for an analogous example.

Section—A recursive section

Synopsis

Content Model

```
Section ::=
(SectionInfo?,
 (Title,Subtitle?,TitleAbbrev?),
 (ToC|LoT|Index|Glossary|Bibliography)*,
 (((CalloutList|GlossList|ItemizedList|OrderedList|SegmentedList|
   SimpleList|VariableList|Caution|Important|Note|Tip|Warning|
   LiteralLayout|ProgramListing|ProgramListingCO|Screen|ScreenCO|
   ScreenShot|Synopsis|CmdSynopsis|FuncSynopsis|FormalPara|Para|
   SimPara|Address|BlockQuote|Graphic|GraphicCO|MediaObject|
   MediaObjectCO|InformalEquation|InformalExample|InformalFigure|
   InformalTable|Equation|Example|Figure|Table|MsgSet|Procedure|
```

```
    Sidebar|QandASet|Anchor|BridgeHead|Comment|Highlights|
    Abstract|AuthorBlurb|Epigraph|IndexTerm)+,
   ((RefEntry)*|
    Section*))|
  (RefEntry)+|
  Section+),
 (ToC|LoT|Index|Glossary|Bibliography)*)
```

Attributes	Common attributes	
Name	**Type**	**Default**
Label	CDATA	*None*
Status	CDATA	*None*

Parameter Entities
`%bookcomponent.content;`

Description

Section is one of the top-level sectioning elements in a component. There are three types of sectioning elements in DocBook:

- Explicitly numbered sections, **Sect1**...**Sect5**, which must be properly nested and can only be five levels deep.
- Recursive **Sections**, which are an alternative to the numbered sections and have unbounded depth.
- **SimpleSects**, which are terminal. **SimpleSects** can occur as the "leaf" sections in either recursive sections or any of the numbered sections, or directly in components.

Sections may be more convenient than numbered sections in some authoring environments because they can be moved around in the document hierarchy without renaming.

None of the sectioning elements is allowed to "float" in a component. You can place paragraphs and other block elements before a section, but you cannot place anything after it.

Processing expectations

Formatted as a displayed block. Sometimes sections are numbered.

Use of deeply nested **Sections** may cause problems in some processing systems.

Attributes

Label

`Label` specifies an identifying string for presentation purposes.

Generally, an explicit `Label` attribute is used only if the processing system is incapable of generating the label automatically. If present, the `Label` is normative; it will used even if the processing system is capable of automatic labelling.

Status

`Status` identifies the editorial or publication status of the **Section**.

Publication status might be used to control formatting (for example, printing a "draft" watermark on drafts) or processing (perhaps a document with a status of "final" should not include any components that are not final).

See Also

BridgeHead, **Sect1**, **Sect2**, **Sect3**, **Sect4**, **Sect5**, **SimpleSect**

Examples

```
<!DOCTYPE chapter PUBLIC "-//OASIS//DTD DocBook V3.1//EN">
<chapter><title>Test Chapter</title>
<para>This chapter uses recursive sections.</para>
<section>
<sectioninfo>
<abstract><para>A trivial example of recursive sections.</para>
</abstract>
</sectioninfo>
<title>Like a Sect1</title>
<subtitle>Or How I Learned to Let Go of Enumeration
and Love to Recurse</subtitle>
<para>This section is like a Sect1.</para>
<section><title>Like a Sect2</title>
<para>This section is like a Sect2.</para>
<section><title>Like a Sect3</title>
<para>This section is like a Sect3.</para>
<section><title>Like a Sect4</title>
<para>This section is like a Sect4.</para>
<section><title>Like a Sect5</title>
<para>This section is like a Sect5.</para>
<section><title>Would be like a Sect6</title>
<para>This section would be like a Sect6, if there was one.</para>
<section><title>Would be like a Sect7</title>
<para>This section would be like a Sect7, if there was one.</para>
</section>
</section>
</section>
</section>
</section>
</section>
</section>
</chapter>
```

SectionInfo—Meta-information for a recursive section

Synopsis

Content Model

```
SectionInfo ::=
((Graphic|MediaObject|LegalNotice|ModeSpec|SubjectSet|KeywordSet|
  ITermSet|Abbrev|Abstract|Address|ArtPageNums|Author|AuthorGroup|
  AuthorInitials|BiblioMisc|BiblioSet|Collab|ConfGroup|
  ContractNum|ContractSponsor|Copyright|CorpAuthor|CorpName|Date|
  Edition|Editor|InvPartNumber|ISBN|ISSN|IssueNum|OrgName|
  OtherCredit|PageNums|PrintHistory|ProductName|ProductNumber|
  PubDate|Publisher|PublisherName|PubsNumber|ReleaseInfo|
  RevHistory|SeriesVolNums|Subtitle|Title|TitleAbbrev|VolumeNum|
  CiteTitle|Honorific|FirstName|Surname|Lineage|OtherName|
  Affiliation|AuthorBlurb|Contrib|IndexTerm)+)
```

Attributes	Common attributes

Description

Like the other "info" elements, **SectionInfo** contains meta-information about the section of the document in which it occurs.

Processing expectations

Suppressed. Many of the elements in this wrapper may be used in presentation, but they are not generally printed as part of the formatting of the wrapper. The wrapper merely serves to identify where they occur.

4.0 *Future Changes*

AuthorBlurb and **Affiliation** will be removed from the inline content of **SectionInfo** in DocBook V4.0. A new wrapper element will be created to associate this information with authors, editors, and other contributors.

See Also

ArtHeader, **BookBiblio**, **BookInfo**, **DocInfo**, **ObjectInfo**, **RefSynopsisDivInfo**, **ScreenInfo**, **Sect1Info**, **Sect2Info**, **Sect3Info**, **Sect4Info**, **Sect5Info**, **SetInfo**

Examples

For examples, see **Section**.

See—Part of an index term directing the reader instead to another entry in the index

Synopsis

Mixed Content Model

```
See ::=
((#PCDATA|FootnoteRef|XRef|Abbrev|Acronym|Citation|CiteRefEntry|
  CiteTitle|Emphasis|FirstTerm|ForeignPhrase|GlossTerm|Footnote|
  Phrase|Quote|Trademark|WordAsWord|Link|OLink|ULink|Action|
  Application|ClassName|Command|ComputerOutput|Database|Email|
  EnVar|ErrorCode|ErrorName|ErrorType|Filename|Function|GUIButton|
  GUIIcon|GUILabel|GUIMenu|GUIMenuItem|GUISubmenu|Hardware|
  Interface|InterfaceDefinition|KeyCap|KeyCode|KeyCombo|KeySym|
  Literal|Constant|Markup|MediaLabel|MenuChoice|MouseButton|
  MsgText|Option|Optional|Parameter|Prompt|Property|Replaceable|
  ReturnValue|SGMLTag|StructField|StructName|Symbol|SystemItem|
  Token|Type|UserInput|VarName|Anchor|Author|AuthorInitials|
  CorpAuthor|ModeSpec|OtherCredit|ProductName|ProductNumber|
  RevHistory|Comment|Subscript|Superscript|InlineGraphic|
  InlineMediaObject)+)
```

Attributes	Common attributes

Description

The use of **See** in an **IndexTerm** indicates that the reader should be directed elsewhere in the index if they attempt to look up this term.

The content of **See** identifies another term in the index which the reader should consult *instead* of the current term.

Processing expectations

Suppressed. This element provides data for processing but it is not rendered in the primary flow of text.

It is possible for multiple **IndexTerms**, taken together, to form an illogical index. For example, given the following **IndexTerms**:

```
<indexterm><primary>Extensible Markup Language</primary>
  <see>XML</see></indexterm>
<indexterm><primary>Extensible Markup Language</primary>
  <secondary>definition of</secondary>
</indexterm>
```

there's no way to construct a logical index because an entry in the index should never have both a **see** and other content.

DocBook cannot detect these errors. You will have to rely on an external process to find them.

4.0 *Future Changes*

The **InterfaceDefinition** element will be discarded in DocBook V4.0. It will no longer be available in the content model of this element.

See Also

IndexEntry, **IndexTerm**, **Primary**, **PrimaryIE**, **Secondary**, **SecondaryIE**, **SeeAlso**, **SeeAlsoIE**, **SeeIE**, **Tertiary**, **TertiaryIE**

Examples

For examples, see **IndexTerm**.

SeeAlso—Part of an index term directing the reader also to another entry in the index

Synopsis

Mixed Content Model

```
SeeAlso ::=
((#PCDATA|FootnoteRef|XRef|Abbrev|Acronym|Citation|CiteRefEntry|
  CiteTitle|Emphasis|FirstTerm|ForeignPhrase|GlossTerm|Footnote|
  Phrase|Quote|Trademark|WordAsWord|Link|OLink|ULink|Action|
  Application|ClassName|Command|ComputerOutput|Database|Email|
  EnVar|ErrorCode|ErrorName|ErrorType|Filename|Function|GUIButton|
  GUIIcon|GUILabel|GUIMenu|GUIMenuItem|GUISubmenu|Hardware|
  Interface|InterfaceDefinition|KeyCap|KeyCode|KeyCombo|KeySym|
  Literal|Constant|Markup|MediaLabel|MenuChoice|MouseButton|
  MsgText|Option|Optional|Parameter|Prompt|Property|Replaceable|
  ReturnValue|SGMLTag|StructField|StructName|Symbol|SystemItem|
  Token|Type|UserInput|VarName|Anchor|Author|AuthorInitials|
  CorpAuthor|ModeSpec|OtherCredit|ProductName|ProductNumber|
  RevHistory|Comment|Subscript|Superscript|InlineGraphic|
  InlineMediaObject)+)
```

Attributes	Common attributes

Description

The use of **SeeAlso** in an **IndexTerm** indicates that the reader should be directed elsewhere in the index for additional information.

The content of **SeeAlso** identifies another term in the index that the reader should consult *in addition to* the current term.

Processing expectations

Suppressed. This element provides data for processing but is not rendered in the primary flow of text.

4.0 *Future Changes*

The **InterfaceDefinition** element will be discarded in DocBook V4.0. It will no longer be available in the content model of this element.

See Also

IndexEntry, **IndexTerm**, **Primary**, **PrimaryIE**, **Secondary**, **SecondaryIE**, **See**, **SeeAlsoIE**, **SeeIE**, **Tertiary**, **TertiaryIE**

Examples

For examples, see **IndexTerm**.

SeeAlsoIE—A "See also" entry in an index, rather than in the text

Synopsis

Mixed Content Model

```
SeeAlsoIE ::=
((#PCDATA|FootnoteRef|XRef|Abbrev|Acronym|Citation|CiteRefEntry|
  CiteTitle|Emphasis|FirstTerm|ForeignPhrase|GlossTerm|Footnote|
  Phrase|Quote|Trademark|WordAsWord|Link|OLink|ULink|Action|
  Application|ClassName|Command|ComputerOutput|Database|Email|
  EnVar|ErrorCode|ErrorName|ErrorType|Filename|Function|GUIButton|
  GUIIcon|GUILabel|GUIMenu|GUIMenuItem|GUISubmenu|Hardware|
  Interface|InterfaceDefinition|KeyCap|KeyCode|KeyCombo|KeySym|
  Literal|Constant|Markup|MediaLabel|MenuChoice|MouseButton|
  MsgText|Option|Optional|Parameter|Prompt|Property|Replaceable|
  ReturnValue|SGMLTag|StructField|StructName|Symbol|SystemItem|
  Token|Type|UserInput|VarName|Anchor|Author|AuthorInitials|
  CorpAuthor|ModeSpec|OtherCredit|ProductName|ProductNumber|
  RevHistory|Comment|Subscript|Superscript|InlineGraphic|
  InlineMediaObject)+)
```

Attributes	Common attributes	
Name	**Type**	**Default**
Linkends	IDREFS	*None*

Description

SeeAlsoIE identifies a "See also" cross-reference in an **IndexEntry**. **IndexEntrys** occur in an **Index**, not in the flow of the text. They are part of a formatted index, not markers for indexing.

Processing expectations

Formatted as a displayed block. **IndexEntrys** that include a **SeeAlsoIE** should be formatted normally, with the "See also" indented below the term.

SeeAlsoIE is usually expected to generate the text "See Also".

The Linkends attribute should point other **IndexEntrys** in the same **Index**. Online systems may use them to form hypertext links.

4.0 *Future Changes*

The **InterfaceDefinition** element will be discarded in DocBook V4.0. It will no longer be available in the content model of this element.

Attributes

Linkends

Linkends points to a the related **IndexEntrys**.

See Also

IndexEntry, **IndexTerm**, **Primary**, **PrimaryIE**, **Secondary**, **SecondaryIE**, **See**, **SeeAlso**, **SeeIE**, **Tertiary**, **TertiaryIE**

Examples

For examples, see **Index**.

SeeIE—A "See" entry in an index, rather than in the text

Synopsis

Mixed Content Model

```
SeeIE ::=
((#PCDATA|FootnoteRef|XRef|Abbrev|Acronym|Citation|CiteRefEntry|
  CiteTitle|Emphasis|FirstTerm|ForeignPhrase|GlossTerm|Footnote|
  Phrase|Quote|Trademark|WordAsWord|Link|OLink|ULink|Action|
  Application|ClassName|Command|ComputerOutput|Database|Email|
  EnVar|ErrorCode|ErrorName|ErrorType|Filename|Function|GUIButton|
  GUIIcon|GUILabel|GUIMenu|GUIMenuItem|GUISubmenu|Hardware|
  Interface|InterfaceDefinition|KeyCap|KeyCode|KeyCombo|KeySym|
  Literal|Constant|Markup|MediaLabel|MenuChoice|MouseButton|
  MsgText|Option|Optional|Parameter|Prompt|Property|Replaceable|
  ReturnValue|SGMLTag|StructField|StructName|Symbol|SystemItem|
  Token|Type|UserInput|VarName|Anchor|Author|AuthorInitials|
  CorpAuthor|ModeSpec|OtherCredit|ProductName|ProductNumber|
  RevHistory|Comment|Subscript|Superscript|InlineGraphic|
  InlineMediaObject)+)
```

Attributes Name	Common attributes Type	**Default**
Linkend	IDREF	*None*

Description

SeeIE identifies a "See" cross reference in an **IndexEntry**. **IndexEntrys** occur in an **Index**, not in the flow of the text. They are part of a formatted index, not markers for indexing.

Processing expectations

Formatted as a displayed block. **IndexEntrys** that include a **SeeIE** should be formatted normally, with the "See also" indented below the term. There should be no other entries for this term.

SeeIE is usually expected to generate the text, "See."

The `Linkend` attribute should point to the referenced **IndexEntrys**, which should be in the same **Index**. Online systems may use the link information to form a hypertext link.

4.0 Future Changes

The **InterfaceDefinition** element will be discarded in DocBook V4.0. It will no longer be available in the content model of this element.

Attributes

Linkend

`Linkend` points to the associated **IndexEntry**.

See Also

IndexEntry, **IndexTerm**, **Primary**, **PrimaryIE**, **Secondary**, **SecondaryIE**, **See**, **SeeAlso**, **SeeAlsoIE**, **Tertiary**, **TertiaryIE**

Examples

For examples, see **Index**.

Seg—An element of a list item in a segmented list

Synopsis

Mixed Content Model

```
Seg ::=
((#PCDATA|FootnoteRef|XRef|Abbrev|Acronym|Citation|CiteRefEntry|
  CiteTitle|Emphasis|FirstTerm|ForeignPhrase|GlossTerm|Footnote|
  Phrase|Quote|Trademark|WordAsWord|Link|OLink|ULink|Action|
  Application|ClassName|Command|ComputerOutput|Database|Email|
  EnVar|ErrorCode|ErrorName|ErrorType|Filename|Function|GUIButton|
  GUIIcon|GUILabel|GUIMenu|GUIMenuItem|GUISubmenu|Hardware|
  Interface|InterfaceDefinition|KeyCap|KeyCode|KeyCombo|KeySym|
  Literal|Constant|Markup|MediaLabel|MenuChoice|MouseButton|
```

```
MsgText|Option|Optional|Parameter|Prompt|Property|Replaceable|
ReturnValue|SGMLTag|StructField|StructName|Symbol|SystemItem|
Token|Type|UserInput|VarName|Anchor|Author|AuthorInitials|
CorpAuthor|ModeSpec|OtherCredit|ProductName|ProductNumber|
RevHistory|Comment|Subscript|Superscript|InlineGraphic|
InlineMediaObject|InlineEquation|Synopsis|CmdSynopsis|
FuncSynopsis|IndexTerm)+)
```

Attributes	Common attributes

Description

A **SegmentedList** consists of a set of headings (**SegTitles**) and a list of parallel sets of elements. Every **SegListItem** contains a set of elements that have a one-to-one correspondence with the headings. Each of these elements is contained in a **Seg**.

Processing expectations

Segmented lists can be formatted in a number of ways. Two popular formats are tabular and as a list of repeated headings and elements. In a tabular presentation, each **Seg** is a cell in the body of the table. In the list presentation, each **Seg** occurs next to the appropriate heading.

DocBook cannot detect errors caused by too many or too few **Segs** in a **SegListItem**. You will have to rely on external processes to find those errors.

4.0 *Future Changes*

The **InterfaceDefinition** element will be discarded in DocBook V4.0. It will no longer be available in the content model of this element.

Examples

For examples, see **SegmentedList**.

SegListItem—A list item in a segmented list

Synopsis

Content Model

```
SegListItem ::=
(Seg,Seg+)
```

Attributes	Common attributes

Description

A **SegmentedList** consists of a set of headings (**SegTitles**) and a list of parallel sets of elements. Each set of elements is stored in a **SegListItem**.

Processing expectations

Segmented lists can be formatted in a number of ways. Two popular formats are tabular and as a list of repeated headings and elements. In a tabular presentation, each **SegListItem** is a row in the table. In the list presentation, each **SegListItem** contains a block of heading/element pairs.

DocBook cannot detect errors caused by too many or too few **Segs** in a **SegListItem**. You will have to rely on external processes to find those errors.

4.0 *Future Changes*

The **InterfaceDefinition** element will be discarded in DocBook V4.0. It will no longer be available in the content model of this element.

Examples

For examples, see **SegmentedList**.

SegmentedList—A segmented list, a list of sets of elements

Synopsis

Content Model

```
SegmentedList ::=
((Title,TitleAbbrev?)?,
 SegTitle*,SegListItem+)
```

Attributes	Common attributes	
Parameter Entities		
`%admon.mix;`	`%bookcomponent.content;`	`%component.mix;`
`%divcomponent.mix;`	`%example.mix;`	`%footnote.mix;`
`%glossdef.mix;`	`%highlights.mix;`	`%legalnotice.mix;`
`%list.class;`	`%para.mix;`	`%qandaset.mix;`
`%refcomponent.mix;`	`%sidebar.mix;`	`%tabentry.mix;`
`%tbl.entry.mdl;`	`%textobject.mix;`	

Description

A **SegmentedList** consists of a set of headings (**SegTitles**) and a list of parallel sets of elements. Every **SegListItem** contains a set of elements that have a one-to-one correspondence with the headings. Each of these elements is contained in a **Seg**.

Processing expectations

Segmented lists can be formatted in a number of ways. Two popular formats are tabular and as a list of repeated headings and elements. In a tabular presentation, the **SegmentedList** is the table. In the list presentation, the **SegmentedList** surrounds the entire list of blocks of heading/element pairs.

4.0 *Future Changes*

In DocBook V4.0, at least two **SegTitles** will be required.

See Also

CalloutList, **ItemizedList**, **ListItem**, **OrderedList**, **SimpleList**, **VariableList**

Examples

```
<!DOCTYPE para PUBLIC "-//OASIS//DTD DocBook V3.1//EN">
<para>
The capitals of the states of the United States of America are:

<segmentedlist><title>State Capitals</title>
<segtitle>State</segtitle>
<segtitle>Capital</segtitle>
<seglistitem><seg>Alabama</seg><seg>Montgomery</seg></seglistitem>
<seglistitem><seg>Alaska</seg><seg>Juneau</seg></seglistitem>
<seglistitem><seg>Arkansas</seg><seg>Little Rock</seg></seglistitem>
</segmentedlist>

&hellip;
</para>
```

The capitals of the states of the United States of America are:

State Capitals

State: Alabama
Capital: Montgomery

State: Alaska
Capital: Anchorage

State: Arkansas
Capital: Little Rock

...

Alternatively:

Table 5-1. State Capitals

State	Capital
Alabama	???
Alaska	Anchorage
Arkansas	Little Rock

...

SegTitle—The title of an element of a list item in a segmented list

Synopsis

Mixed Content Model

```
SegTitle ::=
((#PCDATA|FootnoteRef|XRef|Abbrev|Acronym|Citation|CiteRefEntry|
  CiteTitle|Emphasis|FirstTerm|ForeignPhrase|GlossTerm|Footnote|
  Phrase|Quote|Trademark|WordAsWord|Link|OLink|ULink|Action|
```

```
Application|ClassName|Command|ComputerOutput|Database|Email|
EnVar|ErrorCode|ErrorName|ErrorType|Filename|Function|GUIButton|
GUIIcon|GUILabel|GUIMenu|GUIMenuItem|GUISubmenu|Hardware|
Interface|InterfaceDefinition|KeyCap|KeyCode|KeyCombo|KeySym|
Literal|Constant|Markup|MediaLabel|MenuChoice|MouseButton|
MsgText|Option|Optional|Parameter|Prompt|Property|Replaceable|
ReturnValue|SGMLTag|StructField|StructName|Symbol|SystemItem|
Token|Type|UserInput|VarName|Anchor|Author|AuthorInitials|
CorpAuthor|ModeSpec|OtherCredit|ProductName|ProductNumber|
RevHistory|Comment|Subscript|Superscript|InlineGraphic|
InlineMediaObject|InlineEquation|IndexTerm)+)
```

Attributes Common attributes

Description

Each heading in a **SegmentedList** is contained in its own **SegTitle**.

The relationship between **SegTitles** and **Segs** is implicit in the document; the first **SegTitle** goes with the first **Seg** in each **SegListItem**, the second **SegTitle** goes with the second **Seg**, and so on.

Processing expectations

Segmented lists can be formatted in a number of ways. Two popular formats are tabular and as list of repeated headings and elements. In a tabular presentation, each **SegTitle** is a column heading. In the list presentation, each **SegTitle** is repeated before the corresponding **Seg**.

4.0 *Future Changes*

The **InterfaceDefinition** element will be discarded in DocBook V4.0. It will no longer be available in the content model of this element.

Examples

For examples, see **SegmentedList**.

SeriesInfo—Information about the publication series of which a book is a part

Synopsis

Content Model

```
SeriesInfo ::=
((Abbrev|Abstract|Address|ArtPageNums|Author|AuthorGroup|
  AuthorInitials|BiblioMisc|BiblioSet|Collab|ConfGroup|
  ContractNum|ContractSponsor|Copyright|CorpAuthor|CorpName|Date|
  Edition|Editor|InvPartNumber|ISBN|ISSN|IssueNum|OrgName|
  OtherCredit|PageNums|PrintHistory|ProductName|ProductNumber|
  PubDate|Publisher|PublisherName|PubsNumber|ReleaseInfo|
  RevHistory|SeriesVolNums|Subtitle|Title|TitleAbbrev|VolumeNum|
  CiteTitle|Honorific|FirstName|Surname|Lineage|OtherName|
  Affiliation|AuthorBlurb|Contrib|IndexTerm)+)
```

Attributes Common attributes

Description

In a bibliography entry for a book that was published as part of a series, **SeriesInfo** is a wrapper for bibliographic information about the series as a whole.

Processing expectations

Formatted inline.

4.0 Future Changes

SeriesInfo may be discarded in DocBook V4.0. With the creation of **BiblioSet**, **SeriesInfo** is now simply a special case of **BiblioSet**.

If it persists, **AuthorBlurb** and **Affiliation** will be removed from the inline content of **SeriesInfo**. A new wrapper element will be created to associate this information with authors, editors, and other contributors.

Examples

For examples, see **Bibliography**.

SeriesVolNums—Numbers of the volumes in a series of books

Synopsis

Mixed Content Model	
`SeriesVolNums ::= ((#PCDATA|Link|OLink|ULink|Emphasis|Trademark|Replaceable|Comment| Subscript|Superscript|InlineGraphic|InlineMediaObject|IndexTerm)+)`	
Attributes	Common attributes
Parameter Entities `%bibliocomponent.mix;`	

Description

SeriesVolNums contains the numbers of the volumes of the books in a series. It is a wrapper for bibliographic information.

Processing expectations

Formatted inline. Sometimes suppressed.

See Also

InvPartNumber, **ISBN**, **ISSN**, **IssueNum**, **ProductNumber**, **PubsNumber**, **VolumeNum**

Examples

For examples, see **Bibliography**.

Set—A collection of books

Synopsis

Content Model
```
Set ::=
((Title,Subtitle?,TitleAbbrev?)?,
 SetInfo?,ToC?,
 (Book)+,
 SetIndex?)
```

Attributes	Common attributes	
Name	**Type**	**Default**
Status	CDATA	*None*
FPI	CDATA	*None*

Description

A **Set** is a collection of **Books**. Placing multiple **Books** in a **Set**, as opposed to publishing each of them separately, has the advantage that ID/IDREF links can then be used across all books.

Set is the very top of the DocBook structural hierarchy. There's nothing that contains a **Set**.

Processing expectations

Formatted as a displayed block. A **Set** may generate additional front and back matter (tables of contents and **SetIndex**s, for example) around the **Books** it contains.

Attributes

FPI

`FPI` holds the Formal Public Identifier for the **Set**.

Status

`Status` identifies the editorial or publication status of the **Set**.

Publication status might be used to control formatting (for example, printing a "draft" watermark on drafts) or processing (perhaps a document with a status of "final" should not include any components that are not final).

See Also

Appendix, **Article**, **Book**, **Chapter**, **Colophon**, **Dedication**, **Part**, **PartIntro**, **Preface**

Examples

```
<!DOCTYPE set PUBLIC "-//OASIS//DTD DocBook V3.1//EN">
```

```
<set><title>The Perl Series</title>
<setinfo>
  <corpauthor>O'Reilly &amp; Associates, Inc.</corpauthor>
</setinfo>
<book><title>Learning Perl</title> ... </book>
<book><title>Programming Perl</title> ... </book>
<book><title>Advanced Perl Programming</title> ... </book>
</set>
```

SetIndex—An index to a set of books

Synopsis

Content Model

```
SetIndex ::=
((DocInfo?,Title,Subtitle?,TitleAbbrev?)?,
 (CalloutList|GlossList|ItemizedList|OrderedList|SegmentedList|
  SimpleList|VariableList|Caution|Important|Note|Tip|Warning|
  LiteralLayout|ProgramListing|ProgramListingCO|Screen|ScreenCO|
  ScreenShot|Synopsis|CmdSynopsis|FuncSynopsis|FormalPara|Para|
  SimPara|Address|BlockQuote|Graphic|GraphicCO|MediaObject|
  MediaObjectCO|InformalEquation|InformalExample|InformalFigure|
  InformalTable|Equation|Example|Figure|Table|MsgSet|Procedure|
  Sidebar|QandASet|Anchor|BridgeHead|Comment|Highlights|Abstract|
  AuthorBlurb|Epigraph|IndexTerm)*,
 (IndexDiv*|IndexEntry*))
```

Attributes	Common attributes

Parameter Entities

```
%index.class;
```

Description

A **SetIndex** contains the formatted index of a complete **Set** of **Books**. An index may begin with introductory material, followed by any number of **IndexEntry**s or **IndexDiv**s.

Processing expectations

Formatted as a displayed block. An **Index** in a **Set** usually causes a forced page break in print media.

In many processing systems, indexes are generated automatically or semiautomatically and never appear instantiated as DocBook markup.

Examples

See **Index**.

SetInfo—Meta-information for a Set

Synopsis

Content Model

```
SetInfo ::=
((Graphic|MediaObject|LegalNotice|ModeSpec|SubjectSet|KeywordSet|
  ITermSet|Abbrev|Abstract|Address|ArtPageNums|Author|AuthorGroup|
  AuthorInitials|BiblioMisc|BiblioSet|Collab|ConfGroup|
  ContractNum|ContractSponsor|Copyright|CorpAuthor|CorpName|Date|
  Edition|Editor|InvPartNumber|ISBN|ISSN|IssueNum|OrgName|
  OtherCredit|PageNums|PrintHistory|ProductName|ProductNumber|
  PubDate|Publisher|PublisherName|PubsNumber|ReleaseInfo|
  RevHistory|SeriesVolNums|Subtitle|Title|TitleAbbrev|VolumeNum|
  CiteTitle|Honorific|FirstName|Surname|Lineage|OtherName|
  Affiliation|AuthorBlurb|Contrib|IndexTerm)+)
```

Attributes	Common attributes	
Name	**Type**	**Default**
Contents	IDREFS	*None*

Description

SetInfo contains meta-information about an entire set of **Books**.

Processing expectations

Suppressed. Many of the elements in this wrapper may be used in presentation, but they are not generally printed as part of the formatting of the wrapper. The wrapper merely serves to identify where they occur.

4.0 *Future Changes*

AuthorBlurb and **Affiliation** will be removed from the inline content of **SetInfo** in DocBook V4.0. A new wrapper element will be created to associate this information with authors, editors, and other contributors.

Attributes

Contents

`Contents`, if specified, should contain a list of all the IDs of the book-level subelements in the **Set**, presumably in their natural order.

See Also

ArtHeader, **BookBiblio**, **BookInfo**, **DocInfo**, **ObjectInfo**, **RefSynopsisDivInfo**, **ScreenInfo**, **Sect1Info**, **Sect2Info**, **Sect3Info**, **Sect4Info**, **Sect5Info**, **SectionInfo**

Examples

For examples, see **Set**.

SGMLTag—A component of SGML markup

Synopsis

Mixed Content Model

```
SGMLTag ::=
((#PCDATA|Replaceable|InlineGraphic|InlineMediaObject|IndexTerm)+)
```

Attributes **Name**	Common attributes **Type**	 **Default**
Class	*Enumeration:* Attribute AttValue Element EndTag GenEntity NumCharRef ParamEntity PI SGMLComment StartTag	*None*

Parameter Entities

`%cptr.char.mix;`	`%ndxterm.char.mix;`	`%para.char.mix;`
`%programlisting.content;`	`%refinline.char.mix;`	`%refname.char.mix;`
`%screen.content;`	`%tbl.entry.mdl;`	`%tech.char.class;`
`%title.char.mix;`		

Description

An **SGMLTag** identifies an SGML markup construct. The utility of this element is almost wholly constrained to books about SGML.

SGMLTag is sufficient for most XML constructs, which are identical to the corresponding SGML constructs, it but does not have any provisions for handling the special features of XML markup. A future version of DocBook will address this issue, probably by adding new `Class` values. In the meantime, you may get by by assigning a `Role` attribute for XML.

Processing expectations

Formatted inline. **SGMLTag** generates all the necessary punctuation before and after the construct it identifies. For example, it generates both the leading ampersand and the trailing semicolon when the `Class` is `genentity`.

Attributes

Class

`Class` identifies the specific SGML construct represented.

See Also

ComputerOutput, **Constant**, **Literal**, **Markup**, **Option**, **Optional**, **Parameter**, **Prompt**, **Replaceable**, **UserInput**, **VarName**

Examples

For examples, see **Collab**, **Link**, **Literal**, **RefEntry**, **SimpleList**, **WordAsWord**, **XRef**.

ShortAffil—A brief description of an affiliation

Synopsis

Mixed Content Model

```
ShortAffil ::=
((#PCDATA|Link|OLink|ULink|Emphasis|Trademark|Replaceable|Comment|
  Subscript|Superscript|InlineGraphic|InlineMediaObject|IndexTerm)+)
```

Attributes	Common attributes

Description

ShortAffil contains an abbreviated or brief description of an individual's **Affiliation**.

Processing expectations

May be formatted inline or as a displayed block, depending on context. Sometimes suppressed.

See Also

Affiliation, **CorpName**, **JobTitle**, **OrgDiv**, **OrgName**

Examples

For examples, see **Author**, **AuthorGroup**.

Shortcut—A key combination for an action that is also accessible through a menu

Synopsis

Content Model

```
Shortcut ::=
((KeyCap|KeyCombo|KeySym|MouseButton)+)
```

Attributes	Common attributes	
Name	**Type**	**Default**
OtherAction	CDATA	*None*

Name	Type	Default
Action	*Enumeration:* Click Double-Click Other Press Seq Simul	*None*
MoreInfo	*Enumeration:* None RefEntry	"None"

Description

A **Shortcut** contains the key combination that is a shortcut for a **MenuChoice**. Users that are familiar with the shortcuts can access the functionality of the corresponding menu choice, without navigating through the menu structure to find the right menu item.

Processing expectations

Formatted inline. The `MoreInfo` attribute can help generate a link or query to retrieve additional information.

Attributes

Action

`Action` identifies the nature of the action taken. If **Shortcut** contains more than one action element, `Simul` is default value for `Action`, otherwise there is no default.

If `Other` is specified, `OtherAction` should be used to identify the nature of the action.

MoreInfo

If `MoreInfo` is set to `RefEntry`, it implies that a **RefEntry** exists which further describes the **Shortcut**.

OtherAction

`OtherAction` should be used when `Action` is set to `Other`. It identifes the nature of the action in some application-specific way.

See Also

Accel, **GUIButton**, **GUIIcon**, **GUILabel**, **GUIMenu**, **GUIMenuItem**, **GUISubmenu**, **KeyCap**, **KeyCode**, **KeyCombo**, **KeySym**, **MenuChoice**, **MouseButton**

Examples

```
<!DOCTYPE para PUBLIC "-//OASIS//DTD DocBook V3.1//EN">
<para>
You can exit from GNU Emacs with
<menuchoice>
  <shortcut>
    <keycombo><keysym>C-x</keysym><keysym>C-c</keysym></keycombo>
  </shortcut>
  <guimenu>Files</guimenu>
  <guimenuitem>Exit Emacs</guimenuitem>
</menuchoice>.
</para>
```

You can exit from GNU Emacs with *Files* → *Exit Emacs* (`C-x`+`C-c`).

For additional examples, see also **MenuChoice**.

Sidebar—A portion of a document that is isolated from the main narrative flow

Synopsis

Content Model

```
Sidebar ::=
((Title,TitleAbbrev?)?,
 (CalloutList|GlossList|ItemizedList|OrderedList|SegmentedList|
  SimpleList|VariableList|Caution|Important|Note|Tip|Warning|
  LiteralLayout|ProgramListing|ProgramListingCO|Screen|ScreenCO|
  ScreenShot|Synopsis|CmdSynopsis|FuncSynopsis|FormalPara|Para|
  SimPara|Address|BlockQuote|Graphic|GraphicCO|MediaObject|
  MediaObjectCO|InformalEquation|InformalExample|InformalFigure|
  InformalTable|Equation|Example|Figure|Table|Procedure|Anchor|
  BridgeHead|Comment|Highlights|IndexTerm)+)
```

Attributes	Common attributes	
Parameter Entities		
%admon.mix;	%bookcomponent.content;	%component.mix;
%compound.class;	%divcomponent.mix;	%refcomponent.mix;

Description

A **Sidebar** is a short piece of text, rarely longer than a single column or page, that is presented outside the narrative flow of the main text.

Sidebars are often used for digressions or interesting observations that are related, but not directly relevant, to the main text.

Processing expectations

Formatted as a displayed block. **Sidebars** are sometimes boxed.

DocBook does not specify the location of the **Sidebar** within the final displayed flow of text. The wrapper may float or remain where it is located.

See Also

Abstract, BlockQuote, Epigraph, Highlights

Examples

```
<!DOCTYPE sect1 PUBLIC "-//OASIS//DTD DocBook V3.1//EN">
<sect1><title>An Example Section</title>

<para>
Some narrative text.
</para>

<sidebar><title>A Sidebar</title>
<para>
Sidebar content.
</para>
</sidebar>

<para>
The continuing flow of the narrative text, as if the
sidebar was not present.
</para>

</sect1>
```

SimPara—A paragraph that contains only text and inline markup, no block elements

Synopsis

Mixed Content Model

```
SimPara ::=
((#PCDATA|FootnoteRef|XRef|Abbrev|Acronym|Citation|CiteRefEntry|
  CiteTitle|Emphasis|FirstTerm|ForeignPhrase|GlossTerm|Footnote|
  Phrase|Quote|Trademark|WordAsWord|Link|OLink|ULink|Action|
  Application|ClassName|Command|ComputerOutput|Database|Email|
  EnVar|ErrorCode|ErrorName|ErrorType|Filename|Function|GUIButton|
  GUIIcon|GUILabel|GUIMenu|GUIMenuItem|GUISubmenu|Hardware|
  Interface|InterfaceDefinition|KeyCap|KeyCode|KeyCombo|KeySym|
  Literal|Constant|Markup|MediaLabel|MenuChoice|MouseButton|
  MsgText|Option|Optional|Parameter|Prompt|Property|Replaceable|
  ReturnValue|SGMLTag|StructField|StructName|Symbol|SystemItem|
  Token|Type|UserInput|VarName|Anchor|Author|AuthorInitials|
  CorpAuthor|ModeSpec|OtherCredit|ProductName|ProductNumber|
  RevHistory|Comment|Subscript|Superscript|InlineGraphic|
  InlineMediaObject|InlineEquation|Synopsis|CmdSynopsis|
  FuncSynopsis|IndexTerm)+)
```

Attributes	Common attributes

Parameter Entities		
%admon.mix;	%bookcomponent.content;	%component.mix;
%divcomponent.mix;	%example.mix;	%footnote.mix;
%glossdef.mix;	%highlights.mix;	%indexdivcomponent.mix;
%legalnotice.mix;	%para.class;	%qandaset.mix;
%refcomponent.mix;	%sidebar.mix;	%tabentry.mix;
%tbl.entry.mdl;	%textobject.mix;	

Description

A **SimPara** is a "simple paragraph," one that may contain only character data and inline elements. The **Para** element is less restrictive; it may also contain block level structures (lists, figures, and so on).

Processing expectations

Formatted as a displayed block.

4.0 *Future Changes*

The **InterfaceDefinition** element will be discarded in DocBook V4.0. It will no longer be available in the content model of this element.

See Also

FormalPara, **Para**

Examples

```
<!DOCTYPE simpara PUBLIC "-//OASIS//DTD DocBook V3.1//EN">
<simpara>
Just the text, ma'am.
</simpara>
```

Just the text, ma'am.

For additional examples, see also **Para**.

SimpleList—An undecorated list of single words or short phrases

Synopsis

Content Model		
SimpleList ::= (Member+)		
Attributes	Common attributes	
Name	**Type**	**Default**
Columns	NUMBER	*None*
Type	*Enumeration:* Horiz Inline Vert	"Vert"

Parameter Entities		
%admon.mix;	%bookcomponent.content;	%component.mix;
%divcomponent.mix;	%example.mix;	%footnote.mix;
%glossdef.mix;	%highlights.mix;	%indexdivcomponent.mix;
%legalnotice.mix;	%list.class;	%para.mix;
%qandaset.mix;	%refcomponent.mix;	%sidebar.mix;
%tabentry.mix;	%tbl.entry.mdl;	%textobject.mix;

Description

A **SimpleList** is a list of words or phrases. It offers a convenient alternative to the other list elements for inline content.

Processing expectations

Ironically, the processing expectations of a **SimpleList** are quite complex.

The presentation of a **SimpleList** is controlled by the `Type` attribute, which has three possible values:

`Inline`
: Indicates that the **Members** of the list should be rendered as a comma separated, inline list.

`Horiz`
: Indicates that the **Members** of the list should be rendered in a tabular fashion with members running across the rows.

`Vert`
: Indicates that the **Members** of the list should be rendered in a tabular fashion with members running down the columns. This is the default.

In both of the tabular cases, the number of columns in the table is controlled by the `Columns` attribute.

Attributes

Columns
: `Columns` specifies the number of columns to be used in the presentation of a **SimpleList** with a `Type` of `Vert` or `Horiz`. If `Columns` is unspecified, `1` is assumed.

Type
: `Type` specifies how the **Members** of the **SimpleList** are to be formatted. (This attribute would better fit DocBook semantics if it were named "`Class`").

See Also

CalloutList, **ItemizedList**, **ListItem**, **OrderedList**, **SegmentedList**, **VariableList**

Examples

```
<!DOCTYPE para PUBLIC "-//OASIS//DTD DocBook V3.1//EN">
<para>
Here is a <sgmltag>SimpleList</>, rendered inline:
<simplelist type=inline>
<member>A</>
<member>B</>
<member>C</>
<member>D</>
<member>E</>
<member>F</>
<member>G</>
</simplelist>
</para>
```

Here is a **SimpleList**, rendered inline: A, B, C, D, E, F, G

```
<!DOCTYPE para PUBLIC "-//OASIS//DTD DocBook V3.1//EN">
<para>
Here is the same <sgmltag>SimpleList</> rendered horizontally with
three columns:
<simplelist type=horiz columns=3>
<member>A</>
<member>B</>
<member>C</>
<member>D</>
<member>E</>
<member>F</>
<member>G</>
</simplelist>
</para>
```

Here is the same **SimpleList** rendered horizontally with three columns:

A	B	C
D	E	F
G		

```
<!DOCTYPE para PUBLIC "-//OASIS//DTD DocBook V3.1//EN">
<para>
Finally, here is the list rendered vertically:
<simplelist type=vert columns=3>
<member>A</>
<member>B</>
<member>C</>
<member>D</>
<member>E</>
<member>F</>
<member>G</>
</simplelist>
</para>
```

Finally, here is the list rendered vertically:

A D F
B E G
C

SimpleSect—A section of a document with no subdivisions

Synopsis

Content Model

```
SimpleSect ::=
((Title,Subtitle?,TitleAbbrev?),
 (CalloutList|GlossList|ItemizedList|OrderedList|SegmentedList|
  SimpleList|VariableList|Caution|Important|Note|Tip|Warning|
  LiteralLayout|ProgramListing|ProgramListingCO|Screen|ScreenCO|
  ScreenShot|Synopsis|CmdSynopsis|FuncSynopsis|FormalPara|Para|
  SimPara|Address|BlockQuote|Graphic|GraphicCO|MediaObject|
  MediaObjectCO|InformalEquation|InformalExample|InformalFigure|
  InformalTable|Equation|Example|Figure|Table|MsgSet|Procedure|
  Sidebar|QandASet|Anchor|BridgeHead|Comment|Highlights|Abstract|
  AuthorBlurb|Epigraph|IndexTerm)+)
```

Attributes	Common attributes

Parameter Entities

```
%bookcomponent.content;
```

Description

SimpleSect is one of the top-level sectioning elements in a component. There are three types of sectioning elements in DocBook:

- Explicitly numbered sections, **Sect1**...**Sect5**, which must be properly nested and can only be five levels deep.
- Recursive **Sections**, which are alternative to the numbered sections and have unbounded depth.
- **SimpleSects**, which are terminal. **SimpleSects** can occur as the "leaf" sections in either recursive sections or any of the numbered sections, or directly in components.

SimpleSects may be more convenient than numbered sections in some authoring environments because they can be moved around in the document hierarchy without renaming.

None of the sectioning elements is allowed to "float" in a component. You can place paragraphs and other block elements before a section, but you cannot place anything after it.

Processing expectations

Formatted as a displayed block. Sometimes sections are numbered.

See Also

BridgeHead, **Sect1**, **Sect2**, **Sect3**, **Sect4**, **Sect5**, **Section**

Examples

```
<!DOCTYPE sect1 PUBLIC "-//OASIS//DTD DocBook V3.1//EN">
<sect1><title>Additional Coding</title>

<para>
Support for the additional features requested will be provided.
</para>

<simplesect><title>Estimated Time</title>

<para>
2 to 3 weeks.
</para>

</simplesect>
</sect1>
```

spanspec—Formatting information for a spanned column in a table

Synopsis

Content Model

```
spanspec ::=
EMPTY
```

Attributes

Name	Type	Default
rowsep	NUMBER	*None*
spanname	NMTOKEN	*Required*
colsep	NUMBER	*None*
namest	NMTOKEN	*Required*
nameend	NMTOKEN	*Required*
charoff	NUTOKEN	*None*
align	*Enumeration:* center char justify left right	*None*
char	CDATA	*None*

Parameter Entities

`%tbl.entrytbl.mdl;` `%tbl.tgroup.mdl;`

Description

A **SpanSpec** associates a name with a span between two columns in a table. In the body of the table, cells can refer to the span by name. Cells that refer to a span will span horizontally from the first column to the last column, inclusive.

Cells can also form spans directly, by naming the start and end columns themselves. The added benefit of a **SpanSpec** is that it can associate formatting information (such as alignment and table rule specifications) with the span. This information does not need to be repeated then, on each spanning cell.

Processing expectations

Suppressed. This element is expected to obey the semantics of the *CALS Table Model Document Type Definition*, as specified by *OASIS Technical Memorandum TM 9502:1995* (*http://www.oasis-open.org/html/a502.htm*).

The `NameSt` and `NameEnd` attributes of a **SpanSpec** must refer to named **ColSpecs** in the same table. In other words, if the **SpanSpec**

```
<spanspec spanname="fullyear" namest="jan" nameend="dec">
```

exists in a table, **ColSpecs** named "jan" and "dec" must also exist in the same table.

Attributes

align

`Align` specifies the horizontal alignment of **Entrys** (or **EntryTbls**) in the span. The default alignment is inherited from the enclosing **TGroup**. If `Char` is specified, see also `Char` and `CharOff`. Individual **Entrys** and **EntryTbls** can specify an alternate alignment.

char

`Char` specifies the alignment character when the `Align` attribute is set to `Char`.

charoff

`CharOff` specifies the percentage of the column's total width that should appear to the left of the first occurance of the character identified in `Char` when the `Align` attribute is set to `Char`. This attribute is inherited from the **ColSpec** of the column specified in `Namest` or from the enclosing **TGroup**.

colsep

If `ColSep` has the value 1 (true), then a rule will be drawn to the right of the spanning column described by this **SpanSpec**. A value of 0 (false) suppresses the rule. The rule to the right of the last column in the table is controlled by the `Frame` attribute of the enclosing **Table** or **InformalTable** and the `ColSep` of the last column in the table is ignored. If unspecified, this attribute is inherited from enclosing elements.

nameend

`NameEnd` is the name (defined in a **ColSpec**) of the rightmost column of the span.

namest

`NameSt` is the name (defined in a **ColSpec**) of the leftmost column of the span.

rowsep

If RowSep has the value 1 (true), then a rule will be drawn below all the cells in this **Span**. A value of 0 (false) suppresses the rule. The rule below the last row in the table is controlled by the Frame attribute of the enclosing **Table** or **InformalTable** and the RowSep of the last row is ignored. If unspecified, this attribute is inherited from enclosing elements.

spanname

SpanName specifies a name by which subsequent **Entry** and **EntryTbls** can refer to the span defined in this **SpanSpec**.

See Also

colspec, **entry**, **entrytbl**, **InformalTable**, **row**, **Table**, **tbody**, **tfoot**, **tgroup**, **thead**

Examples

For examples, see **RefEntry**, **Table**.

State—A state or province in an address

Synopsis

Mixed Content Model	
`State ::= ((#PCDATA|Link|OLink|ULink|Emphasis|Trademark|Replaceable|Comment| Subscript|Superscript|InlineGraphic|InlineMediaObject|IndexTerm)+)`	
Attributes	Common attributes

Description

A **State** is the name or postal abbreviation for a state (or province) in an **Address**.

Processing expectations

Formatted inline. In an **Address**, this element may inherit the verbatim qualities of an address.

See Also

Address, **City**, **Country**, **Email**, **Fax**, **OtherAddr**, **Phone**, **POB**, **Postcode**, **Street**

Examples

For examples, see **Address**.

Step—A unit of action in a procedure

Synopsis

Content Model

```
Step ::=
(Title?,
 (((CalloutList|GlossList|ItemizedList|OrderedList|SegmentedList|
   SimpleList|VariableList|Caution|Important|Note|Tip|Warning|
   LiteralLayout|ProgramListing|ProgramListingCO|Screen|ScreenCO|
   ScreenShot|Synopsis|CmdSynopsis|FuncSynopsis|FormalPara|Para|
   SimPara|Address|BlockQuote|Graphic|GraphicCO|MediaObject|
   MediaObjectCO|InformalEquation|InformalExample|InformalFigure|
   InformalTable|Equation|Example|Figure|Table|MsgSet|Procedure|
   Sidebar|QandASet|Anchor|BridgeHead|Comment|Highlights|
   Abstract|AuthorBlurb|Epigraph|IndexTerm)+,
  (SubSteps,
   (CalloutList|GlossList|ItemizedList|OrderedList|SegmentedList|
    SimpleList|VariableList|Caution|Important|Note|Tip|Warning|
    LiteralLayout|ProgramListing|ProgramListingCO|Screen|
    ScreenCO|ScreenShot|Synopsis|CmdSynopsis|FuncSynopsis|
    FormalPara|Para|SimPara|Address|BlockQuote|Graphic|GraphicCO|
    MediaObject|MediaObjectCO|InformalEquation|InformalExample|
    InformalFigure|InformalTable|Equation|Example|Figure|Table|
    MsgSet|Procedure|Sidebar|QandASet|Anchor|BridgeHead|Comment|
    Highlights|Abstract|AuthorBlurb|Epigraph|IndexTerm)*)?)|
 (SubSteps,
  (CalloutList|GlossList|ItemizedList|OrderedList|SegmentedList|
   SimpleList|VariableList|Caution|Important|Note|Tip|Warning|
   LiteralLayout|ProgramListing|ProgramListingCO|Screen|ScreenCO|
   ScreenShot|Synopsis|CmdSynopsis|FuncSynopsis|FormalPara|Para|
   SimPara|Address|BlockQuote|Graphic|GraphicCO|MediaObject|
   MediaObjectCO|InformalEquation|InformalExample|InformalFigure|
   InformalTable|Equation|Example|Figure|Table|MsgSet|Procedure|
   Sidebar|QandASet|Anchor|BridgeHead|Comment|Highlights|
   Abstract|AuthorBlurb|Epigraph|IndexTerm)*)))
```

Attributes	Common attributes	
Name	**Type**	**Default**
Performance	*Enumeration:* Optional Required	"Required"

Description

A **Step** identifies a unit of action in a **Procedure**. If a finer level of granularity is required for some steps, you can embed **SubSteps** in a **Step**. Embedded **SubSteps** contain **Steps**, so that substeps can be nested to any depth.

Processing expectations

Formatted as a displayed block. **Steps** are almost always numbered.

Attributes

Performance

`Performance` specifies whether particular **Step** in a **Procedure** must be performed or is optional.

Examples

For examples, see **Procedure**.

Street—A street address in an address

Synopsis

Mixed Content Model
`Street ::=`
`((#PCDATA|Link|OLink|ULink|Emphasis|Trademark|Replaceable|Comment|`
`  Subscript|Superscript|InlineGraphic|InlineMediaObject|IndexTerm)+)`	

Attributes	Common attributes

Description

In postal addresses, the **Street** element contains the street address portion of the **Address**. If an address contains more than one line of street address information, each line should appear in its own **Street**.

Processing expectations

Formatted inline. In an **Address**, this element may inherit the verbatim qualities of an address.

See Also

Address, **City**, **Country**, **Email**, **Fax**, **OtherAddr**, **Phone**, **POB**, **Postcode**, **State**

Examples

For examples, see **Address**, **Publisher**.

StructField—A field in a structure (in the programming language sense)

Synopsis

Mixed Content Model
`StructField ::=`
`((#PCDATA|Replaceable|InlineGraphic|InlineMediaObject|IndexTerm)+)`	

Attributes	Common attributes

Parameter Entities		
%cptr.char.mix;	%ndxterm.char.mix;	%para.char.mix;
%programlisting.content;	%refinline.char.mix;	%refname.char.mix;
%screen.content;	%tbl.entry.mdl;	%tech.char.class;
%title.char.mix;		

Description

A **StructField** is a wrapper for the name of a field in a `struct` (a syntactic element of the C programming language) or a field in an equivalent construct in another programming language.

Processing expectations

Formatted inline.

See Also

ClassName, **Interface**, **InterfaceDefinition**, **Property**, **StructName**, **Symbol**, **Token**, **Type**

Examples

```
<!DOCTYPE para PUBLIC "-//OASIS//DTD DocBook V3.1//EN">
<para>
The <structfield>tm_isdst</structfield> field is non-zero when
the time reported is in daylight savings time.
</para>
```

The *tm_isdst* field is non-zero when the time reported is in daylight savings time.

StructName—The name of a structure (in the programming language sense)

Synopsis

Mixed Content Model		
StructName ::= ((#PCDATA|Replaceable|InlineGraphic|InlineMediaObject|IndexTerm)+)		
Attributes	Common attributes	
Parameter Entities		
%cptr.char.mix;	%ndxterm.char.mix;	%para.char.mix;
%programlisting.content;	%refinline.char.mix;	%refname.char.mix;
%screen.content;	%tbl.entry.mdl;	%tech.char.class;
%title.char.mix;		

Description

StructName is an inline wrapper for the name of a `struct` (a syntactic element of the C programming language) or an equivalent construct in another programming language.

Processing expectations

Formatted inline.

See Also

ClassName, **Interface**, **InterfaceDefinition**, **Property**, **StructField**, **Symbol**, **Token**, **Type**

Examples

```
<!DOCTYPE para PUBLIC "-//OASIS//DTD DocBook V3.1//EN">
<para>
The <structname>tm</structname> structure, returned by
<function>_get_tm</function>, contains complete information
about the current time of day.
</para>
```

The *tm* structure, returned by *_get_tm*, contains complete information about the current time of day.

Subject—One of a group of terms describing the subject matter of a document

Synopsis

Content Model
`Subject ::=`
`(SubjectTerm+)`		

Attributes **Name**	Common attributes **Type**	**Default**
Weight	NUMBER	*None*

Description

A "subject" categorizes or describes the topic of a document, or section of a document. In DocBook, a **Subject** is defined by the **SubjectTerms** that it contains.

Subject terms should be drawn from a controlled vocabulary, such as the *Library of Congress Subject Headings.* If an outside vocabulary is not appropriate, a local or institutional subject set should be created.

The advantage of a controlled vocabulary is that it places the document into a known subject space. Searching the subject space with a particular subject term will find *all* of the documents that claim to have that subject. There's no need to worry about terms that are synonymous with the search item, or homophones of the search term.

All of the **SubjectTerms** in a **Subject** should describe the same subject, and be from the *same controlled vocabulary*.

Processing expectations

May be formatted inline or as a displayed block, depending on context. Subjects are rarely displayed to a reader. Usually, they are reserved for searching and retrieval purposes.

Unlike **Keywords**, which may be chosen freely, subject terms should come from a controlled vocabulary.

In order to assure that typographic or other errors are not introduced into the subject terms, they should be compared against the controlled vocabulary by an external process.

Attributes

Weight

`Weight` specifies a ranking for this **Subject** relative to other subjects in the same set.

See Also

Keyword, **KeywordSet**, **SubjectSet**, **SubjectTerm**

Examples

For examples, see **SubjectSet**.

SubjectSet—A set of terms describing the subject matter of a document

Synopsis

Content Model
`SubjectSet ::=`
`(Subject+)`		

Attributes **Name**	Common attributes **Type**	**Default**
Scheme	NAME	*None*

Description

A **SubjectSet** is a container for a set of **Subjects**. All of the **Subjects** within a **SubjectSet** should come from the *same* controlled vocabulary.

A document can be described using terms from more than one controlled vocabulary. In order to do this, you should use the `Scheme` attribute to distinguish between controlled vocabularies.

Processing expectations

May be formatted inline or as a displayed block, depending on context. Subjects are rarely displayed to a reader. Usually, they are reserved for searching and retrieval purposes.

DocBook does not specify a relationship between **SubjectSets** in different parts of a document or between a **SubjectSet** and the **SubjectSets** of enclosing parts of the document.

Attributes

Scheme

`Scheme` identifies the controlled vocabulary used by this **SubjectSet**'s terms.

See Also

Keyword, **KeywordSet**, **Subject**, **SubjectTerm**

Examples

```
<!DOCTYPE subjectset PUBLIC "-//OASIS//DTD DocBook V3.1//EN">
<subjectset scheme="libraryofcongress">
<subject>
  <subjectterm>Electronic Publishing</subjectterm>
</subject>
<subject>
  <subjectterm>SGML (Computer program language)</subjectterm>
</subject>
</subjectset>
```

SubjectTerm—A term in a group of terms describing the subject matter of a document

Synopsis

Mixed Content Model
`SubjectTerm ::=`
`(#PCDATA)`	

Attributes	Common attributes

Description

A **SubjectTerm** is an individual subject word or phrase that describes the subject matter of a document or the portion of a document in which it occurs.

Subject terms are not expected to contain any markup. They are external descriptions from a controlled vocabulary.

Processing expectations

May be formatted inline or as a displayed block, depending on context. Subject terms are rarely displayed to a reader. Usually, they are reserved for searching and retrieval purposes.

See Also

Keyword, **KeywordSet**, **Subject**, **SubjectSet**

Examples

For examples, see **SubjectSet**.

Subscript—A subscript (as in H_2O, the molecular formula for water)

Synopsis

Mixed Content Model

```
Subscript ::=
((#PCDATA|Link|OLink|ULink|Emphasis|Replaceable|Symbol|
  InlineGraphic|InlineMediaObject|Anchor|Comment|Subscript|
  Superscript)+)
```

Attributes	Common attributes	
Parameter Entities		
`%cptr.char.mix;`	`%docinfo.char.mix;`	`%ndxterm.char.mix;`
`%other.char.class;`	`%para.char.mix;`	`%programlisting.content;`
`%refinline.char.mix;`	`%screen.content;`	`%tbl.entry.mdl;`
`%title.char.mix;`	`%word.char.mix;`	

Description

Subscript identifies text that is to be displayed as a subscript when rendered.

Processing expectations

Formatted inline. Subscripts are usually printed in a smaller font and shifted down with respect to the baseline.

See Also

Equation, **InformalEquation**, **InlineEquation**, **Superscript**

Examples

```
<!DOCTYPE para PUBLIC "-//OASIS//DTD DocBook V3.1//EN">
<para>
Thirsty?  Have some H<subscript>2</subscript>O.
</para>
```

Thirsty? Have some H_2O.

SubSteps—A wrapper for steps that occur within steps in a procedure

Synopsis

Content Model SubSteps ::= (Step+)		
Attributes **Name**	Common attributes **Type**	 **Default**
Performance	*Enumeration:* Optional Required	"Required"

Description

A **Procedure** describes a sequence of **Steps** that a reader is expected to perform. If a finer level of granularity is required for some steps, you can use **SubSteps** to embed substeps within a **Step**.

SubSteps contain **Steps**, so substeps can be nested to any depth.

Processing expectations

Formatted as a displayed block. **SubSteps** are almost always numbered.

Attributes

Performance

`Performance` specifies whether particular set of **Substep** in a **Procedure** must be performed or is optional.

Examples

For examples, see **Procedure**.

Subtitle—The subtitle of a document

Synopsis

Mixed Content Model

```
Subtitle ::=
((#PCDATA|FootnoteRef|XRef|Abbrev|Acronym|Citation|CiteRefEntry|
  CiteTitle|Emphasis|FirstTerm|ForeignPhrase|GlossTerm|Footnote|
  Phrase|Quote|Trademark|WordAsWord|Link|OLink|ULink|Action|
  Application|ClassName|Command|ComputerOutput|Database|Email|
  EnVar|ErrorCode|ErrorName|ErrorType|Filename|Function|GUIButton|
  GUIIcon|GUILabel|GUIMenu|GUIMenuItem|GUISubmenu|Hardware|
  Interface|InterfaceDefinition|KeyCap|KeyCode|KeyCombo|KeySym|
  Literal|Constant|Markup|MediaLabel|MenuChoice|MouseButton|
  MsgText|Option|Optional|Parameter|Prompt|Property|Replaceable|
  ReturnValue|SGMLTag|StructField|StructName|Symbol|SystemItem|
  Token|Type|UserInput|VarName|Anchor|Author|AuthorInitials|
  CorpAuthor|ModeSpec|OtherCredit|ProductName|ProductNumber|
  RevHistory|Comment|Subscript|Superscript|InlineGraphic|
  InlineMediaObject|InlineEquation|IndexTerm)+)
```

Attributes	Common attributes	
Parameter Entities		
%bibliocomponent.mix;	%bookcomponent.title.content;	%div.title.content;
%refsect.title.content;	%sect.title.content;	

Description

A **Subtitle** identifies the subtitle of a document, or portion of a document.

Processing expectations

Formatted as a displayed block.

See Also

Title, **TitleAbbrev**

Examples

For examples, see **Bibliography**, **Sect1Info**, **Section**.

Superscript—A superscript (as in x^2, the mathematical notation for x multiplied by itself)

Synopsis

Mixed Content Model

```
Superscript ::=
((#PCDATA|Link|OLink|ULink|Emphasis|Replaceable|Symbol|
  InlineGraphic|InlineMediaObject|Anchor|Comment|Subscript|
  Superscript)+)
```

Attributes	Common attributes	
Parameter Entities		
`%cptr.char.mix;`	`%docinfo.char.mix;`	`%ndxterm.char.mix;`
`%other.char.class;`	`%para.char.mix;`	`%programlisting.content;`
`%refinline.char.mix;`	`%screen.content;`	`%tbl.entry.mdl;`
`%title.char.mix;`	`%word.char.mix;`	

Description

Superscript identifies text that is to be displayed as a superscript when rendered.

Processing expectations

Formatted inline. Superscripts are usually printed in a smaller font and shifted up with respect to the baseline.

See Also

Equation, **InformalEquation**, **InlineEquation**, **Subscript**

Examples

```
<!DOCTYPE para PUBLIC "-//OASIS//DTD DocBook V3.1//EN">
<para>
The equation e<superscript>&pi;i</superscript> + 1 = 0 ties together
five of the most important mathematical constants.
</para>
```

The equation $e^{\pi i} + 1 = 0$ ties together five of the most important mathematical constants.

For additional examples, see also **InlineMediaObject**.

Surname—A family name; in western cultures the "last name"

Synopsis

Mixed Content Model	
`Surname ::= ((#PCDATA|Link|OLink|ULink|Emphasis|Trademark|Replaceable|Comment| Subscript|Superscript|InlineGraphic|InlineMediaObject|IndexTerm)+)`	
Attributes	Common attributes
Parameter Entities	
`%bibliocomponent.mix;`	`%person.ident.mix;`

Description

A **Surname** is a family name; in Western cultures, the "last name."

Processing expectations

Formatted inline. In an **Address**, this element may inherit the verbatim qualities of an address.

See Also

Affiliation, **FirstName**, **Honorific**, **Lineage**, **OtherName**

Examples

For examples, see **Ackno**, **Article**, **Author**, **AuthorGroup**, **Bibliography**, **BiblioMSet**, **BiblioSet**, **Book**, **BookInfo**, **OtherCredit**.

Symbol—A name that is replaced by a value before processing

Synopsis

Mixed Content Model
`Symbol ::=`
`((#PCDATA|Replaceable|InlineGraphic|InlineMediaObject|IndexTerm)+)`		

Attributes	Common attributes	
Name	**Type**	**Default**
Class	*Enumeration:* Limit	*None*
Parameter Entities		
`%cptr.char.mix;`	`%ndxterm.char.mix;`	`%para.char.mix;`
`%programlisting.content;`	`%refinline.char.mix;`	`%refname.char.mix;`
`%screen.content;`	`%tbl.entry.mdl;`	`%tech.char.class;`
`%title.char.mix;`		

Description

A **Symbol** is a name that represents a value. It should be used in contexts in which the name will actually be replaced by a value before processing. The canonical example is a `#define`d symbol in a C program where the C preprocessor replaces every occurance of the symbol with its value before compilation begins.

The `Limit` value of the `Class` attribute identifies those symbols that represent system limitations (for example, the number of characters allowed in a path name or the largest possible positive integer). DocBook V3.1 introduced the **Constant** element, which may be more suitable for some of these symbols.

Processing expectations

Formatted inline.

Attributes

Class

`Class` indicates the type of **Symbol**.

See Also

ClassName, **Interface**, **InterfaceDefinition**, **Property**, **StructField**, **StructName**, **Token**, **Type**

Examples

```
<!DOCTYPE para PUBLIC "-//OASIS//DTD DocBook V3.1//EN">
<para>
No filename may be more than <symbol class=limit>MAXPATHLEN</symbol>
characters long.
</para>
```

No filename may be more than **MAXPATHLEN** characters long.

SynopFragment—A portion of a **CmdSynopsis** broken out from the main body of the synopsis

Synopsis

Content Model
`SynopFragment ::=`
`((Arg|Group)+)`	

Attributes	Common attributes

Description

A complex **CmdSynopsis** can be made more manageable with **SynopFragment**s. Rather than attempting to present the entire synopsis in one large piece, parts of the synopsis can be extracted out and presented elsewhere. These extracted pieces are placed in **SynopFragment**s at the end of the **CmdSynopsis**.

At the point in which each piece was extracted, insert a **SynopFragmentRef** that points to the fragment. The content of the reference element will be presented inline.

Processing expectations

Formatted as a displayed block.

The presentation system is responsible for generating text that makes the reader aware of the link. This can be done with numbered bullets, or any other appropriate mechanism. Whatever mark is generated for the reference must also be generated for the fragment.

Online systems have additional flexibility. They may generate hot links between the references and the fragments, for example, or place the fragments in pop-up windows.

See Also

Arg, **CmdSynopsis**, **Group**, **RefSynopsisDiv**, **SBR**, **SynopFragmentRef**

Examples

```
<!DOCTYPE cmdsynopsis PUBLIC "-//OASIS//DTD DocBook V3.1//EN">
<cmdsynopsis>
  <command>cccp</command>
  <arg>-$</arg>
  <arg>-C</arg>
  <arg rep=repeat>-D<replaceable>name</replaceable>
       <arg>=<replaceable>definition</replaceable></arg></arg>
  <arg>-dD</arg>
  <arg>-dM</arg>
  <sbr>
  <arg rep=repeat>-I <replaceable>directory</replaceable></arg>
  <arg>-H</arg>
  <arg>-I-</arg>
  <arg rep=repeat>-imacros <replaceable>file</replaceable></arg>
  <sbr>
  <arg rep=repeat>-include <replaceable>file</replaceable></arg>
  <group>
    <synopfragmentref linkend="langs">languages</synopfragmentref>
  </group>
  <arg>-lint</arg>
  <sbr>
  <group>
    <arg>-M</arg>
    <arg>-MD</arg>
    <arg>-MM</arg>
    <arg>-MMD</arg>
  </group>
  <arg>-nostdinc</arg>
  <arg>-P</arg>
  <arg>-pedantic</arg>
  <sbr>
  <arg>-pedantic-errors</arg>
  <arg>-trigraphs</arg>
  <arg>-U<replaceable>name</replaceable></arg>
  <sbr>
  <arg>-undef</arg>
  <arg choice="plain"><synopfragmentref linkend="warn">warnings
    </synopfragmentref></arg>
  <group choice=req>
    <arg><replaceable>infile</replaceable></arg>
    <arg>-</arg>
  </group>
  <group choice=req>
```

```
    <arg><replaceable>outfile</replaceable></arg>
    <arg>-</arg>
  </group>

  <synopfragment id="langs">
    <group choice="plain">
      <arg>-lang-c</arg>
      <arg>-lang-c++</arg>
      <arg>-lang-objc</arg>
    </group>
  </synopfragment>

  <synopfragment id="warn">
    <arg>-Wtrigraphs</arg>
    <arg>-Wcomment</arg>
    <arg>-Wall</arg>
    <arg>-Wtraditional</arg>
  </synopfragment>

</cmdsynopsis>
```

```
cccp [-$] [-C] [-Dname [=definition]...] [-dD] [-dM]
 [-I directory...] [-H] [-I-] [-imacros file...]
 [-include file...] [❶languages] [-lint]
 [-M | -MD | -MM | -MMD] [-nostdinc] [-P] [-pedantic]
 [-pedantic-errors] [-trigraphs] [-Uname]
 [-undef] ❷warnings      {infile | -} {outfile | -}

❶ -lang-c | -lang-c++ | -lang-objc
❷ [-Wtrigraphs] [-Wcomment] [-Wall] [-Wtraditional]
```

For additional examples, see also **CmdSynopsis**.

SynopFragmentRef—A reference to a fragment of a command synopsis

Synopsis

Declared Content SynopFragmentRef ::= RCDATA		
Attributes **Name**	Common attributes **Type**	**Default**
Linkend	IDREF	*Required*

Description

A complex **CmdSynopsis** can be made more manageable with **SynopFragments**. Rather than attempting to present the entire synopsis in one large piece, parts of the synopsis can be extracted out and presented elsewhere.

At the point where each piece was extracted, insert a **SynopFragmentRef** that points to the fragment. The content of the **SynopFragmentRef** will be presented inline.

The extracted pieces are placed in **SynopFragment**s at the end of the **CmdSynopsis**.

NOTE The content model of **SynopFragmentRef** is unique in the SGML version of DocBook because it contains `RCDATA` declared content. What this means is that all markup inside a **SynopFragmentRef** is ignored, except for entity references.

How, you might ask, is this different from a content model that includes only `#PCDATA`? The difference is only apparent when you consider inclusions. Recall that an inclusion provides a list of elements that can occur *anywhere* inside an element. So, for example, the fact that **Chapter** lists **IndexTerm** as an inclusion means that **IndexTerm** can legally occur inside of a **SynopFragmentRef** that's nested inside a chapter, even if the content model of **SynopFragmentRef** does not explicitly allow **IndexTerm**s. Making the content `RCDATA` ensures that the markup will not be recognized, even if it's allowed by inclusion. A neat trick.

XML does not support `RCDATA`.

Processing expectations

Formatted as a displayed block.

The presentation system is responsible for generating text that makes the reader aware of the link. This can be done with numbered bullets, or any other appropriate mechanism.

Online systems have additional flexibility. They may generate hot links between the references and the fragments, for example, or place the fragments in pop-up windows.

Attributes

Linkend

`Linkend` points to the **SynopFragment** referenced.

See Also

Arg, **CmdSynopsis**, **Group**, **RefSynopsisDiv**, **SBR**, **SynopFragment**

Examples

For examples, see **SynopFragment**.

Synopsis—A general-purpose element for representing the syntax of commands or functions

Synopsis

Mixed Content Model

```
Synopsis ::=
((LineAnnotation|#PCDATA|FootnoteRef|XRef|Abbrev|Acronym|Citation|
  CiteRefEntry|CiteTitle|Emphasis|FirstTerm|ForeignPhrase|
  GlossTerm|Footnote|Phrase|Quote|Trademark|WordAsWord|Link|OLink|
  ULink|Action|Application|ClassName|Command|ComputerOutput|
  Database|Email|EnVar|ErrorCode|ErrorName|ErrorType|Filename|
  Function|GUIButton|GUIIcon|GUILabel|GUIMenu|GUIMenuItem|
  GUISubmenu|Hardware|Interface|InterfaceDefinition|KeyCap|
  KeyCode|KeyCombo|KeySym|Literal|Constant|Markup|MediaLabel|
  MenuChoice|MouseButton|MsgText|Option|Optional|Parameter|Prompt|
  Property|Replaceable|ReturnValue|SGMLTag|StructField|StructName|
  Symbol|SystemItem|Token|Type|UserInput|VarName|Anchor|Author|
  AuthorInitials|CorpAuthor|ModeSpec|OtherCredit|ProductName|
  ProductNumber|RevHistory|Comment|Subscript|Superscript|
  InlineGraphic|InlineMediaObject|InlineEquation|Synopsis|
  CmdSynopsis|FuncSynopsis|IndexTerm|Graphic|MediaObject)+)
```

Attributes Common attributes

Name	**Type**	**Default**
Label	CDATA	*None*
Format	*Enumerated notation:* linespecific	"linespecific"

Parameter Entities

%admon.mix;	%bookcomponent.content;	%component.mix;
%divcomponent.mix;	%example.mix;	%figure.mix;
%footnote.mix;	%glossdef.mix;	%indexdivcomponent.mix;
%para.char.mix;	%programlisting.content;	%qandaset.mix;
%refcomponent.mix;	%screen.content;	%sidebar.mix;
%synop.class;	%tbl.entry.mdl;	

Description

A **Synopsis** is a verbatim environment for displaying command, function, and other syntax summaries.

Unlike **CmdSynopsis** and **FuncSynopsis** which have a complex interior structure, **Synopsis** is simply a verbatim environment.

Processing expectations

This element is displayed "verbatim"; whitespace and linebreaks within this element are significant. **Synopsis** elements are usually displayed in a fixed width font.

4.0 *Future Changes*

The **InterfaceDefinition** element will be discarded in DocBook V4.0. It will no longer be available in the content model of this element.

Attributes

Format

The `Format` attribute applies the `linespecific` notation to all synopses. All white space and line breaks must be preserved.

Label

`Label` specifies an identifying number or string that may be used in presentation.

See Also

CmdSynopsis, **ComputerOutput**, **FuncSynopsis**, **LineAnnotation**, **LiteralLayout**, **ProgramListing**, **Screen**, **ScreenShot**, **UserInput**

Examples

```
<!DOCTYPE synopsis PUBLIC "-//OASIS//DTD DocBook V3.1//EN">
<synopsis>
chgrp [-R [-H | -L | -P] [-f] group file...
</synopsis>
```

```
chgrp [-R [-H | -L | -P] [-f] group file...
```

```
<!DOCTYPE synopsis PUBLIC "-//OASIS//DTD DocBook V3.1//EN">
<synopsis>
int max(int int1, int int2);
</synopsis>
```

```
int max(int int1, int int2);
```

For additional examples, see also **Optional**, **RefEntry**.

SystemItem—A system-related item or term

Synopsis

Mixed Content Model

```
SystemItem ::=
((#PCDATA|Link|OLink|ULink|Action|Application|ClassName|Command|
  ComputerOutput|Database|Email|EnVar|ErrorCode|ErrorName|
  ErrorType|Filename|Function|GUIButton|GUIIcon|GUILabel|GUIMenu|
  GUIMenuItem|GUISubmenu|Hardware|Interface|InterfaceDefinition|
  KeyCap|KeyCode|KeyCombo|KeySym|Literal|Constant|Markup|
  MediaLabel|MenuChoice|MouseButton|MsgText|Option|Optional|
  Parameter|Prompt|Property|Replaceable|ReturnValue|SGMLTag|
  StructField|StructName|Symbol|SystemItem|Token|Type|UserInput|
  VarName|Anchor|Comment|Subscript|Superscript|InlineGraphic|
  InlineMediaObject|IndexTerm|Acronym)+)
```

Attributes Common attributes		
Name	**Type**	**Default**
Class	*Enumeration:* Constant EnvironVar Macro OSname Prompt Resource SystemName	*None*
MoreInfo	*Enumeration:* None RefEntry	"None"

Parameter Entities		
`%cptr.char.mix;`	`%ndxterm.char.mix;`	`%para.char.mix;`
`%programlisting.content;`	`%refinline.char.mix;`	`%refname.char.mix;`
`%screen.content;`	`%tbl.entry.mdl;`	`%tech.char.class;`
`%title.char.mix;`		

Description

A **SystemItem** identifies any system-related item or term. The `Class` attribute defines a number of common system-related terms.

Many inline elements in DocBook are, in fact, system-related. Some of the objects identified by the `Class` attribute on **SystemItem** may eventually migrate out to be inline elements of their own accord…and vice versa.

Processing expectations

Formatted inline. The `MoreInfo` attribute can help generate a link or query to retrieve additional information.

4.0 *Future Changes*

In DocBook V4.0, the content model of **SystemItem** will be constrained to `(#PCDATA | Replaceable | InlineGraphic)`.

Also, the `EnvironVar` and `Prompt` values of `Class` will be discarded (use **EnVar** and **Prompt** instead).

Attributes

Class

`Class` indicates the type of **SystemItem**.

MoreInfo

If `MoreInfo` is set to `RefEntry`, it implies that a **RefEntry** exists which further describes the **SystemItem**.

See Also

ComputerOutput, **EnVar**, **Filename**, **Prompt**, **UserInput**

Examples

```
<!DOCTYPE para PUBLIC "-//OASIS//DTD DocBook V3.1//EN">
<para>
For many years, O'Reilly's primary web server,
<ulink url="http://www.oreilly.com/">http://www.oreilly.com/</ulink>,
was hosted by <application>WN</application> on
<systemitem class="systemname">helio.oreilly.com</systemitem>.
</para>
```

For many years, O'Reilly's primary web server, *http://www.oreilly.com/*, was hosted by WN on *helio.oreilly.com.*

For additional examples, see also **Part**.

Table—A formal table in a document

Synopsis

Content Model

```
Table ::=
(((Title,TitleAbbrev?),
  (IndexTerm)*,
  (Graphic+|MediaObject+|TGroup+)))
```

Attributes Common attributes

Name	Type	Default
Label	CDATA	*None*
pgwide	NUMBER	*None*
rowsep	NUMBER	*None*
shortentry	NUMBER	*None*
colsep	NUMBER	*None*
tabstyle	NMTOKEN	*None*
frame	*Enumeration:* all bottom none sides top topbot	*None*
orient	*Enumeration:* land port	*None*
tocentry	NUMBER	*None*

Parameter Entities

%admon.mix;	%bookcomponent.content;	%component.mix;
%divcomponent.mix;	%footnote.exclusion;	%formal.class;
%formal.exclusion;	%glossdef.mix;	%highlights.exclusion;
%para.mix;	%qandaset.mix;	%refcomponent.mix;
%sidebar.mix;	%tbl.table.excep;	%tbl.table.name;

Description

The **Table** element identifies a formal table. DocBook uses the CALS table model, which describes tables geometrically using rows, columns, and cells.

Tables may include column headers and footers, but there is no provision for row headers.

Processing expectations

Formatted as a displayed block. This element is expected to obey the semantics of the *CALS Table Model Document Type Definition*, as specified by *OASIS Technical Memorandum TM 9502:1995* (*http://www.oasis-open.org/html/a502.htm*).

Attributes

Label

`Label` specifies an identifying string for presentation purposes.

Generally, an explicit `Label` attribute is used only if the processing system is incapable of generating the label automatically. If present, the `Label` is normative; it will used even if the processing system is capable of automatic labelling.

colsep

If `ColSep` has the value 1 (true), then a rule will be drawn to the right of all columns in this table. A value of 0 (false) suppresses the rule. The rule to the right of the last column in the table is controlled by the `Frame` attribute, not the `ColSep`.

frame

`Frame` specifies how the table is to be framed.

orient

`Orient` specifies the orientation of the **Table**. An orientation of `Port` is the "upright", the same orientation as the rest of the text flow. An orientation of `Land` is 90 degrees counterclockwise from the upright orientation.

pgwide

If `Pgwide` has the value 0 (false), then the **Table** is rendered in the current text flow (with flow column width). A value of 1 (true) specifies that the table should be rendered across the full text page.

rowsep

If `RowSep` has the value 1 (true), then a rule will be drawn below all the rows in the **Table** (unless other, interior elements, suppress some or all of the rules). A value of 0 (false) suppresses the rule. The rule below the last row in the table is controlled by the `Frame` attribute and the `RowSep` of the last row is ignored.

shortentry

If **ShortEntry** has the value 1 (true), then the **Table**'s **TitleAbbrev** will be used in the **LoT**, **Index**, etc. A value of 0 (false) indicates that the full **Title** should be used in those places.

tabstyle

`TabStyle` holds the name of a table style defined in a stylesheet (e.g., a FOSI) that will be used to process this document.

tocentry

If `ToCEntry` has the value 1 (true), then the **Table** will appear in a generated List of Tables. The default value of 0 (false) indicates that it will not.

See Also

colspec, **entry**, **entrytbl**, **Equation**, **Example**, **Figure**, **InformalEquation**, **InformalExample**, **InformalFigure**, **InformalTable**, **row**, **spanspec**, **tbody**, **tfoot**, **tgroup**, **thead**

Examples

```
<!DOCTYPE table PUBLIC "-//OASIS//DTD DocBook V3.1//EN">
<table frame=all><title>Sample Table</title>
<tgroup cols=5 align=left colsep=1 rowsep=1>
<colspec colname=c1>
<colspec colname=c2>
<colspec colname=c3>
<colspec colnum=5 colname=c5>
<spanspec spanname=hspan namest=c1 nameend=c2 align=center>
<spanspec spanname=bspan namest=c2 nameend=c3 align=center>
<thead>
<row>
  <entry spanname=hspan>Horizontal Span</entry>
  <entry>a3</entry>
  <entry>a4</entry>
  <entry>a5</entry>
</row>
</thead>
<tfoot>
<row>
  <entry>f1</entry>
  <entry>f2</entry>
  <entry>f3</entry>
  <entry>f4</entry>
  <entry>f5</entry>
</row>
</tfoot>
<tbody>
<row>
  <entry>b1</entry>
  <entry>b2</entry>
  <entry>b3</entry>
```

```
  <entry>b4</entry>
  <entry morerows=1 valign=middle><para>  <!-- Pernicous Mixed Content -->
  Vertical Span</para></entry>
</row>
<row>
  <entry>c1</entry>
  <entry spanname=bspan morerows=1 valign=bottom>Span Both</entry>
  <entry>c4</entry>
</row>
<row>
  <entry>d1</entry>
  <entry>d4</entry>
  <entry>d5</entry>
</row>
</tbody>
</tgroup>
</table>
```

Table 1. Sample Table

Horizontal Span		a3	a4	a5
b1	b2	b3	b4	Vertical Span
c1	Span Both		c4	
d1			d4	d5
f1	f2	f3	f4	f5

tbody—A wrapper for the rows of a table or informal table

Synopsis

Content Model
`tbody ::=`
`(row+)`		

Attributes **Name**	Common attributes **Type**	 **Default**
valign	*Enumeration:* bottom middle top	*None*
Parameter Entities `%tbl.entrytbl.mdl;`	 `%tbl.tgroup.mdl;`	

Description

The **TBody** wrapper identifies the **Rows** of a table that form the body of the table, as distinct from the header (**THead**) and footer (**TFoot**) rows.

In most tables, the **TBody** contains most of the rows.

Processing expectations

This element is expected to obey the semantics of the *CALS Table Model Document Type Definition*, as specified by *OASIS Technical Memorandum TM 9502:1995* (*http://www.oasis-open.org/html/a502.htm*).

Attributes

valign

VAlign specifies the vertical alignment of text (and other elements) within the cells of this **TBody**.

See Also

colspec, **entry**, **entrytbl**, **InformalTable**, **row**, **spanspec**, **Table**, **tfoot**, **tgroup**, **thead**

Examples

For examples, see **entrytbl**, **FootnoteRef**, **InformalTable**, **RefEntry**, **Table**.

Term—The word or phrase being defined or described in a variable list

Synopsis

Mixed Content Model

```
Term ::=
((#PCDATA|FootnoteRef|XRef|Abbrev|Acronym|Citation|CiteRefEntry|
  CiteTitle|Emphasis|FirstTerm|ForeignPhrase|GlossTerm|Footnote|
  Phrase|Quote|Trademark|WordAsWord|Link|OLink|ULink|Action|
  Application|ClassName|Command|ComputerOutput|Database|Email|
  EnVar|ErrorCode|ErrorName|ErrorType|Filename|Function|GUIButton|
  GUIIcon|GUILabel|GUIMenu|GUIMenuItem|GUISubmenu|Hardware|
  Interface|InterfaceDefinition|KeyCap|KeyCode|KeyCombo|KeySym|
  Literal|Constant|Markup|MediaLabel|MenuChoice|MouseButton|
  MsgText|Option|Optional|Parameter|Prompt|Property|Replaceable|
  ReturnValue|SGMLTag|StructField|StructName|Symbol|SystemItem|
  Token|Type|UserInput|VarName|Anchor|Author|AuthorInitials|
  CorpAuthor|ModeSpec|OtherCredit|ProductName|ProductNumber|
  RevHistory|Comment|Subscript|Superscript|InlineGraphic|
  InlineMediaObject|InlineEquation|Synopsis|CmdSynopsis|
  FuncSynopsis|IndexTerm)+)
```

Attributes	Common attributes

Description

The **Term** in a **VarListEntry** identifies the thing that is described or defined by that entry.

Processing expectations

Formatted as a displayed block. **Terms** are usually formatted to make them stand out with respect to the text that follows. The best presentation depends on several factors, including the number and length of the terms. The `TermLength` attribute on the containing **VariableList** may influence the presentation of **Terms**. See **VariableList**.

4.0 *Future Changes*

The **InterfaceDefinition** element will be discarded in DocBook V4.0. It will no longer be available in the content model of this element.

Examples

For examples, see **RefEntry**, **VariableList**.

Tertiary—A tertiary word or phrase in an index term

Synopsis

Mixed Content Model

```
Tertiary ::=
((#PCDATA|FootnoteRef|XRef|Abbrev|Acronym|Citation|CiteRefEntry|
  CiteTitle|Emphasis|FirstTerm|ForeignPhrase|GlossTerm|Footnote|
  Phrase|Quote|Trademark|WordAsWord|Link|OLink|ULink|Action|
  Application|ClassName|Command|ComputerOutput|Database|Email|
  EnVar|ErrorCode|ErrorName|ErrorType|Filename|Function|GUIButton|
  GUIIcon|GUILabel|GUIMenu|GUIMenuItem|GUISubmenu|Hardware|
  Interface|InterfaceDefinition|KeyCap|KeyCode|KeyCombo|KeySym|
  Literal|Constant|Markup|MediaLabel|MenuChoice|MouseButton|
  MsgText|Option|Optional|Parameter|Prompt|Property|Replaceable|
  ReturnValue|SGMLTag|StructField|StructName|Symbol|SystemItem|
  Token|Type|UserInput|VarName|Anchor|Author|AuthorInitials|
  CorpAuthor|ModeSpec|OtherCredit|ProductName|ProductNumber|
  RevHistory|Comment|Subscript|Superscript|InlineGraphic|
  InlineMediaObject)+)
```

Attributes	Common attributes	
Name	**Type**	**Default**
SortAs	CDATA	*None*

Description

Tertiary contains a third-level word or phrase in an **IndexTerm**. The text of a **Tertiary** term is less significant than the **Primary** and **Secondary** terms for sorting and display purposes.

DocBook does not define any additional levels. You cannot use **IndexTerms** to construct indexes with more than three levels without extending the DTD.

In **IndexTerms**, you can only have one primary, secondary, and tertiary term. If you want to index multiple tertiary terms for the same primary and secondary, you must repeat the primary and secondary in another **IndexTerm**. You cannot place several **Tertiarys** in the same primary.

Processing expectations

Suppressed. This element provides data for processing but is not rendered in the primary flow of text.

4.0 *Future Changes*

The **InterfaceDefinition** element will be discarded in DocBook V4.0. It will no longer be available in the content model of this element.

Attributes

SortAs

`SortAs` specifies the string by which the element's content is to be sorted. If unspecified, the proper content is used.

See Also

IndexEntry, **IndexTerm**, **Primary**, **PrimaryIE**, **Secondary**, **SecondaryIE**, **See**, **SeeAlso**, **SeeAlsoIE**, **SeeIE**, **TertiaryIE**

Examples

For examples, see **IndexTerm**.

TertiaryIE—A tertiary term in an index entry, rather than in the text

Synopsis

Mixed Content Model

```
TertiaryIE ::=
((#PCDATA|FootnoteRef|XRef|Abbrev|Acronym|Citation|CiteRefEntry|
  CiteTitle|Emphasis|FirstTerm|ForeignPhrase|GlossTerm|Footnote|
  Phrase|Quote|Trademark|WordAsWord|Link|OLink|ULink|Action|
  Application|ClassName|Command|ComputerOutput|Database|Email|
  EnVar|ErrorCode|ErrorName|ErrorType|Filename|Function|GUIButton|
  GUIIcon|GUILabel|GUIMenu|GUIMenuItem|GUISubmenu|Hardware|
  Interface|InterfaceDefinition|KeyCap|KeyCode|KeyCombo|KeySym|
  Literal|Constant|Markup|MediaLabel|MenuChoice|MouseButton|
  MsgText|Option|Optional|Parameter|Prompt|Property|Replaceable|
  ReturnValue|SGMLTag|StructField|StructName|Symbol|SystemItem|
  Token|Type|UserInput|VarName|Anchor|Author|AuthorInitials|
  CorpAuthor|ModeSpec|OtherCredit|ProductName|ProductNumber|
  RevHistory|Comment|Subscript|Superscript|InlineGraphic|
  InlineMediaObject)+)
```

Attributes	Common attributes	
Name	**Type**	**Default**
Linkends	IDREFS	*None*

Description

TertiaryIE identifies a third-level word or words in an **IndexEntry**.

In **IndexEntrys**, you can specify as many tertiary terms that are necessary. Secondary and tertiary terms can be mixed, following the primary.

Processing expectations

Formatted as a displayed block. **TertiaryIEs** occur below the **SecondaryIE**, and are usually aligned with each other and indented from the secondary.

4.0 *Future Changes*

The **InterfaceDefinition** element will be discarded in DocBook V4.0. It will no longer be available in the content model of this element.

Attributes

Linkends

`Linkends`, if used, points to the **IndexTerms** indexed by this entry.

See Also

IndexEntry, **IndexTerm**, **Primary**, **PrimaryIE**, **Secondary**, **SecondaryIE**, **See**, **SeeAlso**, **SeeAlsoIE**, **SeeIE**, **Tertiary**

Examples

For examples, see **Index**.

TextObject—A wrapper for a text description of an object and its associated meta-information

Synopsis

Content Model

```
TextObject ::=
(ObjectInfo?,
 (Phrase|
  (CalloutList|GlossList|ItemizedList|OrderedList|SegmentedList|
   SimpleList|VariableList|Caution|Important|Note|Tip|Warning|
   LiteralLayout|ProgramListing|ProgramListingCO|Screen|ScreenCO|
   ScreenShot|FormalPara|Para|SimPara|BlockQuote)+))
```

Attributes	Common attributes

Description

A **TextObject** is a wrapper containing a textual description of a media object, and its associated meta-information. **TextObjects** are only allowed in **MediaObjects** as a fall-back option, they cannot be the primary content.

There are two different forms of **TextObject**, and it is not unreasonable for a media object to contain both of them.

In the first form, the content of a **TextObject** is simply a **Phrase**. This form is a mechanism for providing a simple "alt text" for a media object. The phrase might be used, for example, as the value of the `ALT` attribute on an HTML **IMG**, with the primary content of the image coming from one of the other objects in the media object.

In the second form, the content of **TextObject** is a longer, prose description. This form could be used when rendering to devices that are incapable of displaying any of the other alternatives.

Processing expectations

May be formatted inline or as a displayed block, depending on context. It might not be rendered at all, depending on its placement within a **MediaObject** or **InlineMediaObject** and the constraints on the publishing system. For a more detailed description of the semantics involved, see **MediaObject**.

See Also

Alt, **AudioObject**, **Caption**, **Graphic**, **ImageObject**, **InlineGraphic**, **InlineMediaObject**, **MediaObject**, **VideoObject**

Examples

For examples, see **AudioObject**, **ImageObject**, **InformalFigure**, **InlineMediaObject**, **VideoObject**.

---

tfoot—A table footer consisting of one or more rows

Synopsis

Content Model
`tfoot ::=`
`(colspec*,row+)`		

Attributes **Name**	Common attributes **Type**	 **Default**
valign	*Enumeration:* bottom middle top	*None*

Parameter Entities	
%tbl.hdft.name;	%tbl.tgroup.mdl;

Description

The **TFoot** wrapper identifies the **Rows** of a table that form the foot of the table, as distinct from the header (**THead**) and body (**TBody**) rows.

Footer rows are always rendered at the end of the table, despite thier logical placement near the beginning.

Processing expectations

This element is expected to obey the semantics of the *CALS Table Model Document Type Definition*, as specified by *OASIS Technical Memorandum TM 9502:1995* (*http://www.oasis-open.org/html/a502.htm*). Footer rows are often presented in an alternate typographic style, such as boldface.

In paged media, if a table spans across multiple pages, footer rows are printed on the bottom of each page.

In our experience, relatively few formatters handle footer rows correctly.

Attributes

valign

`VAlign` specifies the vertical alignment of text (and other elements) within the cells of this **TFoot**.

See Also

colspec, **entry**, **entrytbl**, **InformalTable**, **row**, **spanspec**, **Table**, **tbody**, **tgroup**, **thead**

Examples

For examples, see **Table**.

tgroup—A wrapper for the main content of a table, or part of a table

Synopsis

Content Model

```
tgroup ::=
(colspec*,spanspec*,thead?,tfoot?,tbody)
```

Attributes Name	Common attributes Type	 Default
rowsep	NUMBER	*None*
colsep	NUMBER	*None*

Name	Type	Default
align	*Enumeration:* center char justify left right	*None*
cols	NUMBER	*Required*
tgroupstyle	NMTOKEN	*None*
charoff	NUTOKEN	*None*
char	CDATA	*None*
Parameter Entities		
`%tbl.table-main.mdl;`	`%tbl.table.mdl;`	

Description

A **TGroup** surrounds a logically complete portion of a table. Most tables consist of a single **TGroup**, but complex tables with widely varying column specifications may be easier to code using multiple **TGroup**s.

The **TGroup** specifies the number of columns in the table, and contains all of the header, body, and footer rows, along with any additional column or span specifications necessary to express the geometry of the table.

Most of the properties of rows, columns, and cells inherit their default characteristics from the enclosing **TGroup**.

Processing expectations

This element is expected to obey the semantics of the *CALS Table Model Document Type Definition*, as specified by *OASIS Technical Memorandum TM 9502:1995* (*http://www.oasis-open.org/html/a502.htm*).

Attributes

align

`Align` specifies the horizontal alignment of **Entry**s (or **EntryTbl**s) in cells of the **TGroup**. If `Char` is specified, see also `Char` and `CharOff`. Individual columns, spans, and cells can provide an alternate alignment.

char

`Char` specifies the alignment character when the `Align` attribute is set to `Char`.

charoff

`CharOff` specifies the percentage of the column's total width that should appear to the left of the first occurance of the character identified in `Char` when the `Align` attribute is set to `Char`.

cols

`Cols` specifies the number of columns in the table.

colsep

If `ColSep` has the value 1 (true), then a rule will be drawn to the right of all columns in this **TGroup**. A value of 0 (false) suppresses the rule. The rule to the right of the last column in the table is controlled by the `Frame` attribute of the enclosing **Table** or **InformalTable** and not the `ColSep`.

rowsep

If `RowSep` has the value 1 (true), then a rule will be drawn below all the rows in this **TGroup** (unless other, interior elements, suppress some or all of the rules). A value of 0 (false) suppresses the rule. The rule below the last row in the table is controlled by the `Frame` attribute of the enclosing **Table** or **InformalTable** and the `RowSep` of the last row is ignored. If unspecified, this attribute is inherited from enclosing elements.

tgroupstyle

`TGroupstyle` holds the name of a table group style defined in a stylesheet (e. g., a FOSI) that will be used to process this document.

See Also

colspec, **entry**, **entrytbl**, **InformalTable**, **row**, **spanspec**, **Table**, **tbody**, **tfoot**, **thead**

Examples

For examples, see **entrytbl**, **FootnoteRef**, **InformalTable**, **RefEntry**, **Table**.

thead—A table header consisting of one or more rows

Synopsis

Content Model
`thead ::=`
`(colspec*,row+)`		

Attributes **Name**	Common attributes **Type**	 **Default**
valign	*Enumeration:* bottom middle top	*None*
Parameter Entities `%tbl.entrytbl.mdl;`	 `%tbl.hdft.name;`	 `%tbl.tgroup.mdl;`

Description

The **THead** wrapper identifies the **Rows** of a table that form the head of the table, as distinct from the body (**TBody**) and foot (**TFoot**) rows.

Header rows are always rendered at the beginning of the table.

Processing expectations

This element is expected to obey the semantics of the *CALS Table Model Document Type Definition*, as specified by *OASIS Technical Memorandum TM 9502:1995* (*http://www.oasis-open.org/html/a502.htm*). Header rows are often presented in an alternate typographic style, such as boldface.

In paged media, if a table spans across multiple pages, header rows are printed at the top of each new page.

Attributes

valign

VAlign specifies the vertical alignment of text (and other elements) within the cells of this **THead**.

See Also

colspec, **entry**, **entrytbl**, **InformalTable**, **row**, **spanspec**, **Table**, **tbody**, **tfoot**, **tgroup**

Examples

For examples, see **RefEntry**, **Table**.

Tip—A suggestion to the user, set off from the text

Synopsis

Content Model

```
Tip ::=
(Title?,
 (CalloutList|GlossList|ItemizedList|OrderedList|SegmentedList|
  SimpleList|VariableList|LiteralLayout|ProgramListing|
  ProgramListingCO|Screen|ScreenCO|ScreenShot|Synopsis|
  CmdSynopsis|FuncSynopsis|FormalPara|Para|SimPara|Address|
  BlockQuote|Graphic|GraphicCO|MediaObject|MediaObjectCO|
  InformalEquation|InformalExample|InformalFigure|InformalTable|
  Equation|Example|Figure|Table|Procedure|Sidebar|Anchor|
  BridgeHead|Comment|IndexTerm)+)
```

Attributes	Common attributes	
Parameter Entities		
%admon.class;	%admon.exclusion;	%bookcomponent.content;
%component.mix;	%divcomponent.mix;	%highlights.mix;
%legalnotice.mix;	%para.mix;	%refcomponent.mix;
%sidebar.mix;	%tabentry.mix;	%tbl.entry.mdl;
%textobject.mix;		

Description

A **Tip** is an admonition set off from the main text.

In some types of documentation, the semantics of admonitions are clearly defined (**Caution** might imply the possibility of harm to equipment whereas **Warning** might imply harm to a person), but DocBook makes no such assertions.

Processing expectations

Formatted as a displayed block. Often outputs the generated text "Tip" or some other visible indication of the type of admonition, especially if a **Title** is not present. Sometimes outputs a graphical icon or other symbol as well.

See Also

Caution, Important, Note, Warning

Examples

```
<!DOCTYPE tip PUBLIC "-//OASIS//DTD DocBook V3.1//EN">
<tip>
<para>
If you tie your shoelaces, you're less likely to trip and
fall down.
</para>
</tip>
```

TIP If you tie your shoelaces, you're less likely to trip and fall down.

Title—The text of the title of a section of a document or of a formal block-level element

Synopsis

Mixed Content Model

```
Title ::=
((#PCDATA|FootnoteRef|XRef|Abbrev|Acronym|Citation|CiteRefEntry|
  CiteTitle|Emphasis|FirstTerm|ForeignPhrase|GlossTerm|Footnote|
  Phrase|Quote|Trademark|WordAsWord|Link|OLink|ULink|Action|
  Application|ClassName|Command|ComputerOutput|Database|Email|
  EnVar|ErrorCode|ErrorName|ErrorType|Filename|Function|GUIButton|
  GUIIcon|GUILabel|GUIMenu|GUIMenuItem|GUISubmenu|Hardware|
  Interface|InterfaceDefinition|KeyCap|KeyCode|KeyCombo|KeySym|
  Literal|Constant|Markup|MediaLabel|MenuChoice|MouseButton|
  MsgText|Option|Optional|Parameter|Prompt|Property|Replaceable|
  ReturnValue|SGMLTag|StructField|StructName|Symbol|SystemItem|
  Token|Type|UserInput|VarName|Anchor|Author|AuthorInitials|
  CorpAuthor|ModeSpec|OtherCredit|ProductName|ProductNumber|
  RevHistory|Comment|Subscript|Superscript|InlineGraphic|
  InlineMediaObject|InlineEquation|IndexTerm)+)
```

Attributes Name	Common attributes Type	 Default
Pagenum	CDATA	*None*

Parameter Entities		
%bibliocomponent.mix;	%bookcomponent.title.content;	%div.title.content;
%formalobject.title.content;	%refsect.title.content;	%sect.title.content;
%tbl.table-titles.mdl;	%tbl.table.mdl;	%titles;

Description

Title is widely used in DocBook. It identifies the titles of documents and parts of documents, and is the required caption on formal objects. It is also allowed as an optional title or caption on many additional block elements.

Processing expectations

Formatted as a displayed block. Titles are often repeated in several locations, for example, at the location where the object occurs, in the *table of contents*, and in running headers and footers.

DocBook does not offer any mechanism for indicating where a line break should occur in long titles. Titles are often repeated and no single line break is likely to be correct in all of the places where a title is used. Instead, you will have to rely on your processing system to provide a mechanism, such as a processing instruction, for identifing the location of forced line breaks.

There are some contexts in which a **Title** can appear more than once. For example, it may appear in both **Book** and **BookInfo**:

```
<book><title>Some Book Title</title>
<bookinfo>
  <title>Some Book Title</title>
  <author><firstname>Some</firstname><surname>Author</surname>
    </author>
</bookinfo>
...
```

In these contexts, if the **Title** occurs more than once, *the same* title must be used in both places. It is an error to use different titles, although DocBook has no way to detect the error.

4.0 *Future Changes*

The **InterfaceDefinition** element will be discarded in DocBook V4.0. It will no longer be available in the content model of this element.

Attributes

Pagenum

PageNum identifies the page on which this **Title** appears in some version of the printed document.

See Also

Subtitle, **TitleAbbrev**

Examples

```
<!DOCTYPE sect1 PUBLIC "-//OASIS//DTD DocBook V3.1//EN">
<sect1><title>A Sect One</title>
<para>
Actual content.
</para>
</sect1>
```

TitleAbbrev—The abbreviation of a **Title**

Synopsis

Mixed Content Model

```
TitleAbbrev ::=
((#PCDATA|FootnoteRef|XRef|Abbrev|Acronym|Citation|CiteRefEntry|
  CiteTitle|Emphasis|FirstTerm|ForeignPhrase|GlossTerm|Footnote|
  Phrase|Quote|Trademark|WordAsWord|Link|OLink|ULink|Action|
  Application|ClassName|Command|ComputerOutput|Database|Email|
  EnVar|ErrorCode|ErrorName|ErrorType|Filename|Function|GUIButton|
  GUIIcon|GUILabel|GUIMenu|GUIMenuItem|GUISubmenu|Hardware|
  Interface|InterfaceDefinition|KeyCap|KeyCode|KeyCombo|KeySym|
  Literal|Constant|Markup|MediaLabel|MenuChoice|MouseButton|
  MsgText|Option|Optional|Parameter|Prompt|Property|Replaceable|
  ReturnValue|SGMLTag|StructField|StructName|Symbol|SystemItem|
  Token|Type|UserInput|VarName|Anchor|Author|AuthorInitials|
  CorpAuthor|ModeSpec|OtherCredit|ProductName|ProductNumber|
  RevHistory|Comment|Subscript|Superscript|InlineGraphic|
  InlineMediaObject|InlineEquation|IndexTerm)+)
```

Attributes	Common attributes	
Parameter Entities		
%bibliocomponent.mix;	%bookcomponent.title.content;	%div.title.content;
%formalobject.title.content;	%refsect.title.content;	%sect.title.content;
%tbl.table.mdl;		

Description

TitleAbbrev holds an abbreviated version of a **Title**. One common use of **TitleAbbrev** is for the text used in running headers or footers, when the proper title is too long to be used conveniently.

Processing expectations

May be formatted inline or as a displayed block, depending on context. Abbreviated titles are usually used only in specific contexts, such as headers and footers, and suppressed everywhere else.

4.0 *Future Changes*

The **InterfaceDefinition** element will be discarded in DocBook V4.0. It will no longer be available in the content model of this element.

See Also

Subtitle, **Title**

Examples

```
<!DOCTYPE chapter PUBLIC "-//OASIS//DTD DocBook V3.1//EN">
<chapter><title>How to Configure the Menu Subsystem
of the Graphical User Interface</title>
<titleabbrev>Configuring Menus</titleabbrev>
<para>
Actual content.
</para>
</chapter>
```

For additional examples, see also **Article**, **Book**, **XRef**.

ToC—A table of contents

Synopsis

Content Model

```
ToC ::=
((DocInfo?,Title,Subtitle?,TitleAbbrev?)?,
 ToCfront*,
 (ToCpart|ToCchap)*,
 ToCback*)
```

Attributes	Common attributes	
Name	**Type**	**Default**
Pagenum	CDATA	*None*

Parameter Entities

%nav.class; %partcontent.mix;

Description

The ToC element defines a *table of contents* in a document.

The general structure of elements in a **ToC** is analogous to the structure of the document described. For example, a **ToC** for a **Book** might contain **TocFront** elements for the front-matter of the book, **TocChap** elements for the body of the book, and **TocBack** elements for the back matter. Inside each of these are additional elements reflecting the structure of each component.

Processing expectations

Formatted as a displayed block.

In real life, ToCs are usually generated automatically by the presentation system and never have to be represented explicitly in the document source.

Attributes

Pagenum

PageNum indicates the page on which this Table of Contents appears in the printed document

Examples

```
<!DOCTYPE toc PUBLIC "-//OASIS//DTD DocBook V3.1//EN">
<toc>
<tocfront pagenum="i">Preface</tocfront>
<tocpart>
  <tocchap>
    <tocentry pagenum="1">Getting Started with SGML/XML</tocentry>
    <toclevel1>
      <tocentry pagenum="1">HTML and SGML vs. XML</tocentry>
    </toclevel1>
    <toclevel1>
      <tocentry pagenum="3">How Does DocBook Fit In?</tocentry>
      <toclevel2>
        <tocentry pagenum="3">A Short DocBook History</tocentry>
      </toclevel2>
    </toclevel1>
    <!-- ... -->
  </tocchap>
</tocpart>
<!-- ... -->
<tocback pagenum="305">Bibliography</tocback>
</toc>
```

ToCback—An entry in a table of contents for a back matter component

Synopsis

Mixed Content Model

```
ToCback ::=
((#PCDATA|FootnoteRef|XRef|Abbrev|Acronym|Citation|CiteRefEntry|
  CiteTitle|Emphasis|FirstTerm|ForeignPhrase|GlossTerm|Footnote|
  Phrase|Quote|Trademark|WordAsWord|Link|OLink|ULink|Action|
  Application|ClassName|Command|ComputerOutput|Database|Email|
  EnVar|ErrorCode|ErrorName|ErrorType|Filename|Function|GUIButton|
```

GUIIcon | GUILabel | GUIMenu | GUIMenuItem | GUISubmenu | Hardware | Interface | InterfaceDefinition | KeyCap | KeyCode | KeyCombo | KeySym | Literal | Constant | Markup | MediaLabel | MenuChoice | MouseButton | MsgText | Option | Optional | Parameter | Prompt | Property | Replaceable | ReturnValue | SGMLTag | StructField | StructName | Symbol | SystemItem | Token | Type | UserInput | VarName | Anchor | Author | AuthorInitials | CorpAuthor | ModeSpec | OtherCredit | ProductName | ProductNumber | RevHistory | Comment | Subscript | Superscript | InlineGraphic | InlineMediaObject | InlineEquation | Synopsis | CmdSynopsis | FuncSynopsis | IndexTerm) +)		
Attributes	Common attributes	
Name	**Type**	**Default**
Label	CDATA	*None*
Linkend	IDREF	*None*
Pagenum	CDATA	*None*

Description

The **ToCback** element is a chapter-level **ToC** element for back matter (**Bibliography**s, **Index**s, and so on).

Processing expectations

Formatted as a displayed block.

In real life, **ToC**s are usually generated automatically by the presentation system and never have to be represented explicitly in the document source.

4.0 *Future Changes*

The **InterfaceDefinition** element will be discarded in DocBook V4.0. It will no longer be available in the content model of this element.

Attributes

Label

`Label` specifies an identifying string for presentation purposes.

Generally, an explicit `Label` attribute is used only if the processing system is incapable of generating the label automatically. If present, the `Label` is normative; it will used even if the processing system is capable of automatic labelling.

Linkend

`Linkend` points to the associated back matter element.

Pagenum

`PageNum` indicates the page on which the element of backmatter appears in some version of the printed document.

Examples

For examples, see **ToC**.

ToCchap—An entry in a table of contents for a component in the body of a document

Synopsis

Content Model
```
ToCchap ::=
(ToCentry+,ToClevel1*)
```

Attributes	Common attributes	
Name	**Type**	**Default**
Label	CDATA	*None*

Description

The **ToCchap** element is a chapter-level **ToC** element for components in the main body of a document.

Processing expectations

Formatted as a displayed block.

In real life, **ToC**s are usually generated automatically by the presentation system and never have to be represented explicitly in the document source.

Attributes

Label

`Label` specifies an identifying string for presentation purposes.

Generally, an explicit `Label` attribute is used only if the processing system is incapable of generating the label automatically. If present, the `Label` is normative; it will used even if the processing system is capable of automatic labelling.

Examples

For examples, see **ToC**.

ToCentry—A component title in a table of contents

Synopsis

Mixed Content Model
```
ToCentry ::=
((#PCDATA|FootnoteRef|XRef|Abbrev|Acronym|Citation|CiteRefEntry|
  CiteTitle|Emphasis|FirstTerm|ForeignPhrase|GlossTerm|Footnote|
  Phrase|Quote|Trademark|WordAsWord|Link|OLink|ULink|Action|
  Application|ClassName|Command|ComputerOutput|Database|Email|
  EnVar|ErrorCode|ErrorName|ErrorType|Filename|Function|GUIButton|
  GUIIcon|GUILabel|GUIMenu|GUIMenuItem|GUISubmenu|Hardware|
  Interface|InterfaceDefinition|KeyCap|KeyCode|KeyCombo|KeySym|
  Literal|Constant|Markup|MediaLabel|MenuChoice|MouseButton|
```

```
MsgText|Option|Optional|Parameter|Prompt|Property|Replaceable|
ReturnValue|SGMLTag|StructField|StructName|Symbol|SystemItem|
Token|Type|UserInput|VarName|Anchor|Author|AuthorInitials|
CorpAuthor|ModeSpec|OtherCredit|ProductName|ProductNumber|
RevHistory|Comment|Subscript|Superscript|InlineGraphic|
InlineMediaObject|InlineEquation|Synopsis|CmdSynopsis|
FuncSynopsis|IndexTerm)+)
```

Attributes	Common attributes	
Name	**Type**	**Default**
Linkend	IDREF	*None*
Pagenum	CDATA	*None*

Description

A **ToCentry** contains the title of an entry in a **ToC**. In entries that allow nested structure, such as **ToCchap**, this additional wrapper is necessary in order to require that a title be present.

Processing expectations

Formatted as a displayed block.

In real life, **ToC**s are usually generated automatically by the presentation system and never have to be represented explicitly in the document source.

4.0 *Future Changes*

The **InterfaceDefinition** element will be discarded in DocBook V4.0. It will no longer be available in the content model of this element.

Attributes

Linkend

`Linkend` points to the associated element in the document.

Pagenum

`PageNum` indicates the page on which this **ToC** element appears in some version of the printed document.

Examples

For examples, see **ToC**.

ToCfront—An entry in a table of contents for a front matter component

Synopsis

Mixed Content Model

```
ToCfront ::=
((#PCDATA|FootnoteRef|XRef|Abbrev|Acronym|Citation|CiteRefEntry|
  CiteTitle|Emphasis|FirstTerm|ForeignPhrase|GlossTerm|Footnote|
```

```
Phrase|Quote|Trademark|WordAsWord|Link|OLink|ULink|Action|
Application|ClassName|Command|ComputerOutput|Database|Email|
EnVar|ErrorCode|ErrorName|ErrorType|Filename|Function|GUIButton|
GUIIcon|GUILabel|GUIMenu|GUIMenuItem|GUISubmenu|Hardware|
Interface|InterfaceDefinition|KeyCap|KeyCode|KeyCombo|KeySym|
Literal|Constant|Markup|MediaLabel|MenuChoice|MouseButton|
MsgText|Option|Optional|Parameter|Prompt|Property|Replaceable|
ReturnValue|SGMLTag|StructField|StructName|Symbol|SystemItem|
Token|Type|UserInput|VarName|Anchor|Author|AuthorInitials|
CorpAuthor|ModeSpec|OtherCredit|ProductName|ProductNumber|
RevHistory|Comment|Subscript|Superscript|InlineGraphic|
InlineMediaObject|InlineEquation|Synopsis|CmdSynopsis|
FuncSynopsis|IndexTerm)+)
```

Attributes	Common attributes	
Name	**Type**	**Default**
Label	CDATA	*None*
Linkend	IDREF	*None*
Pagenum	CDATA	*None*

Description

The **ToCfront** element is a chapter-level **ToC** element for front matter such as **Prefaces**.

Processing expectations

Formatted as a displayed block.

In real life, **ToC**s are usually generated automatically by the presentation system and never have to be represented explicitly in the document source.

[4.0] *Future Changes*

The **InterfaceDefinition** element will be discarded in DocBook V4.0. It will no longer be available in the content model of this element.

Attributes

Label

`Label` specifies an identifying number or string that may be used in presentation.

Generally, an explicit `Label` attribute is used only if the processing system is incapable of generating the label automatically. If present, the `Label` is normative; it will used even if the processing system is capable of automatic labelling.

Linkend

`Linkend` points to the associated front matter element.

Pagenum

`PageNum` indicates the page on which the element of frontmatter appears in som version of the printed document.

Examples

For examples, see **ToC**.

ToClevel1—A top-level entry within a table of contents entry for a chapter-like component

Synopsis

Content Model
`ToClevel1 ::=`
`(ToCentry+,ToClevel2*)`	

Attributes	Common attributes

Description

The **ToClevel1** element is a **ToC** entry for a first-level section in a component.

Processing expectations

Formatted as a displayed block.

In real life, **ToCs** are usually generated automatically by the presentation system and never have to be represented explicitly in the document source.

Examples

For examples, see **ToC**.

ToClevel2—A second-level entry within a table of contents entry for a chapter-like component

Synopsis

Content Model
`ToClevel2 ::=`
`(ToCentry+,ToClevel3*)`	

Attributes	Common attributes

Description

The **ToClevel2** element is a **ToC** entry for a second-level section in a component.

Processing expectations

Formatted as a displayed block.

In real life, **ToCs** are usually generated automatically by the presentation system and never have to be represented explicitly in the document source.

Examples

For examples, see **ToC**.

ToClevel3—A third-level entry within a table of contents entry for a chapter-like component

Synopsis

Content Model
`ToClevel3 ::=`
`(ToCentry+,ToClevel4*)`	

Attributes	Common attributes

Description

The **ToClevel3** element is a **ToC** entry for a third-level section in a component.

Processing expectations

Formatted as a displayed block.

In real life, **ToC**s are usually generated automatically by the presentation system and never have to be represented explicitly in the document source.

Examples

For examples, see **ToC**.

ToClevel4—A fourth-level entry within a table of contents entry for a chapter-like component

Synopsis

Content Model
`ToClevel4 ::=`
`(ToCentry+,ToClevel5*)`	

Attributes	Common attributes

Description

The **ToClevel4** element is a **ToC** entry for a fourth-level section in a component.

Processing expectations

Formatted as a displayed block.

In real life, **ToC**s are usually generated automatically by the presentation system and never have to be represented explicitly in the document source.

Examples

For examples, see **ToC**.

ToClevel5—A fifth-level entry within a table of contents entry for a chapter-like component

Synopsis

Content Model
`ToClevel5 ::=`
`(ToCentry+)`	

Attributes	Common attributes

Description

The **ToClevel5** element is a **ToC** entry for a fifth-level section in a component.

The **ToC** machinery in DocBook has not been extended to handle the infinitely recursive nature of **Sections**. It may never be extended.

Processing expectations

Formatted as a displayed block.

In real life, **ToCs** are usually generated automatically by the presentation system and never have to be represented explicitly in the document source.

Examples

For examples, see **ToC**.

ToCpart—An entry in a table of contents for a part of a book

Synopsis

Content Model
`ToCpart ::=`
`(ToCentry+,ToCchap*)`	

Attributes	Common attributes

Description

The **ToCpart** element is a division-level **ToC** element for **Parts** and **References**.

Processing expectations

Formatted as a displayed block.

In real life, ToCs are usually generated automatically by the presentation system and never have to be represented explicitly in the document source.

Examples

For examples, see **ToC**.

Token—A unit of information

Synopsis

Mixed Content Model
`Token ::=`
`((#PCDATA|Replaceable|InlineGraphic|InlineMediaObject|IndexTerm)+)`		

Attributes	Common attributes	
Parameter Entities		
`%cptr.char.mix;`	`%ndxterm.char.mix;`	`%para.char.mix;`
`%programlisting.con-tent;`	`%refinline.char.mix;`	`%refname.char.mix;`
`%screen.content;`	`%tbl.entry.mdl;`	`%tech.char.class;`
`%title.char.mix;`		

Description

A **Token** identifies a unit of information. Usually, "tokens" are the result of some processing pass that has performed lexical analysis and divided a data set into the smallest units of information used for subsequent processing.

Exactly what constitutes a token varies by context.

Processing expectations

Formatted inline.

See Also

ClassName, **Interface**, **InterfaceDefinition**, **Property**, **StructField**, **StructName**, **Symbol**, **Type**

Examples

```
<!DOCTYPE para PUBLIC "-//OASIS//DTD DocBook V3.1//EN">
<para>
In parsing, line ends are turned into the <token>CRLF</token>, all other
whitespace becomes <token>WHITESP</token>.
</para>
```

In parsing, line ends are turned into the `CRLF`, all other whitespace becomes `WHITESP`.

Trademark—A trademark

Synopsis

Mixed Content Model

```
Trademark ::=
((#PCDATA|Link|OLink|ULink|Action|Application|ClassName|Command|
  ComputerOutput|Database|Email|EnVar|ErrorCode|ErrorName|
  ErrorType|Filename|Function|GUIButton|GUIIcon|GUILabel|GUIMenu|
  GUIMenuItem|GUISubmenu|Hardware|Interface|InterfaceDefinition|
  KeyCap|KeyCode|KeyCombo|KeySym|Literal|Constant|Markup|
  MediaLabel|MenuChoice|MouseButton|MsgText|Option|Optional|
  Parameter|Prompt|Property|Replaceable|ReturnValue|SGMLTag|
  StructField|StructName|Symbol|SystemItem|Token|Type|UserInput|
  VarName|Anchor|Comment|Subscript|Superscript|InlineGraphic|
  InlineMediaObject|Emphasis)+)
```

Attributes	Common attributes	
Name	**Type**	**Default**
Class	*Enumeration:* Copyright Registered Service Trade	"Trade"

Parameter Entities

`%docinfo.char.mix;`	`%gen.char.class;`	`%ndxterm.char.mix;`
`%para.char.mix;`	`%programlisting.content;`	`%refinline.char.mix;`
`%screen.content;`	`%tbl.entry.mdl;`	`%title.char.mix;`
`%word.char.mix;`		

Description

Trademark identifies a legal trademark.

One of the values of the `Class` attribute on **Trademark** is `Copyright`. DocBook also has a **Copyright** element, but it is confined to meta-information. A copyright in running text is best represented as `<trademark class=copyright>`.

Processing expectations

Formatted inline.

In addition to **Trademark**, two of the values of the `Class` attribute on **ProductName** make assertions about trademarks; presumably the same markup is intended for both **Trademark** and **ProductName** when they make assertions about trademarks.

4.0 *Future Changes*

The **InterfaceDefinition** element will be discarded in DocBook V4.0. It will no longer be available in the content model of this element.

Attributes

Class

`Class` indicates the type of **Trademark**. The default is `Trade`.

See Also

Copyright, **LegalNotice**, **ProductName**

Examples

```
<!DOCTYPE para PUBLIC "-//OASIS//DTD DocBook V3.1//EN">
<para>
The name <trademark class=registered>WebSite</trademark> is a
registered trademark of O'Reilly &amp; Associates, Inc.
</para>
```

The name WebSite® is a registered trademark of O'Reilly &Associates, Inc.

For additional examples, see also **AudioObject**, **ProductName**, **ScreenCO**.

Type—The classification of a value

Synopsis

Mixed Content Model
`Type ::=`
`((#PCDATA|Replaceable|InlineGraphic|InlineMediaObject|IndexTerm)+)`		

Attributes	Common attributes	
Parameter Entities		
`%cptr.char.mix;`	`%ndxterm.char.mix;`	`%para.char.mix;`
`%programlisting.content;`	`%refinline.char.mix;`	`%refname.char.mix;`
`%screen.content;`	`%tbl.entry.mdl;`	`%tech.char.class;`
`%title.char.mix;`		

Description

In general usage, **Type** identifies one member of a class of values.

In documenting computer programs, it identifies specifically a "type," as might be declared with `typedef` in the C programming language.

Processing expectations

Formatted inline.

See Also

ClassName, **Interface**, **InterfaceDefinition**, **Property**, **StructField**, **StructName**, **Symbol**, **Token**

Examples

```
<!DOCTYPE para PUBLIC "-//OASIS//DTD DocBook V3.1//EN">
<para>
The <function>geteuid</function> function returns a <type>uid_t</type> that
contains the user's <emphasis>effective</emphasis> user id.
</para>
```

The *geteuid* function returns a *uid_t* that contains the user's *effective* user id.

ULink—A link that addresses its target by means of a URL (Uniform Resource Locator)

Synopsis

Mixed Content Model

```
ULink ::=
((#PCDATA|FootnoteRef|XRef|Abbrev|Acronym|Citation|CiteRefEntry|
  CiteTitle|Emphasis|FirstTerm|ForeignPhrase|GlossTerm|Footnote|
  Phrase|Quote|Trademark|WordAsWord|Link|OLink|ULink|Action|
  Application|ClassName|Command|ComputerOutput|Database|Email|
  EnVar|ErrorCode|ErrorName|ErrorType|Filename|Function|GUIButton|
  GUIIcon|GUILabel|GUIMenu|GUIMenuItem|GUISubmenu|Hardware|
  Interface|InterfaceDefinition|KeyCap|KeyCode|KeyCombo|KeySym|
  Literal|Constant|Markup|MediaLabel|MenuChoice|MouseButton|
  MsgText|Option|Optional|Parameter|Prompt|Property|Replaceable|
  ReturnValue|SGMLTag|StructField|StructName|Symbol|SystemItem|
  Token|Type|UserInput|VarName|Anchor|Author|AuthorInitials|
  CorpAuthor|ModeSpec|OtherCredit|ProductName|ProductNumber|
  RevHistory|Comment|Subscript|Superscript|InlineGraphic|
  InlineMediaObject|InlineEquation|Synopsis|CmdSynopsis|
  FuncSynopsis|IndexTerm)+)
```

Attributes — Common attributes

Name	Type	Default
Type	CDATA	*None*
URL	CDATA	*Required*

Parameter Entities

%cptr.char.mix;	%docinfo.char.mix;	%indexdivcomponent.mix;
%link.char.class;	%ndxterm.char.mix;	%para.char.mix;
%programlisting.content;	%refinline.char.mix;	%screen.content;
%tbl.entry.mdl;	%title.char.mix;	%word.char.mix;

Description

The **ULink** element forms the equivalent of an HTML anchor (<A HREF="...">) for cross reference by a Uniform Resource Locator (URL).

Processing expectations

Formatted inline. When rendered online, it is natural to make the content of the **ULink** element an active link. When rendered in print media, the URL might be ignored, printed after the text of the link, or printed as a footnote.

Linking elements must not be nested within other linking elements (including themselves). Because DocBook is harmonizing towards XML, this restriction cannot easily be enforced by the DTD. The processing of nested linking elements is undefined.

4.0 *Future Changes*

The **InterfaceDefinition** element will be discarded in DocBook V4.0. It will no longer be available in the content model of this element.

Attributes

Type

Type is available for application-specific customization of the linking behavior.

URL

URL specifies the Uniform Resource Locator that is the target of the **ULink**.

See Also

Anchor, **Link**, **OLink**, **XRef**

Examples

```
<!DOCTYPE para PUBLIC "-//OASIS//DTD DocBook V3.1//EN">
<para>
For more information, see the O'Reilly catalog entry for
<ulink url="http://www.ora.com/catalog/tex/"><citetitle>Making TeX
Work</citetitle></ulink>.
</para>
```

For more information, see the O'Reilly catalog entry for *Making TeX Work* (*http://www.ora.com/catalog/tex/*).

For additional examples, see also **BookInfo**, **OLink**, **ProductNumber**, **SystemItem**.

UserInput—Data entered by the user

Synopsis

Mixed Content Model

```
UserInput ::=
((#PCDATA|Link|OLink|ULink|Action|Application|ClassName|Command|
  ComputerOutput|Database|Email|EnVar|ErrorCode|ErrorName|
  ErrorType|Filename|Function|GUIButton|GUIIcon|GUILabel|GUIMenu|
  GUIMenuItem|GUISubmenu|Hardware|Interface|InterfaceDefinition|
  KeyCap|KeyCode|KeyCombo|KeySym|Literal|Constant|Markup|
  MediaLabel|MenuChoice|MouseButton|MsgText|Option|Optional|
  Parameter|Prompt|Property|Replaceable|ReturnValue|SGMLTag|
  StructField|StructName|Symbol|SystemItem|Token|Type|UserInput|
  VarName|Anchor|Comment|Subscript|Superscript|InlineGraphic|
  InlineMediaObject|IndexTerm)+)
```

Attributes Name	Common attributes Type	Default
MoreInfo	*Enumeration:* None RefEntry	"None"

Parameter Entities		
%cptr.char.mix;	%ndxterm.char.mix;	%para.char.mix;
%programlisting.content;	%refinline.char.mix;	%refname.char.mix;
%screen.content;	%tbl.entry.mdl;	%tech.char.class;
%title.char.mix;		

Description

The **UserInput** element identifies words or phrases that the user is expected to provide as input to a computer program.

Note that **UserInput** is not a verbatim environment, but an inline.

Processing expectations

Formatted inline. The `MoreInfo` attribute can help generate a link or query to retrieve additional information. Often presented in a fixed width font.

4.0 *Future Changes*

The **InterfaceDefinition** element will be discarded in DocBook V4.0. It will no longer be available in the content model of this element.

Attributes

MoreInfo

If `MoreInfo` is set to `RefEntry`, it implies that a **RefEntry** exists which further describes the **UserInput**.

See Also

ComputerOutput, **Constant**, **EnVar**, **Filename**, **LineAnnotation**, **Literal**, **LiteralLayout**, **Markup**, **Option**, **Optional**, **Parameter**, **ProgramListing**, **Prompt**, **Replaceable**, **Screen**, **ScreenShot**, **SGMLTag**, **Synopsis**, **SystemItem**, **VarName**

Examples

```
<!DOCTYPE para PUBLIC "-//OASIS//DTD DocBook V3.1//EN">
<para>
At the system prompt, enter <userinput>xyzzy</userinput> to gain
supervisor access to the system.
</para>
```

At the system prompt, enter **`xyzzy`** to gain supervisor access to the system.

VarArgs—An empty element in a function synopsis indicating a variable number of arguments

Synopsis

Content Model
`VarArgs ::=`
`EMPTY`	

Attributes	Common attributes

Description

VarArgs indicates that a function takes a variable number of arguments.

Processing expectations

The **VarArgs** element produces generated text that indicates that the function takes a variable number of arguments. The exact generated text may vary. One common result is “`(...)`”.

See Also

FuncDef, **FuncParams**, **FuncPrototype**, **FuncSynopsisInfo**, **Function**, **ParamDef**, **Parameter**, **ReturnValue**, **Void**

Examples

```
<!DOCTYPE funcsynopsis PUBLIC "-//OASIS//DTD DocBook V3.1//EN">
<funcsynopsis>
<funcsynopsisinfo>
#include &lt;varargs.h&gt;
</funcsynopsisinfo>
<funcprototype>
  <funcdef>int <function>max</function></funcdef>
  <varargs>
</funcprototype>
</funcsynopsis>
```

```
#include <varargs.h>

int max(...);
```

For additional examples, see also **FuncSynopsis**.

VariableList—A list in which each entry is composed of a set of one or more terms and an associated description

Synopsis

Content Model
`VariableList ::=`
`((Title,TitleAbbrev?)?,`
` VarListEntry+)`		

Attributes **Name**	Common attributes **Type**	 **Default**
TermLength	CDATA	*None*
Parameter Entities		
`%admon.mix;`	`%bookcomponent.content;`	`%component.mix;`
`%divcomponent.mix;`	`%example.mix;`	`%footnote.mix;`
`%glossdef.mix;`	`%highlights.mix;`	`%indexdivcomponent.mix;`
`%legalnotice.mix;`	`%list.class;`	`%para.mix;`
`%qandaset.mix;`	`%refcomponent.mix;`	`%sidebar.mix;`
`%tabentry.mix;`	`%tbl.entry.mdl;`	`%textobject.mix;`

Description

A **VariableList** is a list consisting of **Terms** and their definitions or descriptions.

Processing expectations

Formatted as a displayed block.

There are many ways to deal with the problems presented in formatting a variable list with long **Terms**. DocBook does not mandate any particular presentation. The `TermLength` attribute may influence the presentation of **Terms**.

Attributes

TermLength

`TermLength` indicates a length beyond which the presentation engine may consider the **Term**(s) too long and select an alternate presentation of the **Term**(s) and/or, the associated **ListItem**.

See Also

CalloutList, **ItemizedList**, **ListItem**, **OrderedList**, **SegmentedList**, **SimpleList**

Examples

```
<!DOCTYPE variablelist PUBLIC "-//OASIS//DTD DocBook V3.1//EN">
<variablelist><title>Font Filename Extensions</title>
<varlistentry><term><filename>TTF</filename></term>
<listitem>
<para>
```

```
TrueType fonts.
</para>
</listitem>
</varlistentry>
<varlistentry><term><filename>PFA</filename></term>
              <term><filename>PFB</filename></term>
<listitem>
<para>
PostScript fonts.  <filename>PFA</filename> files are common on
<acronym>UNIX</acronym> systems, <filename>PFB</filename> files
are more common on Windows systems.
</para>
</listitem>
</varlistentry>
</variablelist>
```

Font Filename Extensions

TTF
: TrueType fonts.

PFA
PFB
: PostScript fonts. *PFA* files are common on UNIX systems, *PFB* files are more common on Windows systems.

For additional examples, see also **RefEntry**.

VarListEntry—A wrapper for a set of terms and the associated description in a variable list

Synopsis

Content Model	
`VarListEntry ::=` `(Term+,ListItem)`	
Attributes	Common attributes

Description

A **VarListEntry** is an entry in a **VariableList**. Each **VarListEntry** contains one or more **Terms** and their description or definition.

Processing expectations

Formatted as a displayed block.

Terms are usually formatted to make them stand out with respect to the text that follows. The best presentation depends on several factors, including the number and length of the terms. See **VariableList**.

Examples

For examples, see **RefEntry**, **VariableList**.

VarName—The name of a variable

Synopsis

Mixed Content Model VarName ::= (#PCDATA|Replaceable|InlineGraphic|InlineMediaObject|IndexTerm)*		
Attributes	Common attributes	
Parameter Entities		
%cptr.char.mix;	%ndxterm.char.mix;	%para.char.mix;
%programlisting.content;	%refinline.char.mix;	%refname.char.mix;
%screen.content;	%tbl.entry.mdl;	%tech.char.class;
%title.char.mix;		

Description

A **VarName** identifies a variable name in a programming or expression language. Variables most often get their values from **Literals**, **Replaceable** values, **Constants**, or **Symbols**.

Processing expectations

Formatted inline.

See Also

Command, **ComputerOutput**, **Constant**, **Literal**, **Markup**, **Option**, **Optional**, **Parameter**, **Prompt**, **Replaceable**, **SGMLTag**, **UserInput**

Examples

```
<!DOCTYPE para PUBLIC "-//OASIS//DTD DocBook V3.1//EN">
<para>
In Perl, <varname>@ARGV</varname> contains the command line paramters
used when the script was run.
</para>
```

In Perl, `@ARGV` contains the command line paramters used when the script was run.

VideoData—Pointer to external video data

Synopsis

Content Model

```
VideoData ::=
EMPTY
```

Attributes	Common attributes	
Name	**Type**	**Default**
Width	NUTOKEN	*None*
SrcCredit	CDATA	*None*
Scale	NUMBER	*None*
Format	*Enumeration:* BMP CGM-BINARY CGM-CHAR CGM-CLEAR DITROFF DVI EPS EQN FAX GIF GIF87a GIF89a IGES JPEG JPG linespecific PCX PIC PS SGML TBL TEX TIFF WMF WPG	*None*
Scalefit	NUMBER	*None*
Align	*Enumeration:* Center Left Right	*None*
Depth	NUTOKEN	*None*
EntityRef	ENTITY	*None*
FileRef	CDATA	*None*

Description

This element points to an external entity containing video data.

Processing expectations

May be formatted inline or as a displayed block, depending on context. Rendering a video is usually accomplished by reserving a rectangular area on the display and "running" the video in that frame.

There are two ways to provide content for **VideoData**: `EntityRef` or `FileRef`. It is best to use only one of these methods. However, if multiple sources are provided, `EntityRef` will be used in favor of `FileRef`.

Attributes

Align

`Align` specifies the horizontal alignment of the image data on the page or within the element that frames it.

Depth

`Depth` specifies the desired depth (vertical distance, at least in horizontal writing systems) of the video data.

EntityRef

`EntityRef` identifies the general entity which points to the content of the video data.

FileRef

`FileRef` specifies the name of the file which contains the content of the video data.

Format

`Format` identifies the format of the video data. The `Format` must be a defined notation.

Scale

`Scale` specifies integer representing a percentage scaling factor (retaining the relative dimensions of the original video frame). If unspecified, the value 100 (100%) is assumed.

Scalefit

If `ScaleFit` has the value 1 (true), then the video frame is to be scaled (uniformly) to the specified width or depth. The default value of 0 (false) indicates that the image will not be scaled to fit (although it may still be scaled by the `Scale` attribute).

SrcCredit

`SrcCredit` contains details about the source of the video data.

Width

`Width` indicates the width of the graphic.

VideoObject—A wrapper for video data and its associated meta-information

Synopsis

Content Model
`VideoObject ::=`
`(ObjectInfo?,VideoData)`	

Attributes	Common attributes
Parameter Entities `%mediaobject.mix;`	

Description

A **VideoObject** is a wrapper containing **VideoData** and its associated meta-information.

Processing expectations

May be formatted inline or as a displayed block, depending on context. It might not be rendered at all, depending on its placement within a **MediaObject** or **InlineMediaObject** and the constraints on the publishing system. For a more detailed description of the semantics involved, see **MediaObject**.

See Also

Alt, **AudioObject**, **Caption**, **Graphic**, **ImageObject**, **InlineGraphic**, **InlineMediaObject**, **MediaObject**, **TextObject**

Examples

```
<!DOCTYPE mediaobject PUBLIC "-//OASIS//DTD DocBook V3.1//EN">
<mediaobject>
<videoobject>
<videodata fileref='movie.avi'>
</videoobject>
<imageobject>
<imagedata fileref='movie-frame.gif'>
</imageobject>
<textobject>
<para>This video illustrates the proper way to assemble an
inverting time distortion device.
</para>
<warning>
<para>
It is imperative that the primary and secondary temporal
couplings not be mounted in the wrong order. Temporal
catastrophe is the likely result. The future you destroy
may be your own.
</para>
</warning>
</textobject>
</mediaobject>
```

Void—An empty element in a function synopsis indicating that the function in question takes no arguments

Synopsis

Content Model	
`Void ::=` `EMPTY`	
Attributes	Common attributes

Description

The **Void** element indicates explicitly that a **Function** has no arguments.

Processing expectations

The **Void** element produces generated text that indicates the function has no arguments (or returns nothing). The exact generated text may vary. One common result is `void`.

See Also

FuncDef, **FuncParams**, **FuncPrototype**, **FuncSynopsisInfo**, **Function**, **ParamDef**, **Parameter**, **ReturnValue**, **VarArgs**

Examples

For examples, see **FuncDef**, **FuncSynopsis**.

VolumeNum—The volume number of a document in a set (as of books in a set or articles in a journal)

Synopsis

Mixed Content Model	

`VolumeNum ::=`
`((#PCDATA|Link|OLink|ULink|Emphasis|Trademark|Replaceable|Comment|`
`  Subscript|Superscript|InlineGraphic|InlineMediaObject|IndexTerm)+)`	

Attributes	Common attributes
Parameter Entities `%bibliocomponent.mix;`	

Description

VolumeNum identifies the volume number of a **Book** in a **Set**, or a periodical. It is a wrapper for bibliographic information.

Processing expectations

Formatted inline. Sometimes suppressed.

See Also

InvPartNumber, **ISBN**, **ISSN**, **IssueNum**, **ProductNumber**, **PubsNumber**, **SeriesVolNums**

Examples

For examples, see **Article**, **Bibliography**, **BiblioMSet**.

Warning—An admonition set off from the text

Synopsis

Content Model

```
Warning ::=
(Title?,
 (CalloutList|GlossList|ItemizedList|OrderedList|SegmentedList|
  SimpleList|VariableList|LiteralLayout|ProgramListing|
  ProgramListingCO|Screen|ScreenCO|ScreenShot|Synopsis|
  CmdSynopsis|FuncSynopsis|FormalPara|Para|SimPara|Address|
  BlockQuote|Graphic|GraphicCO|MediaObject|MediaObjectCO|
  InformalEquation|InformalExample|InformalFigure|InformalTable|
  Equation|Example|Figure|Table|Procedure|Sidebar|Anchor|
  BridgeHead|Comment|IndexTerm)+)
```

Attributes	Common attributes	
Parameter Entities		
`%admon.class;`	`%admon.exclusion;`	`%bookcomponent.content;`
`%component.mix;`	`%divcomponent.mix;`	`%highlights.mix;`
`%legalnotice.mix;`	`%para.mix;`	`%refcomponent.mix;`
`%sidebar.mix;`	`%tabentry.mix;`	`%tbl.entry.mdl;`
`%textobject.mix;`		

Description

A **Warning** is an admonition, usually set off from the main text.

In some types of documentation, the semantics of admonitions are clearly defined (**Caution** might imply the possibility of harm to equipment whereas **Warning** might imply harm to a person), but DocBook makes no such assertions.

Processing expectations

Formatted as a displayed block. Often outputs the generated text "Warning" or some other visible indication of the type of admonition, especially if a **Title** is not present. Sometimes outputs a graphical icon or other symbol as well.

See Also

Caution, **Important**, **Note**, **Tip**

Examples

```
<!DOCTYPE warning PUBLIC "-//OASIS//DTD DocBook V3.1//EN">
<warning>
<para>
Striking your thumb with a hammer may cause severe pain and discomfort.
</para>
</warning>
```

WARNING Striking your thumb with a hammer may cause severe pain and discomfort.

For additional examples, see also **VideoObject**.

WordAsWord—A word meant specifically as a word and not representing anything else

Synopsis

Mixed Content Model

```
WordAsWord ::=
((#PCDATA|Acronym|Emphasis|Trademark|Link|OLink|ULink|Anchor|
  Comment|Subscript|Superscript|InlineGraphic|InlineMediaObject|
  IndexTerm)+)
```

Attributes	Common attributes	
Parameter Entities		
%gen.char.class;	%ndxterm.char.mix;	%para.char.mix;
%programlisting.content;	%refinline.char.mix;	%screen.content;
%tbl.entry.mdl;	%title.char.mix;	

Description

A lot of technical documentation contains words that have overloaded meanings. Sometimes it is useful to be able to use a word without invoking its technical meaning. The **WordAsWord** element identifies a word or phrase that might otherwise be interpreted in some specific way, and asserts that it should be interpreted simply as a word.

It is unlikely that the presentation of this element will be able to help readers understand the variation in meaning; good writing will have to achieve that goal. The real value of **WordAsWord** lies in the fact that full-text searching and indexing tools can use it to avoid false-positives.

Processing expectations

Formatted inline.

See Also

Abbrev, **Acronym**, **Emphasis**, **ForeignPhrase**, **Phrase**, **Quote**

Examples

```
<!DOCTYPE para PUBLIC "-//OASIS//DTD DocBook V3.1//EN">
<para>
A <wordasword>Term</wordasword> in Algebra has a very different meaning
than a <sgmltag>Term</sgmltag> in DocBook.
</para>
```

A *Term* in Algebra has a very different meaning than a **Term** in DocBook.

XRef—A cross reference to another part of the document

Synopsis

Content Model
`XRef ::=`
`EMPTY`		

Attributes **Name**	Common attributes **Type**	**Default**
Linkend Endterm	IDREF IDREF	*Required* *None*
Parameter Entities `%ndxterm.char.mix;`	`%para.char.mix;`	`%programlisting.content;`
`%refinline.char.mix;`	`%screen.content;`	`%tbl.entry.mdl;`
`%title.char.mix;`	`%xref.char.class;`	

Description

The **XRef** element forms a cross-reference from the location of the **XRef** to the element to which it points. Unlike **Link** and the other cross-referencing elements, **XRef** is empty. The processing system has to generate appropriate cross-reference text for the reader.

Processing expectations

If the `Endterm` attribute is specified, the content of the element pointed to by `Endterm` must be used as the text of the cross-reference, otherwise it is up to the application to generate appropriate cross reference text from the element pointed to by `Linkend`.

If the object *pointed to* has a specified `XRefLabel`, that should be used as the cross-reference text.

Attributes

Endterm

`Endterm` points to the element whose content is to be used as the text of the link.

Linkend

`Linkend` points to the target of the cross reference.

See Also

Anchor, **Link**, **OLink**, **ULink**

Examples

Consider the following example:

```
<!DOCTYPE book PUBLIC "-//OASIS//DTD DocBook V3.1//EN">
<book><title>An Example Book</title>
<chapter id="ch01"><title>XRef Samples</title>
<para>
This paragraph demonstrates several features of
<sgmltag>XRef</>.
</para>
<itemizedlist>
<listitem><para>A straight link generates the
cross-reference text: <xref linkend="ch02">.
</para></listitem>
<listitem><para>A link to an element with an
<sgmltag class="attribute">XRefLabel</sgmltag>:
<xref linkend="ch03">.
</para></listitem>
<listitem><para>A link with an
<sgmltag class="attribute">EndTerm</sgmltag>:
<xref linkend="ch04" endterm="ch04short">.
</para></listitem>
</itemizedlist>
</chapter>

<chapter id="ch02">
  <title>The Second Chapter</title>
  <para>Some content here</para>
</chapter>

<chapter id="ch03" xreflabel="Chapter the Third">
  <title>The Third Chapter</title>
  <para>Some content here</para>
</chapter>
```

```
<chapter id="ch04">
  <title>The Fourth Chapter</title>
  <titleabbrev id="ch04short">Chapter 4</titleabbrev>
  <para>Some content here</para>
</chapter>
</book>
```

One reasonable rendering for the content of the first chapter of this book is the following:

This paragraph demonstrates several features of **XRef**.

- A straight link generates the cross-reference text: Chapter 2, "The Second Chapter"
- A link to an element with an `XRefLabel`: Chapter the Third.
- A link with an `EndTerm`: Chapter 4.

Of course, in an online system, these references would also be links to the appropriate chapters.

For additional examples, see also **Part**.

Year—The year of publication of a document

Synopsis

Mixed Content Model
`Year ::=`
`((#PCDATA|Link|OLink|ULink|Emphasis|Trademark|Replaceable|Comment|`
`Subscript|Superscript|InlineGraphic|InlineMediaObject|IndexTerm)+)`	

Attributes	Common attributes

Description

Year identifies a year. In DocBook V3.0, this is only used in **Copyright**, to identify the year or years in which copyright is asserted.

Processing expectations

Formatted inline.

Examples

For examples, see **Bibliography**, **BiblioSet**, **BookInfo**, **Copyright**.

DocBook Parameter Entity Reference

The reference pages in this section describe each of the parameter entities used in DocBook. This information is most useful when you are writing a customization layer.

In the print version of this book, these reference pages provide only a brief summary of the function of each broad family of parameter entities. There are nearly 2,000 parameter entity declarations in DocBook, and displaying long lists of parameter entity names on paper seemed wasteful. The online version provides more detailed, hyperlinked information about each parameter entity family.

%.attlist; Parameter Entities*—Control individual attribute list declarations

Synopsis

Used to control marked sections around the declarations of individual attribute lists.

Description

The `%*.attlist;` parameter entities provide marked sections around individual attribute list declarations. You can selectively include or remove attribute list declarations from DocBook by changing these parameter entities.

%.attrib; Parameter Entities*—Define attributes on selected elements

Synopsis

Used to parameterize the definition of attribute lists.

Description

The `%*.attrib;` parameter entities contain partial attribute declaration lists. They are used in `<!ATTLIST...>` declarations to parameterize attribute names and values on selected elements.

%.attval; Parameter Entities*—Define attribute values

Synopsis

Used to parameterize attribute values.

Description

The `%*.attval;` and `%*.attvals;` parameter entities contain literal values. They are used in the declaration of attribute types to provide symbolic names for values. For example, `%yes.attval;` is used instead of 1, because it is more meaningful semantically.

CALS Table Model Parameter Entities—Control the CALS Table Model

Synopsis

Used to parameterize the CALS Table Model.

Description

The CALS Table Model is incorporated into DocBook by reference to the standard CALS Table Model DTD. The CALS Table Model DTD, like DocBook, can be customized by defining a number of parameter entities before including it. The following parameter entities are the CALS table-model related parameter entities defined by DocBook:

`%bodyatt;`	`%tbl.entrytbl.mdl;`	`%tbl.table.att;`
`%calstbls;`	`%tbl.hdft.excep;`	`%tbl.table.excep;`
`%paracon;`	`%tbl.hdft.mdl;`	`%tbl.table.mdl;`
`%secur;`	`%tbl.hdft.name;`	`%tbl.table.name;`
`%tabentry.mix;`	`%tbl.row.excep;`	`%tbl.tgroup.att;`
`%tbl.entry.excep;`	`%tbl.row.mdl;`	`%tbl.tgroup.mdl;`
`%tbl.entry.mdl;`	`%tbl.table-main.mdl;`	`%titles;`
`%tbl.entrytbl.excep;`	`%tbl.table-titles.mdl;`	`%yesorno;`

%.class; Parameter Entities*—Define the DocBook "classes"

Synopsis

Used to parameterize the collections of elements that form a single class `%list.class;`.

Description

Classes group elements of a similar type, for example, all the lists are in the `%list.class;`.

If you want to add a new kind of something (a new kind of list or a new kind of verbatim environment, for example), you generally want to add the name of the new element to the appropriate class.

Common Attribute Parameter Entities—Define the common attributes

Synopsis

Used to define the common attributes.

Description

These parameter entities define the attributes that are considered "common." Common attributes occur on every element.

They are provided by either the `%common.attrib;` parameter entity or the `%idreq.common.attrib;` parameter entity. Those parameter entities are defined in terms of other parameter entities that define individual common attributes. The following parameter entities are used to define the common attributes:

`%arch.attrib;`	`%idreq.attrib;`	`%revision.attrib;`
`%common.attrib;`	`%idreq.common.attrib;`	`%revisionflag.attrib;`
`%conformance.attrib;`	`%lang.attrib;`	`%userlevel.attrib;`
`%effectivity.attrib;`	`%os.attrib;`	`%vendor.attrib;`
`%id.attrib;`	`%remap.attrib;`	`%xreflabel.attrib;`

Heavy use of parameter entities for the common attributes makes global changes to common attributes easy.

%.content.module; Parameter Entities*—Control groups of element definitions

Synopsis

Used to control marked sections around groups of element declarations.

Description

The content module parameter entities provide marked sections around groups of related elements. You can selectively include or remove these elements from DocBook by changing these parameter entities.

%*.content; Parameter Entities—Specify content of selected elements

Synopsis

Used to control the content of selected elements.

Description

The content model of several elements in DocBook are controlled by parameter entities. This allows easy, global change of the content model of similar elements (for example, all components).

DocBook Module Parameter Entities—Control inclusion of DocBook modules

Synopsis

These parameter entities control the inclusion of DocBook modules.

Description

The modules listed here are included in DocBook DTD via parameter entity reference. For more information about these modules, and additional modules that can be defined, see Chapter 5, *Customizing DocBook*.

The following parameter entities are used to control the inclusion of DocBook modules:

```
%dbcent;     %dbhier;   %dbpool;
%dbgenent;   %dbnotn;
```

%*.element; Parameter Entities—Control individual element declarations

Synopsis

Used to control marked sections around the declarations of individual elements.

Description

The `%*.element;` parameter entities provide marked sections around individual element declarations. You can selectively include or remove element declarations from DocBook by changing these parameter entities.

%.exclusion; Parameter Entities*—Control SGML exclusions

Synopsis

Used to control the exclusion declarations on elements with exclusions.

Description

The `%*.exclusion;` parameter entities parameterize element exclusions. You can selectively include or remove elements from the exclusion by changing the appropriate parameter entity.

%.inclusion; Parameter Entities*—Control SGML inclusions

Synopsis

Used to control the inclusion declarations on elements with inclusions.

Description

The `%*.inclusion;` parameter entities parameterize element inclusions. You can selectively include or remove elements from the inclusion by changing the appropriate parameter entity. For example, if you remove **BeginPage** from the `%ubiq.inclusion;` parameter entity, it is no longer included everywhere in DocBook.

%local..attrib; Parameter Entities*—Allow attribute extension

Synopsis

Used to extend attribute declarations for each element.

Description

These parameter entities offer a place where you can easily add new attributes to DocBook elements. Each of the local attribute parameter entities is defined as empty by default in DocBook.

%local..class; Parameter Entities*—Allow class extension

Synopsis

Used to extend DocBook classes.

Description

These parameter entities offer a place where you can easily add new elements to the DocBook classes. Each of the local class parameter entities is defined as empty by default in DocBook.

%local..mix; Parameter Entities*—Allow mixture extension

Synopsis

Used to extend DocBook mixtures.

Description

These parameter entities offer a place where you can easily add new elements to the DocBook mixtures. Each of the local mixture parameter entities is defined as empty by default in DocBook.

%.mix; Parameter Entities*—Parameter entities that define the DocBook mixtures

Synopsis

Used to define DocBook mixtures.

Description

Mixtures are collections of classes that appear in content models. For example, the content model of an **Example** element includes the `%example.mix;`. Not every element's content model is a single mixture, but elements in the same class tend to have the same mixture in their content model.

If you want to change the content model of some class of elements (lists or admonitions, perhaps), you generally want to change the definition of the appropriate mixture.

%.module; Parameter Entities*—Control element definitions

Synopsis

Used to control marked sections around the declarations of individual elements and their attribute lists.

Description

The module parameter entities provide marked sections around element definitions. You can selectively include or remove elements from DocBook by changing these parameter entities.

Role Attribute Parameter Entities—Control the definition of role attributes

Synopsis

Used to define the `Role` attribute on each element.

Description

Role contains a string used to classify or subclassify an element.

It is parameterized in such a way that every element's role attribute is defined in its own parameter entity. This provides an easy mechanism for modifying the legal values of the **Role** attribute for particular elements.

DocBook Character Entity Reference

The reference pages in this section describe each of the ISO character entity sets referenced in DocBook.

A Note on Unicode Character References and Glyphs

Most of the glyphs this reference are from the TmsPF Roman font by Production First Software (*http://ourworld.compuserve.com/homepages/profirst/homepagx.htm*). A few glyphs are from Everson Mono (*http://www.indigo.ie/egt/celtscript/*), and are provided with the permission of Michael Everson.

The Unicode character numbers and reference glyphs in this section are examples only. Some characters have more than one Unicode representation and different Unicode characters may be appropriate in different contexts. Similarly, the glyph images offer only one of many possible representations for the specified character.

Unicode support requires much more than a simple character to glyph mapping; for more information on Unicode, consult *The Unicode Standard, Version 2.0* (*http://www.unicode.org/unicode/uni2book/u2.html*) and *Unicode Technical Report #8* (*http://www.unicode.org/unicode/reports/tr8.html*), which describes Unicode Version 2.1.

Added Math Symbols: Arrow Relations Character Entities (%isoamsa;)

%isoamsa;—Added Math Symbols: Arrow Relations Character Entities

Synopsis

The `%isoamsa;` parameter entity includes the ISO character entities with the public identifier:

```
ISO 8879:1986//ENTITIES Added Math Symbols: Arrow Relations//EN
```

Description

The following character entities are defined in this entity set:

Entity	Unicode #	Glyph	Description
cularr	21B6	↶	Anticlockwise top semicircle arrow
curarr	21B7	↷	Clockwise top semicircle arrow
dArr	21D3	⇓	Downwards double arrow
darr2	21CA	⇊	Downwards paired arrows
dharl	21C3	⇃	Downwards harpoon with barb leftwards
dharr	21C2	⇂	Downwards harpoon with barb rightwards
lAarr	21DA	⇚	Leftwards triple arrow
Larr	219E	↞	Leftwards two headed arrow
larr2	21C7	⇇	Leftwards paired arrows
larrhk	21A9	↩	Leftwards arrow with hook
larrlp	21AB	↫	Leftwards arrow with loop
larrtl	21A2	↢	Leftwards arrow with tail
lhard	21BD	↽	Leftwards harpoon with barb downwards
lharu	21BC	↼	Leftwards harpoon with barb upwards
hArr	21D4	⇔	Left right double arrow
harr	2194	↔	Left right arrow
lrarr2	21C6	⇆	Leftwards arrow over rightwards arrow
rlarr2	21C4	⇄	Rightwards arrow over leftwards arrow
harrw	21AD	↭	Left right wave arrow
rlhar2	21CC	⇌	Rightwards harpoon over leftwards harpoon
lrhar2	21CB	⇋	Leftwards harpoon over rightwards harpoon
lsh	21B0	↰	Upwards arrow with tip leftwards
map	21A6	↦	Rightwards arrow from bar
mumap	22B8	⊸	Multimap
nearr	2197	↗	North east arrow
nlArr	21CD	⇍	Leftwards double arrow with stroke
nlarr	219A	↚	Leftwards arrow with stroke
nhArr	21CE	⇎	Left right double arrow with stroke
nharr	21AE	↮	Left right arrow with stroke
nrarr	219B	↛	Rightwards arrow with stroke
nrArr	21CF	⇏	Rightwards double arrow with stroke
nwarr	2196	↖	North west arrow
olarr	21BA	↺	Anticlockwise open circle arrow
orarr	21BB	↻	Clockwise open circle arrow

Entity	Unicode #	Glyph	Description
rAarr	21DB	⇛	Rightwards triple arrow
Rarr	21A0	↠	Rightwards two headed arrow
rarr2	21C9	⇉	Rightwards paired arrows
rarrhk	21AA	↪	Rightwards arrow with hook
rarrlp	21AC	↬	Rightwards arrow with loop
rarrtl	21A3	↣	Rightwards arrow with tail
rarrw	21DD	⇝	Rightwards squiggle arrow
rhard	21C1	⇁	Rightwards harpoon with barb downwards
rharu	21C0	⇀	Rightwards harpoon with barb upwards
rsh	21B1	↱	Upwards arrow with tip rightwards
drarr	2198	↘	South east arrow
dlarr	2199	↙	South west arrow
uArr	21D1	⇑	Upwards double arrow
uarr2	21C8	⇈	Upwards paired arrows
vArr	21D5	⇕	Up down double arrow
varr	2195	↕	Up down arrow
uharl	21BF	↿	Upwards harpoon with barb leftwards
uharr	21BE	↾	Upwards harpoon with barb rightwards
xlArr		⟸	long l dbl arrow
xhArr		⟺	long l&r dbl arr
xharr		⟷	long l&r arr
xrArr		⟹	long rt dbl arr

Added Math Symbols: Binary Operators Character Entities (%isoamsb;)

%isoamsb;—Added Math Symbols: Binary Operators Character Entities

Synopsis

The `%isoamsb;` parameter entity includes the ISO character entities with the public identifier:

```
ISO 8879:1986//ENTITIES Added Math Symbols: Binary Operators//EN
```

Description

The following character entities are defined in this entity set:

Entity	Unicode #	Glyph	Description
amalg		[illegible]	amalgamation or coproduct
Barwed	22BC	⊼	Nand

Entity	Unicode #	Glyph	Description
barwed	22BC	⊼	Nand
Cap	22D2	⋒	Double intersection
Cup	22D3	⋓	Double union
cuvee	22CE	⋎	Curly logical or
cuwed	22CF	⋏	Curly logical and
diam	22C4	⋄	Diamond operator
divonx	22C7	⋇	Division times
intcal	22BA	⊺	Intercalate
lthree	22CB	⋋	Left semidirect product
ltimes	22C9	⋉	Left normal factor semidirect product
minusb	229F	⊟	Squared minus
oast	229B	⊛	Circled asterisk operator
ocir	229A	⊚	Circled ring operator
odash	229D	⊝	Circled dash
odot	2299	⊙	Circled dot operator
ominus	2296	⊖	Circled minus
oplus	2295	⊕	Circled plus
osol	2298	⊘	Circled division slash
otimes	2297	⊗	Circled times
plusb	229E	⊞	Squared plus
plusdo	2214	∔	Dot plus
rthree	22CC	⋌	Right semidirect product
rtimes	22CA	⋊	Right normal factor semidirect product
sdot	22C5	⋅	Dot operator
sdotb	22A1	⊡	Squared dot operator
setmn	2216	∖	Set minus
sqcap	2293	⊓	Square cap
sqcup	2294	⊔	Square cup
ssetmn		∖	sm reverse solidus
sstarf	22C6	⋆	Star operator
timesb	22A0	⊠	Squared times
top	22A4	⊤	Down tack
uplus	228E	⊎	Multiset union
wreath	2240	≀	Wreath product
xcirc	25EF	◯	Large circle
xdtri	25BD	▽	White down-pointing triangle
xutri	25B3	△	White up-pointing triangle

Entity	Unicode #	Glyph	Description
coprod	2210	∐	N-ary coproduct
prod	220F	∏	N-ary product
sum	2211	∑	N-ary summation

Added Math Symbols: Delimiters Character Entities (%isoamsc;)

%isoamsc;—Added Math Symbols: Delimiters Character Entities

Synopsis

The `%isoamsc;` parameter entity includes the ISO character entities with the public identifier:

```
ISO 8879:1986//ENTITIES Added Math Symbols: Delimiters//EN
```

Description

The following character entities are defined in this entity set:

Entity	Unicode #	Glyph	Description
rceil	2309	⌉	Right ceiling
rfloor	230B	⌋	Right floor
rpargt		⦔	right paren, gt
urcorn	231D	⌝	Top right corner
drcorn	231F	⌟	Bottom right corner
lceil	2308	⌈	Left ceiling
lfloor	230A	⌊	Left floor
lpargt		⦓	left parenthesis, gt
ulcorn	231C	⌜	Top left corner
dlcorn	231E	⌞	Bottom left corner

Added Math Symbols: Negated Relations Character Entities (%isoamsn;)

%isoamsn;—Added Math Symbols: Negated Relations Character Entities

Synopsis

The `%isoamsn;` parameter entity includes the ISO character entities with the public identifier:

```
ISO 8879:1986//ENTITIES Added Math Symbols: Negated Relations//EN
```

Description

The following character entities are defined in this entity set:

Entity	Unicode #	Glyph	Description
gnap		⪊	greater, not approximate
gne	2269	≩	Greater-than but not equal to
gnE	2269	≩	Greater-than but not equal to
gnsim	22E7	⋧	Greater-than but not equivalent to
gvnE		≩	gt, vert, not dbl eq
lnap		⪉	less, not approximate
lnE	2268	≨	Less-than but not equal to
lne	2268	≨	Less-than but not equal to
lnsim	22E6	⋦	Less-than but not equivalent to
lvnE		≨	less, vert, not dbl eq
nap	2249	≉	Not almost equal to
ncong	2247	≇	Neither approximately nor actually equal to
nequiv	2262	≢	Not identical to
ngE	2271	≱	Neither greater-than nor equal to
nge		≱	not greater-than-or-equal
nges	2271	≱	Neither greater-than nor equal to
ngt	226F	≯	Not greater-than
nle		≰	not less-than-or-equal
nlE	2270	≰	Neither less-than nor equal to
nles	2270	≰	Neither less-than nor equal to
nlt	226E	≮	Not less-than
nltri	22EA	⋪	Not normal subgroup of
nltrie	22EC	⋬	Not normal subgroup of or equal to
nmid	2224	∤	Does not divide
npar	2226	∦	Not parallel to
npr	2280	⊀	Does not precede
npre		⋠	not precedes, equals
nrtri	22EB	⋫	Does not contain as normal subgroup of
nrtrie	22ED	⋭	Does not contain as normal subgroup or equal
nsc	2281	⊁	Does not succeed
nsce		⋡	not succeeds, equals
nsim	2241	≁	Not tilde
nsime	2244	≄	Not asymptotically equal to
nsmid		∤	nshortmid

Entity	Unicode #	Glyph	Description
nspar		∦	not short par
nsub	2284	⊄	Not a subset of
nsube	2288	⊈	Neither a subset of nor equal to
nsubE	2288	⊈	Neither a subset of nor equal to
nsup	2285	⊅	Not a superset of
nsupE	2289	⊉	Neither a superset of nor equal to
nsupe	2289	⊉	Neither a superset of nor equal to
nvdash	22AC	⊬	Does not prove
nvDash	22AD	⊭	Not true
nVDash	22AF	⊯	Negated double vertical bar double right turnstile
nVdash	22AE	⊮	Does not force
prnap	22E8	⋨	Precedes but not equivalent to
prnE		⪵	precedes, not dbl eq
prnsim	22E8	⋨	Precedes but not equivalent to
scnap	22E9	⋩	Succeed but not equivalent to
scnE		⪶	succeeds, not dbl eq
scnsim	22E9	⋩	Succeed but not equivalent to
subne	228A	⊊	Subset of or not equal to
subnE	228A	⊊	Subset of or not equal to
supne	228B	⊋	Superset of or not equal to
supnE	228B	⊋	Superset of or not equal to
vsubnE		⫋	subset not dbl eq, var
vsubne		⊊	subset, not eq, var
vsupne		⊋	superset, not eq, var
vsupnE		⫌	super not dbl eq, var

Added Math Symbols: Ordinary Character Entities (%isoamso;)

%isoamso;—Added Math Symbols: Ordinary Character Entities

Synopsis

The `%isoamso;` parameter entity includes the ISO character entities with the public identifier:

```
ISO 8879:1986//ENTITIES Added Math Symbols: Ordinary//EN
```

Description

The following character entities are defined in this entity set:

Entity	Unicode #	Glyph	Description
ang	2220	∠	Angle
angmsd	2221	∡	Measured angle
beth	2136	ℶ	Bet symbol
bprime	2035	‵	Reversed prime
comp	2201	∁	Complement
daleth	2138	ℸ	Dalet symbol
ell	2113	ℓ	Script small l
empty		∅	emptyset /varnothing =small o, slash
gimel	2137	ℷ	Gimel symbol
image	2111	ℑ	Fraktur letter capital i
inodot	0131	ı	Latin small letter dotless i
jnodot		ȷ	jmath - small j, no dot
nexist	2204	∄	There does not exist
oS	24C8	Ⓢ	Circled latin capital letter S
planck	0127	ħ	Latin small letter h with stroke
real	211C	ℜ	Fraktur letter capital r
sbsol		∖	sbs - short reverse solidus
vprime	2032	′	Prime
weierp	2118	℘	Script capital p

Added Math Symbols: Relations Character Entities (%isoamsr;)

%isoamsr;—Added Math Symbols: Relations Character Entities

Synopsis

The `%isoamsr;` parameter entity includes the ISO character entities with the public identifier:

```
ISO 8879:1986//ENTITIES Added Math Symbols: Relations//EN
```

Description

The following character entities are defined in this entity set:

Entity	Unicode #	Glyph	Description
ape	224A	≊	Almost equal or equal to
asymp	224D	≍	Equivalent to

Entity	Unicode #	Glyph	Description
bcong	224C	≌	All equal to
bepsi		϶	such that
bowtie	22C8	⋈	Bowtie
bsim	223D	∽	Reversed tilde
bsime	22CD	⋍	Reversed tilde equals
bump	224E	≎	Geometrically equivalent to
bumpe	224F	≏	Difference between
cire	2257	≗	Ring equal to
colone	2254	≔	Colon equals
cuepr	22DE	⋞	Equal to or precedes
cuesc	22DF	⋟	Equal to or succeeds
cupre	227C	≼	Precedes or equal to
dashv	22A3	⊣	Left tack
ecir	2256	≖	Ring in equal to
ecolon	2255	≕	Equals colon
eDot	2251	≑	Geometrically equal to
esdot	2250	≐	Approaches the limit
efDot	2252	≒	Approximately equal to or the image of
egs	22DD	⋝	Equal to or greater-than
els	22DC	⋜	Equal to or less-than
erDot	2253	≓	Image of or approximately equal to
fork	22D4	⋔	Pitchfork
frown	2322	⌢	Frown
gap	2273	≳	Greater-than or equivalent to
gsdot	22D7	⋗	Greater-than with dot
gE	2267	≧	Greater-than over equal to
gel	22DB	⋛	Greater-than equal to or less-than
gEl	22DB	⋛	Greater-than equal to or less-than
ges		⩾	gt-or-equal, slanted
Gg	22D9	⋙	Very much greater-than
gl	2277	≷	Greater-than or less-than
gsim	2273	≳	Greater-than or equivalent to
Gt	226B	≫	Much greater-than
lap	2272	≲	Less-than or equivalent to
ldot	22D6	⋖	Less-than with dot
lE	2266	≦	Less-than over equal to
lEg	22DA	⋚	Less-than equal to or greater-than

Entity	Unicode #	Glyph	Description
leg	22DA	⋚	Less-than equal to or greater-than
les		⩽	less-than-or-eq, slant
lg	2276	≶	Less-than or greater-than
Ll	22D8	⋘	Very much less-than
lsim	2272	≲	Less-than or equivalent to
Lt	226A	≪	Much less-than
ltrie	22B4	⊴	Normal subgroup of or equal to
mid	2223	∣	Divides
models	22A7	⊧	Models
pr	227A	≺	Precedes
prap	227E	≾	Precedes or equivalent to
pre		⪯	precedes, equals
prsim	227E	≾	Precedes or equivalent to
rtrie	22B5	⊵	Contains as normal subgroup or equal to
samalg	2210	∐	N-ary coproduct
sc	227B	≻	Succeeds
scap	227F	≿	Succeeds or equivalent to
sccue	227D	≽	Succeeds or equal to
sce	227D	≽	Succeeds or equal to
scsim	227F	≿	Succeeds or equivalent to
sfrown		⌢	small down curve
smid		∣	
smile	2323	⌣	Smile
spar		∥	short parallel
sqsub	228F	⊏	Square image of
sqsube	2291	⊑	Square image of or equal to
sqsup	2290	⊐	Square original of
sqsupe	2292	⊒	Square original of or equal to
ssmile		⌣	small up curve
Sub	22D0	⋐	Double subset
subE	2286	⊆	Subset of or equal to
Sup	22D1	⋑	Double superset
supE	2287	⊇	Superset of or equal to
thkap		≈	thick approximate
thksim		∼	thick similar
trie	225C	≜	Delta equal to
twixt	226C	≬	Between

Entity	Unicode #	Glyph	Description
vdash	22A2	⊢	Right tack
Vdash	22A9	⊩	Forces
vDash	22A8	⊨	True
veebar	22BB	⊻	Xor
vltri	22B2	⊲	Normal subgroup of
vprop	221D	∝	Proportional to
vrtri	22B3	⊳	Contains as normal subgroup
Vvdash	22AA	⊪	Triple vertical bar right turnstile

Box and Line Drawing Character Entities (%isobox;)

%isobox;—Box and Line Drawing Character Entities

Synopsis

The `%isobox;` parameter entity includes the ISO character entities with the public identifier:

```
ISO 8879:1986//ENTITIES Box and Line Drawing//EN
```

Description

The following character entities are defined in this entity set:

Entity	Unicode #	Glyph	Description
boxh	2500	─	Box drawings light horizontal
boxv	2502	│	Box drawings light vertical
boxur	2514	└	Box drawings light up and right
boxul	2518	┘	Box drawings light up and left
boxdl	2510	┐	Box drawings light down and left
boxdr	250C	┌	Box drawings light down and right
boxvr	251C	├	Box drawings light vertical and right
boxhu	2534	┴	Box drawings light up and horizontal
boxvl	2524	┤	Box drawings light vertical and left
boxhd	252C	┬	Box drawings light down and horizontal
boxvh	253C	┼	Box drawings light vertical and horizontal
boxvR	255E	╞	Box drawings vertical single and right double
boxhU	2568	╨	Box drawings up double and horizontal single
boxvL	2561	╡	Box drawings vertical single and left double

Entity	Unicode #	Glyph	Description
boxhD	2565	╥	Box drawings down double and horizontal single
boxvH	256A	╪	Box drawings vertical single and horizontal double
boxH	2550	═	Box drawings double horizontal
boxV	2551	║	Box drawings double vertical
boxUR	255A	╚	Box drawings double up and right
boxUL	255D	╝	Box drawings double up and left
boxDL	2557	╗	Box drawings double down and left
boxDR	2554	╔	Box drawings double down and right
boxVR	2560	╠	Box drawings double vertical and right
boxHU	2569	╩	Box drawings double up and horizontal
boxVL	2563	╣	Box drawings double vertical and left
boxHD	2566	╦	Box drawings double down and horizontal
boxVH	256C	╬	Box drawings double vertical and horizontal
boxVr	255F	╟	Box drawings vertical double and right single
boxHu	2567	╧	Box drawings up single and horizontal double
boxVl	2562	╢	Box drawings vertical double and left single
boxHd	2564	╤	Box drawings down single and horizontal double
boxVh	256B	╫	Box drawings vertical double and horizontal single
boxuR	2558	╘	Box drawings up single and right double
boxUl	255C	╜	Box drawings up double and left single
boxdL	2555	╕	Box drawings down single and left double
boxDr	2553	╓	Box drawings down double and right single
boxUr	2559	╙	Box drawings up double and right single
boxuL	255B	╛	Box drawings up single and left double
boxDl	2556	╖	Box drawings down double and left single
boxdR	2552	╒	Box drawings down single and right double

Russian Cyrillic Character Entities (%isocyr1;)

%isocyr1;—Russian Cyrillic Character Entities

Synopsis

The `%isocyr1;` parameter entity includes the ISO character entities with the public identifier:

```
ISO 8879:1986//ENTITIES Russian Cyrillic//EN
```

Description

The following character entities are defined in this entity set:

Entity	Unicode #	Glyph	Description
acy	0430	а	Cyrillic small letter a
Acy	0410	А	Cyrillic capital letter A
bcy	0431	б	Cyrillic small letter be
Bcy	0411	Б	Cyrillic capital letter BE
vcy	0432	в	Cyrillic small letter ve
Vcy	0412	В	Cyrillic capital letter VE
gcy	0433	г	Cyrillic small letter ghe
Gcy	0413	Г	Cyrillic capital letter GHE
dcy	0434	д	Cyrillic small letter de
Dcy	0414	Д	Cyrillic capital letter DE
iecy	0435	е	Cyrillic small letter ie
IEcy	0415	Е	Cyrillic capital letter IE
iocy	0451	ё	Cyrillic small letter io
IOcy	0401	Ё	Cyrillic capital letter IO
zhcy	0436	ж	Cyrillic small letter zhe
ZHcy	0416	Ж	Cyrillic capital letter ZHE
zcy	0437	з	Cyrillic small letter ze
Zcy	0417	З	Cyrillic capital letter ZE
icy	0438	и	Cyrillic small letter i
Icy	0418	И	Cyrillic capital letter I
jcy	0439	й	Cyrillic small letter short i
Jcy	0419	Й	Cyrillic capital letter SHORT i
kcy	043A	к	Cyrillic small letter ka
Kcy	041A	К	Cyrillic capital letter KA
lcy	043B	л	Cyrillic small letter el
Lcy	041B	Л	Cyrillic capital letter EL
mcy	043C	м	Cyrillic small letter em
Mcy	041C	М	Cyrillic capital letter EM
ncy	043D	н	Cyrillic small letter en
Ncy	041D	Н	Cyrillic capital letter EN
ocy	043E	о	Cyrillic small letter o
Ocy	041E	О	Cyrillic capital letter O
pcy	043F	п	Cyrillic small letter pe
Pcy	041F	П	Cyrillic capital letter PE

Entity	Unicode #	Glyph	Description
rcy	0440	р	Cyrillic small letter er
Rcy	0420	Р	Cyrillic capital letter ER
scy	0441	с	Cyrillic small letter es
Scy	0421	С	Cyrillic capital letter ES
tcy	0442	т	Cyrillic small letter te
Tcy	0422	Т	Cyrillic capital letter TE
ucy	0443	у	Cyrillic small letter u
Ucy	0423	У	Cyrillic capital letter U
fcy	0444	ф	Cyrillic small letter ef
Fcy	0424	Ф	Cyrillic capital letter EF
khcy	0445	х	Cyrillic small letter ha
KHcy	0425	Х	Cyrillic capital letter HA
tscy	0446	ц	Cyrillic small letter tse
TScy	0426	Ц	Cyrillic capital letter TSE
chcy	0447	ч	Cyrillic small letter che
CHcy	0427	Ч	Cyrillic capital letter CHE
shcy	0448	ш	Cyrillic small letter sha
SHcy	0428	Ш	Cyrillic capital letter SHA
shchcy	0449	щ	Cyrillic small letter shcha
SHCHcy	0429	Щ	Cyrillic capital letter SHCHA
hardcy	044A	ъ	Cyrillic small letter hard sign
HARDcy	042A	Ъ	Cyrillic capital letter HARD sign
ycy	044B	ы	Cyrillic small letter yeru
Ycy	042B	Ы	Cyrillic capital letter YERU
softcy	044C	ь	Cyrillic small letter soft sign
SOFTcy	042C	Ь	Cyrillic capital letter SOFT sign
ecy	044D	э	Cyrillic small letter e
Ecy	042D	Э	Cyrillic capital letter E
yucy	044E	ю	Cyrillic small letter yu
YUcy	042E	Ю	Cyrillic capital letter YU
yacy	044F	я	Cyrillic small letter ya
YAcy	042F	Я	Cyrillic capital letter YA
numero	2116	№	Numero sign

Non-Russian Cyrillic Character Entities (%isocyr2;)

%isocyr2;—Non-Russian Cyrillic Character Entities

Synopsis

The `%isocyr2;` parameter entity includes the ISO character entities with the public identifier:

```
ISO 8879:1986//ENTITIES Non-Russian Cyrillic//EN
```

Description

The following character entities are defined in this entity set:

Entity	Unicode #	Glyph	Description
djcy	0452	ђ	Cyrillic small letter dje
DJcy	0402	Ђ	Cyrillic capital letter DJE
gjcy	0453	ѓ	Cyrillic small letter gje
GJcy	0403	Ѓ	Cyrillic capital letter GJE
jukcy	0454	є	Cyrillic small letter ukrainian ie
Jukcy	0404	Є	Cyrillic capital letter UKRAINIAN ie
dscy	0455	ѕ	Cyrillic small letter dze
DScy	0405	Ѕ	Cyrillic capital letter DZE
iukcy	0456	і	Cyrillic small letter byelorussian-ukrainian i
Iukcy	0406	І	Cyrillic capital letter BYELORUSSIAN-UKRAINIAN i
yicy	0457	ї	Cyrillic small letter yi
YIcy	0407	Ї	Cyrillic capital letter YI
jsercy	0458	ј	Cyrillic small letter je
Jsercy	0408	Ј	Cyrillic capital letter JE
ljcy	0459	љ	Cyrillic small letter lje
LJcy	0409	Љ	Cyrillic capital letter LJE
njcy	045A	њ	Cyrillic small letter nje
NJcy	040A	Њ	Cyrillic capital letter NJE
tshcy	045B	ћ	Cyrillic small letter tshe
TSHcy	040B	Ћ	Cyrillic capital letter TSHE
kjcy	045C	ќ	Cyrillic small letter kje
KJcy	040C	Ќ	Cyrillic capital letter KJE
ubrcy	045E	ў	Cyrillic small letter short u
Ubrcy	040E	Ў	Cyrillic capital letter SHORT u
dzcy	045F	џ	Cyrillic small letter dzhe
DZcy	040F	Џ	Cyrillic capital letter DZHE

Diacritical Marks Character Entities (%isodia;)

%isodia;—Diacritical Marks Character Entities

Synopsis

The `%isodia;` parameter entity includes the ISO character entities with the public identifier:

```
ISO 8879:1986//ENTITIES Diacritical Marks//EN
```

Description

The following character entities are defined in this entity set:

Entity	Unicode #	Glyph	Description
acute	00B4	ó	Acute accent
breve	02D8	ŏ	Breve
caron	02C7	ǒ	Caron
cedil	00B8	o̧	Cedilla
circ	005E	ô	Circumflex accent
dblac	02DD	ő	Double acute accent
die	00A8	ö	Diaeresis
dot	02D9	ȯ	Dot above
grave	0060	ò	Grave accent
macr	00AF	ō	Macron
ogon	02DB	o	Ogonek
ring	02DA	o̊	Ring above
tilde	02DC	õ	Small tilde
uml	00A8	ö	Diaeresis

Greek Letters Character Entities (%isogrk1;)

%isogrk1;—Greek Letters Character Entities

Synopsis

The `%isogrk1;` parameter entity includes the ISO character entities with the public identifier:

```
ISO 8879:1986//ENTITIES Greek Letters//EN
```

Description

The following character entities are defined in this entity set:

Entity	Unicode #	Glyph	Description
agr	03B1	α	Greek small letter alpha
Agr	0391	Α	Greek capital letter ALPHA
bgr	03B2	β	Greek small letter beta
Bgr	0392	Β	Greek capital letter BETA
ggr	03B3	γ	Greek small letter gamma
Ggr	0393	Γ	Greek capital letter GAMMA
dgr	03B4	δ	Greek small letter delta
Dgr	0394	Δ	Greek capital letter DELTA
egr	03B5	ε	Greek small letter epsilon
Egr	0395	Ε	Greek capital letter EPSILON
zgr	03B6	ζ	Greek small letter zeta
Zgr	0396	Ζ	Greek capital letter ZETA
eegr	03B7	η	Greek small letter eta
EEgr	0397	Η	Greek capital letter ETA
thgr	03B8	θ	Greek small letter theta
THgr	0398	Θ	Greek capital letter THETA
igr	03B9	ι	Greek small letter iota
Igr	0399	Ι	Greek capital letter IOTA
kgr	03BA	κ	Greek small letter kappa
Kgr	039A	Κ	Greek capital letter KAPPA
lgr	03BB	λ	Greek small letter lamda
Lgr	039B	Λ	Greek capital letter LAMDA
mgr	03BC	μ	Greek small letter mu
Mgr	039C	Μ	Greek capital letter MU
ngr	03BD	ν	Greek small letter nu
Ngr	039D	Ν	Greek capital letter NU
xgr	03BE	ξ	Greek small letter xi
Xgr	039E	Ξ	Greek capital letter XI
ogr	03BF	ο	Greek small letter omicron
Ogr	039F	Ο	Greek capital letter OMICRON
pgr	03C0	π	Greek small letter pi
Pgr	03A0	Π	Greek capital letter PI
rgr	03C1	ρ	Greek small letter rho
Rgr	03A1	Ρ	Greek capital letter RHO

Entity	Unicode #	Glyph	Description
sgr	03C3	σ	Greek small letter sigma
Sgr	03A3	Σ	Greek capital letter SIGMA
sfgr	03C2	ς	Greek small letter final sigma
tgr	03C4	τ	Greek small letter tau
Tgr	03A4	Τ	Greek capital letter TAU
ugr	03C5	υ	Greek small letter upsilon
Ugr	03A5	Υ	Greek capital letter UPSILON
phgr	03C6	φ	Greek small letter phi
PHgr	03A6	Φ	Greek capital letter PHI
khgr	03C7	χ	Greek small letter chi
KHgr	03A7	Χ	Greek capital letter CHI
psgr	03C8	ψ	Greek small letter psi
PSgr	03A8	Ψ	Greek capital letter PSI
ohgr	03C9	ω	Greek small letter omega
OHgr	03A9	Ω	Greek capital letter OMEGA

Monotoniko Greek Character Entities (%isogrk2;)

%isogrk2;—Monotoniko Greek Character Entities

Synopsis

The `%isogrk2;` parameter entity includes the ISO character entities with the public identifier:

```
ISO 8879:1986//ENTITIES Monotoniko Greek//EN
```

Description

The following character entities are defined in this entity set:

Entity	Unicode #	Glyph	Description
aacgr	03AC	ά	Greek small letter alpha with tonos
Aacgr	0386	Ά	Greek capital letter ALPHA with tonos
eacgr	03AD	έ	Greek small letter epsilon with tonos
Eacgr	0388	Έ	Greek capital letter EPSILON with tonos
eeacgr	03AE	ή	Greek small letter eta with tonos
EEacgr	0389	Ή	Greek capital letter ETA with tonos
idigr	03CA	ϊ	Greek small letter iota with dialytika
Idigr	03AA	Ϊ	Greek capital letter IOTA with dialytika
iacgr	03AF	ί	Greek small letter iota with tonos

Entity	Unicode #	Glyph	Description
Iacgr	038A	Ί	Greek capital letter IOTA with tonos
idiagr	0390	ΐ	Greek small letter iota with dialytika and tonos
oacgr	03CC	ό	Greek small letter omicron with tonos
Oacgr	038C	Ό	Greek capital letter OMICRON with tonos
udigr	03CB	ϋ	Greek small letter upsilon with dialytika
Udigr	03AB	Ϋ	Greek capital letter UPSILON with dialytika
uacgr	03CD	ύ	Greek small letter upsilon with tonos
Uacgr	038E	Ύ	Greek capital letter UPSILON with tonos
udiagr	03B0	ΰ	Greek small letter upsilon with tonos and dialytika
ohacgr	03CE	ώ	Greek small letter omega with tonos
OHacgr	038F	Ώ	Greek capital letter OMEGA with tonos

Greek Symbols Character Entities (%isogrk3;)

%isogrk3;—Greek Symbols Character Entities

Synopsis

The `%isogrk3;` parameter entity includes the ISO character entities with the public identifier:

```
ISO 8879:1986//ENTITIES Greek Symbols//EN
```

Description

The following character entities are defined in this entity set:

Entity	Unicode #	Glyph	Description
alpha	03B1	α	Greek small letter alpha
beta	03B2	β	Greek small letter beta
gamma	03B3	γ	Greek small letter gamma
Gamma	0393	Γ	Greek capital letter GAMMA
gammad	03DC	F	Greek letter digamma
delta	03B4	δ	Greek small letter delta
Delta	0394	Δ	Greek capital letter DELTA
epsi	03B5	ε	Greek small letter epsilon
epsiv	025B	ε	Latin small letter open e
epsis	03B5	ε	Greek small letter epsilon
zeta	03B6	ζ	Greek small letter zeta
eta	03B7	η	Greek small letter eta
thetas	03B8	θ	Greek small letter theta

Entity	Unicode #	Glyph	Description
Theta	0398	Θ	Greek capital letter THETA
thetav	03D1	ϑ	Greek theta symbol
iota	03B9	ι	Greek small letter iota
kappa	03BA	κ	Greek small letter kappa
kappav	03F0	ϰ	Greek kappa symbol
lambda	03BB	λ	Greek small letter lamda
Lambda	039B	Λ	Greek capital letter LAMDA
mu	03BC	μ	Greek small letter mu
nu	03BD	ν	Greek small letter nu
xi	03BE	ξ	Greek small letter xi
Xi	039E	Ξ	Greek capital letter XI
pi	03C0	π	Greek small letter pi
piv	03D6	ϖ	Greek omega symbol
Pi	03A0	Π	Greek capital letter PI
rho	03C1	ρ	Greek small letter rho
rhov	03F1	ϱ	Greek rho symbol
sigma	03C3	σ	Greek small letter sigma
Sigma	03A3	Σ	Greek capital letter SIGMA
sigmav	03C2	ς	Greek small letter final sigma
tau	03C4	τ	Greek small letter tau
upsi	03C5	υ	Greek small letter upsilon
Upsi	03D2	ϒ	Greek upsilon with hook symbol
phis	03C6	φ	Greek small letter phi
Phi	03A6	Φ	Greek capital letter PHI
phiv	03D5	ϕ	Greek phi symbol
chi	03C7	χ	Greek small letter chi
psi	03C8	ψ	Greek small letter psi
Psi	03A8	Ψ	Greek capital letter PSI
omega	03C9	ω	Greek small letter omega
Omega	03A9	Ω	Greek capital letter OMEGA

Alternative Greek Symbols Character Entities (%isogrk4;)

%isogrk4;—Alternative Greek Symbols Character Entities

Synopsis

The `%isogrk4;` parameter entity includes the ISO character entities with the public identifier:

```
ISO 8879:1986//ENTITIES Alternative Greek Symbols//EN
```

Description

The following character entities are defined in this entity set:

Entity	Unicode #	Glyph	Description
b.alpha	03B1	α	Greek small letter alpha
b.beta	03B2	β	Greek small letter beta
b.gamma	03B3	γ	Greek small letter gamma
b.Gamma	0393	Γ	Greek capital letter GAMMA
b.gammad	03DC	F	Greek letter digamma
b.delta	03B4	δ	Greek small letter delta
b.Delta	0394	Δ	Greek capital letter DELTA
b.epsi	03B5	ε	Greek small letter epsilon
b.epsiv	025B	ε	Latin small letter open e
b.epsis	03B5	ε	Greek small letter epsilon
b.zeta	03B6	ζ	Greek small letter zeta
b.eta	03B7	η	Greek small letter eta
b.thetas	03B8	θ	Greek small letter theta
b.Theta	0398	Θ	Greek capital letter THETA
b.thetav	03D1	ϑ	Greek theta symbol
b.iota	03B9	ι	Greek small letter iota
b.kappa	03BA	κ	Greek small letter kappa
b.kappav	03F0	ϰ	Greek kappa symbol
b.lambda	03BB	λ	Greek small letter lamda
b.Lambda	039B	Λ	Greek capital letter LAMDA
b.mu	03BC	μ	Greek small letter mu
b.nu	03BD	ν	Greek small letter nu
b.xi	03BE	ξ	Greek small letter xi
b.Xi	039E	Ξ	Greek capital letter XI
b.pi	03C0	π	Greek small letter pi

Entity	Unicode #	Glyph	Description
b.Pi	03A0	Π	Greek capital letter PI
b.piv	03D6	ϖ	Greek omega symbol
b.rho	03C1	ρ	Greek small letter rho
b.rhov	03F1	ϱ	Greek rho symbol
b.sigma	03C3	σ	Greek small letter sigma
b.Sigma	03A3	Σ	Greek capital letter SIGMA
b.sigmav	03C2	ς	Greek small letter final sigma
b.tau	03C4	τ	Greek small letter tau
b.upsi	03C5	υ	Greek small letter upsilon
b.Upsi	03D2	ϒ	Greek upsilon with hook symbol
b.phis	03C6	φ	Greek small letter phi
b.Phi	03A6	Φ	Greek capital letter PHI
b.phiv	03D5	ϕ	Greek phi symbol
b.chi	03C7	χ	Greek small letter chi
b.psi	03C8	ψ	Greek small letter psi
b.Psi	03A8	Ψ	Greek capital letter PSI
b.omega	03C9	ω	Greek small letter omega
b.Omega	03A9	Ω	Greek capital letter OMEGA

ISO Latin 1 Character Entities (%isolat1;)

%isolat1;—ISO Latin 1 Character Entities

Synopsis

The `%isolat1;` parameter entity includes the ISO character entities with the public identifier:

```
ISO 8879:1986//ENTITIES Added Latin 1//EN
```

Description

The following character entities are defined in this entity set:

Entity	Unicode #	Glyph	Description
aacute	00E1	á	Latin small letter a with acute
Aacute	00C1	Á	Latin capital letter A with acute
acirc	00E2	â	Latin small letter a with circumflex
Acirc	00C2	Â	Latin capital letter A with circumflex
agrave	00E0	à	Latin small letter a with grave
Agrave	00C0	À	Latin capital letter A with grave

Entity	Unicode #	Glyph	Description
aring	00E5	å	Latin small letter a with ring above
Aring	00C5	Å	Latin capital letter A with ring above
atilde	00E3	ã	Latin small letter a with tilde
Atilde	00C3	Ã	Latin capital letter A with tilde
auml	00E4	ä	Latin small letter a with diaeresis
Auml	00C4	Ä	Latin capital letter A with diaeresis
aelig	00E6	æ	Latin small letter ae
AElig	00C6	Æ	Latin capital letter AE
ccedil	00E7	ç	Latin small letter c with cedilla
Ccedil	00C7	Ç	Latin capital letter C with cedilla
eth	00F0	ð	Latin small letter eth
ETH	00D0	Ð	Latin capital letter ETH
eacute	00E9	é	Latin small letter e with acute
Eacute	00C9	É	Latin capital letter E with acute
ecirc	00EA	ê	Latin small letter e with circumflex
Ecirc	00CA	Ê	Latin capital letter E with circumflex
egrave	00E8	è	Latin small letter e with grave
Egrave	00C8	È	Latin capital letter E with grave
euml	00EB	ë	Latin small letter e with diaeresis
Euml	00CB	Ë	Latin capital letter E with diaeresis
iacute	00ED	í	Latin small letter i with acute
Iacute	00CD	Í	Latin capital letter I with acute
icirc	00EE	î	Latin small letter i with circumflex
Icirc	00CE	Î	Latin capital letter I with circumflex
igrave	00EC	ì	Latin small letter i with grave
Igrave	00CC	Ì	Latin capital letter I with grave
iuml	00EF	ï	Latin small letter i with diaeresis
Iuml	00CF	Ï	Latin capital letter I with diaeresis
ntilde	00F1	ñ	Latin small letter n with tilde
Ntilde	00D1	Ñ	Latin capital letter N with tilde
oacute	00F3	ó	Latin small letter o with acute
Oacute	00D3	Ó	Latin capital letter O with acute
ocirc	00F4	ô	Latin small letter o with circumflex
Ocirc	00D4	Ô	Latin capital letter O with circumflex
ograve	00F2	ò	Latin small letter o with grave
Ograve	00D2	Ò	Latin capital letter O with grave
oslash	00F8	ø	Latin small letter o with stroke

Entity	Unicode #	Glyph	Description
Oslash	00D8	Ø	Latin capital letter O with stroke
otilde	00F5	õ	Latin small letter o with tilde
Otilde	00D5	Õ	Latin capital letter O with tilde
ouml	00F6	ö	Latin small letter o with diaeresis
Ouml	00D6	Ö	Latin capital letter O with diaeresis
szlig	00DF	ß	Latin small letter sharp s
thorn	00FE	þ	Latin small letter thorn
THORN	00DE	Þ	Latin capital letter THORN
uacute	00FA	ú	Latin small letter u with acute
Uacute	00DA	Ú	Latin capital letter U with acute
ucirc	00FB	û	Latin small letter u with circumflex
Ucirc	00DB	Û	Latin capital letter U with circumflex
ugrave	00F9	ù	Latin small letter u with grave
Ugrave	00D9	Ù	Latin capital letter U with grave
uuml	00FC	ü	Latin small letter u with diaeresis
Uuml	00DC	Ü	Latin capital letter U with diaeresis
yacute	00FD	ý	Latin small letter y with acute
Yacute	00DD	Ý	Latin capital letter Y with acute
yuml	00FF	ÿ	Latin small letter y with diaeresis

Added Latin 2 Character Entities (%isolat2;)

%isolat2;—Added Latin 2 Character Entities

Synopsis

The `%isolat2;` parameter entity includes the ISO character entities with the public identifier:

```
ISO 8879:1986//ENTITIES Added Latin 2//EN
```

Description

The following character entities are defined in this entity set:

Entity	Unicode #	Glyph	Description
abreve	0103	ă	Latin small letter a with breve
Abreve	0102	Ă	Latin capital letter A with breve
amacr	0101	ā	Latin small letter a with macron
Amacr	0100	Ā	Latin capital letter A with macron
aogon	0105	ą	Latin small letter a with ogonek

Entity	Unicode #	Glyph	Description
Aogon	0104	Ą	Latin capital letter A with ogonek
cacute	0107	ć	Latin small letter c with acute
Cacute	0106	Ć	Latin capital letter C with acute
ccaron	010D	č	Latin small letter c with caron
Ccaron	010C	Č	Latin capital letter C with caron
ccirc	0109	ĉ	Latin small letter c with circumflex
Ccirc	0108	Ĉ	Latin capital letter C with circumflex
cdot	010B	ċ	Latin small letter c with dot above
Cdot	010A	Ċ	Latin capital letter C with dot above
dcaron	010F	ď	Latin small letter d with caron
Dcaron	010E	Ď	Latin capital letter D with caron
dstrok	0111	đ	Latin small letter d with stroke
Dstrok	0110	Đ	Latin capital letter D with stroke
ecaron	011B	ě	Latin small letter e with caron
Ecaron	011A	Ě	Latin capital letter E with caron
edot	0117	ė	Latin small letter e with dot above
Edot	0116	Ė	Latin capital letter E with dot above
emacr	0113	ē	Latin small letter e with macron
Emacr	0112	Ē	Latin capital letter E with macron
eogon	0119	ę	Latin small letter e with ogonek
Eogon	0118	Ę	Latin capital letter E with ogonek
gacute	01F5	ǵ	Latin small letter g with acute
gbreve	011F	ğ	Latin small letter g with breve
Gbreve	011E	Ğ	Latin capital letter G with breve
Gcedil	0122	Ģ	Latin capital letter G with cedilla
gcirc	011D	ĝ	Latin small letter g with circumflex
Gcirc	011C	Ĝ	Latin capital letter G with circumflex
gdot	0121	ġ	Latin small letter g with dot above
Gdot	0120	Ġ	Latin capital letter G with dot above
hcirc	0125	ĥ	Latin small letter h with circumflex
Hcirc	0124	Ĥ	Latin capital letter H with circumflex
hstrok	0127	ħ	Latin small letter h with stroke
Hstrok	0126	Ħ	Latin capital letter H with stroke
Idot	0130	İ	Latin capital letter I with dot above
Imacr	012A	Ī	Latin capital letter I with macron
imacr	012B	ī	Latin small letter i with macron
ijlig	0133	ĳ	Latin small ligature ij

Entity	Unicode #	Glyph	Description
IJlig	0132	Ĳ	Latin capital ligature ij
inodot	0131	ı	Latin small letter dotless i
iogon	012F	į	Latin small letter i with ogonek
Iogon	012E	Į	Latin capital letter I with ogonek
itilde	0129	ĩ	Latin small letter i with tilde
Itilde	0128	Ĩ	Latin capital letter I with tilde
jcirc	0135	ĵ	Latin small letter j with circumflex
Jcirc	0134	Ĵ	Latin capital letter J with circumflex
kcedil	0137	ķ	Latin small letter k with cedilla
Kcedil	0136	Ķ	Latin capital letter K with cedilla
kgreen	0138	ĸ	Latin small letter kra
lacute	013A	ĺ	Latin small letter l with acute
Lacute	0139	Ĺ	Latin capital letter L with acute
lcaron	013E	ľ	Latin small letter l with caron
Lcaron	013D	Ľ	Latin capital letter L with caron
lcedil	013C	ļ	Latin small letter l with cedilla
Lcedil	013B	Ļ	Latin capital letter L with cedilla
lmidot	0140	ŀ	Latin small letter l with middle dot
Lmidot	013F	Ŀ	Latin capital letter L with middle dot
lstrok	0142	ł	Latin small letter l with stroke
Lstrok	0141	Ł	Latin capital letter L with stroke
nacute	0144	ń	Latin small letter n with acute
Nacute	0143	Ń	Latin capital letter N with acute
eng	014B	ŋ	Latin small letter eng
ENG	014A	Ŋ	Latin capital letter ENG
napos	0149	ŉ	Latin small letter n preceded by apostrophe
ncaron	0148	ň	Latin small letter n with caron
Ncaron	0147	Ň	Latin capital letter N with caron
ncedil	0146	ņ	Latin small letter n with cedilla
Ncedil	0145	Ņ	Latin capital letter N with cedilla
odblac	0151	ő	Latin small letter o with double acute
Odblac	0150	Ő	Latin capital letter O with double acute
Omacr	014C	Ō	Latin capital letter O with macron
omacr	014D	ō	Latin small letter o with macron
oelig	0153	œ	Latin small ligature oe
OElig	0152	Œ	Latin capital ligature oe
racute	0155	ŕ	Latin small letter r with acute

Entity	Unicode #	Glyph	Description
Racute	0154	Ŕ	Latin capital letter R with acute
rcaron	0159	ř	Latin small letter r with caron
Rcaron	0158	Ř	Latin capital letter R with caron
rcedil	0157	ŗ	Latin small letter r with cedilla
Rcedil	0156	Ŗ	Latin capital letter R with cedilla
sacute	015B	ś	Latin small letter s with acute
Sacute	015A	Ś	Latin capital letter S with acute
scaron	0161	š	Latin small letter s with caron
Scaron	0160	Š	Latin capital letter S with caron
scedil	015F	ş	Latin small letter s with cedilla
Scedil	015E	Ş	Latin capital letter S with cedilla
scirc	015D	ŝ	Latin small letter s with circumflex
Scirc	015C	Ŝ	Latin capital letter S with circumflex
tcaron	0165	ť	Latin small letter t with caron
Tcaron	0164	Ť	Latin capital letter T with caron
tcedil	0163	ţ	Latin small letter t with cedilla
Tcedil	0162	Ţ	Latin capital letter T with cedilla
tstrok	0167	ŧ	Latin small letter t with stroke
Tstrok	0166	Ŧ	Latin capital letter T with stroke
ubreve	016D	ŭ	Latin small letter u with breve
Ubreve	016C	Ŭ	Latin capital letter U with breve
udblac	0171	ű	Latin small letter u with double acute
Udblac	0170	Ű	Latin capital letter U with double acute
umacr	016B	ū	Latin small letter u with macron
Umacr	016A	Ū	Latin capital letter U with macron
uogon	0173	ų	Latin small letter u with ogonek
Uogon	0172	Ų	Latin capital letter U with ogonek
uring	016F	ů	Latin small letter u with ring above
Uring	016E	Ů	Latin capital letter U with ring above
utilde	0169	ũ	Latin small letter u with tilde
Utilde	0168	Ũ	Latin capital letter U with tilde
wcirc	0175	ŵ	Latin small letter w with circumflex
Wcirc	0174	Ŵ	Latin capital letter W with circumflex
ycirc	0177	ŷ	Latin small letter y with circumflex
Ycirc	0176	Ŷ	Latin capital letter Y with circumflex
Yuml	0178	Ÿ	Latin capital letter Y with diaeresis
zacute	017A	ź	Latin small letter z with acute

Entity	Unicode #	Glyph	Description
Zacute	0179	Ź	Latin capital letter Z with acute
zcaron	017E	ž	Latin small letter z with caron
Zcaron	017D	Ž	Latin capital letter Z with caron
zdot	017C	ż	Latin small letter z with dot above
Zdot	017B	Ż	Latin capital letter Z with dot above

Numeric and Special Graphic Character Entities (%isonum;)

%isonum;—Numeric and Special Graphic Character Entities

Synopsis

The `%isonum;` parameter entity includes the ISO character entities with the public identifier:

```
ISO 8879:1986//ENTITIES Numeric and Special Graphic//EN
```

Description

The following character entities are defined in this entity set:

Entity	Unicode #	Glyph	Description
half	00BD	½	Vulgar fraction one half
frac12	00BD	½	Vulgar fraction one half
frac14	00BC	¼	Vulgar fraction one quarter
frac34	00BE	¾	Vulgar fraction three quarters
frac18	215B	⅛	Vulgar fraction one eighth
frac38	215C	⅜	Vulgar fraction three eighths
frac58	215D	⅝	Vulgar fraction five eighths
frac78	215E	⅞	Vulgar fraction seven eighths
sup1	00B9	^{1}	Superscript one
sup2	00B2	^{2}	Superscript two
sup3	00B3	^{3}	Superscript three
plus	002B	+	Plus sign
plusmn	00B1	±	Plus-minus sign
lt	003C	<	Less-than sign
equals	003D	=	Equals sign
gt	003E	>	Greater-than sign
divide	00F7	÷	Division sign
times	00D7	×	Multiplication sign

Entity	Unicode #	Glyph	Description
curren	00A4	¤	Currency sign
pound	00A3	£	Pound sign
dollar	0024	$	Dollar sign
cent	00A2	¢	Cent sign
yen	00A5	¥	Yen sign
num	0023	#	Number sign
percnt	0025	%	Percent sign
amp	0026	&	Ampersand
ast	002A	*	Asterisk
commat	0040	@	Commercial at
lsqb	005B	[	Left square bracket
bsol	005C	\	Reverse solidus
rsqb	005D	]	Right square bracket
lcub	007B	{	Left curly bracket
horbar	2015	―	Horizontal bar
verbar	007C			Vertical line
rcub	007D	}	Right curly bracket
micro	00B5	µ	Micro sign
ohm	2126	Ω	Ohm sign
deg	00B0	°	Degree sign
ordm	00BA	º	Masculine ordinal indicator
ordf	00AA	ª	Feminine ordinal indicator
sect	00A7	§	Section sign
para	00B6	¶	Pilcrow sign
middot	00B7	·	Middle dot
larr	2190	←	Leftwards arrow
rarr	2192	→	Rightwards arrow
uarr	2191	↑	Upwards arrow
darr	2193	↓	Downwards arrow
copy	00A9	©	Copyright sign
reg	00AE	®	Registered sign
trade	2122	™	Trade mark sign
brvbar	00A6	¦	Broken bar
not	00AC	¬	Not sign
sung			Eighth note
excl	0021	!	Exclamation mark
iexcl	00A1	¡	Inverted exclamation mark

Entity	Unicode #	Glyph	Description
quot	0022	"	Quotation mark
apos	0027	'	Apostrophe
lpar	0028	(	Left parenthesis
rpar	0029	)	Right parenthesis
comma	002C	,	Comma
lowbar	005F	_	Low line
hyphen	002D	-	Hyphen
period	002E	.	Period
sol	002F	/	Solidus
colon	003A	:	Colon
semi	003B	;	Semicolon
quest	003F	?	Question mark
iquest	00BF	¿	Inverted question mark
laquo	00AB	«	Left-pointing double angle quotation mark
raquo	00BB	»	Right-pointing double angle quotation mark
lsquo	2018	‘	Left single quotation mark
rsquo	2019	’	Right single quotation mark
ldquo	201C	“	Left double quotation mark
rdquo	201D	”	Right double quotation mark
nbsp	00A0	▯	No-break space
shy	00AD	-	Soft hyphen

Publishing Character Entities (%isopub;)

%isopub;—Publishing Character Entities

Synopsis

The `%isopub;` parameter entity includes the ISO character entities with the public identifier:

```
ISO 8879:1986//ENTITIES Publishing//EN
```

Description

The following character entities are defined in this entity set:

Entity	Unicode #	Glyph	Description
emsp	2003	▯	Em space
ensp	2002	▯	En space
emsp13	2004	▯	Three-per-em space

Entity	Unicode #	Glyph	Description
emsp14	2005		Four-per-em space
numsp	2007		Figure space
puncsp	2008		Punctuation space
thinsp	2009		Thin space
hairsp	200A		Hair space
mdash	2014	—	Em dash
ndash	2013	–	En dash
dash	2010	‐	Dash
blank	2423	␣	Open box
hellip	2026	…	Horizontal ellipsis
nldr	2025	‥	Two dot leader
frac13	2153	⅓	Vulgar fraction one third
frac23	2154	⅔	Vulgar fraction two thirds
frac15	2155	⅕	Vulgar fraction one fifth
frac25	2156	⅖	Vulgar fraction two fifths
frac35	2157	⅗	Vulgar fraction three fifths
frac45	2158	⅘	Vulgar fraction four fifths
frac16	2159	⅙	Vulgar fraction one sixth
frac56	215A	⅚	Vulgar fraction five sixths
incare	2105	℅	Care of
block	2588	█	Full block
uhblk	2580	▀	Upper half block
lhblk	2584	▄	Lower half block
blk14	2591	░	Light shade
blk12	2592	▒	Medium shade
blk34	2593	▓	Dark shade
marker	25AE	▮	Black vertical rectangle
cir	25CB	○	White circle
squ	25A1	□	White square
rect	25AD	▭	White rectangle
utri	25B5	▵	White up-pointing small triangle
dtri	25BF	▿	White down-pointing small triangle
star		☆	star, open
bull	2022	•	Bullet
squf	25AA	▪	Black small square
utrif	25B4	▴	Black up-pointing small triangle
dtrif	25BE	▾	Black down-pointing small triangle

Entity	Unicode #	Glyph	Description
ltrif	25C2	◂	Black left-pointing small triangle
rtrif	25B8	▸	Black right-pointing small triangle
clubs	2663	♣	Black club suit
diams	2666	♦	Black diamond suit
hearts	2661	♡	White heart suit
spades	2660	♠	Black spade suit
malt	2720	✠	Maltese cross
dagger	2020	†	Dagger
Dagger	2021	‡	Double dagger
check	2713	✓	Check mark
cross	2717	✗	Ballot x
sharp	266F	♯	Music sharp sign
flat	266D	♭	Music flat sign
male	2642	♂	Male sign
female	2640	♀	Female sign
phone	260E	☎	Black telephone
telrec	2315	⌕	Telephone recorder
copysr	2117	℗	Sound recording copyright
caret	2041	⁁	Caret insertion point
lsquor	201A	‚	Single low-nine quotation mark
ldquor	201E	„	Double low-nine quotation mark
fflig	FB00	ff	Latin small ligature ff
filig	007F	fi	Latin small ligature fi
fjlig		fj	small fj ligature
ffilig	FB03	ffi	Latin small ligature ffi
ffllig	FB04	ffl	Latin small ligature ffl
fllig	0090	fl	Latin small ligature fl
mldr	2026	…	Horizontal ellipsis
rdquor	201D	”	Right double quotation mark
rsquor	2019	’	Right single quotation mark
vellip	22EE	⋮	Vertical ellipsis
hybull	2043	⁃	Hyphen bullet
loz	25CA	◊	Lozenge
lozf		⧫	blacklozenge - lozenge, filled
ltri	25C3	◃	White left-pointing small triangle
rtri	25B9	▹	White right-pointing small triangle
starf		★	bigstar - star, filled

Entity	Unicode #	Glyph	Description
natur	266E	♮	Music natural sign
rx	211E	℞	Prescription take
sext	2736	✶	Six pointed black star
target	2316	⌖	Position indicator
dlcrop	230D	⌍	Bottom left crop
drcrop	230C	⌌	Bottom right crop
ulcrop	230F	⌏	Top left crop
urcrop	230E	⌎	Top right crop

General Technical Character Entities (%isotech;)

%isotech;—General Technical Character Entities

Synopsis

The `%isotech;` parameter entity includes the ISO character entities with the public identifier:

```
ISO 8879:1986//ENTITIES General Technical//EN
```

Description

The following character entities are defined in this entity set:

Entity	Unicode #	Glyph	Description
aleph	2135	ℵ	Alef symbol
and	2227	∧	Logical and
ang90	221F	∟	Right angle
angsph	2222	∢	Spherical angle
ap	2248	≈	Almost equal to
becaus	2235	∵	Because
bottom	22A5	⊥	Up tack
cap	2229	∩	Intersection
cong	2245	≅	Approximately equal to
conint	222E	∮	Contour integral
cup	222A	∪	Union
equiv	2261	≡	Identical to
exist	2203	∃	There exists
forall	2200	∀	For all
fnof	0192	ƒ	Latin small letter f with hook
ge	2265	≥	Greater-than or equal to

Entity	Unicode #	Glyph	Description
iff		⇔	iff =if and only if
infin	221E	∞	Infinity
int	222B	∫	Integral
isin	2208	∈	Element of
lang	3008	〈	Left angle bracket
lArr	21D0	⇐	Leftwards double arrow
le	2264	≤	Less-than or equal to
minus	2212	−	Minus sign
mnplus	2213	∓	Minus-or-plus sign
nabla	2207	∇	Nabla
ne	2260	≠	Not equal to
ni	220B	∋	Contains as member
or	2228	∨	Logical or
par	2225	∥	Parallel to
part	2202	∂	Partial differential
permil	2030	‰	Per mille sign
perp	22A5	⊥	Up tack
prime	2032	′	Prime
Prime	2033	″	Double prime
prop	221D	∝	Proportional to
radic	221A	√	Square root
rang	3009	〉	Right angle bracket
rArr	21D2	⇒	Rightwards double arrow
sim	223C	∼	Tilde operator
sime	2243	≃	Asymptotically equal to
square	25A1	□	White square
sub	2282	⊂	Subset of
sube	2286	⊆	Subset of or equal to
sup	2283	⊃	Superset of
supe	2287	⊇	Superset of or equal to
there4	2234	∴	Therefore
Verbar	2016	‖	Double vertical line
angst	212B	Å	Angstrom sign
bernou	212C	ℬ	Script capital b
compfn	2218	∘	Ring operator
Dot	00A8	ö	Diaeresis
DotDot	20DC	⃜	Combining four dots above

Entity	Unicode #	Glyph	Description
hamilt	210B	ℋ	Script capital h
lagran	2112	ℒ	Script capital l
lowast	2217	∗	Asterisk operator
notin	2209	∉	Not an element of
order	2134	ℴ	Script capital o
phmmat	2133	ℳ	Script capital m
tdot	20DB	⃛	Combining three dots above
tprime	2034	‴	Triple prime
wedgeq	2259	≙	Estimates

III

Appendixes

Installation

Installing the DocBook DTD

This appendix describes how to install the DocBook DTD on your system so that popular command-line tools like SP can use it. If you are installing DocBook for use with a commercial application, consult the documentation for your application as well.

This appendix describes the installation of DocBook V3.1. If you are using another distribution, the process should be about the same, but there may be minor differences. DocBook V3.1 is backward compatible with DocBook V3.0, and is the recommended distribution at the time of this writing.

Unpacking the DocBook V3.1 Distribution

DocBook is distributed on the DocBook web site (*http://www.oasis-open.org/docbook/*). You will also find a copy of the distribution on the CD-ROM.

The distribution consists of 14 files:

31chg.txt	Describes the changes in DocBook V3.1 from the preceding version (3.0)
40issues.txt	Summarizes backwards-incompatible changes planned for DocBook V4.0
50issues.txt	Summarizes backwards-incompatible changes planned for DocBook V5.0
cals-tbl.dtd	The CALS Table Model DTD
ChangeLog	A GNU-style ChangeLog summarizing the individual edits made on each file in the distribution since V3.0.
dbcent.mod	The character entity module
dbgenent.mod	The general entity module
dbhier.mod	The document hierarchy module
dbnotn.mod	The notations module
dbpool.mod	The information pool module

docbook.cat	A sample OASIS catalog for DocBook
docbook.dcl	An SGML Declaration suitable for DocBook
docbook.dtd	The DocBook DTD
readme.txt	The DocBook V3.1 "readme" file

Unpack the distribution into a directory on your system. The exact location is irrelevant. On UNIX systems it's common to put it somewhere under */usr/local* or */share* (for example, */usr/local/sgml/docbook* or */share/sgml/docbook*). On a PC, perhaps *c:\sgml\docbook*.

Getting the ISO Entity Sets

DocBook refers to a number of standard entity sets that are not distributed with DocBook. (They aren't distributed with DocBook because they aren't maintained by the DocBook TC. They're maintained by ISO.) If you've installed other SGML DTDs or tools, they may already be on your system.

If you are missing some of them, they are available from Robin Cover's pages at OASIS: *http://www.oasis-open.org/cover/ISOEnts.zip*.* See *http://www.oasis-open.org/cover/topics.html#entities* for more information.

The DocBook Catalog

DocBook uses public identifiers to refer to its constituent parts. In some sense, DocBook *is* DocBook because it has the formal public identifier "`-//OASIS//DTD DocBook V3.1//EN`". In order for tools on your system to find your locally installed copy of DocBook, you must map these public identifiers into system identifiers, i.e., filenames, on your system. For a complete discussion of catalog files, see "Public Identifiers, System Identifiers, and Catalog Files," in Chapter 2, *Creating DocBook Documents*.

The DocBook distribution includes a sample catalog, *docbook.cat*, which provides a mapping for all of the public identifiers referenced by DocBook. This mapping won't work "out of the box" for two reasons: first, your tools won't be able to find it, and second, the mappings for the ISO entity sets probably don't point to the right place on your system.

Finding the Catalog

If you've already got some other SGML DTDs installed, you probably already have a catalog file. In this case, the easiest thing to do is append the DocBook catalog

* The names of the entity files in this distribution do not exactly match the names of the files used in the catalog file distributed with DocBook (*docbook.cat*). Make sure your catalog file points to the right files.

entries to the end of your existing catalog and then change them to point to the files on your system.

If DocBook is the first DTD that you're installing, make a copy of *docbook.cat* and call it *catalog*. Put this file in a higher-level directory and edit the relative pathnames that it contains to point to the actual locations of the files on your system. For example, if you installed DocBook in */share/sgml/docbk30/*, put the *catalog* in */share/sgml/*.

In order for applications to find your catalog file(s), you may have to change the application preferences or set an environment variable. For SP and Jade, set the environment variable *SGML_CATALOG_FILES* to the delimited list of catalog filenames. On my system, this looks like:

```
SGML_CATALOG_FILES=./catalog;n:/share/sgml/catalog;n:/adept80/doctypes/
catalog.jade;j:/jade/catalog
```

(On a UNIX machine, use colons instead of semicolons to delimit the filenames.)

If you don't wish to set the environment variable, you can explicitly pass the name of each catalog to the SP application with the *-c* option, like this:

```
nsgmls -c ./catalog -c n:/share/sgml/catalog -c othercatalogs ...
```

Fixing the Catalog

The basic format of each entry in the DocBook catalog is:

```
PUBLIC "some public id" "some filename"
```

What you have to do is change each of the "some filenames" to point to the actual name of the file on your system.

NOTE Filenames should be supplied using absolute filenames, or paths relative to the location of the *catalog* file.

To continue with the example above, let's say that you've got:

- DocBook in */share/sgml/docbk30/*,
- The ISO entities in */share/sgml/entities/8879/*, and
- Your catalog in */share/sgml/catalog*

Then you would change the catalog entry for the DTD to be:

```
PUBLIC "-//OASIS//DTD DocBook V3.1//EN" "docbk30/docbook.dtd"
```

You would change the catalog entry for the general technical character entities to:

```
PUBLIC "ISO 8879:1986//ENTITIES General Technical//EN" "entities/8879/iso-
tech.gml"
```

And similarly for the other public identifiers used by DocBook. In each case, the filename specified for the public identifier should be the name of the file on your system, specified as an absolute filename, or relative to the location of the *catalog* in which it occurs.

Mapping System Identifiers for XML

Since XML documents are required to have system identifiers, but are not required to have public identifiers, it's likely that some of the documents you want to process will only have system identifiers.

It turns out that you can still take advantage of the catalog in this case. The SYSTEM directive allows you to map the system identifier used in the document to the actual location on your system.

Suppose that you work with a colleague who uses the system identifier "file:///c:/sgml/db3xml/db3xml.dtd" to identify the XML version of DocBook on her system. On your system, you want to map that to "/share/sgml/db3xml/db3xml.dtd". The following entry in your catalog will do the trick:

```
SYSTEM "http://docbook.org/docbook/xml/1.4/db3xml.dtd" "/share/sgml/db3xml/
db3xml.dtd"
```

Unfortunately, this technique only works with applications that read and understand catalog files.

Testing Your Installation

The best way to test your installation is with a simple command-line parser like *nsgmls* from SP. Create a small test document, like this:

```
<!DOCTYPE chapter PUBLIC "-//OASIS//DTD DocBook V3.1//EN">
<chapter><title>Test Chapter</title>
<para>
This is a test document.
</para>
</chapter>
```

and run the following command:

```
nsgmls -sv test.sgm
```

If the *nsgmls* command produces errors, review your catalog and resolve the errors. You can ignore warnings about DTDDECL being unsupported. It is unsupported, and there's no way to disable the warning message. Note, however, that this may also affect which SGML declaration gets used. When in doubt, pass the correct declaration explicitly and see if that corrects any problems. (To parse *test.sgm* with the declaration *docbook.dcl* explicitly, run *nsgmls -sv docbook.dcl test.sgm.*)

For some suggestions about how to work around these problems in SP and Jade, see the next section, "Installing Jade."

Installing Jade

For simplicity, the instructions assume that you are working with Jade on a Microsoft Windows machine. These instructions should be just as useful if you are working on another platform, except for the normal cross-platform idiosyncracies (path and filename separator characters, use of drive letters, etc.).

Download and unpack the Jade (*http://www.jclark.com/jade/*) distribution. Binary distributions are available for some platforms, which makes installation a simple matter of unpacking the distribution. Or you can build Jade from the source (consult the documentation that comes with Jade for more detail about building it from source).

You may wish to add the directory where you installed Jade to your *PATH*. If not, make sure that you use the fully qualified name of the executable when you run the commands below.

Setting Up the Catalog

First, the catalog needs to be set up as described in "The DocBook Catalog" in order for Jade to be able to parse your DocBook documents. In addition, Jade comes with its own *catalog* file that you must add to the *SGML_CATALOG_FILES* environment variable or otherwise make available to Jade.

Testing Jade

Download *jtest.sgm* (*http://nwalsh.com/docbook/dsssl/doc/testdata/jtest.sgm*) and *jtest.dsl* (*http://nwalsh.com/docbook/dsssl/doc/testdata/jtest.dsl*). (Or get them off the CD-ROM in FIXME.) These are self-contained test documents. Test Jade by running:

```
jade -t rtf -d jtest.dsl jtest.sgm
```

This command should silently produce jtest.rtf (*http://nwalsh.com/docbook/dsssl/doc/testdata/jtest.rtf*). If you encounter warnings or errors here, Jade is not installed correctly. One possible culprit is your catalog setup. See "Dealing with Multiple Declarations," in Chapter 4, *Publishing DocBook Documents*.

DTDDECL Warnings

One annoying shortcoming in Jade is that it does not support the `DTDDECL` catalog directive and it complains loudly if it encounters one. In Jade, it's almost always possible to work around the problems that `DTDDECL` would solve, so you can generally ignore the warnings.

If you also use applications that do understand DTDDECL, and find the warnings too distracting to bear, setup alternate catalogs for SP applications, *catalog.jade*, that are identical to your normal catalogs but do not contain any DTDDECL entries. You can then avoid the warnings by putting *catalog.jade* in your *SGML_CATALOG_FILES* path, instead of *catalog*.

Installing the Modular DocBook Stylesheets

Norman Walsh (*http://nwalsh.com/~ndw/*) (one of your intrepid authors ;-) maintains two DSSSL stylesheets for DocBook, one for print and one for online (HTML) output. You can obtain both of these stylesheets from *http://nwalsh.com/docbook/dsssl/*. (A recent version is also on the CD-ROM.)

1. If you have not already done so, download and install the DocBook DTD as described in "Installing the DocBook DTD."
2. Likewise, if Jade is not installed on your system, download and install it as described in "Installing Jade."
3. Download and unpack the stylesheet distribution (*http://nwalsh.com/docbook/dsssl/*).
4. Test the installation by processing *test.sgm* (from the previous section) with Jade:

   ```
   jade -t rtf -d d:\where-you-unpacked-the-stylesheets\docbook\print\docbook.dsl
   test.sgm
   ```

   This command should silently produce *test.rtf* (*http://nwalsh.com/docbook/dsssl/doc/testdata/test.rtf*). If not, and the preceding test succeeded, something has gone wrong—contact the maintainer (*http://nwalsh.com/~ndw/contact.html*).

   To test the HTML stylesheet, run:

   ```
   jade -t sgml -d d:\where-you-unpacked-the-stylesheets\docbook\html\docbook.dsl
   test.sgm
   ```

   This command should silently produce *c01.htm* (*http://nwalsh.com/docbook/dsssl/doc/testdata/c01.htm*). If not, and the preceding test succeeded, something has gone wrong; contact the maintainer (*http://nwalsh.com/~ndw/contact.html*).

B

DocBook and XML

XML, the Extensible Markup Language (*http://www.w3.org/TR/REC-xml*), is a simple dialect of SGML. In the words of the XML specification, "the goal [of XML] is to enable generic SGML to be served, received, and processed on the Web in the way that is now possible with HTML."

XML raises two issues with respect to DocBook:

- Are DocBook SGML instances valid XML instances?
- Can the DocBook DTD be made into a valid XML DTD?

If you have an existing SGML system, and your primary goal is to serve DocBook documents over the Web as XML, only the first of these issues is relevant. As the popularity of XML grows, we will see more and more XML-aware tools that don't implement full ISO 8879 SGML. If your goal is to author DocBook documents with one of this new generation of tools, you will only be able to achieve validity with an XML DocBook DTD.

Although not yet officially adopted by the OASIS DocBook Technical Committee, an XML version of DocBook is available now and provided on the CD-ROM.

DocBook Instances as XML

Most DocBook documents can be made into well-formed XML documents very easily. With few exceptions, valid DocBook SGML instances are also well-formed XML instances. The following areas may need to be addressed.

System Identifiers

It is common for SGML instances to use only a public identifier in document type and parameter entity declarations:

```
<!DOCTYPE chapter PUBLIC "-//OASIS//DTD DocBook V3.1//EN">
<chapter><title>Chapter Title</title>
<para>
This <emphasis>paragraph</emphasis> is important.
</para>
</chapter>
```

XML requires a system identifier:

```
<!DOCTYPE chapter PUBLIC "-//Norman Walsh//DTD DocBk XML V1.4//EN"
                  "http://docbook.org/docbook/xml/1.4/db3xml.dtd">
<chapter><title>Chapter Title</title>
<para>
This <emphasis>paragraph</emphasis> is important.
</para>
</chapter>
```

If you're used to using catalog files to resolve system identifiers, you may be dismayed to learn that system identifiers are required. Because most tools favor system identifiers over public identifiers, all of the portability that was gained by the use of catalog files seems to have been lost. In the long run, it'll be regained by the fact that XML system identifiers can be URNs, which will have a resolution scheme like catalogs, but what about the short run?

Luckily, there are a couple of options. First, you can tell your tools to use the public identifiers even though system identifiers are present. Simply add:

```
OVERRIDE YES
```

to your catalog files. Alternatively, you can remap system identifers with the `SYSTEM` catalog directive. If you are faced with documents that don't use public identifiers at all, this is probably your only option.

Minimization

If you have used SGML minimization features in your instances:

```
<!DOCTYPE chapter PUBLIC "-//OASIS//DTD DocBook V3.1//EN">
<chapter id=❶chap1><title>Chapter Title</title>
<para>
This <emphasis>paragraph❷</> is important.
</para>
</chapter>
```

they will not be well-formed XML instances. In particular, XML

❶ Requires that all attribute values be quoted.

❷ Does not allow short tag minization.

XML also forbids tag omission, and there are probably a half dozen or so more exotic examples of minimization that you have used. They're all illegal. The easiest way to remove these minimizations is probably with a tool like *sgmlnorm* (included in the SP and Jade distributions, on the CD-ROM).

The result will be something like this:

```
<?xml version='1.0'?>
<!DOCTYPE book PUBLIC "-//Norman Walsh//DTD DocBk XML V1.4//EN"
                  "http://docbook.org/docbook/xml/1.4/db3xml.dtd">
<chapter id="chap1"><title>Chapter Title</title>
<para>
This <emphasis>paragraph</emphasis> is important.
</para>
</chapter>
```

Attribute Default Values

Correct processing of this document may require access to the default attributes:

```
<!DOCTYPE chapter PUBLIC "-//OASIS//DTD DocBook V3.1//EN">
<chapter><title>Chapter Title</title>
<para>
Write to us at:
<address❶>
90 Sherman Street
Cambridge, MA 02140
</address>
</para>
</chapter>
```

❶ **Address** expresses that its content is line-specific with an attribute.

Some XML processing environments are going to ignore the doctype declaration in your document, even if it's present. This is relevant when your instance uses elements that have attributes with default values. The default values are expressed in the DTD, but may not be expressed in your instance. In the case of DocBook, there are relatively few of these, and your stylesheet can probably be constructed to do the right thing in either case. (It essentially treats the attributes as if they had implied values.)

The result will be something like this:

```
<?xml version='1.0'?>
<!DOCTYPE book PUBLIC "-//Norman Walsh//DTD DocBk XML V1.4//EN"
                  "http://docbook.org/docbook/xml/1.4/db3xml.dtd">
<chapter><title>Chapter Title</title>
<para>
Write to us at:
<address format="linespecific">
90 Sherman Street
Cambridge, MA 02140
```

```
</address>
</para>
</chapter>
```

Character and SDATA Entities

```
<!DOCTYPE chapter PUBLIC "-//OASIS//DTD DocBook V3.1//EN">
<chapter><title>Chapter Title</title>
<para>
This book was published by O'Reilly❶&trade;.
</para>
</chapter>
```

❶ The DocBook DTD defines all of the standard ISO entities automatically, but the ISO definitions use **SDATA**, which is not allowed in XML. Eventually, ISO (or someone else) will release official ISO standard entity sets that make reference to the appropriate Unicode character for each entity. Until then, DocBk XML DTD is distributed with an unofficial set.

If you use entities in your document, it may be wise to put declarations for them in the internal subset of each instance, because some XML browsers are going to parse the internal subset but not the external subset. If the entity declarations are in your DTD, and the browser does not parse the external subset, the browser won't know how to display the entities in your document.

The result will be something like this:

```
<?xml version='1.0'?>
<!DOCTYPE book PUBLIC "-//Norman Walsh//DTD DocBk XML V1.4//EN"
                "http://docbook.org/docbook/xml/1.4/db3xml.dtd" [
<!ENTITY trade "&#x2122;">
<chapter><title>Chapter Title</title>
<para>
This book was published by O'Reilly&trade;.
</para>
</chapter>
```

Case-Sensitivity

```
❶<!DocType Book PUBLIC "-//OASIS//DTD DocBook V3.1//EN">
❷<book><title>Book Title</title>
<chapter><title>Chapter Title❸</Title>
<para>
Paragraph test.
</para>
❹<PARA>
A second paragraph.
</PARA>
</chapter>
</book>
```

With the standard DocBook SGML declaration, DocBook instances are not case-sensitive with respect to element and attribute names. XML is always case-sensitive. As long as you have used the same case consistently, your XML instances will be well-formed, but it may still be advantageous to do some case-folding because it will simplify the construction of stylesheets.

❶ Keywords in XML are case-sensitive, and must be in uppercase.

❷ The name declared in the document type declaration, like all other names, is case-sensitive.

❸ Start and end tags must use the same case.

❹ In XML, **Para** is not the same as **PARA**. Note that this is a validity error (against the DocBk XML DTD), but it is not an XML well-formedness error. The use of **para** and **PARA** as distinct names is as legitimate as using **foo** and **bar**, as long as they are properly nested.

The result will be something like this:

```
<?xml version='1.0'?>
<!DOCTYPE book PUBLIC "-//Norman Walsh//DTD DocBk XML V1.4//EN"
                  "http://docbook.org/docbook/xml/1.4/db3xml.dtd">
<book><title>Book Title</title>
<chapter><title>Chapter Title</title>
<para>
Paragraph test.
</para>
<para>
A second paragraph.
</para>
</chapter>
</book>
```

No #CONREF Attributes

```
<!DOCTYPE chapter PUBLIC "-//OASIS//DTD DocBook V3.1//EN">
<chapter><title>Chapter Title</title>
<indexterm id="idx-bor"><primary>Something</primary></indexterm>❶
<para>
Paragraph test.
</para>
<indexterm startref="idx-bor">❷
</chapter>
```

The `StartRef` attribute on **indexterm** and the `OtherTerm` attribute on **GlossSee** and **GlossSeeAlso** are **#CONREF** attributes.

In SGML terms, this means that when these attributes are used, the content of the tag is taken to be the same as the content of the tag pointed to by the attribute.

❶❷ If you have used these attributes, your instance will contain both empty and non-empty versions of these tags.

Your best bet is to transform the **#CONREF** version into an empty tag and let your stylesheet deal with it appropriately.

The result will be something like this:

```
<?xml version='1.0'?>
<!DOCTYPE book PUBLIC "-//Norman Walsh//DTD DocBk XML V1.4//EN"
                 "http://docbook.org/docbook/xml/1.4/db3xml.dtd">
<chapter><title>Chapter Title</title>
<indexterm id="idx-bor"><primary>Something</primary></indexterm>
<para>
Paragraph test.
</para>
<indexterm startref="idx-bor"/>
</chapter>
```

Only Explicit CDATA-Marked Sections Are Allowed

```
<!DOCTYPE chapter PUBLIC "-//OASIS//DTD DocBook V3.1//EN" [
<!ENTITY % draft "IGNORE">
<!ENTITY % sourcecode "CDATA">
]>
<chapter><title>Chapter Title</title>
❶<![ %draft; [
<para>
Draft paragraph.
</para>
]]>
<para>
The following code is totally out of context:
<programlisting>
<![ ❷%sourcecode; [
if (x < 3) {
  y = 3;
}
]]>
</programlisting>
</chapter>
```

❶❷ Parameter entities are not allowed in the body of XML documents (they are allowed in the internal subset).

❶ XML instances cannot contain IGNORE, INCLUDE, TEMP, or RCDATA marked sections.

❷ CDATA marked sections must use the "CDATA" keyword literally because parameter entities are not allowed.

The result will be something like this:

```
<?xml version='1.0'?>
<!DOCTYPE book PUBLIC "-//Norman Walsh//DTD DocBk XML V1.4//EN"
                 "http://docbook.org/docbook/xml/1.4/db3xml.dtd">
<chapter><title>Chapter Title</title>
```

```
<para>
The following code is totally out of context:
<programlisting>
<![CDATA[
if (x < 3) {
  y = 3;
}
]]>
</programlisting>
</chapter>
```

No SUBDOC or CDATA External Entities

```
<!DOCTYPE chapter PUBLIC "-//OASIS//DTD DocBook V3.1//EN" [
<!ENTITY % sourcecode SYSTEM "program.c" CDATA>
]>
<chapter><title>Chapter Title</title>
<para>
The following code is totally out of context:
<programlisting>
&sourcecode;
</programlisting>
</chapter>
```

XML instances cannot use CDATA or SUBDOC external entities. One option for integrating external CDATA content into a document is to employ a pre-processing pass that inserts the content inline, wrapped in a CDATA marked section.

SUBDOC entities may be more problematic. If you do not require validation, it may be sufficient to simply put them inline. XML namespaces may offer another possible solution.

The result will be something like this:

```
<?xml version='1.0'?>
<!DOCTYPE book PUBLIC "-//Norman Walsh//DTD DocBk XML V1.4//EN"
                      "http://docbook.org/docbook/xml/1.4/db3xml.dtd">
<chapter><title>Chapter Title</title>
<para>
The following code is totally out of context:
<programlisting>
<![CDATA[
int main () {
..
}
]]>
</programlisting>
</chapter>
```

No Data Attributes on Notations

They're not allowed in XML, so don't add any.

No Attribute Value Specifications on Entity Declarations

They're not allowed in XML, so don't add any.

The DocBook DTD as XML

Converting the DocBook DTD to XML is much more challenging than converting the instances. It is probably not possible to construct an XML DTD that is identical to the validation power of DocBook. The list below identifies most of the issues that must be addressed, and describes how the DocBk XML DTD deals with them:

Comments are not allowed inside markup declarations
: Most of them have been moved to comment declarations preceding the markup declaration that used to contain them. A few small, inline comments that seemed like they would be out of context if moved before the declaration were simply deleted.

Name groups are not allowed in element or attribute list declarations
: The small number of places in which DocBook uses name groups have been expanded.

: There's one downside: DocBook uses `%admon.class;` in a name group to define the content model, and attribute lists for elements in the admonitions class. In DocBk XML DTD, this convenience cannot be expressed. If additional admonitions are added, the element and attribute list declarations will have to be copied for them.

No `CDATA` *or* `RCDATA` *declared content*
: **Graphic** and **InlineGraphic** have been made `EMPTY`. The content model for **SynopFragmentRef**, the only `RCDATA` element in DocBook, has been changed to `(arg | group)+`.

No exclusions or inclusions on element declarations
: They had to be removed.

: In DocBook, exclusions are used to exclude the following:

- Ubiquitous elements (**indexterm** and **BeginPage**) from a number of contexts in which they should not occur (such as metadata, for example).
- Formal objects from **Highlights**, **Examples**, **Figures** and **LegalNotices**.
- Formal objects and **InformalTables** from tables.
- Block elements and **Footnotes** from **Footnotes**
- Admonitions, **EntryTbls**, and **Acronyms** from themselves.

Removing these exclusions from DocBk XML DTD means that it is now valid, in the XML sense, to do some things that don't make a lot of sense (like put a **Footnote** in a **Footnote**). Be careful.

Inclusions in DocBook are used to add the ubiquitious elements (**indexterm** and **BeginPage**) unconditionally to a large number of contexts. In order to make these elements available in DocBk XML DTD, they have been added to most of the parameter entities that include `#PCDATA`. If new locations are discovered where these terms are desired, DocBk XML DTD will be updated.

Elements with mixed content must have `#PCDATA` *first.*
: The content models of many elements have been updated to make them a repeatable OR group beginning with `#PCDATA`.

Many declared attribute types (`NAME`, `NUMBER`, `NUTOKEN`, *and so on) are not allowed*
: They have all been replaced by `NMTOKEN` or `CDATA`.

No `#CONREF` *attributes allowed.*
: The `#CONREF` attributes on **indexterm**, **GlossSee**, and **GlossSeeAlso** were changed to `#IMPLIED`. The content model of **indexterm** was modified so that it can be empty.

Attribute default values must be quoted.
: Quotes were added wherever necessary.

C

DocBook Versions

The OASIS DocBook Technical Committee (TC) is committed to the continued evolution of DocBook. As new needs are expressed by the DocBook-user community, the committee will adapt DocBook so it continues to meet the needs of its users.

The TC observes a very cautious policy regarding changes to the DTD. Backward-incompatible changes can only be introduced:

- In major releases (4.0, 5.0, 6.0, and so on)
- Only if the change was described in comments in the DTD in the previous major release

Changes made at point-releases are always backward-compatible to the previous major release. This policy assures that DocBook users always have time to prepare for any coming changes.

This appendix describes the changes planned for DocBook.

DocBook V3.0

DocBook V3.0 was released in 1997. It has been widely adopted and integrated into several commercial products. It is likely that DocBook V3.0 will be in wide use for a while.

DocBook V3.1

DocBook V3.1, released in February 1999 introduced a number of new elements:

MediaObject

MediaObject is a wrapper around **VideoObject**, **AudioObject**, **ImageObject**, and **TextObject**. The purpose of **MediaObject** is twofold: first, it introduces new element types to include video and audio content; second, it provides the option of alternative representations, including text, for objects in a document. **MediaObjects** also allow **Captions** that may be longer than a simple title.

Parallel to **MediaObject** are **InlineMediaObject**, an inline version, and **MediaObjectCO**, a media object with **Callouts**.

For now, media objects and graphics exist together in version 5.0. **Graphic** and **InlineGraphic** will be removed from DocBook.

InformalFigure
: A figure wrapper without a title. This element was added largely for symmetry.

Colophon
: An end-of-the-book **Colophon**.

Section
: **Section** is a recursive section. It exists parallel to, and must be used as an alternative to, **Sect1**.

QandASet
: A set of questions and answers.

Constant
: The **Constant** inline is for identifying constants. It has a `Class` attribute for identifying "limits" as a specific kind of constant.

VarName
: Many authors have requested a tag for identifying variable names. Most often **Literal** (with or without a role) has been chosen as a compromise, but you can't question the utility of identifying variable names, so **VarName** was added.

A tag for identifying variable values does not seem as necessary. For immutable values, a specific tag other than **Literal** seems unnecessary, and **Replaceable** exists for values that are supposed to be filled in by the user.

DocBook V4.0

DocBook V4.0 will introduce a number of backward-incompatible changes.

The policy of the DocBook TC is that backward-incompatible changes can only be introduced in a full version release. They must also be described in comments in the DTD at least one full version earlier. In other words, all the planned version 4.0 incompatibilities were announced with version 3.0.

Backward-incompatible changes to DocBook that are planned for version 4.0:

- The **DocInfo** element will be split out into **ChapterInfo**, **AppendixInfo**, and so on. **ArtHeader** will be renamed to **ArticleInfo**. **SeriesInfo** may be discarded because it has become a special case of **BiblioSet**. **BookBiblio** will be discarded in favor of a new, more inclusive, structure for **BookInfo** (and for **ArticleInfo**, whose earlier **ArtHeader** form contained **BookBiblio**).

- The `%article.class;` entity may be removed from the **Book** content model, and made part of a new top-level document hierarchy.
- The `%nav.class;` entity, which appears in several divisions, will allow **ToCchap** instead of **ToC**.
- **MsgText** will be moved from `%tech.char.class;` to a more appropriate parameter entity.
- The following elements will have their content constrained to the `%smallcptr.char.mix;` mixture: **Action**, **Command**, **Database**, **Filename**, **Hardware**, **Interface**, **KeyCap**, **Literal**, **Option**, **Parameter**, **Property**, and **SystemItem**.
- **AuthorBlurb** and **Affiliation** will be removed from `%person.ident.mix;` and a new wrapper element will be created to allow association of those two elements with **Author** name information.
- **Epigraph** will not be appearing in **BlockQuote**.
- **Comment** will be renamed to **Remark** and will be excluded from itself.
- **GlossTerm** will be excluded from itself, and may be split into an element that appears in a **Glossary** and an element that can appear in the main text.
- The `Subject` attribute on **GlossDef** will be renamed `Keyword`.
- Two **SegTitle** elements will be required in **SegmentedList**.
- **Graphic** and **InlineGraphic** will be declared EMPTY. This change will require that end tags be removed and that any embedded graphic content be stored outside the SGML source and pointed to from an `Entityref` or `Fileref` attribute.
- The `OptMult` and `ReqMult` values for the `Choice` attribute on **Group** will be removed. Use the `Rep` attribute instead to indicate that the choice is repeatable.
- The content model group inside **FuncSynopsis** starting with **FuncDef** will not be available; you will have to use **FuncPrototype**. Also, you will be able to have a mixture of **FuncPrototypes** and **FuncSynopsisInfos** (this is not backward-incompatible all by itself).
- The `EnvironVar` and `Prompt` values for the `Class` attribute on **SystemItem** will be eliminated; use the **EnVar** and **Prompt** elements instead.

DocBook 5.0

DocBook V5.0 will also introduce backward-incompatible changes.

These changes will be announced in version 4.0, although several were announced with version 3.1 as well.

Backward-incompatible changes to DocBook that are planned for version 4.0:

- DocBook 5.0 will be XML compliant. This will introduce a lot of changes.
- The `Coords` attribute will be removed from **AreaSet**.
- **ArtHeader** will be dropped from **BiblioEntry**.
- The `Contents` attribute will be removed from **BookInfo** and **SetInfo**.
- The `%indexdivcomponent.mix;` entity will be restricted. Numbered figures and other elements inappropriate for an **Index** or **SetIndex** will be removed.
- **RevHistory** will be removed from **GlossTerm**.
- The `Constant Class` will be removed from **SystemItem**.
- **Graphic** and **InlineGraphic** will be removed.

DocBk XML

The DocBk XML DTD is an XML version of DocBook produced by Norman Walsh. It is a faithful translation of DocBook, as described in "The DocBook DTD as XML," in Appendix B, *DocBook and XML*.

Although it has not been officially adopted by the DocBook Technical Committee, the TC does have concrete plans to produce an official XML version of DocBook in version 5.0. This is likely to be based on the DocBk XML DTD, or very closely resemble it.

The DocBk XML DTD is supplied on the CD-ROM. It is also available from *http://nwalsh.com/docbook/xml/*.

D

Resources

The quantity of information about SGML and XML is growing on a daily basis. This appendix strives to provide both a complete bibliography of the references mentioned explicitly in this book, and a sampling of resources for additional information about DocBook and about SGML and XML in general. Although not all of these resources are focused specifically on DocBook, they still provide helpful information for DocBook users.

Latest Versions of DocBook

As of July 1998, responsibility for the advancement and maintenance of the DocBook DTD has been transferred from the Davenport Group, which originated it, to the DocBook Technical Committee of OASIS (Organization for the Advancement of Structured Information Standards) at *http://www.oasis-open.org/*.

The latest releases of DocBook can be obtained from the official DocBook home page at *http://www.oasis-open.org/docbook/*.

Resources for Resources

Here's where to find pointers to the subjects you want to find.

The Most Recent Version of This Book
: The most recent online version of this book can be found at *http://docbook.org/*.

The Most Recent Version of DocBook
: The most recent version of DocBook, and the most recent information about the DTD, can be found at the DocBook home page: *http://www.oasis-open.org/docbook/*.

Robin Cover's SGML/XML Web page

Easily the largest and most up-to-date list of SGML/XML resources; can be found at *http://www.oasis-open.org/cover/*.

comp.text.sgml and comp.text.xml

USENET newsgroups devoted to SGML and XML issues.

FAQs

For pointers to several SGML FAQs, see *http://www.oasis-open.org/cover/general.html#faq*. The XML FAQ is available at *http://www.ucc.ie/xml*.

XML.com (http://www.xml.com/)

XML.com (*http://www.xml.com/*), run jointly by Songline Studios and Seybold, is a site devoted to making XML accessible.

Introductory Material on the Web

These documents provide a good background for a better understanding of SGML and XML.

A Gentle Introduction to SGML

A useful and simple document available in its original form at *http://www-tei.uic.edu/orgs/tei/sgml/teip3sg/index.html*.

A Technical Introduction to XML

A close look at the ins-and-outs of XML is available at *http://nwalsh.com/docs/articles/xml/*.

References and Technical Notes on the Web

Entity Management

OASIS Technical Resolution 9401:1997 (Amendment 2 to TR 9401) (*http://www.oasis-open.org/html/a401.htm*).

This document describes OASIS catalog files.

The SGML Declaration

The SGML Declaration, (*http://www.oasis-open.org/cover/wlw11.html*) by Wayne Wholer.

Table Interoperability: Issues for the CALS Table Model

OASIS Technical Research Paper 9501:1995 (*http://www.oasis-open.org/html/a501.htm*).

Exchange Table Model Document Type Definition
OASIS Technical Resolution TR 9503:1995 (*http://www.oasis-open.org/html/a503.htm*).

CALS Table Model Document Type Definition
OASIS Technical Memorandum TM 9502:1995 (*http://www.oasis-open.org/html/a502.htm*)

XML Exchange Table Model Document Type Definition
OASIS Technical Memorandum TM 9901:1999 (*http://www.oasis-open-org/html/a901.htm*).

Internet RFCs

RFCs ("Request for Comments") are standards documents produced by the Internet Engineering Task Force (IETF).

RFC 1630 (http://www.cis.ohio-state.edu/htbin/rfc/rfc1630.html)
Universal Resource Identifiers in WWW.

RFC 1736 (http://www.cis.ohio-state.edu/htbin/rfc/rfc1736.html)
Functional recommendations for Internet Resource Locators.

RFC 1737 (http://www.cis.ohio-state.edu/htbin/rfc/rfc1737.html)
Functional requirements for Uniform Resource Names.

RFC 1738 (http://www.cis.ohio-state.edu/htbin/rfc/rfc1738.html)
Uniform Resource Locators (URL).

RFC 1766 (http://www.cis.ohio-state.edu/htbin/rfc/rfc1766.html)
Tags for the identification of languages

Specifications

Here are pointers to the specifications.

The XML Specification (http://www.w3.org/TR/REC-xml)
The W3C technical recommendation that defines XML 1.0.

Namespaces in XML (http://www.w3.org/TR/REC-xml-names/)
The W3C technical recommendation that defines XML namespaces.

Mathematical Markup Language (MathML) 1.0 Specification (http://www.w3.org/TR/REC-MathML/)
The W3C technical recommendation that defines MathML, an XML representation of mathematical equations.

The Unicode Standard, Version 2.0 (http://www.unicode.org/unicode/uni2book/u2.html)
The Unicode standard.

Unicode Technical Report #8 (http://www.unicode.org/unicode/reports/tr8.html)
Version 2.1 of the Unicode standard.

Books and Printed Resources

There are also a number of books worth checking out:

Maler, Eve, and Jeanne El Andaloussi. *Developing SGML DTDs: From Text to Model to Markup*. 0-13-309881-8. Upper Saddle River: Prentice-Hall PTR, 1996.

van Herwijnen, Erik. *Practical SGML*, 2d ed. 0-7923-9434-8. Kluwer Academic Press, 1994. An introductory book, but not a simple one.

Goldfarb, Charles, and Yuri Rubinksy. *The SGML Handbook*. 0-7923-9434-8. Oxford University Press, 1991. A reference book by the author of the SGML ISO Standard.

Bryan, Martin. *SGML: an author's guide to the Standard Generalized Markup Language*. 0-201-17535-5. Addison-Wesley Publishing Company, 1988.

Ensign, Chet. *$GML: The Billion Dollar Secret*. 0-13-226705-5. Prentice Hall, 1998. Effective SGML evangelism.

Maden, Chris. *Creating Documents with XML*. 1-56592-518-1. O'Reilly & Associates, 1999. An introductory book about XML.

St. Laurent, Simon. *XML: A Primer*. 1-5582-8592-X. MIS:Press/IDG Books Worldwide, 1998. Another introductory book about XML.

Flynn, Peter. *Understanding SGML and XML Tools*. 0-7923-8169-6. Kluwer Academic Publishers, 1998. The standard work on SGML/XML software.

Goosens, Michel, and Sebastian Rahtz. *The LaTeX Web Companion: Integrating TeX, HTML, and XML*. 0-201-43311-7. Addison-Wesley Publishing Company, 1999.

SGML/XML Tools

An attempt to provide a detailed description of all of the SGML/XML tools available is outside the scope of this book.

For a list of recent of SGML tools, check out Robin Cover's SGML/XML page at OASIS: *http://www.oasis-open.org/cover*.

For a list of XML tools, check out XML.com: *http://www.xml.com/*.

E

What's on the CD-ROM?

The CD-ROM that accompanies the print version of this book contains a number of useful resources.

Please read the *readme.txt* file in the root directory of the CD-ROM. It describes any last-minute changes or additions that were made to the CD-ROM after this appendix was written.

DocBook: The Definitive Guide

/sgml/ contains the sources for this book in SGML.

/html/ contains an online version of this book in HTML.

/help/ contains a compiled HTML Help version of the book.

/examples/ contains the complete examples from this book.

The DocBook DTD

/dtds/docbook/db30 contains DocBook V3.0.

/dtds/docbook/db31 contains DocBook V3.1.

/dtds/docbk/db315 contains DocBk XML V3.1.5.

/dtds/docbk/sdb3151 contains a simplified DocBk XML V3.1.5.1.

/dtds/isoents/ contains ISO entity sets needed for the DTDs.

/dtds/usadod/ contains the CALS table model DTD needed for the SGML DocBook DTDs.

Stylesheets

/style/ contains various stylesheets.

/style/dsssl/docbook/ contains the Modular DocBook DSSSL stylesheets. These are the Jade stylesheets described in Chapter 4, *Publishing DocBook Documents.*

/dtds/dsssl/anotess/ contains the Annotated DSSSL stylesheet DTD and related files.

/style/xsl/ contains various XSL stylesheets.

/style/xsl/docbook/ contains the XSL DocBook Stylesheets V0.12.

Other Programs

The */apps* directory contains source and binary releases of other, related software, such as the Jade and XT distributions. The */bin* directory contains the format script briefly discussed in Chapter 5, *Customizing DocBook.*

Interchanging DocBook Documents

One of the early factors that motivated the development of the DocBook DTD was the desire for companies to interchange documents. In particular, UNIX vendors wanted to be able to interchange common UNIX documentation.

A great deal of effort went into making sure that DocBook could handle most (probably all) of the documents that were likely to be exchanged. This avoids the guaranteed interchange problem of DTD extension.

However, simply using DocBook or a subset of it is not enough to ensure successful interchange. If you send someone your DocBook files, you must also tell the recipient about the markup your documents use and any of your additional markup conventions and processing expectations that impose constraints on processing.

This appendix provides a sample interchange questionnaire to help draw your attention to those areas that might be problematic.

For maximum portability, delivered DocBook documents should be accompanied by a filled-out interchange questionnaire. Because each situation is unique, you may need to supply additional information (such as layout specifications) in order to deliver a complete package.

DocBook and SGML Usage

1. What version of the DTD are you using?
2. Did you use any markup features of the DTD that have been flagged as obsolete (to be removed at the next major version of DocBook)? If so, which ones?
3. Did you extend DocBook in any way, inside or outside the provided customization mechanisms? How? All extensions must be negotiated with the recipient.

4. Did you remove markup from DocBook to create a subset? If you used a subset of DocBook, supply the subset you used. (Note that even the removal of references to ISO entity sets creates a subset.)
5. Did you use the supplied SGML declaration or another one? If you used another one, provide it.
6. Did you use the supplied catalog or another one, or none at all? If you used a catalog other than the one supplied, provide it.
7. If your documents bear no document type declaration, and you parsed them with a document declaration (with or without an internal subset), supply it.
8. Did you add `NOTATION` declarations? If so, what are they? List all data content notations used in your documents.
9. Did you use the `SUBDOC` feature? If so, how did you manage the name spaces of their IDs, if you managed them at all?
10. Did you use character sets other than ISO 8859-1 (Latin 1)? If so, which ones? How did you use them?
11. Did you declare and use character entities and other general entities besides the ISO entity sets? If so, supply the entity declarations and the desired appearance of the additional character entities.
12. Are your document files normalized to include all markup explicitly?
13. Are you supplying a document fragment? If so, have you provided any necessary auxiliary information (such as meta-information) for the fragment? Are there any attribute values that haven't been specified that you expect to inherit from a parent that isn't present?

Processing Requirements and Markup Interpretation

14. What formatting that you applied do you require your interchange partner to apply? For example, where and how must text be generated in order for the documents to make sense?
15. Did you supply your stylesheet and information regarding its format and version?
16. How did you create tables of contents, lists of titles, and indexes? Are they stored in DocBook form? If so, did you generate them (and according to what rules) or create them by hand?
17. If you used the `Lang` common attribute, why, and to what effect?
18. If you used the `Remap` common attribute, why, and to what effect?

19. If you used the `Role` common attribute, why, and to what effect?
20. If you used the effectivity attributes, which did you use, why, and to what effect?
21. What values did you give to the `Label` attribute and how are they to be interpreted for rendering?
22. What values did you give to the `Mark` and `Override` attributes for lists and how are they to be interpreted for rendering?
23. Did you use the `Renderas` attribute on sections and/or **BridgeHeads**?
24. Did you supply all keyword values you used for attributes whose declared values are not enumerated tokens, along with the expected processing for the occurrence of each keyword?
25. Did you use markup to control width, size, and/or positioning settings (such as "fold-out" or "centered") for graphics, line specific regions, and tables? If so, how?
26. For rendering of **Sidebars**, must these appear in the flow of the text where they appear in your files, or may they float?
27. Did you use **Callouts**? If so, what are the processing expectations for callout marks?
28. Did you use **ItemizedLists**? If so, what are the processing expectations for the marks on list items and nested lists?
29. For **Graphic** and **InlineGraphic**, what method(s) did you use for providing graphic data: element content, `Fileref` attribute, or `Entityref` attribute?
30. For **MediaObject** and **InlineMediaObject**, what method(s) did you use for selecting between alternative presentations?
31. How did you specify column widths in tables? Did you use vertical spans? Did you use horizontal spans?
32. Did you use **EntryTbls**?
33. If you used the `Type` attribute on the link elements, why, and to what effect?
34. If you used **XRef**, do your interchange partners need additional information about the semantic of the link? Have you provided it, perhaps with `Role`?
35. Did you use the `Subject` attribute on **GlossDef**? If so, did you use a thesaurus of terms? If so, what is it?
36. If you used the `Class` attribute on **RefMiscInfo**, why and to what effect?
37. If you used **ULink** and provided URLs that are queries, what back-end processing is required to resolve those queries?

38. `FileRef` or `EntityRef` is supplied on every **Graphic**, **InlineGraphic**, **AudioData**, **ImageData**, and **VideoData** element. If one is not present, what is the expectation?
39. If your **Bibliographys** or **Glossarys** have special processing expectations, such as the ability to display only those entries that are cited, have you described them?
40. If your **Bibliographys** contain **BiblioEntrys**, what are the processing expectations? Which fields are selected for display? What punctuation is added, and where?
41. Do **GlossTerms** or other elements have implicit linking relationships that must be obeyed or handled in presentation?
42. Did you use any processing instructions? Why and what for? Are they in entities?
43. What copyfitting have you already done, and for what outputs?

Miscellaneous

44. Have you checked your files for viruses?
45. If you used **BridgeHead**, have you joined a recovery support group?

G

DocBook V3.1 Quick Reference

Element	Brief Description
Abbrev	An abbreviation, especially one followed by a period
Abstract	A summary
Accel	A graphical user interface (GUI) keyboard shortcut
Ackno	Acknowledgements in an **Article**
Acronym	An often pronounceable word made from the initial (or selected) letters of a name or phrase
Action	A response to a user event
Address	A real-world address, generally a postal address
Affiliation	The institutional affiliation of an individual
Alt	Text representation for a graphical element
Anchor	A spot in the document
Answer	An answer to a question posed in a **QandASet**
Appendix	An appendix in a **Book** or **Article**
Application	The name of a software program
Area	A region defined for a **Callout** in a graphic or code example
AreaSet	A set of related areas in a graphic or code example
AreaSpec	A collection of regions in a graphic or code example
Arg	An argument in a **CmdSynopsis**
ArtHeader	Meta-information for an **Article**
ArtPageNums	The page numbers of an article as published
Article	An article
Attribution	The source of a block quote or epigraph
AudioData	Pointer to external audio data
AudioObject	A wrapper for audio data and its associated meta-information
Author	The name of an individual author

Element	Brief Description
AuthorBlurb	A short description or note about an author
AuthorGroup	Wrapper for author information when a document has multiple authors or collabarators
AuthorInitials	The initials or other short identifier for an author
BeginPage	The location of a page break in a print version of the document
BiblioDiv	A section of a **Bibliography**
BiblioEntry	An entry in a **Bibliography**
BiblioMSet	A "cooked" container for related bibliographic information
BiblioMisc	Untyped bibliographic information
BiblioMixed	An entry in a **Bibliography**
BiblioSet	A "raw" container for related bibliographic information
Bibliography	A bibliography
BlockQuote	A quotation set off from the main text
Book	A book
BookBiblio	Meta-information about a book used in a bibliographical citation
BookInfo	Meta-information for a Book
BridgeHead	A free-floating heading
CO	The location of a callout embedded in text
Callout	A "called out" description of a marked **Area**
CalloutList	A list of **Callouts**
Caption	A caption
Caution	A note of caution
Chapter	A chapter, as of a book
Citation	An inline bibliographic reference to another published work
CiteRefEntry	A citation to a reference page
CiteTitle	The title of a cited work
City	The name of a city in an address
ClassName	The name of a class, in the object-oriented programming sense
CmdSynopsis	A syntax summary for a software command
ColSpec	Specifications for a column in a table
Collab	Identifies a collaborator
CollabName	The name of a collaborator
Colophon	Text at the back of a book describing facts about its production
Command	The name of an executable program or other software command
Comment	A comment intended for presentation in a draft manuscript
ComputerOutput	Data, generally text, displayed or presented by a computer
ConfDates	The dates of a conference for which a document was written
ConfGroup	A wrapper for document meta-information about a conference

Element	Brief Description
ConfNum	An identifier, frequently numerical, associated with a conference for which a document was written
ConfSponsor	The sponsor of a conference for which a document was written
ConfTitle	The title of a conference for which a document was written
Constant	A programming or system constant
ContractNum	The contract number of a document
ContractSponsor	The sponsor of a contract
Contrib	A summary of the contributions made to a document by a credited source
Copyright	Copyright information about a document
CorpAuthor	A corporate author, as opposed to an individual
CorpName	The name of a corporation
Country	The name of a country
Database	The name of a database, or part of a database
Date	The date of publication or revision of a document
Dedication	A wrapper for the dedication section of a book
DocInfo	Meta-data for a book component
Edition	The name or number of an edition of a document
Editor	The name of the editor of a document
Email	An email address
Emphasis	Emphasized text
EnVar	A software environment variable
Entry	A cell in a table
EntryTbl	A subtable appearing in place of an **Entry** in a table
Epigraph	A short inscription at the beginning of a document or component
Equation	A displayed mathematical equation
ErrorCode	An error code
ErrorName	An error message
ErrorType	The classification of an error message
Example	A formal example, with a title
Fax	A fax number
Figure	A formal figure, generally an illustration, with a title
Filename	The name of a file
FirstName	The first name of a person
FirstTerm	The first occurrence of a term
Footnote	A footnote
FootnoteRef	A cross reference to a footnote (a footnote mark)

Element	Brief Description
ForeignPhrase	A word or phrase in a language other than the primary language of the document
FormalPara	A paragraph with a title
FuncDef	A function (subroutine) name and its return type
FuncParams	Parameters for a function referenced through a function pointer in a synopsis
FuncPrototype	The prototype of a function
FuncSynopsis	The syntax summary for a function definition
FuncSynopsisInfo	Information supplementing the **FuncDefs** of a **FuncSynopsis**
Function	The name of a function or subroutine, as in a programming language
GUIButton	The text on a button in a GUI
GUIIcon	Graphic and/or text appearing as a icon in a GUI
GUILabel	The text of a label in a GUI
GUIMenu	The name of a menu in a GUI
GUIMenuItem	The name of a terminal menu item in a GUI
GUISubmenu	The name of a submenu in a GUI
GlossDef	A definition in a **GlossEntry**
GlossDiv	A division in a **Glossary**
GlossEntry	An entry in a **Glossary** or **GlossList**
GlossList	A wrapper for a set of **GlossEntry**s
GlossSee	A cross-reference from one **GlossEntry** to another
GlossSeeAlso	A cross-reference from one **GlossEntry** to another
GlossTerm	A glossary term
Glossary	A glossary
Graphic	A displayed graphical object (not an inline)
GraphicCO	A graphic that contains callout areas
Group	A group of elements in a **CmdSynopsis**
Hardware	A physical part of a computer system
Highlights	A summary of the main points of the discussed component
Holder	The name of the individual or organization that holds a copyright
Honorific	The title of a person
ISBN	The International Standard Book Number of a document
ISSN	The International Standard Serial Number of a periodical
ITermSet	A set of index terms in the meta-information of a document
ImageData	Pointer to external image data
ImageObject	A wrapper for image data and its associated meta-information
ImageObjectCO	A wrapper for an image object with callouts

Element	Brief Description
Important	An admonition set off from the text
Index	An index
IndexDiv	A division in an index
IndexEntry	An entry in an index
IndexTerm	A wrapper for terms to be indexed
InformalEquation	A displayed mathematical equation without a title
InformalExample	A displayed example without a title
InformalFigure	A untitled figure
InformalTable	A table without a title
InlineEquation	A mathematical equation or expression occurring inline
InlineGraphic	An object containing or pointing to graphical data that will be rendered inline
InlineMediaObject	An inline media object (video, audio, image, and so on)
Interface	An element of a GUI
InterfaceDefinition	The name of a formal specification of a GUI
InvPartNumber	An inventory part number
IssueNum	The number of an issue of a journal
ItemizedList	A list in which each entry is marked with a bullet or other dingbat
JobTitle	The title of an individual in an organization
KeyCap	The text printed on a key on a keyboard
KeyCode	The internal, frequently numeric, identifier for a key on a keyboard
KeyCombo	A combination of input actions
KeySym	The symbolic name of a key on a keyboard
Keyword	One of a set of keywords describing the content of a document
KeywordSet	A set of keywords describing the content of a document
LegalNotice	A statement of legal obligations or requirements
LineAnnotation	A comment on a line in a verbatim listing
Lineage	The portion of a person's name indicating a relationship to ancestors
Link	A hypertext link
ListItem	A wrapper for the elements of a list item
Literal	Inline text that is some literal value
LiteralLayout	A block of text in which line breaks and white space are to be reproduced faithfully
LoT	A list of the titles of formal objects (as tables or figures) in a document
LoTentry	An entry in a list of titles
ManVolNum	A reference volume number

Element	Brief Description
Markup	A string of formatting markup in text that is to be represented literally
MediaLabel	A name that identifies the physical medium on which some information resides
MediaObject	A displayed media object (video, audio, image, etc.)
MediaObjectCO	A media object that contains callouts
Member	An element of a simple list
MenuChoice	A selection or series of selections from a menu
ModeSpec	Application-specific information necessary for the completion of an OLink
MouseButton	The conventional name of a mouse button
Msg	A message in a message set
MsgAud	The audience to which a message in a message set is relevant
MsgEntry	A wrapper for an entry in a message set
MsgExplan	Explanatory material relating to a message in a message set
MsgInfo	Information about a message in a message set
MsgLevel	The level of importance or severity of a message in a message set
MsgMain	The primary component of a message in a message set
MsgOrig	The origin of a message in a message set
MsgRel	A related component of a message in a message set
MsgSet	A detailed set of messages, usually error messages
MsgSub	A subcomponent of a message in a message set
MsgText	The actual text of a message component in a message set
Note	A message set off from the text
OLink	A link that addresses its target indirectly, through an entity
ObjectInfo	Meta-information for an object
Option	An option for a software command
Optional	Optional information
OrderedList	A list in which each entry is marked with a sequentially incremented label
OrgDiv	A division of an organization
OrgName	The name of an organization other than a corporation
OtherAddr	Uncategorized information in address
OtherCredit	A person or entity, other than an author or editor, credited in a document
OtherName	A component of a persons name that is not a first name, surname, or lineage
POB	A post office box in an address

Element	Brief Description
PageNums	The numbers of the pages in a book, for use in a bibliographic entry
Para	A paragraph
ParamDef	Information about a function parameter in a programming language
Parameter	A value or a symbolic reference to a value
Part	A division in a book
PartIntro	An introduction to the contents of a part
Phone	A telephone number
Phrase	A span of text
Postcode	A postal code in an address
Preface	Introductory matter preceding the first chapter of a book
Primary	The primary word or phrase under which an index term should be sorted
PrimaryIE	A primary term in an index entry, not in the text
PrintHistory	The printing history of a document
Procedure	A list of operations to be performed in a well-defined sequence
ProductName	The formal name of a product
ProductNumber	A number assigned to a product
ProgramListing	A literal listing of all or part of a program
ProgramListingCO	A program listing with associated areas used in callouts
Prompt	A character or string indicating the start of an input field in a computer display
Property	A unit of data associated with some part of a computer system
PubDate	The date of publication of a document
Publisher	The publisher of a document
PublisherName	The name of the publisher of a document
PubsNumber	A number assigned to a publication other than an ISBN or ISSN or inventory part number
QandADiv	A titled division in a **QandASet**
QandAEntry	A question/answer set within a **QandASet**
QandASet	A question-and-answer set
Question	A question in a **QandASet**
Quote	An inline quotation
RefClass	The scope or other indication of applicability of a reference entry
RefDescriptor	A description of the topic of a reference page
RefEntry	A reference page (originally a UNIX man-style reference page)
RefEntryTitle	The title of a reference page
RefMeta	Meta-information for a reference entry

Element	Brief Description
RefMiscInfo	Meta-information for a reference entry other than the title and volume number
RefName	The name of (one of) the subject(s) of a reference page
RefNameDiv	The name, purpose, and classification of a reference page
RefPurpose	A short (one sentence) synopsis of the topic of a reference page
RefSect1	A major subsection of a reference entry
RefSect1Info	Meta-information for a **RefSect1**
RefSect2	A subsection of a **RefSect1**
RefSect2Info	Meta-information for a **RefSect2**
RefSect3	A subsection of a **RefSect2**
RefSect3Info	Meta-information for a **RefSect3**
RefSynopsisDiv	A syntactic synopsis of the subject of the reference page
RefSynopsisDivInfo	Meta-information for a **RefSynopsisDiv**
Reference	A collection of reference entries
ReleaseInfo	Information about a particular release of a document
Replaceable	Content that may or must be replaced by the user
ReturnValue	The value returned by a function
RevHistory	A history of the revisions to a document
RevNumber	A document revision number
RevRemark	A description of a revision to a document
Revision	An entry describing a single revision in the history of the revisions to a document
Row	A row in a table
SBR	An explicit line break in a command synopsis
SGMLTag	A component of SGML markup
Screen	Text that a user sees or might see on a computer screen
ScreenCO	A screen with associated areas used in callouts
ScreenInfo	Information about how a screen shot was produced
ScreenShot	A representation of what the user sees or might see on a computer screen
Secondary	A secondary word or phrase in an index term
SecondaryIE	A secondary term in an index entry, rather than in the text
Sect1	A top-level section of document
Sect1Info	Meta-information for a **Sect1**
Sect2	A subsection within a **Sect1**
Sect2Info	Meta-information for a **Sect2**
Sect3	A subsection within a **Sect2**
Sect3Info	Meta-information for a **Sect3**

Element	Brief Description
Sect4	A subsection within a **Sect3**
Sect4Info	Meta-information for a **Sect4**
Sect5	A subsection within a **Sect4**
Sect5Info	Meta-information for a **Sect5**
Section	A recursive section
SectionInfo	Meta-information for a recursive section
See	Part of an index term directing the reader instead to another entry in the index
SeeAlso	Part of an index term directing the reader also to another entry in the index
SeeAlsoIE	A "See also" entry in an index, rather than in the text
SeeIE	A "See" entry in an index, rather than in the text
Seg	An element of a list item in a segmented list
SegListItem	A list item in a segmented list
SegTitle	The title of an element of a list item in a segmented list
SegmentedList	A segmented list, a list of sets of elements
SeriesInfo	Information about the publication series of which a book is a part
SeriesVolNums	Numbers of the volumes in a series of books
Set	A collection of books
SetIndex	An index to a set of books
SetInfo	Meta-information for a **Set**
ShortAffil	A brief description of an affiliation
Shortcut	A key combination for an action that is also accessible through a menu
Sidebar	A portion of a document that is isolated from the main narrative flow
SimPara	A paragraph that contains only text and inline markup, no block elements
SimpleList	An undecorated list of single words or short phrases
SimpleSect	A section of a document with no subdivisions
SpanSpec	Formatting information for a spanned column in a table
State	A state or province in an address
Step	A unit of action in a procedure
Street	A street address in an address
StructField	A field in a structure (in the programming language sense)
StructName	The name of a structure (in the programming language sense)
SubSteps	A wrapper for steps that occur within steps in a procedure
Subject	One of a group of terms describing the subject matter of a document

Element	Brief Description
SubjectSet	A set of terms describing the subject matter of a document
SubjectTerm	A term in a group of terms describing the subject matter of a document
Subscript	A subscript (as in H_2O, the molecular formula for water)
Subtitle	The subtitle of a document
Superscript	A superscript (as in x^2, the mathematical notation for x multiplied by itself)
Surname	A family name, in western cultures the "last name"
Symbol	A name that is replaced by a value before processing
SynopFragment	A portion of a **CmdSynopsis** broken out from the main body of the synopsis
SynopFragmentRef	A reference to a fragment of a command synopsis
Synopsis	A general-purpose element for representing the syntax of commands or functions
SystemItem	A system-related item or term
TBody	A wrapper for the rows of a table or informal table
TFoot	A table footer consisting of one or more rows
TGroup	A wrapper for the main content of a table, or part of a table
THead	A table header consisting of one or more rows
Table	A formal table in a document
Term	The word or phrase being defined or described in a variable list
Tertiary	A tertiary word or phrase in an index term
TertiaryIE	A tertiary term in an index entry, rather than in the text
TextObject	A wrapper for a text description of an object and its associated meta-information
Tip	A suggestion to the user, set off from the text
Title	The text of the title of a section of a document or of a formal block-level element
TitleAbbrev	The abbreviation of a **Title**
ToC	A table of contents
ToCback	An entry in a table of contents for a back matter component
ToCchap	An entry in a table of contents for a component in the body of a document
ToCentry	A component title in a table of contents
ToCfront	An entry in a table of contents for a front matter component
ToClevel1	A top-level entry within a table of contents entry for a chapter-like component
ToClevel2	A second-level entry within a table of contents entry for a chapter-like component

Element	Brief Description
ToClevel3	A third-level entry within a table of contents entry for a chapter-like component
ToClevel4	A fourth-level entry within a table of contents entry for a chapter-like component
ToClevel5	A fifth-level entry within a table of contents entry for a chapter-like component
ToCpart	An entry in a table of contents for a part of a book
Token	A unit of information
Trademark	A trademark
Type	The classification of a value
ULink	A link that addresses its target by means of a URL (Uniform Resource Locator)
UserInput	Data entered by the user
VarArgs	An empty element in a function synopsis indicating a variable number of arguments
VarListEntry	A wrapper for a set of terms and the associated description in a variable list
VarName	The name of a variable
VariableList	A list in which each entry is composed of a set of one or more terms and an associated description
VideoData	Pointer to external video data
VideoObject	A wrapper for video data and its associated meta-information
Void	An empty element in a function synopsis indicating that the function in question takes no arguments
VolumeNum	The volume number of a document in a set (as of books in a set or articles in a journal)
Warning	An admonition set off from the text
WordAsWord	A word meant specifically as a word and not representing anything else
XRef	A cross reference to another part of the document
Year	The year of publication of a document

Glossary

attribute

Attributes augment the element on which they appear; they also provide additional information about the element.

Attributes appear as name-value pairs in the element's start-tag. For example, to assign the value `hostname` to the `Role` attribute of **SystemItem**, you would use the mark up: `<systemitem role="hostname">`.

callout

A pointer, verbal or graphical or both, to a *component* of an illustration or a text object.

cooked

"Cooked" data, as distinct from "raw," is a collection of elements and character data that's ready for presentation. The processor is not expected to rearrange, select, or suppress any of the elements, but simply present them as specified.

See also **Raw**.

document type declaration (DTD)

A set of declarations that defines the names of the elements and their attributes, and that specifies rules for their combination or sequence.

DSSSL

Document Style Semantics and Specification Language (ISO/IEC 10179:1996). An international standard stylesheet language for SGML/XML documents.

element

Elements define the hierarchical structure of a document. Most elements have start and end tags and contain some part of the document content. Empty elements have only a start tag and have no content.

entity

A name assigned (by means of a declaration) to some chunk of data so it can be referred to by that name; the data can be of various kinds (a special character or a chapter or a set of declarations in a DTD, for instance), and the way in which it is referred to depends on the type of data and where it is being referenced: SGML has parameter, general, external, internal, and data entities.

exclusion

An exclusion is used in a DTD to indicate that, within the element on which the exclusion occurs, the excluded elements are not valid anywhere within the content of the element.

For example, in DocBook, **Footnote** excludes **Footnote**. This means that footnotes cannot nest, even though **Footnote** contains **Para**, and **Footnote** occurs in the proper content model of **Para**.

See "Marked sections," in Chapter 1, *Getting Started with SGML/XML.*

external entity

An external entity is a general entity that refers to another document. External entities are often used to incorporate parsable text documents, like legal notices or chapters, into larger units, like chapters or books.

external subset

Element, attribute, and other declarations that compose (part of) a document type definition that are stored in an external entity, and referenced from a document's document type declaration using a public or system identifier.

float

Text objects like sidebars, figures, tables, and graphics are said to float when their actual place in the document is not fixed. For presentation on a printed page, for instance, a graphic may float to the top of the next page if it is too tall to fit on the page in which it actually falls, in the sequence of words and the sequence of other like objects in a document.

formal public identifier

A public identifier that conforms to the specification of formal public identifers in ISO 8879.

FOSI

Formatting Output Specification Instance, an SGML document that specifies the appearance or presentation of another SGML document in accordance with the Output Specification DTD defined by MIL-STD-28001C.

general entity

An entity referenced by a name that starts with an ampersand (&) and ends with a semicolon. Most of the time general entities are used in SGML documents, not in the DTD. There are two types, external and internal entities, and they refer either to special characters or to text objects like commonly repeated phrases or names or chapters.

GI

Generic identifier, proper term for the actual name of an element; `Para` is the generic identifier of the **para** element.

inclusion

An inclusion is used in a DTD to indicate that, within the element on which the inclusion occurs, the included elements are valid anywhere within the content of the element.

For example, in DocBook, **Chapter** includes **IndexTerm**. This means that **IndexTerms** can occur anywhere inside chapters, even inside elements that do not have **IndexTerms** in their proper content models.

See "Marked sections" in Chapter 1.

internal entity

A general entity that references a piece of text (including its markup and even other internal entities), usually as a keyboard shortcut.

internal subset

Element, attribute, and other declarations that compose (part of) a document type definition that are stored in a document, within the document type declaration.

meta-information

Meta-information is information about a document, such as the specification of its author or its date of composition, as opposed to the content of a document itself.

parameter entity

An entity usually referenced in the DTD by a name that starts with a percent sign (%) and ends with a semicolon. In DocBook, parameter entities are mainly used to facilitate customization of the DTD, but they can also be used to control marked sections of a document.

processing instruction

An essentially arbitrary string preceded by a question mark and delimited by angle brackets that is intended to convey information to an application that processes an SGML instance. For example, the processing instruction `<?linebreak>` might cause the formatter to introduce a line break at the position where the processing instruction occurs.

In XML documents, processing instructions should have the form:

```
<?pitarget param1="value1" param2="value2"?>
```

The ***pitarget*** should be a name that the processing application will recognize. Additional information in the PI should be added using "attribute syntax."

public identifier

An abstract identifier for an SGML or XML document, DTD, or external entity.

raw

"Raw" data is just a collection of elements, with no additional punctation or information about presentation. To continue the cooking metaphor, raw data is just a set of ingredients. It's up to the processor to select appropriate elements, arrange them for display, and add required presentational information.

See also **Cooked**.

SGML

Standard Generalized Markup Language, an international standard (ISO 8879) that specifies the rules for the creation of platform-independent markup languages for electronic texts.

stylesheet

A file that specifies the presentation or appearance of a document; there are several standards for such stylesheets, including CSS, FOSIs, DSSSL, and, most recently, XSL. Vendors often have proprietary stylesheet formats as well.

system identifier

In SGML, a local, system-dependent identifier for a document, DTD, or external entity. Usually a filename on the local system.

In XML, a system identifer is required to be a URI.

tag

An SGML element name enclosed in angle brackets (<>), used to mark up the semantics or structure of a document. `<Para>` is a tag in DocBook used to mark the beginning of a paragraph.

URI

Uniform Resource Identifier, the W3C's codification of the name and address syntax of present and future objects on the Internet. In its most basic form, a URI consists of a scheme name (such as file, http, ftp, news, mailto, gopher) followed by a colon, followed by a path whose nature is determined by the scheme that precedes it (see RFC 1630).

URI is the umbrella term for URNs, URLs, and all other Uniform Resource Identifiers.

URL

Uniform Resource Locator, a name and address for an existing object accessible over the Internet. `http://www.docbook.org` is an example of a URL (see RFC 1738).

URN

Uniform Resource Name, the result of an evolving attempt to define a name and address syntax for *persistent* objects accessible over the Internet; `urn:foo:a123,456` is a legal URN consisting of three colon-separated fields: `urn` followed by a namespace identifier, followed by a namespace specifier (see RFC 1737 and RFC 2141 for details).

W3C

The World Wide Web Consortium (*http://www.w3.org/*).

wrapper

Some elements, such as **Chapter**, have important semantic significance. Other elements serve no obvious purpose except to contain a number of other elements. For example, **BookInfo** has no important semantics; it merely serves as a container for the meta-information about a book. Elements that are just containers are sometimes called "wrappers."

XML

The Extensible Markup Language (*http://www.w3.org/TR/REC-xml*), a subset of SGML designed specifically for use over the Web.

XSL

XML Style Language, an evolving language for stylesheets to be attached to XML documents. The stylesheet is itself an XML document.

Index

D

E

F

J

K

L

M

S

T

U

V

W

X

Z

About the Authors

Norman Walsh is a Principal Software Engineeer with Arbortext Inc., the world's leading provider of content creation and management software for enterprise XML applications. As a member of the Engineering Group, Norman works on both the next generation of Arbortext products and with Arbortext's consultants and customers to develop and implement the standards-based solutions that best meet their unique needs.

Norm is an active participant in several standards efforts, including the DocBook Technical Committee of OASIS, where he is a member of the Editorial Board. He is also the chair of the OASIS Tables Technical Committee and a member of the W3C XSL Working Group.

Prior to joining Arbortext, Norman developed online books and web technologies for a publishing company and developed a number of large web resources. Norman received his M.S. in Computer Science from the University of Massachusetts, Amherst.

Leonard Muellner has been implementing and supporting the production of O'Reilly books marked up in DocBook since 1994.

Colophon

Our look is the result of reader comments, our own experimentation, and feedback from distribution channels. Distinctive covers complement our distinctive approach to technical topics, breathing personality and life into potentially dry subjects.

The bird on the cover of *DocBook: The Definitive Guide* is a wood duck. Often considered one of the most beautiful ducks in North America, the male wood duck has a metallic purple and green head with white streaks extending from its bill around the eyes and down to its blue and green, gold-flecked wings. It has a white neck, chestnut-colored chest, a white or red bill, and yellow-orange legs and feet. Females have more brown, gray, and subdued hues.

Wood ducks nest off the ground in tree cavities, commonly with narrow openings originally used by a woodpecker, owl, or other small bird. Their nests can be as high as thirty feet off the ground, and they prefer to nest over or beside water, but will nest up to a couple of miles from water if necessary. Many people have successfully attracted wood ducks to unwooded wetlands by building nesting boxes, which can even be purchased from several birding groups.

A large conservation effort in the early 1900s helped bring this colorful duck back from the brink of extinction, and wood ducks can now be found in 38 states in the United States and eight provinces in Canada.

Edie Freedman designed the cover of this book, using a 19th-century engraving from the Dover Pictorial Archive. Kathleen Wilson produced the cover layout using QuarkXPress 3.32 and Adobe's ITC Garamond font. Alicia Cech designed the inside layout, based on a series design by Nancy Priest. Hanna Dyer designed the CD label; Kathleen Wilson produced the label using QuarkXPress 4.0. The text was formatted from SGML into FrameMaker 5.5 with Jade, using a DSSSL conversion stylesheet written by Chris Maden. The interior fonts are ITC Garamond Light, Garamond Book, and ConstantWillison.

Whenever possible, our books use RepKover™, a durable and flexible lay-flat binding. If the page count exceeds RepKover's limit, perfect binding is used.

The illustrations that appear in this book were produced by Robert Romano and Rhon Porter using Macromedia Freehand 8 and Adobe Photoshop 5. David Futato was the production editor; Madeleine Newell guided the book through the early stages of production. Mark Nigara was the copyeditor for *DocBook: The Definitive Guide*. Abigail Myers provided production assistance and typesetting. Ellie Cutler was the proofreader, and quality assurance was provided by Jeff Holcomb and Claire Cloutier LeBlanc. Ellen Troutman indexed the book. This colophon was written by Nicole Arigo.

More Titles from O'Reilly

Web Programming

Writing Apache Modules with Perl and C

By Lincoln Stein & Doug MacEachern
1st Edition March 1999
746 pages, ISBN 1-56592-567-X

This guide to Web programming teaches you how to extend the capabilities of the Apache Web server. It explains the design of Apache, mod_perl, and the Apache API, then demonstrates how to use them to rewrite CGI scripts, filter HTML documents on the server-side, enhance server log functionality, convert file formats on the fly, and more.

Webmaster in a Nutshell, 2nd Edition

By Stephen Spainhour & Robert Eckstein
2nd Edition June 1999
540 pages, ISBN 1-56592-325-1

This indispensable book takes all the essential reference information for the Web and pulls it together into one volume. It covers HTML 4.0, CSS, XML, CGI, SSI, JavaScript 1.2, PHP, HTTP 1.1, and administration for the Apache server.

Java Servlet Programming

By Jason Hunter with William Crawford
1st Edition November 1998
528 pages, ISBN 1-56592-391-X

Java servlets offer a fast, powerful, portable replacement for CGI scripts. *Java Servlet Programming* covers everything you need to know to write effective servlets. Topics include: serving dynamic Web content, maintaining state information, session tracking, database connectivity using JDBC, and applet-servlet communication.

JavaScript Application Cookbook

By Jerry Bradenbaugh
1st Edition September 1999
478 pages, ISBN 1-56592-577-7

JavaScript Application Cookbook literally hands the Webmaster a set of ready-to-go, client-side JavaScript applications with thorough documentation to help them understand and extend the applications. By providing such a set of applications, *JavaScript Application Cookbook* allows Webmasters to immediately add extra functionality to their Web sites.

Practical Internet Groupware

By Jon Udell
1st Edition October 1999 (est.)
384 pages (est.), ISBN 1-56592-537-8

This revolutionary book tells users, programmers, IS managers, and system administrators how to build Internet groupware applications that organize the casual and chaotic transmission of online information into useful, disciplined, and documented data.

How to stay in touch with O'Reilly

1. Visit Our Award-Winning Web Site

http://www.oreilly.com/

★"Top 100 Sites on the Web" —*PC Magazine*
★"Top 5% Web sites" —*Point Communications*
★"3-Star site" —*The McKinley Group*

Our web site contains a library of comprehensive product information (including book excerpts and tables of contents), downloadable software, background articles, interviews with technology leaders, links to relevant sites, book cover art, and more. File us in your Bookmarks or Hotlist!

2. Join Our Email Mailing Lists

New Product Releases

To receive automatic email with brief descriptions of all new O'Reilly products as they are released, send email to:
listproc@online.oreilly.com
Put the following information in the first line of your message (*not* in the Subject field):
subscribe oreilly-news

O'Reilly Events

If you'd also like us to send information about trade show events, special promotions, and other O'Reilly events, send email to:
listproc@online.oreilly.com
Put the following information in the first line of your message (*not* in the Subject field):
subscribe oreilly-events

3. Get Examples from Our Books via FTP

There are two ways to access an archive of example files from our books:

Regular FTP

- ftp to:
  ftp.oreilly.com
  (login: anonymous
  password: your email address)
- Point your web browser to:
  ftp://ftp.oreilly.com/

FTPMAIL

- Send an email message to:
  ftpmail@online.oreilly.com
  (Write "help" in the message body)

4. Contact Us via Email

order@oreilly.com
To place a book or software order online. Good for North American and international customers.

subscriptions@oreilly.com
To place an order for any of our newsletters or periodicals.

books@oreilly.com
General questions about any of our books.

software@oreilly.com
For general questions and product information about our software. Check out O'Reilly Software Online at **http://software.oreilly.com/** for software and technical support information. Registered O'Reilly software users send your questions to: **website-support@oreilly.com**

cs@oreilly.com
For answers to problems regarding your order or our products.

booktech@oreilly.com
For book content technical questions or corrections.

proposals@oreilly.com
To submit new book or software proposals to our editors and product managers.

international@oreilly.com
For information about our international distributors or translation queries. For a list of our distributors outside of North America check out:
http://www.oreilly.com/www/order/country.html

O'Reilly & Associates, Inc.
101 Morris Street, Sebastopol, CA 95472 USA
TEL 707-829-0515 or 800-998-9938
(6am to 5pm PST)
FAX 707-829-0104

International Distributors

UK, Europe, Middle East and Africa (except France, Germany, Austria, Switzerland, Luxembourg, Liechtenstein, and Eastern Europe)

INQUIRIES

O'Reilly UK Limited
4 Castle Street
Farnham
Surrey, GU9 7HS
United Kingdom
Telephone: 44-1252-711776
Fax: 44-1252-734211
Email: josette@oreilly.com

ORDERS

Wiley Distribution Services Ltd.
1 Oldlands Way
Bognor Regis
West Sussex PO22 9SA
United Kingdom
Telephone: 44-1243-779777
Fax: 44-1243-820250
Email: cs-books@wiley.co.uk

France

Orders

GEODIF
61, Bd Saint-Germain
75240 Paris Cedex 05, France
Tel: 33-1-44-41-46-16 (French books)
Tel: 33-1-44-41-11-87 (English books)
Fax: 33-1-44-41-11-44
Email: distribution@eyrolles.com

Inquiries

Éditions O'Reilly
18 rue Séguier
75006 Paris, France
Tel: 33-1-40-51-52-30
Fax: 33-1-40-51-52-31
Email: france@editions-oreilly.fr

Germany, Switzerland, Austria, Eastern Europe, Luxembourg, and Liechtenstein

Inquiries & Orders

O'Reilly Verlag
Balthasarstr. 81
D-50670 Köln
Germany
Telephone: 49-221-973160-91
Fax: 49-221-973160-8
Email: anfragen@oreilly.de (inquiries)
Email: order@oreilly.de (orders)

Canada (French language books)

Les Éditions Flammarion ltée
375, Avenue Laurier Ouest
Montréal (Québec) H2V 2K3
Tel: 00-1-514-277-8807
Fax: 00-1-514-278-2085
Email: info@flammarion.qc.ca

Hong Kong

City Discount Subscription Service, Ltd.
Unit D, 3rd Floor, Yan's Tower
27 Wong Chuk Hang Road
Aberdeen, Hong Kong
Tel: 852-2580-3539
Fax: 852-2580-6463
Email: citydis@ppn.com.hk

Korea

Hanbit Media, Inc.
Sonyoung Bldg. 202
Yeksam-dong 736-36
Kangnam-ku
Seoul, Korea
Tel: 822-554-9610
Fax: 822-556-0363
Email: hant93@chollian.dacom.co.kr

Philippines

Mutual Books, Inc.
429-D Shaw Boulevard
Mandaluyong City, Metro
Manila, Philippines
Tel: 632-725-7538
Fax: 632-721-3056
Email: mbikikog@mnl.sequel.net

Taiwan

O'Reilly Taiwan
No. 3, Lane 131
Hang-Chow South Road
Section 1, Taipei, Taiwan
Tel: 886-2-23968990
Fax: 886-2-23968916
Email: taiwan@oreilly.com

China

O'Reilly Beijing
Room 2410
160, FuXingMenNeiDaJie
XiCheng District
Beijing, China PR 100031
Tel: 86-10-86631006
Fax: 86-10-86631007
Email: beijing@oreilly.com

India

Computer Bookshop (India) Pvt. Ltd.
190 Dr. D.N. Road, Fort
Bombay 400 001 India
Tel: 91-22-207-0989
Fax: 91-22-262-3551
Email: cbsbom@giasbm01.vsnl.net.in

Japan

O'Reilly Japan, Inc.
Kiyoshige Building 2F
12-Bancho, Sanei-cho
Shinjuku-ku
Tokyo 160-0008 Japan
Tel: 81-3-3356-5227
Fax: 81-3-3356-5261
Email: japan@oreilly.com

All Other Asian Countries

O'Reilly & Associates, Inc.
101 Morris Street
Sebastopol, CA 95472 USA
Tel: 707-829-0515
Fax: 707-829-0104
Email: order@oreilly.com

Australia

WoodsLane Pty., Ltd.
7/5 Vuko Place
Warriewood NSW 2102
Australia
Tel: 61-2-9970-5111
Fax: 61-2-9970-5002
Email: info@woodslane.com.au

New Zealand

Woodslane New Zealand, Ltd.
21 Cooks Street (P.O. Box 575)
Waganui, New Zealand
Tel: 64-6-347-6543
Fax: 64-6-345-4840
Email: info@woodslane.com.au

Latin America

McGraw-Hill Interamericana
Editores, S.A. de C.V.
Cedro No. 512
Col. Atlampa
06450, Mexico, D.F.
Tel: 52-5-547-6777
Fax: 52-5-547-3336
Email: mcgraw-hill@infosel.net.mx

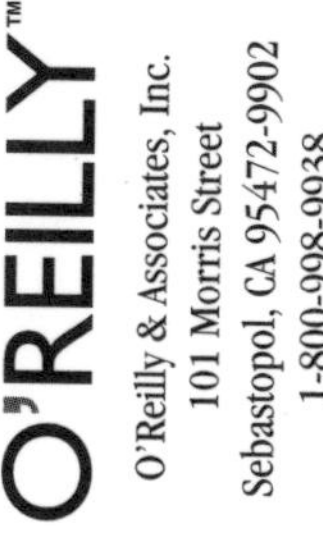

O'REILLY™

O'Reilly & Associates, Inc.
101 Morris Street
Sebastopol, CA 95472-9902
1-800-998-9938

Visit us online at:
http://www.ora.com/

O'REILLY WOULD LIKE TO HEAR FROM YOU

Which book did this card come from?

____

Where did you buy this book?

- ❑ Bookstore
- ❑ Computer Store
- ❑ Direct from O'Reilly
- ❑ Class/seminar
- ❑ Bundled with hardware/software
- ❑ Other ________________

What operating system do you use?

- ❑ UNIX
- ❑ Macintosh
- ❑ Windows NT
- ❑ PC(Windows/DOS)
- ❑ Other ________________

What is your job description?

- ❑ System Administrator
- ❑ Programmer
- ❑ Network Administrator
- ❑ Educator/Teacher
- ❑ Web Developer
- ❑ Other ________________

❑ Please send me O'Reilly's catalog, containing a complete listing of O'Reilly books and software.

Name ____________ Company/Organization ____________

Address ____________

City ______ State ______ Zip/Postal Code ______ Country ______

Telephone ____________ Internet or other email address (specify network) ____________

neteenth century wood engraving
a bear from the O'Reilly &
sociates Nutshell Handbook®
sing & Managing UUCP.

PLACE
STAMP
HERE

NO POSTAGE
NECESSARY IF
MAILED IN THE
UNITED STATES

BUSINESS REPLY MAIL

FIRST CLASS MAIL PERMIT NO. 80 SEBASTOPOL, CA

Postage will be paid by addressee

O'Reilly & Associates, Inc.
101 Morris Street
Sebastopol, CA 95472-9902